Lecture Notes in Computer Science 15527

The series Lecture Notes in Computer Science (LNCS), including its subseries Lecture Notes in Artificial Intelligence (LNAI) and Lecture Notes in Bioinformatics (LNBI), has established itself as a medium for the publication of new developments in computer science and information technology research, teaching, and education.

LNCS enjoys close cooperation with the computer science R & D community, the series counts many renowned academics among its volume editors and paper authors, and collaborates with prestigious societies. Its mission is to serve this international community by providing an invaluable service, mainly focused on the publication of conference and workshop proceedings and postproceedings. LNCS commenced publication in 1973.

Xu Chen · Geyong Min · Deke Guo · Xia Xie ·
Lingjun Pu
Editors

Network and Parallel Computing

20th IFIP WG 10.3 International Conference, NPC 2024
Haikou, China, December 7–8, 2024
Proceedings, Part I

Springer

Editors
Xu Chen
Sun Yat-sen University
Guangzhou, China

Geyong Min
University of Exeter
Exeter, UK

Deke Guo
National University of Defense Technology
Changsha, China

Xia Xie
Hainan University
Haikou, China

Lingjun Pu
Nankai University
Tianjin, China

ISSN 0302-9743   ISSN 1611-3349 (electronic)
Lecture Notes in Computer Science
ISBN 978-981-96-2829-2   ISBN 978-981-96-2830-8 (eBook)
https://doi.org/10.1007/978-981-96-2830-8

Preface

Welcome to the proceedings of the twentieth edition of the International Conference on Network and Parallel Computing (NPC 2024), held in Haikou, China, from December 7–8, 2024. NPC is a prestigious annual gathering that serves as a global platform for researchers, academics, and industry professionals to explore and exchange cutting-edge ideas, research findings, and innovative solutions in the fields of network, distributed, and parallel computing. Topics of interest include, but are not limited to, parallel and distributed applications and algorithms, parallel and distributed architectures and systems, and parallel and distributed software environments and tools.

A total of 200 submissions were received in response to our call for papers. These papers originated from Asia, Australia, Europe, and North America. Each submission was sent to at least three reviewers (four reviewers per submission on average) to evaluate its originality, innovation, readability, and relevance to the expected audience. Based on the reviews received, 76 papers were accepted for inclusion in the technical conference program, with an acceptance rate of about 38%.

We sincerely thank the authors for contributing their outstanding research work to NPC 2024. We also want to thank every member of the NPC 2024 Organizing Committee, Program Committee, and Steering Committee for their great efforts in putting together such an exciting program. Finally, we thank all the attendees and volunteers for NPC 2024.

December 2024

Xu Chen
Geyong Min
Deke Guo
Xia Xie
Lingjun Pu

Organization

General Chair

Deke Guo   National University of Defense Technology,
                                  China

Program Co-chairs

Xu Chen   Sun Yat-sen University, China
Geyong Min   University of Exeter, UK

Local Chair

Xia Xie   Hainan University, China

Publicity Co-chairs

Shiqiang Wang   IBM T. J. Watson Research Center, USA
Cheng Li   University of Science and Technology of China,
                                  China
Tingting Yuan   University of Göttingen, Germany

Registration Chair

Xiaohui Peng   Institute of Computing Technology, CAS, China

Publication Chair

Lingjun Pu   Nankai University, China

Web and Information System Chair

Tao Ouyang   Sun Yat-sen University, China

Finance Chair

Ran Zheng   Huazhong University of Science and Technology,
                                                 China

Steering Committee

Hai Jin (Co-chair)   Huazhong University of Science and Technology,
                                                 China
Jean-Luc Gaudiot (Co-chair)   University of California, Irvine, USA
Stéphane Zuckerman (Vice Chair)   Université de Cergy-Pontoise, France
Chen Ding   University of Rochester, USA
Kemal Ebcioglu   Global Supercomputing, USA
Jack Dongarra   University of Tennessee, USA
Tony Hey   Science and Technology Facilities Council, UK
Yoichi Muraoka   Waseda University, Japan
Viktor Prasanna   University of Southern California, USA
Daniel Reed   University of Utah, USA
Weisong Shi   University of Delaware, USA
Ninghui Sun   Institute of Computing Technology, CAS, China
Zhiwei Xu   Institute of Computing Technology, CAS, China

Program Committee

Amir Taherkordi   University of Oslo, Norway
Anna Kobusinska   Poznań University of Technology, Poland
Aravind Sankaran   RWTH Aachen University, Germany
Bing Luo   Duke Kunshan University, China
Bo Mao   Xiamen University, China
Bo Gu   Sun Yat-sen University, China
Changkun Jiang   Shenzhen University, China
Chao Li   Shanghai Jiao Tong University, China
Chao Qiu   Tianjin University, China
Chaojie Gu   Zhejiang University, China
Chen Chen   University of Cambridge, UK
Zhiguang Chen   National University of Defense Technology,
                                                 China
Chen Chen   Xidian University, China
Chengxi Gao   Shenzhen Institute of Advanced Technology,
                                                 China

Chentao Wu	Shanghai Jiao Tong University, China
Chenyang Wang	Shenzhen University, China
Chundian Li	Meta Platforms, USA
Cong Wang	Zhejiang University, China
Dan Huang	Sun Yat-sen University, China
Dazhao Cheng	Wuhan University, China
Deze Zeng	China University of Geosciences, China
Dezun Dong	National University of Defense Technology, China
En Shao	Institute of Computing Technology, China
Fan Wu	Central South University, China
Fang Dong	Southeast University, China
Fangxin Wang	Chinese University of Hong Kong, Shenzhen, China
Fei Xu	East China Normal University, China
Feifei Chen	Deakin University, Australia
Gang Chen	Sun Yat-sen University, China
Geyao Cheng	National University of Defense Technology, China
Geyong Min	University of Exeter, UK
Giuseppe Tricomi	Università di Messina, Italy
Gongming Zhao	University of Science and Technology of China, China
Guangjing Huang	Sun Yat-sen University, China
Guocheng Liao	Sun Yat-sen University, China
Haisheng Tan	University of Science and Technology of China, China
Hengshan Yue	Jilin University, China
Hongju Cheng	Fuzhou University, China
Honglong Chen	China University of Petroleum, China
Houqun Yang	Hainan University, China
Huaming Wu	Tianjin University, China
Huan Zhou	Northwestern Polytechnical University, China
Huawei Huang	Sun Yat-sen University, China
Jiang Wenchao	Guangdong University of Technology, China
Jianxiong Guo	Beijing Normal University, China
Jiawen Kang	Guangdong University of Technology, China
Jie Gong	Sun Yat-sen University, China
Jingpu Duan	Pengcheng Laboratory, China
Jingwen Leng	Shanghai Jiao Tong University, China
Jingyi Li	Sun Yat-sen University, China
Jixian Zhang	University of Electronic Science and Technology, China

Jun Zhao	Nanyang Technological University, Singapore
Ke Luo	Sun Yat-sen University, China
Keren Zhou	OpenAI/George Mason University, USA
Konglin Zhu	Beijing University of Posts and Telecommunications, China
Lailong Luo	National University of Defense Technology, China
Laiping Zhao	Tianjin University, China
Lars Nagel	Loughborough University, UK
Lei Gong	University of Science and Technology of China, China
Lei Liu	Xidian University, China
Lei Yang	South China University of Technology, China
Lei Yang	University of Nevada, Reno, USA
Leyi Xiao	Hainan University, China
Liekang Zeng	Sun Yat-sen University, China
Lin Wang	Paderborn University, Germany
Lingjun Pu	Nankai University, China
Liu Daibo	Hunan University, China
Long Chen	Guangdong University of Technology, China
Long Zheng	Huazhong University of Science and Technology, China
Lu Liu	University of Leicester, UK
Mariano Scazzariello	KTH Royal Institute of Technology, Sweden
Menghao Zhang	Beihang University, China
Mengwei Xu	Beijing University of Posts and Telecommunications, China
Mengyuan Zhang	Beihang University, China
Miao Hu	Sun Yat-sen University, China
Minghua Shen	Sun Yat-sen University, China
Minghui Min	China University of Mining and Technology, China
Mingxing Zhang	Tsinghua University, China
Minxian Xu	Shenzhen Institutes of Advanced Technology, China
Nan Ji	Hainan University, China
Peng Li	University of Aizu, Japan
Peng Liu	Hangzhou Dianzi University, China
Peng Sun	Hunan University, China
Peng Zhao	Xi'an Jiaotong University, China
Pengfei Chen	Sun Yat-sen University, China
Qian Ma	Sun Yat-sen University, China

Qiang He	Huazhong University of Science and Technology, China
Qianyi Huang	Sun Yat-sen University, China
Qiong Wu	Sun Yat-sen University, China
Qiufen Xia	Dalian University of Technology, China
Qiushi Li	Tsinghua University, China
Quan Chen	Shanghai Jiao Tong University, China
Rong Gu	Nanjing University, China
Rongfei Zeng	Northeastern University, China
Sen Lin	University of Houston, USA
Shad Kirmani	Ebay Inc., USA
Sheng Zhang	Nanjing University, China
Shengyuan Ye	Sun Yat-sen University, China
Shigang Li	Beijing University of Posts and Telecommunications, China
Shigeng Zhang	Central South University, China
Shihong Hu	Jiangnan University, China
Shimin Gong	Sun Yat-sen University, China
Shuai Yu	Sun Yat-sen University, China
Song Yang	Beijing Institute of Technology, China
Songwen Pei	University of Shanghai for Science and Technology, China
Stephan Sigg	Aalto University, Finland
Sven Groppe	University of Lübeck, Germany
Tao Ouyang	San Yet-sen University, China
Tengjiao He	Jinan University, China
Tian Wang	Beijing Normal University, China
Tianxi Ji	Texas Tech University, USA
Tingting Yuan	University of Göttingen, Germany
Wanchun Jiang	Central South University, China
Wen Xia	Harbin Institute of Technology, Shenzhen, China
Wenfei Wu	Peking University, China
Wenzheng Xu	Sichuan University, China
Xianwei Zhang	AMD Inc., China
Xiao Ma	Beijing University of Posts and Telecommunications, China
Xiao Zhang	Shandong University, China
Xiaobo Zhou	Tianjin University, China
Xiaofei Wang	Tianjin University, China
Xiaofeng Gao	Shanghai Jiao Tong University, China
Xiaofeng Hou	Shanghai Jiao Tong University, China
Xiaohui Peng	Institute of Computing Technology, China

Xiaolong Xu	Nanjing University, China
Xiaomin Ouyang	Hong Kong University of Science and Technology, Hong Kong, China
Xiaowen Gong	Auburn University, USA
Xiaoxi Zhang	Sun Yat-sen University, China
Ximing Wu	Sun Yat-sen University, China
Xin Li	Nanjing University of Aeronautics and Astronautics, China
Xingzhou Zhang	Institute of Computing Technology, China
Xinyi Li	Northwest University, China
Xiuhua Li	Chongqing University, China
Xu Chen	Sun Yat-sen University, China
Xuebin Ren	Xi'an Jiaotong University, China
Yalan Wu	Guangdong University of Technology, China
Yali Yuan	Southeast University, China
Yanchao Zhao	Nanjing University of Aeronautics and Astronautics, China
Yanni Yang	Shandong University, China
Yi Wang	Shenzhen University, China
Yibo Huang	University of Michigan, USA
Yifan Wang	Institute of Computing Technology, China
Yifei Zhu	Shanghai Jiao Tong University, China
Yifei Zou	Hong Kong University, China
Yin Zhang	University of Electronic Science and Technology, China
Yongheng Deng	Tsinghua University, China
Yongmin Zhang	Central South University, China
Yuan Wu	University of Macau, Macau, China
Zeke Wang	Zhejiang University, China
Zhi Liu	University of Electro-Communications, Japan
Zhi Zhou	Sun Yat-sen University, China
Zhiping Cai	National University of Defense Technology, China
Zhiqing Tang	Beijing Normal University, China
Zhiwei Zhao	University of Electronic Science and Technology, China
Zhiying Feng	Sun Yat-sen University, China
Zhu Xiao	Hunan University, China
Zhuozhao Li	Southern University of Science and Technology, China

Contents – Part I

High-performance and Parallel Computing

Novel Memory and Storage Systems

Emerging Architectures and Systems

Contents – Part II

Edge Computing and Intelligence

Federated Learning Algorithms and Systems

Emerging Networks

In-network Computing and Processing

High-performance and Parallel Computing

A Novel Consensus Mechanism Based on Dynamic Sharding

Jingyu Zhang[1,2], Yilong Teng[1], Yongtao Sun[1], Shi Zhu[3], Fangliao Yang[3], and Lailong Luo[2(✉)]

[1] School of Computer and Communication Engineering,
Changsha University of Science and Technology, Changsha, China
zhangzhang@csust.edu.cn , syongtao@stu.csust.edu.cn
[2] Science and Technology on Information Systems Engineering Laboratory,
School of Systems Engineering, National University of Defense Technology,
Changsha, China
luolailong09@nudt.edu.cn
[3] Data Operations Center, State Grid Hunan Electric Power Information
and Communication Corporation, Changsha, Hunan, China

Abstract. Blockchain, as an emerging technology, has been widely studied by the researchers from academia and industry. Alliance chain, as an important form of blockchain, is often applied to smart grids, smart city and the Internet of Things to ensure the authenticity and reliability of data. Practical Byzantine Fault Tolerance (PBFT) algorithm is a key technology to ensure data consistency in the alliance chains, and it plays a critical role in improving system performance, security and scalability. However, with the increase of the number of nodes and transactions, the ability of PBFT to process transactions is challenged. In particular, PBFT's linear transaction processing also limits its ability to process transactions in parallel. In view of the problems existing in PBFT, this paper studies the consensus mechanism optimization, and puts forward a consensus mechanism with better performance. In this paper, in order to solve the problem of weak parallel transaction processing capability of PBFT, we propose a novel Consensus Mechanism based on Dynamic Sharding (CMDS). CMDS firstly constructs a dynamic fragmentation model based on consistent hash algorithm to segment nodes, and then constructs a voting consensus mechanism based on reputation weight to achieve global state consistency. The experimental results show that CMDS can significantly improve the ability of parallel transaction processing and the performance of blockchain system.

Keywords: Blockchain technology · Consensus mechanism · Reputation evaluation · Sharding mechanism

1 Introduction

Blockchain technology, as an emerging technology, was first proposed in 2008 by Satoshi Nakamoto, and nowadays it has been widely used in various fields.

© IFIP International Federation for Information Processing 2025
Published by Springer Nature Switzerland AG 2025
X. Chen et al. (Eds.): NPC 2024, LNCS 15527, pp. 3–15, 2025.
https://doi.org/10.1007/978-981-96-2830-8_1

The blockchain is a decentralized ledger system that utilizes cryptographic techniques, consensus mechanisms, and smart contract technology to securely record transactional data [1]. As shown in Fig. 1, the decentralization, traceability, tamper-proof and other characteristics of blockchain technology [2] make it have broad application prospects in many fields such as supply chain finance [3], smart power [4,5], intelligent transportation [6,7], and Internet of things [8]. This cross-domain application demonstrates the diversity of blockchain technology and its ability to solve complex problems. As the core technology of blockchain system to achieve decentralized consistency, has become a research hotspot in academia and industry.

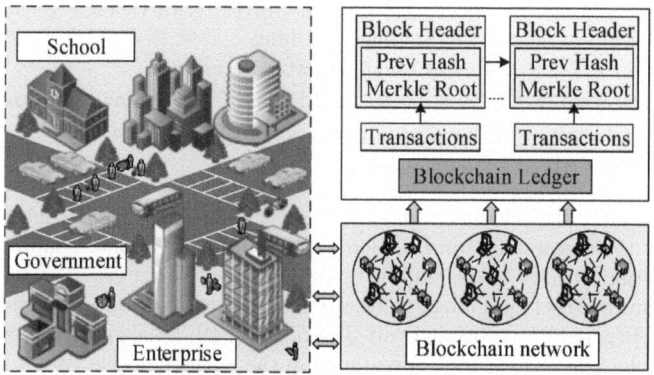

Fig. 1. The typical application scenarios of blockchain system.

Due to the high latency of peer-to-peer networks, each node observes an inconsistent order of transactions. To solve this problem, consensus mechanisms have been proposed to make all nodes reach consensus on the content and order of created transactions within a certain time [9]. The alliance blockchain system is the typical and wildly used blockchain system, and the most commonly used consensus mechanism in alliance blockchains is the Practical Byzantine Fault Tolerance (PBFT) algorithm. The PBFT consensus algorithm can efficiently and securely achieve consensus in scenarios with a small number of nodes. However, PBFT faces challenges in complex large-scale application scenarios, and the ability to process transactions in parallel is weak. The PBFT algorithm is not well designed to support the parallel processing of transactions. It requires that all transactions must be processed and confirmed in sequence, which means that even if multiple transactions can be processed simultaneously, the system must process them in a certain order, thus limiting the processing efficiency. In large-scale transaction scenarios, this sequential requirement can lead to significant performance bottlenecks and latency issues, especially when large amounts of data need to be processed quickly. Therefore, in this paper we try to design better consensus algorithms to improve the parallel processing performance. Our main contributions are summarized as follows:

- To further enhance the parallel transaction processing capability, we propose a novel Consensus Mechanism based on Dynamic Sharding (CMDS) by leveraging the Node Comprehensive Reputation Evaluation model (NCRE) reputation.
- Furthermore, we construct a Voting Consensus based on Reputation Weight (VCRW) to complete the global consensus, so as to achieve the consistency of the data status of each sharding.
- Finally, we conduct simulation experiments to validate the proposed CMDS. The experimental results show that CMDS significantly improves the ability of the blockchain system to process transactions in parallel, thereby improving the throughput of the blockchain system.

In the rest of this paper, Sect. 2 investigates the related work. Section 3 provides the design implementation, and Sect. 4 provides the experimental evaluation. Section 5 summarises this work.

2 Related Work

2.1 Consensus Mechanism Research

Consensus mechanism optimization has become an important research direction nowadays. Tian et al. [10] proposed a high-performance and scalable Byzantine Fault Tolerant (BFT) protocol, which secretly selects block proposers and uses threshold signatures as a multi-round voting mechanism to confirm the validity of the proposed blocks. Alqahtani et al. [11] pointed out that communication complexity is an important reason for the performance and throughput bottleneck of consensus protocols. Gai et al. [12] introduced a protocol to alleviate the leader bottleneck in BFT consensus through a robust shared memory pool to improve the scalability and robustness of the blockchain consensus mechanism. Deng et al. [13] introduced a consensus algorithm derived from directed acyclic graphs and backpropagation neural networks to address the scalability, concurrency, and security challenges faced by existing consortium blockchain consensus algorithms. Swathi et al. [14] proposed a system to solve the scalability problem of permissioned chains by adopting data science techniques. Xiang et al. [15] proposed an efficient Byzantine fault-tolerant consensus algorithm, which uses gossip protocol for message communication and improves the throughput of the system.

2.2 Sharding Mechanism

Optimizing the consensus mechanism of blockchain based on sharding technology is also an important direction in the field of blockchain research. Shen et al. proposed a node fragmentation model based on guarantee tree, which effectively improves system security while maintaining a certain degree of decentralization [16]. The SG-PBFT consensus algorithm uses the score grouping mechanism to optimize the traditional PBFT consensus algorithm to improve the consensus efficiency [17]. Cheng et al. [18] proposed SharDAG mechanism, which uses

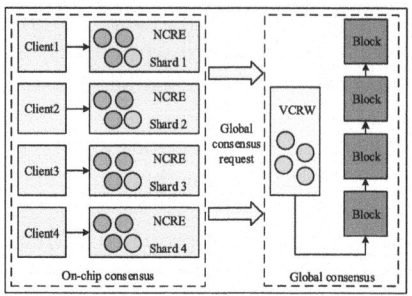   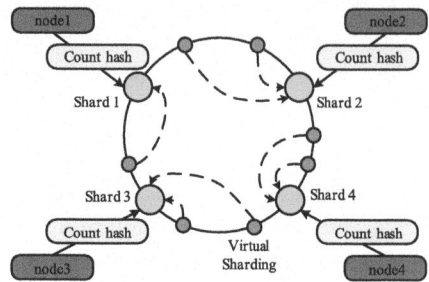

Fig. 2. CMDS framework.   **Fig. 3.** Dynamic sharding.

adaptive sharding to achieve high performance and strong consistency for DAG-based blockchains, which can improve throughput and reduce storage overhead of cross-shard transactions.

From the above related research, although the existing research work has solutions to optimize performance through node selection and grouping mechanism, these solutions tend to ignore the high latency and low efficiency problems caused by PBFT linear consensus and do not consider the dynamic fragmentation of nodes. Therefore, we combine the consistent hash algorithm and the node reputation mechanism to construct a dynamic sharding model in the blockchain to achieve the balance of node distribution. In the sharding model, the intra-shard consensus and the global consensus are carried out, which effectively improves the consensus efficiency and system security.

3   Design Implementation

We propose CMDS to improve the ability of the PBFT consensus mechanism to process transactions in parallel. As shown in Fig. 2, the mechanism first constructs a dynamic sharding model based on consistent hashing algorithm. This model uses hash mapping and virtual sharding to allocate nodes in the blockchain system, ensuring a balanced number of nodes in each shard. On the basis of building a stable sharding foundation, the CMDS mechanism designed intra-shard consensus and global consensus. For intra-shard consensus, the CMDS mechanism adopts a reputation aware randomized consensus mechanism NCRE to ensure fast transaction verification within the shard. After completing intra-shard consensus, the leader nodes of each shard initiate proposals and execute global consensus through the reputation weight based voting consensus mechanism VCRW to achieve consistency in data states between shards. Table 1 shows the relevant symbols used in the consensus mechanism based on dynamic sharding.

Table 1. CMDS symbol definition

Symbol	Explanation
n	Total number of system nodes
n_{id}	Node number
S_c	The number of shards
ϖ	Expected number of fragmentation nodes
S_r	Number of virtual shards
S_t	Number of nodes within the slice
S_n	The number of fragmentation threshold
ts	Nodes join the timestamp of the system
w_i	The credit weight of the node
r_i	Node reputation value

3.1 Dynamic Sharding Model

We construct a dynamic sharding model based on consistent hash algorithm to achieve the balance of node distribution. Figure 3 illustrates the dynamic sharding process based on the consistent hashing algorithm, and it includes the following steps:

1) **Determine the number of shards.** The number of shards is determined according to the total number of nodes in the blockchain network and the expected number of nodes in each shard. The number of shards can be obtained by the following formula:

$$S_c = \lfloor n/\varpi \rfloor + 1 \tag{1}$$

where S_c represents the number of shards, n is the total number of nodes in the blockchain system, and ϖ represents the expected number of shard nodes. In order to deal with the change impact of the total number of nodes on the number of shards, this study designs a node periodic detection mechanism to regularly monitor the total number of nodes n in the current network. When the change ratio Δn of the number of nodes exceeds the set threshold θ, the system will recalculate the number of shards according to the expression (1). The change ratio of the number of nodes is calculated as follows:

$$\Delta n = \left| \frac{n - n_{prev}}{n} \right| \tag{2}$$

where n is the total number of nodes after the last shard counting period.

2) **Virtual shard creation.** After determining the number of shards, multiple virtual shards are created for each real shard to achieve a more balanced node distribution. The hash value corresponding to each shard number is calculated

by the hash algorithm, and the shard and its virtual shard are mapped to the hash ring according to these hash values. We have:

$$H\left(i\right) = hash\left(i\right) mod\vartheta \tag{3}$$

where i is the identifier of the real shard or virtual shard, $H\left(i\right)$ is the hash value of the corresponding shard, $hash$ represents the hash function, and ϑ represents the size of the hash ring.

3) **Node mapping to the hash ring.** When a node enters the alliance blockchain system, the admission authority will assign a unique number to each node and generate an initial hash value according to the time series. The hash value of a node determines its position on the hash ring, and the node position is calculated as follows:

$$p_i = hash\left(n_{id} + ts\right) mod\vartheta \tag{4}$$

where p_i represents the position of the node in the hash ring, n_{id} represents the node number, and ts represents the timestamp when the node enters the system.

4) **Shard allocation of nodes.** According to Step 3, the position of the node on the hash ring can be calculated, and subsequently the virtual shard whose hash value is greater than the node position p can be searched in a clockwise direction. That is, find the smallest $H\left(i\right)$ satisfying $P\left(i\right) < H\left(i\right)$. When a node finds its virtual shard, it is mapped back to the real shard it belongs to.

5) **Number verification of shard nodes.** In order to ensure that the number of nodes in each shard satisfies fault tolerance and security, this study designs a verification strategy for the number of nodes. When the node shard allocation is completed, the system checks whether the number of nodes within each shard satisfies the preset lower threshold S_t. If the number of nodes in a shard is below the threshold S_t, the mechanism of re-sharding is triggered. At this time, the system reduces the number of virtual shards and reallocates the nodes to ensure that all shards have enough nodes to maintain the stability and security of the network.

3.2   Node Comprehensive Reputation Evaluation Model

The Node Comprehensive Reputation Evaluation (NCRE) model evaluates the nodes comprehensively and divides them into common nodes and candidate nodes based on their reputation values. Then, node selection strategies are designed for candidate nodes to filter out the set of excellent consensus nodes. The comprehensive reputation value of a node is categorized into node's base reputation, consensus reputation and historical reputation. The base reputation is mainly determined by the base performance of the node, and the base reputation value is normalized and calculated as shown below:

$$R_d\left(id\right) = \frac{1}{1 + e^{-(\beta + \chi + \gamma)}} \tag{5}$$

where β represents the node processor efficiency score, χ represents the node sensor performance score, and γ represents the node memory performance score.

The consensus reputation of a node represents the specific performance of the node's participation in the consensus process during t rounds. Firstly, a feature matrix is established for the consensus indicators of the nodes participating in the consensus $C = (c_{ij})_{m \times n}$. For the indicators of positive directivity (e.g., the data quality, the success rate), and the expression is as follows:

$$c_{ij} = \frac{c_{ij} - \min_{i=1}^{n} c_{ij}}{\max_{i=1}^{n} c_{ij} - \min_{i=1}^{n} c_{ij}} \tag{6}$$

For the indicators of negative directivity (e.g., the processing delay, response delay), and the expression is as follows:

$$c_{ij} = \frac{\max_{i=1}^{n} c_{ij} - c_{ij}}{\max_{i=1}^{n} c_{ij} - \min_{i=1}^{n} c_{ij}} \tag{7}$$

where m represents the number of consensus indicators, n represents the number of nodes, and c_{ij} represents the normalized value of the jth indicator of node i.

After getting the normalized value of each indicator, the reputation of each node is calculated, and the consensus reputation of each node in round t is obtained as follows:

$$Rc_t(id) = \frac{\sum_{j=1}^{m} c_{ij}}{m} \tag{8}$$

where $Rc_t(id)$ represents the consensus reputation value of the node in round t, and c_{ij} represents the normalized value of the jth index of node i.

Finally, the node's comprehensive reputation is calculated by combining its historical reputation and preliminary comprehensive reputation. The calculation of a node's comprehensive reputation is as follows:

$$R_t(id) = \frac{1}{1 + e^{-\lambda\left(\frac{R_d(id) + Rc_t(id)}{2} - R_{t-1(id)}\right)}} \tag{9}$$

where λ is a positive number that indicates the slope of the function, which is the rate indicating the reputation value changes. $R_{t-1(id)}$ represents the reputation value of the node in the last caculation round, and $R_0(id)$ is set to 0.

3.3 Voting Consensus Mechanism

After the nodes are allocated through the dynamic sharding model based on consistency hashing algorithm, the blockchain system begins to execute the consensus process, as shown in Fig. 4. This process is divided into two main parts: intra-shard consensus and global consensus. First, the nodes within a shard utilize the NCRE to screen out high-quality consensus nodes for intra-shard transaction consensus. After the consensus within the shard is completed, the leader nodes of each shard need to conduct a global consensus to achieve the consistency of the whole network state.

After the intra-shard consensus is completed, VCRW operations need to be performed between each shard leader node in order to synchronize the global state. This process consists of the following detailed steps:

1) **Global state proposal generation.** In order to ensure the integrity and uniqueness of the proposal information, the leader node calculates the proposal identifier based on the summary of the transaction information and the time of the proposal generation. The calculation method is as follows:

$$PID = hash\left(Tx_{digest} + Ts\right) \tag{10}$$

where PID represents the proposal identifier, Tx_{digest} represents the summary of transaction information, and Ts is the time when the proposal is generated.

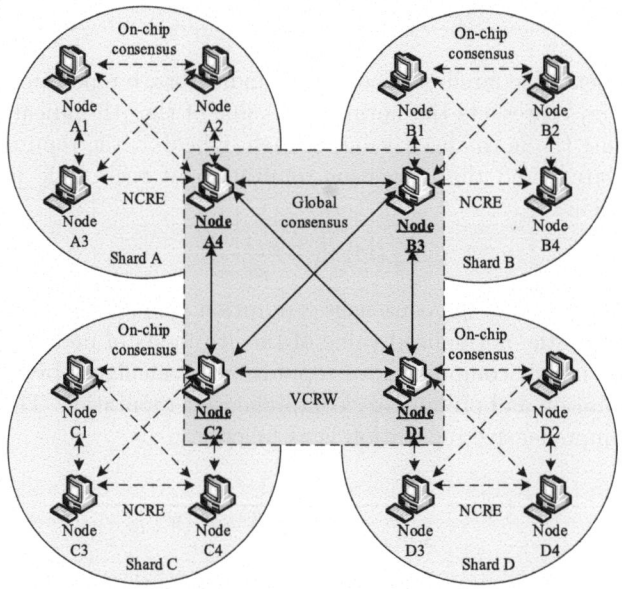

Fig. 4. Voting consensus.

2) **Proposal broadcast and collection.** The leader node of each shard broadcasts its proposal and proposal identifier to the leaders of other shards. At the same time, it collects proposals from other shard leaders and processes them for the voting phase.

3) **Reputation weight calculation.** According to the constructed node reputation comprehensive evaluation model, the comprehensive reputation value of each shard leader node can be obtained, and the weight of each node in the voting can be calculated by the following formula:

$$w_i = \frac{r_i}{\sum_{j-1}^{n} r_j} \tag{11}$$

where w_i represents the voting weight of node i, r_i is the reputation score of node i, and n represents the total number of leader nodes.

4) **Voting execution and aggregation.** Each leader validates the proposal it receives, evaluates the proposal, and votes on it. If the following expression is satisfied, then the proposal is approved:

$$sum\,(Vote_i \times w_i) > Threshold \tag{12}$$

where $Vote_i$ is the vote of node i on a proposal (1 means yes, 0 means no), and $Threshold$ is the minimum weighted proportion of votes needed for the proposal to pass, and the threshold is set to $2/3$. If the above equation does not pass, the progress will repeat.

5) **Global state update and broadcast.** Once a proposal is approved, each shard leader sends the proposal to the client, and when the client receives more than $2/3$ of the number of leaders, it can process the proposal for this transaction. At this point, the global state is updated, and the shard leader will broadcast the approved proposals to all shards to ensure that each node is in sync with the latest global state.

4   Experimental Evaluation

As a prominent Byzantine consensus algorithm, PBFT serves as a valuable baseline due to its credibility. To comprehensively evaluate the performance of CMDS, we compare the performance of CMDS, PBFT, and RARC [19] in terms of throughput and measured the average processing time per transaction. The experimental settings are as follows: different network node numbers (40, 60, 80, 100, and 120) and different batch sizes (200, 400, 600, or 800 transactions).

4.1   Throughput

In blockchain systems, throughput refers to the number of transactions successfully processed and confirmed by the system per time slot. This metric reflects the efficiency of a blockchain system in processing transaction data.

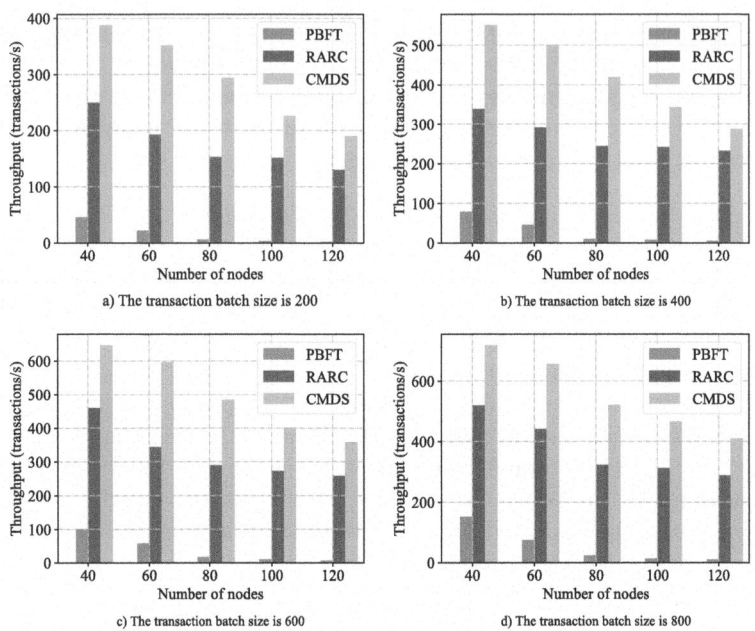

Fig. 5. Throughput comparisons of the different consensus mechanisms.

To measure the throughput of CMDS, we conduct experiments with different nodes as well as with different batch size Settings. In the throughput measurement experiments, the number of shards Sc is set to 4. Figure 5 illustrates the throughput of CMDS, RARC as well as PBFT under different experimental conditions. It can be seen from the figure that, with the increase of the number of nodes, the throughput of the three consensus mechanisms shows a downward trend, but CMDS has the best throughput under the condition of more nodes. When the batch size is 800, the throughput of CMDS and RARC are 409.557 transactions/s and 287.563 transactions/s respectively. When the number of nodes is 120, the throughput of CMDS is 42.42% higher than that of RARC. From the above analysis, it can be seen that CMDS can significantly improve the efficiency of the blockchain system by processing transactions in parallel, which is more suitable for application scenarios with large-scale nodes and massive transactions.

4.2   Average Processing Time Per Transaction

The Average Processing Time Per Transaction (APTPT) is a key indicator of the processing efficiency of a blockchain system. Similar to consensus latency, the lower APTPT, the more efficient the blockchain system is in processing transactions.

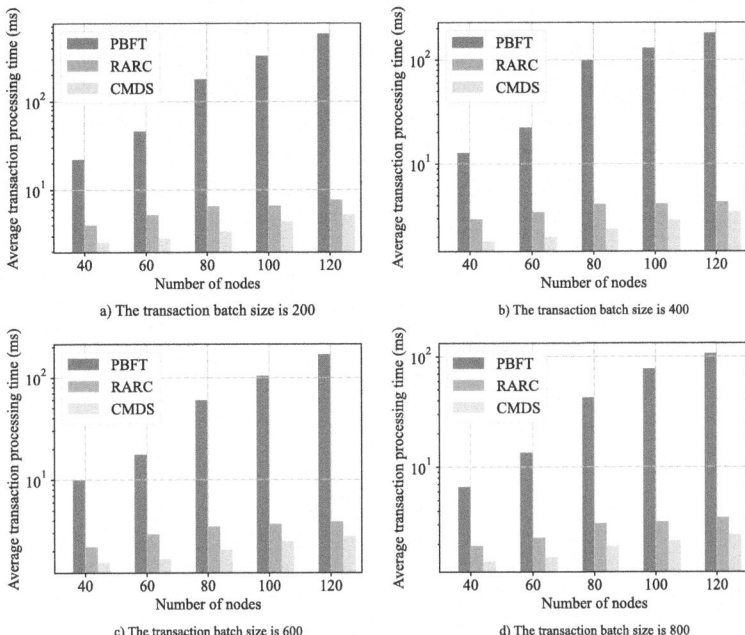

Fig. 6. Comparisons of the average processing time per transaction with different consensus mechanisms.

In order to evaluate the processing efficiency of different blockchain consensus mechanisms, we conduct the experiments measuring the average processing time per transaction under different batch sizes (200, 400, 600, 800) and different numbers of nodes. The experimental results are shown in Fig. 6. From the figure, it can be seen that the APTPT increases for all three consensus mechanisms as the number of nodes increases, but the processing time increases more slowly for CMDS compared with PBFT and RARC. This demonstrates that CMDS improves the transaction processing efficiency of the blockchain system by processing transactions in parallel through the sharding mechanism. When the number of nodes is 120 and the transaction batch size is 200, the APTPT of CMDS is 5.264 ms, while the APTPT of RARC is 7.703 ms, and the APTPT of CMDS is reduced by 31.66% compared with that of RARC, which can be seen from the above analysis that CMDS significantly improves the performance of blockchain system and is suitable for large-scale blockchain systems.

5   Conclusion

The PBFT consensus mechanism's limited ability to process transactions in parallel motivates the introduction of a novel consensus mechanism CMDS based on dynamic sharding. Our proposed CMDS initially constructs a node dynamic shard model using the consistent hash algorithm to evenly distribute nodes across shards. For CMDS, we further proposed a voting consensus mechanism based on reputation weight for global data synchronization. Through simulation experiments, we demonstrated that CMDS significantly enhances the blockchain system's capacity for parallel transaction processing, thereby increasing its throughput and overall performance.

Acknowledgments. This research is supported by the National Natural Science Foundation of China (Nos. U23B2004, 62072056, 62473146), the Hunan Provincial Natural Science Foundation Key Program (No. 2024JJ3017), the Hunan Provincial Key Research and Development Program (Nos. 2024JK2005, 2022GK2019, 2022SK2107), the Natural Science Foundation of Hunan Province (No. 2023JJ30054), and the Research Foundation of Education Bureau of Hunan Province (No. 23B0303).

References

1. Palacios, R.C., Sánchez-Gordón, M., Arias-Aranda, D.: A critical review on blockchain assessment initiatives: a technology evolution viewpoint. J. Softw. Evol. Process. **32**(11) (2020)
2. Liu, H., Zhang, P., Pu, G., Yang, T., Maharjan, S., Zhang, Y.: Blockchain empowered cooperative authentication with data traceability in vehicular edge computing. IEEE Trans. Veh. Technol. **69**(4), 4221–4232 (2020)
3. Yang, W., Wang, Z., Zhou, X., Yao, J.: The optimisation research of Blockchain application in the financial institution-dominated supply chain finance system. Int. J. Prod. Res. **61**(11), 3735–3755 (2023)
4. Sun, W., et al.: Data privacy protection and sharing in smart grid based on blockchain technology. In: ICCSIE, pp. 350–355 (2023)
5. Enescu, F.-M., Bizon, N., Stirbu, C.: Smart Energy Grids used in irrigation systems using the blockchain applications. In: ECAI, pp. 1–6 (2019)
6. Das, D., Banerjee, S., Chatterjee, P., Ghosh, U., Biswas, U.: Blockchain for intelligent transportation systems: applications, challenges, and opportunities. IEEE Internet Things J. **10**(21), 18961–18970 (2023)
7. Astarita, V., Giofrè, V.P., Mirabelli, G., Solina, V.: A review of blockchain-based systems in transportation. Inf. **11**(1), 21 (2020)
8. Mathur, S., Kalla, A., Gür, G., Bohra, M.K., Liyanage, M.: A survey on role of blockchain for IoT: applications and technical aspects. Comput. Networks **227**, 109726 (2023)
9. Kelkar, M., Zhang, F., Goldfeder, S., Juels, A.: Order-fairness for byzantine consensus. In: CRYPTO (3), pp. 451–480 (2020)
10. Tian, J., Tian, J., Hongwei, X.: TSBFT: a scalable and efficient leaderless byzantine consensus for consortium blockchain. Comput. Netw. **222**, 109541 (2023)
11. Alqahtani, S., Demirbas, M.: Bottlenecks in blockchain consensus protocols. In: COINS, pp. 1–8 (2021)
12. Gai, F., Niu, J., Beschastnikh, I., Feng, C., Wang, S.: Scaling blockchain consensus via a robust shared mempool. In: ICDE, pp. 530–543 (2023)
13. Deng, X., Li, K., Wang, Z., Liu, H., Leng, J.: A novel consensus algorithm based on segmented DAG and BP neural network for consortium blockchain. Secur. Commun. Netw. **2022** (2022). https://doi.org/10.1155/2022/1060765

14. Swathi, P., Venkatesan, M.: Scalability improvement and analysis of permissioned-blockchain. ICT Express **7**(3), 283–289 (2021)
15. Fu, X., Wang, H., Shi, P., Ma, X., Zhang, X.: TeeGraph: trusted execution environment and directed acyclic graph-based consensus algorithm for IoT blockchains. Sci. China Inf. Sci. **65**(3) (2022)
16. Shen, T., Li, T., Zhuo, Yu., Bai, F., Zhang, C.: GT-NRSM: efficient and scalable sharding consensus mechanism for consortium blockchain. J. Supercomput. **79**(17), 20041–20075 (2023)
17. Xu, G., et al.: SG-PBFT: a secure and highly efficient distributed blockchain PBFT consensus algorithm for intelligent Internet of vehicles. J. Parallel Distrib. Comput. **164**, 1–11 (2022)
18. Cheng, F., et al.: SharDAG: scaling DAG-based blockchains via adaptive sharding. In: ICDE, pp. 2068–2081 (2024)
19. Zhang, J., Sun, Y., Zhang, Z., Ren, W., Luo, L.: A reputation-aware randomization consensus algorithm for performance optimization in blockchain systems. In: CSCWD, pp. 1615–1620 (2024)

AsymFB: Accelerating LLM Training Through Asymmetric Model Parallelism

Jiawei Zhang[1,2], En Shao[1,2(✉)], Leping Wang[1], Guangming Tan[1,2], and Ninghui Sun[1,2]

[1] Institution of Computing Technology, Chinese Academy of Sciences, Beijing, China
{zhangjiawei21b,shaoen,wangleping,tgm,snh}@ict.ac.cn
[2] University of Chinese Academy of Sciences, Beijing, China

Abstract. Transformer-based large language models (LLMs) have become a dominant force in natural language processing, advancing both research and industry. As model sizes have grown from billions to hundreds of billions of parameters, training them on a single GPU is no longer feasible, making distributed training essential. Existing distributed training methods partition models into non-overlapping segments of equal-size to cut memory usage on each device, but this creates cross-device data dependencies. These dependencies lead to delays and reduced throughput, particularly during the forward phase. This paper introduces AsymFB, a novel model parallelism algorithm designed to address these limitations. By adopting an asymmetric partitioning approach, AsymFB assigns varying numbers of devices to different training phases—forward, recompute, and backward—optimizing resource allocation and minimizing performance penalties. Our approach demonstrates up to a 1.25× speedup compared to traditional methods, significantly improving the efficiency of training large-scale LLMs and mitigating common performance bottlenecks.

Keywords: LLM training · model parallelism · throughput

1 Introduction

Transformer-based large language models (LLMs) have become dominant in natural language processing, showing impressive effectiveness in both research and industry [4,16,19,23]. Recently, their parameter counts have surged from billions to hundreds of billions, making single-GPU training infeasible. This has led to the development of various parallelism methods [6,7,9,12,13,17,18,21,22] for distributed training across multiple GPUs.

Current LLM training systems use various model parallelism strategies that partition models into non-overlapping, equal-sized sets to lower per-device memory needs during the backward phase. However, this approach creates cross-device data dependencies during the forward phase, leading to performance penalties like delays from data fetching and waiting for inputs. These issues, known as non-overlapping communication and bubbling, can cause GPU under-utilization and reduced throughput.

We introduce AsymFB, a new model parallelism algorithm designed to overcome the limitations of existing methods. Our approach optimizes the trade-off between performance penalties by differentiating the forward, recompute, and backward phases of training. Each phase is assigned to varying numbers of devices in asymmetric patterns to meet specific resource and locality needs. AsymFB achieves up to 1.25× speedup over baseline methods by recalibrating this trade-off. Below, we outline three key insights into AsymFB.

- Concentrate on locality along critical path: Cross-device data dependencies impact training efficiency differently across phases, most significantly during the forward phase. By reorganizing the training flow and shifting dependencies from critical to non-critical paths, we can create more opportunities for overlapping operations.
- Asymmetric duplication brings flexibility: Model parallelism methods need specific data layouts. By duplicating the model with different layouts, the training process can adaptively utilize various parallelism strategies based on resource availability and locality requirements during training.
- Recomputation allows separation: Recomputation [2] is crucial for managing out-of-memory (OOM) errors in LLMs, as it reduces the memory footprint of reused data across phases. This allows for the separation and flexible scheduling of training phases.

Our approach features two main innovations. First, a computation scheduler orchestrates different phases of the training process—forward, recomputation, and backward—by reorganizing them to minimize unnecessary data transfers and remote fetches along critical path. Second, a data manager oversees the transfer of activation data and model weights based on data dependencies. This manager strategically schedules these transfers, as most are non-blocking and can occur at any point within an extended time window.

We summarize our contributions as follows:

- A new model parallelism method for LLM training (Sect. 3), which explores parallelizing different phases of the training process and enhances locality on critical path.
- A computation scheduler (Sect. 4) and a data manager (Sect. 5), which work together to minimize idle periods and overlap computation with communication.
- An implementation within the widely adopted LLM training framework Megatron-LM, along with an evaluation across various workloads that highlights the advantages of AsymFB (Sect. 6).

We implemented our method on the versatile Megatron-LM framework, using additional primitives from torch.distributed with PyTorch 1.13 [14]. The evaluation was conducted on 4 Nvidia V100 GPUs with a PCIe 3.0 bus, covering LLM training workloads such as OPT, LLaMA, and Bloom.

2   Background

2.1   LLM Training and Activation Recomputation.

The exponential increase in LLM parameter scale has heightened hardware resource demands, especially for training due to excessive activation memory. Activation recomputation [2] addresses this by reducing activation memory at the cost of extra computation. For LLMs, it involves storing only the inputs of each transformer layer and recomputing intermediate activations before the backward phase, making it widely adopted in training systems [11,18].

2.2   Model Parallelism

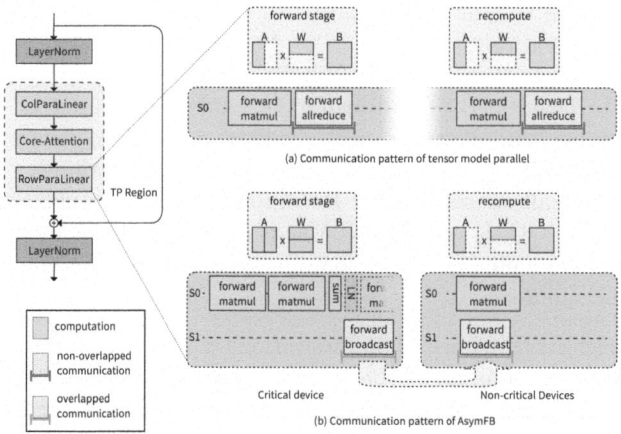

Fig. 1. the computation and communication pattern of tensor model parallelism and AsymFB.

Training large LLMs on a single GPU is impractical due to memory and time constraints. Model parallelism methods partition the model into non-overlapping, equal-sized segments distributed across devices, determining the execution patterns for all training phases, including forward, backward, initialization, and finalization, regardless of resource requirements.

Tensor model parallelism [18,21,22] applies to matrix multiplication between activation tensors and model weights. Tensor model parallelism shards and distributes model weight across devices. When result tensor of multiplication is replicated, communication is required to collect result from different devices.

Pipeline model parallelism [6,7,12,13,15] divides the model into stages, each containing an equal number of consecutive layers. During the forward phase, each stage depends on the output of the previous one, while in the backward phase, stages rely on the gradients of the inputs in reverse order. This approach allows different stages to be executed in parallel, operating in a pipeline manner.

2.3   Challenges of Model Parallelism

Challenges in model parallelism arise from cross-device data dependencies on the critical path. Dividing the model into non-overlapping sets leads to performance penalties as devices wait for each other. Below, we outline specific instances of these data dependencies.

Challenge 1. Collective Communication in Tensor Model Parallel. Figure 1-(a) illustrates tensor model parallelism in Megatron-LM. During the forward and recompute phases of the self-attention layer, communication occurs after row-parallel matrix multiplication, affecting the critical path. The multi-layer perceptron (MLP) faces similar challenges with this parallel strategy.

Challenge 2. Warmup and Cooldown in Pipeline Parallel. In pipeline model parallelism, stages are interdependent, necessitating synchronization during warm-up and cool-down phases. With each stage having the same number of layers and no overlap, bubble time remains uniform across devices. This rigid partitioning leads to a higher bubble rate and increased time penalties.

This paper explores solutions to consolidate the forward phase on a single device to minimize costly communication on critical paths, while distributing other phases across more devices for greater parallelism.

3   Overview of AsymFB

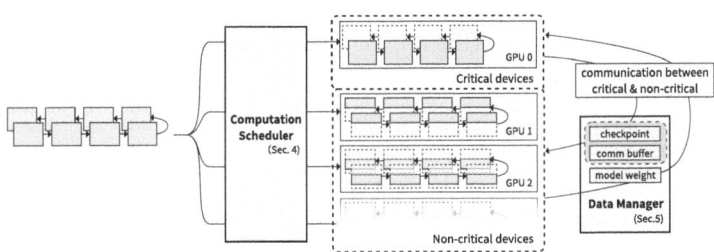

Fig. 2. Research content overview of AsymFB.

Figure 2 illustrates AsymFB, which includes a computation scheduler and a data manager. These components collaborate to minimize remote data fetching along the critical path. AsymFB distinguishes between locality-sensitive and other phases, scheduling them on different devices separately, as defined below.

Definition. A **critical phase** is a training phase where communication cannot be overlapped with computation in tensor model parallelism. A **critical device** is a device used specially for critical phases execution in AsymFB.

The computation scheduler (Sect. 4) assigns different phases (forward, recomputation, and backward) to specific device groups. We use asymmetric model duplication and schedule these phases in varied patterns, allowing the two groups to operate in parallel using a pipeline approach.

The data manager (Sect. 5) manages data storage and transfers between device groups, considering activation recomputation. It identifies reused activation data and model weights, temporarily storing them in a buffer for transfer. Non-blocking communications are initiated to meet data dependency deadlines.

4   AsymFB Computation Scheduling

In this section, we propose a computational scheduler that assigns different phases of the training process to two device groups. Model parameters are duplicated on two device groups asymmetrically to support different parallel methods used for different phases. We further utilize the asymmetric duplication to flexibly reduce warm-up/cool-down bubbles.

4.1   Model Modification

To enable flexible scheduling, AsymFB modifies the execution pattern of LLM models, as illustrated in Fig. 1-(b). Model parameters are duplicated and distributed across two device groups. On non-critical devices, AsymFB shards the model following tensor model parallelism. On the critical device, weight tensors are divided into N parts corresponding to N non-critical devices. Weights are sharded along the output direction for column parallelism and along the input direction for row parallelism. Different shards are multiplied with corresponding data tensors sequentially. In row parallelism, results are aggregated locally after the N sharded matrix multiplications, avoiding the all-reduce method used in tensor model parallelism.

4.2   Pipelined Forward and Backward

As shown in Fig. 3, data dependency exists between the forward phase on the critical device and the recompute phase on non-critical devices, requiring serial execution on two device groups. AsymFB divides input data into multiple chunks, feeding them to the model sequentially, similar to pipeline parallelism. However, unlike traditional pipeline parallelism, each data chunk is processed continuously on each device, allowing AsymFB to implement a direct pipeline approach without interleaving.

4.3   Flexibly Schedule Computation with Asymmetric Duplication

AsymFB uses varying numbers of critical and non-critical devices in a pipeline. During the warmup phase, only critical devices are utilized, causing non-critical devices to idle and create extra bubbling. To enhance resource utilization,

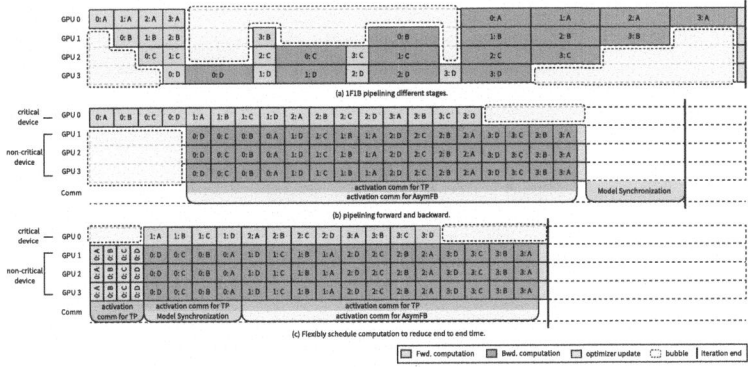

Fig. 3. the scheduling pattern of forward and backward in AsymFB.

AsymFB flexibly schedules the forward phase of the warmup stage on non-critical devices, as shown in Fig. 3. This modified warmup phase operates similarly to tensor model parallelism, leveraging asymmetric duplication to reduce bubble rates. Additionally, activation tensors from the first data chunk are generated on non-critical devices during this phase, allowing recomputation without extra data transfer and improving data locality.

4.4   Performance Modeling

The longest stage of a pipeline dictates the overall performance of the schedule. Therefore, we carefully select the number of devices to balance the length of the stages. The computational workload for the forward phase equals to that of the recompute phase and half that of the backward phase. As a result, non-critical devices handle three times the computation of critical devices. We recommend a 3:1 ratio between the two device groups to maintain balanced stages.

5   AsymFB Data Managing

The recomputation technique significantly alters the pattern of data reuse during LLM training. AsymFB leverages this technique by carefully managing the remote fetching of reused data. This data fetching overlaps with computations and is interleaved to minimize contention.

5.1   Checkpoint Data Managing

The recomputation technique preserves crucial activation tensors as checkpoints during the forward phase while temporarily discarding other activation tensors. Abandoned tensors are recomputed in the recompute phase using these checkpoints. See Fig. 4-(a), in AsymFB, checkpoints are generated on critical devices

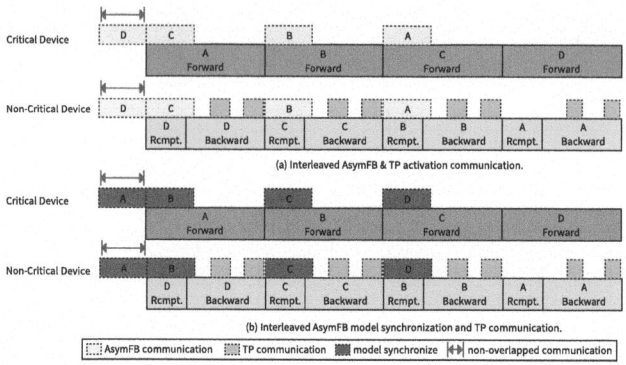

Fig. 4. Data managing pattern in AsymFB.

and utilized by non-critical devices during recomputation. This data dependency necessitates periodic broadcasting of each checkpoint tensor to non-critical devices. AsymFB transmits checkpoints in reverse order of layers, ensuring they are consumed promptly after being sent.

5.2   Intermediate Tensor Data Managing

A complete re-execution between two checkpoints is conveyed during recomputation, including communication. To prevent communication from blocking computation, AsymFB saves intermediate result tensors from these communications during the forward process and sends them to non-critical devices. This approach replaces blocking communications during the recompute phase with non-blocking broadcasts. AsymFB transmits intermediate tensors in reverse order of layers, following the same rationale as for checkpoints.

5.3   Update Weight Data Managing

Model weights on non-critical devices are updated each cycle, while those on critical devices are not. As shown in Fig. 4-(b), the consistency requirement necessitates periodically sending weight tensors from non-critical devices to the critical device. AsymFB's data management overlaps this sending process with the first chunk of the critical device and the second chunk of the non-critical device. The collaboration between data management and computation scheduling (Sect. 4.3) eliminates interference between weight updating and the broadcasting of checkpoints and intermediate tensors. AsymFB transmits the updated weights in the forward order of layers.

6   Evaluation

In this section, we evaluate the overall throughput of AsymFB and compare it with baseline model parallelism approaches. Besides, in order to explain the effectiveness of this method, we analyze the details of latency breakdown in LLM training. Subsequently, an ablation study was conducted to verify the effectiveness of different components of the method.

6.1 Experiment Setup

Table 1. Different model hyper-parameters used for evaluation.

	#Layers	#Heads	Hidden Size	GBS	LBS
OPT-6.7B*	16	36	4608	8	2
LLaMA-7B*	12	36	4608		
Bloom-7B*	8	36	4608		
OPT-13B*	8	48	6144		
OPT-30B*	4	60	7680		

[1]GBS & LBS stand for global/local batch size.

Software Implementation. We implement AsymFB based on the widely adopted LLM training framework Megatron-LM [18]. Our wheel execute with Pytorch 1.13 [14], Python 3.10 and CUDA 11.7.

Hardware Platform. We evaluate AsymFB on a server with 4 Nvidia V100-PCIE 32GB GPUs and Intel Xeon Gold 6330 56-core CPU. The GPUs connect to each other with PCIe 3.0 ×16.

Workload. As shown in Table 1, we evaluate AsymFB on 5 different large language models, varying in model types and sizes. We modified the hidden_size and reduced the number of layers for each model to ensure that the models can be equally divided to different number of GPUs and fit in GPU memory. We set global batch size to 8 and split it into four chunks with a micro batch size of 2.

Baselines. We choose three different Baselines, 1F1B pipeline model parallelism (PP), Megatron-LM's tensor model parallelism (TP), and Megatron-LM's TP+PP. The mathematical form of AsymFB training on N devices is strictly equivalent to tensor model parallel training on $N-1$ devices, so we focus only on the evaluation of throughput.

6.2 Overall Performance

We train different LLMs under the same conditions and compare AsymFB with the results of each baseline. Due to training on 4 GPUs, Megatron-TP+PP selected only tensor model parallelism size 2 and pipeline model parallelism size 2. We use iteration per second to represent throughput.

Figure 5-(a) shows the overall performance during training. Among them, when training Bloom-7B using 1F1B pipeline parallelism causes out-of-memory.

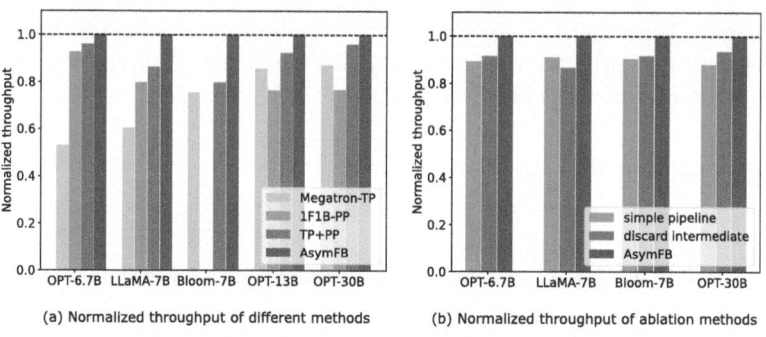

(a) Normalized throughput of different methods   (b) Normalized throughput of ablation methods

Fig. 5. Normalized Overall throughput comparison.

AsymFB outperformed all baselines in all other testcases. The performance gain of AsymFB varies greatly across different models, reaching 1.04–1.26× over the best baseline when the model parameter scale is around 7B. When fixing the model to be OPT and changing the model size, the performance gain of AsymFB relative to Megatron-TP+PP reaches 1.04–1.08×. It is worth noting that the performance ratio of TP and PP fluctuates greatly when the model size changes, but their throughput are smaller than AsymFB in the whole range, which proves the robustness of AsymFB's performance.

6.3   Detailed Performance

Table 2. breakdown of performance critical path for each system.

	Method	non-overlapping Fwd. comm ratio	non-overlapping Bwd. comm ratio	bubble rate	utilization
OPT-6.7B	Ours	15.8%	34.2%	8.0%	64.7%
	Megatron-TP	62.4%	53.0%	0	44.6%
	1F1B-PP	<1%	<1%	42.0%	58.0%
	TP+PP	36.2%	19.1%	22.2%	59.1%
OPT-30B	Ours	10.0%	31.5%	11.3%	63.7%
	Megatron-TP	58.4%	45.6%	0	49.9%
	1F1B-PP	3.1%	1.2%	51.45%	47.7%
	TP+PP	31.4%	13.7%	30.4%	56.3%

We further analyze the performance gain of AsymFB by comparing it with other baselines on OPT-6.7B and OPT-30B in the details of latency breakdown. Latency of an LLM training process is decomposed into computation time, non-overlapping communication time and scheduling bubble time. Computation time and non-overlapping communication time are additionally analyzed in forward, recompute and backward phases. Table 2 exhibits the numerical result of the evaluation. Non-overlapping Fwd./Bwd. comm ratio represents the average ratio of non-overlapping communication cost in forward phase or recomputation and backward phase combined.

As in the table, AsymFB's performance gain comes from better tradeoff between communication time and scheduling bubbles. Taking OPT-6.7B as an example, AsymFB reduces the bubble rate from 42.0% to 8.0% compared to pipeline model parallelism. Besides, compared to the tensor model parallelism, AsymFB greatly reduces idle due to communication by overlapping computation and communication, especially for forward phase. Megatron-TP+PP also makes a tradeoff between communication and bubbles, but it fails to do overlapping and losses optimization opportunity. When model size increase to OPT-30B, proportion of non-overlapping communication in training process decreases. This is because larger hidden size brings higher ratio between computation and communication time, and leads to more thorough overlapping.

6.4   Ablation Study

To verify the performance gains from AsymFB's computation scheduler and data manager, we constructed two AsymFB versions: (1) For computation scheduler, simply pipelined forward and backward as in Fig. 3-(b) in the computation scheduler. (2) For data manager, discard all intermediate tensors in Sect. 5.2 and restore all-reduce at recompute phase. We evaluate AsymFB and the two additional versions on testcases to show the effect of these components.

As shown in Fig. 5-(b), AsymFB achieved the best performance on all testcases. A performance improvement of 1.10–1.14× is achieved compared to the first version, and 1.07–1.15× compared to the second version. This proves that both optimization components in AsymFB play a role in improving throughput.

7   Related Work

Pipeline model parallelism [6,7,12,13,15] partitions the model along layers into stages and distribute them across devices. These works focus on reducing bubble rate with intricate scheduling of the model, such as layer slicing [13] or out-of-order kernel execution [15].

Tensor model parallelism [18,21,22] distributes model weights and computation of each layer on different devices and use frequent communication of activation tensors to fulfill data dependency.

ZeRO [17] like distributed data parallel methods shards model weights of each layer on different devices, and collect required parameters with communication before doing computation. Works are done to overlap these communication with computations [1,20].

Hybrid parallel methods [3,10,18] combine data/tensor/pipeline parallel methods and do tradeoffs between the cost of them. Automated optimization systems [5,8,9,24] further formalize the optimization possibilities of each layer as cost model and search space, and use intricate searching algorithms to find the best combination.

8   Conclusion

We propose AsymFB, which accelerates LLM training. This is achieved by asymmetrically duplicating the model and co-designing computation and data scheduling. AsymFB achieves up to 1.25× speedup compared to state-of-art model parallelism methods and proved robust in different model type and scale.

Acknowledgments. This work was sponsored in part by NKRDP under Grant No.2021YFB0300202, and in part by NSFC under Grant No.62102396, Beijing Nova Program under Grant No.Z211100002121143,20220484217, Youth Innovation Promotion Association of Chinese Academy of Sciences under Grant No.2021099, CCF-Ant Research Fund CCF-AFSGRF under Grant No.20230207, Pilotfor Major Scientific Research Facility of Jiangsu Province of China under Grant No.BM2021800. Supported by the Innovation Funding of ICT, CAS under Grant No. E461030

References

1. Chen, C., et al.: Centauri: enabling efficient scheduling for communication-computation overlap in large model training via communication partitioning. In: Proceedings of the 29th ACM International Conference on Architectural Support for Programming Languages and Operating Systems, vol. 3, pp. 178–191 (2024)
2. Chen, T., Xu, B., Zhang, C., Guestrin, C.: Training deep nets with sublinear memory cost. arXiv preprint arXiv:1604.06174 (2016)
3. Cheng, Y., et al.: Accelerating end-to-end deep learning workflow with codesign of data preprocessing and scheduling. IEEE Trans. Parallel Distrib. Syst. **32**(7), 1802–1814 (2020)
4. Chowdhery, A., et al.: PaLM: scaling language modeling with pathways. J. Mach. Learn. Res. **24**(240), 1–113 (2023)
5. Fan, S., et al.: DAPPLE: a pipelined data parallel approach for training large models. In: Proceedings of the 26th ACM SIGPLAN Symposium on Principles and Practice of Parallel Programming, pp. 431–445 (2021)
6. He, C., Li, S., Soltanolkotabi, M., Avestimehr, S.: PipeTransformer: automated elastic pipelining for distributed training of transformers. arXiv preprint arXiv:2102.03161 (2021)
7. Huang, Y., et al.: GPipe: efficient training of giant neural networks using pipeline parallelism. In: Advances in Neural Information Processing Systems, vol. 32 (2019)
8. Jia, Z., Lin, S., Qi, C.R., Aiken, A.: Exploring hidden dimensions in accelerating convolutional neural networks. In: International Conference on Machine Learning, pp. 2274–2283. PMLR (2018)
9. Jia, Z., Zaharia, M., Aiken, A.: Beyond data and model parallelism for deep neural networks. Proc. Mach. Learn. Syst. **1**, 1–13 (2019)
10. Korthikanti, V.A., et al.: Reducing activation recomputation in large transformer models. Proc. Mach. Learn. Syst. **5**, 341–353 (2023)

11. Li, F., et al.: Fold3D: rethinking and parallelizing computational and communicational tasks in the training of large DNN models. IEEE Trans. Parallel Distrib. Syst. **34**(5), 1432–1449 (2023)
12. Li, Z., et al.: TeraPipe: token-level pipeline parallelism for training large-scale language models. In: International Conference on Machine Learning, pp. 6543–6552. PMLR (2021)
13. Narayanan, D., et al.: PipeDream: generalized pipeline parallelism for DNN training. In: Proceedings of the 27th ACM Symposium on Operating Systems Principles, pp. 1–15 (2019)
14. Paszke, A., et al.: PyTorch: an imperative style, high-performance deep learning library. In: Advances in Neural Information Processing Systems, vol. 32 (2019)
15. Qi, P., Wan, X., Huang, G., Lin, M.: Zero bubble pipeline parallelism. arXiv preprint arXiv:2401.10241 (2023)
16. Radford, A., et al.: Language models are unsupervised multitask learners. OpenAI blog **1**(8), 9 (2019)
17. Rajbhandari, S., Rasley, J., Ruwase, O., He, Y.: ZeRO: memory optimizations toward training trillion parameter models. In: SC20: International Conference for High Performance Computing, Networking, Storage and Analysis, pp. 1–16. IEEE (2020)
18. Shoeybi, M., Patwary, M., Puri, R., LeGresley, P., Casper, J., Catanzaro, B.: Megatron-LM: training multi-billion parameter language models using model parallelism. arXiv preprint arXiv:1909.08053 (2019)
19. Touvron, H., et al.: LLaMA: open and efficient foundation language models. arXiv preprint arXiv:2302.13971 (2023)
20. Wang, H., Wang, L., Xu, H., Wang, Y., Li, Y., Han, Y.: PrimePar: efficient spatial-temporal tensor partitioning for large transformer model training. In: Proceedings of the 29th ACM International Conference on Architectural Support for Programming Languages and Operating Systems, vol. 3, pp. 801–817 (2024)
21. Xu, Y., et al.: GSPMD: general and scalable parallelization for ML computation graphs. arXiv preprint arXiv:2105.04663 (2021)
22. Yuan, J., et al.: OneFlow: redesign the distributed deep learning framework from scratch. arXiv preprint arXiv:2110.15032 (2021)
23. Zhang, S., et al.: OPT: open pre-trained transformer language models. arXiv preprint arXiv:2205.01068 (2022)
24. Zheng, L., et al.: Alpa: automating inter-and {intra-operator} parallelism for distributed deep learning. In: 16th USENIX Symposium on Operating Systems Design and Implementation (OSDI 22), pp. 559–578 (2022)

DaCP: Accelerating Synchronization-Free SpTRSV via GPU-Friendly Data Communication and Parallelism Strategies

Mingfeng Guo[1], Liang Deng[1(✉)], Zhe Dai[1], Ruitian Li[1,2], Gaofeng Lin[1], and Jie Liu[2]

[1] Computational Aerodynamics Institute, China Aerodynamics Research and Development Center, Mianyang, China
{dengliang11,daizhe17}@nudt.edu.cn
[2] Science and Technology on Parallel and Distributed Processing Laboratory, National University of Defense Technology, Changsha, China
liujie@nudt.edu.cn

Abstract. Sparse triangular solve (SpTRSV) is a vital component in various scientific applications, and numerous GPU-based SpTRSV algorithms have been proposed. Synchronization-free SpTRSV is currently the mainstream algorithm on GPU due to its short preprocessing time and outstanding performance. However, we observed that this algorithm still has two performance bottlenecks. Firstly, the thread-level parallel mode can introduce to thread divergence issues within GPU warps during the writing phase. Secondly, the thread-level and warp-level fusion mode may struggles to fully exploit GPU resources due to suboptimal mapping relationships between rows and threads. To address these issues, this paper proposes DaCPSpTRSV, a new synchronization-free algorithm with GPU-friendly data communication and parallelism strategies. Specifically, we first develop a fast-forward thread-level approach, incorporating an efficient global memory access pattern and a light-weight dependency control mechanism, to optimize data communication and alleviate thread divergence. A fine-grained fusion strategy is then proposed to maximize GPU parallelism by adaptively selecting the suitable thread-level or warp-level modes. Moreover, the commonly-used compressed sparse row (CSR) format is employed in our DaCPSpTRSV, enhancing the versatility of our algorithm. We evaluate our approach using 245 matrices from the SuiteSparse Matrix Collection on two NVIDIA GPUs, demonstrating speedup ratios of up to 4.77×, 4.94×, 1.67×, and 1.62× compared to cuSPARSE, Sync-Free, CapelliniSpTRSV, and YuenyeungSpTRSV, respectively. The project is open-sourced at https://github.com/gmfff12334/DaCP.

Keywords: Synchronization-free · SpTRSV · GPU · CSR

© IFIP International Federation for Information Processing 2025
Published by Springer Nature Switzerland AG 2025
X. Chen et al. (Eds.): NPC 2024, LNCS 15527, pp. 28–40, 2025.
https://doi.org/10.1007/978-981-96-2830-8_3

1   Introduction

The sparse triangular solve (SpTRSV) operation is a crucial component in solving sparse matrix linear systems, typically expressed as $Lx = b$. Here, L represents a lower triangular sparse matrix, b is a dense matrix vector, and x is the target vector that needs to be solved. This operation holds significant importance across various scientific and engineering domains, including the least squares method [1], direct methods [2] and sparse iterative solvers [3]. Owing to its high parallel computing capabilities and low energy consumption, the GPU has played a significant role in many sparse matrix operations [4–6], including SpTRSV [8,9]. However, implementing an efficient SpTRSV algorithm remains challenging due to inherent internal data dependencies.

To effectively parallelize SpTRSV on GPU, researchers commonly address the dependency problem during the preprocessing stage. Anderson and Saad [7] introduced the level-set method, which divides components of the same level into a set. Although the level-set method allows components in the same set to be processed in parallel, preprocessing usually takes a lot of time. In addition, due to the dependencies between different sets, the cost of global synchronization will also increase. To tackle the preprocessing and synchronization challenges, Liu [8] proposed a synchronization-free SpTRSV algorithm. This method resolves the high global synchronization overhead through atomic operations on the GPU, eliminating the need for excessive preprocessing operations. Building on this, Su et al. introduced CapelliniSpTRSV [10] and YuenyeungSpTRSV [11], optimizing the synchronization-free SpTRSV algorithm by integrating thread-level and warp-level parallel modes. It processes rows with a substantial number of non-zero elements at the warp-level, while handling rows with a smaller number of non-zero elements at the thread-level. Nowadays, YuenyeungSpTRSV is the state-of-the-art SpTRSV algorithm, which outperforms other algorithms on a wide range of workloads. However, this algorithm still suffers from unreasonable thread allocation and requires addressing the following two issues. First, a significant number of thread divergences arises in thread-level parallel mode, wherein each thread in a warp processes different rows. Second, selecting between warp-level or thread-level modes based on the average number of non-zero elements in sub-matrix may prevent some rows from achieving optimal parallelism.

To address the above issues, we propose DaCPSpTRSV, a new synchronization-free algorithm with GPU-friendly data communication and parallelism strategies. In particular, we initially design a fast-forward thread-level approach, integrating an efficient global memory access pattern and a lightweight dependency control mechanism, to enhance data communication efficiency and mitigate the effects of thread divergence. Subsequently, DaCPSpTRSV introduces a fine-grained strategy for selecting either thread-level and warp-level modes to improve data parallelism. Consequently, our DaCPSpTRSV minimizes the performance degradation caused by thread divergence and ensures that each row of the sparse matrix receives sufficient computing resources for parallel computation. Finally, we evaluate DaCPSpTRSV with 245 matrices from the University of SuiteSparse Matrix Collection [12] on NVIDIA V100 and

A100 GPUs, and compare our approach with cuSPARSE [13], Sync-Free [8], CapelliniSpTRSV [10], and YuenyeungSpTRSV [11]. The experimental results demonstrate the superior performance of DaCPSpTRSV, with speedup factors of 4.77×, 4.94×, 1.67×, and 1.62×, respectively, when compared to the aforementioned algorithms. These findings underscore the efficacy of DaCPSpTRSV in outperforming other algorithms.

To summarize our contributions in this paper:

- We present our perspective on existing synchronization-free SpTRSV parallel algorithms and propose DaCPSpTRSV, an efficient CSR-based SpTRSV kernel on GPU.
- We introduce the fast-forward thread-level approach, fine-grained thread-level and warp-level fusion method, which optimize data communication and improve data parallelism, leading to address the performance bottlenecks in previous SpTRSV algorithms.
- We evaluated DaCPSpTRSV using 245 matrices and demonstrated its advantages over the current state-of-the-art SpTRSV solutions.

2   Preliminaries

2.1   Basic SpTRSV

SpTRSV is expressed as $Lx = b$, where L is a sparse matrix, usually stored in compressed sparse row (CSR) format. CSR is the most popular sparse matrix storage format, which uses three arrays to store non-zero elements in the matrix. As shown in Fig. 1, the *row_ptr* indicates the beginning index in the values and column indices arrays for each row. *col_idx* keeps track of the column indices corresponding to the non-zero elements in the values array. *Val* stores the non-zero elements of the matrix in a consecutive manner.

Algorithm 1 presents the serial implementation of CSR-SpTRSV. The solution procedure commences with an iteration through each row of the matrix. Within each row, the algorithm computes the non-zero elements, excluding the last one, and aggregates the results in the variable *left_sum*. This computation involves considering contributions from the previously solved variable x in the same column. Finally, armed with the variables b_i and *left_sum*, the algorithm solves for x_i in the vector.

2.2   Level-Set SpTRSV

Anderson and Saad proposed the level-set method for parallel SpTRSV. The level-set SpTRSV algorithm begins by organizing the non-zero elements of the sparse matrix into levels, ensuring that the elements within the same level can be processed in parallel, then iterates through these levels in a sequential manner. As shown in the Fig. 1, the matrix L is divided into 3 levels. For instance, rows 0, 1 and 6, having no dependencies within level 0, can be caculated concurrently. However, it is crucial to synchronize dependency information between levels, necessitating a sequential execution across levels.

Algorithm 1: Basic CSR-SpTRSV Algorithm

Data: Matrix L,Vector b
Result: Vector x

1 **for** $i = 0$ **to** $m - 1$ **do**
2   **for** $j = row\_ptr[i]$ **to** $row\_ptr[i + 1] - 2$ **do**
3        $\left|$ left_sum[i] $\leftarrow$ left_sum[i] + val[j] * x[col_ind[j]];
4   **end**
5   x[i] $\leftarrow$ (b[i]-left_sum)/val[row_ptr[j+1]-1];
6 **end**

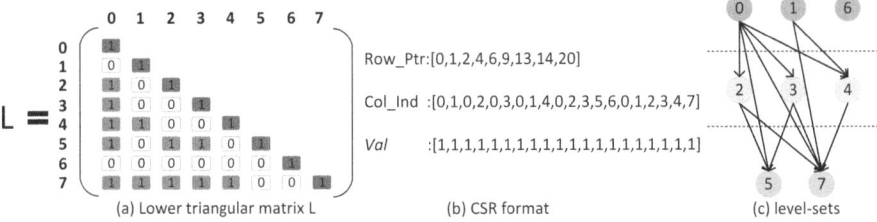

(a) Lower triangular matrix L   (b) CSR format   (c) level-sets

Fig. 1. An example of Lx = b, (a) lower triangular matrix L; (b) CSR representation format of matrix L; (c) dependency between components of the x: there are three level-sets in the L matrix.

2.3 Synchronization-Free SpTRSV

The initial synchronization-free algorithm devised by Liu, named Sync-Free [8], is specifically designed for parallel execution, harnessing the full potential of GPUs. In contrast to conventional SpTRSV methods reliant on global synchronization points, Sync-Free SpTRSV empowers threads to operate independently, thereby substantially mitigating synchronization overhead. Algorithm 2 shows synchronization-free CSR-SpTRSV, the algorithm exploits warp-level parallelism, enabling each GPU warp to process an individual row of the sparse matrix.

Recognizing that warp-level SpTRSV may underutilize GPU resources under certain conditions. Su et al. introduced the thread-level synchronization-free SpTRSV algorithm CapelliniSpTRSV [10], marking a significant breakthrough in the field. This parallel method optimizes GPU utilization, particularly when faced with high average components per level and sparse rows. Furthermore YuenyeungSpTRSV [11], another innovation by Su et al., takes a hybrid approach, combining both thread-level and warp-level synchronization-free SpTRSV algorithms. The outstanding experimental performance of these algorithms solidifies CapelliniSpTRSV and YuenyeungSpTRSV as the state-of-the-art synchronization-free SpTRSV algorithms available.

Algorithm 2: Synchronization-Free CSR-SpTRSV Algorithm

Data: Matrix L,Vector b,Array get_value
Result: Vector x
1 for $i = 0$ to $m - 1$ **in parallel do**
2   for $thread\_id = 0$ to $warp\_size - 1$ **in parallel do**
3   for $j = row\_ptr[i] + thread\_id$ **to** $row\_ptr[i + 1] - 2$ **do**
4   **while** $get\_value[j] \neq true$ **do**
5   __threadfence_block();//busy wait
6   **end**
7   left_sum $\leftarrow$ left_sum + val[j] * x[col_ind[j]];
8              $j + =$ warp_size;
9   **end**
10   **end**
11   __shfl_down_sync(left_sum,offset);
12   **if** $thread\_id==0$ **then**
13   x[i] $\leftarrow$ (b[i]-left_sum)/val[row_ptr[j+1]-1];
14   __threadfence();
15   get_value[i] $\leftarrow$ 1;
16   **end**
17 **end**

2.4 Motivation

The previous synchronization-free SpTRSV algorithm addressed several performance bottlenecks but revealed some shortcomings during implementation with certain matrices. Specifically, 1) Due to the SIMT (single instruction, multiple threads) architecture of GPUs, threads that perform write operations can cause other threads to pause. This issue is especially pronounced in thread-level parallelism, leading to significant thread divergence. 2) When selecting a parallel strategy based on the average number of non-zero elements in sub-matrices, inappropriate parallel granularities are often chosen for certain rows. In experiments, we frequently observe that rows with very few non-zero elements select warp-level parallelism, while rows with many non-zero elements select thread-level parallelism.

We illustrate the workflow of the state-of-the-art synchronization-free algorithm in Fig. 2. In this example, we utilize the L matrix depicted in Fig. 1 as input. Assuming there are 4 warps with 3 threads in each warp, we initially divide the matrix L into 3 sub-matrices. The thread-level and warp-level selection thresholds are set to 3. During parallel processing, distinct stages include reading, writing, and waiting or idle phases. It is evident that there are excessive idle phases in the thread-level parallelism. For instance, within warp1, the write phase of each thread occurs at different intervals. Consequently, while one thread executes a write operation, the remaining threads are forced into suspension, resulting in idle states. Moreover, the parallel strategies selected by rows 5 and 6 in the matrix are not optimal. Row 5, with a large number of non-zero elements, is more suitable for a warp-level strategy, while row 6, with only one non-zero element, should use a thread-level strategy.

Therefore, there is still room for improving the performance of GPU-based synchronization-free parallel algorithms. We can try to reduce thread divergence and improve parallelism in our algorithm design.

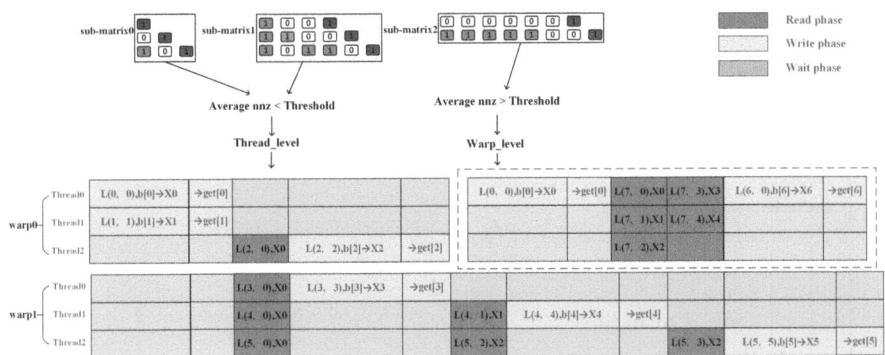

Fig. 2. An example of synchronization-free SpTRSV strategy based on GPU.

3   DaCPSpTRSV

3.1   Fast-Forward Thread-Level Approach Design

First, we aim to optimize memory access during the write phase in the thread-level algorithm. As previously mentioned, in the CapelliniSpTRSV algorithm, each thread computes a row in the sparse matrix, involving primarily two phases: reading and writing. The writing phase involves calculating and setting the relevant components $x[i]$. Specifically, during the writing phase, we need to fetch the right dense vector $b[i]$ and the last element of the row $Val[row\_ptr[i+1]-1]$ from global memory. Since each thread enters the write phase at a different time, multiple global memory access instructions are required to obtain these variables. In our approach, we streamline global memory access for these two variables using a single instruction. To elaborate, the algorithm loads these variables from global memory into registers before read and write operations. This allows each thread in the warp to obtain these two variables in parallel, enhancing the efficiency of global memory access. Furthermore, during the write phase, having direct access to these variables in faster registers, thereby improving the efficiency of write operations. This efficient data communication in memory will decrease the wait time for other threads in the warp, consequently enhancing parallel efficiency.

Secondly, we aim to design a dependency control mechanism that is not only faster but also ensures correct results. In the previous algorithm, after resolving the pertinent component x, the thread was required to set *get_value*

Algorithm 3: Efficient thread-level Synchronization-Free CSR-SpTRSV Algorithm

---

Data: Matrix L, Vector b
Result: Vector x
1 cudaMALLOC(&x,m);
2 cudaMEMSET(x,0xFF,m);
3 **for** $i = 0$ to $m - 1$ **in parallel do**
4 | left_sum ← b[i];
5 | diag ← Val[row_ptr[i+1]-1];
6 | j ← row_ptr[i]; col ←col_ind[j];
7 | **if** $col{=}{=}i$ **then**
8 | | x[i] = left_sum/diag;
9 | **end**
10 | **while** col_ji **do**
11 | | **while** $\_\_double2hiint(x[col]){\neq}(int)0xFFFFFFFF$ **do**
12 | | | left_sum←left_sum-Val[j]*x[col];
13 | | | j++;
14 | | | col←Col_Ind[j];
15 | | **end**
16 | | **if** $col{=}{=}i$ **then**
17 | | | x[i]= left_sum/diag;
18 | | **end**
19 | **end**
20 **end**

---

to 1. Signaling to all other threads that the component has been successfully resolved. This was followed by employing __threadfence()_ to enforce sequentially-consistent ordering on memory accesses. In our method, we have eliminated the setting of *get_value* and removed the __threadfence()_ procedures. Our algorithm directly determines whether the dependency is resolved based on the change in the value of x. Before the calculation begins, we initialize the value of x to its maximum value. During the writing phase, once the algorithm completes its calculations, the relevant value is stored in the corresponding x, indicating that the component x for that row is now available for use by other threads. At the start of the read phase, in line 11 of the algorithm, it will be judged whether x still holds its original value. If not, this indicates that the dependency's value has been resolved. If it does retain the initial value, monitoring changes in its value continues. This rapid data communication in dependent control will further enhance the parallel efficiency between threads.

As depicted in Fig. 3, the advantages of employing our optimization strategy are unmistakable, showcasing a marked improvement over the previous algorithm. While our approach doesn't entirely eradicate thread divergence, we mitigate its impact through refined memory access patterns and enhanced dependency control mechanisms.

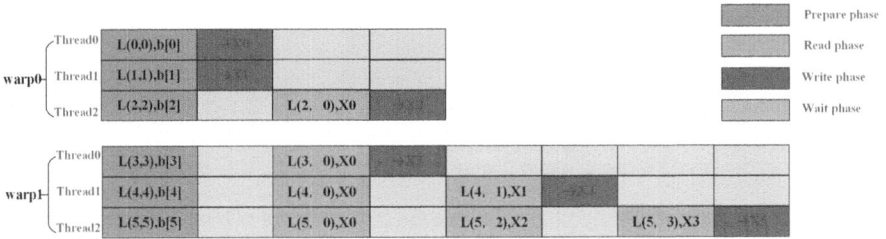

Fig. 3. Benefits of thread-level parallelism after Fast-Forward strategy optimization.

3.2 Fine-Grained Thread-Level and Warp-Level Fusion Method

We have devised a finely-tuned selection strategy to discern whether to employ thread-level or warp-level parallelism. This approach determines the level of parallelism based on the number of non-zero elements in each row. When a row contains a substantial number of non-zero elements, it is assigned to warp-level processing. The remaining consecutive rows are grouped together, forming row groups that are processed using the thread-level algorithm.

We describe the flowchart of Fine-grained thread-level and warp-level fusion strategy in Fig. 4. For long rows, the algorithm directly classifies the row into warp-level parallelism. For short rows, we combine short rows into row groups, and the rows in the row group use thread-level parallelism. There are two types of row groups in the thread-level. The first type selects thread-level processing for a consecutive set of 32 (warp_size) rows. The second type selects thread-level processing for consecutive $ptr(ptr < 32)$ rows. Given that Row i selects warp-level, rows $row[i\text{-}ptr\text{-}1]$ to $row[i\text{-}1]$ constitute a row group. We did a lot of testing on the GPU to determine the threshold. Finally, we found that the threshold setting is still related to the warp size, and set the threshold to $warp\_size/2$.

In our algorithm, the $warp\_row$ array is used to record the index of the starting row being processed by a warp. This array serves a dual purpose: it identifies the first row of the row group at the thread-level and the current row at the warp-level. It is worth mentioning that within the thread-level algorithm, each thread should process rows that fall within the range of $warp\_start[i]$ and $warp\_start[i+1]$. If a thread encounters a row that exceeds this range, it will terminate immediately.

4 Evaluation

4.1 Experimental Setup

We have conducted performance measurements of DaCPSpTRSV and four other SpTRSV algorithms on two NVIDIA GPUs. The platforms evaluated encompass the Volta-based NVIDIA V100, and Ampere-based NVIDIA A100. Baseline methods analyzed include the NVIDIA cuSPARSE library v11.4, classic synchronization-free SpTRSV, as well as optimized Synchronization-Free CapelliniSpTRSV and YuenyeungSpTRSV algorithms.

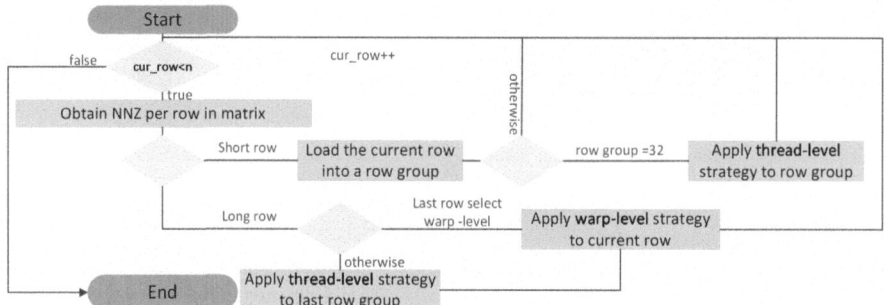

Fig. 4. Flowchart of the Fine-grained thread-level and warp-level fusion strategy.

We selected 245 sparse matrices from the SuiteSparse Matrix Collection [12], which have been used in the experiments of CapelliniSpTRSV and Yuenye-ungSpTRSV. These matrices were selected to represent diverse fields, including graphics applications, circuit simulation, and more. The matrix rows (n) ranged from 25,605 to 55,042,369, with non-zero elements (nnz) varying from 103,167 to 113,651,169, and levels spanned from 1 to 4,283.

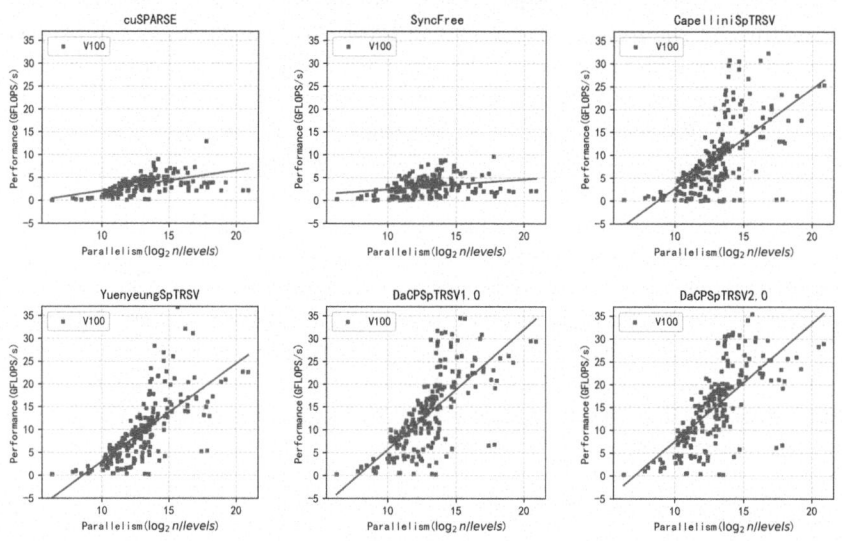

Fig. 5. Performance comparison of DaCPSpTRSV and other four state-of-the-art synchronization-free SpTRSV methods on V100 GPUs.

4.2   Overall Performance

In Fig. 5, we present a performance comparison of five algorithms on NVIDIA
V100. All 245 matrices were tested in double precision. The x-axis of the graph is
the parallelism ($\log_2 n/levels$) of each matrix, and the y-axis is the performance
(GFLOPS/s) of the matrix. To illustrate the advantages of our two optimization strategies more effectively, we divided DaCPSpTRSV into versions 1.0 and
2.0. Version 1.0 incorporates only the fast-forward optimization strategy, while
version 2.0 integrates both fast-forward and fine-grained fusion strategies.

As depicted in Fig. 5, our DaCPSpTRSV exhibits significant performance
advantages over the other four algorithms. Specific performance metrics are
detailed in Table 2. First of all, the average performance of our DaCPSpTRSV
on V100 and A100 reached 15.16 and 17.56 GFLOPS/s respectively. In contrast, the average performance of the state-of-the-art Yuenyeung was 9.38 and
9.56 GFLOPS/s. Notably, DaCPSpTRSV achieved its peak performance of 77.32
GFLOPS/s on A100 (with the matrix parabolic_fem). Furthermore, compared
to cuSPARSE, our DaCPSpTRSV outperforms 99% of matrices, with only
4 matrices showing inferior performance. This further underscores the broad
applicability of our approach. Additionally, DaCPSpTRSV 2.0 marginally surpasses the results of DaCPSpTRSV 1.0. Both our fast-forward strategy and fine-
grained fusion strategy prove effective in yielding significant benefits. Finally,
our DaCPSpTRSV achieved acceleration ratios of 4.77×, 4.94×, 1.67×, and
1.62× respectivel5y compared to cuSPARSE, Sync-Free, CapelliniSpTRSV, and
YuenyeungSpTRSV (Table 1).

Table 1. Two GPU platforms and five evaluated algorithms

Algorithm	cuSPARSE	Sync-Free	Cape	Yy	DaCP1.0	DaCP2.0
Avg Perf (GFLOPS/s) on V100	3.42	3.07	9.16	9.38	13.44	15.16
Avg Perf (GFLOPS/s) on A100	4.04	2.82	10.21	9.38	14.81	17.56
Perc vs. cuSPARSE on V100	–	41%	84%	95%	96%	99%
DaCP2.0's Speedup on V100	4.77×	4.97×	1.67×	1.62×	1.21×	–

4.3   Detailed Analysis

To further scrutinize the benefits of our DaCP, we conducted a comprehensive
analysis of six representative matrices. Table 3 outlines the characteristics and
performance effects of these matrices, while Fig. 6 illustrates a comparison of
bandwidth for the same set. Our performance measurements were obtained using
NVIDIA's Nsight Compute tool. In terms of bandwidth, while the other four
algorithms fail to exceed 60GB/s across the six matrices, our DaCP surpasses
100 GB/s on four of them.

Table 2. Six representative matrix properties, and performance comparison of cuS-PARSE, YuenyeungSpTRSV, and our DaCPSpTRSV algorithm on V100 GPU

Matrix	Plot	n	nnz	levels	Performance(GFLOPS/s)			Speedup	
					cuSP.	Yuen.	Our.	vs.cuSP.	vs.Yuen.
c-57		37833	221515	2	5.30	5.20	**14.76**	**2.78x**	**2.83x**
watson_1		201155	389672	35	1.88	3.34	**20.92**	**11.12x**	**6.26x**
trans4		116835	441781	14	2.96	3.34	**14.45**	**4.88x**	**4.32x**
IG5-18		41550	106092	117	0.12	0.35	**3.05**	**25.41x**	**8.71x**
roadNet-TX		1393383	3315043	344	3.89	4.32	**9.74**	**2.50x**	**2.25x**
asia_osm		11950757	24662360	4283	1.33	1.32	**4.20**	**3.16x**	**3.18x**

Specifically, DaCP achieves speedup ratios of $25.41\times$ and $8.71\times$ relative to cuSPARSE and Yuenyeung, respectively, for the matrix "IG5-18". Despite its low parallelism, measured at only 335.13, DaCP still performs exceptionally well. Conversely, the matrix "c-57", which has high parallelism with 2 levels, also benefits significantly from our focus on efficient memory access. Initially, the performance of DaCP1.0 on the matrices "watson_1" and "trans4" was not outstanding. However, after implementing the fine-grained fusion strategy, there was a notable improvement. The bandwidth of DaCP2.0 on these matrices is now six times greater than that of DaCP1.0. Furthermore, DaCP demonstrates remarkable applicability even for matrices with larger levels. Both "RoadNet-TX" and "asia_osm" exceed one million in size, with "asia_osm" having an impressive 4283 levels.

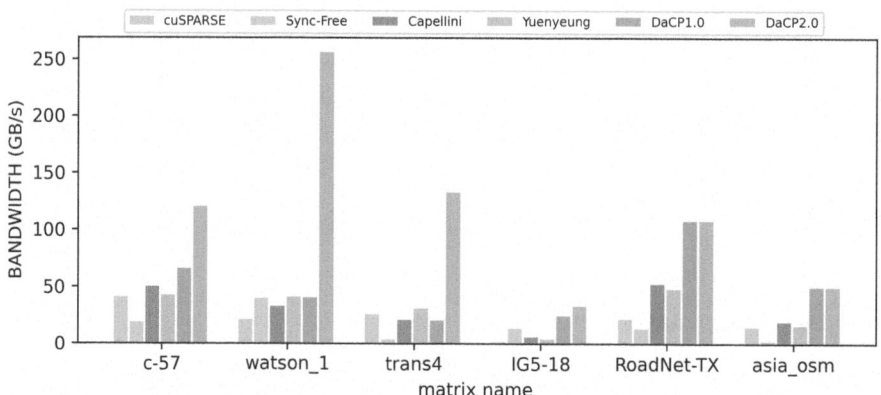

Fig. 6. Bandwidth and performance of 6 representative matrices on V100 GPU

5   Conclusion

In this paper, we introduce a novel synchronization-free SpTRSV algorithm called DaCPSpTRSV, which incorporates GPU-friendly data communication and parallelism strategies. We tackle the limitations of existing synchronization-free algorithms through the design of a fast-forward thread-level approach and a fine-grained fusion strategy. Experimental results conducted on NVIDIA V100 and A100 GPUs demonstrate that our DaCPSpTRSV algorithm achieves significant speedup compared to state-of-the-art GPU-based SpTRSV methods. Furthermore, our approach maintains compatibility with the common CSR storage format, thereby improving the algorithm's applicability.

Acknowledgments. This work was supported by Sichuan Science and Technology Program (Grant No. 2023YFG0152) and the National Key Research, Development Program of China (Grant No. 2021YFB0300101) and ghfund202407023572.

References

1. Björck, Å.: Numerical Methods for Least Squares Problems. Society for Industrial and Applied Mathematics (1996)
2. Duff, I.S., Erisman, A.M., Reid, J.K.: Direct Methods for Sparse Matrices. Oxford University Press (2017)
3. Saad, Y.: Iterative Methods for Sparse Linear Systems. Society for Industrial and Applied Mathematics (2003)
4. Yang, C., Buluç, A., Owens, J.D.: Design principles for sparse matrix multiplication on the GPU. In: Aldinucci, M., Padovani, L., Torquati, M. (eds.) Euro-Par 2018. LNCS, vol. 11014, pp. 672–687. Springer, Cham (2018). https://doi.org/10.1007/978-3-319-96983-1_48
5. Huang, G., Dai, G., Wang, Y., et al.: GE-SpMM: general-purpose sparse matrix-matrix multiplication on GPUs for graph neural networks. In: SC20: International Conference for High Performance Computing, Networking, Storage and Analysis, pp. 1–12. IEEE (2020)
6. Niu, Y., Lu, Z., Ji, H., et al.: TileSpGEMM: a tiled algorithm for parallel sparse general matrix-matrix multiplication on GPUs. In: Proceedings of the 27th ACM SIGPLAN Symposium on Principles and Practice of Parallel Programming, pp. 90–106 (2022)
7. Anderson, E., Saad, Y.: Solving sparse triangular linear systems on parallel computers. Int. J. High Speed Comput. **1**(01), 73–95 (1989)
8. Liu, W., Li, A., Hogg, J., Duff, I.S., Vinter, B.: A synchronization-free algorithm for parallel sparse triangular solves. In: Dutot, P.-F., Trystram, D. (eds.) Euro-Par 2016. LNCS, vol. 9833, pp. 617–630. Springer, Cham (2016). https://doi.org/10.1007/978-3-319-43659-3_45
9. Dufrechou, E., Ezzatti, P.: Solving sparse triangular linear systems in modern GPUs: a synchronization-free algorithm. In: 2018 26th Euromicro International Conference on Parallel, Distributed and Network-based Processing (PDP), pp. 196–203. IEEE (2018)

10. Su, J., Zhang, F., Liu, W., et al.: CapelliniSpTRSV: a thread-level synchronization-free sparse triangular solve on GPUs. In: Proceedings of the 49th International Conference on Parallel Processing, pp. 1–11 (2020)
11. Zhang, F., Su, J., Liu, W., et al.: YuenyeungSpTRSV: a thread-level and warp-level fusion synchronization-free sparse triangular solve[J]. IEEE Trans. Parallel Distrib. Syst. **32**(9), 2321–2337 (2021)
12. Davis, T.A., Hu, Y.: The University of Florida sparse matrix collection. ACM Trans. Math. Softw. (TOMS) **38**(1), 1–25 (2011)
13. Naumov, M., Chien, L., Vandermersch, P., et al.: Cusparse library. In: GPU Technology Conference (2010)

Diagnosability of the Lexicographic Product of Paths and Complete Bipartite Graphs Under PMC Model

Bu Chen(ID) and Feng Li$^{(\boxtimes)}$(ID)

Computer College, Qinghai Normal University, Xi'ning, China
li2006369@126.com

Abstract. The processors within a multiprocessor system use an interconnection network for communication and data transmission, hence the structure of the interconnection network determines various aspects of the system's performance. In the event of processor failures within the system, the system's fault diagnosis capability is very significant. Diagnosability is the crucial parameter for evaluating the fault diagnosis capability of the interconnection network in multiprocessor systems. Studying diagnosability using diagnosis model such as the PMC model is beneficial for improving and optimizing multiprocessor systems. This paper uses the lexicographic product to generate a network structure $P_m \circ K_{x,y}$ which helps maintain the system's parallel processing capability and high-performance computing. When $m \geq 4$, $x + y \geq 5$ and $y > x$, the diagnosability of $P_m \circ K_{x,y}$ under the PMC model is found to be $2x + y$, and when $0 \leq h < 2x + y$, its h-edge fault tolerance diagnosability is $2x + y - h$.

Keywords: fault diagnosis · diagnosability · h-edge tolerable diagnosability · PMC model · lexicographic product · multiprocessor system · complete bipartite graphs · paths

1 Introduction

In large multiprocessor systems, the interconnection network connects thousands of processors within the system, facilitating their communication and data transmission. As the path for sharing resources among processors, the interconnection network requires high connectivity to support data exchange and collaborative computing between processors. Furthermore, when certain processors fail, the assigned tasks may not be completed. If the faulty processors cannot be promptly diagnosed and repaired or replaced, they can significantly affect the system's parallel processing capability. Since high-performance multiprocessor systems often contain a large number of processors, only an interconnection network with advanced fault diagnosis capabilities can quickly identify faulty

© IFIP International Federation for Information Processing 2025
Published by Springer Nature Switzerland AG 2025
X. Chen et al. (Eds.): NPC 2024, LNCS 15527, pp. 41–52, 2025.
https://doi.org/10.1007/978-981-96-2830-8_4

processors and reassign tasks to fault-free processors. This ensures the system's parallel processing capability and reliability.

In related research, a system's fault diagnosis capability is often referred to as diagnosability, which indicates the maximum number of faulty processors that the system can diagnose independently. Over the past two decades, research on diagnosability has been highly abundant. Given the complexity of practical systems, graph theory are commonly employed to model interconnection networks, analyzed using appropriate system-level diagnosis models to determine their diagnosability. Chang et al. [1] applied graph theory to simulate regular networks, successfully determining the diagnosability of several widely used multiprocessor systems under both precise and pessimistic diagnostic strategies, their work highlighted the potential of graph theory in diagnosability research. Additionally, specific interconnection network structures have been studied for their diagnosability under various fault conditions, further enriching the understanding of this field. For example, Zhu [2] explored the h-edge tolerable diagnosability of hypercubes, which applies to systems with hybrid faults, where both processor and physical connection faults occur simultaneously. Furthermore, Lai's research on conditional diagnosability [3], which assumes that every processor must have at least one fault-free neighbor. Besides, the conditional diagnosability has also been extended by Peng's proposal of g-good-neighbor diagnosability which assumes that each processor must have at least g fault-free neighbors [4]. Many interconnection network structures also have had their diagnosability established, as detailed in [5–15].

In the aforementioned research, system-level diagnosis models are of great importance. The most widely used model is the PMC model proposed by Preparata, Metze, and Chien [16]. The PMC model uses a simple graph $G = (V, E)$ to represent the test graph of a system, where the vertex set $V(G)$ represent processors, and the edge set $E(G)$ represent tests between pairs of vertices. Under the PMC model, test results are either 1 or 0, with only fault-free processors providing accurate test results; faulty processors give unreliable test results. If q is fault-free and the result of $(q, w) \in E(G)$ is 0, then w is fault-free. If $(q, w) = 1$, then w is faulty. If q is a faulty processor, then the test results obtained by q will be 1 or 0 randomly. The syndromes of graph G refer to the set of all test results of G. Since the results given by faulty processors are different, different syndromes are commonly used in the PMC model to diagnose faulty processors. Suppose there is a faulty vertex set F in G. The syndromes generated by F are denoted as $\sigma(F)$. Under the PMC model, if F_1 and F_2 are two distinct faulty vertex sets of $V(G)$ and $\sigma(F_1) \cap \sigma(F_2) = \emptyset$, then F_1 and F_2 are considered distinguishable under the PMC model; otherwise, they are indistinguishable.

Next, we introduce the relevant concepts and definitions of graph theory. Necessary concepts are as follows. In a graph $G = (V(G), E(G))$, the order of G is the number of vertices it contains, denoted as $|V(G)|$, and the number of edges is denoted as $|E(G)|$. Consider any two vertices x, y in G. If there exists an edge $(x, y) \in E(G)$, then x and y are adjacent. Consider a vertex a in graph

G, the set of all vertices adjacent to a is called the neighborhood of a, denoted as $N_G(a)$ and $N_G(a) = \{b | (a, b) \in E(G)\}$. In G, the number of vertices adjacent to a is the degree of a, denoted as $d_G(a)$. The minimum and maximum degree of G are denoted as $\delta(G)$ and $\Delta(G)$ respectively, that is:

$$\begin{aligned} \delta(G) &= min\{d_G(x) | x \in V(G)\}, \\ \Delta(G) &= max\{d_G(x) | x \in V(G)\}. \end{aligned} \tag{1}$$

For any subsets F_1, $F_2 \subseteq V(G)$ in graph G, the symmetric difference of F_1 and F_2 is denoted as $F_1 \triangle F_2$. Specifically, $F_1 \triangle F_2 = (F_1 - F_2) \cup (F_2 - F_1) = (F_1 \cup F_2) - (F_1 \cap F_2)$.

In graph theory, there are methods suitable for generating new networks. Sabidussi [17] proposed four graph products: the Cartesian product, the strong product, the direct product and the lexicographic product. Many excellent networks are generated by the graph products of some certain graphs. For example, hypercubes and mesh networks can be obtained through the Cartesian product of paths, while ring networks can be generated by the Cartesian product of cycles, and these networks exhibit good diagnosability. Unlike the Cartesian product, the networks obtained from the lexicographic product have more edges. If two finite undirected graphs $G_1 = (V(G_1), E(G_1))$ and $G_2 = (V(G_2), E(G_2))$ are used as factors, the lexicographic product of G_1 and G_2 is denoted as $G_1 \circ G_2$ and $V(G_1 \circ G_2) = V(G_1) \times V(G_2)$. In $G_1 \circ G_2$, suppose there are two distinct vertices (x_1, y_1) and (x_2, y_2) where $x_1, x_2 \in V(G_1)$, $y_1, y_2 \in V(G_2)$, they are adjacent if and only if $x_1 = x_2$ and $(y_1, y_2) \in E(G_2)$, or $(x_1, x_2) \in E(G_1)$. The properties of the lexicographic product have been explored in detail in [18–20].

Apparently, graphs generated by the lexicographic product generally have higher connectivity and may perform exceptionally well in terms of diagnosability. So we have reason to believe that the lexicographic product is highly suitable for designing large interconnection networks. Therefore, this paper uses the lexicographic product to generate a network structure $P_m \circ K_{x,y}$ suitable for multiprocessor systems and determines its diagnosability as well as its h-edge tolerable diagnosability under hybrid faults circumstances. This paper contributes to the design of networks for high-performance and parallel computing systems and provides valuable insights for the design and analysis of these systems.

2   Main Results

The important concepts involved in this section have been provided in the previous text, with more detailed information available in [21]. First, the definitions of diagnosability and h-edge tolerable diagnosability are given.

Definition 1 [1]. *Given a multiprocessor system $G = (V, E)$ and two distinct faulty vertex sets F_1 and F_2, if $|F_1| \leq t$, $|F_2| \leq t$ with F_1 and F_2 are distinguishable, then the system is t-diagnosable. The maximum integer t such that the system G is t-diagnosable based on the PMC model is called the diagnosability of the system, denoted as $t(G)$.*

Definition 2 [2]. *Given a multiprocessor system $G = (V, E)$ and two non-negative integers h and t, if for any edge set $A \subseteq E(G)$ with $|A| \leq h$, there exist two distinct faulty vertex sets F_1 and F_2 with $|F_1| \leq t$ and $|F_2| \leq t$ such that F_1 and F_2 are distinguishable in $G - A$, then G is h-edge tolerable t-diagnosable under the PMC model. The maximum integer t for which G is h-edge toleable t-diagnosable is called the h-edge toleable diagnosability of G, denoted as $t_h(G)$.*

Determining whether two vertex sets are distinguishable is crucial for establishing the diagnosability of the interconnection network. Lemma 3 addresses the conditions for determining distinguishable subsets in the graph.

Lemma 3 [16]. *For a multiprocessor system $G = (V, E)$ and any two distinct faulty vertex sets $F_1, F_2 \in V(G)$. Under the PMC model, F_1 and F_2 are distinguishable if and only if there exists a vertex $y \in V - (A \cup B)$ such that $N_G(y) \cap (A \triangle B) \neq \emptyset$ (see Fig. 1).*

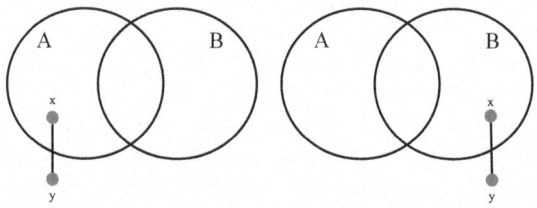

Fig. 1. Two indistinguishable faulty vertex subsets under the PMC Model.

Based on the number of vertices in the network, Lemma 4 provides an natural bound on the diagnosability of an interconnection network under the PMC model. So it is commonly used to verify whether the diagnosability value is reliable and is very useful in the process of determining the diagnosability of an interconnection network.

Lemma 4 [16]. *Given a multiprocessor system $G = (V, E)$, if it is t-diagnosable under the PMC model, then $|V| \geq 2t + 1$.*

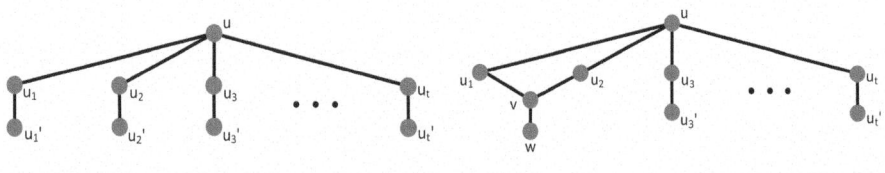

(a) A structure 1 of order t.   (b) A structure 2 of order t.

Fig. 2. Two diagnosis structures.

In [22], Hsu and Tan proposed two excellent structures (illustrated in Fig. 2), these two structures cleverly establishes a connection between the diagnosability of the network and the vertices of it.

Lemma 5 [22]. *Given a multiprocessor system $G = (V, E)$, if there is an structure 1 or 2 of order t rooted at any vertex of G, then the diagnosability of G is t.*

Figure 3 illustrate the structures of P_m and $K_{x,y}$. For two vertices p_1, p_m, an m order path between them can be denoted as $P_m = p_1 p_2 \cdots p_m$, where (p_i, p_{i+1}) is an edge and $i \in (1, 2, \cdots, m-1)$ and all edges of P_m are distinct. In a bipartite graph, the vertices can be divided into two disjoint vertex subsets X and Y such that edges only exist between vertices in X and vertices in Y, there are no edges between vertices within X or within Y. A complete bipartite graph $K_{x,y}$ is a specific type of bipartite graph where if $|X| = x$, $|Y| = y$ and every vertex in X is connected to every vertex in Y with an edge. In other words, all possible edges in the complete bipartite graph are present. Due to the strong structural properties and symmetry of bipartite graphs and paths, they provide clear models and effective solutions in practical applications such as network design, matching problems, and social networks. Based on the structural analysis of complete bipartite graphs and paths, we can further explore their lexicographic product. Based on the previously introduced lemmas and definitions, the problem of determining the diagnosability of $P_m \circ K_{x,y}$ can be transformed into finding the largest indistinguishable faulty vertex sets in $P_m \circ K_{x,y}$ by utilizing the properties of the vertices. Therefore, we will next focus on the structure and properties of $P_m \circ K_{x,y}$ to identify the largest indistinguishable faulty vertex sets.

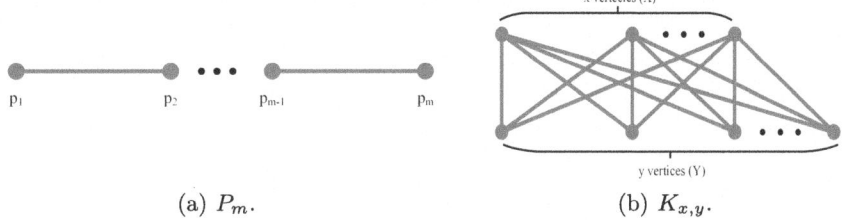

(a) P_m.   (b) $K_{x,y}$.

Fig. 3. The structure of P_m and $K_{x,y}$.

Selecting specific examples for in-depth analysis often reveals the essential characteristics of more general cases. We will further study $P_m \circ K_{x,y}$ by examining $P_3 \circ K_{2,2}$. Assume $V(P_3) = \{p_1, p_2, p_3\}$ and $V(K_{2,2}) = \{1, 2, 3, 4\}$. Based on the definition of the lexicographic product, the structure of $P_3 \circ K_{2,2}$ can be derived, as shown in Fig. 4, $P_3 \circ K_{2,2}$ also exhibits excellent structural properties and symmetry.

By closely observing Fig. 3, Fig. 4 and referring to the definition of the lexicographic product, we can see that the structure of $P_m \circ K_{x,y}$ is obtained by

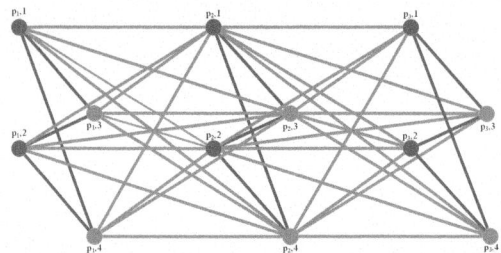

Fig. 4. The structure of $P_3 \circ K_{2,2}$.

replacing each of the m vertices in P_m with $K_{x,y}$. For clarity, the copies of $K_{x,y}$ denoted as $nK_{x,y}$ where $1 \leq n \leq m$. Then connect all vertices of $nK_{x,y}$ with all vertices of $n + 1K_{x,y}$ if $(n, n + 1) \in E(P_m)$. Therefore, it is easy to derive the maximum and minimum degrees of $(P_m \circ K_{x,y})$.

Theorem 6. *Let* $G = P_m \circ K_{x,y}$ *where* $y \geq x$. *Then in* $P_m \circ K_{x,y}$, $\delta(P_m \circ K_{x,y}) = 2x + y$, *and* $\Delta(P_m \circ K_{x,y}) = 2x + 3y$.

Proof. Assume $V(P_m) = \{p_1, p_2, \cdots, p_m\}$ and $V(K_{x,y}) = \{a_1, a_2, \cdots, a_x, b_1, b_2, \cdots, b_y\}$. According to the definition of the lexicographic product, the vertex set of $P_m \circ K_{x,y}$ is:

$$V(P_m \circ K_{x,y}) = \{p_1a_1, \cdots p_1b_y; p_2a_1, \cdots p_2b_y; \cdots; p_ma_1, \cdots p_mb_y\}. \quad (2)$$

According to the previous discussion, it can be seen that in P_m, p_1 and p_m have the fewest adjacent vertices. Therefore, the vertices with the minimum degree in $P_m \circ K_{x,y}$ are located in those $K_{x,y}$'s copies that replace p_1 and p_m. Since $y \geq x$, the vertices with the minimum degree in $P_m \circ K_{x,y}$ are (p_1, i) and (p_m, i) where $i \in (b_1, b_2, \cdots, b_y)$. By applying the definition of lexicographic product, we can deduce that $\delta(P_m \circ K_{x,y}) = x + x + y = 2x + y$, similarly, the vertices with the maximum degree in G are (p_j, i), where $j \in (2, \cdots, m - 1)$ and $i \in (a_1, a_2, \cdots, a_x)$. therefore, $\Delta(P_m \circ K_{x,y}) = y + 2(x + y) = 2x + 3y$.

After understanding the construction of $P_m \circ K_{x,y}$, we can use definition 1, definition 2, and lemma 3 to derive the specific values of the diagnosability and h-edge tolerable diagnosability of $P_m \circ K_{x,y}$.

Corollary 7. *Given a multiprocessor system* $P_m \circ K_{x,y}$ *under the PMC model,* $t(P_m \circ K_{x,y}) \leq 2x + y$.

Proof. Let the vertex with the minimum degree in $P_m \circ K_{x,y}$ be denoted as a. According to Theorem 6, we have $\delta(P_m \circ K_{x,y}) = d_{P_m \circ K_{x,y}}(a) = 2x + y$. Based on vertex a, we construct two vertex sets F_1 and F_2 where $F_1 = \{a\} \cup N_{P_m \circ K_{x,y}}(a)$ and $F_2 = N_{P_m \circ K_{x,y}}(a)$. It is clear that $|F_1| = 2x + y + 1$, $|F_2| = 2x + y$ and $F_1 \triangle F_2 = \{a\}$. Since a is the vertex with the minimum degree, we have $N_{P_m \circ K_{x,y}}(F_1 \triangle F_2) \cap (P_m \circ K_{x,y} - F_1 \cup F_2) = \emptyset$. According to lemma 3, F_1 and F_2 are indistinguishable. Therefore, based on definition 1, we conclude that $t(P_m \circ K_{x,y}) \leq 2x + y$.

Next, it is only necessary to prove the lower bound of $t\left(P_m \circ K_{x,y}\right)$ in order to determine the exact value of $t\left(P_m \circ K_{x,y}\right)$.

Theorem 8. *Given a multiprocessor system $P_m \circ K_{x,y}$ where $m \geq 4, x+y \geq 5$, and $y > x$, then under the PMC model, $t\left(P_m \circ K_{x,y}\right) = 2x + y$.*

Proof. By Lemma 5, to obtain the lower bound of $t\left(P_m \circ K_{x,y}\right)$, we only need to determine the minimum order of the diagnosis structures that can be formed at each vertex in $P_m \circ K_{x,y}$. Divided the vertices of $K_{x,y}$ into two disjoint vertex sbusets X, and Y, and let the vertices in $P_m \circ K_{x,y}$ be denoted as $p_i q_{x,y}$, where $i \in (1, 2, \cdots, m)$, $q_x \in V(X)$, $q_y \in V(Y)$, $m \geq 4$, $x + y \geq 5$ and $y > x$.

When $i = 1$ (the same applies when $i \in (2, 3, \cdots, m)$), if we take $p_i q_y$ as the root node, we can select $p_{i+1} q_{x,y}$ and $p_i q_x$ for a total of $2x + y$ distinct vertices. Since $m \geq 4$, $x + y \geq 5$ and $y > x$, based on the definition of the lexicographic product and the properties of $K_{x,y}$, obviously $p_i q_y$ are connected to $p_i q_x$ and $p_{i+1} q_{x,y}$, both $p_{i+1} q_{x,y}$ and $p_{i+2} q_{x,y}$ are connected as well. We can construct a structure 1 of order $2x + y$ here (see Fig. 5(a)). If we take $p_i q_x$ is the root node, then based on the definition of the lexicographic product and the properties of $K_{x,y}$, we can construct a structure of order $2x + y$ as structure 2 (see Fig. 5(b)).

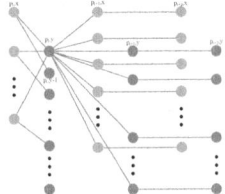   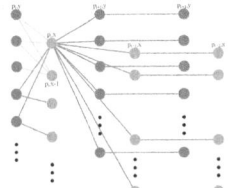

(a) Structure 1 with order $2x + y$.   (b) Structure 2 with order $2x + y$.

Fig. 5. The ways to construct diagnosis structures.

In summary, when $m \geq 4, x + y \geq 5$, and $y > x$, each vertex in $P_m \circ K_{x,y}$ can construct an structure 1 or 2 of at least order $2x + y$. Thus, by Lemma 5 and Corollary 7, Theorem 8 is proven.

In the event of physical connection failures, the h-edge tolerable diagnosability is clearly more suitable for assessing the system's fault diagnosis capability under hybrid fault circumstances. Therefore, the h-edge tolerable diagnosability of $P_m \circ K_{x,y}$ is also worth investigating. In a multiprocessor system, the location of physical connection failures is random. However, if the failures occur in the physical connections incident to the processors with the minimum degree in the interconnection network, it may result in isolated processors. The system cannot diagnose these isolated processors, making such physical connection failures the most impactful on the system. To address this issue, we define a worst-case scenario where physical connection failures in the multiprocessor system preferentially occur at the processors with the minimum degree. The h-edge tolerable diagnosability under the worst-case scenario can effectively measure the system's minimum fault diagnosis capability when physical connection failures occur at any location.

Corollary 9. *Given a multiprocessor system* $P_m \circ K_{x,y}$*, when* $0 \leq h < 2x + y$*, under the worst-case scenario,* $t_h\left(P_m \circ K_{x,y}\right) \leq 2x + y - h$*.*

Proof. We will discuss this proof based on the value of h in two cases.

Case 1: When $h = 0$, it is evident that $t_h\left(P_m \circ K_{x,y}\right) = t\left(P_m \circ K_{x,y}\right)$. From the proof process of Corollary 7, we obtain that when $h = 0$, $t_h\left(P_m \circ K_{x,y}\right) \leq 2x + y - h = 2x + y$.

Case 2: When $0 < h < 2x + y$, let $E_f \subset E\left(P_m \circ K_{x,y}\right)$ be the faulty physical connection set of the system with $|E_f| \leq h$. Consider a vertex with the minimum degree in $P_m \circ K_{x,y}$, denoted as q. According to Theorem 6, $d_{P_m \circ K_{x,y}}(q) = 2x + y$. Under the worst-case scenario, the physical connections incident to q fail first, the degree of q in $P_m \circ K_{x,y} - E_f$ becomes $d_{P_m \circ K_{x,y} - E_f}(q) = 2x + y - h$.

Next, we construct two faulty vertex sets F_1 and F_2 based on the vertex q, defined as follows:

$$F_1 = N_{P_m \circ K_{x,y} - E_f}(q).$$
$$F_2 = \{q\} \cup N_{P_m \circ K_{x,y} - E_f}(q). \tag{3}$$

It is clear that $|F_1| = 2x + y - h$ and $|F_2| = 2x + y - h + 1$ with $F_1 \triangle F_2 = \{q\}$. Since q is the vertex with the minimum degree, in $P_m \circ K_{x,y} - E_f$, we have $N_{P_m \circ K_{x,y} - E_f}(F_1 \triangle F_2) \cap (P_m \circ K_{x,y} - E_f - F_1 \cup F_2) = \emptyset$. According to Lemma 3, F_1 and F_2 are evidently indistinguishable.

Combining this results with Definition 2, we conclude that when $0 \leq h < 2x + y$, $t_h\left(P_m \circ K_{x,y}\right) \leq 2x + y - h$. Next we determine the $t_h\left(P_m \circ K_{x,y}\right)$ based on Corollary 9.

Theorem 10. *Given a multiprocessor system* $P_m \circ K_{x,y}$ *where* $m \geq 4$*,* $x + y \geq 5$*, and* $y > x$*, when* $0 \leq h < 2x + y$*, under the worst-case scenario,* $t_h\left(P_m \circ K_{x,y}\right) = 2x + y - h$*.*

Proof. Under the PMC model, suppose that $E_f \subset E\left(P_m \circ K_{x,y}\right)$ is the faulty physical connection set of $P_m \circ K_{x,y}$ with $|E_f| \leq h$. Additionally, assume that two distinct faulty vertex sets F_1 and F_2 in $P_m \circ K_{x,y} - E_f$ are indistinguishable. From the results of definition 2 and corollary 9, it suffices to prove that $|F_1| \geq 2x + y - h + 1$ or $|F_2| \geq 2x + y - h + 1$ in order to conclude that $t_h\left(P_m \circ K_{x,y}\right) = 2x + y - h$. Given the assumption that F_1 and F_2 are indistinguishable under the PMC model, by lemma 3, we have $N_{P_m \circ K_{x,y} - E_f}(F_1 \triangle F_2) \cap (P_m \circ K_{x,y} - E_f - F_1 \cup F_2) = \emptyset$. Therefore, $N_{P_m \circ K_{x,y} - E_f}(F_1 \triangle F_2) \subseteq (F_1 \cap F_2)$, so it follows that $|F_1 \triangle F_2| + |F_1 \cap F_2| \geq |F_1 \triangle F_2| + |N_{P_m \circ K_{x,y} - E_f}(F_1 \triangle F_2)|$.

Since $F_1 \triangle F_2 \neq \emptyset$, we will proceed by discussing the number of elements in $F_1 \triangle F_2$.

Case 1: When $|F_1 \triangle F_2| = 1$, let the vertex in $F_1 \triangle F_2$ be q, and assume $F_1 - F_2 = \{q\}$. Since F_1 and F_2 are indistinguishable, and $N_{P_m \circ K_{x,y} - E_f} (F_1 \triangle F_2) \subseteq F_1 \cap F_2$, we have:

$$\begin{aligned}
|F_1| &= |F_1 - F_2| + |F_1 \cap F_2| \\
&\geq 1 + \left| N_{P_m \circ K_{x,y} - E_f} (F_1 \triangle F_2) \right| \\
&\geq 1 + \left| N_{P_m \circ K_{x,y}} (q) \right| - |E_f| \\
&\geq 1 + 2x + y - h.
\end{aligned} \tag{4}$$

Clearly, when $|F_1 \triangle F_2| = 1$, we have $|F_1| \geq 2x + y - h + 1$.

Case 2: When $|F_1 \triangle F_2| = 2$, suppose $F_1 \triangle F_2 = \{a, b\}$. If $ab \in E(P_m \circ K_{x,y} - E_f)$, then we have $\left| N_{P_m \circ K_{x,y} - E_f} (F_1 \triangle F_2) \right| \geq 2x + 2y - 2 - h$. However, if $ab \notin E(P_m \circ K_{x,y} - E_f)$, then naturally we have $\left| N_{P_m \circ K_{x,y} - E_f} (F_1 \triangle F_2) \right| \geq 2x + y - h$. Since $N_{P_m \circ K_{x,y} - E_f} (F_1 \triangle F_2) \subseteq (F_1 \cap F_2)$, $x + y \geq 5$ and $y > x$, it is evident that:

$$\begin{aligned}
|F_1| + |F_2| &= |F_1 \cup F_2| + |F_1 \cap F_2| \\
&= |F_1 \triangle F_2| + |F_1 \cap F_2| + |F_1 \cap F_2| \\
&\geq 2 + 2 \left| N_{P_m \circ K_{x,y} - E_f} (F_1 \triangle F_2) \right| \\
&\geq 2 + 2min \{2x + 2y - 2 - h, 2x + y - h\} \\
&\geq 2 + 2(2x + y - h).
\end{aligned} \tag{5}$$

So it follows that $|F_1| \geq 2x + y - h + 1$ or $|F_2| \geq 2x + y - h + 1$. Therefore, when $|F_1 \triangle F_2| = 2$, the proof is completed.

Case 3: When $|F_1 \triangle F_2| \geq 3$, suppose that $|F_1| \leq 2x + y - h$ and $|F_2| \leq 2x + y - h$, according to the assumption before, we have $|F_1 \cap F_2| < 2x + y - h$. Based on the structural analysis of $P_m \circ K_{x,y}$ above, we conclude that when $x + y \geq 5$, $y > x$ and $0 \leq h < 2x + y$, $\left| N_{P_m \circ K_{x,y} - E_f} (F_1 \triangle F_2) \right| \geq 2x + y - h$, obviously contradict to $N_{P_m \circ K_{x,y} - E_f} (F_1 \triangle F_2) \subseteq (F_1 \cap F_2)$. So when $|F_1 \triangle F_2| \geq 3$, we have $|F_1| > 2x + y - h$ or $|F_2| > 2x + y - h$. In conclusion, theorem 10 is proven.

3   Application and Numerical Simulation

As the number of processors in the system increases, accurately identifying faulty processors becomes exceedingly difficult. Additionally, physical connections within the system may also fail, further testing the system's fault diagnosis capabilities. As a result, studying the diagnosability of new interconnection networks obtained through graph products is beneficial for the development of high-performance computing systems. Using the research results presented in this paper, we can easily determine the diagnosability and h-edge tolerable diagnosability of $P_m \circ K_{x,y}$ where $m \geq 4$, $x + y \geq 5$, and $y > x$.

Example 1. Given a multiprocessor system $P_4 \circ K_{2,3}$, according to Theorem 8 and Theorem 10, its diagnosability is 7, when $0 \leq h < 7$, its h-edge tolerable diagnosability is $7 - h$ in the worst-case scenario.

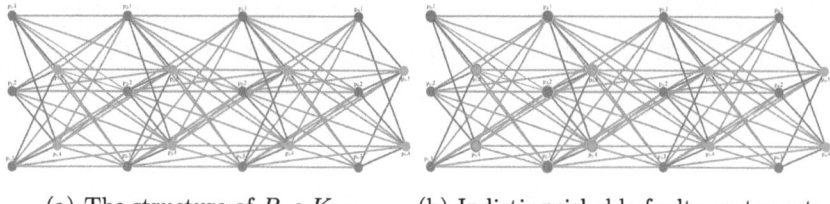

(a) The structure of $P_4 \circ K_{2,3}$.   (b) Indistinguishable faulty vertex sets.

Fig. 6. Illustration of Example 1.

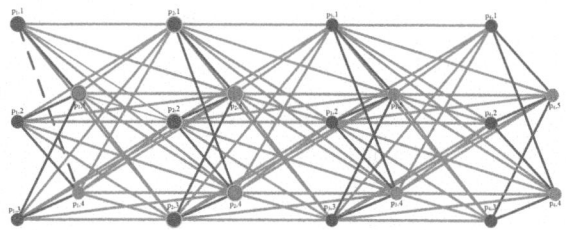

Fig. 7. Two indistinguishable faulty vertex sets in $P_4 \circ K_{2,3}$.

Proof. First, let's present the structure diagram of $P_4 \circ K_{2,3}$. Assume $V(P_4) = \{p_1, p_2, p_3, p_4\}$ and $V(K_{2,3}) = \{1, 2, 3, 4, 5\}$ as shown in Fig. 6(a).

To prove that its diagnosability is 7, we only need construct two faulty vertex sets based on $(p_1, 1)$, the vertices of F_1 and F_2 are marked by red and yellow circles in Fig. 6(b) respectively. By definition 1 and lemma 3, it follows that $t(P_4 \circ K_{2,3}) < 8$. Additionally, in $P_4 \circ K_{2,3}$, any two faulty vertex sets containing 7 vertices are distinguishable. Therefore, we conclude that $t(P_4 \circ K_{2,3}) = 7$. In the worst-case scenario, physical connection failures occur preferentially at the minimum degree vertex. Thus, when $h = 1$, the network topology of $P_4 \circ K_{2,3}$ can be represented as shown in Fig. 7, the red dashed lines indicate the physical connection failure. Similarly, in $P_4 \circ K_{2,3} - \{(p_1, 1), (p_1, 4)\}$, we identify a pair of indistinguishable faulty vertex sets F_1 and F_2, marked with red and yellow circles in Fig. 7, respectively. By definition 2 and lemma 3, we conclude that $t_1(P_4 \circ K_{2,3}) < 7$. Additionally, in $P_4 \circ K_{2,3} - \{(p_1, 1), (p_1, 4)\}$, all faulty vertex sets containing 6 vertices are distinguishable. Therefore, $t_1(P_4 \circ K_{2,3}) = 6$, in summary, we have verified Example 1.

After studying the fault diagnosis capability of $P_m \circ K_{x,y}$ using the PMC model, we conducted simulation experiments in Matlab to analyze the diagnosability and the h-edge tolerable diagnosability of $P_m \circ K_{x,y}$ (see Fig. 8(a) and Fig. 8(b), where the value of h in Fig. 8(b) is randomly generated and satisfies $0 \leq h < 2x + y$). In these figures, t and t_h represent $t(P_m \circ K_{x,y})$ and $t_h(P_m \circ K_{x,y})$, respectively. The results demonstrate that $P_m \circ K_{x,y}$ ($m \geq 4$, $x + y \geq 5$, $y > x$) has excellent fault diagnosis capabilities, making this network structure suitable for parallel processing systems and high-performance computing systems.

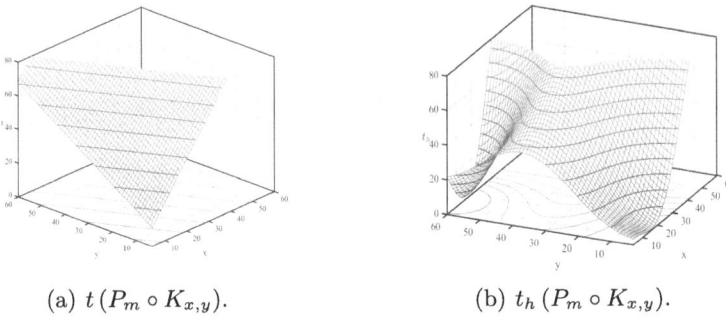

(a) $t\,(P_m \circ K_{x,y})$.   (b) $t_h\,(P_m \circ K_{x,y})$.

Fig. 8. Simulation of diagnosis capability of $P_m \circ K_{x,y}$.

4   Conclusion

This paper introduces a new network structure $P_m \circ K_{x,y}$ based on the lexico-graphic product and using the PMC model determines that its diagnosability is $2x + y$, and its h-edge tolerable diagnosability is $2x + y - h$ under the conditions $0 \le h < 2x + y$, $m \ge 4$, $x + y \ge 5$, and $y > x$. Simulation experiments fur-ther demonstrate that $P_m \circ K_{x,y}$ exhibits excellent fault diagnosis capabilities, making it well-suited for both parallel processing systems and high-performance computing systems. The findings provide valuable insight for the design of large-scale interconnection networks for multiprocessor systems, and indicate that structures derived from the lexicographic product possess favorable properties, particularly in terms of enhanced fault diagnosis capabilities.

Acknowledgments. This work was founded by the National Natural Science Foun-dation of China (grant number 11551002), founded by the Natural Science Foundation of Qinghai Province (grant number $2019 - ZJ - 7093$), founded by students' innovation and entrepreneurship training program of Qinghai Normal University (grant number $qhnucxcy2024024$).

Disclosure of Interests. The authors have no competing interests to declare that are relevant to the content of this article.

References

1. Chang, G.Y., Chang, G.J., Chen, G.H.: Diagnosabilities of regular networks. IEEE Trans. Parallel Distrib. Syst. **16**(4), 314–323 (2005)
2. Zhu, Q., Li, L., Liu, S., et al.: Hybrid fault diagnosis capability analysis of hyper-cubes under the PMC model and MM* model. Theoret. Comput. Sci. **758**, 1–8 (2019)
3. Lai, P.L., Tan, J.J.M., Chang, C.P., et al.: Conditional diagnosability measures for large multiprocessor systems. IEEE Trans. Comput. **54**(2), 165–175 (2005)
4. Peng, S.L., Lin, C.K., Tan, J.J.M., et al.: The g-good-neighbor conditional diag-nosability of hypercube under PMC model. Appl. Math. Comput. **218**(21), 10406–10412 (2012)

5. Liu, H., Hu, X., Gao, S.: The g-good-neighbor conditional diagnosability of locally exchanged twisted cubes. Comput. J. **63**(1), 80–90 (2020)
6. Yuan, J., Liu, A., Wang, X.: The relationship between the g-extra connectivity and the g-extra diagnosability of networks under the MM* model. Comput. J. **64**(6), 921–928 (2021)
7. Sardroud, A.A.A., Ghasemi, M.: The g-good-neighbor diagnosability of triangle-free graphs. J. Supercomput. **79**(7), 7272–7285 (2023)
8. Wang, X., Li, H., Sun, Q., et al.: The g-good-neighbor conditional diagnosability of exchanged crossed cube under the MM* model. Symmetry **14**(11), 2376 (2022)
9. Zhang, S., Yang, W.: The g-extra conditional diagnosability and sequential t/k-diagnosability of hypercubes. Int. J. Comput. Math. **93**(3), 482–497 (2016)
10. Chen, C.A., Hsieh, S.Y.: t/t-diagnosability of regular graphs under the PMC model. ACM Trans. Design Autom. Electron. Syst. (TODAES) **18**(2), 1–13 (2013)
11. Sheu, J.J., Huang, W.T., Chen, C.H.: Strong diagnosability of regular networks under the comparison model. Inf. Process. Lett. **106**(1), 19–25 (2008)
12. Xu, M., Thulasiraman, K., Zhu, Q.: Conditional diagnosability of a class of matching composition networks under the comparison model. Theoret. Comput. Sci. **674**, 43–52 (2017)
13. Hsieh, S.Y., Kao, C.Y.: The conditional diagnosability of k-ary n-cubes under the comparison diagnosis model. IEEE Trans. Comput. **62**(4), 839–843 (2012)
14. Wei, Y., Xu, M.: Hybrid fault diagnosis capability analysis of regular graphs. Theoret. Comput. Sci. **760**, 1–14 (2019)
15. Chen, M., Habib, M., Lin, C.K.: Diagnosability for a family of matching composition networks. J. Supercomput. **79**(7), 7584–7608 (2023)
16. Preparata, F.P., Metze, G., Chien, R.T.: On the connection assignment problem of diagnosable systems. IEEE Trans. Electron. Comput. **16**, 848–854 (2014)
17. Sabidussi, G.: Graph multiplication. Math. Z. **72**(1), 446–45 (1959)
18. Li, F., Wang, W., Xu, Z., et al.: Some results on the lexicographic product of vertex-transitive graphs. Appl. Math. Lett. **24**(11), 1924–1926 (2011)
19. Li, F., Xu, Z.B., Zhao, H.X., et al.: On the number of spanning trees of the lexicographic product of networks. Scientia Sinica Inform. **42**(8), 949–959 (2012)
20. Liang, D., Li, F., Xu, Z.B.: The number of spanning trees in a new lexicographic product of graphs. Sci. China Inf. Sci. **57**(11), 1–9 (2014). https://doi.org/10.1007/s11432-014-5110-z
21. Xu, J.M.: Combinatorial Network Theory, 1st edn. Beijing Science Press (2007)
22. Hsu, G.H., Tan, J.J.M.: A local diagnosability measure for multiprocessor systems. IEEE Trans. Parallel Distrib. Syst. **18**(5), 598–607 (2007)

DTuner: A Construction-Based Optimization Method for Dynamic Tensor Operators Accelerating

Wenxin Chen[1,2], Boyu Diao[1(✉)], Hangda Liu[1,2], RuiSheng Wang[1], and Yongjun Xu[1]

[1] Institute of Computing Technology, Chinese Academy of Sciences, Beijing, China
`diaoboyu2012@ict.ac.cn`
[2] University of Chinese Academy of Sciences, Beijing, China

Abstract. Auto-optimization of tensor programs is a crucial technique in deep learning compilers. Traditional tensor program optimization methods rely on the known fixed shape of the tensor, but when inputs of tensor program are only determined at runtime, these traditional methods cannot optimize in advance. To overcome this challenge, we introduce DTuner, a dynamic shape tensor program optimization method based on a constructive algorithmic. By optimizing for a broad variety of potential input forms, DTuner leverages highly focused and quick optimization methods to increase the efficiency of dynamic shape tensor programs, resulting in notable gains in average performance. Specifically, modern advanced GPUs are composed of general-purpose computing cores and specialized computing cores. Since different input shapes can yield varying performance outcomes across different cores, we incorporate a sampling and prediction method in the optimizer to guide the selection of computing cores. Evaluation results demonstrate that our method is 2 to 3 orders of magnitude faster in tuning time compared to the existing state-of-the-art dynamic tensor program optimization methods (Dietcode). Additionally, the optimization performance of the algorithm is comparable to that of state-of-the-art methods. On the Nvidia A100 and Orin platforms, DTuner can enhance the inference performance of commonly used NLP models by up to 27.5%, with average performance improvements of 6% to 7% for dynamic inputs. For typical single dynamic tensor programs, our method can also achieve a maximum performance improvement of 25.7% and an average improvement of 9%.

Keywords: auto tuning · dynamic shape tensor · AI compiler

1 Introduction

In recent years, the scale and complexity of machine learning models have continuously increased, necessitating more powerful hardware for training and inference. Different models require various types of hardware accelerators, such as

ⓒ IFIP International Federation for Information Processing 2025
Published by Springer Nature Switzerland AG 2025
X. Chen et al. (Eds.): NPC 2024, LNCS 15527, pp. 53–64, 2025.
https://doi.org/10.1007/978-981-96-2830-8_5

GPUs [13] and TPUs [1]. To achieve optimal performance across diverse hardware, the concept of machine learning compilers [3,7,12,15,16] has been proposed in academia. Machine learning compilers enable automated optimization and adaptation, allowing models to better utilize resources across different hardware platforms, thereby accelerating the training and inference processes of machine learning models.

Operator auto-tuning is a core component of the machine learning compiler workflow, aiming at optimizing the computational efficiency of various operators on specific hardware. Although automatic optimization for operators [8] with static shapes is fairly developed, more work is needed because dynamic shapes are becoming more common in natural language processing models, like BERT [5], where batch sizes and input sequence lengths directly affect the input and output dimensions of Q, K, and V computations in the transformer [17] architecture. Since transformers are foundational to current state-of-the-art models [10,11], optimizing these dynamic shape operators is crucial for adapting machine learning compiler technology to more advanced models.

In summary, this paper makes the following three core contributions:

1. It introduces a tiling-based construction algorithm for dynamic shape tensor program auto-optimization, enabling rapid optimization across a wider range of sampled shapes, thereby improving average performance for varying input shapes.
2. During the calculation of tiling sizes, it prunes inefficient branches, thereby reducing auto-tuning time.
3. It considers the varying computational capabilities of different GPU cores during the auto-tuning process and proposes a decision-making method based on sampling and prior knowledge, further enhancing the performance of tensor programs.

2   Related Work

AI Compiler. To address the unique characteristics of deep learning models, a series of specialized compiler frameworks such as TensorFlow XLA [15], TVM [3], MLIR [7], and Glow [12] have been developed. These compilers enhance the execution efficiency of deep learning models through techniques like graph optimization, automatic code generation, and hardware acceleration. For instance, TVM [3] supports a variety of hardware backends via its Relay [6] intermediate representation and utilizes auto-tuning to select the most efficient operator implementation. XLA [15], on the other hand, optimizes the execution performance of TensorFlow [2] computational graphs through static compilation.

Auto Tuning. Auto-tuning is a crucial optimization technique in deep learning compilers [3,7,15,16], designed to automatically identify the optimal configuration parameters during the compilation process, thereby improving model performance on specific hardware platforms. Given the high-dimensionality and complexity of deep learning computational graphs, manual tuning of these parameters is both time-consuming and error-prone, which has led to widespread interest in auto-tuning techniques. AutoTVM [4], a module within Apache TVM, employs a search-based strategy to optimize operators within deep learning models. It supports multiple hardware backends and significantly improves tuning efficiency through techniques such as task decomposition and parallelization. Ansor [21], an additional tuning framework in the TVM ecosystem, enhances AutoTVM's search methodology. With task partitioning and layer-by-layer optimization, it provides more efficient tuning, which is particularly useful for complex neural network architectures. Roller [24] is a technique created especially to optimize static shape tensor algorithms. It uses a tiling-based strategy to handle memory wall difficulties that arise during operator execution.

Dynamic Shape Tensor Program Auto-Tuning. Dynamic shape tensor program auto-tuning presents new challenges compared to static shape optimization. As model structures evolve, operators within these models may exhibit dynamic input shapes. To tackle this problem, Nimble [14] optimizes using a larger input shape and applies this optimization strategy across all input shapes. DISC [22] handles the computation of dynamic shape operators by leveraging vendor-specific operator libraries. DietCode [19] adapts Ansor [21] to optimize by sampling a small number of input shapes, generating several optimization strategies, and mapping these strategies to the corresponding input shapes. The slow optimization speed limits the number of samples, leading to good optimization performance for the sampled shapes but poorer average performance for the many shapes that were not sampled. By reducing optimization time and increasing the number of sampled input shapes, the overall efficiency of dynamic tensor programs can be significantly improved.

3   Background and Motivation

In the forward inference process of traditional deep learning models, the input dimensions are typically fixed, and the input shape of specific layers does not change with varying input data. For a particular model, since each layer has a consistent input shape, optimizing the operator for each layer can be considered as completing the inference optimization for the entire model. However, with the rapid advancement of large language models the input shape of a model and the input shape of its internal layers are no longer necessarily fixed. For example, in the BERT [5] base model, the input size can vary between 1 and 128. We refer to the same operator with the same input as a workload, meaning that a single layer's input can generate multiple workloads. Therefore, to optimize the operator for this layer, it is necessary to optimize all possible workloads. Evidently, as the permissible input length of a model expands, the cost of optimization also increases.

Most existing automatic optimization techniques [14,19] that support dynamic input shapes are based on search algorithms. The vast search space results in slow tuning speeds and a very limited number of input shapes that can be sampled. Consequently, these techniques often fail to achieve optimal results across all possible input shapes.

In a general GPU architecture, the GPU computing cores are divided into CUDA cores and Tensor cores. CUDA cores serve as general-purpose cores capable of handling most tasks on the GPU, while Tensor cores, designed specifically for deep learning, excel in computations like matrix multiplication, offering a natural architectural advantage for many tasks. During model inference optimization, experts typically schedule operators—after mixed precision processing—to the Tensor cores. In response, Bolt [18] has developed a static operator optimization scheme that automatically generates code using the CUTLASS library [13]. Figure 1 has shown that Tensor cores generally perform better with larger input shapes but may not perform optimally with smaller input shapes. To address this, we design a more efficient optimization scheme capable of performing CUDA-level optimizations for a wide range of shapes, thereby improving average performance. Additionally, we utilize prior data and a hardware resource scheduling decision tree to determine the final optimization strategy for specific input shapes.

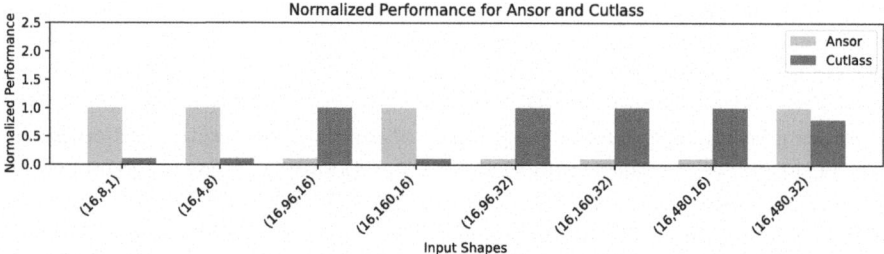

Fig. 1. Different input sizes for dense layers (fully connected layers) are best handled by different types of compute cores (Ansor represents CUDA cores, while Cutlass represents Tensor cores), depending on the hardware architecture.

4   Method

4.1   Overview

As shown in Fig. 2, our approach consists of four main components: a shape sampler, a shape-specific tuner based on construction, hardware dispatcher, and a kernel dispatcher. We determine the number of shapes required for fine-tuning a dynamic shape operator by setting a threshold. The shape-specific tuner optimizes the shapes selected by the sampler. At this stage, we achieve an optimized solution for generic computing cores. For GPUs, which have more efficient specialized computing cores, we use Bolt technology to construct an optimized solution for the specific shape, and select the final optimization scheme through performance sampling and a dispatching method. After automatic optimization of all sampled shapes, we obtain several optimized solutions. A decision tree is used to match an input shape with its most suitable optimization scheme.

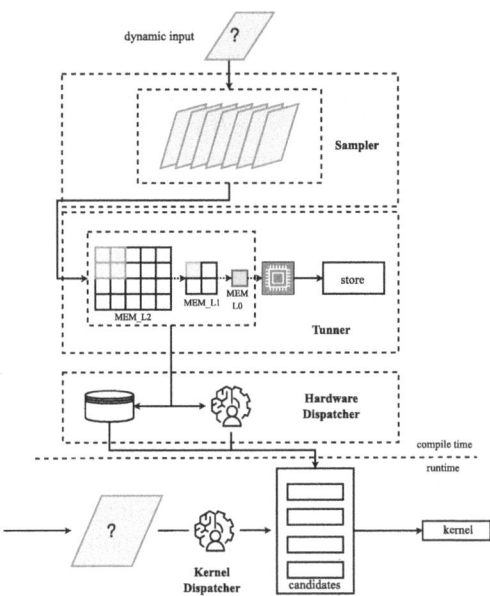

Fig. 2. Dtuner Architectural Overview.

4.2 Sampler

Dynamic shape operators, where the input shapes may vary according to the model's input, are common in models such as large language models (LLMs) due to the varying sequence lengths [5]. Although the input shapes of dynamic shape operators are not infinite, they are constrained within a specific range, with varying probabilities of occurrence. Therefore, optimizing the most probable shapes to perfection is crucial. Additionally, it is important to balance optimization time with performance: Optimizing too many shapes may extend the tuning time, while optimizing too few shapes may degrade overall performance. The most likely shapes are typically specified by model users and developers. Furthermore, thresholds can be designed to determine the number of shapes to optimize.

4.3 Construction-Based Specific Shape Operator Tuner

The optimizer uses a constructive algorithm that draws inspiration from Roller's [23] methodology. The memory wall, where data retrieval from memory is slower than computation speed and hence computational cores are underutilized, is the main source of bottleneck for compute-intensive operators. *load*, *compute*, and *store* are the three steps that we abstract the entire computation process into to solve this, and our goal is to optimize the total computational process by concentrating on the data loading stage.

As shown in Fig. 3, we employ the concept of tiling, combined with the underlying hardware architecture, to sequentially load data from the cache layers furthest from the compute cores to the registers closest to them. For instance, in matrix multiplication $C[m, n] = A[m, k] \times B[n, k]$ executed on a GPU, the matrices A and B initially reside in global memory (HBM_2). The process begins by loading a block $Tile\_A[tile\_m, tile\_k]$ from A and a block $Tile\_B[tile\_n, tile\_k]$ from B into shared memory (HBM_1).

Subsequently, smaller blocks $Tile\_Tile\_A[tile\_tile\_m, tile\_tile\_k]$ from $Tile\_A$ and $Tile\_Tile\_B[tile\_tile\_n, tile\_tile\_k]$ from $Tile\_B$ are loaded into registers (HBM_0), where the processor performs the computations on these blocks. The optimization objective is thus to determine the optimal values for the tiling parameters $tile\_m$, $tile\_n$, $tile\_k$, $tile\_tile\_m$, $tile\_tile\_n$, and $tile\_tile\_k$.

To guide the search for these tiling parameters, we utilize the data reuse rate—a higher rate indicates reduced memory transfer and consequently lower memory overhead. By employing a backtracking algorithm, we enumerate all potential tiling factors and select the one with the highest data reuse rate as the auto-tuner's output. Furthermore, if the maximum potential tile size is large, the range of tiling factors will also be extensive, increasing the depth of backtracking. To expedite the search, we implement tree pruning strategies.

1. Constraining the tiling factors according to hardware limitations, pruning paths where the total size exceeds the HBM's capacity.
2. Instead of directly computing the data reuse rate, we calculate the rate of change in data reuse to guide the pruning process, continuing the search only along the branches with the highest rate of change at each level of the backtracking tree.

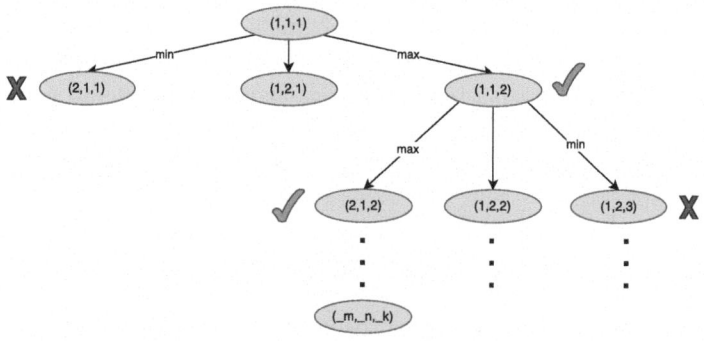

Fig. 3. Example of tiling factor generation.

The rate of change in data reuse is calculated as follows:

$$S_i = \frac{Traffic(T) - Traffic(T_i')}{Footprint(T_i') - Footprint(T)} \tag{1}$$

where:S_i represents the rate of change in data reuse. Traffic(T) and Traffic(T_i') are the memory traffic values for the current and new tiling configurations, respectively. Footprint(T) and Footprint(T_i') are the memory footprints for the current and new tiling configurations, respectively.

A higher value of S_i indicates a greater reduction in memory traffic per unit increase in memory footprint, which corresponds to more efficient data reuse. This rate of change is used to guide the search for optimal tiling configurations. Algorithm 1 provides the pseudocode outlining the entire process.

Algorithm 1. Optimizing Data Reuse for Matrix Multiplication with Best-First Search

---

1: **Input:** Ranges $[0, m]$, $[0, n]$, $[0, k]$ for tiling factors a, b, c
2: **Output:** Maximum Data Reuse Change and corresponding (a, b, c)
3: **function** BACKTRACK(a, b, c)
4:     $mem \leftarrow$ ComputeMem(a, b, c)
5:     **if** $mem > hardware\_mem\_max$ **then return**
6:     **end if**
7:     $reuse \leftarrow$ ComputeDataReuseChange(a, b, c)
8:     **if** $reuse > max\_reuse$ **then** $max\_reuse \leftarrow reuse$, $best\_solution \leftarrow (a, b, c)$
9:     **end if**
10:    $best\_direction \leftarrow$ None, $max\_local\_reuse \leftarrow -\infty$
11:    **for all** (da, db, dc) in $\{(1, 0, 0), (0, 1, 0), (0, 0, 1)\}$ **do**
12:        **if** $a + da \leq m$ **and** $b + db \leq n$ **and** $c + dc \leq k$ **then**
13:            $reuse\_new \leftarrow$ ComputeDataReuseChange($a + da, b + db, c + dc$)
14:            **if** $reuse\_new > max\_local\_reuse$ **then** $max\_local\_reuse \leftarrow reuse\_new$, $best\_direction \leftarrow (a + da, b + db, c + dc)$
15:            **end if**
16:        **end if**
17:    **end for**
18:    **if** $best\_direction \neq$ None **then** BACKTRACK($best\_direction$)
19:    **end if**
20: **end function**
21: **function** SOLVE BACKTRACK($0, 0, 0$)
22:    **Output:** max_reuse, $best\_solution$
23: **end function**

After obtaining the partitioning factors for a sampled shape using a tuner, we construct CUDA kernels using the construction-based algorithm shown as Algorithm 2, with the final CUDA kernel generated by TVM.

Algorithm 2. Tiling Factor to Kernel by Construction-based Algorithm

---

1: **for** each $L1\_input$ in $L2\_inputs$ split by $(tile\_m, tile\_n, tile\_k)$ **do**
2:    $L1\_inputs\_tiles \leftarrow$ Load($inputs[L1\_input]$)
3:    **for** each $l0\_input$ in $L1\_inputs\_tiles$ split by $(tile\_tile\_m, tile\_tile\_n, tile\_tile\_k)$ **do**
4:        $l0\_inputs \leftarrow$ Load($inputs[l0\_input]$)
5:        $l0\_output \leftarrow$ Compute($l0\_inputs$)
6:        Store($l0\_output, l2\_output$)
7:    **end for**
8: **end for**

4.4 Hardware Dispatcher

In practical model deployment scenarios, to leverage more efficient computational units (such as Tensor Cores in GPUs) or to meet model size constraints, it is often necessary to perform quantization or use mixed precision. In these cases, the computation units may be either general CUDA cores or specialized Tensor Cores. To address this, we design a forecaster that leverages prior data and classification predictions to select the appropriate computation core. Tensor Core kernels are generated using the Bolt technology integrated within TVM. When the dynamic input operator's current shape have not been recorded, kernels for both types of computation units are generated, performance data is sampled, and stored in a database. When encountering the same workload in the future, prior data can be retrieved from the database. Once sufficient samples are collected, we use a binary classification model trained on the available data to determine the most suitable deployment hardware core during the compilation phase.

4.5 Kernel Dispatcher

When the dynamic shape operator has a relatively small range of possible input shapes, the sampler will exhaustively sample all possible shapes. Consequently, the optimized kernels in the 'candidates' list are mapped to the corresponding input shapes. At runtime, the operator will automatically map to the appropriate kernel based on the input shape, ensuring execution on the appropriate computational core. However, when the range of possible input shapes is large, the sampler may not cover all operators. In such cases, we train a decision tree to map input shapes to their respective optimization strategies.

5 Experiments

Workloads. In this study, we selected the BERT [5] model as our end-to-end model for evaluation. As one of the pioneering large language models to introduce the Transformer architecture, BERT has had a profound impact on contemporary mainstream models. Its support for dynamic input lengths makes it a representative example of a typical dynamic model. In large language models (LLMs), dynamic shape operators predominantly arise in matrix multiplication operations within Q, K and V computations. Consequently, we have chosen batch matmul and dense operations, which are related to matrix multiplication, as the single-operation workloads for evaluating dynamic input shapes. Given that BERT's token lengths range from 1 to 128, we sampled 12 different input shapes within this range for our evaluation. This choice allows us to comprehensively assess the impact of dynamic input shapes on model performance.

Environment. We conducted this evaluation on two platforms. First, in a general computing environment, we selected server-grade CPUs and GPUs [13]. Second, to facilitate the deployment of the model in resource-constrained environments, we utilized edge devices to perform our evaluation. The detailed configurations of both platforms are as follows: In the cloud server, we used an Intel Xeon Gold 6248R processor and an NVIDIA A100 GPU [13], with the GPU toolkit version being CUDA 12.2, and the operating system was Ubuntu 18.04.6 LTS. On the edge device, we used an ARMv8 Processor rev 1 (v8l) and an NVIDIA Orin NX GPU [9], with the GPU toolkit version being CUDA 11.4, and the operating system was Linux 5.10.104 running on Ubuntu 20.04.

5.1 Single Operator Performance

For the evaluation of a single operator, we selected the batch MatMul operator, simulating a scenario where large language models (LLMs) handle dynamic input. In this scenario, with a fixed batch size and hidden size, the operator dynamically adjusts based on the input sequence length. We fixed the batch size at 192 and the hidden size at 64, selecting 12 different sequence lengths to construct the evaluation benchmark, represented as BatchMatMul([192,L,64], [192,L,64]). We conducted the evaluation on both the Nvidia A100 and Orin platforms, as illustrated in Figs. 4, On the Nvidia A100 platform, DTuner outperformed DietCode by up to 19.3%, with an average improvement of 9.0%. On the Orin platform, DTuner outperformed DietCode by up to 25.7%, with an average improvement of 9.0%.

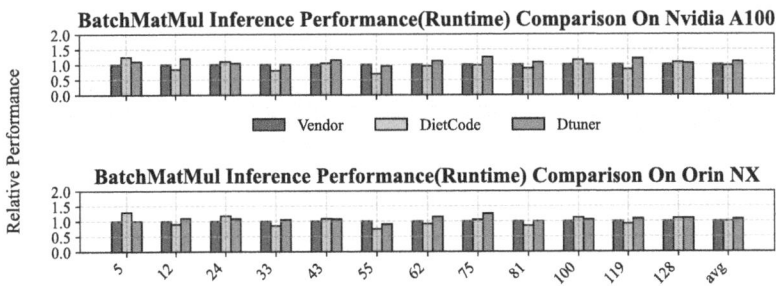

Fig. 4. Performance (the relative speedup of inference latency compared to the vendor) of BatchMatMul ([192, L, 64], [192, L, 64]) (y-axis: higher is better).

5.2   End-to-End Model Performance

We assessed our method by evaluating the inference performance of the BERT base model. After applying compilation optimizations to the BERT base model using DTuner and DietCode, we conducted tests under varying input conditions, with the input sequence length ranging from 0 to 128. Specifically, 12 different inputs were randomly sampled, and each input was used for inference five times. We recorded the inference performance relative to that of the vendor's operator library. On the Nvidia A100 platform, the inference performance of the BERT base model optimized with DTuner averaged a 7.0% improvement over DietCode, with a maximum observed improvement of 24.3%, according to the experimental results, which are shown in Figs. 5. On the Orin platform, DTuner showed an average improvement of 6.0% over DietCode, with a maximum improvement of 27.5%.

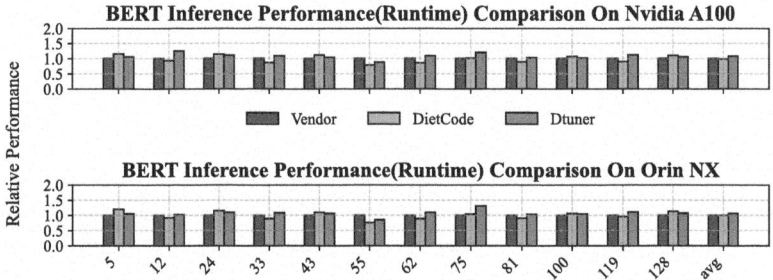

Fig. 5. Performance (the relative speedup of inference latency compared to the vendor) of bert_base varies with different inputs (y-axis: higher is better).

5.3   Compilation Time

Compilation time is a critical metric for evaluating the usability of optimization algorithms. When the optimization time for a single operator is too slow, it can severely impact user experience and significantly reduce the efficiency of deployment. As shown in Fig. 6, due to their extensive search spaces, DietCode and Ansor [20] have optimization times that are 2 to 3 orders of magnitude slower than DTuner. This allows DTuner to sample and optimize more shapes for operators with dynamic input shapes, resulting in better average performance.

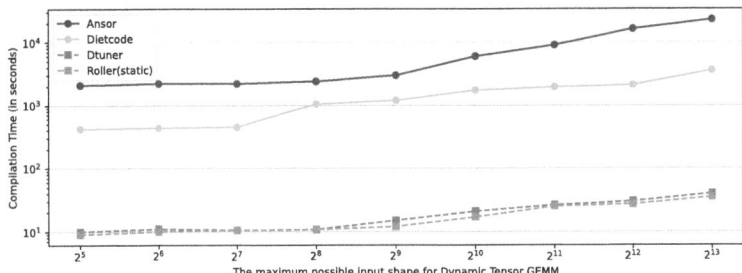

Fig. 6. The impact of input shape changes on optimization time.

6   Conclusion

With the advancement of models like large language models, optimizing dynamic shape tensor programs has become increasingly important. Traditional optimization methods, which are primarily based on search algorithms, do not support the fast tuning required for extensive sampling of specific shapes. As a result, they fail to achieve good average performance across all input shapes. We propose a constructive operator optimization approach that limits the search space to tiling sizes, allowing for efficient optimization of more sampled shapes and achieving better overall performance. Although DTuner offers better average performance for dynamic shape tensor programs, its peak performance for certain shapes is still inferior to search-based optimization algorithms like Ansor. Therefore, the challenge lies in optimizing these cases to match the performance of static shape operator optimization algorithms.

References

1. Google cloud TPU. https://cloud.google.com/tpu. Information on Google's Tensor Processing Units. Accessed 24 Aug 2024
2. Abadi, M., et al.: {TensorFlow}: a system for {Large-Scale} machine learning. In: 12th USENIX Symposium on Operating Systems Design and Implementation (OSDI 2016), pp. 265–283 (2016)
3. Chen, T., et al.: {TVM}: An automated {End-to-End} optimizing compiler for deep learning. In: 13th USENIX Symposium on Operating Systems Design and Implementation (OSDI 2018), pp. 578–594 (2018)
4. Chen, T., et al.: Learning to optimize tensor programs. In: Advances in Neural Information Processing Systems, vol. 31 (2018)
5. Devlin, J., Lee, K., Toutanova, K.: BERT: pre-training of deep bidirectional transformers for language understanding. arXiv preprint arXiv:1810.04805 (2018)
6. Lai, R., et al.: Relax: composable abstractions for end-to-end dynamic machine learning (2023). https://arxiv.org/abs/2311.02103
7. Lattner, C., et al.: MLIR: scaling compiler infrastructure for domain specific computation. In: 2021 IEEE/ACM International Symposium on Code Generation and Optimization (CGO), pp. 2–14. IEEE (2021)

8. Liu, H., Diao, B., Chen, W., Xu, Y.: A resource-aware workload scheduling method for unbalanced GEMMs on GPUs. Comput. J. bxae110 (2024)
9. Mittal, S.: A survey on optimized implementation of deep learning models on the NVIDIA Jetson platform. J. Syst. Architect. **97**, 428–442 (2019)
10. Radford, A., Wu, J., Child, R., Luan, D., Amodei, D., Sutskever, I.: Language models are unsupervised multitask learners (2019)
11. Radford, A.: Improving language understanding by generative pre-training (2018)
12. Rotem, N., et al.: Glow: graph lowering compiler techniques for neural networks. arXiv preprint arXiv:1805.00907 (2018)
13. Sanzharov, V.V., Frolov, V.A., Galaktionov, V.A.: Survey of NVIDIA RTX technology. Program. Comput. Softw. **46**, 297–304 (2020)
14. Shen, H., Chen, T., Liu, Y., Guestrin, C.: Nimble: a compiler and runtime for efficient dynamic neural networks. In: Proceedings of Machine Learning and Systems (MLSys), pp. 1–13. MLSys Organization, Virtual (2021)
15. TensorFlow Development Team: XLA: Tensorflow, compiled. https://www.tensorflow.org/xla
16. Tillet, P.: Triton: an intermediate language and compiler for tiled neural network computations. In: Proceedings of the 3rd ACM SIGPLAN International Workshop on Machine Learning and Programming Languages, pp. 1–12 (2019)
17. Vaswani, A.: Attention is all you need. In: Advances in Neural Information Processing Systems (2017)
18. Xing, J., Wang, L., Zhang, S., Chen, J., Chen, A., Zhu, Y.: Bolt: bridging the gap between auto-tuners and hardware-native performance. Proc. Mach. Learn. Syst. **4**, 204–216 (2022)
19. Zheng, B., et al.: DietCode: automatic optimization for dynamic tensor programs. Proc. Mach. Learn. Syst. **4**, 848–863 (2022)
20. Zheng, L., Yan, E., Chen, T., Moreau, T., Zhang, Z.: Ansor: Generating high-performance tensor programs for deep learning. In: 14th USENIX Symposium on Operating Systems Design and Implementation (OSDI), pp. 863–879. USENIX Association, Virtual (2020)
21. Zheng, L., et al.: Ansor: generating {High-Performance} tensor programs for deep learning. In: 14th USENIX symposium on operating systems design and implementation (OSDI 2020), pp. 863–879 (2020)
22. Zheng, Z., et al.: BladeDISC: optimizing dynamic shape machine learning workloads via compiler approach. Proc. ACM Manage. Data **1**(3), 1–29 (2023)
23. Zhu, H., et al.: ROLLER: fast and efficient tensor compilation for deep learning. In: 16th USENIX Symposium on Operating Systems Design and Implementation (OSDI), pp. 599–616 (2022)
24. Zhu, H., et al.: {ROLLER}: fast and efficient tensor compilation for deep learning. In: 16th USENIX Symposium on Operating Systems Design and Implementation (OSDI 2022), pp. 233–248 (2022)

Efficient Implementation of the LOBPCG Algorithm on a CPU-GPU Cluster

Yang Liu[1,2], Yonghua Zhao[1(✉)], Zexin Wang[1,2], Rongfeng Huang[3],
Dingye Zhang[1,2], and Xinyin Zhang[1,2]

[1] Computer Network Information Center, Chinese Academy of Science,
Beijing, China
yhzhao@sccas.cn
[2] University of Chinese Academy of Sciences, Beijing, China
[3] School of Information Science and Technology, Shijiazhuang Tiedao University,
Shijiazhuang, Hebei, China

Abstract. The Locally Optimal Block Preconditioned Conjugate Gradient (LOBPCG) algorithm is an effective algorithm for solving large-scale sparse eigenvalue problems in various scientific and engineering applications. Based on a distributed CPU-GPU heterogeneous environment, this paper presents an optimized approach for the efficient solution of sparse eigenvalue problems utilizing the LOBPCG algorithm. To conceal intra-node data transfer and reduce the influence of the cross-node MPI communication overhead, we employ a sparse matrix regular two-dimensional partitioning scheme. To enhance GPU data throughput and data reuse, we consolidate multiple sparse matrix-vector multiplications (SPMV) into a single sparse matrix-matrix multiplication (SPMM). Furthermore, for the irregular dense matrix-matrix multiplication (GEMM) involved in the LOBPCG algorithm, we design an adaptive batched GEMM technique for GPU execution. Extensive experimental results demonstrate the computational efficiency and scalability of our approach. Our implementation achieves a significant speedup in solving typical matrices compared to the SLEPc library. The strong scalability performance exceeds 58%.

Keywords: LOBPCG · Eigenvalue Solver · Distributed Heterogeneous

1 Introduction

Large-scale sparse symmetric eigenvalue solvers are critically needed in various application domains, such as electromagnetics [22], hydrodynamics [24], quantum mechanics [26], machine learning [14] and spectral clustering [27]. Typically, these problems are addressed using iterative methods, such as subspace methods [20] and Conjugate Gradient (CG) methods. The Locally Optimal Block Preconditioned Conjugate Gradient (LOBPCG) method [16] is a subspace CG iterative approach specifically designed for solving symmetric eigenvalue problems.

© IFIP International Federation for Information Processing 2025
Published by Springer Nature Switzerland AG 2025
X. Chen et al. (Eds.): NPC 2024, LNCS 15527, pp. 65–76, 2025.
https://doi.org/10.1007/978-981-96-2830-8_6

The LOBPCG algorithm integrates block techniques with the conjugate gradient approach, employing various preconditioning strategies to efficiently solve the smallest (or largest) eigenvalues of sparse symmetric matrices. Its widespread effectiveness has led to implementations in several prominent solver libraries, including SLEPc [15], MAGMA [1,23], BLOPEX [17], PRIMME [21], and Anasazi [4]. SLEPc relies on PETSc [5] for parallel linear algebra operations, and recent enhancements in PETSc for GPU computing have enabled SLEPc to offload certain matrix and vector computations to GPUs. MAGMA supports single-node CPUs/GPUs parallelism and includes optimized BLAS routines [8,23]. The introduction of SELL-P data format for sparse matrix computations and optimized BLAS-routines has improved the computational efficiency of the LOBPCG algorithm [2,3].

With the increasing adoption of large-scale CPU-GPU clusters, efficiently implementing algorithms in these complex environments has become a critical area of focus. However, research on applying the LOBPCG algorithm to solve eigenvalue problems in such environments remains limited.

In this paper, we present an efficient LOBPCG algorithm with significant scalability tailored for distributed CPU-GPU heterogeneous environments. The key contributions of our work are as follows:

- We develop an efficient and scalable LOBPCG algorithm optimized for distributed CPU-GPU heterogeneous environments. Our implementation demonstrates significant speedups, achieving up to 50x performance improvement over SLEPc implementation.
- We design a regular two-dimensional partitioning scheme for sparse matrices in distributed environment to conceal intra-node data transfers and reduce cross-node MPI communication overhead influence.
- We enhance GPU data throughput and reuse by leveraging block-based computations. We also design new computation kernels and an adaptive framework to improve computational efficiency on GPU processors.

2   LOBPCG Algorithm

The generalized eigenvalue problem is defined for the $N \times N$ symmetric matrices A and B. If there exists a set of scalars Φ and a set of orthogonal vectors X such that $AX = \Phi BX$, then the vectors X are referred to as eigenvectors, and the corresponding Φ are their eigenvalues. Here, each $\Phi^i \in \mathbb{R}$, and each vector X^i is an element of $\mathbb{R}^N$. The LOBPCG algorithm is characterized by several key components: preconditioning, search subspace construction, orthogonalization, and the Rayleigh-Ritz (R-R) method.

Preconditioners are employed to enhance the convergence rate of the LOBPCG algorithm. Commonly used preconditioners include the approximate inverse preconditioners [10], incomplete LU factorization [19], and algebraic multigrid methods [18], etc. The selection of an appropriate preconditioner, tailored to the properties of the matrix A, can significantly reduce the spectral range and thus expedite convergence.

The search subspace S is spanned by a set of dense vectors, including the current approximate eigenvectors X, the preconditioned residual vectors R, and the previous approximate eigenvectors P. This subspace captures the eigenvalue information of the original sparse matrix A. The R-R method projects the matrix A onto the smaller-scale subspace S, effectively reducing the eigenvalue problem to a smaller-scale problem. The iterative update of the subspace vectors continues until the residual norm satisfies the convergence criterion.

Orthogonalization is employed to maintain numerical stability by ensuring the subspace vectors remain linearly independent, allowing for an accurate and stable solution of the projected matrix. Common orthogonalization methods include Gram Schmidt orthogonalization [7], Householder transformations [25], etc.

As depicted in Algorithm 1, the LOBPCG algorithm includes two principal computations: dense matrix multiplications, which are computation-intensive, and sparse matrix multiplications, which are memory-bound. The efficient execution of these operations, in conjunction with the strategic selection of preconditioners and orthogonalization method, is crucial for the performance of the LOBPCG algorithm in solving large-scale eigenvalue problems.

3   Implementation in the Distributed CPU-GPU Cluster

In this section, we detail the implementation of the LOBPCG algorithm specifically designed for a distributed CPU-GPU cluster. Figure 1 illustrates the flowchart, covering specific calculations involved in a single processor, cross-node

---

Algorithm 1. LOBPCG Algorithm

1: **Input:** A: Sparse matrix of size $N \times N$; nBs: Block size; $neig$: Number of desired eigenvalues; τ: Convergence tolerance; X^0: Initial orthonormal vectors of size $N \times nBs$; K: Preconditioner.

2: **Output:** Φ: Eigenvalues; Σ: Eigenvectors.

3: Allocate memory for $\Phi \in \mathbb{R}^{nBs}$, and $\Theta, P, W, R \in \mathbb{R}^{nBs \times N}$; initialize $i \leftarrow 0$

4: $[\Phi^0, \Theta^0] \leftarrow$ **Rayleigh-Ritz**$(A, X^0, 3 \times nBs)$

5: $X^0 \leftarrow X^0 \Theta^0$, $R^0 \leftarrow AX^0 - X^0 \Phi^0$

6: **while** $convs < neig$ **do**

7:     $W^i \leftarrow K^{-1} R^i$

8:     $S \leftarrow [X^i, W^i, P^i]$

9:     $[\Phi^i, \Theta^i] \leftarrow$ **Rayleigh-Ritz**$(A, S, 3 \times nBs)$

10:     $X^{i+1} \leftarrow S\Theta^i$, $R^{i+1} \leftarrow AX^{i+1} - X^{i+1}\Phi^i$, $P^{i+1} \leftarrow [0, R^i, P^i]\Theta^i$

11:     **if** $\|R^{i+1}\|_2 < \tau$ **then**

12:         Store the approximate eigenvectors in Σ, $convs \leftarrow convs + 1$

13:     **end if**

14:     $i \leftarrow i + 1$

15: **end while**

16: Output eigenvalues Φ and eigenvectors Σ

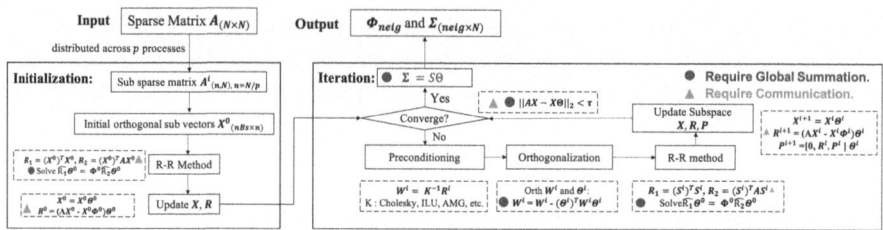

Fig. 1. The distributed cross-node implementation of the LOBPCG algorithm.

communication and the global summation operation. The majority of computations are performed on the GPUs, while the CPUs primarily manage communication tasks. Before and after inter-node communication handled by the CPUs, data must be copied from the GPU to the CPU, and then transferred back to the target GPU.

The input sparse matrix A is typically stored in the widely utilized Compressed Sparse Row (CSR) format [9], with the row blocks evenly distributed across processes. Based on this row partitioning scheme, the matrix A^i is further partitioned into column blocks within each processor, where $A^{(i,i)}$ represents the diagonal blocks and $A^{(i,j),i\neq j}$ represents the off-diagonal blocks (see Fig. 3(a)). Correspondingly, the vectors are also distributed across each process according to the same row partitioning scheme.

In the R-R method, the projection requires the computation of the projection matrices $R_1 = S^T S$ and $R_2 = S^T AS$. Within each process, the sparse matrix multiplication for computing R_2 necessitates intra-node CPU-GPU data transfers and inter-node CPU-CPU data exchanges to obtain the correct right-hand side vectors(see Fig. 3(c)). After R_1 and R_2 are computed, each process holds a portion of the complete projection matrices $\hat{R}_1$ and $\hat{R}_2$. To construct the full projection matrices, the partial results R_1 and R_2 from all processes must be combined (summation), which involves GPU-CPU data transfers followed by a CPU-CPU global summation operation.

3.1 Computational and Communication Overlap

Due to inherent memory access limitations in Sparse Matrix-Vector Multiplication (SPMV), the GPU implementation of the LOBPCG algorithm leverages block vector operations to increase computational intensity. This approach replaces SPMV with Sparse Matrix-Matrix Multiplication (SPMM) [2]. The distributed SPMM operation can be described by the following equation:

$$Y^{(i,k)} = \sum_{j=0}^{p-1} A^{(i,j)} X^{(j,k)} = A^{(i,i)} X^{(i,k)} + \sum_{\substack{j=0 \\ j\neq i}}^{p-1} A^{(i,j)} X^{(j,k)} \qquad (1)$$

where $i, j = 1, \ldots, p, i \neq j, \quad k = 1, \ldots, nBs.$

Data transfer between cross-node CPUs is typically managed using MPI communication, with non-blocking MPI operations (e.g., MPI_Isend and MPI_Irecv) utilizing data buffers to avoid waiting time between CPUs. PCIe serves as the primary communication interface between CPU and GPU, offering high bandwidth and low latency with multi-channel bidirectional data transfer. The GPU hardware scheduler can concurrently manage multiple task queues, allowing GPU computations to proceed while data transfers to and from the CPU are ongoing. Leveraging these CPU and GPU hardware support, we efficiently organize computations and communications to achieve computation-communication overlap.

By the sparse matrix row and column two-dimensional partitioning scheme, during the SPMM computation, diagonal block computations do not require communication, enabling overlap with non-blocking MPI communications, achieving the off-diagonal block communications are hidden behind diagonal block computations. Furthermore, communication overhead between CPUs and data transfers between CPU and GPU can be masked by GPU kernel computations. The ideal optimal computation and communication overlap is illustrated in Fig. 2(b), where communication expenses are exactly hidden by computational costs. Generally, when using a small number of nodes, the computational kernel overhead exceeds the communication overhead. As the number of nodes increases, the proportion of communication overhead gradually rises while the kernel execution time decreases, leading to the GPU computational kernel waiting for data transfers and memory access.

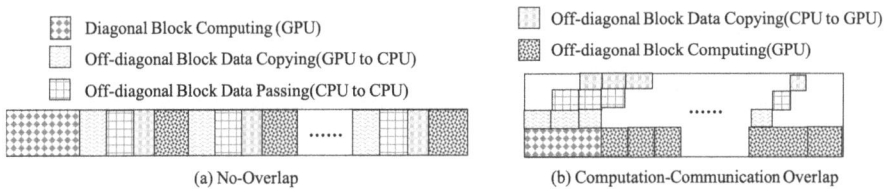

(a) No-Overlap   (b) Computation-Communication Overlap

Fig. 2. Schematic diagram illustrating the difference between no-overlap and computation-communication overlap in a distributed CPU-GPU environment.

To minimize unnecessary data transfers, we perform a preprocessing step to extract communication information for off-diagonal blocks $A^{(i,j)}$. Instead of collecting non-zero column indices from individual rows, we aggregate them across row blocks. This block-based compression strategy leverages the typically higher densities of non-zero elements in certain regions of sparse matrices, often yielding significant efficiency gains. We collect the indices of non-zero columns in blocks and disseminate this information to other processes. Each process receives indices for elements that need to be sent to or received from other processes, ensuring that only relevant elements are transmitted during MPI communication. To facilitate this process, we employ six additional arrays beyond the standard CSR format, as depicted in Fig. 3(b). Although this block-based compression scheme reduces redundant data in MPI communication, it requires reindexing elements within each row for computation. Fortunately, this overhead can be partly mitigated by overlapping computation and communication.

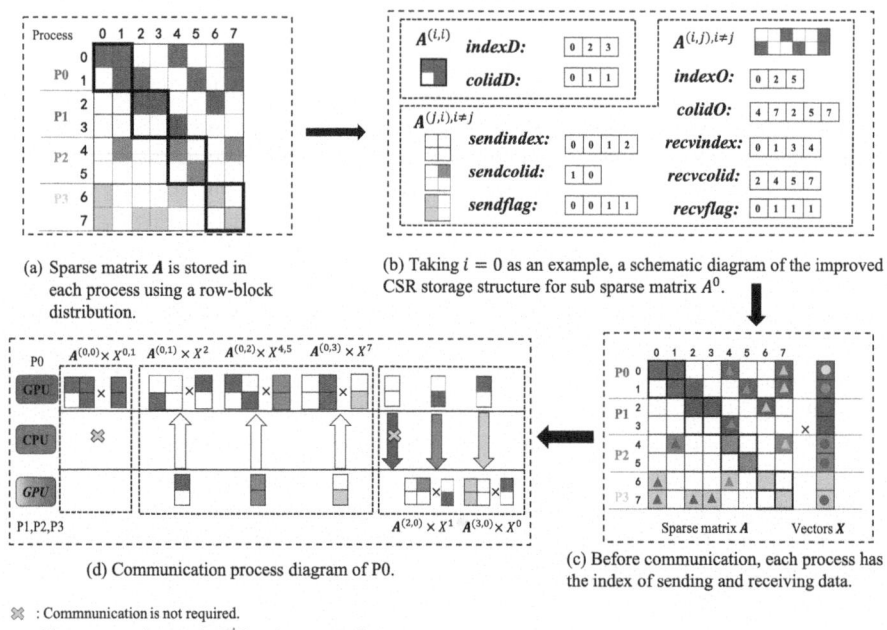

(a) Sparse matrix A is stored in each process using a row-block distribution.

(b) Taking $i = 0$ as an example, a schematic diagram of the improved CSR storage structure for sub sparse matrix A^0.

(d) Communication process diagram of P0.

(c) Before communication, each process has the index of sending and receiving data.

✵ : Commnunication is not required.

▲ : The process needs to receive X^i from the corresponding process.

● : The process needs to send X^i to the corresponding process.

Fig. 3. Schematic diagram of distributed SPMM.

3.2   SPMM GPU Kernel Design

SPMM is typically a memory-bound operation, where the irregular distribution of non-zero elements often results in inefficient access to the vector X, leading to a low ratio of floating-point operations to memory accesses. To address this inefficiency, we designed an optimized computational kernel that combines the CSR-vector [6] and the CSR-adaptive method [11]. The CSR-vector approach assigns a configurable number of threads to process each matrix row, utilizing reduction to aggregate results. The CSR-adaptive method allocates rows or row blocks to thread blocks, with each block handles a roughly equal number of non-zero elements.

In our implementation of the SPMM kernel, matrix rows are classified as either "long" or "short" based on the number of non-zero elements they contain. Long rows with a large number of non-zero elements tend to be a bottleneck as processing them with a single thread block would be inefficient. To alleviate this, we assign multiple threads to process long rows, aggregating results using atomic operations. The Single Instruction Multiple Thread execution model of GPUs schedules threads in warps. Within a Streaming Multiprocessor(SM), only one warp from a block is executed at a time. If a warp is stalled, for example, while waiting for memory access, the SM switches to another warp to avoid idle time. To minimize warp divergence and reduce latency, we ensure that the number of threads processing each long row is a multiple of the warp size. This parallel processing of long rows mitigates the imbalance in thread workload. For short rows, we employ CSR-vector approach to handle them efficiently. This classification of rows into long and short addresses thread workload imbalance and provides adaptability for matrices with unknown sparsity patterns compared to fixed-row partitioning.

Additionally, we exploit the three-level memory hierarchy of the GPU by storing computation data in registers and shared memory. These high-bandwidth storage structures offer superior performance for discontinuous memory access. Threads leverage shared memory to cache intermediate results, while the relatively small "nBs" value allows us to store the same positions of subspace vectors in register memory, thereby improving data reuse during sparse matrix computations.

3.3 GEMM Adaptive Batched Framework

In the LOBPCG algorithm, the "block" computation involves multiplying "wide" matrices ($nBs \ll n$) with "tall" matrices ($n \gg nBs$). Although the large value of n results in a significant computational workload, the block size (nBs) is relatively small (typically less than 10). Vendor-provided BLAS routines often underutilize GPU resources due to fixed thread block sizes and inefficient handling of irregular matrix sizes.

Certain BLAS libraries include batched routines for operations like LU factorization [13], which are designed to handle a set of small matrices in parallel. To address the inefficiencies caused by irregular matrix sizes in BLAS-level matrix multiplications, we leverage batched operations. Specifically, for GEMM in LOBPCG and similar operations, we introduce an adaptive "k-partitioned" batched computation framework. This framework improves GPU kernel data throughput and enhances thread utilization for irregular matrix structures.

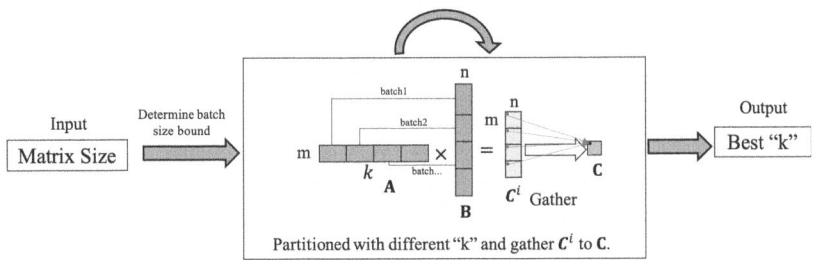

Fig. 4. The "k-partitioned" Batched Computing Framework.

The adaptive "k-partitioned" batched framework (as shown in Fig. 4) consists of three main steps: (1) Determine the maximum batch size upper bound. (2) Uniformly partition the matrix based on the largest k dimension. Each batch contains matrices of the same size, zero-padding or separate handling of excess blocks can be employed. (3)Aggregate results from each batch.

To determine the optimal batch size, it is sufficient to iterate through the "k-partitioned" framework with various batch sizes just once, prior to running the solver. The cost of this iterative process is negligible compared to the overall iteration cost and the resulting performance benefits. Furthermore, the additional memory overhead introduced is insignificant, as the size of C^i is typically small. This framework is flexible and can be extended to other computational kernels, significantly improving GPU utilization and overall performance of such BLAS calculation. Experimental results validate the effectiveness of this framework.

4   Experimental Results

4.1   Experimental Setup and Test DataSet

Our experimental platform consists of a cluster with over 4000 computing nodes. Each node is equipped with a 32-core AMD Zen architecture processor, accompanied by four AMD Instinct MI60 GPUs. The processors are organized into four complex core dies, forming a Non-Uniform Memory Access (NUMA) node configuration. The cluster nodes are interconnected via HDR InfiniBand, offering a bandwidth capacity of 200 Gbps. For the purposes of our experiments, a one-to-one binding between CPU cores and GPUs was enforced, with no direct communication between GPUs.

The test dataset includes matrices from the SuiteSparse Matrix Collection [12] and various sizes of three-dimensional 7-point Laplacian matrices [17]. Details of the matrices are listed in Table 1. For the cross-node CPU implementation of the LOBPCG algorithm, we consider the latest SLEPc as the SOTA benchmark for eigenvalue solving. The convergence criterion is set to $\tau = \|Ax - \lambda x\| < 1e - 6$, and the number of desired eigenvalues $neig = 5$, with identical initial random vectors. Although the preconditioner is a important component of the LOBPCG algorithm, it was not utilized in these experimental tests.

4.2   Performance of Execution Time

We compared the solving times of our implementation with SLEPc. Figure 5 presents the timing results. Our implementation demonstrates significant performance gains, achieving solving times up to 50 times faster. Additionally, as the block size (nBs) increases, a slight performance improvement is observed for certain matrices. This enhancement can be attributed to the batched computing

Table 1. Matrices from the SuiteSparse Matrix Collection and Laplacian matrices. NNZ_Row denotes NNZ(A)/N(A), It(nBs) denotes the average iterations for our implementation.

Name	N	NNZ	NNZ_Row	Application kind	It(5)	It(10)
Si87H76	240,369	10,661,631	44.36	Chemistry Problem	390	280
tmt_sym	726,713	5,080,961	6.99	Electromagnetics Problem	3,217	2,001
SiO2	155,331	11,283,503	72.64	Chemistry Problem	314	198
H2O	67,024	2,216,736	33.07	Chemistry Problem	405	287
apache2	715,176	4,817,870	6.74	Structural Problem	10,601	5,211
Si5H12	19,896	738,598	37.12	Chemistry Problem	158	124
roadNet-TX	1,393,383	5,236,703	3.75	Undirected Graph	2,942	1,880
dblp-2010	326,186	1,615,400	4.95	Undirected Graph	799	662
Laplacian-50^3	125,000	860,000	6.88	Undirected Graph	302	221
Laplacian-100^3	1,000,000	6,940,000	6.94	Undirected Graph	537	395

capabilities of GPU environments, where an increased subspace size has a minimal impact on matrix computation time but significantly reduces the number of required iterations.

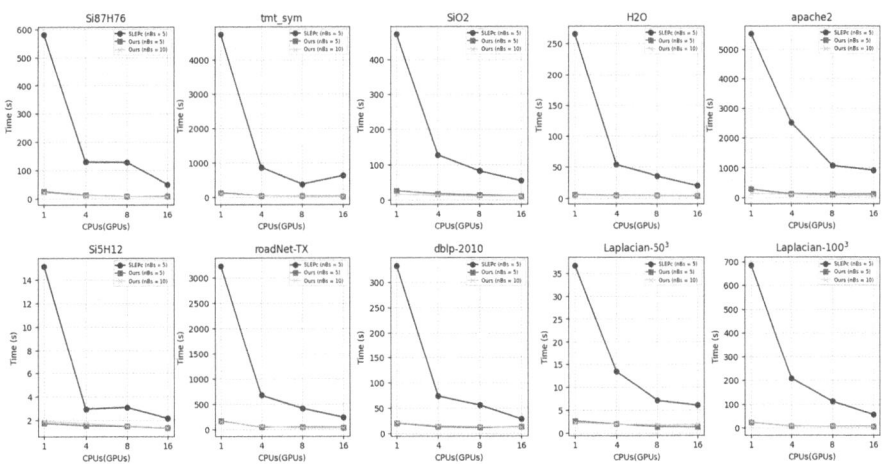

Fig. 5. Performance comparison between our implementation and SLEPc in eigenvalue solving with different numbers of CPUs(GPUs).

We further evaluated the effectiveness of the adaptive "k-partitioned" batched computing framework. Table 2 compares the performance of $X^T X$ between `rocblas_dgemm` (non-batched) and our framework across different matrix sizes. The experimental results demonstrate that the GEMM operation

Table 2. Execution time comparison between `rocblas_dgemm` and our framework with $nBs = 5$ and $nBs = 10$.

X Size	rocblas_dgemm (s)	Ours (s)	X Size	rocblas_dgemm (s)	Ours (s)
5×10^3	0.052	0.052	10×10^3	0.053	0.053
5×10^4	3.861	0.086	10×10^4	3.861	0.084
5×10^5	38.379	0.092	10×10^5	38.404	0.098
5×10^6	383.632	0.240	10×10^6	383.851	0.276

using the batched framework achieves an acceleration ratio of up to 119x compared to the non-batched implementation. Increasing the nBs value has a slight impact on GPU kernel execution time but significantly reduces the number of iterations, leading to further performance improvements.

4.3   Performance of Scalability

We analyzed the scalability of our implementation across multiple nodes using several matrices. The experimental results (Fig. 6) reveal that the SPMM and GEMM operations account for 70% to 97% of the total computation time. Additionally, to evaluate scalability across multiple nodes, we tested a Laplacian matrix of order 64 million, and the strong scalability performance for this matrix exceeded 58%.

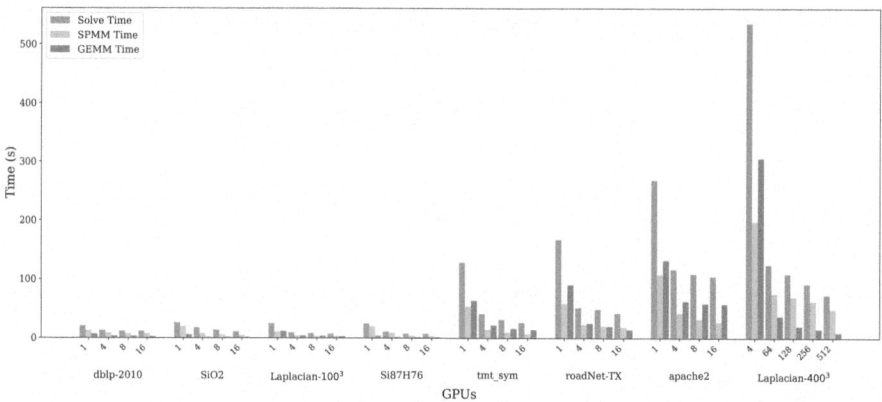

Fig. 6. Performance of SPMM and GEMM in eigenvalue solving for several matrices.

5   Conclusion

In this paper, we introduce an efficient implementation of the LOBPCG algorithm in a distributed CPU-GPU heterogeneous environment for solving symmetric eigenvalue problems. We have developed a two-dimensional partitioning scheme using the CSR format and designed a multi-layer computation communication overlap strategy for SPMM. Additionally, we optimized the GEMM by an adaptive batched framework. Our experimental results demonstrate that these optimizations significantly enhance the performance of the LOBPCG algorithm on a CPU-GPU cluster for eigenvalue solving, achieving speedups multiple times over the SLEPc implementation.

Acknowledgments. This study was supported by the Strategic Priority Research Program of the Chinese Academy of Sciences (No. XDB0500101).

References

1. Anzt, H., Sawyer, W., Tomov, S., Luszczek, P., Yamazaki, I., Dongarra, J.: Optimizing krylov subspace solvers on graphics processing units. In: Fourth International Workshop on Accelerators and Hybrid Exascale Systems (AsHES), IPDPS 2014, Phoenix, AZ. IEEE (2014)
2. Anzt, H., Tomov, S., Dongarra, J.J.: Accelerating the LOBPCG method on GPUs using a blocked sparse matrix vector product. In: SpringSim (HPS), pp. 75–82 (2015)
3. Anzt, H., Tsai, Y.M., Abdelfattah, A., Cojean, T., Dongarra, J.: Evaluating the performance of Nvidia's a100 ampere GPU for sparse and batched computations. In: 2020 IEEE/ACM Performance Modeling, Benchmarking and Simulation of High Performance Computer Systems (PMBS), pp. 26–38. IEEE (2020)
4. Baker, C.G., Hetmaniuk, U.L., Lehoucq, R.B., Thornquist, H.K.: Anasazi software for the numerical solution of large-scale eigenvalue problems. ACM Trans. Math. Softw. (TOMS) **36**(3), 1–23 (2009)
5. Balay, S., et al.: PETSc Web (2024). https://petsc.org/
6. Bell, N., Garland, M.: Implementing sparse matrix-vector multiplication on throughput-oriented processors. In: Proceedings of the Conference on High Performance Computing Networking, Storage and Analysis, pp. 1–11 (2009)
7. Björck, Å.: Numerics of gram-schmidt orthogonalization. Linear Algebra Appl. **197**, 297–316 (1994)
8. Brown, C., Abdelfattah, A., Tomov, S., Dongarra, J.J.: Design, optimization, and benchmarking of dense linear algebra algorithms on AMD GPUs. In: 2020 IEEE High Performance Extreme Computing Conference, HPEC 2020, Waltham, MA, USA, 22–24 September 2020, pp. 1–7. IEEE (2020). https://doi.org/10.1109/HPEC43674.2020.9286214
9. Buluç, A., Fineman, J.T., Frigo, M., Gilbert, J.R., Leiserson, C.E.: Parallel sparse matrix-vector and matrix-transpose-vector multiplication using compressed sparse blocks. In: Proceedings of the Twenty-First Annual Symposium on Parallelism in Algorithms and Architectures, pp. 233–244 (2009)
10. Chow, E., Saad, Y.: Approximate inverse preconditioners via sparse-sparse iterations. SIAM J. Sci. Comput. **19**(3), 995–1023 (1998)
11. Daga, M., Greathouse, J.L.: Structural agnostic SPMV: adapting CSR-adaptive for irregular matrices. In: 2015 IEEE 22nd International conference on high performance computing (HiPC), pp. 64–74. IEEE (2015)
12. Davis, T.A., Hu, Y.: The University of Florida sparse matrix collection. ACM Trans. Math. Softw. (TOMS) **38**(1), 1–25 (2011)

13. Dong, T., Haidar, A., Luszczek, P., Tomov, S., Abdelfattah, A., Dongarra, J.: Magma batched: a batched BLAS approach for small matrix factorizations and applications on GPUs. Technical report (2016)
14. Fortin, A., Jardak, M., Gervais, J., Pierre, R.: Localization of Hopf bifurcations in fluid flow problems. Int. J. Numer. Meth. Fluids **24**(11), 1185–1210 (1997)
15. Hernandez, V., Roman, J.E., Vidal, V.: SLEPc: a scalable and flexible toolkit for the solution of eigenvalue problems. ACM Trans. Math. Softw. (TOMS) **31**(3), 351–362 (2005)
16. Knyazev, A.V.: Toward the optimal preconditioned eigensolver: locally optimal block preconditioned conjugate gradient method. SIAM J. Sci. Comput. **23**(2), 517–541 (2001)
17. Knyazev, A.V., Argentati, M.E., Lashuk, I., Ovtchinnikov, E.E.: Block locally optimal preconditioned eigenvalue xolvers (BLOPEX) in HYPRE and PETSc. SIAM J. Sci. Comput. **29**(5), 2224–2239 (2007)
18. Ruge, J.W., Stüben, K.: Algebraic multigrid. In: Multigrid Methods, pp. 73–130. SIAM (1987)
19. Saad, Y.: ILUT: a dual threshold incomplete LU factorization. Numer. Linear Algebra Appl. **1**(4), 387–402 (1994)
20. Saad, Y.: Numerical Methods for Large Eigenvalue Problems: Revised Edition. SIAM (2011)
21. Stathopoulos, A., McCombs, J.R.: PRIMME: PReconditioned Iterative Multi-Method Eigensolver: Methods and software description. ACM Trans. Math. Softw. **37**(2), 21:1–21:30 (2010)
22. Sun, L., Ji, S., Ye, J.: A least squares formulation for a class of generalized eigenvalue problems in machine learning. In: Proceedings of the 26th Annual International Conference on Machine Learning, pp. 977–984 (2009)
23. Tomov, S., Dongarra, J., Baboulin, M.: Towards dense linear algebra for hybrid GPU accelerated manycore systems. Parallel Comput. **36**(5–6), 232–240 (2010). https://doi.org/10.1016/j.parco.2009.12.005
24. Turbiner, A.: The eigenvalue spectrum in quantum mechanics and the nonlinearization procedure. Soviet Physics Uspekhi **27**(9), 668 (1984)
25. Walker, H.F.: Implementation of the GMRES method using householder transformations. SIAM J. Sci. Stat. Comput. **9**(1), 152–163 (1988)
26. Zhou, P.: Numerical Analysis of Electromagnetic Fields. Springer, Cham (2012)
27. Zhuzhunashvili, D., Knyazev, A.: Preconditioned spectral clustering for stochastic block partition streaming graph challenge. In: 2017 IEEE High Performance Extreme Computing Conference (HPEC), pp. 1–6. IEEE (2017)

HP-CSF: An GPU Optimization Method for CP Decomposition of Incomplete Tensors

Guanxiong Liu[1] and Hao Wu[2(✉)]

[1] School of Computer Science and Technology, Chongqing University of Posts and
Telecommunications, Chongqing 400065, China
[2] College of Computer and Information Science, Southwest University,
Chongqing 400715, China
haowuf@gmail.com

Abstract. A tensor is multi-dimensional generalization of a vector and a matrix in high-dimensional space. Tensor decomposition can represent a high-order tensor into many low-dimensional factors, which can reduce computation and storage complexity during data processing. Canonical Polyadic (CP) decomposition is one of the most widely used decomposition frameworks, which decomposes a N-order tensor into N factor matrices via operating Matricized Tensor Times Khatri-Rao Product (MTTKRP) computation. However, the MTTKRP is the computational bottleneck for algorithms computing CP decomposition of incomplete tensors due to intermediate product of feature matrices. To reduce the computation complexity of MTTKRP, this paper presents Hyperparameter-CSF (HP-CSF). Its main idea is to increase the balance of load at thread-level and set up an allocation rule for parallel deployment. Compared to state-of-the-art works, our method achieves 100.7% speedup across NVIDIA Geforce RTX 4090 on a range of sparse tensors.

Keywords: MTTKRP · tensor decomposition · parallel deployment · CP

1 Introduction

Big data mining is an effective technology in industries. As numerous attributes can be labeled with tensor, it is valuable to achieve a complete tensor for data analysis. However, most tensors constructed from daily information are sparse. It is difficult to fill all the blanks of a high dimensional tensor. Therefore, exploring the missing data based on the known parts becomes a major task [1]. Tensor decomposition is an effective method for completing sparse tensors. It fills unknown elements of tensors based on the known data through dimensionality reduction.

Canonical Polyadic Decomposition (CPD) is widely used in tensor completion. It brings an idea that a single tensor can be divided into several sub-tensors and these sub-tensors could be merged to approximate the original tensor. As the distances from the merged tensor to the original tensor getting smaller on known elements, the confidence of filling positions getting stronger [2–4]. Given a rank-R sparse tensor, CPD model

© IFIP International Federation for Information Processing 2025
Published by Springer Nature Switzerland AG 2025
X. Chen et al. (Eds.): NPC 2024, LNCS 15527, pp. 77–90, 2025.
https://doi.org/10.1007/978-981-96-2830-8_7

constructs R rank-one tensors and calculates the summation from outer product of feature vectors to achieve the approximate tensor. To solve out the values filling in rank-one tensors, Alternating Least Squares (ALS) is a popular method to iteratively optimize CPD, which is called CP-ALS. Each iteration of CP-ALS updates one of the feature matrices with the other matrices fixed [5]. The calculation process includes two parts. The former is a multiplication of a matricized tensor and a Khatri-Rao product, and the second part is a pseudo-inverse of Hadamard product. Finally, multiply the products to achieve a new rank-one tensor. During this process, Matricized Tensor Times Khatri-Rao Product (MTTKRP) costs most of the time computation.

As Khatri-Rao product within MTTKRP requires lots of computation for intermediate results, [2] proposes an optimized equivalent calculation to avoid the large intermediate results. It uses known indices of nonzero elements for MTTKRP calculations rather than finishes the whole Khatri-Rao product. Further, [3] creates a structure called SPLATT to reduce additional multiplications. This structure creates a Compressed Sparse Fiber (CSF) storage format by compressing the repetitive indices on both slice and fiber levels [4]. For improving the performance on MTTKRP calculation, CSF-based format has been improved as B-CSF, HB-CSF [6], MM-CSF [7] and some local optimizations from [8–10]. The current proposed methods have contributions either on controlling load balance or reducing atomic conflicts. But there is still some practicability for improving.

In this paper, we propose an optimized approach based on HB-CSF data structure and improve the speed of calculation for GPU kernels. The contributions can be summarized as below:

- We propose a fine-grained parallel strategy on thread-level of GPU to decrease the atomic operations and improve the performance.
- We optimize a binning method on how to regroup the original dataset into different bins.
- We utilize a parallelism on multiple streams for kernel-level parallel computing.

2   Background

Assume that X is a third-order tensor with the sizes I, J, K of dimensions. CPD decomposes X into several small tensors and X is equivalent to the summation of these small tensors. The number of small tensors is named rank, denoted as R, and the small tensors are called rank-one tensors. A rank-one tensor could be constructed as an outer product of several vectors, and the original tensor X could be approximated by a summation of R rank-one tensors [11]. The structure of CPD is shown in Fig. 1 and the formulation can be written as (1). $\mathbf{A}, \mathbf{B}$ and $\mathbf{C}$ denote feature matrices. a, b and c denote vectors.

$$X \approx \sum_{r=1}^{R} \lambda_r a_r \circ b_r \circ c_r \equiv [\![\lambda; \mathbf{A}, \mathbf{B}, \mathbf{C}]\!] \tag{1}$$

Along different dimensions to convert X into unfolding matrices, the mode-1 matrices of X can be built as $X_1 \approx \mathbf{A}(\mathbf{C} \odot \mathbf{B})^{\mathrm{T}}$. As an approximation of X, the calculated dense tensor is denoted as $\tilde{X}$. $\left\|X - \tilde{X}\right\|_F$ is defined as the evaluating index for completion. Suppose mode-1 unfolding as an example, minimize $\left\|X - \tilde{X}\right\|_F$ is equivalent to minimize $\left\|X_1 - \hat{A}(C \odot B)^{\mathrm{T}}\right\|_F$. X_1 is a matricized tensor with elements unchanged. All the parameters without $\hat{A}$ are constants, then $\hat{A}$ can be solved as (2). $C \odot B$ is a Khatri-Rao product of C and B which requires JKR calculations. Because of the sparseness of X_1, most elements of $C \odot B$ won't be utilized. Consider an element of X_1 is at (i, y), there has column index $y = j + k * J$. [2] provides an optimization on $C \odot B$ and the element-based computation is shown as (3). $N_{i,:}$ is row i of intermediate matrix N.

$$\hat{A} = X_1 \left[(C \odot B)^{\mathrm{T}}\right]^\dagger = X_1(C \odot B)\left(C^{\mathrm{T}}C * B^{\mathrm{T}}B\right)^\dagger \tag{2}$$

$$N_{i,:} = \sum_{k=0}^{K} C(k,:) \sum_{j=0}^{J} X_{i,j,k} B(j,:) \tag{3}$$

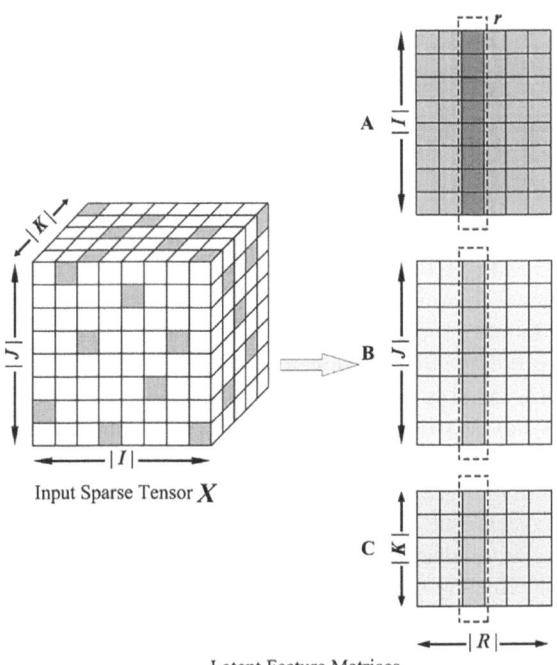

Input Sparse Tensor X

Latent Feature Matrices

Fig. 1. Structure of CPD model

3   Related Work

Related works have advanced a lot in parallel MTTKRP computing. As a common storage format, coordinate-based (COO) format is widely used. A third-order tensor stores each index of dimensions for elements, and extracts coordinate value to get slice and fiber. As another kind format, Compressed Sparse Fiber (CSF) is proposed in [4]. CSF contains six arrays and begins with reordering the COO data following an ascending order of dimension size. Then respectively counts the elements of each fiber and counts the fibers of each slice. Both formats are shown in Fig. 2. For COO-MTTKRP, each thread carries the same load for calculation, but it generates significant atomic conflicts which inhibits the performance. In CSF-MTTKRP, each thread works on a single slice without conflicts, but the slices referring to Fig. 2(c) have different loads on slices and fibers. As a result, the threads couldn't finish their jobs at the same moment and the completed threads within warps are idle, having a great waste of hardware.

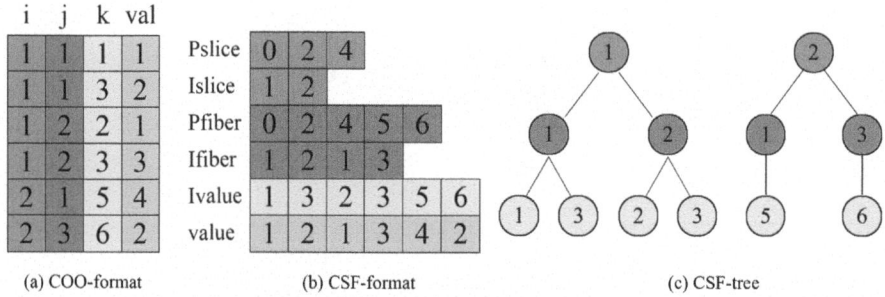

(a) COO-format   (b) CSF-format   (c) CSF-tree

Fig. 2. COO and CSF formats

To reduce load imbalance and threads conflicts, some parallel methods have been developed on COO and CSF formats. [12] proposes HICOO data format based on COO, rebuilding the original coordinates with double indices to reduce storage and grouping several small blocks into a superblock. [13] creates a new permutation format based on COO format and records the true position of initial permutation. [14] proposes a flagged-coordinate (F-COO) and uses two flags to indicate whether changes happen on slice or fiber. [15] replaces the COO format with HLS format by saving data in bitmap format and proposes a TCU optimization. [8] splits the original tensor into several subtensors and provides a vertex weighting scheme. [9] divides elements equally to each thread on CSF and stores intermediate result to reduce computation. [7] MM-CSF compares the fiber lengths of each mode for element and assigns it to the longest partition. [10] proposes an optimization on reducing repeated calculation. The current methods mainly reduce the calculations by merging similar fibers and reduce load balance with slice cutting. However, these two optimization ideas will cause negative impact on the opposite side. How to reduce the coupled effect is the focus of research.

4 Proposal Method

Our research is focused on Hybrid Balanced-CSF format (HB-CSF) from [6]. HB-CSF has a hybriding-phase, a balancing-phase and a binning-phase. In the hybriding-phase, HB-CSF divides the original data into three parts, expressed as COO, CSL and CSF. The slice with a single nonzero will be pushed into COO set; the slice with a single element of each fiber will be piled in CSL set; the other slices are placed in CSF set. Our proposed method is called hyperparameter-CSF (HP-CSF) and the overall process is shown in Fig. 3. We extend a testing phase to execute our method and set up an optimized parallel strategy. The time consumption of testing phase is not included in the experimental results.

4.1 Multiplying the Thread Load

To solve the problem of thread load balancing, [6] proposed Balance-CSF (B-CSF) to redistribute the elements from the original slices. Figure 4 shows the balancing phase with fiber threshold 1. B-CSF splits a heavy fiber into several light fibers and splits the slices into several light slices. In this way, slices will be reconstructed into more balanced slice-segments. That is a fiber-level operation which requires a threshold of fiber length.

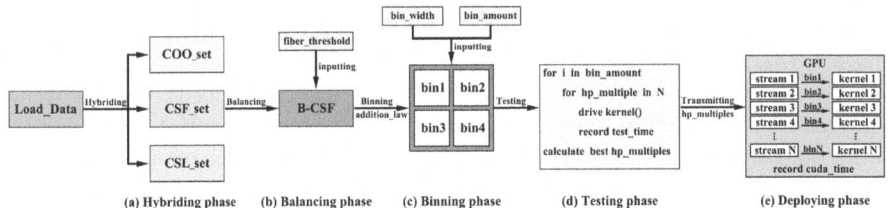

Fig. 3. Overall flow of proposed method HP-CSF

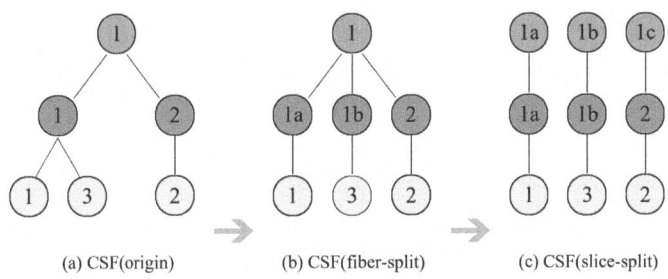

Fig. 4. Balancing phase of CSF

While different threads updating the same row of feature matrix, there would generate conflicts on reading and writing [16]. As a single slice is divided into several slices for different threads, there will decrease the load difference but generate more thread conflicts. To reduce the waste caused by atomic operation locking, HP-CSF multiplies the loads for threads to decrease the locking frequency. Figure 5 shows the differences between single load and multiple loads for threads. In Fig. 5(a), thread_1 and thread_2 will respectively execute the single load in cycle_1 referring to slice 1 and then take the other load referring to slice 6 in cycle_2. That will generate conflicts twice. In Fig. 5(b), both threads take double loads in cycle_1. If each thread could carry double loads for same slice, that means the threads idle from atomic conflicts would be reduction by half.

82   G. Liu and H. Wu

HP-CSF imports a hyperparameter *hp_multiple* to multiple the thread load on slice. Assume the best condition that all the loads from a thread are referring to the same slice, there will achieve the most speedup for least thread idle. In fact, it is difficult to set a rule for setting *hp_multiple*, because different datasets would generate a variety of B-CSF bins with various lengths. Consider each kind of GPU has a specific adaptability of computing for special dataset, the best *hp_multiple* is different for datasets and hard to be designed. Therefore, we test a series of parameters for *hp_multiple* to update feature matrix before training and get the time consumption. The testing phase is shown in Fig. 3(d). From the test results, we extract the best *hp_multiple* for each bin training.

4.2 Addition-Law for Datasets Binning

Another method to minimum load imbalance of CSF is binning. Suppose *fiber_threshold* is F. After being processed of balancing, the lengths of slices maybe 1, 2, 3, ..., F. Consider that threads from same block would deal slices of high deviation lengths. [6] and [17] use a power-law binning method to filter the slices with similar lengths in the same bin. To keep the load balance of threads, each slice is pushed into the corresponding bin according to its length. Bin-range is important for binning. It sets the maximum and minimum for each bin. The slice length should be within bin-range. If it adopts power-law for bin-range setting, the maximum for each bin is m^{n-1} and the minimum is m^{n-2}. Figure 6(a) shows the power-law binning. The white blanks with numbers are denoted as slices with their lengths and pushed into corresponding bins. The range of bin6 is (16, 32] with $m = 2$ and $n = 6$.

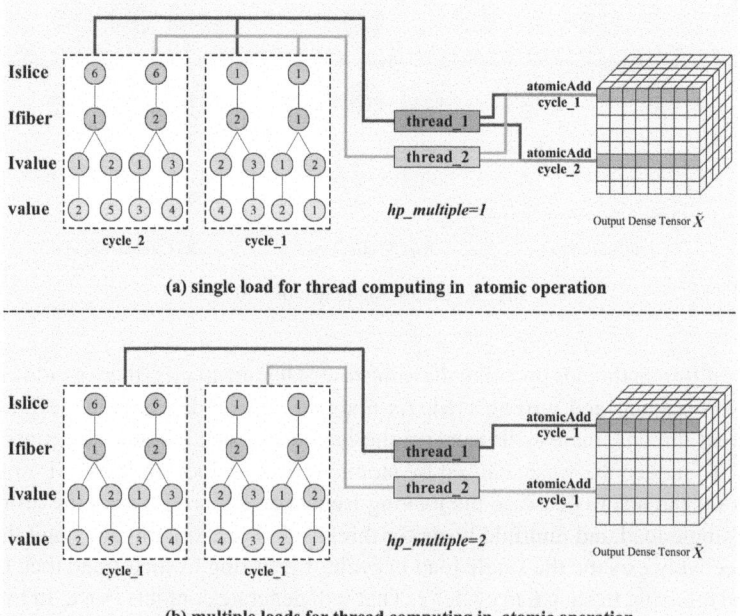

(a) single load for thread computing in atomic operation

(b) multiple loads for thread computing in atomic operation

Fig. 5. The difference between single load and multiple loads on thread computing

In the most ideal condition, improving *fiber_threshold* to achieve a larger bin of balanced slice-segments is helpful for calculation. But it is difficult to guarantee the balance of slice length in larger bin. Inputting *fiber_threshold* 128 provided by [6] and achieving the upper threshold of bins as [1, 2, 4, 8, 16, 32, 64, 128] from power-law binning. For the first bin and second bin, the slice-segments of each bin keep balance on slice length. The higher bins would include various lengths of slice-segments, which force an imbalance in thread load. Especially the last bin, the lengths of slice-segments are distributed from 65 to 128 and have great distinctions. Assume each slice from same bin could keep balance on slice length, then the longer length of slice will provide better performance in single thread computing. If each thread couldn't keep balance of load, it will generate a difference in calculation speed.

To decrease the imbalance on slice length from larger bins, HP-CSF replaces power-law with addition-law in binning phase. In Fig. 6(a), bin6 has the largest difference of 13 on thread load. To decrease the influence of load imbalance, HP-CSF sets adjacent bins with same distance between upper threshold and lower threshold. There requires another hyperparameter *bin_width* to set the bin size. In Fig. 6(b), *bin_width* is 10 for binning. To compare the performance between addition-law and power-law, keep bin amounts fixed, and the comparison results are shown in Sect. 5.

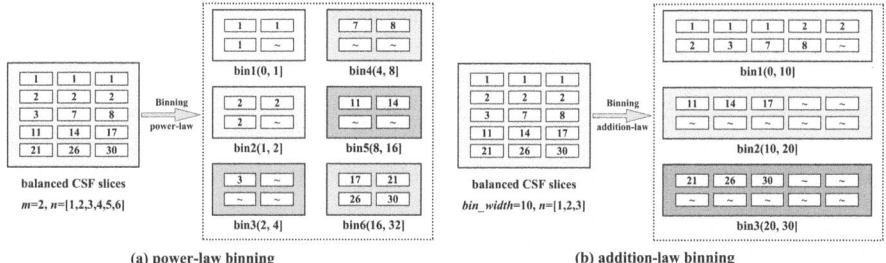

(a) power-law binning   (b) addition-law binning

Fig. 6. Power-law binning and addition-law binning

4.3 Deployment with Multiple Streams

At the sight of kernels deployment, each kernel of CSF and CSL will be driven in order. It will cause a waste of hardware while a few SMs are working but the others have finished their jobs. If separate the SMs from a single kernel to different kernels, it will reduce the time from thread idle. For achieving this purpose, HP-CSF adopts multiple streams for deployment and creates a single stream for each bin to compute CSF and CSL tasks. COO arrays will be computed by an independent stream. The deployment difference between default stream and multiple streams are shown in Fig. 7.

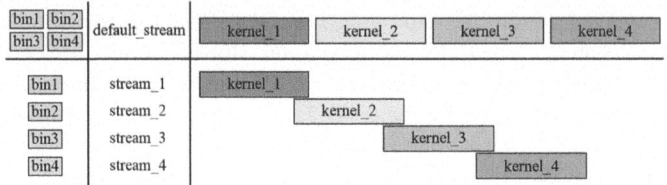

Fig. 7. Difference between default stream and multiple streams

5 Experiments

5.1 Experimental Settings

We compile the CPU codes in Python 3.9 to preprocess data and implement the GPU kernels in CUDA C. These two parts are compiled by pybind11 module. We evaluate our work on GPU NVIDIA Geforce RTX 4090. RTX 4090 device contains 128 SMs, with 16384 CUDA cores, 24 GB global memory, 72 MB L2 cache, a peak single-precision performance of 82.6 TFLOPS, and a peak memory bandwidth 1008 GB/s. The CPU codes are conducted on Intel Core i9-13900KF with 128G RAM. The CUDA version is 11.8. We have selected 10 parallel methods from related research for comparisons in GPU cuda programming. Table 1 introduces the FROSTT datasets information used in our experiments. The rank is 32 for all the experiments.

In high performance computing research of GPU, the runtime of cuda kernel is the most important index which directly evaluates the method. We use cudaEvent to record the start and end of kernel and achieve the cuda runtime. After testing 1000 epochs to update each matrix along different modes, we collect the runtime of each method.

Table 1. Sparse tensor datasets

Dataset	Tensor	Order	Dimensions	Nonzeros	Density
D1	nell2	3	12.1K × 9.2K × 28.8K	76.9M	2.4E−5
D2	nell1	3	2.9M × 2.1M × 25.5M	143.6M	9.05E−13
D3	deli_3D	3	0.5M × 17.3M × 2.5M	140.1M	6.14E−12
D4	flickr_3D	3	0.3M × 28.2M × 1.6M	112.9M	7.8E−12
D5	enron	4	6.1K × 5.7K × 0.2M × 1.2K	54.2M	5.46E−9
D6	flickr_4D	4	0.3M × 28.2M × 1.6M × 0.7K	112.9M	1.07E−14
D7	chicago_crime	5	6K × 24 × 0.4K × 0.4K × 32	6M	8.87E−16
D8	vast_5D	5	0.2M × 11.4K × 2 × 0.1K × 0.1K	26M	7.77E−7

5.2   Optimization with Omitting *Pslice* Arrays

In our preliminary optimization, we achieve HB-CSF by omitting *Pslice* to reduce a cycle. To verify the effectiveness, we deployed the experiments with the parameters *block_size* 512 and *fiber_threshold* 128 for power-law. Considering *Pslice* reorders slice increasing by one, we optimize the calculation by omitting *Pslice*. Figure 8 shows the comparison results. The method using power-law with *Pslice* is marked as P1, and the other one omitting *Pslice* marked as P2. After updating feature matrices for 1000 iterations, we have received that omitting *Pslice* has 3.7% speedup averagely than using *Pslice* for power-law.

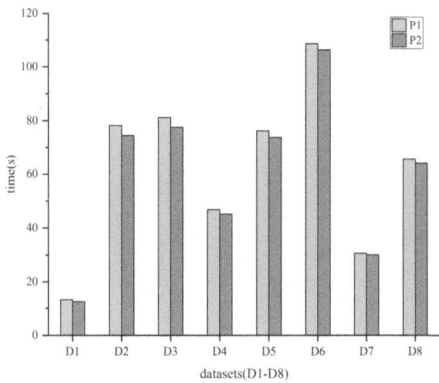

Fig. 8. Comparisons between using Pslice and omitting Pslice in power-law

5.3   Multiplying the Thread Load

We introduce a hyperparameter *hp_multiple* for multiplying the thread load. We iteratively set *hp_multiple* from 1 to 20 for each bin and take 100 iterations to record the time

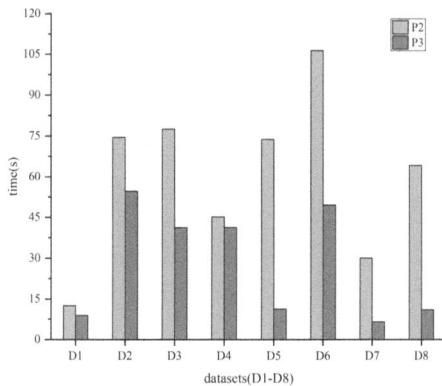

Fig. 9. Power-law comparisons between P2 and P3

consumption. After all the tests, the *hp_multiple* referring to the least time consumption will be taken out for updating feature matrices. The proposed multiplying-load method is represented as P3 and the comparisons with P2 are shown in Fig. 9. Compared to P2, we have received that multiple-load method has 211.12% speedup averagely than single load for power-law.

5.4 Replacing Power-Law with Addition-Law

To compare the performances of addition-law and power-law, we guarantee same bin amounts for two methods. We respectively input [1, 2, 4, 8, 16, 32, 64, 128, 256, 512] for *fiber_threshold* to get a time consumption with power-law binning method. Figure 10 shows the comparison of various *fiber_threshold* settings, and the best parameters of each dataset are displayed in Table 2.

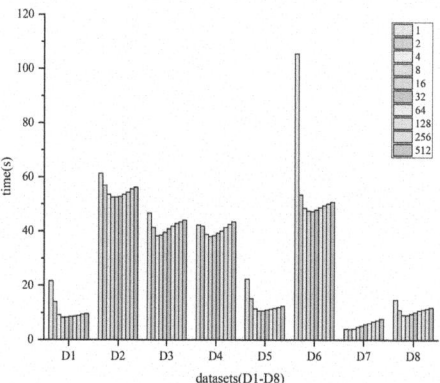

Fig. 10. Different setting for fiber threshold in Power-law of P3

Table 2. The fiber threshold and bin amounts from the best performances in power-law

Dataset	Least Duration	Fiber Threshold	Bin Amount
D1	8.2465	8	4
D2	52.4006	8	4
D3	38.1914	4	3
D4	37.98	8	4
D5	10.7547	8	4
D6	47.2094	16	5
D7	3.8254	2	2
D8	9.2446	8	4

Take the same bin amounts shown in Table 2 for addition-law binning, we create bins with equidistant distance on upper threshold. For the same bin amount of each dataset, we test *bin_width* from 1 to 20 and get time consumption. We pick the best performance with the corresponding parameters of *bin_width*. Then, the best performances from power-law binning and addition-law of each dataset are shown in Fig. 11. P4 shows the best performance with corresponding *fiber_threshold* in power-law binning and A1 denotes the best performance of addition-law binning. We receive a computation speedup from power-law binning to addition-law binning with 6.24% in average. It illustrates that the addition-law binning method could represent a better performance with balancing the thread loads of bins. The best performances with corresponding hyperparameters with addition-law are shown in Table 3.

Table 3. The fiber threshold and bin amounts from the best performances in addition-law

Dataset	Least Duration	Bin Width	Bin Amount
D1	7.8886	20	4
D2	51.4172	9	4
D3	34.9691	16	3
D4	37.0834	10	4
D5	9.7798	18	4
D6	45.2611	13	5
D7	3.3754	10	2
D8	8.869	20	4

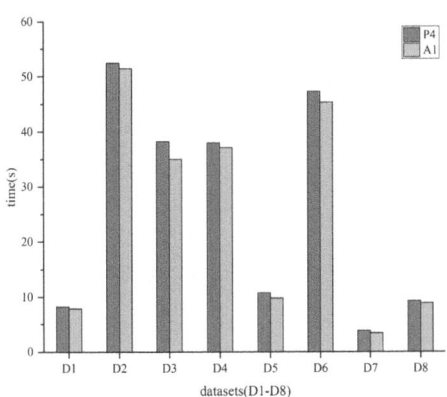

Fig. 11. Comparisons from best performances between power-law and addition-law binning

5.5 Optimization with Multiple Streams

We test multiple streams for each bin of CSF, CSL and COO to achieve parallel kernels driving. Figure 12 shows the difference of performance on speed. In Fig. 12, A1 denotes the deployment with default stream driving each kernel and A2 denotes multiple streams deployment. We achieved an average acceleration of 12.67%.

5.6   Comparison of Kernel Speedup

Figure 13 shows the time summation of all the mode consumption. COO and CSF are two based methods. FCOO [14] limits the length of partition for thread. HICOO [12] groups small blocks for threads. MMCSF [7] assigns each element to its longest fiber. CFCOO [13] distributes all the tasks to each thread equivalently. STEF [9] applies for large amount of memory space to save intermediate results and improve overall computing speed. On D2-D4, our system couldn't support enough additional memory for STEF and the results are vacant. HLS [15] utilizes TCU to deploy a single tile for each warp. From the result, HP-CSF gets the most improvement with 269.8% in D8 and receives an average acceleration with 100.7% in D1-D8.

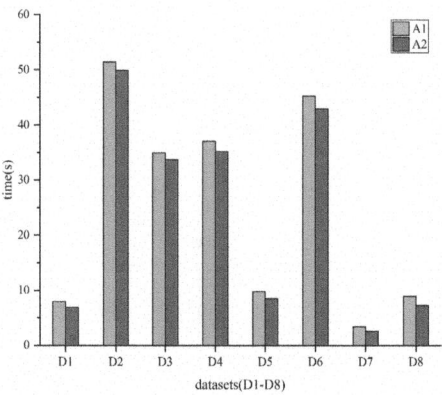

Fig. 12. Comparisons between single stream and multiple streams on each dataset

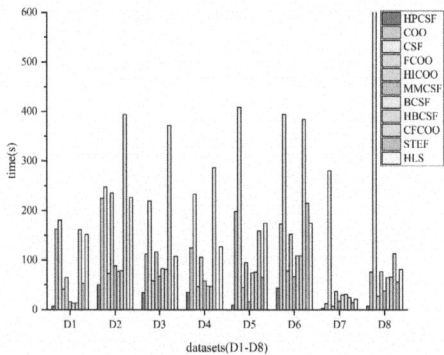

Fig. 13. Comparisons of runtime summation from mode1 to mode5

6   Conclusion

In this paper, we base on HB-CSF and propose an improved method called HP-CSF. We introduce a hyperparameter to multiply the thread loads and reduce the atomic conflicts amounts. Besides, we replace the power-law binning method with addition-law to bin the balanced CSF data. As the slices distributed to threads are getting closer in length, the situation of threads idle has been alleviated. Compared to 10 classical methods, our method has achieved speedup of 100.7%.

Acknowledgments. This work is supported by the National Natural Science Foundation of China under grant 62302402, and the Science and Technology Research Program of Chongqing Municipal Education Commission under grant KJQN202300210, KJZD-K202400209.

References

1. Wu, H., Luo, X., Zhou, M., et al.: A PID-incorporated latent factorization of tensors approach to dynamically weighted directed network analysis. IEEE/CAA J. Automatica Sinica **9**(3), 533–546 (2022)
2. Kang,U., Papalexakis, E., Harpale, A., et al.: GigaTensor: scaling tensor analysis up by 100 times - algorithms and discoveries. In: Proceedings of the 18th ACM SIGKDD International Conference on Knowledge Discovery and Data Mining, pp. 308–316 (2012)
3. Smith, S., Ravindran, N., Sidiropoulos, N., et al.: SPLATT: efficient and parallel sparse tensor-matrix multiplication. In: 2015 IEEE International Parallel and Distributed Processing Symposium, pp. 61–70 (2015)
4. Smith, S., Karypis, G.: Tensor-matrix products with a compressed sparse tensor. In: Proceedings of the 5th Workshop on Irregular Applications: Architectures and Algorithms, pp. 1–7 (2015)
5. Wu, H., Wu,X., Luo, X.: Dynamic Network Representation Based on Latent Factorization of Tensors. Springer, Cham (2023)
6. Nisa, I., Li, J., Sukumaran-Rajam, A., et al.: Load-balanced sparse MTTKRP on GPUs. In: 2019 IEEE International Parallel and Distributed Processing Symposium (IPDPS), pp. 123–133 (2019)
7. Nisa,I., Li, J., Sukumaran-Rajam, A., et al.: An efficient mixed-mode representation of sparse tensors. In: IEEE International Conference on High Performance Computing, Data, and Analytics, pp. 1–25. ACM (2019)
8. Abubaker, N., Acer, S., Aykanat, C.: True load balancing for matricized tensor times Khatri-Rao product. IEEE Trans. Parallel Distrib. Syst. **32**(8), 1974–1986 (2021)
9. Kurt, S., Raje, S., Sukumaran-Rajam, A., et al.: Sparsity-aware tensor decomposition. In: 2022 IEEE International Parallel and Distributed Processing Symposium (IPDPS), pp. 952–962 (2022)
10. Subramaniyan, S., Wang, X.: OptiCPD: optimization for the canonical polyadic decomposition algorithm on GPUs. In: 2023 IEEE International Parallel and Distributed Processing Symposium Workshops (IPDPSW), pp. 403–412 (2023)
11. Wu, H., Luo, X.: Instance-frequency-weighted regularized, nonnegative and adaptive latent factorization of tensors for dynamic QoS analysis. In: Proceedings of the 2021 IEEE International Conference on Web Services (ICWS2021) (Regular), Chicago, IL, USA, pp. 560–568 (2021)
12. Li, J., Sun, J., Vuduc, R.: HiCOO: hierarchical storage of sparse tensors. In: SC18: International Conference for High Performance Computing, Networking, Storage and Analysis, pp. 238–252 (2018)
13. Nagasaka, Y., Fukumoto, N.: Efficient collision-free MTTKRP algorithm for multi-core CPUs with less memory usage. In: 2022 22nd IEEE International Symposium on Cluster, Cloud and Internet Computing (CCGrid), pp. 534–543 (2022)

14. Liu, B., Wen, C., Sarwate, A., et al.: A unified optimization approach for sparse tensor operations on GPUs. In: 2017 IEEE International Conference on Cluster Computing (CLUSTER), pp. 47–57 (2017)
15. Wang, H., Yang, W., Hu, R., et al.: A novel parallel algorithm for sparse tensor matrix chain multiplication via TCU-acceleration. IEEE Trans. Parallel Distrib. Syst. **34**(8), 2419–2432 (2023)
16. Wu, H., Luo, X., Zhou, M.: Advancing non-negative latent factorization of tensors with diversified regularization schemes. IEEE Trans. Serv. Comput. **15**(3), 1334–1344 (2022)
17. Ashari, A., Sedaghati, N., Eisenlohr, J., et al.: Fast sparse matrix-vector multiplication on GPUs for graph applications. In: SC 2014: Proceedings of the International Conference for High Performance Computing, Networking, Storage and Analysis, pp. 781–792 (2014)

JediGAN: A Fully Decentralized Training of GAN with Adaptive Discriminator Averaging and Generator Selection

Xiaoming Han[1], Boan Liu[2], and Dazhao Cheng[1(✉)]

[1] Department of Computer Science, Wuhan University, Wuhan, China
{hanxiaoming,dcheng}@whu.edu.cn
[2] Department of Computing, Hong Kong Polytechnic University,
Kowloon, Hong Kong

Abstract. Existing decentralized learning of Generative Adversarial Network (GAN) suffers from a slower convergence rate and training instability due to the changes in the gradient-sharing approach among workers. It requires more iterations to achieve convergence and deteriorates the GAN training, consequently leading to slow down training speed and accuracy degradation. We propose JediGAN, the novel distributed GAN system that achieves optimal benefits by balancing accuracy and communication overheads through adaptive scheduling strategies. Jedi-GAN reduces overall consensus variance by incorporating adaptive global updates for the discriminators. Additionally, JediGAN effectively leverages the internal characteristics of the GAN to decouple the training processes of the discriminators and generators during the search. It employs the concept of evolutionary selection to update the generators, thereby improving training stability. Through extensive experiments, we show that JediGAN outperforms state-of-the-art decentralized GAN systems, with 13.1% accuracy and 36.6% training speed improvement.

Keywords: Distributed GANs · Adaptive Global Update · Stable Training · Training Speed

1 Introduction

The generative models have gained a considerable amount of attention in unsupervised learning via a framework called Generative Adversarial Network (GAN) [4] due to their outstanding data generation capability. The success of GAN-based models in various applications has been widely recognized, as evidenced by numerous surveys and reviews on GANs, such as computer vision [26], face synthesis [18], text-to-image synthesis [31]. It is well known that high-quality GAN requires a significant amount of training data to fit the target application [12]. However, it has become increasingly difficult to obtain such data in a central location over the past few years due to new data protection rules [22],

© IFIP International Federation for Information Processing 2025
Published by Springer Nature Switzerland AG 2025
X. Chen et al. (Eds.): NPC 2024, LNCS 15527, pp. 91–107, 2025.
https://doi.org/10.1007/978-981-96-2830-8_8

even data cannot be shared or pooled centrally with each other. In many actual scenarios where data is distributed across multiple sources, they are too limited in size to locally train an accurate GAN for the entire population of the distributed data resource. Therefore, a distributed GAN that decentralizes the workloads to the proximate of the data source, i.e. workers, to fit the distribution of data as much as possible has become a research hotspot and challenge. Distributed GAN is a system in which the generator or the discriminator in GAN is deployed in distributed workers according to design requirements which expands and accelerates the training of GAN.

In recent studies, federated learning proposed training statistical models directly on remote workers [14] has been used in distributed GAN applications. It is similar to the parameter server (PS) architecture which selects the workers and updates the parameters with the averages of the trained models through the server [3]. The distributed GAN with federated learning also deploys generators and discriminators on the server and workers according to the deployment strategy such as MDGAN [10] and FedGAN [21]. These strategies exacerbate the inherent communication bottleneck problem [8] on the server side, significantly impacting the scalability of the system and the efficiency of communication due to the neglect of the characteristic that the GAN workload consists of two models and mutual dependence. An alternative approach to avoid such a bottleneck problem is to apply decentralized learning to GAN workloads. Gossiping GANs [9], as a decentralized GAN which the size of communication between workers in a large-scale network is constant, greatly alleviates this problem. It enjoys the benefits of gossip learning, significantly *cheaper scalability and better robustness*, as it doesn't require infrastructure for democratized training and eliminates the risk of a single point of failure. Similarly, decentralized GAN with a swarm communication protocol exists as well [23]. However, these approaches suffer from a slower convergence rate and training instability due to the changes in the gradient-sharing approach among workers, that is, updating the gradient locally instead of globally. In other words, these approaches require more iterations for GAN to achieve convergence and deteriorate the training, consequently leading to slow down training speed and accuracy degradation.

Motivated by the wider acceptance of Serverless Machine Learning Training, We propose JediGAN, a fully decentralized training of GAN system that takes a global update of the discriminator to improve training speed and accuracy and decouples the training process of the discriminator and generator during the search to improve training stability. The contributions of this paper are as follows:

- We adopt global updating of the discriminators to accelerate the convergence rate of decentralized GAN and remedy the accuracy degradation in Gossiping GANs (Sect. 4.2). As per our best knowledge, this is the first work that combines the internal mechanisms of GAN to optimize distributed GAN, which enables JediGAN resilient to GAN-specific issues.
- We greatly reduce the search complexity and the instability of GAN training by decoupling the search of generator and discriminator. Inspired by the evo-

lutionary algorithm, we utilize a consensus global discriminator to select the best generator thus far (Sect. 4.2).

– We further propose a cooperative scheduling strategy that can effectively balance worker consensus and communication overheads. Experiments have verified the effectiveness of our proposed approach that JediGAN outperforms state-of-the-art decentralized GAN systems, with 13.1% accuracy and 36.6% training speed improvement (Sect. 4.4).

2   Background and Motivation

2.1   Background on Distributed Generative Adversarial Networks(GAN)

GAN Architectures: GAN consists of two interdependent neural networks called the discriminator and the generator. They improve their "abilities" through adversarial game strategies: the discriminator learns to distinguish real samples from fake samples, improving its discrimination ability, while the generator learns from the discriminator's feedback to generate high-quality fake samples that can deceive the discriminator. Formally, this is accomplished through a min-max game:

$$\min_{G} \max_{D} \mathbb{E}_{\mathbf{x} \sim p_{\mathrm{data}}} [\log D(\mathbf{x})] + \mathbb{E}_{\mathbf{z} \sim p_{\mathbf{z}}}[\log(1 - D(G(\mathbf{z})))] \tag{1}$$

where the discriminator's output $D(\mathbf{x}) \in [0, 1]$ is the probability that $\mathbf{x}$ is real data and the generator's output $G(\mathbf{z})$ is a generated synthetic sample from a latent vector z. The objective of the generator is to minimize $1 - D(G(\mathbf{z}))$ to estimate the real sample distribution while the objective of the discriminator is to maximize $1 - D(G(\mathbf{z}))$ and $D(\mathbf{x})$.

Distributed GAN Systems:

Distributed GAN with Federated Learning: As an intuitive research example, FedGAN employs the method of federated learning to directly utilize GAN as the computational load. It relies on the central server to periodically aggregate and update the GAN parameters of the workers for distributed training. Obviously, it ignores the internal characteristics of GAN, which has to upload or download the parameters of both the generator and discriminator and makes the inherent communication bottleneck [17] in federated networks more "prominent". Another manner to deploy is to separate the discriminator and generator, e.g. MDGAN, in which the central server only hosts the generator and the worker only hosts the discriminator. Although we believe that this manner benefits from the calculation and memory overhead of the workers, it increases the communication frequency between the server and the worker since both the generator and the discriminator rely on each other's calculation results during the training.

Distributed GAN with Gossip Learning: Gossiping GAN is a method that uses the gossip protocol for decentralized training, and the discriminator and generator are deployed on each worker under decentralized control. Each worker periodically updates its local discriminator/generator with the local dataset and sends it to another using gossip communication in the network. The worker receives the discriminator/generator and merges it. Merging is typically achieved by averaging the model parameters. This decentralized communication topology successfully addresses the communication bottleneck problem arising from federated learning based on the PS structure, thereby eliminating the need for waits in all computing nodes due to synchronization issues with the central node. However, the reduced synchronization communication in Gossiping GAN comes at a cost: a slower convergence rate. While algorithms are proven to have convergence linear speedup asymptotically, it is sensitive to network topology and synchronization period. Similar to that, there is also GAN distributed training with swarm communication protocol [23]. The approach proposed in this paper focuses on addressing the cost resulting from such decentralized GAN gradient-sharing methods.

2.2   Motivation and Case Study

Motivated by the above background of different communication strategies to aggregate and update the GAN parameters, following the communication advantages of decentralized training, we further conduct a measurement study on the state-of-art distributed GANs of fully decentralized. The aim was to demonstrate the impact of communication strategies on the convergence of GANs as training workloads. We also investigated the underlying reasons.

Measurement Setup: We deploy GAN workloads over 10 machines equipped with a GeForce RTX-3080 GPU, 10 GB memory. The machines connect with each other with an Ethernet network with an average speed of 10 Gbps.

Communication Configuration: We compared the gradient update strategies of FedGAN and GossipingGAN, which correspond to global updates and local updates, respectively. Without loss of generality, we replace the server synchronization method in FedGAN based on the PS structure with the Ring All-Reduce approach to avoid communication bottlenecks. In the one-peer exponential network, the exact global update can be achieved via $\ln(n)$ gossip communications, which generally takes more wall-clock time than a single Ring All-Reduce operation. This enables us to focus on the relationship between communication overheads and convergence by setting the local training times K In the case study, we set FedGAN with $K = 1$ as the upper limit of communication overhead, and GossipingGAN with $K = 50$ as the lower limit of communication overhead.

Datasets and Workloads: We utilize two typical GAN models and datasets: OriginalGAN workload [4] with a parameter size of 8.17M is applied to the Mnist dataset [16], and WGAN-gp workload [7] with a parameter size of 26.07M is applied to the Cifar10 dataset [15].

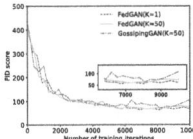 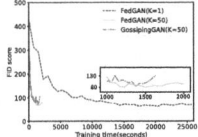 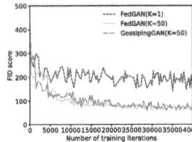 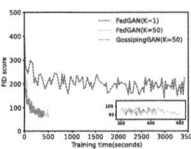

Fig. 1. FID score over iteration rounds loaded as WGAN-gp

Fig. 2. FID score over time loaded as WGAN-gp

Fig. 3. FID score over iteration rounds loaded as origanGAN

Fig. 4. FID score over time loaded as origanGAN

Communication Overhead vs Convergence: Figure 1 illustrates the iteration rounds of the WGAN-gp workload and its corresponding FID scores when employing the FedGAN and GossipingGAN strategies for aggregating and updating parameters. We can see that FedGAN(K = 1) has the highest accuracy, that is, it can achieve the best FID score during the convergence phase, which is 62.56. On the other hand, GossipingGAN performs the worst despite having the lowest communication overhead. It requires more iterations to improve accuracy, which undoubtedly incurs additional computational overhead. This is because the gossip communication strategy can only achieve local consensus between workers at each iteration. However, in terms of training time shown in Fig. 2, both FedGAN(K = 50) and GossipingGAN can converge faster, and take significantly less time (about 1400 s) to achieve their respective best FID scores compared to FedGAN(K = 1) (about 20400 s). This indicates that FedGAN(K = 1) incurs significant communication costs while obtaining the best FID score. Undoubtedly, this exacerbates the convergence performance.

Instability vs Convergence: Contrary to WGAN-gp workloads, GossipingGAN with the origanGAN workload is the best-performing in both training time and accuracy shown as Fig. 3 and Fig. 4. GossipingGAN achieved the best FID score of 57.46, which is close to FedGAN(K = 50) (58.91), while FedGAN(K = 1) performed poorly with a score of 139.95. Furthermore, GossipingGAN reached convergence in about 370 s, faster than FedGAN(K = 1) (about 2900 s) and FedGAN(K = 50) (about 410 s). This indicates that simply aggregating and updating the parameters of these discriminators and generators in the GAN game, as done with a single DNN workload, may result in poor performance. This is because the architectures of the generator and discriminator are deeply coupled, increasing search complexity and the instability of GAN training. Obviously, FedGAN ignores the internal characteristics of GAN, particularly making its instability more pronounced during the distributed training process. Please note that although FedGAN did not exhibit instability issues on the WGAN-gp workload, this is due to the utilization of a redesigned loss function within the generator or discriminator. However, this approach costs additional computational overhead as a trade-off to achieve convergence.

2.3 Potential Approach

Communication overhead of distributed GAN based on PS structure hinders the scalability of large-scale federated learning. This prompted us to combine the gossip protocol with SGD [2] to efficiently train GANs without the need for a central server i.e., we use the time-varying one-peer exponential graph following [1], it is fully asynchronous avoiding all kinds of idling, then the exchanges are pairwise and benefit from the faster communication channel CPI. More importantly, we should also consider the relationship between communication overhead and the convergence of GAN workloads. Reviewing GAN systems, the strategy of efficiently assigning GANs to distributed datasets is still an open research topic due to the mutual dependence of generators and discriminators to consider. This requires refinement of gossip techniques in the specific context of GANs to bridge the gap between local consensus (e.g., GossipingGAN) and global consensus (e.g., FedGAN) in gradient-sharing approaches without incurring additional overhead.

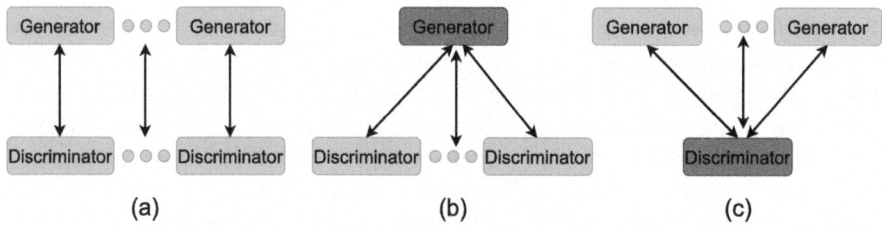

Fig. 5. Game types in distributed GAN system

GossipingGAN is an instance of N-versus-N games that puts both the discriminator and generator networks on distributed nodes for training, as depicted in Fig. 5(a). Some recent research, such as MDGAN [10], exploits the advantage of 1-versus-N games that decouple pairs of generators and discriminators, as shown Fig. 5(b), using the results feedback by a set of discriminators to update a generator. The same goes for multiple generator-one discriminator, i.e. N-versus-1, such as EAGAN [27], shown as Fig. 5(c). These decoupled game types consider the computation dependency between the discriminator and generator, aiming to reduce computation overhead without compromising accuracy.

Motivated by the above observations, we adopt a decentralized network topology with a gossip communication protocol to address the expensive communication overhead in distributed GAN training. Additionally, we utilize the Ring All-Reduce approach for periodic global aggregating and updating to accelerate convergence for the GAN workload. Finally, we decouple the generator and discriminator in distributed GANs to enhance training stability.

3 Design Overview

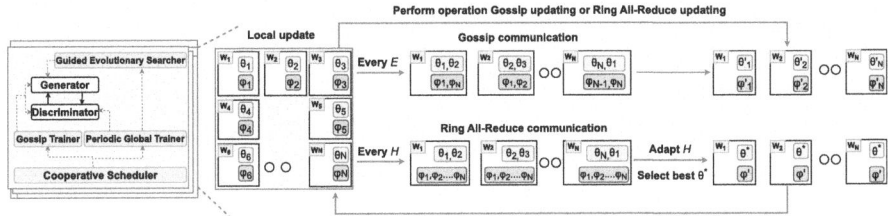

Fig. 6. The Modular Design

3.1 Modular Design

JediGAN (see Fig. 6) has a set of *control modules* and a *cooperative scheduler*,
The control modules schedule the generators and discriminators for performing
GAN training tasks, including a **Gossip Trainer**, a **Periodic Global Trainer**,
and a **Guided Evolutionary Searcher** on each worker. The Gossip trainer and
Periodic Global trainer execute the operation of gossip and Ring All-Reduce,
respectively, to control how consensus is achieved among the generators and
discriminators. The Guided Evolutionary Searcher selects the top-performing
generator to reset the generators of all workers, aiming to alleviate the instability of GAN training during the search process. The **Cooperative Scheduler**
adaptively optimizes when to schedule the control modules based on the current
communication overhead and convergence results.

3.2 JediGAN Learning Procedure

We present the learning procedure of JediGAN which consists of an initialization
stage and training stages. At the initialization stage, the generators and discriminators initialize the parameters to the same value respectively. Then it starts
the following training process until the convergence of the worker generator:

(a) *Gossip updating:* The Cooperative Scheduler first invokes the Gossip Trainer
    to conduct internal warm-up training on each pair of generator and discrim-
    inator within the workers. Every M rounds, the generator and discriminator
    in each worker aggregate and update parameter information by indepen-
    dently and randomly selecting their respective target machines (send or
    receive) based on the sum-weighted gossip rule using Bernoulli variables
    (see Algorithm 1).

(b) *Ring All-Reduce updating:* The Cooperative Scheduler invokes the Periodic Global Trainer at the Kth round to perform a Ring All-Reduce operation, globally averaging the discriminator parameters of all workers. Please note that the generators on the workers still aggregate and update parameters using the Gossip trainer. The global averaging period K is initialized to a small value K_{init}.

(c) *Generator updating:* After all discriminators on the workers have completed the global synchronization update, the Cooperative Scheduler continues to invoke the Guided Evolutionary Searcher to select the best generator for resetting and updating all generators. Specifically, the Guided Evolutionary Searcher utilizes the globally updated discriminators to fairly discriminate the fake data generated by all generators at this point. Additionally, we collect FID scores of the fake data generated by the best generators for flexible period adjustment K.

3.3   The JediGAN Algorithm

We consider a decentralized GAN system consisting of N workers. Let $\mathcal{N} = \{n_1, n_2, \ldots, n_N\}$ denote the set of workers. The worker n_i has its private dataset d_i. We denote the total datasets of all workers as $\mathcal{D} = \{d_1, d_2, \ldots, d_N\}$. Each worker has a generator and a discriminator. Let $G_i(\theta, z)$ and $D_i (\varphi, d)$ be the generator and discriminator of worker n_i respectively, where θ and φ denotes their parameters respectively. The generator takes input z (i.e., the noise signal), while the discriminator takes input d (i.e., the fake or real samples).

Problem Formulation. JediGAN train D_i to maximize the probability of assigning the correct label to both training data and samples from G_i. JediGAN simultaneously train G_i to minimize $log(1 - D_i(\varphi, G_i(\theta, \mathbf{z})))$. The objective is for decentralized cooperative workers to come up with a consensus on a set of G_i parameters θ (although during training each worker operates on its own copy of θ) and it can be formulated as the following minimax objective function:

$$\min_{G_{1:N}} \max_{D_{1:N}} \mathbb{E}_{\mathbf{x} \sim p_{\text{data}}} [\log D_i(\varphi, \mathbf{x})] + \mathbb{E}_{\mathbf{z} \sim p_{\mathbf{z}}}[\log(1 - D_i(\varphi, G_i(\theta, \mathbf{z})))] \quad (2)$$

where φ or θ denotes the parameters received and processed by worker n_i through Gossip trainer, Periodic Global trainer, Guided Evolutionary Searcher, or local iterative training. The generated samples from G_i (θ, z) and the local training data $\mathbf{X}_r$ are used as inputs $D_i(\varphi, G_i(\theta, \mathbf{z}))$ and $D_i(\varphi, \mathbf{x}_i)$ respectively to update the gradients of D_i $(\forall i \in \mathcal{N})$. $D_i(\varphi, G_i(\theta, \mathbf{z}))$ focuses on training the G_i to generate more realistic training data. We define the gradient function of D_i and G_i as follows:

$$\mathbf{g}_{\varphi,i}(\theta, \varphi, \mathbf{z}, \mathbf{X}_r) = \nabla_\varphi [\log D_i(\varphi, \mathbf{x}_i) + \log(1 - D_i(\varphi, G_i(\theta, \mathbf{z})))] \quad (3)$$

$$\mathbf{g}_{\theta,i}(\theta, \varphi, \mathbf{z}) = \nabla_\theta \log(1 - D_i(\varphi, G_i(\theta, \mathbf{z}))) \quad (4)$$

where ∇ is the gradient operator, $\mathbf{x}_i$ is a batch of $\mathbf{d}_i$.

The training process relies on the chosen optimizer algorithm like stochastic gradient descent (SGD) [5], Momentum [24], and Adam [13]. They are used to update φ_i and θ_i with $\mathbf{g}_{\varphi,i}$ and $\mathbf{g}_{\theta,i}$, respectively.

Algorithm 1. Cooperative Scheduling Optimization Algorithm

1: **Initialize**: Unified parameters θ_i for G_i, φ_i for D_i, N for number of workers
2: **Input**: Learning rate η_d,η_g, Local iterations E, Warmup iterations K ,$C \leftarrow 0$, $Signal \leftarrow 0$, Averaging period $H \leftarrow H_{init}$, $Optimizer_D, Optimizer_G$
3: **repeat**
4: $\quad z_{i,D}, z_{i,G} \leftarrow \{z_1,\ldots,z_N\}$ $\quad \triangleright$sample noise data
5: $\quad d_i =\leftarrow \{d_1,\ldots,d_N\}$ $\quad \triangleright$training data batch
6: $\quad$ Get update gradient $\mathbf{g}_{\varphi_i,i}(\theta_i,\varphi_i,z_{i,D},d_i)$ of D_i via Eq.(3) $\quad i \in \{1,\ldots,N\}$
7: $\quad \varphi_i \leftarrow Optimizer_D(\eta_d,\mathbf{g}_{\varphi_i,i})$ $\quad \triangleright$ update local weights of D_i
8: $\quad$ **if** $Signal == 1$ **then**
9: $\quad\quad \theta_i\leftarrow GuidedEvolutionarySearcher(D_i^H, G_i)$
10: $\quad\quad Signal = 0$
11: $\quad$ Get update gradient $\mathbf{g}_{\theta_i,i}(\theta_i,\varphi_i,z_{i,G})$ of G_i via Eq.(4)
12: $\quad \theta_i \leftarrow Optimizer_G(\eta_g,\mathbf{g}_{\theta,i})$ $\quad \triangleright$ update local weights of G_i
13: $\quad C \leftarrow C+1$
14: $\quad$ **if** $C\%H == 0$ **then**
15: $\quad\quad \varphi_i\leftarrow PeriodicGlobaltrainer(D_i)\triangleright$Ring All Reduce operation on all D_i
16: $\quad\quad \theta_i\leftarrow Gossiptrainer(G_i)$ $\quad \triangleright$gossip operation on all G_i
17: $\quad\quad H \leftarrow AdaptiveGlobalAverage(samples, C, K)$
18: $\quad\quad Signal = 1$
19: $\quad\quad$ **continue**
20: $\quad$ **end if**
21: $\quad$ **if** $C\%E == 0$ **then**
22: $\quad\quad \theta_i,\varphi_i \leftarrow Gossiptrainer(D_i, G_i)$ $\quad \triangleright$ gossip operation on all D_i and G_i
23: $\quad$ **end if**
24: **until** G_i reaches convergence
25: **Output**:φ_i, θ_i

Algorithm 2. Adaptive Global Average and Guided Evolutionary Searcher functions

---

1: **function** Adaptive Global Average($samples, C, K$)
2: $\quad Fid\_Score \leftarrow calculate\_fid(samples, testdata)$
3: $\quad$ **if** $C < K$ **then**
4: $\quad\quad Previous\_Fid \leftarrow Fid\_Score$
5: $\quad$ **else**
6: $\quad\quad H \leftarrow \left\lceil e^{(Previous\_Fid - Fid\_score)} H_{init} \right\rceil$
7: $\quad$ **return** H
8: **function** Guided Evolutionary Searcher(D_i^H,G_i)
9: $\quad$ Select the best θ_i^* from fixed and unified D^H result:
10: $\quad \{D^H(\varphi^H, G_1(\theta_1, z_1)),\ldots,D^H(\varphi^H, G_N(\theta_N, z_N))\}$
11: $\quad \theta_1 = \ldots = \theta_N = \theta_i^* \leftarrow$ Weight-resetting

---

3.4   Cooperative Scheduling Optimization

JediGAN comprises two learning modes: one mode involves the averaging of G_i and D_i parameters based on gossip communication, and the other mode involves the periodic global averaging of D_i parameters through Ring All-Reduce communication. To address the slow convergence rate of gossip learning, we propose a **Cooperative Scheduling Optimization(CSO)** algorithm (Algorithm 1) with Cooperative Scheduler. This algorithm can combine the advantages of these two modes to perform fine-grained adaptive scheduling of G_i and D_i on workers. Our goal is to mitigate the slow convergence rate and enhance the performance of the decentralized GAN system.

Each worker's D_i and G_i solely depend on each other's parameters θ_i, φ_i, along with the local d_i, to train themselves. The training process involves training D_i first (lines 4–7) and then training G_i (lines 11–12) in each iteration round. Similar to federated learning in the 'PS' structure, we perform gossip training using Gossiptrainer after training locally on the worker n_i for E rounds (lines 21–23). A well-known example of a decentralized algorithm is gossip averaging. It is very fast to make different workers converge toward a consensus by exchanging information in a one-peer exponential graph way [1]. This family of algorithms presents many advantages like being fully asynchronous and decentralized as they do not require a central variable. In this paper, we focus on improving the system performance of decentralized GAN system through gossip training along with periodic global averaging D_i by Periodic Global trainer exploiting Ring All-Reduce operations (lines 14–20). Therefore, we assume that the resources and data are homogeneous. The Adaptive Global Average function is listed in the Algorithm 2. We use a counter C to record the number of iteration rounds. The global averaging period H is initialized to a small value H_{init} (e.g. 2 4). Once C modulus H equals 0, global averaging happens. In the global average step, workers synchronize parameters φ_i of its D_i using the efficient Ring All-Reduce primitives. JediGAN requires manual tuning of H, which can be burdensome. As $H \to \infty$, JediGAN becomes equivalent to Gossiping GANs [9]. Conversely, as $H \to 0$, JediGAN becomes equivalent to FedGAN [21]. In practice, we indirectly evaluate the H via FID scores (Fr'echet Inception Distance [11]) based on generators and sample FID scores for the K iterations. Inspired by [25], If we discover the influence of the initial value H_{init} and adjust the next H period, the better the score of FID, the larger the value of H. Furthermore, we consider the GAN's internal features during global averaging and incorporate a Guided Evolutionary Searcher (Guided Evolutionary Searcher function in Algorithm 2), to mitigate the instability of training. We decouple the pairs of D_i and G_i into two stages. In stage 1, we fix the D^H and select best G_i(lines 10). All G_i are paired with the same D^H, i.e., the candidate G_i and the fixed D^H are in a many-to-one relationship. In stage 2, the best G_i^* of stage 1 is used to provide supervision signals for training D^H. Specifically, in stage 2, we create N copies of the best G_i^* of stage 1 instead of G_i(lines 11), and each G_i copy is paired with a different D_i and trained independently. Thus, the G_i^* and candidate D_i of stage 2 are in a one-to-many relationship.

4   Evaluation

In this section, we experimentally evaluate the performance of JediGAN with the aim to answer the following questions:

- How does JediGAN compare to existing distributed GANs? (Sect. 4.2)
- How do the internal factors, such as Periodic Global trainer, Guided Evolutionary Searcher, and Cooperative Scheduler, affect the performance? (Sect. 4.2)
- How is JediGAN scalability to learning settings? (Sect. 4.4)

4.1   Methodology

Testbed. We evaluate JediGAN using 10 machines, each of which is equipped with one GeForce RTX-3080 GPU with 3.70 GHz i9-10900X Intel CPU, 64 GB RAM, and 10 Gbps Ethernet.

Datasets and Models. We employ four public datasets: Mnist [16], Cifar10 [15],100-Shot-Panda [29]. Without loss of generality, we use four representative models with increasing model sizes: OriginalGAN [4], DCGAN [20], WGAN-gp [7], and FastGAN [19] as distributed GAN workloads. See Table 1 for details.

Baselines. We compare JediGAN against two state-of-the-art distributed GANs: 1) *FedGAN*, where each worker owns a generator and a discriminator, and parameters are periodically synchronized globally via a server. We compare the cases where periodic K is equal to 1 and N respectively; 2) *GossipGAN*, uses the gossip protocol for decentralized training of distributed GANs where the parameters of the generator and discriminator may not be sent to the same machine during each communication step (independent destination selection).

Evaluation Metrics. We use the Fr'echet inception distance (FID) and training speed as the metrics to evaluate the performance of JediGAN and the baselines. FID characterizes the difference between the synthesized data distribution and the real data distribution [11]. A smaller FID value implies the diversity and quality of generated data and thus represents a better performance. We present the empirical studies on Mnist, Cifar10, 100-Shot-Panda. In our experiments, we randomly sampled 20% of images from test data and generated data to compute FID scores.

Table 1. Parameter settings for GAN workload.

Setting	Workload			
	OriginalGAN(Mnist)	DCGAN(Mnist)	WGAN-gp(Cifar10)	FastGAN(Panda)
Parameter	8.17M	14.37M	26.07M	162.6M
Input Size	28 * 28	28 * 28	64 * 64 * 3	256 * 256 * 3

4.2   Overall Performance

Table 2. Performance evaluation results of various systems under different GAN workloads

System	Workload							
	OriginalGAN(Mnist)		DCGAN(Mnist)		WGAN-gp(Cifar10)		FastGAN(Panda)	
	Accurcy	Runtime	Accurcy	Runtime	Accuracy	Runtime	Accuracy	Runtime
FedGAN(K=1)	139.95	2965.95	42.82	3321.96	62.56	20395.8	**17.08**	507.77
FedGAN	58.91	411.51	44.47	624.26	63.87	1382.27	17.82	186.85
GossipingGAN	57.46	368.90	68.17	**448.52**	68.63	1428.60	17.87	96.50
JediGAN	54.49	471.62	41.43	711.20	59.30	**1073.05**	18.80	131.28
JediGAN*	**53.73**	**283.60**	**40.78**	742.95	**59.23**	1569.61	17.51	**87.12**

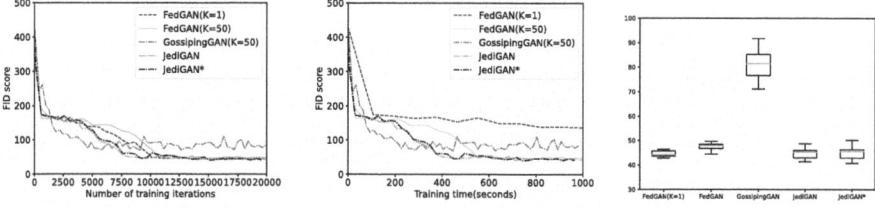

Fig. 7. FID score over iteration rounds loaded as DCGAN

Fig. 8. FID score over time loaded as DCGAN

Fig. 9. FID score over iteration rounds loaded as DCGAN

Table 2 illustrates the best FID scores and training runtimes of the aforementioned approaches over the four GAN workloads. JediGAN manually adjusts H for periodic global averaging, while JediGAN* represents our proposed method that adaptively adjusts H. Overall, our proposed approach shows the best performance compared to the baseline, with an average improvement of 13.1% in accuracy and an average improvement of 36.6% in training speed. In the FastGAN workload, JediGAN* can achieve FID scores comparable to FedGAN (K=1), which are 17.51 and 17.08 respectively, but the training time is accelerated by 5.83 times. In the DCGAN workload, The convergence speed of JediGAN* is slower than that of GossipingGAN, which are 742.95 and 448.52 respectively, but the accuracy is improved by 40.2%. On the other hand, FedGAN (K=1) performs worst with the OriginalGAN workload which confirms the instability of the GAN network itself. The utilization of frequent synchronous updates of discriminator and generator parameters in FedGAN(K=1) exacerbates the negative impact of this instability. Many works have improved the stability of GAN training by manually modifying the GAN workload architecture, which requires human expertise.

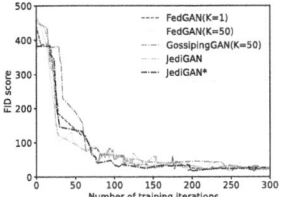 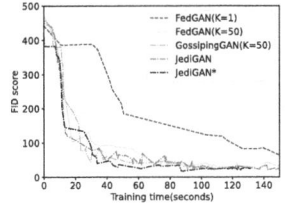 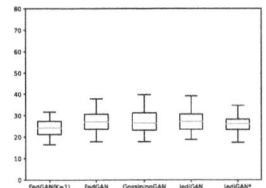

Fig. 10. FID score over iteration rounds loaded as FastGAN

Fig. 11. FID score over time loaded as FastGAN

Fig. 12. FID score over iteration rounds loaded as FastGAN

Convergence Analysis: Figure 7 and Fig. 8 show the FID score of the DCGAN workload changes with the number of iterations and training time. Despite having almost the same convergence as FedGAN after 10,000 epoch, our approach reaches convergence with fewer iterations and faster speed. Although GossipingGAN converges quickly (about 7500 epoch), its accuracy is not satisfactory. This is because our approach has the ability to explore the optimal performance of the system by balancing the consensus advantage of global updates and the communication overhead advantage of local updates[1].

Stability Analysis: Figure 10 and Fig. 11 show the FID score of the Fast-GAN workload changes with the number of iterations and training time. For the FastGAN workload, unlike the DCGAN workload, GossipingGAN achieves nearly the same final accuracy as other methods (only slightly lower), especially after 240 epochs. Furthermore, it also significantly lags behind FedGAN and even JediGAN in terms of training speed shown in Table 2. This indicates that while coarse-grained global updates enhance global consensus, they neglect the deep coupling characteristics within the GAN, increasing search complexity and making early-stage training convergence difficult, resulting in instability. Jedi-GAN* achieves fast and stable convergence by dynamically adjusting the timing of global aggregation, significantly reducing unnecessary communication costs like in FedGAN, while also enhancing global consensus. We also validated the stability of various approaches after the convergence of DCGAN and FastGAN workloads, as shown in Fig. 9 and Fig. 12. JediGAN* performs exceptionally well compared to FedGAN, reducing a significant amount of communication costs while maintaining a high level of performance (See Footnote 1).

---

[1] Experiments on other workloads show similar results.

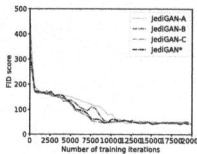 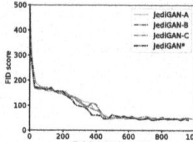 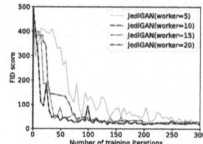 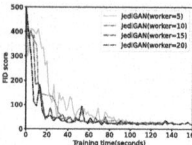

Fig. 13. Training accuracy for component analysis.   **Fig. 14.** Training speed for component analysis   **Fig. 15.** FID score over iteration rounds loaded as Fast-GAN.   **Fig. 16.** FID score over time loaded as FastGAN.

4.3 Component Ablation Analysis

In this section, we explore JediGAN's internal components better to understand their contributions to the performance of the system. We implemented three breakdown versions of JediGAN to take a closer look at the contribution of each component: 1) JediGAN-A has the Cooperative Scheduler and Guided Evolutionary Searcher but does not have Periodic Global Trainer; 2) JediGAN-B has the Cooperative Scheduler and the Periodic Global Trainer but does not have the Guided Evolutionary Searcher; and 3) JediGAN-C has the Periodic Global Trainer and the Guided Evolutionary Searcher but does not have the Cooperative Scheduler. We evaluate these approaches on the DCGAN workload (See Footnote 1).

Figure 13 shows the FID score over the number of iterations of JediGAN*, JediGAN-A, JediGAN-B and JediGAN-C. We can intuitively observe that in the case of the same number of training iterations, that is, the same computation overhead, the FID score of JediGAN* before convergence is better than JediGAN-A, JediGAN-B, but slightly worse than JediGAN-C. Figure 14 shows their FID score over the training time. The results show that JediGAN converges faster than others, including JediGAN-C, which is reduced by 150 s. Specifically, the best FID score for JediGAN* is 40.78 which is better than JediGAN-A (42.69), JediGAN-B (41.36) and JediGAN-C (41.43). This demonstrates that the Periodic Global Trainer and the Guided Evolutionary Searcher can significantly improve training performance. Meanwhile, the cooperative scheduling strategy balances the FID score and the communication overhead (i.e., accuracy and training speed) caused by global updates to achieve optimal performance benefits.

4.4 Scalability Analysis

We use more workers to illustrate the scalability of JediGAN, as well as its accuracy, set to $\mathcal{N} = \{5, 10, 15, 20\}$. We distribute the dataset to each worker in an independent and identically distributed (iid) manner. Figure 15 and Fig. 16 demonstrate the FID score of JediGAN* with the number of iterations and training time for different numbers of workers under FastGAN workload (See

Footnote 1). We can intuitively observe that with the same number of training iterations or training time, the FID score is lower with the increase of workers. Specifically, the best FID scores for JediGAN* with 5 workers, 10 workers, 15 workers, and 20 workers are 23.52,17.51,17.39,17.03, respectively. It means that JediGAN performs better in terms of training accuracy as the number of workers increases. It can be further explained that although the communication overhead will increase with the increase of workers using all-reduce for global updates, our approach can effectively balance the worker consensus and communication cost, thus having good scalability. Experiments have verified the effectiveness of our proposed approach.

5 Related Work

Centralized Distributed GAN System: Recent advances in distributed GAN systems with Federated learning involve [21] [6] which aggregates and updates models through a central server. [10] extends the algorithm of the original generator and discriminator 1-versus-1 game to the algorithm of the 1-versus-N game. it aims at reducing the computation of edge devices by relying on a single generator, hosted on the central server, with only the discriminator kept on the workers. [30] implemented 1-versus-N game in medical scenereconstruct. It focuses on the privacy of user data on the edge device and aims to synthesize data from similarly distributed real data for diagnosis. RYonetani, [28] solves the non-independent-and-identically-distributed data (non-iid) problem-based on the MDGAN framework which has also one single generator. However, the nature of GANs being composed of dual networks with interdependent computations, exacerbates the communication bottleneck issue in PS structure methods. Furthermore, in certain scenarios, like learning over a distributed sensor network spanning a wide area it is often unfeasible to maintain continuous communication with a central parameter server [8].

Decentralized Distributed GAN System: GossipGAN proposed by [9] is the first work to study decentralized GANs using the Gossip communication protocol. The approach simply incorporates the GAN load into gossip learning, resulting in reduced consensus among the local GAN workload and disregarding the intrinsic characteristics of GAN. Building upon this, JediGAN utilizes the Ring All-Reduce method for periodic global aggregation and update of the discriminator, aiming to accelerate the convergence of GAN workloads. Additionally, JediGAN decouples the generator and discriminator in distributed GAN, enhancing training stability.

6 Conclusion

In this paper, we further explore a fully decentralized GAN training system without reducing the overall convergence rate. We developed JediGAN, a fine-grained task scheduling system that enables us to apply a global update and the intrinsic mechanism of GAN to distributed GAN based on gossip learning. Experiments show that we reasonably utilize the intrinsic mechanism of GAN and the advantages of periodic global averaging to mitigate the impact of communication and aggregation costs without affecting accuracy which improves the performance of the system.

Acknowledgment. This work was supported by the National Key Research and Development Program of China (2023YFE0205700), National Natural Science Foundation of China (62341410, 62302348), and Wuhan University - Duke Kunshan University Joint Research Platform Seed Fund (XXWHUDKUZZJJ202311, XXWHUDKUZ-ZJJ202313).

References

1. Assran, M., Loizou, N., Ballas, N., Rabbat, M.: Stochastic gradient push for distributed deep learning. In: International Conference on Machine Learning, pp. 344–353. PMLR (2019)
2. Blot, M., Picard, D., Cord, M., Thome, N.: Gossip training for deep learning. arXiv preprint arXiv:1611.09726 (2016)
3. Dean, J., et al.: Large scale distributed deep networks. In: Advances in Neural Information Processing Systems, vol. 25 (2012)
4. Goodfellow, I., et al.: Generative adversarial nets. In: Advances in Neural Information Processing Systems, vol. 27 (2014)
5. Goyal, P., et al.: Accurate, large minibatch SGD: training imagenet in 1 hour. arXiv preprint arXiv:1706.02677 (2017)
6. Guerraoui, R., Guirguis, A., Kermarrec, A.M., Merrer, E.L.: FeGAN: scaling distributed GANs. In: Proceedings of the 21st International Middleware Conference, pp. 193–206 (2020)
7. Gulrajani, I., Ahmed, F., Arjovsky, M., Dumoulin, V., Courville, A.C.: Improved training of Wasserstein GANs. In: Advances in Neural Information Processing Systems, vol. 30 (2017)
8. Haghighat, A.K., Ravichandra-Mouli, V., Chakraborty, P., Esfandiari, Y., Arabi, S., Sharma, A.: Applications of deep learning in intelligent transportation systems. J. Big Data Anal. Transp. **2**, 115–145 (2020)
9. Hardy, C., Le Merrer, E., Sericola, B.: Gossiping GANs: position paper. In: Proceedings of the Second Workshop on Distributed Infrastructures for Deep Learning, pp. 25–28 (2018)
10. Hardy, C., Le Merrer, E., Sericola, B.: MD-GAN: multi-discriminator generative adversarial networks for distributed datasets. In: 2019 IEEE International Parallel and Distributed Processing Symposium (IPDPS), pp. 866–877. IEEE (2019)
11. Heusel, M., Ramsauer, H., Unterthiner, T., Nessler, B., Hochreiter, S.: GANs trained by a two time-scale update rule converge to a local Nash equilibrium. In: Advances in Neural Information Processing Systems, vol. 30 (2017)
12. Jiang, L., Dai, B., Wu, W., Loy, C.C.: Deceive D: adaptive pseudo augmentation for GAN training with limited data. In; Advances in Neural Information Processing Systems, vol. 34 (2021)
13. Kingma, D.P., Ba, J.: Adam: a method for stochastic optimization. arXiv preprint arXiv:1412.6980 (2014)

14. Konečnỳ, J., McMahan, H.B., Yu, F.X., Richtárik, P., Suresh, A.T., Bacon, D.: Federated learning: strategies for improving communication efficiency. arXiv preprint arXiv:1610.05492 (2016)
15. Krizhevsky, A., Hinton, G., et al.: Learning multiple layers of features from tiny images (2009)
16. LeCun, Y., Bottou, L., Bengio, Y., Haffner, P.: Gradient-based learning applied to document recognition. Proc. IEEE **86**(11), 2278–2324 (1998)
17. Li, T., Sahu, A.K., Talwalkar, A., Smith, V.: Federated learning: challenges, methods, and future directions. IEEE Signal Process. Mag. **37**(3), 50–60 (2020)
18. Li, Z., Jiang, R., Aarabi, P.: Continuous face aging via self-estimated residual age embedding. In: Proceedings of the IEEE/CVF Conference on Computer Vision and Pattern Recognition, pp. 15008–15017 (2021)
19. Liu, B., Zhu, Y., Song, K., Elgammal, A.: Towards faster and stabilized GAN training for high-fidelity few-shot image synthesis. arXiv preprint arXiv:2101.04775 (2021)
20. Radford, A., Metz, L., Chintala, S.: Unsupervised representation learning with deep convolutional generative adversarial networks. arXiv preprint arXiv:1511.06434 (2015)
21. Rasouli, M., Sun, T., Rajagopal, R.: FedGAN: federated generative adversarial networks for distributed data. arXiv preprint arXiv:2006.07228 (2020)
22. Regulation, G.D.P.: General data protection regulation (GDPR). Intersoft Consulting, Accessed in October **24**(1) (2018)
23. Shreeharsha, K., Korde, C.G., Vasantha, M., Kumar, Y.N.: Training of generative adversarial networks using particle swarm optimization algorithm. In: 2021 IEEE International Symposium on Smart Electronic Systems (iSES), pp. 127–130. IEEE (2021)
24. Sutskever, I., Martens, J., Dahl, G., Hinton, G.: On the importance of initialization and momentum in deep learning. In: International Conference on Machine Learning, pp. 1139–1147. PMLR (2013)
25. Wang, S., et al.: Adaptive federated learning in resource constrained edge computing systems. IEEE J. Sel. Areas Commun. **37**(6), 1205–1221 (2019)
26. Wang, Z., She, Q., Ward, T.E.: Generative adversarial networks in computer vision: a survey and taxonomy. ACM Comput. Surv. (CSUR) **54**(2), 1–38 (2021)
27. Ying, G., He, X., Gao, B., Han, B., Chu, X.: EAGAN: efficient two-stage evolutionary architecture search for GANs. In: European Conference on Computer Vision, pp. 37–53. Springer, Cham (2022)
28. Yonetani, R., Takahashi, T., Hashimoto, A., Ushiku, Y.: Decentralized learning of generative adversarial networks from non-IID data. arXiv preprint arXiv:1905.09684 (2019)
29. Zhao, S., Liu, Z., Lin, J., Zhu, J.Y., Han, S.: Differentiable augmentation for data-efficient GAN training. Adv. Neural. Inf. Process. Syst. **33**, 7559–7570 (2020)
30. Zhao, Y., Chen, J., Zhang, J., Wu, D., Teng, J., Yu, S.: PDGAN: a novel poisoning defense method in federated learning using generative adversarial network. In: International Conference on Algorithms and Architectures for Parallel Processing, pp. 595–609. Springer, Cham (2019)
31. Zhou, R., Jiang, C., Xu, Q.: A survey on generative adversarial network-based text-to-image synthesis. Neurocomputing **451**, 316–336 (2021)

Optimizing V_o-V_{iso}: A Modified Methodology to Parallel Computing with Isolating Data in Memristor Arrays

Wenqing Wang[1] , Yabo Chen[1], Nuo Xu[1(✉)], Yihong Hu[1], Chenglong Huang[1], Shaojun Wei[2], and Liang Fang[1(✉)]

[1] National University of Defense Technology, Changsha 410073, China
{wangwenqing,xunuo,lfang}@nudt.edu.cn
[2] Tsinghua University, Beijing 100084, China

Abstract. The MAGIC NOR gate-based memristor array is a promising processing-in-memory (PIM) approach due to its massive parallelism, flexible logical operation, and non-volatile memory characteristics. The V_o-V_{iso} MAGIC NOR gate operation mode is proposed to achieve high-throughput parallel computing and isolate other data within a memristor array. However, V_{iso} has a cumulative effect on the node voltage of the active row, calling into question the feasibility of V_o-V_{iso} operation mode. In this paper, circuit analysis defines the necessary circuit parameter conditions for enabling parallel computing and isolation units in the MAGIC NOR gate array. By algorithms in Python and CUDA C++ exploration, we determined that achieving the necessary conditions within the array parameters ranges—including the tolerance margin V_Δ, array size, V_o, V_{iso} and memristor parameters suitable for real-world circuit requirements—is unfeasible. In response to these challenges, we modified the memristor array architecture. The modified architecture employs transistors to activate compute units while safeguarding the rest selectively. The feasibility of this architecture is validated by SPICE with selected transistors fabricated using a 65 nm process, taking into account transistor resistance and the fluctuations in V_{set} and V_{reset} in the 8×8 modified memristor array. To accommodate the design requirement of the state-of-the-art memristor array, the feasibility of 64×64 modified memristor array, taking into account the impact of wire resistance, is further verified. This paper bridges the gap between reliable high-throughput parallel computing operation and MAGIC NOR PIM architecture.

Keywords: PIM · MAGIC NOR gate · Memristor array · Parallel computing · Isolating voltage · Feasibility · Architecture

1 Introduction

Processing-in-Memory (PIM) has gained significant traction due to its ability to minimize data movement by performing computations within the memory

© IFIP International Federation for Information Processing 2025
Published by Springer Nature Switzerland AG 2025
X. Chen et al. (Eds.): NPC 2024, LNCS 15527, pp. 108–120, 2025.
https://doi.org/10.1007/978-981-96-2830-8_9

[1,2]. Among various PIM, the MAGIC NOR gate stands out for its complete logic functionality, operational simplicity, and suitability for parallel computing within arrays [2–4]. High-throughput parallel computing and isolating data is fundamental to the MAGIC NOR memristor array. Based on this parallel computing and isolating data operation, the MAGIC NOR array can implement high-throughput synthetic mapping [5–7]. For example, Rotem Ben Hu proposed a SIMPLE flow for synthesizing logical functions based on this parallel computing and isolating data operation. These high-throughput synthetic mappings underpin the design of the MAGIC NOR memristor PIM architectures [2–4].

Previous research implemented parallel computing and data isolation using isolation voltages on unselected rows and columns [5–7]. However, these isolation voltages have a cumulative effect on the node voltages, potentially leading to logic operation errors. This issue has been minimally explored in the literature. Anne Siemon's study, for example, simulated a 3×5 MAGIC NOR memristor crossbar and identified logic errors. However, this research only examined one operation mode error in a small array size. It does not show the requirement of the correct logic operation in the memristor array and whether adjustment of the parameters of the memristor array can get a suitable memristor array. In this paper, we employ formula derivation to calculate the node voltages for each row, considering the effect of array size, operating voltage, isolation voltage, and other memristor parameters. We determine that no matter how to adjust the operating voltage, isolation voltage, and other memristor parameters, they can not conform to actual circuit requirements.

To further solve the problem that isolation voltages have a cumulative effect on node voltage, we take transistors to modify the memristor array. Although there are transistors used to solve the sneak current problem in the stateful logic memristor circuit [8], they are used to solve one logic operation without parallel computing and isolating data. In this paper, we design the transistor-modified memristor array to support parallel computing and isolating data, which is the foundation of parallel synthetic mapping.

However, the practical problem is that a transistor is not an ideal switch. It still has resistance when the transistor is in an open state. Thus, when doing parallel computing and isolating data, we need to consider the effect of transistor resistance. We carefully select transistor and memristor parameters to ensure parallel computing and data isolation operations are correct.

Furthermore, synthetic mapping based on parallel computing and isolating other data is used for PIM architecture. Then we need to ensure the modified memristor array satisfies the array size requirements of state-of-the-art MAGIC NOR PIM architecture, such as RACER [3]. However, when the array size increases, the resistance of the wire in the array is non-negligible. In this paper, we verify that the modified memristor array meets the requirements of the state-of-the-art MAGIC NOR PIM architecture's array size while accounting for wire resistance, transistor resistance, and fluctuations in memristor parameters.

This work bridges the gap between the actual circuit design of the memristor array and massive throughout synthetic mapping for the PIM architecture-based MAGIC NOR. The primary contributions of this research are outlined as follows:

– We identify the challenge of V_o-V_{iso} operation in MAGIC NOR array by conducting quantitative simulations of the V_o-V_{iso} operation in an 8×8 memristor array, revealing its errors. We establish the conditions under which V_o-V_{iso} operation is completely logic correct in the MAGIC NOR array. By aligning the prerequisites for the logically correct V_o-V_{iso} operation, we derive constraints on V_{iso}, V_o, array size, and memristor parameters.
– We systematically explore parameters of memristor array including array size, V_o, V_{iso}, V_{set}, V_{reset}, high/low resistance of memristor, and tolerance margin V_Δ by Python and CUDA C++, aims to identify combinations that satisfy logically correct V_o-V_{iso} operation. Results indicate that even with adjustments to the parameters of a memristor array, V_o-V_{iso} operation mode can not work effectively in the memristor array.
– To address the limitations of the V_o-V_{iso} operation mode, we propose a transistor-modified memristor array structure. We simulate parallel computing with data isolation operation using an 8×8 transistor-modified memristor array in SPICE, incorporating 65 nm process transistors. Our simulations account for transistor resistance and fluctuations in V_{set} and V_{reset}. We further extend the parallel computing with data isolation operation simulation to a 64×64 array, considering the impact of wire resistance. The results demonstrate the robustness of the proposed structure in executing parallel computing while isolating data.

2   Background and Motivation

This section provides an overview of the foundational knowledge and the driving forces behind this research.

2.1   MAGIC NOR Logic Gate and V_o-V_{iso} Operation within Memristor Arrays

The memristor, used for logic operation has a high resistance state (HRS) and low resistance state (LRS). These states are determined by the applied voltage, and crucially, the memristor retains its resistance state even after power is discontinued. Therefore, circuits built with digital memristors offer both computational and storage capabilities. Figure 1(a) shows the circuit diagram of the MAGIC NOR gate. Logic 0 and 1 correspond to the HRS and LRS of the memristor, respectively. The out memristor is initially in the LRS, that is, logic 1. When the operating voltage pulse V_o is applied to the terminals of memristors a and b, the output memristor, connected to ground (GND), adopts a logic state equivalent to a NOR b [9].

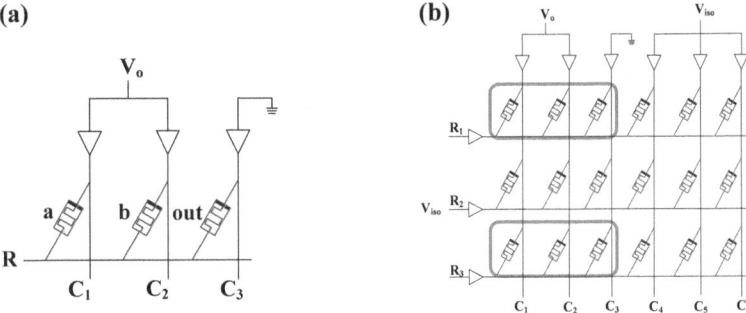

Fig. 1. (a) Schematic diagram of a two-input MAGIC NOR logic gate. (b) The V_o-V_{iso} operation to parallel computing and isolating data in a memristor array.

The process for parallel computing NOR logic and data isolation within a MAGIC NOR crossbar is to apply the operating voltage V_o to the operation columns, connect GND to the output column, and apply the isolation voltage V_{iso} to the rows and columns that do not participate in the operation as illustrated in Fig. 1(b). According to previous studies, this operational mode is viable as long as $0 < |V_{iso}| < |V_{reset}| < \frac{V_o}{2}$ [6,9]. Numerous articles have explored the mapping and synthesis of various algorithms on arrays based on this parallel computing NOR logic and data isolation operation mode [2,5–7,9–13].

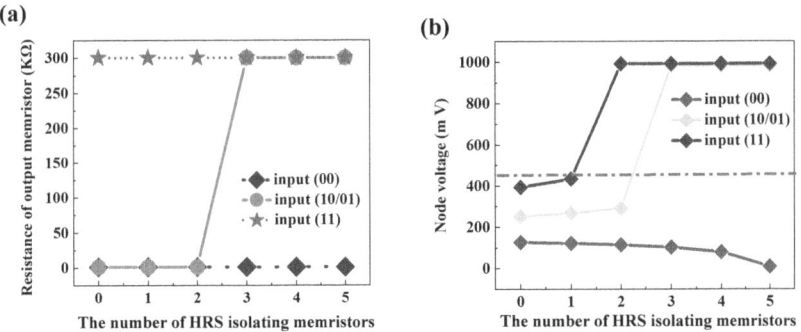

Fig. 2. (a) The resistance of output after V_o-V_{iso} NOR operation in the 8×8 memristor array. (b) The node voltage after V_o-V_{iso} NOR operation in the 8 × 8 memristor array.

2.2   Motivation

Table 1. The typical memristor parameters.

V_{set} (V)	V_{reset} (V)	$R_h(k\Omega)$	$R_l(k\Omega)$
-1.5	0.3	300	1

However, the practical scenario reveals that the implementation of V_{iso} alters the node voltage (V_n) of the row, potentially causing logical misoperations. We simulate it in an 8×8 memristor array by SPICE. The memristor parameters are shown in Table 1. We set V_{iso} as 0.15 V and V_o as 1 V, which conforms to $0 < |V_{iso}| < |V_{reset}| < \frac{V_o}{2}$. The node voltage V_n, which determines whether the memristors in a row can correctly change or maintain their states, is determined solely by the voltages and resistances of the memristors in the row during the V_o-V_{iso} operation, without considering the resistance of the array wire. Due to the V_n of the isolated row being equal to V_{iso}, the voltage applied on memristors in the isolated rows is -0.85 V, 0.15 V, and 0 V respectively. Thus, the voltage applied to memristors in isolated rows will not change the resistances of memristors and cause logic errors in isolated rows.

Consequently, we analyzed the output memristor's resistance and node voltage of these operational rows under various input conditions (00, 10/01, and 11), with the number of HRS isolating memristors in these operational rows ranging from 0 to 5 in an 8×8 memristor array. The selection of isolated rows was randomized, as were the logic states of the memristors within these rows. As demonstrated in Fig. 2(a), the inputs of 10/01 have output logic error when the count of isolating HRS memristors in the operational row totals 0, 1, or 2. As shown in Fig. 2(b), when $V_n > 0.45$ V, the voltage applied on LRS of isolating memristors in the operational row > 0.3 V, prompting their transition to HRS. Our simulation quantitatively reveals the inaccuracies of the V_o-V_{iso} operation in an 8×8 typical memristor array.

Therefore, detailed research is required to verify whether the V_o-V_{iso} operation can function correctly by adjusting array size, operating voltage, isolation voltage, and memristor parameters. if can't, the new parallel computing and isolating data methodology need to be proposed.

3   The Feasibility of V_o-V_{iso} Operation

To evaluate the feasibility of the V_o-V_{iso} operation, we first establish the necessary conditions for logical correctness within the memristor array. We then determine suitable values for V_o, V_{iso}, array dimensions, and memristor parameters that meet these conditions. Additionally, we ignore wire resistance in the array model, as it is negligible for small arrays. For larger arrays, wire resistance can be considered later.

3.1   Requirement for Correct Logic Operation

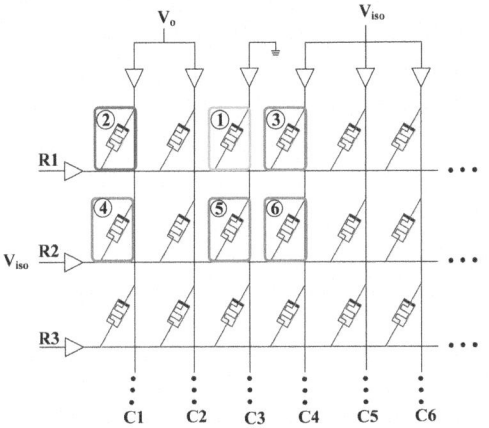

Fig. 3. A V_o-V_{iso} operation in an m × n memristor array. ①, ②, and ③ respond to different cases of memristors in these operation rows. ④, ⑤, and ⑥ respond to different cases of memristors in these isolation rows.

Ensuring logical accuracy in the V_o-V_{iso} operation within a memristor array necessitates the following conditions:

- The resistance state of output memristors in the operational rows must logically transition.
- The resistance state of input memristors, memristors that are not input or output memristors in those operational rows, and memristors in isolating rows should remain unchanged during and after the operation.

The memristor's resistance state depends on the magnitude and direction of the voltage applied. So analyzing the voltage across these memristors when V_o-V_{iso} operation can derive various necessary inequalities. Considering the circuit's inherent properties and disregarding wire resistance for initial simplification, column-to-column swaps do not alter the circuit's topology, meaning there's no impact on the voltage-current relationships within the circuit. For calculation simplicity, we configure the array size as m × n, with input memristors located in the first and second columns and output memristors in the third column, as illustrated in Fig. 3. For ①, it necessitates $V_n(001) < V_{reset}$, $V_n(101) > V_{reset}$, and $V_n(111) > V_{reset}$. V_n represents the node voltage of the row, the first two elements in brackets of V_n represent the logic state of input memristors, and the last element signifies the logic state of output memristor. The V_n at the logic operation row is derived using Millman's theorem as follows:

$$V_n = \frac{G_1 * V_o + G_2 * V_o + G_4 * V_{iso}... + G_n * V_{iso}}{G_1 + G_2 + G_3 + G_4 + ... + G_n} \tag{1}$$

This equation demonstrates that V_n for operation rows is solely dependent on the resistances of memristors in that row, V_o and V_{iso}, assuming wire resistance within the array is negligible.

For ②, we must ensure that $(V_o\text{-}V_n) < |V_{set}|$. For ③, we should guarantee that $(V_n\text{-}V_{iso}) < V_{reset}$. The different states of V_n concludes $V_n(001)$, $V_n(101)$, $V_n(100)$, $V_n(111)$ and $V_n(110)$.

The memristors in isolating rows respond to ④, ⑤, and ⑥. ④ is that one end of the memristor is V_o and the other end is V_{iso}. ⑤ is that one end of the memristor is V_{iso} and the other end is GND. ⑥ is that the voltage at both ends of the memristor is V_{iso}. Therefore, the resistances of these memristors in those isolating rows remain unchanged as long as $(V_o - V_{iso}) < |V_{set}|$, $(V_{iso} - V_o) < V_{reset}$, and $V_{iso} < V_{reset}$.

Acknowledging that V_{set} and V_{reset} may vary across different devices or even within the same device across different operations, we introduce a tolerance margin, V_Δ, to accommodate these fluctuations. The larger the V_Δ implies greater tolerance to device variability but imposes stricter inequality requirements.

Combining all these conditions for executing the $V_o\text{-}V_{iso}$ operation in a memristor array, can be simplified as the following inequalities:

$$V_{reset} - V_n(001) > V_\Delta$$
$$V_n(101) - V_{reset} > V_\Delta$$
$$V_n(111) - V_{reset} > V_\Delta$$
$$|V_{set}| + V_n(001) - V_o > V_\Delta$$
$$|V_{set}| + V_n(101) - V_o > V_\Delta$$
$$|V_{set}| + V_n(111) - V_o > V_\Delta \tag{2}$$
$$V_{reset} - V_n(001) + V_{iso} > V_\Delta$$
$$V_{reset} - V_n(100) + V_{iso} > V_\Delta$$
$$V_{reset} - V_n(110) + V_{iso} > V_\Delta$$
$$|V_{set}| + V_{iso} - V_o > V_\Delta$$
$$V_{reset} - V_{iso} > V_\Delta$$

$V_n(001)$ can be deduced as:

$$V_n(001) = \frac{V_o * (G_h + G_h) + V_{iso} * (q * G_h + p * G_l)}{2 * G_h + G_l + q * G_h + p * G_l} \tag{3}$$

$V_n(101)$, $V_n(111)$, $V_n(100)$, and $V_n(110)$ can be deduced similarly. The variables q and p denote the number of isolated memristors in the active row that are in the HRS and LRS, respectively. G_h and G_l represent the conductance of the HRS and LRS memristor respectively. To ensure the $V_o\text{-}V_{iso}$ operation remains logically accurate under all circumstances, the inequalities must be consistently fulfilled for q as any natural number up to $n - 3$. The value of p is determined by $n - 3 - q$.

3.2   Finding Suitable Array Dimensions, V_o, V_{iso} for Typical Memristor Arrays

To assess the practicality of implementing V_o-V_{iso} parallel MAGIC NOR execution mode in a memristor array, the typical memristor is utilized in MAGIC NOR operation. Its parameters are detailed in Table 1. Our objective is to determine an array size, along with corresponding V_o, V_{iso} values, that meets all inequalities in Sect. 3.1. Considering the constraints of real-world circuits, V_o and V_{iso} were limited to [0.1 V, 3 V] with 0.1 V increments. Array sizes ranged from 4 to 512 columns. V_Δ was set to 0.1 V. We utilize Python to evaluate each variable combination and satisfy the inequalities in Sect. 3.1. Our findings indicate that within the specified parameter space and adhering to typical memristor properties, there exists no combination of array size, V_o, and V_{iso} that simultaneously satisfies all requisite conditions. This outcome highlights the challenges inherent to realizing V_o-V_{iso} operations within arrays based on typical memristors.

3.3   Finding Suitable Array Size, V_o, V_{iso} with Adjusting Memristor Parameters and V_Δ

Due to the lack of a viable configuration for array size, V_o and V_{iso} with typical memristor parameters, we explore adjusting memristor parameters and tolerance margin V_Δ. Since memristor parameters can be fine-tuned during manufacturing [14], and a smaller V_Δ may relax constraints, we aim to identify memristor parameters and V_Δ values that meet the required conditions within a predefined parameter space. To handle the computational demands of this search, we use CUDA C++ for parallel processing. V_{set} and V_{reset} parameters range from 0.1 V to 3 V in 0.1 V increments. Low resistance (R_l) varies from 1 KΩ to 10 KΩ in 100 Ω steps, while high resistance (R_h) ranges from $10 * R_l$ to $10000 * R_l$, with increments of $(10000 * R_l - 10 * R_l)/100$.

Our findings indicate that at $V_\Delta = 0.1$, no suitable memristor parameters meet all conditions. Reducing V_Δ to 0.01 allows for potential configurations, but only for arrays with four columns. The reason is that the more columns there are, the more stringent the inequalities need to be satisfied. As V_Δ approaches zero, more parameter sets become feasible, but such small values are impractical for real circuits. Conclusively, the cumulative effect of isolation voltage on node voltage significantly challenges the implementation of V_o-V_{iso} operations within the considered parameter ranges for practical circuits.

4   Transistor-Modified Memristor Array for Parallel Computing and Data Protection

In this section, we proposed the transistor-modified array design to do parallel computing and data isolating. We make simulations to verify the feasibility of the modified array design considering the effect of the resistance of the transistor, the fluctuation of the memristor parameters, and the wire resistance in the memristor array by SPICE. The wire delay is not considered due to it can be hidden by the operating voltage pulse considering the array size.

4.1   Transistor-Modified Memristor Array Design

Figure 4(a) demonstrates parallel NOR and data isolation operation in this modified array. V_o is applied to the first and second columns, with the third column connected to GND. Source voltage is applied to selectors R_1, R_2, C_1, C_2, and C_3 to open control transistors, while other selectors are grounded to keep transistors closed. This setup allows memristors in columns 1,2, and 3 of rows 1 and 2 to perform NOR operations while others are isolated. The basic unit, shown in the insert of Fig. 4(a), includes two transistors and a memristor. These two transistors are controlled by R and C selectors respectively.

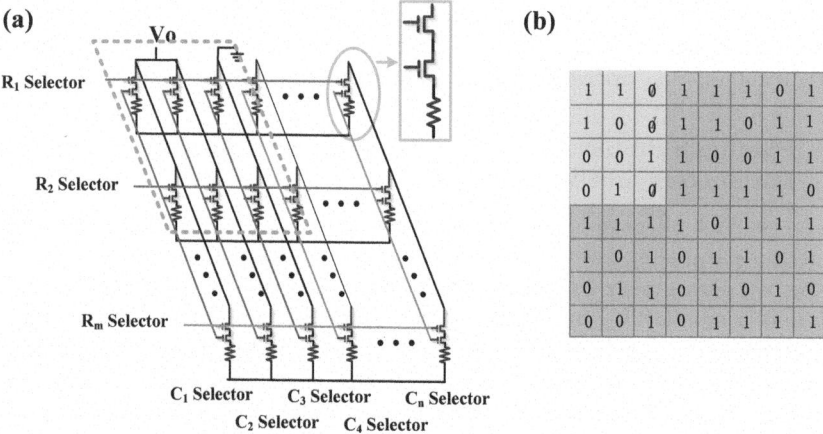

Fig. 4. (a) The modified memristor array structure. (b) The memristor logic state before and after parallel NOR with isolated data operation in the modified 8 × 8 MAGIC memristor array.

To the best of our knowledge, this is the first use of a transistor-modified memristor array to address parallel computing and data protection. It can tolerate the voltage fluctuation of V_{set} and V_{reset}. The area of transistors can be hidden by the back-end-of-line (BEOL) process. Furthermore, the logic operation Min and NAND [13] parallel computing are also suitable in this modified structure because they have similar logic error reasons. In addition, this modified structure can also combine the partition design in [14] to further improve parallelism in the memristor array.

4.2   Simulation of the Modified 8 × 8 MAGIC Memristor Array

To verify the feasibility of the transistor-modified memristor array design, we conducted simulations on a modified 8 × 8 MAGIC memristor array by SPICE. The NMOS transistors, fabricated using a 65 nm process, have dimensions W

= 650 nm and L = 65 nm. A voltage of 2.5 V is applied to the parallel computing R and C selectors to activate the transistors, while other selectors are grounded to keep transistors closed. In the active state, the transistors act as low-resistance paths, whereas in the inactive state, they present very high resistance. We adjusted the low resistance of the typical memristor to 5 KΩ to ensure most of the voltage is applied to the memristor when transistors in its unit are open, ensuring the accuracy of MAGIC NOR logic gate operations.

The logic state of the 8 × 8 memristor array, both before and after parallel computations with isolated data, is shown in Fig. 4(b). The yellow-highlighted regions indicate units performing parallel MAGIC NOR operations. Columns 1 and 2 are input columns, and the third column is the output column. The red numbers in the third column represent the output memristor logic states before the operation. The inputs of 00, 01/10, and 11 in the parallel operation row change or maintain the output logic state correctly. The isolating memristors do not change their logical value because the isolating unit has at least one off-state transistor, which significantly increases the unit's resistance, minimally affecting the parallel computational units. The high resistance of transistors in isolating units ensures that most of the applied voltage is dropped across the transistors, leaving insufficient voltage across the memristor to alter its resistance state. Furthermore, considering a voltage fluctuation of ±0.1 V for both V_{set} and V_{reset}, the correctness of the operations within the array remains unaffected, demonstrating the robustness of this configuration under slight voltage variations.

4.3 Simulation of the Modified 64 × 64 MAGIC Memristor Array

To meet the requirements of memristor PIM structures like RACER, which uses a 64 × 64 memristor array as its compute core, we simulated a modified structure within the same array. The simulation considered a 0.1 V fluctuation in V_{set} and V_{reset}, and the impact of array wiring and transistor resistance. The memristor array model, including wiring resistance (R_{wire}), is shown in Fig. 5(a). Each segment of R_{wire} was assigned a resistance value of 25 Ω [15].

From the analysis in Sect. 4.2, we learned that due to the high resistance of turned-off transistors, the corresponding units do not alter their memristor states during operation and have minimal impact on parallel compute units. Therefore, we focused solely on the parallel compute units, specifically considering the effects of R_{wire}. A parallel MAGIC NOR logic gate, incorporating R_{wire}, is simplified in Fig. 5(b). Here, WR_1 denotes the column wire resistance, ranging from 25 Ω and 1600 Ω. WR_2 and WR_3 represent the row wire resistances, with their combined values ranging from 50 Ω to 1600 Ω. Our simulation aimed to determine whether the MAGIC NOR logic gate can function correctly when WR_1, WR_2 and WR_3 fluctuate within their respective ranges, alongside a 0.1 V fluctuation in V_{set} and V_{reset}. By SPICE simulating the worst-case scenario for R_{wire}, we validated that the parallel logic operations within the array remain accurate.

This outcome demonstrates the practicality of a parameter-optimized structure in a 64 × 64 memristor array, considering fluctuations in V_{set} and V_{reset}, wire resistance, and transistor resistance. It verifies that the structure can effectively execute parallel MAGIC NOR gates and isolate data under realistic conditions, making it well-suited for integrating massively parallel algorithm mapping with logical memristor array architecture.

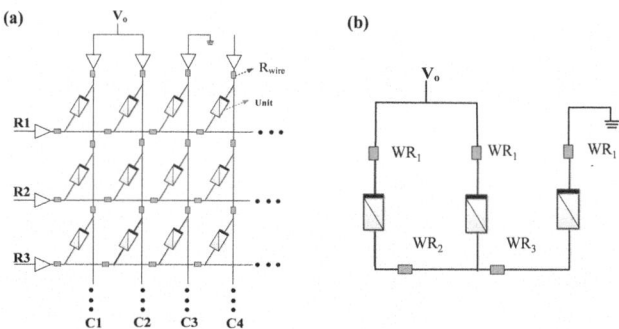

Fig. 5. (a) The modified 64×64 MAGIC memristor array considering R_{wire}. (b) The simplified mode of a parallel execution MAGIC NOR logic gate with R_{wire} in this array.

5   Conclusion

This study tackles the challenge of the V_o-V_{iso} operation in memristor arrays, where cumulative node voltage effects can cause logic errors. We began by defining the necessary circuit parameters for parallel computing and isolation in non-involved units of MAGIC NOR gate array operations. Through adjusting memristor parameters, tolerance margin V_Δ, array size, V_o, and V_{iso}, we found that meeting these conditions within practical parameter ranges is infeasible. To address these challenges, we proposed a transistor-modified memristor array that uses transistors to selectively activate compute units while protecting the rest. We validated this architecture considering fluctuations in V_{set} and V_{reset}, as well as the effects of wire and transistor resistance. Our proposed structure resolves the identified issue of parallel computing and isolating other data in the MAGIC NOR memristor array. It also has the potential to parallel Min and NAND logical operations and integration with the partition design, thereby enhancing computational efficiency and parallelism in memristor arrays.

Acknowledgments. This research is supported by NSFC-62202483, 22-ZZCX046-02, NSFC-62172155, U22A2027, NSFC-62202481, ZK22-05 and 22-TDRCJH02-006.

References

1. He, M., et al.: Newton: a dram-maker's accelerator-in-memory (aim) architecture for machine learning. In: 2020 53rd Annual IEEE/ACM International Symposium on Microarchitecture (MICRO), pp. 372–385 (2020)
2. Imani, M., Gupta, S., Kim, Y., Rosing, T.: Floatpim: in-memory acceleration of deep neural network training with high precision. In: Proceedings of the 46th International Symposium on Computer Architecture, pp. 802–815 (2019)
3. Truong, M.S.Q., et al.: Racer: bit-pipelined processing using resistive memory. In: MICRO-54: 54th Annual IEEE/ACM International Symposium on Microarchitecture, MICRO 2021, pp. 100–116. Association for Computing Machinery, New York (2021)
4. Imani, M., Gupta, S., Rosing, T.: Ultra-efficient processing in-memory for data intensive applications. In: 2017 54th ACM/EDAC/IEEE Design Automation Conference (DAC), pp. 1–6 (2017)
5. Ben Hur, R., Wald, N., Talati, N., Kvatinsky, S.: Simple magic: synthesis and in-memory mapping of logic execution for memristor-aided logic. In: 2017 IEEE/ACM International Conference on Computer-Aided Design (ICCAD), pp. 225–232 (2017)
6. Thangkhiew, P.L., Gharpinde, R., Datta, K.: Efficient mapping of Boolean functions to memristor crossbar using magic nor gates. IEEE Trans. Circuits Syst. I Regul. Pap. **65**(8), 2466–2476 (2018)
7. Haj-Ali, A., Ben-Hur, R., Wald, N., Kvatinsky, S.: Efficient algorithms for in-memory fixed point multiplication using magic. In: 2018 IEEE International Symposium on Circuits and Systems (ISCAS), pp. 1–5. IEEE (2018)
8. Li, Z., Zhu, X., Li, N., Long, H.: SCMOS: series-connected memristor-only stateful logic. In: 2020 IEEE 15th International Conference on Solid-State & Integrated Circuit Technology (ICSICT), pp. 1–3 (2020)
9. Talati, N., Gupta, S., Mane, P., Kvatinsky, S.: Logic design within memristive memories using memristor-aided logic (magic). IEEE Trans. Nanotechnol. **15**(4), 635–650 (2016)
10. Ben-Hur, R., et al.: Simpler magic: synthesis and mapping of in-memory logic executed in a single row to improve throughput. IEEE Trans. Comput. Aided Des. Integr. Circuits Syst. **39**(10), 2434–2447 (2020)
11. Gupta, S., Imani, M., Rosing, T.: Felix: fast and energy-efficient logic in memory. In: 2018 IEEE/ACM International Conference on Computer-Aided Design (ICCAD), pp. 1–7. IEEE (2018)
12. Leitersdorf, O., Ronen, R., Kvatinsky, S.: Multpim: fast stateful multiplication for processing-in-memory. IEEE Trans. Circuits Syst. II Express Briefs **69**(3), 1647–1651 (2021)
13. Lu, Z., Arafin, M.T., Qu, G.: Rime: a scalable and energy-efficient processing-in-memory architecture for floating-point operations. In: 2021 26th Asia and South Pacific Design Automation Conference (ASP-DAC), pp. 120–125 (2021)

14. Song, Y., et al.: Reconfigurable and efficient implementation of 16 Boolean logics and full-adder functions with memristor crossbar for beyond von Neumann in-memory computing. Adv. Sci. **9**(15), 2200036 (2022)
15. Huang, C., Xu, N., Qiu, K., Zhu, Y., Ma, D., Fang, L.: Efficient and optimized methods for alleviating the impacts of IR-drop and fault in RRAM based neural computing systems. IEEE J. Electron Dev. Soc. **9**, 645–652 (2021)

Parallel Computation of the Combination of Two Point Operations in Conic Curves Cryptosystem over $GF(2^n)$ Using Tile Self-assembly

Yongnan Li[✉]

School of National Security, People's Public Security University of China,
Beijing 100038, China
liyongnan@ppsuc.edu.cn

Abstract. How to accomplish the basic operations in cryptosystem becomes a hot research direction in the field of DNA-based cryptography. This paper proposes a DNA computing model that could fulfill parallel computation of point-addition and point-doubling, two fundamental point operations in conic curves cryptosystem, using tile self-assembly. The combination of the two operations is a key step to compute point-multiplication, a point operation to generate intractability of conic curve discrete logarithm problem. Point-addition is deduced by division in one sub-model and another sub-model calculates point-doubling directly and generates the parameters for division. The assembly time complexity of this model is $2n^2 + 3n - 3$, and the space complexity is $n^4 + 3n^3 - 3n + 1$.

Keywords: Point-addition · Point-doubling · Conic curves · Finite field GF(2^n) · DNA computing

1 Introduction

DNA computing model is the mathematical abstraction for researchers proposing algorithms to accomplish corresponding functions such as sticker model [11], tile assembly model [10], splicing model [4], etc. Tile assembly model uses tile self-assembly to fulfill autonomous molecular computations [12]. There was research that has proved tile assembly model was possible to simulate Turing machine [13] in theory. The algorithm over finite field GF(2^n), in which carry bits are not necessary to be considered and all valid parameters are coded as 1 or 0, is very suitable to be accomplished based on tile assembly model. This typical mathematic set is also very common used to construct cryptosystem such as elliptic curves cryptosystem [9] and conic curves cryptosystem [3].

This paper proposes a DNA computing model to compute point-addition and point-doubling simultaneously in conic curves cryptosystem over finite field GF(2^n) using tile self-assembly. The final results are obtained by two different sub-models performing different functions. The models of point-addition [6] and point-doubling [8] are combined by re-designing the assembly rules and sharing some common parameters. A previous model of division [7] is used as one sub-model by adding some functions of transferring parameters. This paper mainly focus on designing the computation tiles in another sub-model. All parameters in the assembly process are encoded as bits to solve the variables matching problem in some early research [1,2]. All possible cases of inputs are covered by this model.

Due to page limitation, we will not introduce the basic theories of tile self-assembly and point-operations on conic curves over finite field $GF(2^n)$. For more detail about them, please refer [6,8]. Section 2 will describe our tile assembly model which could calculate two operations in parallel. Last section will provide a conclusion of the contributions.

2   Model to Compute Point-Addition and Point-Doubling

In point-addition, two continuous additions comprise the divisor while the dividend is consisted of a modular-multiplication and an addition expressed as bitwise *xor* operation [6]. The result of point-addition could be obtained with the operation of division using the dividend and divisor. While two point-parameters are same, the divisor of point-doubling is always 1 and the dividend is the result [8]. According to these features of point-addition and point-doubling, the process of computing two point operations could be divided into two parts accomplished by two sub-models. The first one computes point-doubling, the dividend of point-addition and the divisor of point-addition in parallel. The second one calculates the division in point-addition and transfers necessary parameters. Figure 1 shows the structure of this model, which denotes the sub-model *PDPA* to compute point-multiplication [5]. *A* part and *B* part consist of the first sub-model while *C* part represents the second sub-model. The computation tiles in the second sub-model will be discussed firstly. Then the first sub-model will be designed to match the second one.

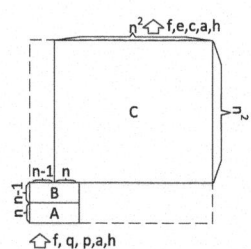

Fig. 1. The structure of the model.

2.1   The Computation Tiles in the Second Sub-model

The computation tiles in the model of division need 6 bits in every side [7]. There still need 1 bit to identify the second sub-model and 3 bits in every side to transfer the constant number 1, the coefficient *a* of conic curves, the result of point-addition expressed as e. 10 bits are enough in every side of the computation tile. Figure 2 shows the tile template used in the second sub-model. The first 6 bits remain the same encoding ways with the computation tiles in the model of division, while the 7th, 8th and 9th bits transfer the three parameters by acting $N_7N_8N_9 = W_7W_8W_9$ and $E_7E_8E_9 = S_7S_8S_9$. The 10th bits are 0 in N side and S side, and they are coded as # in W side and E side. The first sub-model also adopts the tile with 10 bits in every side and the 10th bits are # in N side and S side to label the difference. Figure 3 shows the computation tiles in the bottom assembly row of the second sub-model. The top assembly row of the first sub-model have to match it. In order to make the whole model be used repeatedly, seed configuration of the first sub-model containing input parameters also needs to match the top assembly row of the second sub-model.

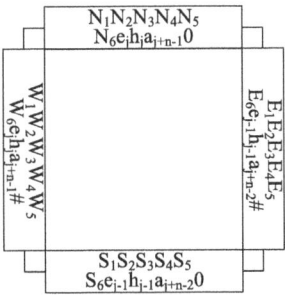

Fig. 2. The tile sample of the second sub-model.

2.2 Seed Configuration

Let $\Gamma = \{\alpha_{00uvvwxyz\#} = <00uvvwxyz\#, null, null, null>, \beta_{\#\#\#\#\#\#1\#\#0} = <null, null, null, \#\#\#\#\#\#1\#\#0>, \beta_{\#\#\#\#\#\#1\#\#1} = <null, null, null, \#\#\#\#\#\#1\#\#1>, \beta_{\#\#\#\#\#\#1\#\#\#} = <null, null, null, \#\#\#\#\#\#1\#\#\#>, \beta_{\#\#\#\#\#\#\#\#00} = <null, null, null, \#\#\#\#\#\#\#\#00>, \beta_{\#\#\#\#\#1\#\#\#\#} = <null, null, null, \#\#\#\#\#1\#\#\#\#>, \beta_{\#\#\#\#\#\#\#\#\#\#} = <null, null, null, \#\#\#\#\#\#\#\#\#\#>\}$ be the set of all boundary tiles, where $u,v,w,x,y,z \in \{0,1\}$, the number of which is 70. Seed configuration of the model to compute the first sub-model is such that

- $\forall i \in \{0, \ldots, n-2\}, S(i,-1) =$

  $\alpha_{c_{2n-2-i}e_{2n-2-i}f_{n-1-i}s_{n-1-i}s_{n-1-i}q_{n-1-i}p_{n-1-i}h_{n-1-i}a_{2n-2-i}\#} = \alpha_{00f_{n-1-i}s_{n-1-i}s_{n-1-i}q_{n-1-i}p_{n-1-i}00\#},$
- $S(n-1,-1) = \alpha_{c_{n-1}e_{n-1}f_0s_0s_0q_0p_0h_0a_{n-1}\#} =$

  $\alpha_{c_{n-1}e_{n-1}1s_0s_0q_0p_01a_{n-1}\#},$
- $\forall i \in \{n, \ldots, 2n-2\}, S(i,-1) =$

  $\alpha_{c_{2n-2-i}e_{2n-2-i}00000h_{n-1-i}a_{2n-2-i}\#},$
- $\forall j \in \{0, \ldots, 2n-2\}, S(-1,j) =$
  - $\beta_{\#\#\#\#\#\#1\#\#\#}$, if $j = 0$,
  - $\beta_{\#\#\#\#\#\#1\#\#0}$, if $0 < j < n-1$,
  - $\beta_{\#\#\#\#\#\#1\#\#1}$, if $j = n-1$,
  - $\beta_{\#\#\#\#\#\#\#\#00}$, if $n-1 < j < 2n-2$.

For the whole model to compute the two point operations in parallel, the seed configuration adds more boundary tiles in position (i,j) as

- $\forall i \in \{2n-1,\ldots,n^2+n-2\}$, $S(i,-1) = \alpha_{000000000\#}$,
- $\forall j \in \{2n-1,\ldots,n^2+2n-2\}$, $S(-1,j) =$
  - $\beta_{\#\#\#\#00\#\#\#\#}$, if $j = 3n-2$,
  - $\beta_{\#\#\#1\#\#\#\#\#\#}$, if $(j+2)mod\ n = 0\&j \neq 3n-3$,
  - $\beta_{\#\#\#\#\#\#\#\#\#\#}$, other cases.

The meaning of the subscript will be explained in further detail below. Therefore, the assembly time complexity of this model is $T(n) = 2n^2 + 3n - 3$, and the space complexity is $S(n) = (n^2+n-1) \cdot (n^2+2n-1) = n^4 + 3n^3 - 3n + 1$. If only considering the first sub-model, their values are $4n - 3$ and $4n^2 - 4n + 1$, respectively.

2.3   Algorithm for Computing Point-Addition and Point-Doubling

Algorithm 1, extended from the original algorithm of modular-multiplication [7], shows parallel computing steps of point-addition and point-doubling. ∞ is coded as $\{\#,\cdots,\#\}$ in the algorithm. The computation tiles are designed based on this algorithm. There are 4 different cases in this algorithm:

- case 1: $P(p) \neq O_{2^n}(0,0)$ and $Q(q) \neq O_{2^n}(0,0)$,
- case 2: $P(p) \neq O_{2^n}(0,0)$ and $Q(q) = O_{2^n}(0,0)$,
- case 3: $P(p) = O_{2^n}(0,0)$ and $Q(q) \neq O_{2^n}(0,0)$,
- case 4: $P(p) = O_{2^n}(0,0)$ and $Q(q) = O_{2^n}(0,0)$.

The rest part of this section will propose the computation tiles for four different cases.

2.4   The Computation Tiles for Case 1 in the First Sub-model

Case 1 maps from line 12 to line 25 in Algorithm 1. The main operations in the first sub-model include modular-multiplication, modular-square and addition. In Algorithm 1, p, q, f', a, h, c, d and e respectively map to the first point-parameter for $P(p)$ in $C_{2^n}(a,b)$, the second point-parameter for $Q(q)$ in $C_{2^n}(a,b)$, the modulus number without the highest bit, the coefficient of $C_{2^n}(a,b)$, constant number 1 in divisor, the dividend, the divisor and the point-parameter for $E(e) = 2P(p)$.

Figure 4 shows the computation tiles considering the cases that both of the two points are not $O_{2^n}(0,0) \in C_{2^n}(a,b)$. The bits represent the same meanings with them in Algorithm 1. Most instructions are already demonstrated inside different tiles. In order to reduce the number of tile encoding way, some computation tiles contain the bits with their subscripts smaller than zero and the corresponding bit means 0 in such circumstances.

In the first assembly step, the computation tiles in Figs. 4(a) and 4(b) obtain d, and merge a in to c and e while $i = n - 1$. Their S sides map the bit order of the N sides of the top row in the second sub-model that computes division and transfers parameters. The initial value of divisor d is zero and it is not input from the S side. Two additions expressed as $p \oplus q \oplus h$ are calculated by executing $E_6 = xor(S_6,S_7,S_8)$ and they are

Algorithm 1. The computing process of the first sub-model

Input: $p = \{p_{n-1}, \cdots, p_0\}$, $q = \{q_{n-1}, \cdots, q_0\}$, $a = \{a_{n-1}, \cdots, a_0\}$, $A = \{a_{2n-2}, \cdots, a_n\}$, $h = \{h_{n-1}, \cdots, h_0\}$, $f' = \{f_{n-1}, \cdots, f_0\}$, $c = \{c_{2n-2}, \cdots, c_0\}$, $d = \{d_{n-1}, \cdots, d_0\}$, $e = \{e_{2n-2}, \cdots, e_0\}$.

Output: $\{c_{n-1}, \cdots, c_0\} = (q \cdot p + a) \bmod f$, $\{d_{n-1}, \cdots, d_0\} = (q + p + h) \bmod f$, $\{e_{n-1}, \cdots, e_0\} = (p \cdot p + a) \bmod f$.

1: $\{h_{n-1}, \cdots, h_0\} \leftarrow 1$.
2: $\{a_{2n-2}, \cdots, a_n\} \leftarrow 0$.
3: $\{c_{2n-2}, \cdots, c_0\} \leftarrow \{a_{2n-2}, \cdots, a_0\}$.
4: $\{e_{2n-2}, \cdots, e_0\} \leftarrow \{a_{2n-2}, \cdots, a_0\}$.
5: $\{d_{n-1}, \cdots, d_0\} \leftarrow \{p_{n-1}, \cdots, p_0\} \oplus \{q_{n-1}, \cdots, q_0\} \oplus \{h_{n-1}, \cdots, h_0\}$.
6: **if** $q_{n-1} = \#\&p_{n-1} \in \{0, 1\}$, **then**
7: $\quad$ $\{c_{n-1}, \cdots, c_0\} \leftarrow \{p_{n-1}, \cdots, p_0\}, \{d_{n-1}, \cdots, d_0\} \leftarrow \{h_{n-1}, \cdots, h_0\}$.
8: **if** $p_{n-1} = \#\&q_{n-1} \in \{0, 1\}$, **then**
9: $\quad$ $\{c_{n-1}, \cdots, c_0\} \leftarrow \{q_{n-1}, \cdots, q_0\}, \{d_{n-1}, \cdots, d_0\} \leftarrow \{h_{n-1}, \cdots, h_0\}$.
10: **if** $p_{n-1} = \#\&q_{n-1} = \#$, **then**
11: $\quad$ $\{c_{n-1}, \cdots, c_0\} \leftarrow \{1, \cdots, 1\}, \{d_{n-1}, \cdots, d_0\} \leftarrow \{0, \cdots 0\}$.
12: **for** i from $n-1$ to 1 **do**
13: $\quad$ **if** $q_i = 1$, **then**
14: $\quad\quad$ $\{c_{n-1+i}, \cdots, c_i\} \leftarrow \{c_{n-1+i}, \cdots, c_i\} \oplus \{p_{n-1}, \cdots, p_0\}$.
15: $\quad$ **if** $c_{n-1+i} = 1$, **then**
16: $\quad\quad$ $\{c_{n-2+i}, \cdots, c_{i-1}\} \leftarrow \{c_{n-2+i}, \cdots, c_{i-1}\} \oplus \{f_{n-1}, \cdots, f_0\}$.
17: $\quad$ **if** $p_i = 1$, **then**
18: $\quad\quad$ $\{e_{n-1+i}, \cdots, e_i\} \leftarrow \{e_{n-1+i}, \cdots, e_i\} \oplus \{p_{n-1}, \cdots, p_0\}$.
19: $\quad$ **if** $e_{n-1+i} = 1$, **then**
20: $\quad\quad$ $\{e_{n-2+i}, \cdots, e_{i-1}\} \leftarrow \{e_{n-2+i}, \cdots, e_{i-1}\} \oplus \{f_{n-1}, \cdots, f_0\}$.
21: **end for**
22: **if** $q_0 = 1$, **then**
23: $\quad$ $\{c_{n-1}, \cdots, c_0\} \leftarrow \{c_{n-1}, \cdots, c_0\} \oplus \{p_{n-1}, \cdots, p_0\}$.
24: **if** $p_0 = 1$, **then**
25: $\quad$ $\{e_{n-1}, \cdots, e_0\} \leftarrow \{e_{n-1}, \cdots, e_0\} \oplus \{p_{n-1}, \cdots, p_0\}$.
26: **Return** $\{c_{n-1}, \cdots, c_0\}, \{d_{n-1}, \cdots, d_0\}, \{e_{n-1}, \cdots, e_0\}$.

Algorithm 2. Making right side move for c

Input: $c = \{c_{2n-2}, \cdots, c_0\}$.
Output:
1: **for** i from $n-1$ to 0 **do**
2: $\quad$ $c_i \leftarrow c_{i+n-1}$.
3: **end for**
4: **for** i from $2n-2$ to n **do**
5: $\quad$ $c_i \leftarrow \#$.
6: **end for**
7: **Return** $\{c_{2n-2}, \cdots, c_0\}$.

---

transferred to N side by acting $N_6 = W_6$. The initial bit values of c and e are 0, while the first two bits are constant number 0 in the N sides of the top row in the second sub-model. The first two bits are shared by different parameters with no conflicts. s

denotes the result of modular-square in division and it will not be used in the first sub-model even it appears in the S side bottom computation tiles. q in S sides representing the result of modular-multiplication in division inputs into the first sub-model as the point-parameter of $Q(q)$ in $C_{2^n}(a,b)$. Other valid bits use the same arguments in the two sub-models.

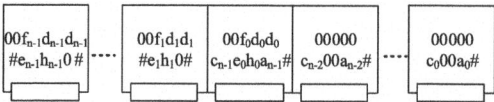

Fig. 3. The first $2n - 1$ computation tiles containing valid input bits in the bottom assembly row in the second sub-model.

The first assembly row starts from the blue tile fulfilling the condition judgements in *line*s 13&15&17&19. E_1 mapping *line* 15 in Algorithm 1 means the highest bit of the dividend c of the division in point-addition. E_2 denotes the highest bit of point-doubling e to map *line* 19 in Algorithm 1. E_2 and E_4 indicate q_{n-1} in *line* 13 and p_{n-1} in *line* 17 in Algorithm 1. Blue tile assigns $E_1E_2E_3E_4$ to make the green tiles mapping lines 14&16&18&20 on its E side perform different instructions for computing the corresponding bits of c and e. S_9 in green tiles signifying the relevant bit of constant parameter a is merged into N_1 in all four cases. There are four different cases to compute c and the instructions depend on W_1W_3 in green tiles. 00, 10, 01 and 11 respectively map to $N_1 = xor(S_1, S_9)$, $N_1 = xor(S_1, S_9, W_7)$, $N_1 = xor(S_1, S_9, S_7)$ and $N_1 = xor(S_1, S_9, W_7, S_7)$. W_2 and W_4 control 4 similar cases using N_2S_2 to replace N_1S_1.

The computation tiles in Figs. 4(d) and 4(e) consider the cases of i varies from $n - 2$ to 1. N_1 denoting the bits in c depends on W_1, W_3, S_1, S_5 and W_7 with the instructions inside the green tile. Compared with the green tiles in the first assembly row in Fig. 4(b), the instructions are $N_1 = S_1$, $N_1 = xor(S_1, W_7)$, $N_1 = xor(S_1, S_5)$ and $N_1 = xor(S_1, W_7, S_5)$ for four different values of W_1 and W_3. In the green tiles in Fig. 4(e), W_2 and W_4 control the instructions that use N_2S_2 to replace N_1S_1 to compute e. $q_{i+j-n+1}$ and $p_{i+j-n+1}$ in green tile transferring from S side to N side identify the remaining bits in two multipliers, which will be used in the upper assembly rows to compute c and e. The other bits on S side and W side are respectively assigned to the corresponding bits on E side and N side. They are moved into the computation tiles on its *northeast* side.

Blue tile in Fig. 4(g) maps *line*s 22&24 and also computes the highest bits of c and e to reduce the assembly complexity. Therefore, subscript j varies from $n - 2$ to 0 in green tiles in Fig. 4(h) mapping *line*s 23&25 in Algorithm 1. Figure 3 shows computation tiles including the necessary input bits in the bottom assembly row of the second sub-model designed based on the model of division [7]. For $i = 0$ in Algorithm 1, the N side bits of computation tiles have to be re-arranged to match the S side of the computation tiles in Fig. 3. Except c in the 6th bits of N side, all other bits could be matched as shown in Figs. 4(g) and 4(h). There still need $n - 1$ assembly row to make n bits in c move right-shift $n - 1$ tiles and other bits move from S side to N side directly. Three types of white tiles on the S side of gray tile in Fig. 4(i) fulfill this function using $n - 1$ assembly row. The process could be demonstrated in Algorithm 2.

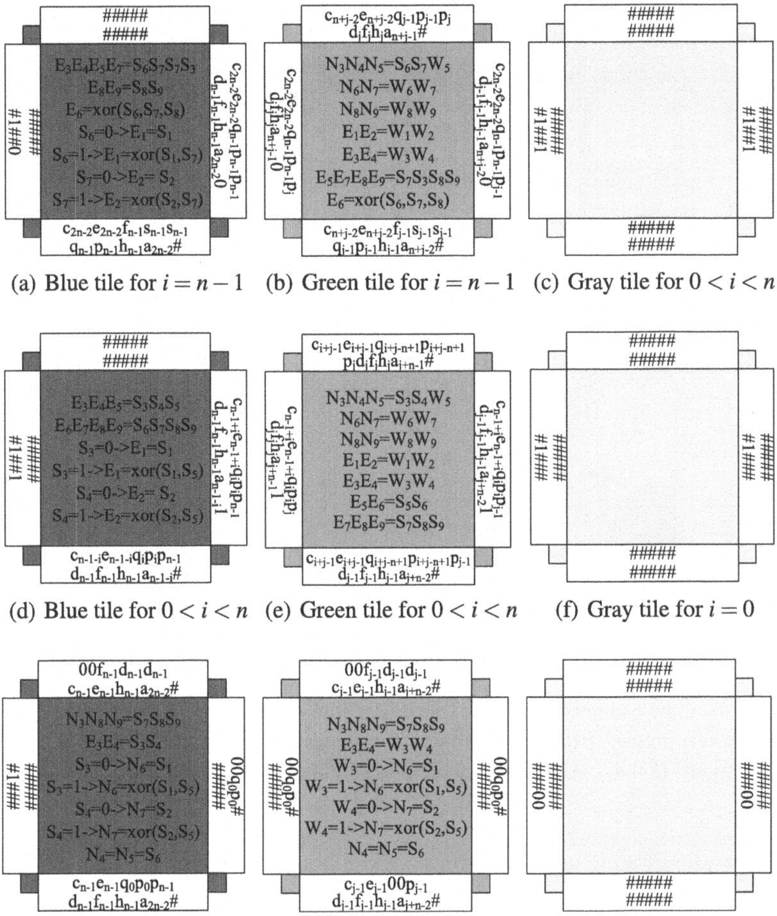

(a) Blue tile for $i = n-1$
$E_3E_4E_5E_7=S_6S_7S_7S_3$
$E_8E_9=S_8S_9$
$E_6=xor(S_6,S_7,S_8)$
$S_6=0\text{->}E_1=S_1$
$S_6=1\text{->}E_1=xor(S_1,S_7)$
$S_7=0\text{->}E_2=S_2$
$S_7=1\text{->}E_2=xor(S_2,S_7)$

(b) Green tile for $i = n-1$
top: $c_{n+j-2}e_{n+j-2}q_{j-1}p_j$ $d_jf_jh_ja_{n+j-1}\#$
$N_3N_4N_5=S_6S_7W_5$
$N_6N_7=W_6W_7$
$N_8N_9=W_8W_9$
$E_1E_2=W_1W_2$
$E_3E_4=W_3W_4$
$E_5E_7E_8E_9=S_7S_3S_8S_9$
$E_6=xor(S_6,S_7,S_8)$
bottom: $c_{n+j-2}e_{n+j-2}f_{n-1}s_{j-1}$ $q_{j-1}p_{j-1}h_{j-1}a_{n+j-1}\#$

(c) Gray tile for $0 < i < n$

(d) Blue tile for $0 < i < n$
$E_3E_4E_5=S_3S_4S_5$
$E_6E_7E_8E_9=S_6S_7S_8S_9$
$S_3=0\text{->}E_1=S_1$
$S_3=1\text{->}E_1=xor(S_1,S_5)$
$S_4=0\text{->}E_2=S_2$
$S_4=1\text{->}E_2=xor(S_2,S_5)$
bottom: $c_{n-1-i}e_{n-1-i}q_ip_{n-1}$ $d_nf_{n-1}h_{n-1}a_{n-1-i}\#$

(e) Green tile for $0 < i < n$
top: $c_{i+j-1}e_{i+j-1}q_{i+j-n+1}p_{i+j-n+1}$ $p_jd_jf_jh_ja_{i+n-1}\#$
$N_3N_4N_5=S_3S_4W_5$
$N_6N_7=W_6W_7$
$N_8N_9=W_8W_9$
$E_1E_2=W_1W_2$
$E_3E_4=W_3W_4$
$E_5E_6=S_5S_6$
$E_7E_8E_9=S_7S_8S_9$
bottom: $c_{i+j-1}e_{i+j-1}q_{i+j-n+1}p_{i+j-n+1}p_{j-1}$ $d_{j-1}f_{j-1}h_{j-1}a_{i+n-2}\#$

(f) Gray tile for $i = 0$

(g) Blue tile for $i = 0$
top: $00f_{n-1}d_{n-1}d_{n-1}$ $c_ne_nh_{n-1}a_{2n-2}\#$
$N_3N_8N_9=S_7S_8S_9$
$E_3E_4=S_3S_4$
$S_3=0\text{->}N_6=S_1$
$S_3=1\text{->}N_6=xor(S_1,S_5)$
$S_4=0\text{->}N_7=S_2$
$S_4=1\text{->}N_7=xor(S_2,S_5)$
$N_4=N_5=S_6$
bottom: $c_{n-1}e_{n-1}q_0p_0p_{n-1}$ $d_{n-1}f_{n-1}h_{n-1}a_{2n-2}\#$

(h) Green tile for $i = 0$
top: $00f_{j-1}d_{j-1}d_{j-1}$ $c_je_{j-1}h_{j-1}a_{j+n-2}\#$
$N_3N_8N_9=S_7S_8S_9$
$E_3E_4=W_3W_4$
$W_3=0\text{->}N_6=S_1$
$W_3=1\text{->}N_6=xor(S_1,S_5)$
$W_4=0\text{->}N_7=S_2$
$W_4=1\text{->}N_7=xor(S_2,S_5)$
$N_4=N_5=S_6$
bottom: $c_{j-1}e_{j-1}00p_{j-1}$ $d_{j-1}f_{j-1}h_{j-1}a_{j+n-2}\#$

(i) Gray tile for moving c

Fig. 4. Computation tiles for both points are not $O_{2^n}(0,0) \in C_{2^n}(a,b)$. Subscript j varies from $n-1$ to 0 in these figures. $a_k = 0$ if its subscript is bigger than $n-1$. (Color figure online)

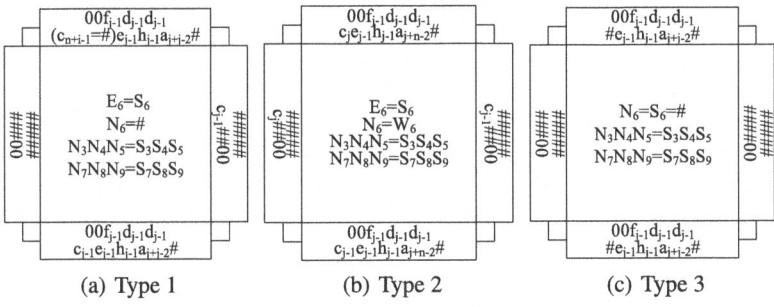

(a) Type 1
top: $00f_{j-1}d_{j-1}d_{j-1}$ $(c_{n+i-1}=\#)e_{j-1}h_{j-1}a_{j+i-2}\#$
$E_6=S_6$
$N_6=\#$
$N_3N_4N_5=S_3S_4S_5$
$N_7N_8N_9=S_7S_8S_9$
bottom: $00f_{j-1}d_{j-1}d_{j-1}$ $c_{j-1}e_{j-1}h_{j-1}a_{j+i-2}\#$

(b) Type 2
top: $00f_{j-1}d_{j-1}d_{j-1}$ $c_je_{j-1}h_{j-1}a_{j+n-2}\#$
$E_6=S_6$
$N_6=W_6$
$N_3N_4N_5=S_3S_4S_5$
$N_7N_8N_9=S_7S_8S_9$
bottom: $00f_{j-1}d_{j-1}d_{j-1}$ $c_{j-1}e_{j-1}h_{j-1}a_{j+n-2}\#$

(c) Type 3
top: $00f_{j-1}d_{j-1}d_{j-1}$ $\#e_{j-1}h_{j-1}a_{j+i-2}\#$
$N_6=S_6=\#$
$N_3N_4N_5=S_3S_4S_5$
$N_7N_8N_9=S_7S_8S_9$
bottom: $00f_{j-1}d_{j-1}d_{j-1}$ $\#e_{j-1}h_{j-1}a_{j+i-2}\#$

Fig. 5. The white tile making right shift move for c in the 6th bits. Other bits transfer to N side directly without adjustment.

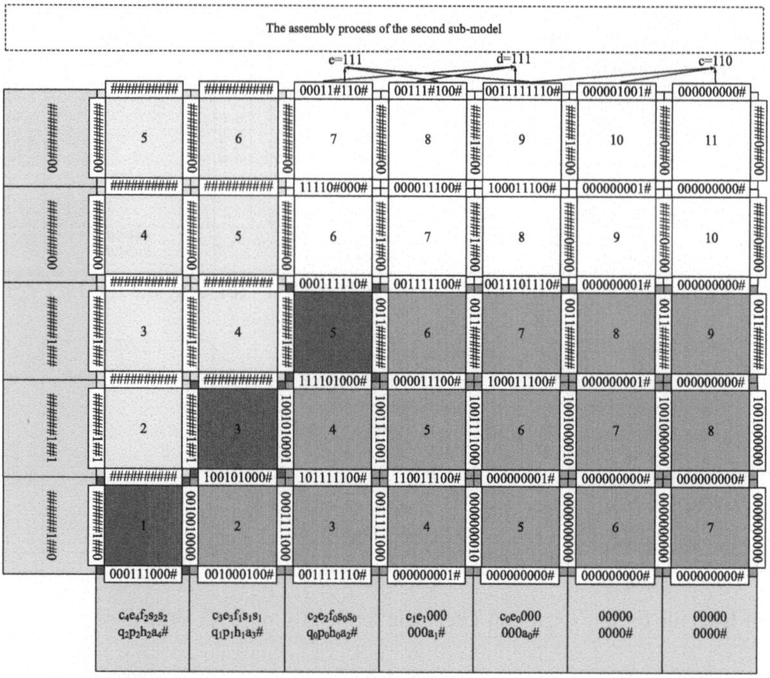

The assembly process of the second sub-model

		e=111		d=111		c=110
########	#########	00011#110#	00111#100#	0011111110#	000001001#	000000000#
5	6	7	8	9	10	11
########	#########	11110#000#	000011100#	100011100#	000000001#	000000000#
4	5	6	7	8	9	10
########	#########	000111110#	001111100#	0011101110#	000000001#	000000000#
3	4	5	6	7	8	9
########	#########	111101000#	000011100#	100011100#	000000001#	000000000#
2	3	4	5	6	7	8
########	100101000#	101111100#	110011100#	000000001#	000000000#	000000000#
1	2	3	4	5	6	7
000111000#	001000100#	001111110#	000000001#	000000000#	000000000#	000000000#
$c_4e_4f_2s_2s_2$ $q_2p_2h_2a_4$#	$c_3e_3f_1s_1s_1$ $q_1p_1h_1a_3$#	$c_2e_2f_0s_0s_0$ $q_0p_0h_0a_2$#	c_1e_1000 $000a_1$#	c_0c_0000 $000a_0$#	00000 0000#	00000 0000#

Fig. 6. The assembly example of the first sub-model with the inputs $s = 101$, $f' = 011$, $q = 101$, $p = 011$, $h = 001$ and $a = 010$. The top row shows the result $e = 111$, $c = 110$ and $d = 111$. The second sub-model in the N side will calculate point-addition and the result is $c/d = 101$.

Figure 6 shows an assembly example of the first sub-model that both points $P(p)$ and $Q(q)$ are not $O_{2^n}(0,0) = O(\infty)$. It costs 11 assembly steps and the assembly order is depicted inside the computation tiles.

2.5 The Computation Tiles for Case 2 in the First Sub-model

While $Q(q)$ is $O_{2^n}(0,0) = O(\infty)$ and $p \neq \infty$, the process of computing point-doubling remains unchanged. Figure 7 shows the computation tiles for $q = \infty$ in the first sub-model. The cyan tiles and orange tiles are respectively updated from blue tiles and green tiles in Fig. 4. The white tiles in Fig. 5 in the k_{th} assembly row, where $n-1 < k < 2n-2$, could cover case 2 in the first sub-model. According to the definition of point-addition, the result of $P(p) \oplus O(\infty)$ is $P(p)$. In the first sub-model, let $c = p$ and $d = h = 1$ to make the result of division be p in the second sub-model. In the first assembly row for $i = n-1$, set $c = p$ by acting $E_1 = S_7$ and $N_1 = W_1$. For $i \in [1, n-2]$, the instructions for transferring c are $E_1 = S_1$ and $N_1 = W_1$. The instructions for c are the same with the case of two non-zero points. The bits for h and q are set as # to enable it in the assembly process. In the n_{th} assembly row for $i = 0$, assign $d = h = 1$ directly by acting $N_4 = N_5 = S_8$.

2.6 The Computation Tiles for Case 3 in the First Sub-model

If $q \neq \infty$ and $P(p)$ is $O_{2^n}(0,0) = O(\infty)$, point-addition and point-doubling—e in the first sub-model—are respectively $Q(q)$ and $O(\infty)$. c and d could be q and 1. The assembly principle is similar with the case that $Q(q)$ is $O(\infty)$ and $p \neq \infty$. Figure 8 shows the computation tiles for $q = \infty$ mapping *line* 9 in Algorithm 1 in the first sub-model. The white tiles in Fig. 5 still work without changing in the k_{th} assembly row, where $n - 1 < k < 2n - 2$.

2.7 The Computation Tiles for Case 4 in the First Sub-model

If $P(p)$ and $Q(q)$ are both $O_{2^n}(0,0) = O(\infty)$, the results of two types of point operations are both $O_{2^n}(0,0) = O(\infty)$. e is assigned as $\{\# \cdots \#\}$ to denote ∞. d must be 0 and c could be an arbitrary nonzero value to ensure that point-addition is $O_{2^n}(0,0) = O(\infty)$. Figure 9 shows the computation tiles replacing blue tile and green tile in Fig. 4 that work for two input point are not $O_{2^n}(0,0) = O(\infty)$. Except h, a and f, three constant values that will be transferred to the second sub-model, all parameters are set as # in the assembly process. For $i = 0$ in the n_{th} assembly row, d and c are assigned as $\{0, \cdots, 0\}$ and $\{1, \cdots, 1\}$ as shown in *line* 11 in Algorithm 1. The white tiles could still play a role and there is no need to be updated.

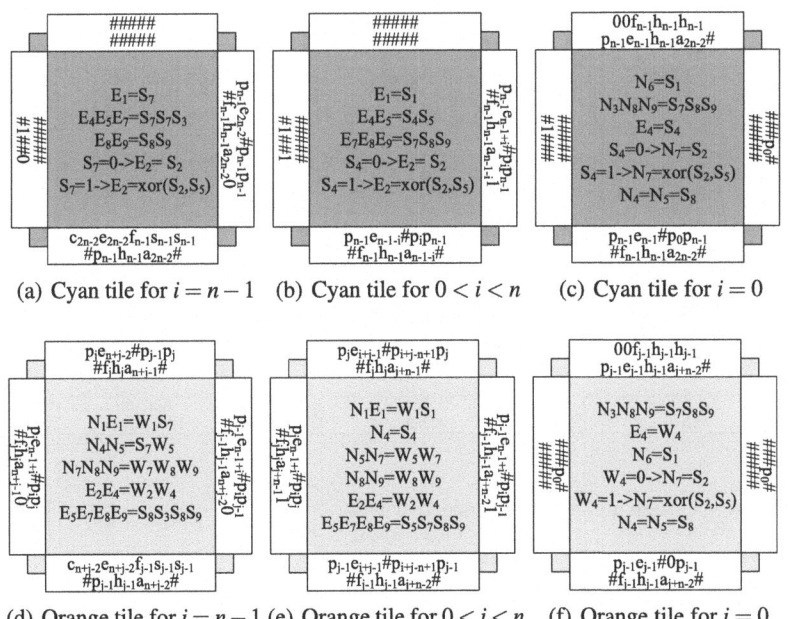

(a) Cyan tile for $i = n - 1$ (b) Cyan tile for $0 < i < n$ (c) Cyan tile for $i = 0$

(d) Orange tile for $i = n - 1$ (e) Orange tile for $0 < i < n$ (f) Orange tile for $i = 0$

Fig. 7. Computation tiles for $Q(q)$ is $O_{2^n}(0,0) \in C_{2^n}(a,b)$ and $P(p)$ is not $O_{2^n}(0,0)$. (Color figure online)

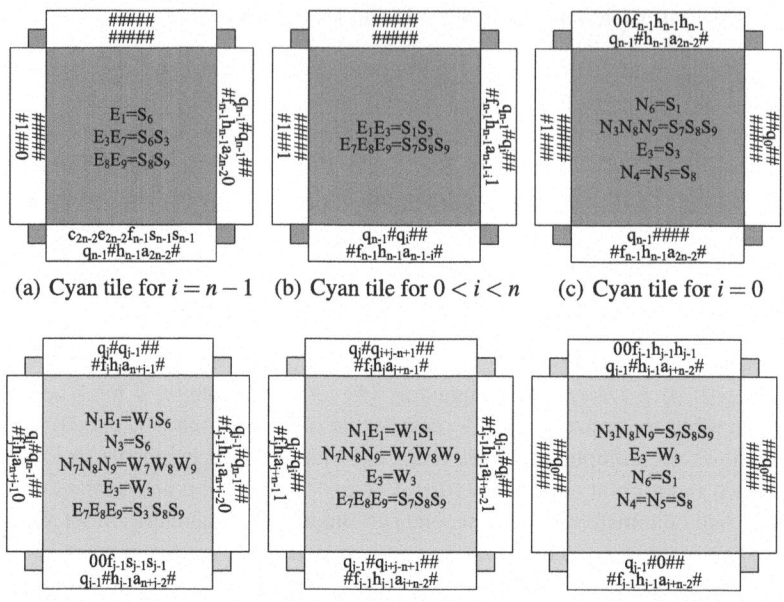

Fig. 8. Computation tiles for $P(p)$ is $O_{2^n}(0,0) \in C_{2^n}(a,b)$ and $Q(q)$ is not $O_{2^n}(0,0)$. (Color figure online)

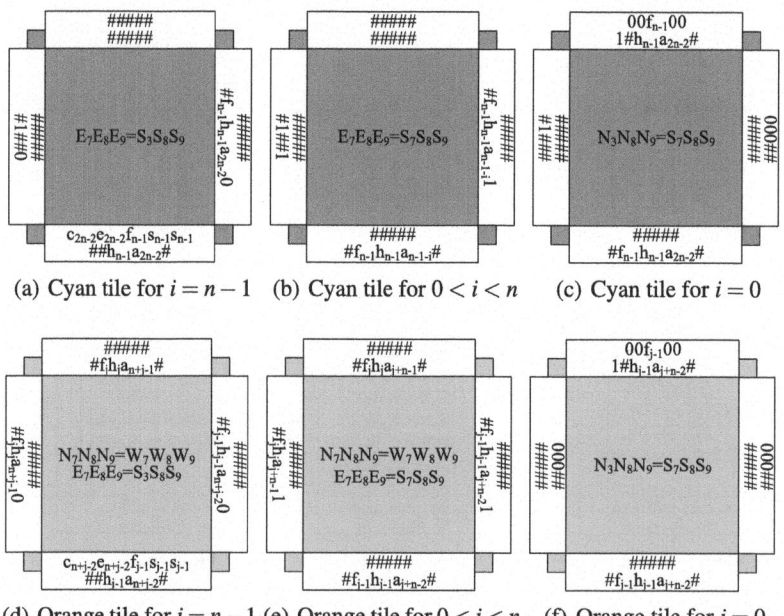

Fig. 9. Computation tiles for both points are $O_{2^n}(0,0)$. (Color figure online)

3   Conclusions

This paper proposes a tile assembly model that could compute point-addition and point-doubling in parallel in conic curves cryptosystem over finite field $GF(2^n)$. This model is updated from the sub-models proposed in previous researches [6–8] by redesigning the computation tiles and assembly steps. A sub-model calculates point-doubling and generates the parameters to compute point-addition. Another sub-model designed based on a previous model of division obtains the final result of point-addition with the outputs of the first sub-model as inputs and transfers other parameters containing point-doubling to its top assembly row. Four possible cases of inputs are all considered in this model which could be used continually for its N side of top assembly row matching the S side of bottom row. The assembly time complexity of this model is $2n^2 + 3n - 3$, and the space complexity is $n^4 + 3n^3 - 3n + 1$.

Acknowledgements. This study is sponsored by Double First-Class Innovation Research Project for People's Public Security University of China (No. 2023SYL20).

References

1. Barua, R., Das, S.: Finite field arithmetic using self-assembly of DNA tilings. In: Proceeding of the 2003 Congress on Evolutionary Computation (CEC 2003), vol. 4, pp. 2529–2536. IEEE (2003)
2. Cheng, Z.: Computation of multiplicative inversion and division in gf(2(n)) by self-assembly of DNA tiles. J. Comput. Theor. Nanosci. **9**(3), 336–346 (2012)
3. Daniel, R.M., Rajsingh, E.B., Silas, S.: A forward secure signcryption scheme with ciphertext authentication for e-payment systems using conic curve cryptography. J. King Saud Univ.-Comput. Inf. Sci. (2018)
4. Heng, F.W., Ismail, N.I.: Generalisations of DNA splicing systems with one palindromic restriction enzyme. Matematika **34**(1), 59–71 (2018)
5. Li, Y.: A tile assembly model to calculate point-multiplication on conic curves over finite field $GF(2^n)$. In: Proceeding of 18th IEEE International Symposium on Parallel and Distributed Processing with Applications (ISPA 2020), Exeter, UK, pp. 41–48. IEEE (2020)
6. Li, Y., Xiao, L.: Arithmetic computation using self-assembly of DNA tiles: point-addition on conic curves over finite field $GF(2^n)$. In: Proceeding of 25th International Conference on Parallel and Distributed Systems (IPCADS 2019), Tianjin, China, pp. 888–895. IEEE (2019)
7. Li, Y., Xiao, L.: Parallel computation of division over $GF(2^n)$ covering divide-by-zero based on tile assembly model. In: Proceeding of 17th IEEE International Symposium on Parallel and Distributed Processing with Applications (ISPA 2019), Xiamen, China, pp. 499–506. IEEE (2019)
8. Li, Y., Xiao, L.: Parallel DNA computing model of point-doubling in conic curves cryptosystem over finite field $GF(2^n)$. In: Proceeding of The 21st IEEE International Conference on High Performance Computing and Communications (HPCC 2019), Zhangjiajie, China, pp. 1564–1571. IEEE (2019)
9. Mahmood, K., Chaudhry, S.A., Naqvi, H., Kumari, S., Li, X., Sangaiah, A.K.: An elliptic curve cryptography based lightweight authentication scheme for smart grid communication. Futur. Gener. Comput. Syst. **81**, 557–565 (2018)

10. Meunier, P.É., Woods, D.: The non-cooperative tile assembly model is not intrinsically universal or capable of bounded turing machine simulation. In: Proceedings of the 49th Annual ACM SIGACT Symposium on Theory of Computing, pp. 328–341. ACM (2017)
11. Sarkar, M., Ghosal, P., Mohanty, S.P.: Exploring the feasibility of a DNA computer: design of an ALU using sticker-based DNA model. IEEE Trans. Nanobiosci. **16**(6), 383–399 (2017)
12. Winfree, E.: Algorithmic self-assembly of DNA. Ph.D. thesis, California Institute of Technology (1998)
13. Winfree, E., Yang, X., Seeman, N.C.: Universal computation via self-assembly of DNA: some theory and experiments. DNA Based Comput. II 191–213 (1998)

Parallel Construction of Independent Spanning Trees on 3-ary n-cube Networks

Yuzhen Xu, Weibei Fan$^{(\boxtimes)}$, Mengjie Lv, Xueli Sun, Lei Han, and Fu Xiao

School of Computer Science, Nanjing University of Posts and Telecommunications,
Nanjing, China
{wbfan,mjlv,sunxueli,hanlei,xiaof}@njupt.edu.cn

Abstract. As networks grow larger and more intricate, failures become unavoidable. Interconnection networks need continual and reliable functioning, as well as effective routing methods for transmitting data among processors. Ensuring fault tolerance in routing, especially through independent spanning trees (ISTs), is crucial. The 3-ary n-cube network (Q_n^3) boasts numerous properties such as low vertex degree, regularity, and straightforward implementation. In this paper, We have presented an effective parallel constructive approach for ISTs on Q_n^3 relying on the ascending sequence. Derived from the ISTs constructed before, we obtain a fault-tolerant routing system that utilizes those as its routing table. Following this, we evaluate the effectiveness of the fault-tolerant routing mechanism through simulated data. Simulated data reveals a progressive escalation in transmission success rates as dimensionality increases, approaching near-perfection at almost 100%. Its findings can provide a valuable benchmark and offer insights into the efficacy of fault-tolerant communication within a broad spectrum of cube-based systems.

Keywords: Independent spanning tree · 3-ary n-cube networks · fault-tolerant routing · parallel algorithm

1 Introduction

The rapid development of artificial intelligence technology has put forward new demands for high-performance computing (HPC), leading to an increasing demand for computing resources. Nowadays, HPC is a key research tool for achieving significant scientific progress, mainly in parallel and distributed systems, where interconnected networks play a crucial role [1,5]. An interconnection network (network for short), often depicted as a graph, illustrates processors as vertices and communication links between processors as edges [6].

Hypercube is a classic interconnection network structure known for its advantageous features like low diameter, symmetrical design, scalability, and recursive nature. However, a drawback of the hypercube is that as its dimensionality grows, so does the node degree. This increase in node degree can pose challenges in parallel computing systems [9]. The 3-ary n-cube, designated as Q_n^3, emerged as a

© IFIP International Federation for Information Processing 2025
Published by Springer Nature Switzerland AG 2025
X. Chen et al. (Eds.): NPC 2024, LNCS 15527, pp. 133–145, 2025.
https://doi.org/10.1007/978-981-96-2830-8_11

significant extension of the hypercube, retaining its outstanding characteristics while introducing new advantages like reduced message latency and simplified implementation. Q_n^3 has captured the attention of both the academic community for research purposes and has been actively employed in the practical construction of parallel computers. The Blue Gene/L and Cray XT5 supercomputers are notable examples. Moreover, the utilization of Q_n^3 extends to the development of data center networks, including systems like CamCube and NovaCube [4].

As interconnection networks expand, the likelihood of network failures rises. To alleviate issues caused by processor or link failures, fault-tolerant communication technology has become crucial [8]. Solutions involve efficient algorithm design and equipment updates. Leveraging the network's inherent traits to craft high-performance algorithms is key to enhancing communication performance. Employing ISTs for designing high-performance communication algorithms is a highly effective approach in improving interconnection network communication performance [2]. Moreover, ISTs also play a vital role in reliable communication protocols, one-to-all broadcasting, multinode broadcasting, reliable broadcasting, and secure message distribution. Consequently, the construction of multiple ISTs on a network has emerged as a significant and pressing concern. Yet, there exist a conjecture regarding the existence of ISTs in any given graph:

Conjecture. Given an n-vertex-connected graph G with $n \leq 1$, there exist n-vertex-ISTs rooted at an arbitrary vertex on G.

Khuller and Schieber demonstrated that in the case where any n-vertex-connected graph possesses n-vertex-ISTs [10]. Although the conjecture has been proved correct for $k \leq 5$, it is still open for $k \geq 5$ for a graph G of arbitrary topologies [13]. Consequently, researchers have been focusing on the study of ISTs on various special graphs. However, the conjecture has been solved on some restricted classes of graphs, such as product graphs [11], hypercubes [6], locally twisted cubes [14] and crossed cubes [12], etc.

As the Q_n^3 is a kind of product graph and is a $2n$-vertex-connected graph, the maximum number of ISTs that can be constructed on a Q_n^3 is $2n$. Nevertheless, the establishment of ISTs encounters several hurdles.

1) Expanding the network's size increases the complexity associated with constructing ISTs. For expansive networks, finding an optimal solution can require a significant investment of time, highlighting the critical need for developing efficient algorithms to address this challenge effectively.
2) In various interconnection networks, aligning the number of ISTs with the vertex connectivity presents a significant obstacle. Vertex connectivity typically represents the maximum number of ISTs attainable within a graph; however, achieving parity between these quantities remains challenging in numerous network scenarios.

In this paper, we explore the generation of ISTs on the Q_n^3 and introduce a effective parallel algorithm for building $2n$ ISTs. The number of ISTs $2n$ is optimal, representing the maximum number allowed in Q_n^3.

Apart from studying the effective generation of ISTs on Q_n^3 when vertex failures occur, we performed simulations to assess fault-tolerant routing utilizing these ISTs as routing tables. Our evaluation encompassed analyzing key performance metrics like Average Path Length (APL) and Transmission Failure Rate (TFR). The main contributions of this paper can be summarized as:

1. We propose a parallel algorithm with a time complexity of $O(N)$ ($N = 3^n$) to construct $2n$ ISTs on Q_n^3, where each tree can be constructed concurrently.
1. By establishing a total of $2n$ ISTs on Q_n^3, a number considered optimal due to the graph's $2n$-vertex connectivity, we achieve the maximum number of vertex-disjoint paths, which facilitate fault-tolerant routing strategies.
2. In a simulated experiment, we delve into two key dimensions: the Transmission Failure Rate (TFR), which quantifies unsuccessful transmissions in relation to the total, and the Average Path Length (APL). Our data simulations reveal a pattern of increasing transmission success rates with higher dimensions, nearing almost perfect success rates.

The rest of this paper is organized as follows. Section 2 gives some definitions and notations. Section 3 proposes an algorithm for Q_n^3 to construct $2n$ independent spanning trees and then proves the correctness of existence of ISTs. Section 4 conducts simulations to evaluate fault-tolerant routing using these ISTs as routing tables. The final section concludes this paper.

2   Preliminaries

In this section, we first give some definitions and notations and then we will introduce the definition of the 3-ary n-cube and the dimension-backbone walk.

An interconnection architecture plays a crucial role in parallel computing systems, represented as a basic graph G comprising the vertex set $V(G)$ and the edge set $E(G)$. For vertices x and y in G, a path P connecting these two vertices can be denoted as $Path(P, x, y)$. Correspondingly, $V(P)$ and $E(P)$ designate the vertex set and edge set of P, respectively, and $ancestor(P, x)$ represents the ancestor set of a vertex x in P. Two paths P and Q are considered *vertex-disjoint* if $E(P) \cap E(Q) = \emptyset$ and $V(P) \cap V(Q) = \{x, y\}$. When it comes to two spanning trees T_i and T_j rooted at the same vertex x in graph G, they are said to be independent if, for every vertex $y \in V(G) \setminus x$, the path $Path(P, x, y)$ in T_i and the path in $Path(Q, x, y)$ T_j are internally vertex-disjoint. A collection of spanning trees on graph G is classified as independent if they are mutually independent. For other terminologies and notations not mentioned above, please refer to [15].

Then, we give the definition of 3-ary n-cube, denoted by Q_n^3.

Definition 1. [3] A 3-ary n-cube contains 3^n vertices for $n \geq 1$. A vertex x of Q_n^3 can be represented as a binary string $x_{n-1}x_{n-2}\ldots x_1x_0$, where $x_i \in \{0, 1, 2\}$ for any integer $i \in \{0, 1, \ldots, n-1\}$. Vertices x and y are adjacent if and only if:

- $x_j = (y_j \pm 1) \bmod 3$ for $0 \leq j \leq n-1$,
- $x_i = y_i$ for $i \in \{0, 1, 2, \ldots, n-1\} - \{j\}$.

The bit x_i, representing the i-th position from right to left in the binary string of a vertex $x = x_{n-1}x_{n-2}\cdots x_1 x_0$, is referred to as the i-dimension. An edge (x, y) that satisfies $x_j = (y_j \pm 1) \bmod 3$ for $0 \leq j \leq n - 1$ is termed a j-dimensional edge or j-edge and we say that x and y have a leftmost differing bit at position j. A j-dimensional vertex is a vertex incident to a j-edge. We also denote all the j-dimensional vertices of x as $N_\pm(x, j)$, also called j-neighbor vertices where $N_+(x, j) = x_{n-1}x_{n-2}\cdots [(x_j + 1) \bmod 3]\cdots x_0$ and $N_-(x, j) = x_{n-1}x_{n-2}\cdots [(x_j - 1) \bmod 3]\cdots x_0$. Let $Q_{n-1}^3(s)$ denote the subgraph of Q_n^3 induced by $\{(u_{n-1}u_{n-2}\cdots u_i u_{i-1}\cdots u_j \cdots u_0) \in V(Q_n^3)|s = u_i u_{i-1}\cdots u_j\}$, where $0 \leq i < j \leq n - 1$. Figure 1 illustrates 3-ary 1-cube, 3-ary 2-cube, and 3-ary 3-cube.

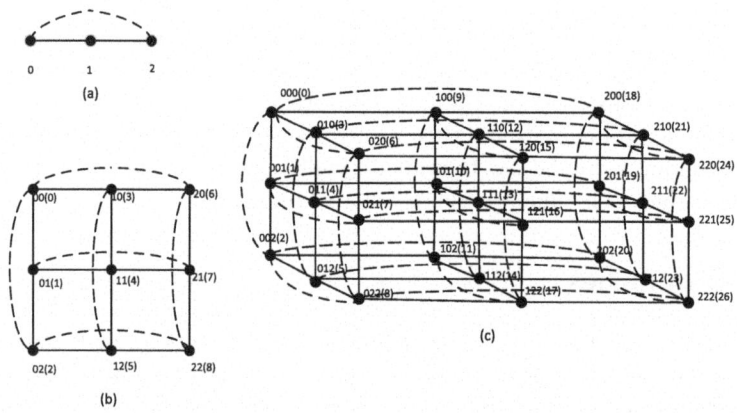

Fig. 1. (a) 3-ary 1-cube. (b) 3-ary 2-cube. (c) 3-ary 3-cube.

Definition 2. [7] Let $P : u^{(0)}, u^{(1)}, \ldots, u^{(k)}$ be a path in Q_n^3 for $n \leq 2$. For each vertex $u^{(i)} = N_\pm(u^{(i-1)}, m_i) \in V(P) \setminus \{u^{(0)}\}$, we replace $u^{(i)}$ with m_i. Then we obtain a *dimension-backbone walk* : $u^{(0)}, m_1, m_2, \ldots, m_k$. Let DM(P) denote the dimension-backbone walk of P.

In a similar manner, the *reverse dimension-backbone walk* is defined as follows: For each vertex $u^{(i-1)} = N_\pm(u^{(i)}, m_i) \in V(P) \setminus \{u^{(0)}\}$, we replace $u^{(i-1)}$ with m_i. This replacement results in a reverse dimension-backbone walk: $u^{(k)}, m_k, m_{k-1}, \ldots, m_1$. Let ReDM(P) represent the reverse dimension-backbone walk of P.

3   Construction of Independent Spanning Trees

This section begins with the introduction of a parallel algorithm for constructing ISTs rooted at any vertex on Q_n^3. Subsequently, we establish the validity of $2n$

ISTs and conduct a time complexity analysis. Hereafter, we consistently employ $x = x_{n-1}x_{n-2}\cdots x_0$ to represent any root vertex of ISTs on Q_n^3.

Algorithm 1. PTIST

Input: An integer n with $n \geq 1$, root vertex x, $x = x_{n-1}x_{n-2}\cdots x_0$, and an integer
   array $A = \{0, 1, 2, \ldots, n-1\}$;
Output: $2n$ independent spanning trees $T_0, T_1, \ldots$, and T_{2n-1} rooted at x on Q_n^3.
1: **for** $i = 0$ to $2n - 1$ **do**
2:     **in parallel**
3:     **if** $i \bmod 2 == 0$ **then**
4:         Let $a = \lfloor i/2 \rfloor$;
5:         Let $u = x_{n-1}x_{n-2}\cdots (x_a + 1) \bmod 3 \cdots x_0$;
6:     **else**
7:         Let $u = x_{n-1}x_{n-2}\cdots (x_a - 1) \bmod 3 \cdots x_0$;
8:         $V(T_i) = \{u\}$;
9:         $E(T_i) = \emptyset$;
10:    **end if**
11:    **for** level$= 0$ to $n - 1$ **do**
12:       **for** each vertex $v \in V(T_i)$ **do**
13:          Let $t = A[(level + a + 1 + n) \bmod n]$;
14:          $y_1 = x_{n-1}\cdots (x_t + 1) \bmod 3 \cdots x_0$;
15:          $y_2 = x_{n-1}\cdots (x_t - 1) \bmod 3 \cdots x_0$;
16:          $E(T_i) = E(T_i) \cup \{(v, y_1), (v, y_2)\}$;
17:          $V(T_i) = V(T_i) \cup \{y_1, y_2\}$;
18:       **end for**
19:    **end for**
20: **end for**

3.1   Algorithm to Construct ISTs

Given n integers $0, 1, \ldots, n - 1$, we can obtain an ascending sequence $A = \{0, 1, 2, \ldots, n - 1\}$. Initially, we present a parallel algorithm named PTIST (see Algorithm 1) for building $2n$ ISTs rooted at an arbitrary vertex x on Q_n^3, utilizing the ascending sequence $A = \{0, 1, 2, \ldots, n - 1\}$.

Consider the scenario where the inputs are $n = 2$, $x = 0$, and $A = \{0, 1\}$. Let's illustrate this with T_0 on Q_n^3 as a specific instance (see Fig. 2). The construction steps are outlined as follows.

Initially, there is only one vertex, 1, in the tree T_0. In the first iteration (level=0), $t = A[(level+a+1+n) \bmod n] = 1$ (see line 14 of PTIST), connecting vertex 0 in T_0 to its 1-neighbor vertices, 4 and 7. Consequently, $V(T_0) = \{1, 4, 7\}$ and $E(T_0) = \{(1, 4), (1, 7)\}$.

In the second iteration (level=1), $t = A[(level + a + 1 + n) \bmod n] = 0$ (see line 14), leading to each vertex $y \in V(T_0)$ being linked to its 0-neighbor vertices $N_\pm(y, 0)$. As a result, vertices 0 and 2 connect to vertex 1. Similarly, vertices 1 and 5, vertices 6 and 8, are connected to vertices 4 and 5 respectively. Consequently, the edges $(1, 0), (2, 1), (3, 4), (5, 4), (6, 7)$ and $(8, 17)$ are added to

T_0, with $V(T_0)$ encompassing all vertices of Q_2^3. Thus, a spanning tree T_0 rooted at vertex 0 on Q_2^3 is obtained. The construction processes of T_1, T_2, and T_3 on Q_2^3 in Fig. 2 are similar to that of T_0. It should be noted that each tree is constructed in parallel.

3.2   Correctness of Algorithm PTIST

In this section, we mainly prove the correctness of the construction of independent spanning trees. According to the definition of Q_n^3, it is obvious that a walk $P : u^{(0)}, u^{(1)} = N_\pm(u^{(0)}, m_1), u^{(2)} = N_\pm(u^{(1)}, m_2), \ldots, u^{(k)} = N_\pm(u^{(k-1)}, m_k),$ $u^{(k+1)} = N_\pm(u^{(k)}, m_1)$ in Q_n^3 is a path, where k is an integer satisfying $1 \le k \le n$, $m_1, m_2, \ldots, m_k$ are all distinct from each other and $0 \le m_i \le n - 1$ for $i = 1, 2, \ldots, k$. Then, we define a vector $\langle \alpha_1, \alpha_2, \ldots, \alpha_n \rangle$ as a nonnegative vector if $\alpha_1, \alpha_2, \ldots, \alpha_n \ge 0$. In the following, we consistently set the nonnegative vector $\langle \alpha_1, \alpha_2, \ldots, \alpha_n \rangle$ to be $\langle 1, 2, \ldots, n - 1 \rangle$. Before giving the proof, we first give the following lemma.

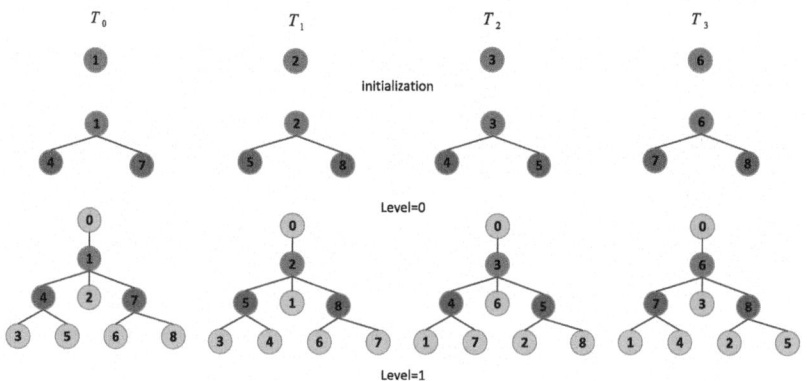

Fig. 2. Construction of ISTs on Q_2^3.

Lemma 1. Suppose that $P : u^{(0)}, u^{(1)} = N_\pm(u^{(0)}, m_1), u^{(2)} = N_\pm(u^{(1)}, m_2),$ $\ldots, u^{(k)} = N_\pm(u^{(k-1)}, m_k) = y$, and $Q : u^{(0)}, v^{(1)} = N_\pm(u^{(0)}, n_1), v^{(2)} = N_\pm(v^{(1)}, n_2), \ldots, v^{(t)} = N_\pm(u^{(t-1)}, n_t) = y$ are two paths in Q_n^3 for any two integers k, t with $1 \le k, t \le n$ and $m_k \ne n_t$. If the following conditions hold:

1. $\langle \alpha_{i_1}, \alpha_{i_2}, \ldots, \alpha_{i_k} \rangle = \langle m_1, m_2, \ldots, m_k \rangle$, where $1 \le i_1 < i_2 < \cdots < i_k \le n$,
2. $\langle \alpha_{j_1}, \alpha_{j_2}, \ldots, \alpha_{j_k} \rangle = \langle n_1, n_2, \ldots, n_t \rangle$, where $1 \le j_1 < j_2 < \cdots < j_t \le n$,

then, we have $V(path(P, u^{(0)}, u^{(k)})) \cap V(path(Q, u^{(0)}, v^{(t)})) = \{y\}$.

Proof. We establish the lemma through a proof by contradiction. Referring to Definition 2, we denote the reverse dimension-backbone walk ReDM(P) as: $y, m_k, m_{k-1}, \ldots, m_1$, and the ReDM(Q) as: $y, n_t, n_{t-1}, \ldots, n_1$. Consequently, there exist a and b satisfying $u^{(a)} = v^{(b)}$, where $0 \le a \le k-1$ and $0 \le b \le t-1$. Consider $A = m_k, m_{k-1}, \ldots, m_{a+1}$ and $B = n_t, n_{t-1}, \ldots, n_{b+1}$. Since $m_k \neq n_t$, it follows that $A \neq B$. Let $l = \max((A \cup B) \setminus (A \cap B))$. Thus, we can deduce that the l-th bit of $u^{(a)}$ differs from that of $v^{(b)}$. This leads to a contradiction, thus establishing the lemma.

Lemma 2. Suppose that $P : u^{(0)}$, $u^{(1)} = N_{\pm}(u^{(0)}, m_1)$, $u^{(2)} = N_{\pm}(u^{(1)}, m_2)$, $\ldots, u^{(k)} = N_{\pm}(u^{(k-1)}, m_k)$, and $Q : u^{(0)}$, $v^{(1)} = N_{\pm}(u^{(0)}, n_1)$, $v^{(2)} = N_{\pm}(v^{(1)}, n_2)$, $\ldots$, $v^{(t)} = N_{\pm}(u^{(t-1)}, n_t)$ are two paths in Q_n^3 for any two integers k, t with $1 \le k, t \le n$ and $m_1 \neq n_1$. If the following conditions hold:

1. $\langle \alpha_{i_1}, \alpha_{i_2}, \ldots, \alpha_{i_k} \rangle = \langle m_1, m_2, \ldots, m_k \rangle$, where $1 \le i_1 < i_2 < \cdots < i_k \le n$,
2. $\langle \alpha_{j_1}, \alpha_{j_2}, \ldots, \alpha_{j_k} \rangle = \langle n_1, n_2, \ldots, n_t \rangle$, where $1 \le j_1 < j_2 < \cdots < j_t \le n$,

then, we have $V(path(P, u^{(1)}, u^{(k)}) \cap V(path(Q, u^{(1)}, v^{(t)}) = \emptyset$.

Proof. By the conditions in the lemma, $u^{(1)}$ is m_1-neighbor of $u^{(0)}$ and $v^{(1)}$ is n_1-neighbor of $v^{(0)}$. It is clear that $u^{(1)} \in V(Q_n^3(x_{(m_1 \pm 1) \bmod 3}) \cdots x_1 x_0)$ and $v^{(1)} \in V(Q_n^3(x_{(n_1 \pm 1) \bmod 3}) \cdots x_1 x_0)$. Similarly, we have $\{u^{(2)}, u^{(3)}, \ldots, u^{(k)}\} \subseteq V(Q_n^3(x_{(m_1 \pm 1) \bmod 3}) \cdots x_1 x_0)$ and $\{v^{(2)}, v^{(3)}, \ldots, v^{(t)}\} \subseteq V(Q_n^3(x_{(n_1 \pm 1) \bmod 3}) \cdots x_1 x_0)$. Since $m_1 \neq n_1$, we have $V(Q_n^3(x_{(m_1 \pm 1) \bmod 3} \cdots x_1 x_0) \cap V(Q_n^3(x_{(n_1 \pm 1) \bmod 3}) \cdots x_1 x_0) = \emptyset$, which implies that $\{u^{(1)}, u^{(2)}, u^{(3)}, \ldots, u^{(k)}\} \cap \{v^{(1)}, v^{(2)}, v^{(3)}, \ldots, v^{(t)}\} = \emptyset$. As a result, $V(path(P, u^{(1)}, u^{(k)}) \cap V(path(Q, u^{(1)}, v^{(t)}) = \emptyset$.

In the subsequent discussion, we define a non-negative vector as $\langle \beta_1, \beta_2, \ldots, \beta_n \rangle = \langle q+1, \ldots, n-1, 0, 1, \ldots, q \rangle$, where q is an integer satisfying $0 \le q \le n-1$.

Lemma 3. T_i is obtained by algorithm PTIST, $|V(T_i)| = 3^n$, where $0 \le i \le 2n-1$.

Proof. After n-time iterations in algorithm PTIST, it is clear that we have

$$1 + 1 \times 2 + 3 \times 2 + 3^2 \times 2 + 3^3 \times 2 + \cdots + 3^{n-1} \times 2 = 3^n$$

vertices in $V(T_i)$ for any integer i with $0 \le i \le n-1$.

Theorem 1. For any integer i with $0 \le i \le 2n-1$, T_i obtained by algorithm PTIST is a spanning tree rooted at vertex x on Q_n^3.

Proof. According to algorithm PTIST, we obtain $2n$ trees $T_0, T_1, \ldots$ and T_{2n-1} rooted at x on Q_n^3 and it is obvious no common vertices in T_i for $i = 0, 1, \ldots, 2n-1$. $V(T_i) \subseteq V(Q_n^3)$ for $i = 0, 1, \ldots, 2n-1$. According to Lemma 3, $|V(T_i)| = 3^n$ for $i = 0, 1, \ldots, 2n-1$. As a result, for any integer i with $0 \le i \le 2n-1$, T_i obtained by algorithm PTIST is a spanning tree rooted at vertex x on Q_n^3.

Lemma 4. [7] Let T_i and T_j with $0 \le i, j \le 2n-1$ and $i \neq j$, be two spanning trees rooted at vertex x on a Graph G. T_i and T_j are independent if and only if for every vertex $v \in V(G) \setminus \{x\}$, $ancestor(v, T_i) \cap ancestor(v, T_j) = \{x\}$ and $ancestor(v, T_i) \cup ancestor(v, T_j) \supset \{x\}$.

We let nonnegative vector $\langle \gamma_1, \gamma_2, \ldots, \gamma_n \rangle = \langle r+1, r+2, \ldots, n-1, 0, 1, \ldots, r-1, r \rangle$ for any integer r with $0 \leq r \leq n-1$. Now we give the following lemma, which is helpful to prove the correctness of ISTs obtained by algorithm PTIST.

Lemma 5. Assume that $P: u^{(0)}$, $u^{(1)} = N_{\pm}(u^{(0)}, q)$, $u^{(2)} = N_{\pm}(u^{(1)}, m_1)$, $u^{(3)} = N_{\pm}(u^{(2)}, m_2)$, $\ldots$, $u^{(k+1)} = N_{\pm}(u^{(k)}, m_k)$ and $Q: u^{(0)}$, $v^{(1)} = N_{\pm}(u^{(0)}, q)$, $v^{(2)} = N_{\pm}(v^{(1)}, n_1)$, $v^{(3)} = N_{\pm}(v^{(2)}, n_2)$, $\ldots$, $v^{(t+1)} = N_{\pm}(v^{(t)}, n_t)$ are two paths in Q_n^3 for any two integers k, t with $2 \leq k, t \leq n$ and $r \neq q$. If the following conditions hold:

1. $\langle \beta_{i_1}, \beta_{i_2}, \ldots, \beta_{i_k} \rangle = \langle m_1, m_2, \ldots, m_k \rangle$, where $1 \leq i_1 < i_2 < \cdots < i_k \leq n$, and $\beta_{i_1} \neq q$
2. $\langle \gamma_{j_1}, \gamma_{j_2}, \ldots, \gamma_{j_t} \rangle = \langle n_1, n_2, \ldots, n_t \rangle$, where $1 \leq j_1 < j_2 < \cdots < j_t \leq n$ and $\gamma_{j_1} \neq r$ and
3. $y \in V(P) \cap V(Q) \setminus \{u^{(0)}\}$

then, we have $ancestor(y, P) \cap ancestor(y, Q) = \{u^{(0)}\}$ and $ancestor\ (y, P) \cap ancestor(y, Q) \supset \{u^{(0)}\}$.

Proof. Without loss of generality, we suppose $r \geq q$. It is obvious that $ancestor(y, P) \cup ancestor(y, Q) \supset \{u^{(0)}\}$. Since $r \neq q$, we have $u^{(1)} \neq v^{(1)}$. If $y = u^{(1)}$ or $y = v^{(0)}$, then it is evident that $ancestor(y, P) \cap ancestor(y, Q) = u^{(0)}$. Therefore, in the subsequent analysis, our sole task is to demonstrate that $ancestor(y, P) \cap ancestor(y, Q) = u^{(0)}$ with $y = u^{(a)} = v^{(b)} \in V(p) \cup V(Q) \setminus \{u^{(0)}, u^{(1)}, v^{(1)}\}$. Let $A = \{m_1, m_2, \ldots, m_{a-1}\}$ and $B = \{n_1, n_2, \ldots, n_{b-1}\}$, where $1 \leq a \leq k+1$ and $1 \leq b \leq t+1$. Assume that $l = \max((A \cup B) \setminus (A \cap B))$. We have the following three cases:

Case (1) $l > r$. The l-bit of $u^{(a)}$ is different from that of $v^{(b)}$. Thus, $u^{(a)} \neq v^{(b)}$. We get a contradiction.

Case (2) $l < r$. Since $v^{(1)} = N_{\pm}(u^{(0)}, r)$, the r-bit of $u^{(a)}$ is different from that of $v^{(b)}$. Thus, $u^{(a)} \neq v^{(b)}$. We get a contradiction.

Case (3) $l = r$. We partition A into two subsets $A_1 = \{m_1, m_1, \ldots, m_i\}$ and $A_2 = \{m_{i+1}, m_{i+}, \ldots, m_{a-1}\} \supseteq \{m_{a-1}\}$, Then, we partition B into $B_1 = \{n_1, n-2, \ldots, n_k\}$ and $B_2 = \{n_{j+1}, n_{j+2}, \ldots, n_{b-1}\} \supseteq \{n_{b-1}\}$, which are all arranged in ascending orders. Then, we have the following subcases.

Case (3.1) $r \in B$ and $r \notin A$. $\min(B_1) > r$ and $\max(B_2) \leq r$. Thus, $n_{b-1} = r$. Since $r \notin A$, $m_{a-1} \neq r$, we have $\max(A_2) = m_{a-1} < r$. By Lemma 1, we have $V(path(P, u^{(i+2)}, u^{(a)})) \cap V(path(Q, v^{(j+2)}, v^{(b)})) = \{y\}$. According to Lemma 2, we have $V(path(P, u^{(1)}, u^{(i+1)})) \cap V(path(Q, v^{(1)}, v^{(j+1)})) = \emptyset$. Then, we discuss whether $path(P, u^{(i+2)}, y)$ intersects with $path(Q, v^{(1)}, v^{(j+1)})$ and whether $path(P, u^{(1)}, u^{(i+1)})$ intersects with $path(Q, v^{(j+2)}, y)$. Since $\max(A_2) = m_{a-1} < r$ and $\min(B_1) > r$, and it is clear that $\max((A_2 \cup B_1) \setminus (A_2 \cap B_1)) = n_j$, the n_jth bit of each vertex in $V(path(P, u^{(i+2)}, y))$ is different from that in $V(path(Q, v^{(1)}, v^{(j+1)}))$. Thus, $V(path(P, u^{(i+2)}, y)) \cap V(path(Q, v^{(1)}, v^{(j+1)})) = \emptyset$. When it comes to $V(path(P, u^{(1)}, u^{(i+1)})) \cap V(path(Q, v^{(j+2)}, y)) = \emptyset$, We will divide our discussion into two categories. $\min(A_1) > r$. It is obvious that $\max((A_1 \cup B_2) \setminus (A_1 \cap B_2)) = m_i$, thus, the m_ith bit of each vertex in $V(path(P, u^{(1)}, u^{(i+1)}))$ is different from that in $V(path(Q, v^{(j+2)}, y))$. Thus, when $\min(A_1) > r$, $V(path(P, u^{(1)}, u^{(i+1)})) \cap V(path(Q, v^{(j+2)}, y)) = \emptyset$. When $\min(A_1) \leq r$. Similarly to $\min(A_1) > r$, the conclusion also holds.

Case (3.2) $r \in A$ and $r \notin B$. It is obvious that $r \in A_1$, $\max(A_2) \leq q < r$, $\max(B_1) > r$ and $\max(B_2) < r$. Similar to Case (3.1), we also have $ancestor(y, P) \cap ancestor(y, Q) = \{u^{(0)}\}$.

Based on the aforementioned outcomes, the subsequent theorem validates the accuracy of independent spanning trees on Q_n^3.

Theorem 2. For any integer n with $n \geq 2$ and an arbitrary vertex x on Q_n^3, $T_0, T_1, \ldots, T_{2n-1}$ obtained by algorithm PTIST are $2n$ ISTs rooted at vertex x on Q_n^3.

Proof. According to Theorem 1, for any integer i such that $0 \leq i \leq 2n - 1$, T_i represents a spanning tree rooted at vertex x in Q_n^3. We now aim to demonstrate the independence of $T_0, T_1, \ldots, T_{2n-1}$ derived from the PTIST algorithm. For any pair of integers i and j satisfying $0 \leq i < j \leq 2n - 1$ and for any vertex $y \in V(Q_n^3) \setminus x$, consider P as the path $x, u^{(1)}, u^{(2)}, \ldots, y$ in T_i and Q as the path $x, v^{(1)}, v^{(2)}, \ldots, y$ in T_j. It can be verified that P and Q adhere to the conditions outlined in Lemma 5. Consequently, $ancestor(y, T_i) \cap ancestor(y, T_j) = \{x\}$ and $ancestor(y, T_i) \cup ancestor(y, T_j) \supset \{x\}$. By virtue of Lemma 4, T_i and T_j exhibit independence.

Hence, the $2n$ ISTs T_0, T_1, ..., T_{2n-1} generated by the PTIST algorithm serve as independent spanning trees rooted at vertex x on Q_n^3.

Theorem 3. The time complexity of algorithm PTIST is $O(N)$, where $N = 3^n$ and $n \geq 2$.

Proof. According to Theorem 2, for any integer n such that $n \geq 2$ and for any vertex x on Q_n^3, the $2n$ independent spanning trees $T_0, T_1, \ldots, T_{2n-1}$ produced by the PTIST algorithm act as independent spanning trees rooted at vertex x on Q_n^3. As per Lemma 3, $|V(T_i)| = 3^n$, where $0 \leq i \leq 2n - 1$ and T_i is obtained through the PTIST algorithm. Through the PTIST algorithm, all independent spanning trees are concurrently generated. Consequently, the theorem holds.

4   Performance Evaluations

In this section, we evaluate the performance of fault-tolerant routing by utilizing the IST as the routing table while simulating vertex failures. This assessment enables us to scrutinize the efficacy of our routing strategy in handling component failures effectively.

4.1   Evaluation Environment

In a tree structure, any two vertices uniquely define the path connecting them, making the previously established IST function as the routing table for communication within the 3-ary n-cube. The presence of multiple ISTs guarantees fault tolerance in our routing infrastructure, imparting resilience against failures.

We implemented all the algorithms for building IST and necessary fault-tolerant routing algorithms using the Python programming language. The simulations took place on a system running Windows 11, equipped with a 2.60 GHz 13th Gen Intel Core i9-13900H CPU and 16 GB RAM. This hardware configuration offered the required computational power and memory capacity for efficient simulation execution. Our experiments are concentrated on two primary directions: the *Transmission Failure Rate* (TFR), indicating the ratio of failed transmissions to overall transmissions, and *Average Path Length* (APL).

4.2   Evaluation Results

In reference to Theorem 2, the collection $T_0, T_1, \ldots, T_{2n-1}$ is established as the $2n$ ISTs constructed of a Q_n^3. Defining P_i as the transmission path determined by T_i ($0 \leq i \leq 2n-1$) for each transmission instance within a Q_n^3 from s to d, we categorize paths containing at least one faulty vertex as *failure routes* and those without faults as *regular routes*. The path length for each regular route can be calculated specifically. It is essential to highlight that for fault-tolerant routing, the transmission from s to d can be simultaneously executed in each P_i within the range of 0 to $2n - 1$. Notably, for any pair of unique nodes, s and d, within the network, assuming the count of faulty nodes is below the available ISTs, a dependable fault-free path for data transmission will always be present. Given a specific instance (s, d) and the set of faulty vertices F, the path length for each regular route can be determined. Through 10,000 iterations of the simulation, the APL for all regular routes can be calculated. Furthermore, the number of failed routes of P_i can be ascertained, facilitating the computation of the TFR in Q_n^3 across 10,000 experiments.

We commence the simulation with no vertex failures and progressively introduce a single vertex failure to set F until a specific condition is satisfied. The count of faulty vertices, represented as $|F|$, included in F, is limited to the span of 6 to 27 for $3 \leq n \leq 5$ and 50 to 400 for $6 \leq n \leq 8$ when calculating the TFR based on the scale of Q_n^3. Simultaneously, for the APL computation, we maintain the count of faulty vertices introduced in F within the range of 6 to 27 for $3 \leq n \leq 6$, and vary it between 50 to 400 for $7 \leq n \leq 10$. Based on the experimental results, we can draw the following conclusions:

With a fixed scale of Q_n^3, the TFR increases as the number of faulty nodes in Q_n^3 grows, as shown in Fig. 3(a) and Fig. 3(b). When $|F|$ is less than $2n$, there is a fault-free path between any two distinct nodes in Q_n^3 for reliable data transmission, leading to a TFR of 0 in this scenario. As $|F|$ increases to 27, the TFR in Q_4^3 increases to 24.96%, attributed to the rise in the number of faulty nodes.

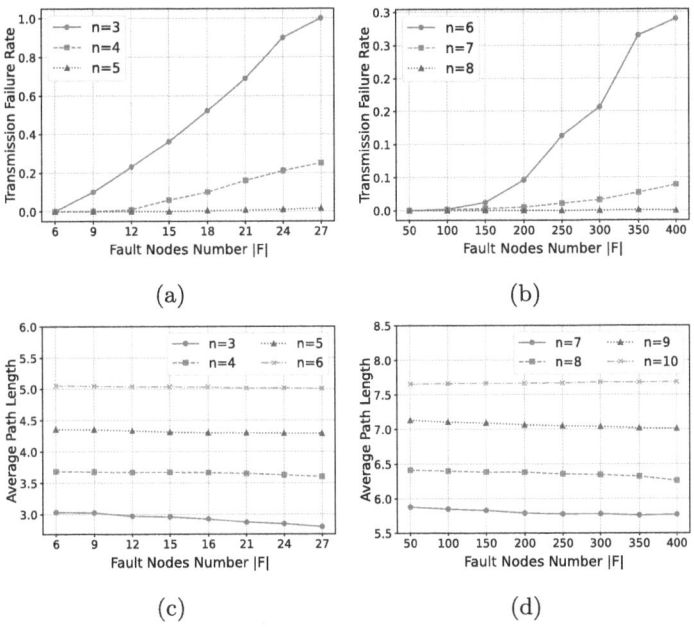

Fig. 3. TFR and APL of different scales of Q_n^3.

Based on the fixed number of faulty nodes, the TFR decreases as the scale of Q_n^3 increases, as illustrated in Fig. 3(a) and Fig. 3(b). For example, at $|F| = 400$, the TFR is 28.91% in Q_6^3, while it drops to 3.2% in Q_7^3. Notably, Q_8^3 shows a TFR of 0, signifying no transmission failures in these setups. This trend can be attributed to the reduced likelihood of failures occurring in the $2n$ paths responsible for data transmission as the network size expands.

When the number of faulty nodes is fixed, the APL increases as the scale of Q_n^3 expands, as shown in Fig. 3(c) and Fig. 3(d). This increase can be attributed to the larger network sizes causing greater average distances between nodes. For instance, at $|F| = 15$, the APL of Q_4^3 is observed to be 2.957 ($n = 3$), 3.667 ($n = 4$), 4.3829 ($n = 5$), and 5.0667 ($n = 6$).

When the scale of Q_n^3 is fixed, the APL diminishes as the number of faulty nodes increases. For instance, with $200, 250, 300, 350$, and 400 faulty nodes in Q_8^3, the APL is observed to be $7.092, 7.047, 7.038, 7.017$, and 7.004 respectively. This phenomenon is primarily due to the rise in faulty nodes within the network, potentially leading to the isolation of a subset of nodes forming a smaller connected component. In this reduced component, path lengths are consequently shortened.

5 Conclusions

In this paper, we have given a parallel constructive method of ISTs on Q_n^3 based on the ascending sequence. At last, simulations were conducted to evaluate fault-tolerant routing using these ISTs as routing tables. In detail, in our initial phase, we designed an algorithm with a time complexity of $O(N)$ designed to produce $2n$ ISTs within an Q_n^3, where N is the total number of nodes on Q_n^3. Leveraging the fact that Q_n^3 is n-vertex-connected, we were able to maximize the number of ISTs generated. Following this, we presented a formal proof, utilizing the adjacency relationship to establish the existence of $2n$ ISTs rooted at a single vertex in Q_n^3. Subsequently, we proceeded to implement a simulation of the algorithm using Python, and the outcomes obtained from the experiment were in alignment with the theoretical predictions.

Acknowledgment. This work is supported by the Major Scientific Instruments and Equipments Development Project of National Natural Science Foundation of China under grant (62427809), Key Program of Natural Science Foundation of Jiangsu under grant (BK20243053, 24KJA520006), Natural Science Foundation of China under Grants (62102193, 62372248, 62302235, 62402241).

References

1. Xu, L., Zhou, S.: Reliability assessment of interconnection networks based on link fault patterns. IEEE Trans. Reliab. **73**(2), 1302–1309 (2024)
2. Wang, G., Yu, J., Zou, Y., Fan, J., Cheng, W.: A new measure of fault-tolerance for network reliability: double-structure connectivity. IEEE/ACM Trans. Netw. **32**(1), 874–889 (2024)
3. Fan, W., Fan, J., Lin, C.-K.: Optimally embedding 3-ary n-cubes into grids. J. Comput. Sci. Technol. **34**, 372–387 (2019)
4. Bauer, D., Carothers, C.: Scalable: RF propagation modeling on the IBM blue gene/L and cray XT5 supercomputers. In: Proceedings of the Winter Simulation Conference, pp. 779–787 (2009)
5. Song, J., Lin, L., Huang, Y., Hsieh, S.-Y.: Intermittent fault diagnosis of split-star networks and its applications. IEEE Trans. Parallel Distrib. Syst. **34**(4), 1253–1264 (2023)
6. Werapun, J., Intakosum, S., Boonjing, V.: An efficient parallel construction of optimal independent spanning trees on hypercubes. J. Parall. Distrib. Comput. **72**(12), 1713–1724 (2012)
7. Cheng, B., Fan, J., Jia, X.: Parallel construction of independent spanning trees and an application in diagnosis on Möbius cubes. J. Supercomput. **65**, 1279–1301 (2013)
8. Li, X., Lin, W., Liu, X.: Completely independent spanning trees on BCCC data center networks with an application to fault-tolerant routing. IEEE Trans. Parallel Distrib. Syst. **33**(8), 1939–1952 (2021)
9. Wang, S., Li, J., Wang, R.: Hamiltonian paths and cycles with prescribed edges in the 3-ary n-cube. Inf. Sci. **181**(14), 3054–3065 (2011)

10. Khuller, S., Schieber, B.: On independent spanning trees. Inf. Process. Lett. **42**(6), 321–323 (1992)
11. Obokata, K., Iwasaki, Y., Bao, F.: Independent spanning trees of product graphs and their construction. IEICE Trans. Fundam. Electron. Commun. Comput. Sci. **79**(11), 1894–1903 (1996)
12. Cheng, B., Fan, J., Jia, X.: Independent spanning trees in crossed cubes. Inf. Sci. **233**, 276–289 (2013)
13. Curran, S., Lee, O., Yu, X.: Finding four independent trees. SIAM J. Comput. **35**(5), 1023–1058 (2006)
14. Liu, Y., Chou, W., Lan, J., Chen, C.: Constructing independent spanning trees for locally twisted cubes. Theor. Comput. Sci. **412**(22), 2237–2252 (2011)
15. Bondy, J.: USR Murty Graph Theory. Graduate Texts in Mathematics, vol. 244 (2008)

SpecInF: Exploiting Idle GPU Resources in Distributed DL Training via Speculative Inference Filling

Cunchi Lv[1,2,4], Xiao Shi[1,5(✉)], Dong Liang[1], Wenting Tan[1], and Xiaofang Zhao[1,3,4]

[1] Institute of Computing Technology, Chinese Academy of Sciences, Beijing, China
{lvcunchi21s,shixiao,liangdong,tanwenting,zhaoxf}@ict.ac.cn
[2] University of Chinese Academy of Sciences, Beijing, China
[3] University of Chinese Academy of Sciences, Nanjing, China
[4] Zhongguancun Laboratory, Haidian, China
[5] Nanjing Institute of InforSuperbahn, Nanjing, China

Abstract. Deep Learning (DL), especially with Large Language Models (LLMs), brings benefits to various areas. However, DL training systems usually yield prominent idling GPU resources due to many factors, such as resource allocation and collective communication. To improve GPU utilization, we present SpecInF, which adopts a **Spec**ulative **In**ference **F**illing method to exploit idle GPU resources. It collocates each primary training instance with additional inference instances on the same GPU, detects the training bubbles and adaptively fills with online or offline inference workloads. Our results show that SpecInF can effectively enhance GPU utilization under mainstream parallel training modes, delivering additional up to 14× offline inference throughputs than TGS and 67% reduction in online inference p95 latency than MPS, while guaranteeing collocated training throughput.

Keywords: Distributed Training · Collocation · Speculative Inference Filling

1 Introduction

The rapid progress in deep learning (DL) has significantly benefitted various areas, like manufacturing [15], artistic creation [2], and online services [19], especially with the emergence of the Large Language Models (LLMs). For example, ChatGPT [19] facilitates a remarkable breakthrough in this evolution. Alongside this, the growth in LLM training has led to a surge in demand for GPUs, with substantially considerable costs. For example, OpenAI used approximately 25,000 Nvidia A100 GPUs for about 90 to 100 days to train GPT-4 [10], costing around 63 million dollars. The cost efficiency is more non-negligible than ever.

© IFIP International Federation for Information Processing 2025
Published by Springer Nature Switzerland AG 2025
X. Chen et al. (Eds.): NPC 2024, LNCS 15527, pp. 146–158, 2025.
https://doi.org/10.1007/978-981-96-2830-8_12

However, GPU utilization in DL training is considerably low due to many factors in distributed patterns, such as well-known communication overheads [24], which largely pulls down the cost efficiency. Although various distributed training patterns greatly shorten the training time, they can also cause GPU resource wastage. For instance, when training GPT-4, the average GPU utilization only ranged between 32% and 36% [10]. This low usage is primarily due to communication overhead, despite significant optimizations in frameworks(e.g., DeepSpeed [13], Colossal [1], NVIDIA Megatron [21], and PyTorch.DDP [12]). Thus, instead of directly optimizing the training workflow, we argue that the idling GPU resources can be reassigned to serve DL inferences. We observe that there exists a complementarity in both memory and compute resource consumption between small- or medium-sized inference and distributed training. Therefore, it can significantly improve GPU utilization by filling DL training idling phases with inference workloads.

In this paper, we present **SpecInF**, a system that leverages a **Spec**ulative **Inf**erence **F**illing mechanism, to exploit idling GPU resources of distributed training and increase aggregated throughputs of GPUs. First, it allows inference instances to collocate with training instances according to their memory demands and GPU idling characteristics. Second, it adopts a Bubble Monitor to detect GPU idling timing in real time. Third, it builds a CUDA Kernel Scheduler to issue tokens to collocated inference instances, in which the Kernel Barrier decides to release inference CUDA kernels to fill training bubbles. In summary, our contributions are as follows:

- We analyze the GPU fragmentation in distributed training, especially for LLMs, and propose to collocate it with inference instances to improve the utilization.
- We design the speculative inference filling mechanism, allowing adaptive kernel scheduling to efficiently serve both online and offline inferences.
- We build and evaluate the SpecInF system. The experiments show that SpecInF significantly improves GPU utilization of various distributed training modes, delivering additional up to 14× offline inference throughputs than TGS and 67% reduction in online inference p95 latency than MPS, while guaranteeing training throughput.

2   Background and Motivation

2.1   Distirubted DL Training and Idle GPU Resources

Distributed DL training has been widely used to accelerate and improve throughput by utilizing multiple GPUs in parallel, mainly including Data Parallelism (DP) [8], Model Parallelism (MP) [21], Pipeline Parallelism (PP) [14], and Hybrid Parallelism (HP) [3]. The parallel strategies divide datasets (e.g., DP) or models (e.g., MP, PP) into multiple GPUs, and complete the forward and backward propagation with explicit communication among GPUs. However, the

GPUs of training clusters are usually underutilized due to many factors, including unreasonable resource allocation, communication overhead and failure recovery. Consequently, idle GPU resources may exist on both compute and memory aspects.

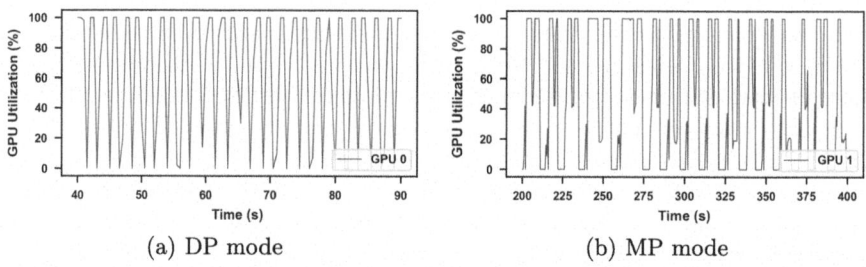

(a) DP mode   (b) MP mode

Fig. 1. The GPU compute utilization timeline of two modes, as monitored by the nvml APIs. (a) training RoBERTa-large model in DP mode via PyTorch.DDP; (b) fine-tuning LLaMA2-7B in MP mode via DeepSpeed. Both two cases involve 4 GPU workers.

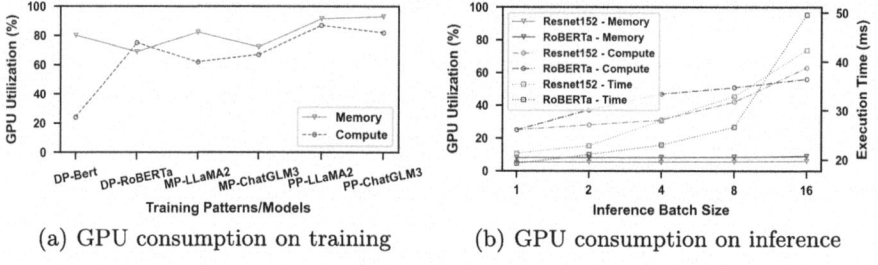

(a) GPU consumption on training   (b) GPU consumption on inference

Fig. 2. GPU occupying characteristics of distributed training and inference.

Idle GPU Computing Resources. The communication among GPUs causes explicit temporal idling in GPU computing resources. Despite the optimizations (e.g., torch.DDP [12], DeepSpeed [13], and ColossalAI [1]), it is still hard to fully overlap computation with communication. Figure 1(a) illustrates that there is nearly 30% GPU-time is waiting for communication in the DP mode. Figure 1(b) depicts that GPU utilization of MP shows similar situations. Furthermore, we observe that the average compute utilization across various training tasks ranges from 20% to 80%, as shown in the purple line of Fig. 2(a).

GPU Memory Fragments. Although training tasks are typically memory-bound [4,11,23,24], there exist various GPU memory fragments in practice, since

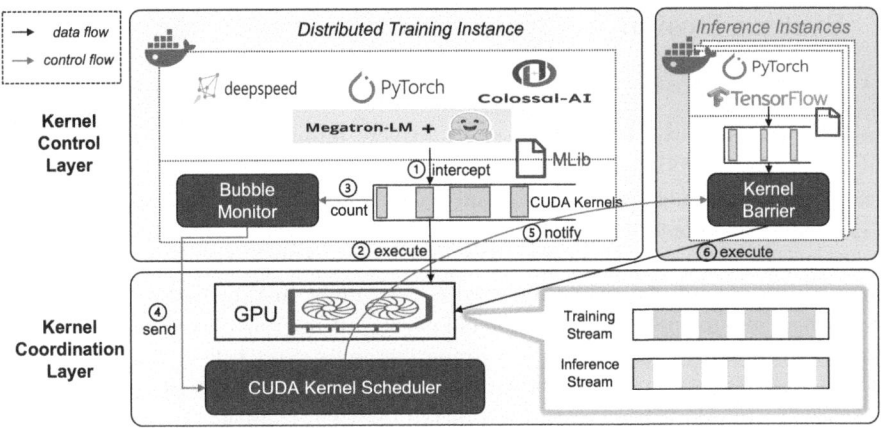

Fig. 3. The system architecture of SpecInF.

the local batch size is often set with powers of 2, aiming to ensure training convergence and maximize GPU performance [9,20]. As illustrated by the orange line in Fig. 2(a), an average memory fragmentation of 10–20% across three training modes is observed. For the GPU with 40 GB memory, the idle memory resource can be 4 to 8 GB.

2.2 Insight and Challenges

Insight. Considering the temporal (compute resource) and spatial (memory resource) fragments of GPUs, we argue that these unused resources can be adequate to serve moderate DL inference workloads. As shown in Fig. 2(b), with the inference batch size increasing, the memory resource consumption stays stable due to the unnecessity of storing gradients and activations, and built-in memory pooling mechanism [8], while the utilization of GPU compute resources notably increases, by 25% to 56% of RoBERTa. The corresponding inference latencies (at the 50 ms level) are much shorter than the training iteration (as shown in Fig. 1(a)). Thus, we propose a speculative inference filling method to improve the GPU utilization of specific training clusters, allowing to reassign idling GPU resources to handle moderate inference workloads.

Goals and Challenges. To improve the GPU utilization of training clusters, we attempt to build a speculative inference filling mechanism integrated into the training system. This mechanism aims to maintain the training throughput while concurrently providing additional inference services. The challenges include two aspects. First, it is difficult to decide the speculative filling timing. Second, it is necessary to avoid interference between the training and inference workloads. The timing accuracy and interference may affect the performance of both training and inference workloads.

3 System Design

3.1 Overview

SpecInF builds on the key idea of speculatively filling inference workloads into bubble periods[1] produced by distributed training tasks, as illustrated in Fig. 3. It consists of a kernel control layer and a coordination layer.

At the kernel control layer, training and inference workloads can be observed and manipulated in the view of CUDA kernels. First, SpecInF collocates one or more additional inference instances with a training instance to share a GPU, preparing the runtime context to speculatively fill inference workloads. Second, to observe the GPU utilization of training instances, SpecInF initiates the Bubble Monitor (BM) for each training worker to detect idle periods. It is suitable for general communication-optimized distributed DL frameworks, such as Deep-Speed [13], Megatron-LM [21]. BM intercepts ❶ and counts ❸ the CUDA kernels, issued at runtime by training instances, which are dispatched to GPU for execution ❷. Third, SpecInF leverages the Kernel Barrier (KB) to take charge of either blocking or forwarding CUDA kernels of inference instances to the GPU.

At the coordination layer, the CUDA Kernel Scheduler (CKS) on each node is responsible for recognizing training bubbles ❹ and deciding speculative inference execution timings of collocated inference instances ❺. SpecInF introduces two distinct mechanisms tailored for offline and online inference tasks, acknowledging their varying degrees of SLO-sensitivity (Service Level Objective), which is explained in Sect. 3.3.

3.2 Collocation Basics

Before running the speculative filling workflow, collocation should be done in advance. There are several factors explicitly affecting the collocation policies, including distinct spatial and temporal GPU requirements of tasks (as shown in Sect. 2.1), risks of OOM errors, training interruptions and throughput degradation due to severe resource contention. According to profilings, SpecInF adheres to the following principles:

- **Principle-I:** The sum of GPU memory occupied at the peak of each collocated instance must be less than the upper limit (e.g., 40 GB) of a specific GPU. Based on it, SpecInF collocates inference instances as much as possible to enhance aggregated throughput and GPU utilization.
- **Principle-II:** The minimal execution time (i.e., batch size = 1) of collocated online inference must be shorter than the maximal bubble of the primary training task, to at least serve one inference request.

---

[1] For simplicity, we refer to the GPU-idling period in training mentioned above as bubbles.

Algorithm 1. Adaptive Kernel Scheduling Algorithm

1: **Input:**
2:      Z_c: The kernel zero-count from the Bubble Monitor.
3:      α, β: The thresholds of two phases.
4:      γ: The multiplicative coefficient for offline inference tasks.
5:      m: The number of collocated inference instances.
6:      UL, LL: The upper and lower limit of tokens.
7: **Output:**
8:      *tokens* for offline inference and *status* for online, used by speculation execution.
9: **if** $Z_c \leq \alpha$ **then**
10:      $tokens \leftarrow 0$, $status \leftarrow busy$ ▷ conservative phase
11: **else if** $Z_c \leq \beta$ **then**
12:      $tokens \leftarrow \min(LL, tokens * \gamma)/m$, $status \leftarrow busy$ ▷ incremental phase
13: **else**
14:      $tokens \leftarrow \min(UL, tokens * \gamma)/m$, $status \leftarrow idle$ ▷ stable phase
15: **end if**

3.3 Speculative Inference Filling

Bubble Monitor. The bubble monitor detects the possible GPU idling time by observing the CUDA kernel issuing ratio of training instances. A straightforward method to monitor GPU utilization is leveraging tools such as nvml [18] at the application level. However, this approach has two issues. First, the statistical data collection presents a non-negligible delay. The sampling period may vary between 1 and 1/6 s, depending on the devices used. Second, the data is updated at fixed intervals, e.g., every 200ms. Thus, the tools may fail to quickly and accurately recognize training bubbles, hindering effective speculative filling.

SpecInF employs a hijacking statistics method. Specifically, it mounts the monitoring library (MLib) to training instances. The MLib intercepts the CUDA kernels and records the counts periodically (e.g., 2 ms), which are saved to a sliding window maintained by the BM. Concurrently, the BM calculates the number of continuous zero-counts of sliding windows and then sends it to the CUDA Kernel Scheduler on the node.

CUDA Kernel Scheduler. The CKS can oversee all GPUs within the node. It acts as a bridge to coordinate the bubble monitoring and speculative filling. It evaluates the GPU busy/idle status information sent by a specific BM and determines the timing and amount of speculative filling.

The Algorithm 1 outlines the adaptive scheduling logic for a specific GPU. It is divided into three phases: the *conservative phase*, the *incremental phase*, and the *stable phase*. During the conservative phase (line 9–10), CKS maintains the GPU *logically* busy to prevent interfering with ongoing CUDA execution of relatively longer training kernels. In the incremental phase (line 11–12), CKS opts to gradually increase tokens allocated to each offline inference instance, instead of maximizing them immediately, to mitigate interference associated with asynchronous execution. The *busy* status setting for online inference stems from the same reason. In the stable phase (lines 13–14), CKS capitalizes on a relatively steady bubble period, typically characterized by intense communication workloads, to maximize GPU utilization.

Kernel Barrier. Both online and offline inference workloads can be used to fill training bubbles by the KB, while online workloads need explicit SLO guarantees. For *offline inference* workloads, the KB receives allocated tokens from the CKS to serve corresponding inference workloads. Each kernel, when forwarded to the GPU, consumes tokens proportionate to its size. It also collects CUDA kernel count information, similar to the BM. If the remaining tokens during a given period are insufficient, the KB blocks subsequent inference kernel issuing in the queue. Conversely, when collocated training resumes, the tokens sent by CKS may decrease to zero. It is crucial to note that despite the asynchronous nature of CUDA kernel execution, our observations via the Nsight System indicate that for inference tasks, the CUDA APIs issued by CPU are almost synchronously triggered. The preceding CUDA API waits for its corresponding kernel to complete on the GPU before launching the next one, with most kernel execution times under 1 ms. In summary, the token release and block mechanism effectively minimizes resource contention with collocated training, thereby ensuring throughput.

For *online inference* workloads, KB additionally adopts a real-time pull-and-execute mechanism to meet the demands of stringent SLOs, since it is challenging to fill online requests into training bubbles without mutual interference due to the unpredictability of workloads. In this case, KB proactively pulls online requests one by one from the request queue, upon receiving the *idle* signal (set by Algorithm 1). Based on Principle-II in Sect. 3.2, SpecInF ensures to handle at least one request during bubbles of each training iteration. Moreover, to avoid training resuming immediately after pulling one request, CKS preemptively sets the status to *busy*, according to profiling information on training iteration time (e.g., 1.5 s). During the *busy* status, requests are handled by other inference instances.

4   Implementation

We implement a prototype of SpecInF with 2k C LOCs and 2k Python LOCs for evaluations. In the prototype, all training and inference tasks run with *NVIDIA-docker* runtime.

The MLib is based on Linux LD_PRELOAD mechanism, where the interception libraries are written in /etc./ld.so.preload file, allowing the hook logic to be loaded before the standard CUDA APIs. The BM is running as a *pthread* within the MLib process. The KB follows the same implementation logic as MLib, while the difference is that it sets up a *pthread* to forward or block the inference kernels. The CUDA Kernel Scheduler, running as a daemon, actively establishes a *UNIX socket* with each collocated instance to receive or send information.

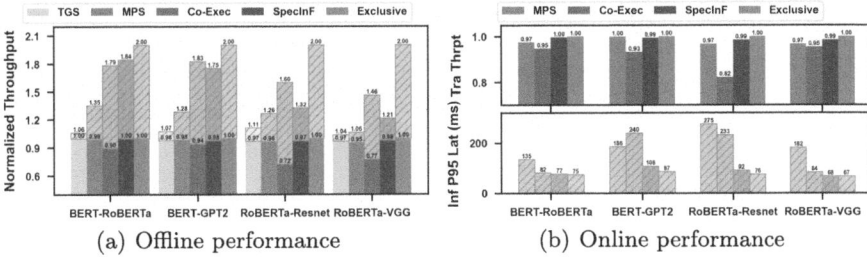

(a) Offline performance   (b) Online performance

Fig. 4. DP performance comparison: (a) the solid bar represents normalized training throughput and the light bar with dashed lines represents normalized offline inference throughput. (b) bars in the upper subfigure indicate normalized training throughputs, and the lower subfigure shows p95 latency of online inference. TGS is excluded due to excessive tail latencies.

5   Evaluation

5.1   Methodology

Experiment Testbed. We evaluate SpecInF on a GPU server with 4 * NVIDIA A100-40GB, equipped with PyTorch v1.11, DeepSpeed v0.11.1, CUDA v11.7.

Workloads. For the training workloads, we adopt BERT-base and RoBERTa-large training based on Pytorch.DDP for DP mode, LLaMA2-7B and ChatGLM-6B fine-tuning with DeepSpeed for MP and PP modes. For inference workloads, we employ medium-sized models, such as Resnet152, BERT-base, VGG19, RoBERTa-large, and GPT2-large. Poisson distribution [22] is used for generating online inference workloads. For the collocation cases of RoBERTa-Resnet and RoBERTa-VGG in Sect. 5.2, the mean value is set to 30. In other scenarios, we use a mean value of 10 across 2000 total requests.

Metrics. For evaluating distributed training and offline inference, the primary metrics include tokens per second (tokens/s) for NLP models and samples per second (samples/s) for CV models. To facilitate direct comparisons, we normalize these metrics to throughputs without GPU sharing. For online inference, we focus on tail latency (i.e., p95).

Baselines. We compare SpecInF with the following methods.

- **MPS** [17]. A popular spatial GPU sharing technique developed by NVIDIA. It is used by many works [5,25].
- **TGS** [23]. A transparent GPU sharing mechanism between DL jobs, focuses on guaranteeing productive job throughputs.
- **Co-Exec.** The strawman GPU sharing method despite resource contention.
- **Exclusive.** Each training or inference instance monopolizes the whole GPU.

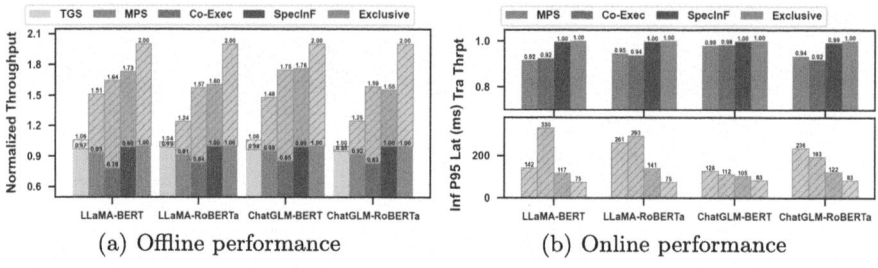

(a) Offline performance   (b) Online performance

Fig. 5. MP performance comparison.

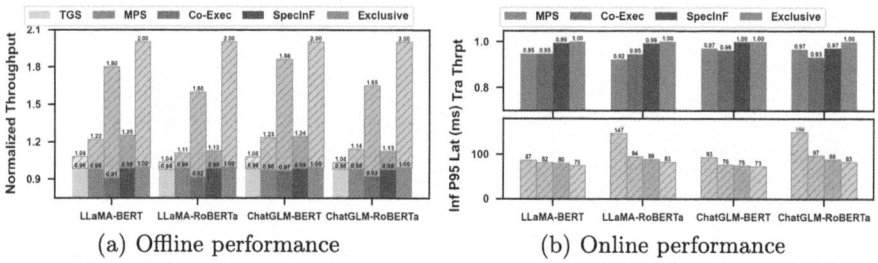

(a) Offline performance   (b) Online performance

Fig. 6. PP performance comparison.

5.2 Speculative Inference Filling Performance

Offline Inference Filling. Figures 4(a), 5(a) and 6(a) demonstrate that SpecInF delivers high throughputs for offline inferences with training throughput guarantees in DP, MP and PP modes. Considering the primary training workload, all baselines, except Co-Exec, generally maintain the performance. For the collocated offline inference workloads, SpecInF provides 23–84% throughput of Exclusive and 33–94% of Co-Exec, best in other baselines. However, the Exclusive requires one additional GPU, and Co-Exec significantly reduces collocated training throughput (e.g., up to 28% in the RoBERTa-Resnet case), failing to meet the goals in Sect. 2.2.

In DP cases, inference throughput is 1.23×–3.5× of MPS, and 2.9×–14× of TGS. The underperformance of TGS is mainly due to its inadequate bubble detection and relatively conservative time-share strategy, while MPS statically limits GPU resources available to the inference process. In MP cases, SpecInF achieves the highest aggregated throughputs in the first three cases with training throughput guarantees. Specifically, the inference throughput increases by up to 80% and 11× compared to MPS and TGS, respectively. In PP cases, the advantages of SpecInF become relatively marginal to DP and MP cases. Co-Exec achieves significantly higher inference throughput but sacrifices 3%–9% of training throughput. SpecInF's performance is comparable to MPS and superior to TGS. The underlying reason is that though dividing a mini-batch into small micro-batches shortens bubbles, it leaves GPU consistently underutilized, thus allowing it to sufficiently

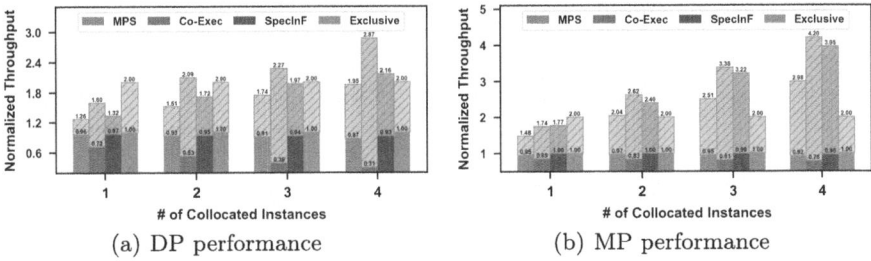

Fig. 7. Performance comparison under different sizes of collocated inference instances. Here we regard the single instance throughput on the exclusive GPU as the normalized one. (a) the RoBERTa-Resnet collocation case; (b) the ChatGLM-BERT collocation case.

handle inference workloads in Co-Exec mode. In the future, for the PP scenario, we aim to execute inference workloads concurrently as much as possible until the BM observes that training iterations have lengthened.

Online Inference Filling. Figures 4(b), 5(b), 6(b) demonstrate that SpecInF can deliver low p95 latencies of online inference with training throughput guarantees. SpecInF consistently shows the lowest p95 latency of inferences, trailing only behind the Exclusive mode, while maintaining standard training throughputs. This advantage is owing to the proactive pull-and-execute mechanism. In DP cases, shown in Fig. 4(b), SpecInF reduces p95 by up to 61% and 67% compared to Co-Exec and MPS, respectively. In MP cases, it lowers p95 by an average of 40% compared to Co-Exec and 33% compared to MPS. Similar to offline cases above, the gains in PP modes diminish, but SpecInF still maintains the best tail latency performance except Exclusive.

5.3   Multi-instance Support

Aggregated Throughput Improvement with Multiple Inference Instances Support. As Principle-I in Sect. 3.2 mentions, SpecInF supports collocating multiple inference instances to enhance GPU utilization. Figure 7 shows that SpecInF achieves a sub-linear growth in inference throughput while ensuring training throughput, with increasing collocated inference instances. In DP cases depicted in Fig. 7(a), SpecInF outperforms Exclusive by achieving an additional 35%–123% in inference throughput when the number of instances ranges from 1 to 4, with a maximum training throughput reduction of less than 7%. Although Co-Exec surpasses all other baselines in aggregated throughput, it leads to a substantial degradation in training, up to 61%. Consistent trends are observed in the MP scenario shown in Fig. 7(b). Specifically, SpecInF matches the offline throughput performance of Co-Exec while avoiding the latter's detrimental impact on training, which can reach up to 22%. Notably, with 4 instances, the inference throughput soars to 299% more than that of Exclusive.

5.4   System Overhead

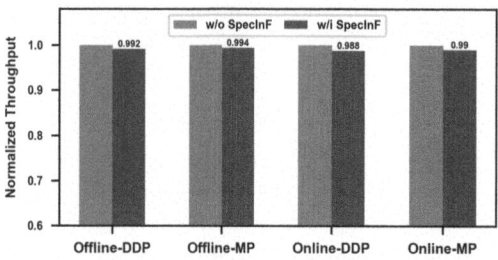

Negligible System Overhead.
We evaluate the system overhead by collocating the training
instance with inference instances, but without triggering any
inference requests. These scenarios include BERT-RoBERTa
in Fig. 4 and ChatGLM-
RoBERTa in Fig. 5). The results
show in Fig. 8. Figures indicate the overheads of speculative filling including bubble
monitoring, kernel scheduling and kernel barrier, are minimal (i.e., 1%), which
is considered acceptable.

Fig. 8. The System Overhead Speedup.

6   Related Work

DL Scheduling. As DL evolves, systems adopt various scheduling methods.
Tiresias [6] provides elastic training, without explicit resource scheduling, to
improve throughput or reduce Job Completion Time. Works like [5,25] focus on
supporting GPU-efficient and high-throughput inference serving. Mixing them
up, Lyra [7] loan inference GPUs to train models in the long run (i.e., at hours
level). Orion [22] collocates small-sized training and inference tasks but at the
thread level, which is not suitable for cloud containers.

GPU Sharing. The straightforward method to enhance GPU utilization effectively is to share a single GPU with multiple DL tasks. Existing works can be
categorized into temporal and spatial sharing approaches. For temporal sharing,
Antman [24] implicitly inserts training jobs during iterations. Based on this,
TGS [23] provides high transparency. However, both methods are not suitable
for LLMs due to large memory footprints. As for spatial sharing, MIG [16] supports the physical isolation of GPU devices but lacks adaptability. MPS [17] is
widely used in DL systems [5,25], while it can not dynamically consume idle
compute resources completely due to static allocation. Aiming at distributed
training, SpecInF detects bubbles timely and speculatively fills inference workloads to improve GPU utilization.

7   Conclusion

Nowadays, Deep Learning revolutionizes various aspects of life. However, GPUs
used for training these DL applications are usually underutilized, yielding massive compute and memory fragments. We observe that moderate inference workloads are well-suited to fill up these GPU fragmentations. In this paper, we
present SpecInF, which collocates distributed training with online/offline inference instances, to speculatively serve inference workloads, significantly improving GPU utilization. The results show that SpecInF can exploit the idling GPU

resources in various distributed training modes, delivering additional up to 14×
offline inference throughputs than TGS and 67% reduction in online inference
p95 latency than MPS, while guaranteeing collocated training throughput.

Acknowledgement. We thank our colleague Xiaohong Wang for her kind support
in this study. This work is supported by the Innovation Funding of ICT, CAS under
Grant No. E461040, No. E361060, and the Pilot for Major Scientific Research Facility
of Jiangsu Province of China under Grant No. BM2021800.

References

1. Clossal AI. Pytorch DDP (2024). https://github.com/hpcaitech/ColossalAI
2. Stability AI. Stable diffusion (2024). https://stability.ai/
3. DeepSpeed. Hybrid parallelism (2024). https://www.deepspeed.ai/tutorials/pipeline/
4. Tsinghua University Knowledge Engineering and Data Mining Group. Thudm chatglm3 (2024). https://github.com/THUDM/ChatGLM3
5. Gu, J., Zhu, Y., Wang, P., Chadha, M., Gerndt, M.: FaST-GShare: enabling efficient spatio-temporal GPU sharing in serverless computing for deep learning inference. In: Proceedings of the 52nd International Conference on Parallel Processing, pp. 635–644 (2023)
6. Gu, J., et al.: Tiresias: a {GPU} cluster manager for distributed deep learning. In: 16th USENIX Symposium on Networked Systems Design and Implementation (NSDI 2019), pp. 485–500 (2019)
7. Li, J., Xu, H., Zhu, Y., Liu, Z., Guo, C., Wang, C.: Lyra: elastic scheduling for deep learning clusters. In: Proceedings of the Eighteenth European Conference on Computer Systems, pp. 835–850 (2023)
8. Li, S., et al.: PyTorch distributed: experiences on accelerating data parallel training. Proc. VLDB Endow. **13**(12) (2020)
9. Masters, D., Luschi, C.: Revisiting small batch training for deep neural networks. arXiv preprint arXiv:1804.07612 (2018)
10. Medium. All GPT-4 details (2024). https://openai.com/chatgpt/
11. Meta. Meta LLaMA2 (2024). https://llama.meta.com/llama2/
12. Meta. Pytorch DDP (2024). https://pytorch.org/tutorials/intermediate/ddp_tutorial.html
13. Microsoft. Microsoft deepspeed (2024). https://github.com/microsoft/DeepSpeed
14. Narayanan, D., et al.: PipeDream: generalized pipeline parallelism for DNN training. In: Proceedings of the 27th ACM Symposium on Operating Systems Principles, pp. 1–15 (2019)
15. Nvidia. Industry AI (2024). https://www.nvidia.cn/industries/industrial/
16. NVIDIA. Nvidia MIG (2024). https://www.nvidia.com/en-us/technologies/multi-instance-gpu/
17. NVIDIA. Nvidia MPS (2024). https://docs.nvidia.com/deploy/mps/
18. NVIDIA. NVML library (2024). https://developer.nvidia.com/management-library-nvml
19. OpenAI. OpenAI ChatGPT (2024). https://openai.com/chatgpt/
20. Park, S.J., Fried, J., Kim, S., Alizadeh, M., Belay, A.: Efficient strong scaling through burst parallel training. Proc. Mach. Learn. Syst. **4**, 748–761 (2022)

21. Shoeybi, M., Patwary, M., Puri, R., LeGresley, P., Casper, J., Catanzaro, B.: Megatron-LM: training multi-billion parameter language models using model parallelism. arXiv preprint arXiv:1909.08053 (2019)
22. Strati, F., Ma, X., Klimovic, A.: Orion: interference-aware, fine-grained GPU sharing for ml applications. In: Proceedings of the Nineteenth European Conference on Computer Systems, pp. 1075–1092 (2024)
23. Wu, B., Zhang, Z., Bai, Z., Liu, X., Jin, X.: Transparent {GPU} sharing in container clouds for deep learning workloads. In: 20th USENIX Symposium on Networked Systems Design and Implementation (NSDI 2023), pp. 69–85 (2023)
24. Xiao, W., et al.: {AntMan}: dynamic scaling on {GPU} clusters for deep learning. In: 14th USENIX Symposium on Operating Systems Design and Implementation (OSDI 2020), pp. 533–548 (2020)
25. Yang, Y., et al.: INFless: a native serverless system for low-latency, high-throughput inference. In: Proceedings of the 27th ACM International Conference on Architectural Support for Programming Languages and Operating Systems, pp. 768–781 (2022)

swDarknet: A Heterogeneous Parallel Deep Learning Framework Suitable for SW26010 Pro Processor

Huazeng Liu[1,2], Min Tian[1,2(✉)], Xiaoming Wu[1,2], Meihong Yang[1,2], Zenghui Ren[1,2], and Yanlong Li[2]

[1] Key Laboratory of Computing Power Network and Information Security, Ministry of Education, Shandong Computer Science Center (National Supercomputer Center in Jinan), Qilu University of Technology (Shandong Academy of Sciences), Jinan, China
[2] Jinan Key Laboratory of High Performance Computing, Shandong Provincial Key Laboratory of Computer Networks, Shandong Fundamental Research Center for Computer Science, Jinan, China
tianm@sdas.org

Abstract. As the size of AI models grows dramatically to achieve higher accuracy, more and more models are trained on supercomputers with massive computing and memory. However, it is still challenging to accelerate deep learning applications on supercomputer systems with many-core architectures. In this paper, we propose swDarknet: a Darknet-based heterogeneous parallel deep learning framework on the SW26010 Pro processor. First, We designed three heterogeneous parallel DNN layers: adaptive block-splitting strategy for matrix-multiplication layer, optimized memory access for convolutional layer, and block-based parallel pooling layer. Second, we proposed a model averaging (MA) method to efficiently scale swDarknet across many processors. Finally, we evaluated the performance of swDarknet on a core group. As compared with darknet, the convolutional layers achieved an average speedup of 32x. When training AlexNet and VGG-16, swDarknet can achieve up to $36.79\times$ and $181.35\times$ speedup, respectively.

Keywords: deep learning · high performance computing · convolutional neural networks

1 Introduction

In recent years, deep learning technology has triggered revolutionary changes across numerous fields, such as computer vision [1], natural language processing [2], and autonomous driving [3]. This has driven the emergence of a series of deep learning frameworks, such as Darknet [4], Caffe [5], MXNet [6], and TensorFlow [7]. As the depth and number of parameters in visualization models increase, the

© IFIP International Federation for Information Processing 2025
Published by Springer Nature Switzerland AG 2025
X. Chen et al. (Eds.): NPC 2024, LNCS 15527, pp. 159–171, 2025.
https://doi.org/10.1007/978-981-96-2830-8_13

demand for computational resources grows exponentially. Therefore, utilizing supercomputing platforms to train DNN models is expected to become a trend in future developments.

Traditional supercomputers are primarily targeted towards scientific computing, engineering simulations, etc. Many supercomputers like the Sunway Bluelight II lack direct optimization and support for deep learning training. Therefore, fully utilizing the computational power of supercomputers to train DNN faces significant challenges.

Darknet is a framework particularly suited for image processing and visual analysis, compared with Caffe and TensorFlow. Currently, swCaffe [8] and swDNN [9] have optimized CNNs for the characteristics of the Sunway supercomputer. swFlow [10] has also proposed a distributed deep learning framework and optimized the allocation and transfer of computational resources.

We have improved the Darknet framework to fully utilize SW26010 Pro. Our main contributions are as follows:

- We develop a swDarknet heterogeneous parallel deep learning frame. To leverage the performance of SW26010 Pro processor, we adopt a series of optimization strategies and redesign multiple deep neural network layers.
- We propose an adaptive block-splitting strategy for matrix multiplication on SW26010 Pro processor.
- We implement a model averaging (MA) method to scale swDarknet across multiple Sunway nodes.
- Compared with Darknet, swDarknet achieves a 36.79× to 181.35× speedup on a core group.

The rest of this paper is organized as follows. Section 2 introduces the background of the SW26010 Pro processor and the software architecture of Darknet. Section 3 details the optimization of various DNN layers in swDarknet. Section 4 discusses how to extend swDarknet to multiple nodes. Section 5 evaluates the swDarknet framework. Section 6 discusses related work. Section 7 provides some conclusions.

2   Backgrounds

2.1   The Architecture of SW26010 Pro Processor

The SW26010 Pro is a many-core processor equipped on the Sunway Bluelight II supercomputer. As shown in Fig. 1, SW26010 Pro is composed of 6 core groups (CGs). Each core group is connected through a ring network and includes a Management Processing Unit (MPE), an array of Computing Processing Units (CPEs), and a DDR4 main memory. The CPE array consists of 8×8 Computing Processing Units, and the core groups are interconnected through a high-speed network. The processor connects to other external devices through a System Interface (SI).

The MPE adopts the proprietary SW64 instruction set and features a 32 KB L1 instruction cache, a 32 KB L1 data cache, and a 512 KB L2 cache. The CPE

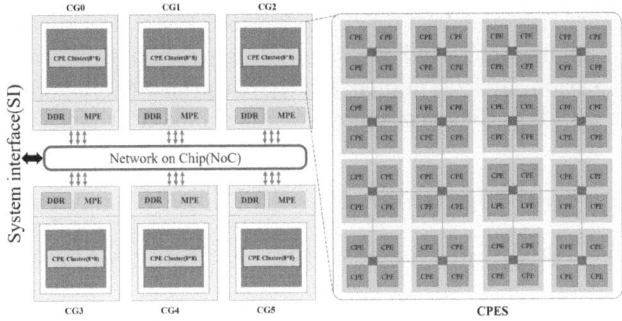

Fig. 1. The architecture of SW26010 Pro many-core processor.

also uses the proprietary SW64 instruction set, with a 512-bit Single Instruction Multiple Data (SIMD) vector unit supporting double-precision, single-precision, half-precision floating-point computations, and integer operations. Each CPE has a 32 KB dedicated instruction cache and a 256 KB Local Data Memory (LDM). The LDM can be fully controlled by the user, and part of the space can also be configured as a hardware-managed Local Data Cache (LDcache).

2.2 Software Architecture

Darknet is known for its excellence in computer vision tasks, especially target detection. It also supports various deep learning tasks such as image classification, semantic segmentation, and generative adversarial networks.

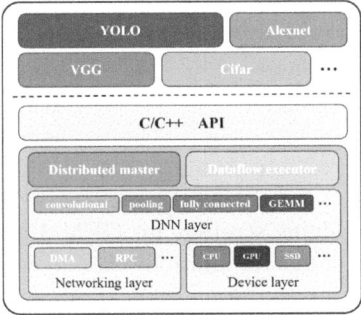

Fig. 2. Darknet Software Architecture.

Darknet is an open-source neural network framework. It adopts a unified software architecture and implements common deep neural network layers such as convolutional, pooling, and fully connected layers, as well as activation functions like ReLU and Logistic, and loss functions. It also includes model series such as

YOLO [4], alexnet [11], and VGG [12], as shown in Fig. 2. Darknet implements a large number of highly optimized core computing operators, such as convolution, matrix multiplication, im2col, and col2im. It performs array operations directly in C language, avoiding the overhead of languages like Python.

3   Redesign and Optimize Parallel DNN Layers

3.1   Adaptive Block-Splitting Strategy for Matrix-Multiplication Layer

we analyzed the hotspots of Darknet on the SW26010 processor. Table 1 shows the running time and percentage of time spent for each layer of the DNN and its functions. The convolutional layer is the major hot spot of GEMM and reaches 98.72% of the total running time. In this section, we focus on optimizing the matrix multiplication layer, which is also the implementation layer for GEMM operations.

Table 1. Darknet hotspot function on a core group.

Function	Subfunction	Time(%)	Time(s)
Forward_convolutional_layer		83.20	2079.99
	gemm	75.71	1892.79
	im2col	6.16	127.91
Backward_convolutional_layer		15.52	387.98
	gemm	14.43	360.82
	im2col	0.62	15.52
	col2im	0.31	7.76
Backward_connected_layer		0.15	3.66
Forward_maxpool_layer		0.11	2.78
Forward_connected_layer		0.05	1.20
Parse_network_cfg		0.08	2.08

We propose a hybrid solving strategy for GEMM based on different matrix shapes. We find two cases of matrix multiplication in convolution operations. As shown in Fig. 3. Case 1 involves the multiplication of an approximately square matrix with a rectangular matrix. Case 2 involves the multiplication of two rectangular matrices.

Process-Level Optimization. In Case 1, where the K dimension is relatively large, we ensure that the data partitioned to each CPE can be stored in the LDM. Therefore, matrix A is partitioned by rows. In Case 2, where the K dimension is small, it is suitable to partition by columns, facilitating the thread-level computation of vector multiplication. Therefore, matrix B is partitioned

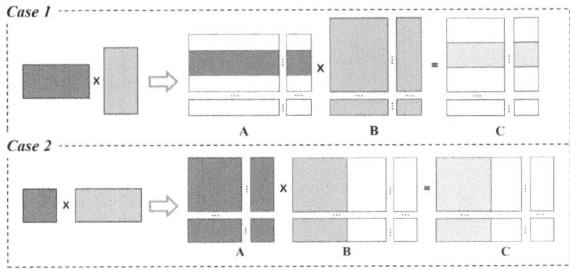

Fig. 3. an adaptive block-splitting strategy for matrix multiplication.

by columns. Specifically, the master process performs the partitioning and sends the data, while each process receives its corresponding row and column blocks. After receiving the data, each process invokes the CPEs for computation and then sends the results back to the master process for aggregation.

Thread-Level Optimization. We partition the data received by each process into sub-blocks and assign them to CPEs. The GEMM operation is mapped onto an 8×8 grid of CPE on the processor. Specifically, we partition the matrix $A \in \mathbb{R}^{m \times k}$ and the matrix $B \in \mathbb{R}^{k \times n}$ into multiple sub-blocks, with each CPE responsible for computing one sub-block $C(i,j) = A(i,:) \cdot B(:,j)$. To reduce data transfer across CPE, we use a row-column register communication mechanism. This allows CPE in the same row and column to share data, thereby improving data reuse.

3.2 Optimized Memory Access for Convolutional Layer

Since Im2col and col2im use irregular memory access patterns, avoiding repeated memory access is crucial for optimization. The im2col function can convert the dimensions of a three-dimensional image array into a two-dimensional matrix, suitable for efficient matrix multiplication in convolution operations. However, as the convolution filter size varies, each sliding window operation results in irregular memory access.

We consider the rows of the image output array as the total task quantity. The total task quantity is evenly distributed across the 8×8 CPE computing units. Specifically, the MPE is responsible for initializing parameters and task partitioning, and then launching the CPEs to execute the computations. Since we have numerous CPE units, we use an integer rounding-up strategy for task allocation. This strategy ensures that each processing unit is assigned a roughly equal number of tasks, avoiding situations where some units are overloaded while others remain idle.

As shown in Fig. 4, within the CPEs, we optimized the memory access pattern by using the direct DMA technique for batch data transfer and storing the data in the LDM. This minimizes the overhead associated with frequent memory access.

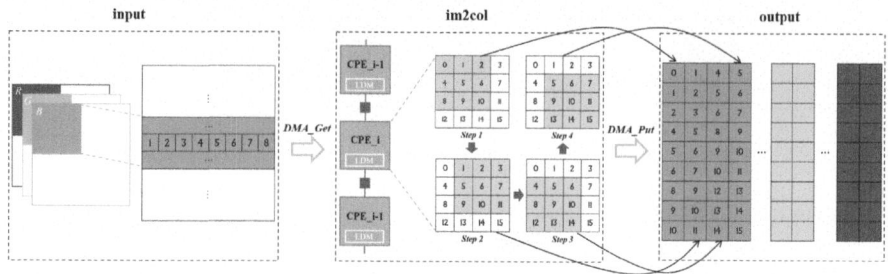

Fig. 4. Optimized memory access parallel im2col On one CG.

We copy the im2col parameters from the MPE to the LDM using DMA_get. Each CPE allocates the channels it needs to process based on its thread ID and the total number of threads. For each channel, the CPE calculates the column offset and row offset, and then computes the input image pixel values for each position based on these offsets. By following this approach, we can efficiently cache data in the LDM and reduce memory bandwidth demands through register communication.

3.3 Block-Based Parallel Pooling Layer

In this section, we accelerate the pooling operation using a master-slave core parallel approach. The pooling layer reduces the spatial dimensions of the feature maps, lowering computational complexity and memory requirements. Simultaneously, it preserves important feature information on a smaller scale, enhancing the model's efficiency and generalization ability. The pooling operation slides a window over each channel and performs a maximum or average operation on the elements within the window. These operations do not involve significant computations but require substantial memory copying. Therefore, during optimization, we should avoid fine-grained memory access and use large data block transfers to increase available memory bandwidth.

In the pooling process, we partition the input feature map into multiple sub-blocks and assign them to different CPEs, enabling parallel execution of the pooling operation. We ensure that each CPE transfers contiguous data blocks as much as possible, storing as many data blocks as possible in the LDM. When a data block cannot be read into the LDM at once, we use distributed DMA for data transfer.

4   Scaling swDarknet on SW26010 Pro

4.1   Process-Level Optimization

In this section, we propose a two-level parallel Model Averaging (MA) algorithm scheme for extending the swDarknet model. The MA algorithm is widely used

Algorithm 1. Parallel MA algoithm

Input: function f($\cdot$), mini-batch size B per process, global parameters w^0, nodes K, number of iterations T, Communication interval M
1: **for** $t = 0, 1, ..., T - 1$ **do**
2:     Initialize K processes;
3:     **for** $k = 0, 1, \ldots, K - 1$ in parallel **do**
4:         Receiving model w_t, and let $w_k^t = w^t$
5:         **for** $m = 0, 1, \ldots, M - 1$ **do**
6:             randomly sample mini-batch as τ_m^k ;
7:             update $w_k^t = w_k^t - \eta^m \nabla f \tau_k^m(w_k^t)$;
8:         **end for**
9:     **end for**
10:    All-reduce $\frac{1}{k} \sum_{k=1}^{K} w^t$;
11:    Update global parameters: $w^{t+1} = \frac{1}{K} \sum_{k=1}^{K} w_k^t$;
12: **end for**

in HPC clusters due to its low communication frequency and ideal acceleration effect [14]. In the MA algorithm, each node performs multiple rounds of iterative updates on the local model based on local data. When the local model converges or the number of local iterations exceeds a preset threshold, a global model averaging is performed. The next iteration continues training using the latest model. Our MA algorithm is described in Algorithm 1.

The implementation of the MA algorithm includes two synchronization methods: parameter server and All-reduce. The parameter server has better fault tolerance for network environments. The overall training is not affected by some nodes. However, when the number of computing nodes reaches a certain level, the parameter server may become a performance bottleneck for the system. Therefore, we use the All-reduce synchronization method, which is more suitable for the high-speed network of the Sunway system.

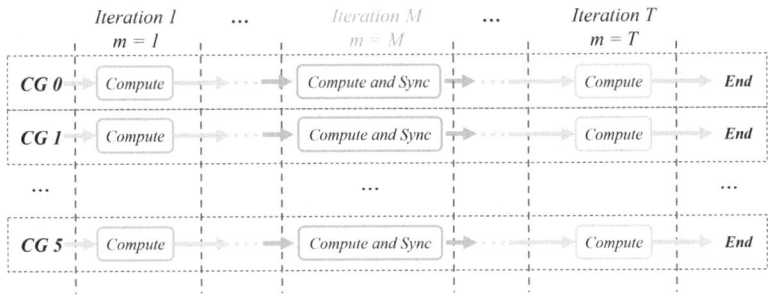

Fig. 5. Iterative details of distributed swDarknet on 6 CGs.

Taking a sw26010 Pro processor as an example, we calculate the average gradient $\frac{1}{K}\sum_{k=1}^{K}w_k^t$ across 6 CGs, as shown in Fig. 5. Specifically, we first partition the corresponding dataset range for each CG. When launching the program, we simultaneously launch 6 CGs. The 6 CGs iterate in parallel for T times. In each iteration, each CG randomly selects a mini-batch τ_k^m based on its dataset for iteration, where k represents the current CG.

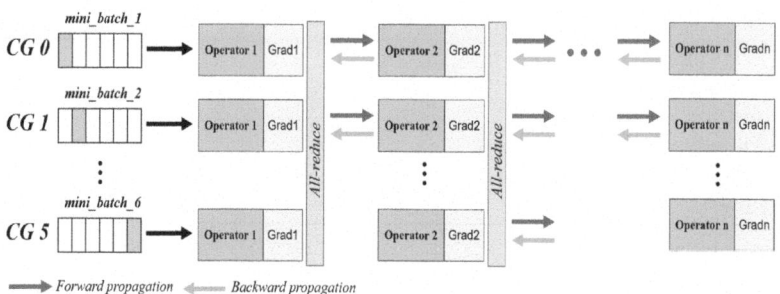

Fig. 6. All-reduce synchronisation details of MA algorithm on 6 CGs.

4.2   Thread-Level Optimization

We set a threshold M at the start of the iteration, as shown in Fig. 6. When m is not equal to M, we only perform local gradient updates $w_k^t = w^t$ without synchronization. When m equals M, during each iteration, every CG performs an Allreduce operation to synchronize the gradients during the forward and backward propagation processes. Each CG receives the globally averaged gradient $\frac{1}{k}\sum_{k=1}^{K}w^t$. Finally, the averaged gradient is used as the new gradient for the next round. This process continues iteratively until N iterations or model convergence is reached.

Data loading is a critical issue in distributed training. Due to the typically large size of datasets used in model training, we have designed an asynchronous data prefetching scheme. At the start of each iteration, every CG calls pthread to launch a thread, which then invokes a CPE thread to asynchronously execute the data loading task. The CPE thread loads 1/6 of the data for each mini-batch, after which the main thread collects and merges the loaded data from all threads, forming a complete mini-batch as the dataset for the current iteration.

5   Evaluation

In our experiments, we utilized the Sunway Bluelight II Supercomputer, which operates under the Sunway Linux 4.4.15 system. The software was compiled using the mpicc and sw9gcc compilers in a hybrid compilation approach to construct swDarknet. For our empirical evaluation, we employed the publicly available CIFAR-10 dataset.

5.1   Optimization Evaluation of Different DNN Layers

In this section, we will introduce the evaluation of the acceleration effects of different DNN layers on the CIFAR model. The experiment includes convolutional layers and max pooling layers. The bar graphs display the processing times of the original program (in seconds) and the optimized program, while the line graphs demonstrate the speedup ratio between the two in Fig. 7.

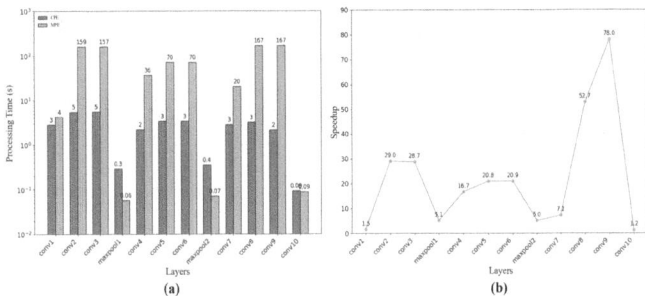

Fig. 7. Comparison of CPE and MPE acceleration of convolutional and Maxpool layers on the Cifar model

With the enhancements from the Matrix-Multiplication Layer, im2col layer, and col2im layer, the convolutional layers achieved a maximum speedup ratio of 78x, with an average speedup of 32x. The max pooling layers also reached a speedup ratio of 5x. This is due to the inherently lower computational complexity of pooling operations, which involve relatively modest computational demands but substantial memory copying activities. These memory operations do not significantly differ in execution time between single-core and many-core environments. Overall, swDarknet achieved a cumulative speedup ratio of 27x on the CIFAR model.

5.2   Optimization Evaluation of Different DNN Models

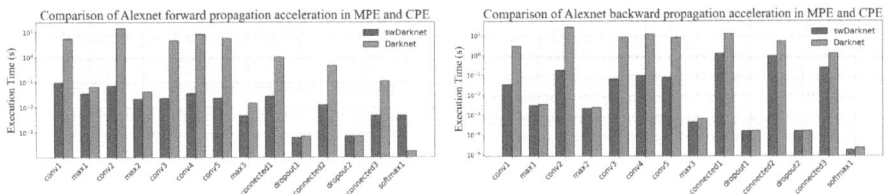

Fig. 8. Forward and Backward Time of Alexnet on CPE and MPE.

In this section, we present the overall performance of the AlexNet and VGG-16 models, as shown in Fig. 8 and Fig. 9. In the AlexNet model, the speed of swDarknet increased by 36.79×, and similarly in the VGG-16 model, the speed of swDarknet increased by 181.35×. The convolutional layers are the most accelerated parts. For large-sized images and models with multiple channels, the im2col and col2im operations can provide an additional 20% acceleration for convolution operations. This is why CPE acceleration makes the convolution layers the highest speedup portion of the entire model.

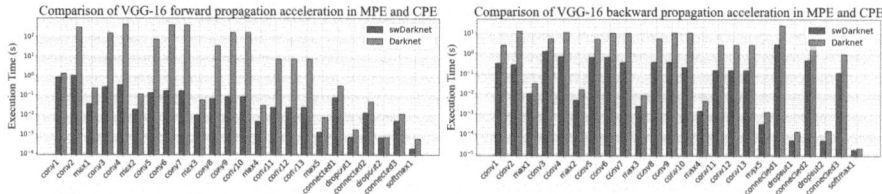

Fig. 9. Forward and Backward Time of VGG-16 on CPE and MPE.

In contrast to convolution layers, the MaxPool layers did not achieve the same high speedup ratio. Pooling operations involve a significant amount of irregular memory access, and when multiple CPEs and MPEs access the main memory simultaneously, they are constrained by bandwidth limitations. Even though we strive to ensure that each CPE transfers continuous data blocks, a substantial amount of time is still consumed by data transfer overhead.

5.3   Optimized Evaluation of Scalability Results

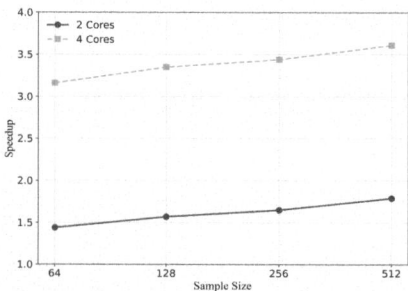

Fig. 10. Scalability of swDarknet.

Since we adopted a distributed strategy using the parallel MA algorithm, the model did not spend much time on the All-reduce operation. We trained the

CIFAR model on 4 processes, with mini-batch sizes of 64, 128, and 256, compared to training on a single node. The experimental results are shown in Fig. 10. The highest speedup was obtained with a mini-batch size of 64, where training on 2 processes was 1.65 times faster. Training on 4 nodes achieved a 3.41 times speedup.

This result indicates that as the number of processes increases, the inter-process communication overhead also increases, thereby slowing down the convergence speed of the model. In large-scale distributed training, communication overhead can significantly impact training efficiency, requiring a balance between the number of parallel processes and communication overhead.

6 Related Work

6.1 Deep Learning Frameworks

With the development of artificial intelligence, many deep learning frameworks are not short of emerging. Jia et al. developed Caffe [5], a modular framework excelling in convolutional neural networks (CNNs), known for its speed and broad adoption in computer vision. Abadi et al. launched TensorFlow [7], a versatile framework with a comprehensive ecosystem, suitable for both research and production due to its scalability and distributed computing support. Chen et al. presented MXNet [6], recognized for its scalability and performance, and integrated into the Apache project, supporting various programming paradigms. Paszke et al. Robbins and Monro's paper [13] introduced a stochastic approximation method, providing foundational techniques for iterative optimization in statistics. created PyTorch [14], popular for its dynamic computation graph and intuitive interface, becoming a preferred tool for deep learning research and rapid prototyping.

6.2 Deep Learning on the Sunway Supercomputer

Fang et al. introduced swDNN [8], a library designed to enhance the performance of deep learning applications on the Sunway Supercomputer by optimizing computation and data transfers. They also developed swCaffe [9], a parallel framework that accelerates the execution of Caffe models on the supercomputer, achieving significant improvements in training speed and efficiency. Li et al. proposed swFLOW, a dataflow-based framework tailored for the Sunway platform, optimizing resource allocation and data transfers to improve efficiency. Lastly, BaGuaLu [15] focused on optimizing large-scale pre-trained models, demonstrating the potential for training brain-scale models efficiently on over 37 million cores of the Sunway Supercomputer.

7 Conclusion

In this paper, we present our experience designing swDarknet, a highly efficient parallel DNN training framework, on sw26010 pro processor architecture. We present a parallel block-splitting matrix multiplication strategy. We have implemented a series of parallel strategies to redesign and optimize three DNN layers. Additionally, we introduce methods for efficiently scaling swDarknet to multiple nodes, including a parallel MA algorithm for gradient synchronization and an asynchronous data prefetching scheme. Our experimental results demonstrated a $36.79\times$ to $181.35\times$ speedup on a core group.

Our future work will primarily focus on two aspects: 1) Enhancing the scalability of swDarknet to support large-scale distributed training. 2) Optimizing synchronous communication. As the number of nodes increases, the communication overhead of All-reduce could become a bottleneck for swDarknet.

Acknowledgments. This research was partly supported by the Pilot Project for Integrated Innovation of Science, Education and Industry of Qilu University of Technology (Shandong Academy of Sciences) (2024GH24).

References

1. Li, X., Wu, Y., Jiang, X., et al.: Enhancing visual document understanding with contrastive learning in large visual-language models[J]. arXiv preprint arXiv:2402.19014 (2024)
2. Yin, F., Ye, X., Durrett, G.: LoFiT: localized Fine-tuning on LLM Representations[J]. arXiv preprint arXiv:2406.01563 (2024)
3. Kirillov, A., Mintun, E., Ravi, N., et al.: Segment anything. In: Proceedings of the IEEE/CVF International Conference on Computer Vision, pp. 4015–4026 (2023)
4. Redmon, J., Divvala, S., Girshick, R., et al.: You only look once: Unified, real-time object detection. In: Proceedings of the IEEE Conference on Computer Vision and Pattern Recognition, pp. 779–788 (2016)
5. Jia, Y., Shelhamer, E., Donahue, J., et al.: Caffe: convolutional architecture for fast feature embedding. In: Proceedings of the 22nd ACM International Conference on Multimedia, pp. 675–678 (2014)
6. Chen, T., Li, M., Li, Y., et al.: Mxnet: a flexible and efficient machine learning library for heterogeneous distributed systems[J]. arXiv preprint arXiv:1512.01274 (2015)
7. Abadi, M., Agarwal, A., Barham, P., et al.: Tensorflow: large-scale machine learning on heterogeneous distributed systems[J]. arXiv preprint arXiv:1603.04467 (2016)
8. Fang, J., Fu, H., Zhao, W., et al.: SWDNN: a library for accelerating deep learning applications on sunway taihulight. In: 2017 IEEE International Parallel and Distributed Processing Symposium (IPDPS), pp. 615–624. (2017)
9. Li, L., Fang, J., Fu, H., et al.: SWCAFFE: a parallel framework for accelerating deep learning applications on sunway taihulight. In: 2018 IEEE International Conference on Cluster Computing (CLUSTER), pp. 4133–422. IEEE (2018)
10. Li, M., Lin, H., Chen, J., et al.: swFLOW: a large-scale distributed framework for deep learning on Sunway TaihuLight supercomputer. Inf. Sci. **570**, 831–847 (2021)
11. Krizhevsky, A., Sutskever, I., Hinton, G.E.: ImageNet classification with deep convolutional neural networks. Commun. ACM **60**(6), 84–90 (2017)
12. Simonyan, K., Zisserman, A.: Very deep convolutional networks for large-scale image recognition[J]. arXiv preprint arXiv:1409.1556 (2014)

13. Robbins, H., Monro, S.: A stochastic approximation method. Ann. Math. Stat. 400–407 (1951)
14. Al-Rfou, R., Alain, G., Almahairi, A., et al.: Theano: a Python framework for fast computation of mathematical expressions[J]. arXiv e-prints. arXiv:1605.02688 (2016)
15. Paszke, A., Gross, S., Massa, F., et al.: Pytorch: an imperative style, high-performance deep learning library. Adv. Neural Inf. Process. Syst. **32** (2019)
16. Ma, Z., He, J., Qiu, J., et al.: BaGuaLu: targeting brain scale pretrained models with over 37 million cores. In: Proceedings of the 27th ACM SIGPLAN Symposium on Principles and Practice of Parallel Programming, pp. 192–204 (2022)

VConv: Autotiling Convolution Algorithm Based on MLIR for Multi-core Vector accelerators

Xiaorong Chen, Cheng Li, and Zhong Liu[✉]

College of Computer, National University of Defense Technology, Changsha 410073, Hunan, China
zhongliu@nudt.edu.cn

Abstract. The convolution is a crucial and computationally intensive operation in machine learning models. Under limited resource and energy budget constraints, vector accelerators are gaining popularity due to their high performance and low power consumption. However, three challenges are of concern to efficiently implement the convolution on vector accelerators. (1) A lot of extra memory may be generated during the data conversion process of traditional matrix multiplication-based convolution algorithms. (2) It has been laborious and error-prone to employ manual vectorization methods. (3) Some existing deep learning compilers (e.g., TVM) have limited adaptability in handling convolutions of different sizes. Therefore, the VConv is proposed in this study. This is an automatic tiled convolution algorithm based on the MLIR code-generation toolchain that can be integrated into machine-learning compilers. It consists of three key components. (1) The data format conversion method, which can avoid the extra memory and data conversion overhead. (2) The automatic tiling algorithm, which can reduce data transfer and improve resource utilization efficiency. (3) The algorithm that automatically generates vectorized kernel code. Experimental results show that the VConv can achieve a computational efficiency of up to 80% on convolutions of different sizes. Besides, the VConv achieves $5\times$ to $15\times$ in computational efficiency and $2\times$ to $3\times$ in energy efficiency in performing convolutions of the AlexNet, the GoogleNet, the VGG16, the YOLOv5s, and the ResNet50 compared to the state-of-the-art methods. Simultaneously, the VConv method has good adaptability and high efficiency, making it more valuable in practical applications.

Keywords: Convolution · Automatic tiling · Multi-core vector accelerator · Code generation · MLIR

1 Introduction

Convolution is a mathematical tensor operation that is commonly used in image processing and convolutional neural network (CNN) models. It is also computationally intensive and takes up most of the execution time in classic CNN models. [10]. Therefore, many methods have been proposed to speed up convolution

X. Chen et al. (Eds.): NPC 2024, LNCS 15527, pp. 172–190, 2025.
https://doi.org/10.1007/978-981-96-2830-8_14

[4,7,20]. Among them, the matrix multiplication convolution algorithm converts convolution calculations into general matrix multiplication operations. It is a general algorithm for implementing convolution calculations [2]. However, data conversion (e.g., im2col [6]) is required from convolution calculation to matrix multiplication. During this period, a large amount of intermediate data may be generated, resulting in a large amount of memory overhead and additional data conversion overhead. In order to reduce data operation overhead, Ferrari et al. [3] proposed SConv. They used a specific cache tiling technology to reduce the number of cache misses and improve performance. However, cache misses have still occurred.

Vector accelerators have the characteristics of fast operation speed, low power consumption, powerful parallel computing units, and strong multi-core processing capabilities [14]. With the rapid growth of computationally intensive applications, vector accelerators are becoming more and more popular to achieve high processing speed under limited resources and energy budgets. However, the storage structure of vector accelerators is different from that of mainstream processors. Traditional computer architectures use hardware-managed caches to solve the storage wall problem, while vector accelerators usually use software-managed on-chip memory to explicitly manage all on-chip and off-chip memories. In order to fully utilize the hardware resources of vector accelerators and improve computing efficiency, many studies have been conducted to directly or indirectly accelerate convolution optimization algorithms through manual vectorization methods [13,21]. However, manual vectorization requires a lot of human resources and is prone to introducing errors, leading to low development efficiency.

Prior studies have addressed the above issues by adopting carefully hand-optimized operator libraries or deep-learning compilers. For instance, mainstream inference engines or frameworks (e.g., OnnxRuntime [15]) use high-performance operator libraries (e.g., CuDNN [2]) to optimize convolutional layers, thereby achieving fast and efficient inference on specific hardware platforms. Although these operator libraries achieve high performance, they relieds on manual tuning and are usually not cross-platform compatible [22]. Deep learning compilers (e.g., TVM [1]) perform platform-specific compilation to accelerate deep learning training/inference. However, these compilers are primarily targeted at mainstream processor platforms and often rely on compiler toolchains (e.g., LLVM). Moreover, they currently lack adaptability for convolutions with different sizes.

In order to address the above-mentioned challenges, we proposed an automated tiling convolution algorithm VConv. Firstly, it provides a LASM dialect (Sect. 4) to integrate the LASM assembler into the MLIR ecosystem. Secondly, it provides a novel and efficient data conversion method. The data conversion method defines the index mapping rule using *affine_maps* and converts it into a large matrix (Sect. 5.1) to match the row-by-row data processing mode of the vector processor. Thirdly, according to the convolutions of different sizes and the storage structure of vector accelerators, the VConv provides a Convolution Automatic Tiling algorithm (CAT) (Sect. 5.2) and a double buffer transfer strategy (Sect. 5.3). Finally, it also provides the Vectorized Kernel Code Generation algorithm (VKGG) for automatically generating kernel vectorized code. Experimental results have shown that VConv is suitable for convolutions of different sizes and has high computational and energy efficiency.

2   Background and Motivation

This section mainly analyzes the architectural characteristics of vector accelerators, the research progress of convolution optimization algorithms, MLIR ecology, and finally reveals the research motivation of the VConv.

2.1   Vector Accelerator

Vector accelerators(as shown in Fig. 1) have unique architectural features that differ from mainstream processors and are primarily composed of clusters of DSPs [21]. Each DSP is mainly composed of a Scalar Process Unit (SPU) and a Vector Process Unit (VPU). The storage structure consists of Scalar Memory (SM), Array Memory (AM), and Direct Memory Access (DMA). The accelerator cores share on-chip Global Shared Memory (GSM) and off-chip DDR memory systems over a high-speed on-chip network. The L1D and AM accessed by the core computing both use SRAM mode. It completely avoids the storage access delay caused by cache data misses.

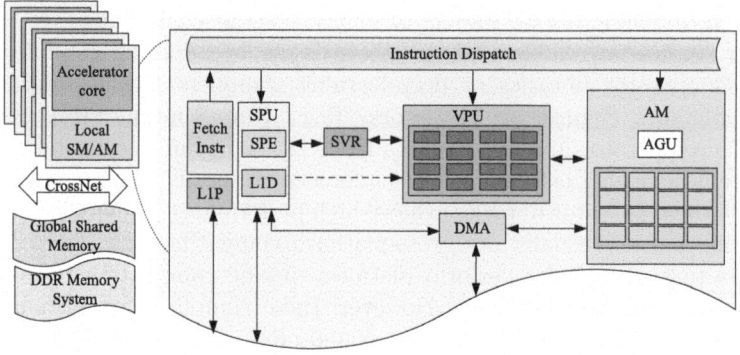

Fig. 1. Architecture diagram of vector accelerator.

In order to make full use of the hardware resources of vector accelerators and improve computing efficiency, a large number of studies have been conducted to directly or indirectly implement accelerated convolution optimization algorithms through manual vectorization methods [13,21]. These research methods propose different optimization strategies and techniques, which significantly improve the computational performance and efficiency of matrix multiplication and convolutional neural networks on multi-core vector processors. However, manual vectorization methods require complex programming skills and a deep understanding of DSP architecture to optimize code while taking full advantage of the hardware's parallel processing capabilities. Moreover, this process requires a lot of human resources and is prone to errors, resulting in low development efficiency. In addition, due to the diversity of deep learning models and the continuous evolution of DSP hardware architecture, manual vectorization methods are difficult to adapt to rapidly changing technical requirements, and lack scalability and portability.

LASM [23] is a compiler optimization framework of high performance for vector accelerators with linear assembly as its front-end language. It generated efficient machine code with a carefully designed optimization strategy. However, it is mainly positioned at the linear assembly level, which is still some distance away from processing complex advanced deep learning models.

2.2   Convolution

The computation of the convolutional layer is defined as Eq. (1). The F is the number of convolution kernels of the convolutional layer. H_o and W_o are the height and width of the output image, respectively. The input image of the current convolutional layer is represented by $img[i * S + x, j * S + y, c]$, the convolution kernel is represented by $weight[f, x, y, c]$, the bias is represented by $b[f]$, and the output image is represented by $output[f, i, j]$.

$$output[f, i, j] = \sum_{y=0}^{W_k - 1} \sum_{x=0}^{H_k - 1} \sum_{c=0}^{C - 1} weight[f, x, y, c] * img[i * S + x, j * S + y, c] + b[f],$$

$$f \in [0, F), i \in [0, H_o), j \in [0, W_o)$$

$$\tag{1}$$

The matrix multiplication convolution algorithm converts the convolution calculation into a general matrix multiplication operation. Many mainstream deep learning frameworks (e.g., Pytorch, TensorFlow) and neural network libraries (e.g., cuDNN [2]) also use the matrix multiplication convolution algorithm. Although it can improve performance, we found three issues that affect the efficiency of the algorithm. (1) Data conversion (e.g., im2col [6]) may generate a large amount of intermediate data, which increases memory and computational costs. (2) Universal data layout may fail to fully utilize hardware parallelism, which reduces resource utilization. (3) A lot of engineering work is required to adapt hardware features and to improve resource utilization, which increases development difficulty and workload.

We found that the convolution kernel sizes are diverse (e.g., 1, 3, 5, 7, 11) by analyzing AlexNet [11], VGG [18], GoogleNet [19], ResNet [5] and yolov5s [9]. The image scale (width and height) varies from 6 to 640, the input channel sizes of the convolution kernel and the image vary from 3 to 2048, and the output channel sizes of the convolution kernel vary from 16 to 2048. This brings adaptation difficulties to fixed-length vector processing units (such as the VPE length is 16). Although TVM and its AutoTVM module provide compiler frameworks and automatic tuning capabilities for a variety of hardware, they are mainly targeted at mainstream processors and rely on compiler toolchains such as LLVM. At the same time, TVM and AutoTVM have limited adaptability to convolutions of different sizes. Therefore, previous convolution optimization algorithms cannot run directly on vector accelerators or have very low execution efficiency.

2.3   MLIR Ecosystem

MLIR [12] is a compiler infrastructure. It provides different levels of abstractions (also known as dialects) across application domains, hardware targets, and execution environments, as well as conversions through these abstractions. Many deep learning frameworks and compilers have leveraged MLIR to deploy deep learning models on high-performance and embedded cpus/gpus, such as TensorFlow, Torch, and ONNX [8]. Unfortunately, the MLIR ecosystem only supports mature hardware targets, including ARM CPUs, x86 CPUs, Nvidia GPUs, AMD GPUs, and other SPIR-V compatible targets. As far as we know, a few researchers are currently researching vector accelerations [16,17]. Although Da et al. [17] and Qiu et al. [16] made a preliminary exploration of digital signal processor (DSP) optimization, they did not elaborate on key technologies such as data blocking, data transmission, and vectorization in detail. This means that emerging vector accelerators cannot yet connect to the MLIR ecosystem and share the benefits.

2.4   Motivation

Based on the above statements, it can be seen that automatic mapping of matrix multiplication convolution algorithm to vector accelerators still needs to face the following challenges. (1) Convolution kernels vary in size, making it difficult to load and store data in the form of vectors. As a result, previous convolution optimization algorithms cannot be run directly or have very low execution efficiency on vector accelerators, and are not adaptable to convolutions of different sizes. (2)The LASM assembler is mainly located at the linear assembly level, and can not handle complex advanced deep learning models. (3) Data transformation may lead to large memory overhead and additional data conversion overhead. Besides, exploring data segmentation strategies and manual vectorization requires a lot of engineering effort, which leads to low development efficiency. (4) Few studies have explored the support of vector accelerators in the MLIR ecosystem, and similar vector accelerator-oriented software (e.g. LASM assembler) has not been able to connect to the MLIR ecosystem.

Therefore, the motivation of this paper is to (1) design a new dialect that can integrate the LASM assembler into the MLIR ecosystem. (2) Design a data layout and format conversion strategy to adapt to the row-by-row data processing mode of vector processors without incurring additional memory overhead. (3) Design an automatic data tiling algorithm and an efficient data transfer mechanism to support convolutions of different sizes and make full use of the computing resources of vector processors. (4) Provide a method to automatically generate kernel vectorization code to improve development efficiency.

3   Overview of VConv

In order to efficiently perform convolution operations on vector accelerators, we propose the sVConv, which is an efficient convolution algorithm designed for vector accelerator hardware based on the MLIR framework. The overview of VConv is shown in Fig. 2.

The architecture design of VConv in the MLIR ecosystem is shown in Fig. 2(a), which is mainly divided into three parts, namely front-end, middle-end, and backend-end. In the front-end, VConv focuses on high-level intermediate representation (hlir) of deep learning model operators. The dialects involved include linalg, onnx, and krnl, which provide high-level abstract representations of convolution operators. At the middle-end, VConv uses MLIR's common core dialects such as affine, vector, memref, and back-end specific IR to implement algorithm logic (alog). This layer is the core of the VConv optimization process. It implements conversions between dialects through defined conversion rules such as "-convert-conv-to-alog" and "-convert-alog-to-lasm". A series of passes are also used for convolution optimization for vector accelerators. These passes are covered in detail in Chap. 5. At the back end, semantic mapping through the lasm dialect generates lasmIR, and lasmIR is finally converted into execution code by the lasm assembler.

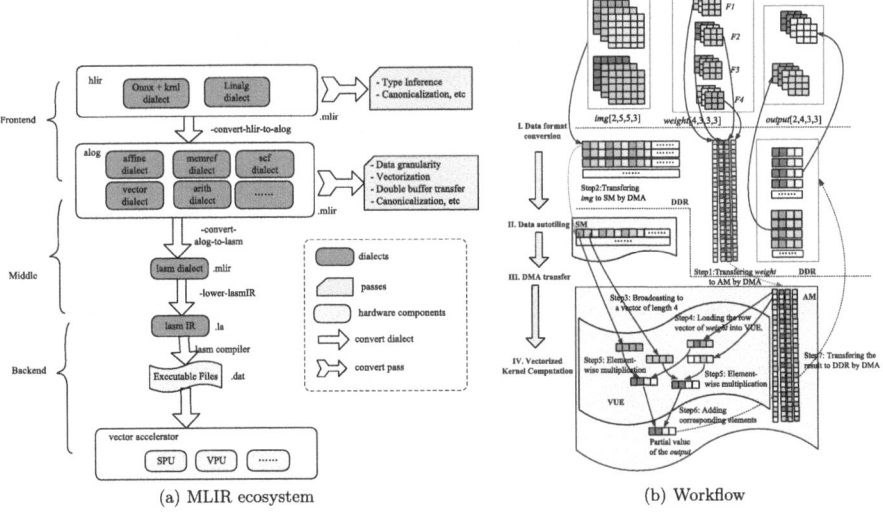

Fig. 2. Overview of VConv.

The compilation process of VConv is shown in Fig. 2(b). It mainly realizes efficient calculation of convolution through passes. Each pass is aimed at a specific calculation optimization goal. The whole process can be divided into 4 stages. In the I stage, is data format conversion. It is implemented through the *convert-hlir-alog* pass, which converts the multi-dimensional tensor into a two-dimensional matrix form according to a specific data arrangement to match the row processing data mode of the vector accelerator. The detailed process is discussed in detail in Sect. 5.1 of the literature. In the II stage, the data is fine-grained through pass, and the data is fine-grained according to the convolution size parameters. Different sizes automatically adapt different segmentation strategies to fit the storage structure of vector accelerators. This is described in detail in Sect. 5.2. In the III stage, the DMA double buffering transmission pass is adopted to reduce the impact of data access on computing performance. The implementation details are covered in Sect. 5.3. In the IV stage, vectorized kernel computation code generation. When compiled, VConv automatically generates vectorized logic code to perform large-scale matrix multiplication calculations. A detailed analysis of this process is included in Sect. 5.4.

4   Lasm Dialect Abstraction

In order to integrate vector accelerators into the MLIR ecosystem, VConv designed the lasm dialect based on the characteristics of vector accelerators and lasm assemblers. The front-end language of Lasm mainly consists of two parts, pseudo-instructions and assembly instructions. The design of the Lasm dialect can be divided into data types, module/function call operations, control operations, calculation operations, memory access operations and others from the perspective of program execution. As shown in Tables 1, the following is a detailed introduction to each category.

Table 1. Lasm dialect cases.

Category	Example
Type of data	*bn, bf, bh, bd*
Function operations	*lasm.main, lasm.func, lasm.ret, lasm.import, lasm.call, lasm.icall*
Calculation operations	*lasm.sadd, lasm.ssub, lasm.smul, lasm.vfmuls32, lasm.vfadds32, lasm.vfmulas32, lasm.sor, lasm.sand, lasm.sshflr*
Control operations	*lasm.if, lasm.loop, lasm.cond_br, lasm.seq, lasm.slt*
Memory access operation	*lasm.load, lasm.store, lasm.dma_start, lasm.svbcast, lasm.smov*
Other operations	*lasm.sect, lasm.usect, lasm.align, lasm.label, lasm.icp, lasm.mdep, lasm.asg, lasm.dreg*

Data types include the bit data type lasm.bn, the 16-bit half-precision type lasm.bh, the 32-bit single-precision floating-point type lasm.bf, and the 64-bit double-precision floating-point type lasm.bd.

Function operations make up the IR structure of lasmIR and are implemented as operations in the lasm dialect. These operations follow a similar design to the built-in dialects.

Computational operations support bitwise, arithmetic, and logical operations. Arithmetic operations are expressed by scalar and vector values. Bitwise and logical operations generally accept scalar values as input.

Control operations are designed to express "if-then-else" and "if" branches and "for" loops.

Memory access operations are mainly used for memory access. For example, lasm.svbcast broadcasts a scalar value to a vector value, lasm.dma_start is used to start DMA data transfer.

Other operations including segment operations and label operations. For example, lasm.sect is used to declare the initialization segment and indicate the storage location of subsequent instructions or data.

The lasm dialect was originally designed as a high-level abstraction of lasmIR to express and manipulate vector calculations more efficiently.

5 Compiling

The compilation process of VConv can be divided into data format conversion, convolution automatic tiling, DMA double buffer transfer and vectorized kernel calculation. These processes are mainly implemented based on MLIR conversion and passes. To realize efficient computation of convolution on vector accelerators and improve the productivity of program development.

5.1 Data Format Conversion

The conversion of data formats is crucial for optimizing computational performance. The traditional optimization method is to convert the convolution product into matrix multiplication, which may generate a lot of redundant data. Moreover, the size of the transformed matrix is small and not suitable for large-scale vector calculations. VConv first designed a data layout strategy that matched the vectorization capabilities of vector processors. Then the multidimensional tensor data structure is transformed into a two-dimensional matrix form to fit the row-by-row data processing mode of the vector processor.

As can be seen from Sect. 2.2, convolutions have different scales. If C, H, or W is used as the vector dimension, data alignment problems may occur. However, most of the values of F are powers of 2, which is more consistent with the vector dimension of the hardware. Therefore, this paper uses the F direction as the vectorization direction and adopts a channel-first data layout method. The convolution kernel is stored in the AM and the image is stored in the SM.

Data format conversion is mainly achieved through the convert-hlir-alog pass. VConv parses the data layout according to the tensor dimension of hlir and converts the format of data that does not conform to the above dimensional rules. First, an index mapping rule is defined using affine mapping (affine_map).

This mapping rule allows us to reorganize the layout of the data, paving the way for data dimension conversion. Then the memref.transpose operation is used to transpose the data dimension. Finally, we apply the memref.collapse_shape operation to convert the four-dimensional tensor into a two-dimensional matrix.

This data layout and data format conversion strategy transforms a large number of inefficient small-scale convolutions into large-scale matrix multiplications. On the other hand, it ensures that all data accesses are performed according to the rows of the matrix. They are very suitable for vector accelerators. It is worth noting that the conversion process does not perform explicit data migration, thus avoiding additional data storage overhead.

5.2   Data Autotiling

The core of the matrix multiplication convolution algorithm is an effective data tiling solution. Its purpose is to minimize the number of data transfers and maximize the utilization of vector processing resources. VConv achieves efficient automatic tiling through compilation. Convolution Automatic Tiling (CAT) is responsible for calculating the size, distribution and scheduling of tiling. The Index Mapping Algorithm (IMA) generates the corresponding loop structure according to the tiling strategy determined by CAT.

In vector accelerators, the efficiency of convolution calculation is mainly affected by the delay slot of floating-point multiply-add (FMAC) instructions and the tail of the vector. The more SNOPs caused by the delay slot, the larger the tail of the vector, and the lower the resource utilization. The known hardware platform parameters include the storage size of SM and AM, respectively M_{sm} and M_{am}, the vector length vl, and the optimal number of delay slot filling p. The convolution parameters include C, H_i, W_i, F, C, H_k, H_k, the data type sizes in bytes is B. The output dimensions are $H_o = \lceil \frac{H_i+2*P-H_k}{S} \rceil + 1$ and $W_o = \lceil \frac{W_i+2*P-W_k}{S} \rceil + 1$.

Assuming that the block sizes transmitted in each iteration are $block_{img}[n, m]$ and $block_w[m, f]$, the value ranges of n, m, and f are shown in formula (2).

$$n \in \{1, 2, ..., H_o * W_o\}, f \in \{1, 2, ..., \min(F, vl)\}, m \in \{1, 2, ..., H_k * W_k * C\} \quad (2)$$

Since the size of $block_{img}[n, m]$ and $block_w[m, f]$ cannot be larger than the storage size of AM and SM, the constraint of the following formula (3) needs to be satisfied.

$$\begin{cases} 0 < nm < \frac{M_{sm}}{2*B} \\ 0 < mf < \frac{M_{am}-nf*B}{2*B} \end{cases} \quad (3)$$

The number of empty beats generated by each iteration delay slot is $y_1 = n\%p$, and the wasted vector computing resources is $y_2 = f\%vl$. The numbers of transmission of img and $weight$ is shown in formulas (4) and (5). The total number of cycles y_5 is shown in formula (6).

$$y_3 = \frac{H_o * W_o * H_k * W_k * C}{n * m} \tag{4}$$

$$y_4 = \frac{F * H_k * W_k * C}{m * f} \tag{5}$$

$$y_5 = \frac{H_o * W_o * F}{f * \frac{n}{(\frac{H_k * W_k * C}{m})}} = \frac{H_o * W_o * F * H_k * W_k * C}{n * m * f} \tag{6}$$

The cost model is shown in formula. (7). The smaller Y is, the smaller the memory access overhead and wasted computing resources are.

$$Y(n, m, f) = y_5 * (y_1 + y_2) + y_3 + y_4 \tag{7}$$

Therefore, our goal is to find a solution (n,m,f) that minimizes the objective function Y. That is, to solve the following optimization issue (8). This paper uses the genetic algorithm (GA) to solve the optimization issue.

$$\min_{n,m,f} Y(n, m, f) \tag{8}$$

After getting the values of n, m, and f, IMA starts to create the circular index mapping rule $forMaps$ (shown as in Algorithm 2). The pseudo-code of the IMA algorithm is shown in Algorithm 1. The input is the convolution scale and the tiling parameters. The output is the circular index mapping $forMaps$.

Algorithm 1: IMA algorithm

Input: N,C,H_i,W_i,F,C,H_k,H_k, n, m, f;
Output: $forMaps$;
1 **if** $(m \geq H_k * W_k * C)$ **then**
2   apply $index\_map$ ① to $forMaps$;
3 **if** $(W_k * C \leq m < H_k * W_k * C)$ **then**
4   apply $index\_map$ ② to $forMaps$;
5 **if** $(m < W_k * C)$ **then**
6   apply $index\_map$ ③ to $forMaps$;
7 output $forMaps$;

Algorithm 2: $forMaps$

1 **for** $i_1 == 0$ to F step f **do**
2   **for** $i_2 == 0$ to H_o step 1 **do**
3   **for** $i_3 == 0$ to W_o step n **do**
4   ①
5 **for** $i_1 == 0$ to F step f **do**
6   **for** $i_2 == 0$ to H_k step 1 **do**
7   **for** $i_3 == 0$ to H_o step 1 **do**
8   **for** $i_4 == 0$ to W_o step n **do**
9   ②
10 **for** $i_1 == 0$ to F step f **do**
11   **for** $i_2 == 0$ to H_k step 1 **do**
12   **for** $i_3 == 0$ to W_k step 1 **do**
13   **for** $i_4 == 0$ to H_o step 1 **do**
14   **for** $i_5 == 0$ to W_o step n **do**
15   ③

The CAT implements automatic tiling of data according to hardware configuration and convolution size to reduce the engineering effort of data segmentation. At the same time, the IMA algorithm defines complex index mapping rules by the *index_map* of the affine dialect. The tiled data will be transmitted to AM or SM by the *index_map* operation to provide the necessary data support for the subsequent vectorization calculation.

5.3 DMA Transfer Strategy

In order to reduce the overhead of data moving delay and avoid the wait between data transmission and computation, this paper proposes a double buffering pass. We use memref.alloc to design two buffers for input data or weight data in SM and AM, respectively. Between computation and data transfer, allowing one buffer to wait for data to be processed while another buffer can be used for new data transfers to hide latency and improve computation performance.

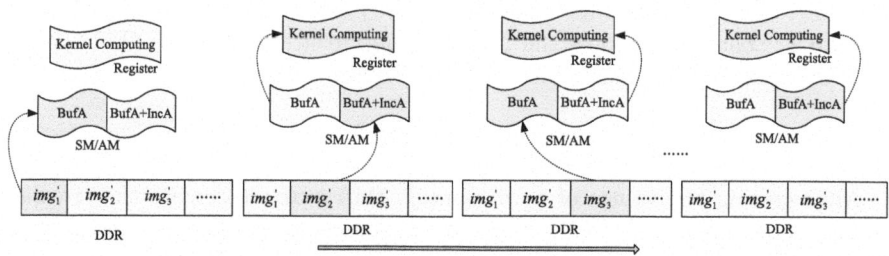

Fig. 3. Double buffering transfer process of *img*.

The pseudo code of the double buffering double buffering algorithm is shown in Algorithm 3, and the transmission process is shown in Fig. 3. Assuming that $m = H_k * W_k * C$. The input is the two-dimensional image $img[H_i * W_i * C]$ and the convolution kernel $weight[H_k * W_k * C, F]$ after tiling. The output also is a two-dimensional tensor $output[H_o * W_o, F]$. In step 1, *memref.alloc* is used to apply for five temporary memory blocks, namely $BufA$, $IncA$, $BufC$, $IncC$, $BufB$. Parameters are initialized in step 2. In step 3 to step 16, the calculation and data transmission are separated through iteration, where the loop structure is obtained according to $forMaps$ in Sect. 5.3. In step 17, returning the result $output[N * H_o * W_o, F]$.

Algorithm 3: Double buffering algorithm

Input: $img[H_i * W_i * C]$, $weight[H_k * W_k * C, F]$;

Output: $output[N * H_o * W_o, F]$;

1 memref.alloc buffers: $BufA$, $IncA$, $BufC$, $IncC$, $BufB$;

2 Initializating parameters: $j = 0$;

3 **for** i_1 *to* F *step* vl **do**

4   apply dma_start $weight[, *vl : (i_1 + 1) * vl]$ to $BufB$;

5   apply dma_wait ;

6     $img[H_i * W_i * C]$ transfor to $img'[H_o * W_o, H_k * W_k * C]$;

7   **for** i_3 *to* H_o *step* 1 **do**

8   **for** i_4 *to* W_o *step* $2n$ **do**

9             $i = index\_map(i_2 * i_3 * i_4 + i_3 * i_4 + i_4)$;

10   apply dma_start $img'[i : (i + n - 1),]$ to $BufA + (j\&1) * IncA$;

11   apply dma_wait ;

12   call $conv\_kernel(BufA + (j\&1) * IncA, BufB)$ to $BufC+(j\&1) * IncC$;

13   apply dma_start $img'[(i + n) : (i + 2n - 1),]$ to $BufA+((j+1)\&1) * IncA$; apply dma_wait ;

14   apply dma_start $BufC + (j\&1) * IncC$ to $output[i : (i + n - 1), i_1 * vl : (i_1 + 1) * vl]$;

15   apply dma_wait ;

16   j=j+1 ;

17 return $output$;

Algorithm 4: VKCG algorithm

Input: $hlir.mlir$, vl;

Output: $alog.mlir$;

1 Reading and parsing the $hlir.mlir$ file;

2 Gettting the location loc and context ctx of the $conv\_kernel$ operation, and creating the $rewriter$;

3 Defining data types of $f32$ and $vectorTy32$;

4 Retrieving the img, $weight$ and $output$ from the $conv\_kernel$ operation;

5 Getting the dimensions of $weight$ and $output$ by using $memref::DimOp$;

6 Creating a loop using $AffineMap$ and $affine::buildAffineLoopNest$;

7   Loading the $weightValue$;

8   Broadcasting the $weightValue$ to $weightVector$;

9   Loading the $imgVector$ and $outputVector$;

10   Performing the FMA operation to obtain the $resultVector$;

11   Storing the $resultVector$ into the $output$;

12 Performing all modifications using the $rewriter$;

13 Writing the modified codes into $alog.mlir$;

14 Return $alog.mlir$.

5.4 Vectorized Kernel Computation

In order to give full play to the potential of the functional computing unit of the vector accelerator and reduce the engineering effort of manual vectorization, this paper proposes a vectorized kernel code generation algorithm (VKCG). VKCG realizes automatic vectorization, data is effectively mapped to the physical memory of the vector accelerator and the computing power of the VPU is fully utilized.

The vectorized kernel computation is performed after tiling data and transferring DMA. The seven steps of vectorized computing logic are shown in Fig. 2(b). The pseudo code of the VKCG algorithm is shown in Algorithm 4. The input is the high-level intermediate representation file *hlir.mlir* and the vector length *vl*, and the output is the algorithm logic intermediate code file *alog.mlir*. In step 1, reading and parsing *hlir.mlir*. In step 2, get the location *loc* and context *ctx* of the *conv_kernel* operation, and create a *rewriter* at the same time. In steps 3 to 4, define the data types and get the *conv_kernel* operation parameters, such as *img*, *weight*, and *output*. In step 5, use *memref::DimOp* to get the dimensions of *weight* and *output*. In step 6, use *AffineMap* and *affine::buildAffineLoopNest* to create the loop. In steps 7–10, create the loop body vector calculation flow. In steps 7 to 8, first load the *weightValue* and broadcast it as the vector *weightVector*. In step 9, load *imgVector* and *outputVector*. In steps 10 to 11, the vector multiplication plus *FMA* operation is performed and the result is stored in the *output*. In step 12, use *rewriter* to make all modifications. In steps 13 to 14, write the modified code to *alog.mlir* and return it.

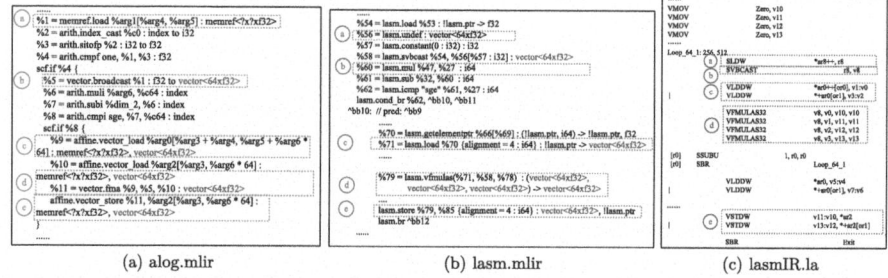

(a) alog.mlir   (b) lasm.mlir   (c) lasmIR.la

Fig. 4. Intermediate pseudocodes after vectorization ($vl = 64$).

The Fig. 4 shows three intermediate codes after vectorization. The vector length is 64. The Fig. 4(a) shows alog.mlir expressed in the MLIR built-in dialects. The Fig. 4(b) shows lasm.mlir expressed in the LASM dialect, which is translated from alog.mlir. Figure 4(c) shows the lasmIR intermediate code translated from lasm.mlir. It can be seen from these three figures that there is a one-to-one correspondence between the conversions of dialects, including operations such as scalar load ⓐ, scalar broadcast ⓑ, vector load ⓒ, vector multiplication and addition ⓓ, vector store ⓔ and so on.

The vectorized kernel computing code generation technology improves the productivity of manual vectorization. At the same time, the computational efficiency of convolution is improved by making full use of the wide vector computing resources of the vector accelerator.

6 Evaluation

6.1 Experimental Setup

Experiment platforms. All experiments were conducted on FT-Matrix32 (named as computer-1) and a laptop equipped with NVIDIA RTX 2050 (named as computer-2). The computer-1 is a high-performance vector processor independently developed by the National University of Defense Technology. Its AM capacity is 512 KB, SM size is 32 KB, floating-point computing performance peak is 512 GFLOPS, and power consumption is from 12 W to 16 W. For the hardware architecture of computer-1, the parameters are configured as follows: $vl = 64$, $p = 6$. The computer-2 has 4 GB of video memory and a peak performance of 5100 GFLOPS, with a power consumption from 30 W to 45 W.

Benchmark Data. In order to evaluate the universality of the method on convolution kernels of different sizes, this paper uses the controlled variable method to design experiments based on a set of commonly used convolution scales ($C=256$, $H_i=W_i=256$, $F=256$, $H_k=W_k=3$, $P=S=1$). The experimental variables include C, F, and H_k (or W_k, $H_k=W_k$, collectively referred to as K in the following text). In addition, the experiment has also been extended to convolution operators in AlexNet, VGG16, YOLOv5s, ResNet50, and GoogleNet.

Comparison Methods and Evaluation Indicators. In order to comprehensively evaluate the performance of the target code generated by the VConv compiler in terms of computational efficiency and energy efficiency. This paper selects three advanced technologies as comparison benchmarks, namely TVM, AutoTVM and OnnxRuntime. Since these methods are specially optimized for GPUs, they are chosen to be experimentally operated on computer-2. At the same time, this paper adopts the evaluation indicators of execution time (T), computational efficiency and energy efficiency ratio (EER). Computational efficiency reflects the ratio of actual performance to its peak performance. Its mathematical symbolic expression is shown in Eq. (9).

$$Efficiency = \frac{Performance_{actual}}{Performance_{peak}} \tag{9}$$

where $Performance_{actual}$ indicates the actual performance and $Performance_{actual} = \frac{C}{T}$, C represents the total floating point calculation amount. Besides, $Performance_{peak}$ indicates the peak performance value.

Energy Efficiency Ratio (EER) refers to the number of floating point operations actually performed per unit of electrical energy consumed. It is an important indicator for measuring energy efficiency. The larger the EER, the higher the energy efficiency. Its mathematical expression is shown in Equation (10), where P represents the power of the target processor.

$$EER = \frac{Performance_{actual}}{P} \tag{10}$$

6.2   Experimental Comparison

Table 2 shows the selected $forMaps$ and the corresponding execution time and computational efficiency of VConv under different F, different C and different K. It can be seen from the table that $forMaps$ is mainly affected by C and K. As C and K increase, $forMaps$ selects more loop levels. However, the computational efficiency of the VConv does not change with the change in the computational scale. The convolution computation efficiency at other scales is between 69.57% and 82.22% except when $C=3$. Therefore, VConv has high computational efficiency for convolutions of different scales in vector processors.

Figure 5 shows the computational efficiency and energy efficiency of VConv, TVM, AutoTVM and OnnxRuntime methods for convolutions of different scales and various classic neural network models. Among them, Fig. 5(a) shows the test results of F from 32 to 2048. It can be seen from the figure that VConv has the highest computational efficiency, and the OnnxRuntime method has the lowest. AutoTVM has the highest energy efficiency, followed by VConv. In addition, the TVM method is greatly affected by F, and the other three methods do not change much. The computational efficiency of TVM, AutoTVM, OnnxRuntime and VConv is 13.78% to 32.56%, 27.97% to 34.04%, and 69.57% to 82.31% respectively. The energy efficiency ratio ranges are 17.56 to 41.51 GFLOPS/W, 35.66 to 43.40 GFLOPS/W, 8.90 to 10.43 GFLOPS/W, and 25.44 to 29.81 GFLOPS/W. Therefore, VConv is suitable for convolution calculations at different F scales.

Figure 5(b) shows the results of C from 3 to 1024. It can be seen from the figure that the computational efficiency of VConv is higher than that of the other three methods except when $C=3$, and OnnxRuntime is the lowest. As C increases, the computational efficiency and energy efficiency of these four methods do not change significantly. Therefore, VConv is suitable for convolution calculations at different C scales.

Figure 5(c) shows the results of K from 1 to 11. As can be seen from the figure, the computational efficiency and energy efficiency ratio of VConv are the highest except when $K=3$. TVM and AutoTVM are relatively efficient only when $K=3$. However, when $K¿3$, as K increases, their computational efficiency and energy efficiency ratio decrease. The efficiency and EER of VConv and OnnxRuntime methods do not change significantly. Therefore, the VConv is suitable for convolution calculations at different K scales.

Figure 6 shows the computational efficiency and energy efficiency of the four methods in AlexNet, GoogleNet, VGG16, YOLOv5s and ResNet50 convolution. As can be seen from the figure, the computational efficiency and energy efficiency of VConv are mostly higher thans the other three methods. In the AlexNet model, the average computational efficiency of TVM, AutoTVM, OnnxRuntime and VConv (the same order below) are 7.54%, 8.11%, 10.95%, 54.22%, and the average energy efficiency is 9.61 GFLOPS/W,

10.34 GFLOPS/W, 6.94 GFLOPS/W, 19.83 GFLOPS/W, respectively. In the VGG16 model, the average computational efficiency is 10.39%, 6.16%, 17.91%, 66.58%, respectively. The average energy efficiency ratios are 13.25 GFLOPS/W, 7.85 GFLOPS/W, 8.52 GFLOPS/W, and 24.35 GFLOPS/W, respectively. In the YOLOv5s model, the average computational efficiency is 2.3%, 2.18%, 4.03%, and 61.28%, respectively; the average energy efficiency ratios are 2.93 GFLOPS/W, 2.78 GFLOPS/W, 7.84 GFLOPS/W, and 22.41 GFLOPS/W, respectively. In the GoogleNet model, the average computational efficiency is 1.15%, 1.11%, 2.07%, and 35.33%, respectively; the average energy efficiency ratios are 1.46 GFLOPS/W, 1.41 GFLOPS/W, 4.52 GFLOPS/W, and 12.92 GFLOPS/W, respectively. In the ResNet50 model, the average computing efficiency is 2.01%, 1.78%, 3.9%, 46.29% respectively; the average energy efficiency ratio is 2.56 GFLOPS/W, 2.27 GFLOPS/W, 5.93 GFLOPS/W, 16.93 GFLOPS/W respectively. Therefore, VConv also has high efficiency and EER in computing the convolution operator in the classic neural network model.

Table 2. The time and efficiency of different F, C and K

id	C	H_i	W_i	F	K	forMaps	Time(ms)	Efficiency	id	C	H_i	W_i	F	K	forMaps	Time(ms)	Efficiency	id	C	H_i	W_i	F	K	forMaps	Time(ms)	Efficiency
1	256	224	224	32	3	①	20.77	69.57%	8	3	224	224	256	3	①	9.99	13.57%	15	256	224	224	256	1	–	18.59	70.35%
2	256	224	224	64	3	②	38.42	75.23%	9	32	224	224	256	3	①	20.24	71.40%	16	256	224	224	256	3	②	144.32	80.10%
3	256	224	224	128	3	②	73.57	78.56%	10	64	224	224	256	3	①	35.46	81.50%	17	256	224	224	256	5	②	409.88	76.95%
4	256	224	224	256	3	②	144.33	80.10%	11	128	224	224	256	3	①	72.21	80.05%	18	256	224	224	256	7	②	738.42	82.22%
5	256	224	224	512	3	②	285.58	80.96%	12	256	224	224	256	3	②	144.33	80.10%	19	256	224	224	256	9	③	1280.25	76.97%
6	256	224	224	1024	3	②	568.19	81.38%	13	512	224	224	256	3	②	286.70	80.65%	20	256	224	224	256	11	③	1836.28	78.70%
7	256	224	224	2048	3	②	1134.65	81.51%	14	1024	224	224	256	3	③	576.08	80.27%									

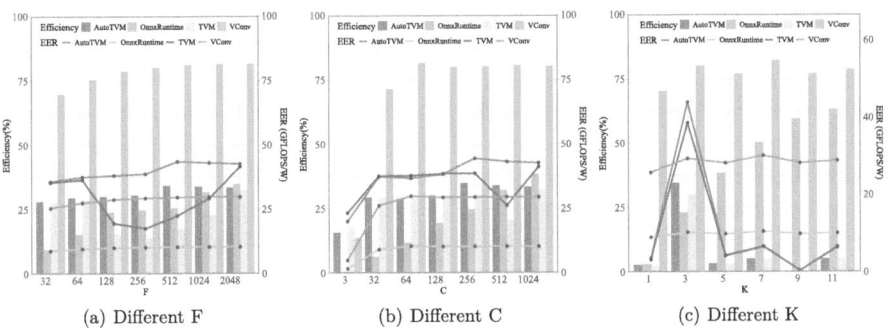

(a) Different F   (b) Different C   (c) Different K

Fig. 5. The efficiency and EER of convolutions of different sizes.

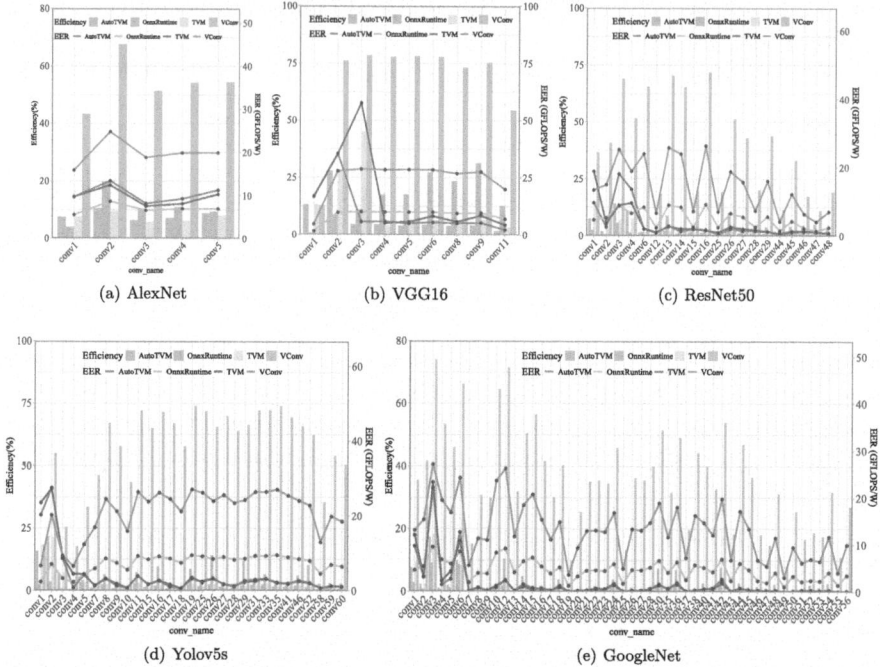

Fig. 6. The efficiency and *EER* of classic neural network models.

6.3   Conclusion

In this paper, we proposed an automated tiling convolution algorithm with high performance to deploy convolutional applications, which is designed for multi-core vector accelerators based on MLIR. Experimental results show that the VConv has stronger universality under convolutions of different sizes compared with other methods. At the same time, it also has higher computational efficiency and energy efficiency. Finally, we believe that the Vconv algorithm can provide strong technical support for the efficient deployment of machine learning models in vector accelerators.

Acknowledgments. We would like to thank the NPC reviewers for their insightful feedback. This work was supported by the NUDT Research Project (No.23-ZZCX-JDZ-11).

Disclosure of Interests. The authors have no competing interests to declare that are relevant to the content of this article.

References

1. Chen, T., et al.: {TVM}: an automated {End-to-End} optimizing compiler for deep learning. In: 13th USENIX Symposium on Operating Systems Design and Implementation (OSDI 2018), pp. 578–594 (2018)
2. Chetlur, S., et al.: cudnn: efficient primitives for deep learning. arXiv preprint arXiv:1410.0759 (2014)
3. Ferrari, V., et al.: Advancing direct convolution using convolution slicing optimization and isa extensions. ACM Trans. Arch. Code Optim. **20**(4), 1–26 (2023)
4. Hao, R., et al.: Towards effective depthwise convolutions on armv8 architecture. arXiv preprint arXiv:2206.12124 (2022)
5. He, K., Zhang, X., Ren, S., Sun, J.: Deep residual learning for image recognition. In: Proceedings of the IEEE Conference on Computer Vision and Pattern Recognition, pp. 770–778 (2016)
6. Heide, F., Heidrich, W., Wetzstein, G.: Fast and flexible convolutional sparse coding. In: Proceedings of the IEEE Conference on Computer Vision and Pattern Recognition, pp. 5135–5143 (2015)
7. Huang, X., Wang, Q., Lu, S., Hao, R., Mei, S., Liu, J.: Evaluating fft-based algorithms for strided convolutions on armv8 architectures? ACM SIGMETRICS Perf. Eval. Rev. **49**(3), 28–29 (2022)
8. Jin, T., et al.: Compiling onnx neural network models using mlir. arXiv preprint arXiv:2008.08272 (2020)
9. Jocher, G., et al.: ultralytics/yolov5: v6. 2-yolov5 classification models, apple m1, reproducibility, clearml and deci.ai integrations. Zenodo (2022)
10. Krizhevsky, A.: One weird trick for parallelizing convolutional neural networks. arXiv preprint arXiv:1404.5997 (2014)
11. Krizhevsky, A., Sutskever, I., Hinton, G.E.: Imagenet classification with deep convolutional neural networks. Adv. Neural Inf. Process. Syst. **25** (2012)
12. Lattner, C., et al.: Mlir: Scaling compiler infrastructure for domain specific computation. In: 2021 IEEE/ACM International Symposium on Code Generation and Optimization (CGO), pp. 2–14. IEEE (2021)
13. Liu, Z., Xiao, X., Li, C., Ma, S., Rangyu, D.: Optimizing convolutional neural networks on multi-core vector accelerator. Parallel Comput. **112**, 102945 (2022)
14. Lu, K., et al.: Mt-3000: a heterogeneous multi-zone processor for hpc. CCF Trans. High Perfor. Comput. **4**(2), 150–164 (2022)
15. Microsoft: Onnx runtime (2019). https://github.com/microsoft/onnxruntime
16. Qiu, C., Wu, J., Ren, H., Zhang, Z.: Optimization of tensor operation in compiler. In: International Conference on Communications and Networking in China, pp. 207–219. Springer, Heidelberg (2022)
17. da Silva, M.C., Sousa, L., Paulino, N., Bispo, J.: A dsl and mlir dialect for streaming and vectorisation. In: International Symposium on Applied Reconfigurable Computing, pp. 181–190. Springer, Heidelberg (2024). https://doi.org/10.1007/978-3-031-55673-9_13
18. Simonyan, K., Zisserman, A.: Very deep convolutional networks for large-scale image recognition. arXiv preprint arXiv:1409.1556 (2014)
19. Szegedy, C., et al.: Going deeper with convolutions. In: Proceedings of the IEEE Conference on Computer Vision and Pattern Recognition, pp. 1–9 (2015)
20. Wang, Q., Mei, S., Liu, J., Gong, C.: Parallel convolution algorithm using implicit matrix multiplication on multi-core cpus. In: 2019 International Joint Conference on Neural Networks (ijcnn), pp. 1–7. IEEE (2019)

21. Xu, J., et al.: Parallel optimization of convolution algorithm for multi-core digital signal processing. J. Natl. Univ. Defense Technol./Guofang Keji Daxue Xuebao **46**(1) (2024)
22. Zhang, H., Xing, M., Wu, Y., Zhao, C.: Compiler technologies in deep learning co-design: a survey. Intell. Comput. **2**, 0040 (2023)
23. Zhong, H., Liu, Z.: Long-life sensitive modulo scheduling with adaptive loop expansion. In: 2022 IEEE 28th International Conference on Parallel and Distributed Systems (ICPADS), pp. 530–537. IEEE (2023)

Novel Memory and Storage Systems

ACH-Code: An Efficient Erasure Code to Reduce Average Repair Cost in Cloud Storage Systems of Multiple Availability Zones

Yucheng Kang, Jiawei Li[✉], Chenming Chang, Keqiang Li, Yupeng Chen, and Yi Zhang

China Telecom eSurfing Cloud, Beijing, China
lijiawei1@chinatelecom.cn

Abstract. In modern cloud storage systems, data is routinely dispersed across distinct availability zones (AZ) to ensure resilience and accessibility. Erasure codes, known for their high reliability and low storage overhead, are preferred over replication. However, the data recovery procedure by erasure codes would suffer from a large amount of data transfer among multiple network-separated storage devices. Although a number of new erasure codes have been proposed to minimize the repair costs, the average repair cost remains high in multi-AZ environments due to the expensive consumption of bandwidth and high latency between availability zones.

To address this problem, we propose AZ-Clay-Hitchhiker-Code (ACH-Code), a novel erasure code tailored for multi-AZ cloud storage systems. By integrating the strengths of Clay code and Hitchhiker code, ACH-Code effectively reduces data transmission across availability zones during repairs. We conduct rigorous mathematical analysis, implement the ACH plugin in Ceph, and evaluate its performance through extensive experiments. Results indicate that ACH-Code achieves a 92.5% reduction in average repair cost compared to AZ-Code and a remarkable 97.5% decrease compared to traditional erasure codes, significantly enhancing the efficiency and cost-effectiveness of data recovery in multi-AZ environments.

Keywords: Erasure Code · Availability Zone · Repair

1 Introduction

In a cloud storage system, providing fault tolerance at the availability zone level is a fundamental capability that ensures the continued operation of the system, even in the face of hardware or software faults, errors, or failures. This capability enhances the system's resilience, allowing it to withstand localized disruptions without compromising the overall availability and accessibility of stored data.

ⓒ IFIP International Federation for Information Processing 2025
Published by Springer Nature Switzerland AG 2025
X. Chen et al. (Eds.): NPC 2024, LNCS 15527, pp. 193–206, 2025.
https://doi.org/10.1007/978-981-96-2830-8_15

An availability zone is a geographic area within the same service region where power and network infrastructure are independent of each other. This design enables cloud storage systems to have stronger fault tolerance. Erasure codes and replication are two of the most common fault tolerance approaches in multi-AZ cloud storage systems. Replication refers to the process of writing one copy of data to multiple storage nodes in a distributed system. In comparison, erasure codes encode the original data to provide redundancy and store the data along with the redundancy to achieve fault tolerance. Many cloud storage systems such as Windows Azure Storage (WAS) [2] and Zettabyte Object Storage (ZOS) in eSurfing Cloud [1] apply erasure codes to provide fault tolerance capabilities across multiple availability zones. Erasure codes offer significantly higher reliability with much lower storage overhead. In the past decades, many erasure codes have been proposed: traditional erasure codes such as RS [9] and LRC [5], some optimized erasure codes such as RGRC [17], optional-LRC [10] and Hitchhiker [8], some Minimum Storage Regenerating (MSR) [3] erasure codes such as Butterfly [6] and Clay [11], and some multiple layers erasure codes such as ECWide [4], XHR-Code [15], Hybrid-RC [16] and AZ-Code [13].

However, these existing erasure codes have some drawbacks in multi-AZ cloud storage systems. Firstly, traditional erasure codes are widely used but resource-intensive for chunk failure repair. Secondly, some optimized erasure codes add additional parity chunks or computations to reduce the cost of repairing single chunk failures, but the repairing efficiency remains low. Thirdly, although MSR erasure codes require minimal resources for chunk repair, they still require a lot of cross-AZ data transfers for chunk repair in multi-AZ environments. Fourthly, although some multi-level erasure codes have been designed to improve data distribution, they do not fully consider the overall recovery efficiency.

To address the above problems, in this paper, we propose a novel erasure code called ACH-Code, which combines the advantages of Clay code and Hitchhiker code. It encodes local parity chunks with both data chunks and global parity chunks within each availability zone. Consequently, ACH-Code enhances the faulty chunk repair efficiency of multi-AZ cloud storage systems without increasing storage overhead, resulting in a significant reduction in cross-AZ data transmission and average repair cost during the repair process.

2   Background and Motivation

To simplify our description, we summarize the notation of this paper in Table 1.

Table 1. Symbols used in this paper

Symbols	Description
n	the number of all chunks in a stripe
k	the number of data chunks in a stripe
m	the number of parity chunks in a stripe
g	the number of global parity chunks in a stripe
z	the number of availability zones (the group of ACH-Code)
p	the number of local parity chunks in a local group
g_p	the number of global parity chunks without XOR operations
D	the data chunk
Q	the global parity chunk in ACH-Code
G	the global parity chunk in other erasure codes
P	the local parity chunk in ACH-Code

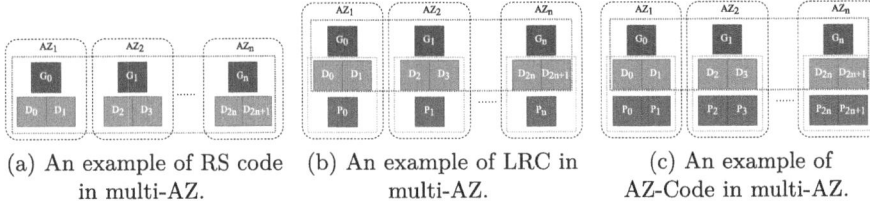

(a) An example of RS code in multi-AZ.   (b) An example of LRC in multi-AZ.   (c) An example of AZ-Code in multi-AZ.

Fig. 1. Example of RS code, LRC and AZ-Code in multi-AZ.

2.1 Existing Erasure Codes in Multi-AZ Cloud Storage Systems

Traditional Code. RS code and LRC are the most traditional erasure codes. RS code utilizes polynomial operations in mathematics to achieve redundant encoding of data. It generates m parity chunks based on k data chunks, ensuring that the original data can be recovered through decoding algorithms as long as any k out of the total $k + m$ data chunks are intact. An example of RS code applied in multi-AZ is shown in Fig. 1(a). LRC divides parity chunks into global parity chunks and local parity chunks, enabling grouped calculations during data recovery. This approach confines the scope of failure recovery within individual groups, thereby reducing data transmission during the recovery process. An example of LRC applied in multi-AZ is shown in Fig. 1(b).

MSR Code. MSR code is a type of regenerating code. Regenerating codes aim to decrease the amount of data transferred from each of the remaining chunks by contacting more chunks during the repair process. When a regenerating code strive to minimize repair traffic without adding any extra storage overhead, we say that the code is a MSR code. The minimum number of surviving chunks in a stripe that can be used to repair the single faulty chunk is $(m+k-1)/m$. Clay Code is an implementation of MSR code, which realizes efficient recovery after data loss by means of coupled-layer and linear combination techniques.

AZ-Code. AZ-Code provides zone-level erasure codes with high fault tolerance in cloud storage systems. It employs a specific MSR code to generate local parity chunks, and utilizes RS code to generate global parity chunks. AZ-Code divides the k data chunks into z availability zones, with k/z data chunks in each availability zone. Generate p local parity chunks for each availability zone by MSR code method and generate g global parity chunks for all k data chunks by RS code. Let n denote the total number of chunks, thus $n = k + z*p + g$. Compared to traditional erasure code, AZ-Code can save recovery bandwidth. An example of AZ-Code applied in multi-AZ is shown in Fig. 1(c).

2.2   Cross-AZ Repair Problem

In multi-AZ cloud storage systems, extensive communication between remote nodes is required. However, the network latency between availability zones is inevitably high due to geographic location and network architecture [14]. When repairing a faulty chunk, multiple chunks distributed across different availability zones need to be transferred, necessitating multiple rounds of remote network communication. This results in poor performance in faulty chunk repair, slowing down data repair speed, and ultimately compromising the overall system stability. Consequently, minimizing the cost of faulty chunk repair emerges as a crucial research problem.

Existing erasure codes repair methods exhibit various drawbacks in multi-AZ environments. In RS codes, any chunk failure requires a minimum of k surviving chunks for repair, which impacts the performance of chunk repair. Although MSR codes can decrease the overall number of data transfers needed for the recovery of individual chunks, they are still unable to eliminate cross-AZ data transfers. LRC codes can perform data chunk repairs locally, but for the single data chunk failure, all the data within the group is still required. AZ-Code has been proposed to be applied in multi-AZ environments, which can reduce the repair cost of the single data chunk. However, repair for global parity chunks still requires cross-AZ data transfer, resulting in poor average repair cost performance.

Table 2. Comparisons among various erasure codes (DT: Data Transfer, RC: Repair Cost, SCR: Single Chunk Repair, DCR: Double Chunks Repair, MCR: Multiple Chunks Repair)

Name	Reliability	Storage Efficiency	Cross-AZ DT For SCR	Cross-AZ DT For DCR	Avg. RC For SCR	Avg. RC For MCR
RS	high	high	high	high	high	high
LRC	high	low	medium	high	medium	high
AZ-Code	high	low	medium	medium	medium	high
ACH-Code	high	low	low	low	low	high

2.3 Motivation

As demonstrated in Sect. 2.2, the current erasure codes exhibit several limitations in multi-AZ environments. In Table 2, we provide a summary and comparison of erasure codes in multi-AZ environments. In this paper, we propose a new erasure code called ACH-Code, which, in multi-AZ cloud storage systems, enables the grouping of both data chunks and global parity chunks by availability zones, along with the generation of local parity chunks. This unique design confines the repair of any faulty chunk solely within its availability zone, eliminating the need for cross-AZ data transmission. Consequently, the efficiency of faulty chunk repair is significantly enhanced. Furthermore, ACH-Code integrates the strengths of both Clay code and Hitchhiker code in the context of faulty chunk repair, resulting in a further reduction in the total amount of data required for the repair process.

3 ACH-Code

3.1 Overview of ACH-Code

The efficiency of faulty chunk repair is pivotal in determining the overall performance of the erasure code storage system. However, existing erasure codes exhibit poor repair performance in multi-AZ environments due to the necessity of multi-rounds network communications. To enhance the repair performance of multi-AZ cloud storage systems, we propose ACH-Code, which combines two different erasure codes (i.e., Hitchhiker code [8] and Clay code [11]) to help us reduce the cost of chunk repairing. More specifically, in the design of ACH-Code, Hitchhiker code employs a novel substripe structure, which reduces the cost of chunk repair. Consequently, we utilize the Hitchhiker code to generate global parity chunks. Clay code adopts the coupled-layer technique, minimizing the repair bandwidth. Therefore, we employ the Clay code to generate local parity chunks. For the sake of simplicity in presentation, we denote ACH-Code using the notation $ACH(k, g, z, p)$, as exemplified in Fig. 2. In this notation, the data within a stripe is partitioned into k data chunks, denoted by D. These k data

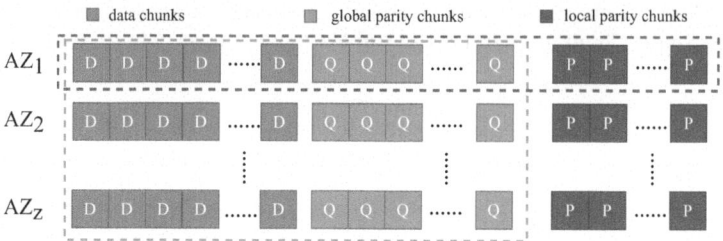

Fig. 2. Overview of $ACH(k, g, z, p)$ in multiple availability zones. Global parity chunks are generated by the Hitchhiker code from all data chunks. Local parity chunks are generated by the Clay code from data chunks and global parity chunks within an availability zone.

chunks are then encoded using the Hitchhiker code to generate g global parity chunks, represented by Q. Subsequently, all chunks are partitioned into z groups, each of which is distributed in a separate availability zone, with each group containing $(k + g)/z$ chunks. Within each group, the Clay code is applied to generate p local parity chunks, denoted by P.

3.2   Hitchhiker Code Layer

In order to tolerate AZ-level faults, we use Hitchhiker code to construct global parity chunks. Hitchhiker code and RS code share the same fault tolerance capability, yet Hitchhiker code consumes less resources for repair compared to RS codes. The Hitchhiker code layer construction of $ACH(12, 6, 3, 2)$ is shown in Fig. 3, which comprises the following steps. Firstly, the stripe is partitioned into two parts, denoted as substripe A and substripe B, respectively. RS encoding calculations are performed on both substripe A and substripe B, generating g global parity chunks for each substripe. Secondly, the k data chunks of substripe A are evenly partitioned into $g - g_p$ groups, and each group of data chunks undergoes XOR operations with the corresponding $g - g_p$ parity chunks generated by substripe B. The resulting $g - g_p$ parity chunks, along with the remaining g_p parity chunks that have not undergone XOR operations, serve as the global parity chunks for substripe B. Finally, substripe A and substripe B are merged to form the global parity chunks of Hitchhiker code. After encoding, the data chunks yield g global parity chunks, and the $k + g$ chunks are evenly partitioned into z groups. This encoding method make substripe B decoding single chunk require only half of $g - g_p$ chunks.

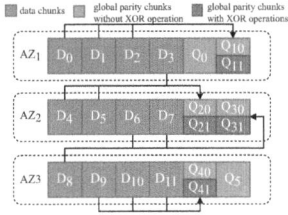
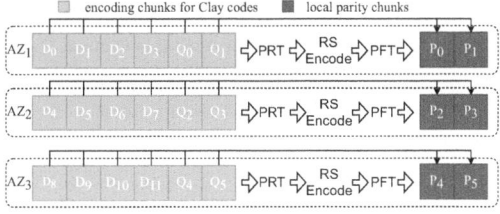

Fig. 3. The Hitchhiker code layer construction of $ACH(12,6,3,2)$.

Fig. 4. The Clay code layer construction of $ACH(12,6,3,2)$.

3.3 Clay Code Layer

To minimize repair costs, we select the Clay code, which exhibits optimal performance in single chunk repairs. The Clay layer construction of $ACH(12,6,3,2)$ is shown in Fig. 4, which encompasses the following steps. Firstly, the data chunk is partitioned into multiple smaller sub-chunks and layered. Secondly, the uncoupled code is calculated using the pairwise reverse transformation (PRT) method. Thirdly, the RS code is computed on the uncoupled code to generate the temporary parity chunk. Finally, the temporary parity chunk is converted into the final local parity chunk using the pairwise forward transformation (PFT) method. Each availability zone is calculated to obtain p parity chunks. This encoding method makes any single chunk decoding require only half of $(k+g)/z+p-1$ chunks in same availability zone.

3.4 Encoding with ACH-Code

The encoding process of $ACH(12,6,3,2)$ is shown in Fig. 5. We summarize the encoding process into the following steps.

(1) Determine the encoding parameters including k, m, g, p, z, and g_p. z is determined based on the number of availability zones. Only when k and m satisfy $(k+m)/z \leq m*(z-1)$ can fault tolerance at the AZ-level be guaranteed. At the same time, $m = g + p*z$, $2 \leq g_p \leq z$.
(2) Divide the stripe into k chunks.

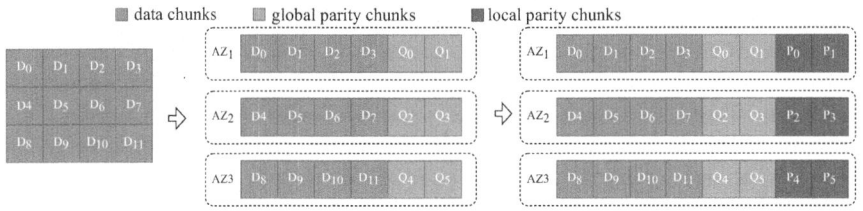

Fig. 5. An example of the encoding process of $ACH(12,6,3,2)$.

Algorithm 1. Algorithm of ACH_Decode Function

Input: W:Lost Chunks Set; A:Available Chunks Map; $ACH(k, z, p, g)$:Configuration of ACH-Code;
Output: D:Decoded Chunks Map
1: **if** $size(W) = 0$ or $\forall (i \in W$ and $i \in A)$ **then**
2:     copy i from A to D;
3:     **return** Outputs;
4: **end if**
5: $w \leftarrow$ new array of z empty sets ; $a \leftarrow$ new array of z empty maps
6: **for** each $i \in W$,each $j \in A$ **do**
7:     compute z_i form i; compute z_j form j;
8:     add i to $w[z_i]$; add j to $a[z_j]$;
9: **end for**
10: **for** each $i \in [0, z)$ **do**
11:     **if** $size(w[i]) \in (0, p]$ **then**
12:         Clay_Decode($w[i]$,$a[i]$,D);
13:     **end if**
14: **end for**
15: **if** $size(W) \neq 0$ **then**
16:     Hitchhiker_Decode(W,A,D);
17: **end if**
18: **if** $size(W) \neq 0$ **then**
19:     ACH_Decode(W,A,D);
20: **end if**
21: **return** Outputs;

---

(3) Utilize the modified Hitchhiker code encoding method to generate global parity chunks. Consequently, the data chunks and global parity chunks are partitioned into z groups in a specific order.

(4) Encode each group individually and employ the data chunks and global parity chunks of each group as the encoding input for the Clay code. Generate p local parity chunks for each availability zone.

3.5   Decoding with ACH-Code

Algorithm 1 shows the decoding method of the ACH-Code, which contains the following four steps.

1. Preprocessing. If the Lost Chunk Set is empty or any missing chunk is contained within the available chunks, no decoding computation is required, and merely data copying is performed. Otherwise, the sets of missing chunks and available chunks are allocated to distinct availability zones based on the encoding grouping method.

2. Repair within AZ. If the number of missing parity chunks within an availability zone is no more than p, the repair of this group of chunks entirely circumvents the need for cross-AZ operations, achieving repair through the Clay decode method instead. Once a chunk is repaired, it is removed from the Lost Chunk Set and subsequently added to the Available Chunks Map.

3. Repair across AZ. If available chunks within an availability zone are insufficient to complete the repair of all chunks, for instance, when the number of faulty chunks within a specific availability zone exceeds p, then global parity chunks are required to participate in the repair process, which is achieved through the Hitchhiker decode method.

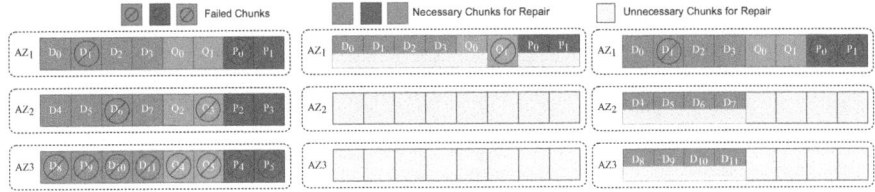

Fig. 6. $ACH(12, 6, 3, 2)$ decoding process under various failure conditions.

4. Final repair. If the data chunks and global parity chunks are repaired, but some local parity chunks remain unrepaired, a recursive call is needed to return to the first step and perform the decoding method again.

Three examples of failed chunks repair for $ACH(12, 6, 3, 2)$ are shown in Fig. 6. In the leftmost image, a total of 12 chunk failures are observed, representing the maximum number of faulty chunks that $ACH(12, 6, 3, 2)$ can accommodate. During the decoding process, all surviving chunks participate. Initially, the Clay code is utilized to repair the faulty chunks in AZ_1 and AZ_2, followed by the Hitchhiker code to repair chunks D and Q in AZ_3. Lastly, P_{5-6} are repaired within AZ_3 using the Clay code. In the middle image, only the global parity chunk Q_1 is faulty, and its repair requires only half of the surviving data within AZ_1, achieved through the Clay code. In the rightmost image, AZ_1 has three faulty chunks. First, the Hitchhiker decoding method is employed to repair chunk D_1, which necessitates only surviving chunks within AZ_1 and half of D_{4-11} for the repair process. Subsequently, the Clay code utilizes the D and Q chunks within AZ_1 to decode the P chunks.

4   Evaluation

In multi-AZ cloud storage systems, where typically three availability zones are employed, z is set to 3. We set p to 2 considering that single chunk failures and double chunk failures are the most common scenarios. To tolerate AZ-level failures, we set g to $k/(z-1)$. Therefore, all evaluations are performed as $ACH(k, k/2, 3, 2)$.

4.1   Mathematical Analysis

Metrics For Evaluating Repair Cost. The average repair cost (ARC) has been used in previous studies [2], based on the assumption that the probability of repair due to failure is the same for all chunks. We perform a comprehensive mathematical analysis of different failure scenarios for four different erasure codes cross-AZ repair cost and analyze the ARC for chunk failures. It is defined as follows where b_i, b_j, b_k represent chunks in the code, and the *cost* method determines the number of chunks required for the repair of b_i, b_j, b_k.

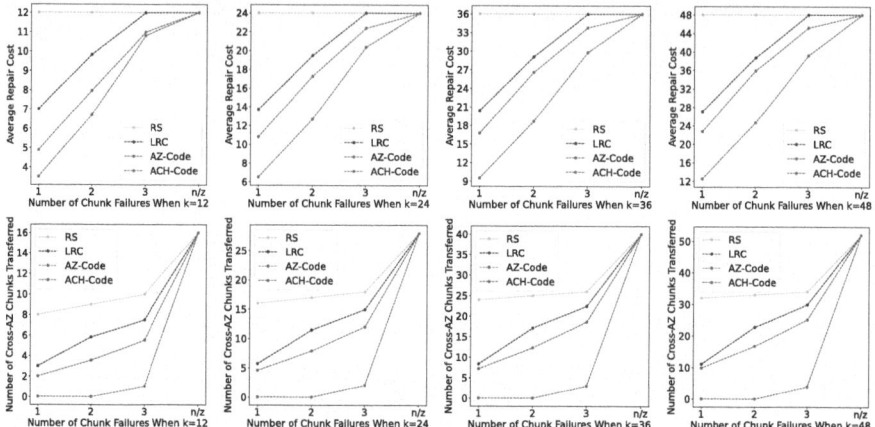

Fig. 7. Comparisons of average repair cost and cross-AZ chunks transferred during repair process among ACH-code, AZ-Code, LRC, and RS code with the same number of chunks (n) and data chunks (k).

$$
\mathrm{ARC} =
\begin{cases}
\dfrac{\sum_{i=1}^{n} cost(b_i)}{n} & \text{when single chunk failed,} \\[2ex]
\dfrac{\sum_{i=1}^{n-1} \sum_{j=i+1}^{n} cost(b_i, b_j)}{C_n^2} & \text{when double chunks failed,} \\[2ex]
\dfrac{\sum_{i=1}^{n-2} \sum_{j=i+1}^{n-1} \sum_{k=j+1}^{n} cost(b_i, b_j, b_k)}{C_n^3} & \text{when triple chunks failed.}
\end{cases}
\tag{1}
$$

Mathematical Analysis Results. We analyze four erasure codes: ACH-Code, AZ-Code, LRC, and RS code, from the perspective of mathematical computation. We calculate the average repair cost and cross-AZ repair cost for various scenarios, including single, double, triple, and multiple chunk failures. These calculations are performed for k values of 12, 24, 36, and 48. The results are shown in Fig. 7.

Cross-AZ Repair Cost. In both single chunk and double chunk failure scenarios, ACH-Code does not involve cross-AZ data transmission. This can be attributed to its capability of repairing global parity chunks through local parity chunks. Although ACH-Code may necessitate more chunks from the same availability zone than AZ-Code for data chunk repairs, it significantly reduces the need for cross-AZ chunk transfers and efficiently utilizes fewer surviving chunks for the repair of global parity chunks.

Average Repair Cost. Apart from the scenario of an entire availability zone failure, ACH-Code demonstrates robust performance by avoiding cross-AZ data transmission. In examining chunk failures recovery, ACH-Code stands out with notable advantages as k increases. At k=48, it reduces ARC by 45–74% compared to AZ-Code, LRC, and RS code for single chunk failures, by 31–49% for double chunk failures, and by 13-18% for triple chunk failures.

4.2 Experiments

Experimental Setup. We implemented ACH-Code and a plugin called ACH based on Ceph [12]. In order to compare with AZ-Code, we also implemented the AZ-Code plugin, which simulates the data transmission and computation of AZ-Code. We selected Jerasure [7] as the plugin for the RS code experiments. LRC has also been implemented in Ceph, and we maintained the same values for the number of groups, k, and m as in ACH-Code and AZ-Code during the experiment. Our experiments are performed on three physical machines in the eSurfing Cloud environment, each of which is equipped with Intel Xeon 4214R CPU cores, 2.4 GHz, 512 GB memory, 12×7 TB disks partitioned and 10Gbps network links. The servers ran CTyunOS 2.0.1 Release. We deployed a Ceph cluster consisting of one Monitor and 72 OSDs. To achieve the desired distribution of data chunks across different availability zones, we replaced the CRUSH algorithm in Ceph and devised a new data distribution algorithm.

Experimental Results. We simulated a realistic multi-AZ environment by introducing a latency of 20ms between machines. Under various configurations of k and chunk sizes, we conducted a comparative analysis of the average repair time for single, double, and triple chunk failure scenarios. The results are shown in Fig. 8. Furthermore, we varied the bandwidth and latency settings to simulate diverse environmental conditions. All improvements of ACH-Code over AZ-Code, RS code, and LRC are listed in Table 3. We observed that ACH-Code achieves better repair performance in all experiments.

Analysis. In scenarios with smaller chunk sizes, ACH demonstrates exceptionally superior repair performance. This is attributed to the fact that during the repair process of ACH-Code, under both single and double chunk failures, there is no cross-AZ data transmission, resulting in significantly reduced data transmission time and thus achieving the best overall repair performance. Notably, for 4 KB chunk sizes, ACH-Code achieves an average repair time reduction of up to 94.8% compared to RS code. In scenarios with 32 MB chunk sizes, ACH-Code offers substantial advantages in average repair time, with the advantage growing more pronounced as k increases. Notably, at $k = 24$, ACH-Code significantly outperforms, particularly versus RS code, reducing the single chunk average repair time by nearly 95.5%.

There are several reasons for these gains. Firstly, we utilize Clay code to recover the lost chunk as much as possible. Secondly, ACH-Code has less network transmission overhead across availability zones because global parity chunks can

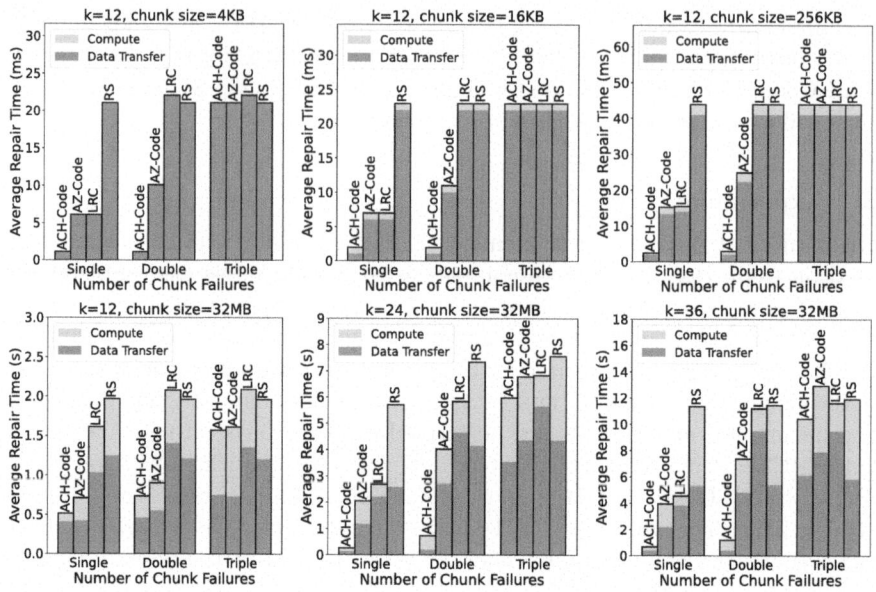

Fig. 8. Comparisons of average repair time for ACH-Code, AZ-Code, LRC, and RS Code in various configurations within a 10 Gbps bandwidth and 20 ms latency environment.

Table 3. Improvement of ACH-code under different conditions

k-chunk size-bandwidths-latency	AZ-Code			RS			LRC		
	1 Fail	2 Fail	3 Fail	1 Fail	2 Fail	3 Fail	1 Fail	2 Fail	3 Fail
12 - 4 KB - 10 Gbps - 20 ms	82.0%	89.1%	0.0%	94.8%	94.8%	0.0%	82.0%	95.0%	4.5%
12 - 16 KB - 10 Gbps - 20 ms	71.4%	81.8%	0.0%	91.3%	91.3%	0.0%	71.4%	1.3%	0.0%
12 - 256 KB - 10 Gbps - 20 ms	86.5%	87.9%	0.0%	94.3%	93.2%	0.0%	86.8%	93.2%	0.0%
12 - 32 MB - 10 Gbps - 20 ms	27.5%	18.5%	2.4%	73.8%	62.5%	19.8%	68.0%	64.7%	24.8%
24 - 32 MB - 10 Gbps - 20 ms	87.6%	81.9%	12.1%	95.5%	90.1%	21.0%	90.5%	87.5%	12.6%
36 - 32 MB - 10 Gbps - 20 ms	79.4%	80.1%	27.8%	92.5%	89.8%	36.7%	75.7%	86.2%	4.2%
36 - 32 MB - 500 Mbps - 0.1 ms	92.2%	84.2%	4.2%	97.5%	91.8%	15.6%	92.6%	91.1%	8.5%
24 - 32 MB - 500 Mbps - 0.1 ms	68.0%	84.0%	2.4%	92.7%	92.3%	23.0%	84.4%	94.3%	44.0%
12 - 32 MB - 500 Mbps - 0.1 ms	67.2%	55.0%	11.5%	87.0%	80.9%	18.3%	77.3%	87.8%	44.2%
36 - 32 MB - 1 Gbps - 0.1 ms	74.8%	81.6%	5.8%	92.1%	91.1%	14.6%	72.3%	88.8%	2.4%
36 - 32 MB - 10 Gbps - 40 ms	91.9%	92.5%	4.5%	96.9%	95.5%	2.6%	91.0%	96.0%	11.1%

also be repaired within the same availability zones. Thirdly, we employed Hitch-hiker code to generate the global parity chunks, which increases computation but reduces the number of chunks needed for repairs.

5 Conclusion

This paper proposes a novel erasure code, ACH-Code, which substantially mitigates the consumption during chunk failure repair across multiple availability zones. ACH-Code integrates the strengths of Hitchhiker code and Clay code, leveraging an optimized chunk distribution strategy to minimize both the average repair cost and cross-AZ data transfers during the recovery process. Through rigorous mathematical analysis and extensive experimental evaluations, we conclusively demonstrate that ACH-Code surpasses existing erasure codes by achieving a notable reduction in both the average data transfers and the average repair time incurred during repair operations. These findings robustly underscore the effectiveness of ACH-Code in augmenting the performance and efficiency of cloud storage systems in multiple availability zone environments.

References

1. eSurfing Cloud, C.T.: Zettabyte object storage. https://www.esurfingcloud.com/document/10026735. Accessed 07 Aug 2023
2. Copeland, M., et al.: Microsoft azure and cloud computing. In: Microsoft Azure: Planning, Deploying, and Managing Your Data Center in the Cloud, pp. 3–26 (2015)
3. Cullina, D., Dimakis, A.G., Ho, T.: Searching for minimum storage regenerating codes. arXiv preprint arXiv:0910.2245 (2009)
4. Hu, Y., Cheng, L., Yao, Q., Lee, P.P., Wang, W., Chen, W.: Exploiting combined locality for {Wide-Stripe} erasure coding in distributed storage. In: 19th USENIX Conference on File and Storage Technologies (FAST 21), pp. 233–248 (2021)
5. Huang, C., et al.: Erasure coding in windows azure storage. In: 2012 USENIX Annual Technical Conference (USENIX ATC 2012), pp. 15–26 (2012)
6. Pamies-Juarez, L., Blagojevic, F., Mateescu, R., Gyuot, C., Gad, E.E., Bandic, Z.: Opening the chrysalis: on the real repair performance of {MSR} codes. In: 14th USENIX Conference on File and Storage Technologies (FAST 2016), pp. 81–94 (2016)
7. Plank, J.S., Simmerman, S., Schuman, C.D.: Jerasure: a library in c/c++ facilitating erasure coding for storage applications. Technical Report CS-07–603, University of Tennessee (2007)
8. Rashmi, K.V., Shah, N.B., Gu, D., Kuang, H., Borthakur, D., Ramchandran, K.: A "hitchhiker's" guide to fast and efficient data reconstruction in erasure-coded data centers. In: Proceedings of the 2014 ACM Conference on SIGCOMM, pp. 331–342 (2014)
9. Reed, I.S., Solomon, G.: Polynomial codes over certain finite fields. J. Soc. Ind. Appl. Math. **8**(2), 300–304 (1960)
10. Tamo, I., Barg, A.: A family of optimal locally recoverable codes. IEEE Trans. Inf. Theory **60**(8), 4661–4676 (2014). https://doi.org/10.1109/TIT.2014.2321280
11. Vajha, M., et al.: Clay codes: Moulding {MDS} codes to yield an {MSR} code. In: 16th USENIX Conference on File and Storage Technologies (FAST 2018), pp. 139–154 (2018)
12. Weil, S., Brandt, S.A., Miller, E.L., Long, D.D., Maltzahn, C.: Ceph: a scalable, high-performance distributed file system. In: Proceedings of the 7th Conference on Operating Systems Design and Implementation (OSDI 2006), pp. 307–320 (2006)

13. Xie, X., et al.: Az-code: an efficient availability zone level erasure code to provide high fault tolerance in cloud storage systems. In: 2019 35th Symposium on Mass Storage Systems and Technologies (MSST), pp. 230–243. IEEE (2019)
14. Xie, X., et al.: Az-recovery: an efficient crossing-az recovery scheme for erasure coded cloud storage systems. In: 2020 International Symposium on Reliable Distributed Systems (SRDS), pp. 236–245 (2020). https://doi.org/10.1109/SRDS51746.2020.00031
15. Yang, G., et al.: Xhr-code: an efficient wide stripe erasure code to reduce cross-rack overhead in cloud storage systems. In: 2022 41st International Symposium on Reliable Distributed Systems (SRDS), pp. 273–283. IEEE (2022)
16. Ye, L., Feng, D., Hu, Y., Wei, X.: Hybrid codes: flexible erasure codes with optimized recovery performance. ACM Trans. Storage (TOS) **16**(4), 1–26 (2020)
17. Zhang, H., Liu, S., Tang, D., Cai, H.: Erasure code with low recovery-overhead in distributed storage systems. J. Comput. Appl. **40**(10), 2942 (2020)

CMS: A Computility Resource Status Management and Storage Framework

Xiaohui Peng[1,2,3], Xudong Luo[1,2,3], Kuo Chang[1,2], and Yifan Wang[1,2,3(✉)]

[1] Institute of Computing Technology, Chinese Academy of Sciences, Beijing, China
{pengxiaohui,changkuo21s,wangyifan2014}@ict.ac.cn
[2] University of Chinese Academy of Sciences, Beijing, China
[3] Nanjing Institute of InforSuperBahn, Nanjing, China

Abstract. With the increasing demand for computility, managing distributed computility resources is crucial for improving service quality and performance of the cross-region computility infrastructure. In order to ensure timely and accurate scheduling of computing tasks on such infrastructure, a distributed computility status storage and query system is needed to achieve millisecond-level performance in terms of multidimensional sort query and multidimensional range query for computility status. Thus, we propose CMS, a computility resource status management and storage framework, which leverages specialized multidimensional indexes to support millisecond-level resource status reporting and querying, as well as sort and range queries. In addition, we developed BCQL and a set of querying algorithms to enhance throughput and reduce query latency. Experimental results show that the average query latency of the multidimensional sorting queries and range queries of the CMS system is 2.499 ms and 2.014 ms, respectively. While, the latency of those queries in Redis-based framework reach 25.66 ms and 25.13 ms, which are 10× higher than the CMS.

Keywords: Distributed System · Computility Resource · Resource Management

1 Introduction

Computility is a new term composed of *compute* and *utility* [14]. It refers to the computational performance provided by a device or system for its applications, serving as a metric of the computing tasks that the device or system can accomplish within a certain period. It represents the ability of the combined hardware and software to serve applications.

As computing technology advances into various sectors of the economy, the existing networked computing infrastructure is unable to meet the demand for computility from emerging applications such as massive sensed big data processing, large-scale model training, and AI for Science. There is an urgent need to construct a more unified and efficient cross-region computility infrastructure

X. Chen et al. (Eds.): NPC 2024, LNCS 15527, pp. 207–218, 2025.
https://doi.org/10.1007/978-981-96-2830-8_16

to provide high-quality computing services for various industries. The management of computility status is a fundamental issue in distributed systems, and the geo-distribution nature increases the difficulty of cross-region computility status management. They reliably assume the accuracy and real-time nature of computility status [8]. There are several fully functional, out-of-the-box real-time computility measurement systems in the industrial field, such as Nagios [2], Ganglia [9], and Prometheus [11]. Meanwhile, the designers of distributed systems often prefer to implement solutions tailored to the specific requirements of their systems.

Distributed computility status management typically consists of two modules: computility status storage and querying. The storage module is responsible for collecting real-time computility status reported by each node and storing it in databases, which are usually a memory-based storage engine. The querying module provides millisecond-level query services of computility status for real-time computing task scheduling decisions. In this paper, we present the design and implementation of a Computility Resource Status Management and Storage Framework (CMS). It provides millisecond-level status reporting and querying while addressing the requirements of multidimensional sorting and range queries. The primary contributions are as follows:

– **BCQL.** We proposed a Basic Computility Query Language (BCQL), which meets all computility query requirements while maintaining a syntax similar to SQL, thereby minimizing the learning curve for users.
– **Multidimensional query index.** We designed a multidimensional query index equipped with a key calculation algorithm that swiftly delivers approximate results for multidimensional queries.
– **CMS.** We implemented a Computility Resource Status Management and Storage Framework (CMS) to store and index real-time computility status. The framework features an optimized internal heuristic index cache to address multidimensional query requirements.

2   Related Work

2.1   Computility Status Management Systems

Table 1 shows four typical computility status management systems in grid computing and cloud computing. Borg [15] is Google's large-scale cluster management system, which uses the centralized Borgmaster to unify resource management and scheduling [3]. Its resource manager on a master node continuously tracks worker nodes' resource usage by periodically collecting reported usage information from each node. Mesos [7] is also a centralized resource management system designed to provide flexible resource sharing and scheduling for large-scale clusters. During operation, the master node passively gathers computility status from each slave node and sends resource offers to frameworks, presenting available computility. This centralized architecture for managing computility resources and status is prone to a single point of failure.

Sparrow [10] is a decentralized distributed scheduling system designed for low-latency tasks. Sparrow's schedulers randomly select a small number of nodes to check their loads and assign tasks to the least-loaded nodes, and each node manages resources locally. However, Sparrow does not support multidimensional queries. Prometheus [11] is a typical time series database that collects computility status across layered clusters. However, its layered data collection method compromises the freshness of data. Moreover, because the data is stored with time as the primary key, Prometheus's querying capabilities are limited in other data fields.

Table 1. Classic computility resource management systems

System	Architecture	Resource Management	Schedule	Cross-Region
Borg [15]	Centralized	Unified	Unified	×
Sparrow [10]	Decentralized	Independent	Independent	×
Mesos [7]	Centralized	Unified	Independent	×
Globus [6]	Grid	Unified	Unified	✓

The Globus Toolkit [6] is a set of components used to build grid computing environments, providing distributed resource management capabilities from different organizations and regions. Users can securely share computility resources across multiple organizations through role-based access control and single sign-on. The Globus task scheduling system dynamically allocates computing nodes based on resource availability.

2.2 Computility Status Storage and Query

The storage and query performance of distributed computility resources plays a crucial role in task scheduling in the cross-region computility infrastructure. Relational database management systems (RDBMS) like MySQL [16] use SQL, which supports comprehensive querying functionalities. They are typically designed for single-machine systems, leading to scalability issues when storing computility status in distributed systems.

Table 2. Current computility resource table.

Instance	Simple Query	Sort Query	Range Query
RDBMS [16]	–	–	–
Redis [13]	✓	1-Dim	1-Dim
Memcached [5]	✓	×	×
Prometheus [11]	×	1-Dim	Time-Dim
etcd [4]	✓	1-Dim	1-Dim

NoSQL is a new type of database paradigm, including key-value data model and time-series model. The most commonly used key-value databases are Redis [13], Memcached [5], and etcd [4]. Redis supports complex querying functionalities through its ordered list data structure, such as sorting and range queries at key dimension. Memcached is a lightweight, high-speed memory database that only supports simple key-value queries. Etcd uses B+tree to support sorting and range queries along a single field.

Table 2 lists the support of query functionalities provide by RDBMS and NoSQL database management systems. From the above analysis, we can conclude that NoSQL databases are more suitable for storing distributed computility status than RDBMS. However, enhancement of the querying module is needed to support more efficient and complex querying. Time series databases struggle to support multidimensional query requirements. Therefore, CMS focuses on the storage and multidimensional query needs of distributed computility status, aiming to achieve millisecond-level storage and querying performance.

3   Design and Implementation

3.1   BCQL

We propose the Basic Computility Query Language (BCQL) for querying computility from CMS. The primary goal of BCQL is to simplify external query calls and reduce usage costs, which led us to modify traditional SQL. To describe the basic syntax of BCQL, we employ the Extended Backus-Naur Form (EBNF) [1].

$$
\begin{aligned}
command &\Leftarrow \text{SELECT } field \text{ FROM } scope \ [clause] \\
&\quad [\text{LIMIT } number] \ [\text{FAST}] \\
clause &\Leftarrow \text{WHERE } restriction \mid \text{ORDER BY } key['] \\
fields &\Leftarrow field \ \{, field\} \mid * \\
scope &\Leftarrow \text{LOCAL}|\text{WIDE} \\
restriction &\Leftarrow expression \ \{\&\& \ expression\} \\
field &\Leftarrow key \mid aggregation(key) \\
aggregation &\Leftarrow \text{AVG} \mid \text{MIN} \mid \text{MAX} \mid \text{SUM} \\
expression &\Leftarrow key \ operator \ value \\
operator &\Leftarrow > \mid < \mid == \mid <= \mid >=
\end{aligned}
$$

In general, BCQL statements can be categorized into four types, each corresponding to different query scenarios. Table 3 illustrates the distinctions among these four query types, where ✓ indicates the presence of a specific feature in BCQL.

3.2   CMS Architecture

As illustrated in Fig. 1, CMS is divided into two components: the front-end and the back-end. The front-end is designed for user interaction, while the back-end focuses on kernel-level operations.

Currently, the front-end features four implemented clients: the CLI client, script client, reporter client, and RPC client. The CLI and script clients handle

Table 3. Four query in BCQL

Type	WHERE	ORDER BY	Equivalent Restrict	Scenarios
Simple Query	×	×	×	base function
Sort Query	×	✓	×	resource schedule
Regular Range Query	✓	×	×	locate or filter nodes
Equivalent Range Query	✓	×	✓	locate or filter nodes
Invalid Query	✓	✓	–	–

user interactions, while the reporter client, deployed on each node, collects the computility status and reports it to the back-end in a timely manner. The RPC client is responsible for managing RPC calls.

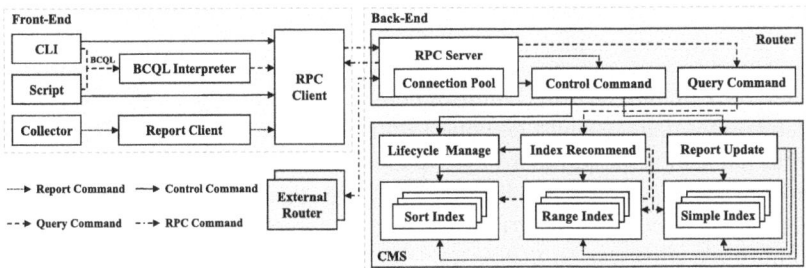

Fig. 1. CMS Architecture

In the back-end of CMS, the router receives requests from the front-end and determines whether to forward or process them. The CMS module executes the request commands and consists of three submodules. The *lifecycle management* module manages the lifecycle of the index, overseeing both its creation and destruction. The *index recommendation* module suggests the most appropriate index for a query based on specific requirements and utilizes caching to enhance search speed. Finally, the *report update* module is tasked with inserting computility data into the index.

3.3   Multidimensional Index

All indexes are implemented using a skiplist [12]. While skiplist is effective for 1D queries, its application in multidimensional scenarios poses challenges. To address this, we designed an algorithm (as shown in Algorithm 1) to map multidimensional keys to a 1D format, referred to as **key calculation**, enabling the use of skiplist for multidimensional queries. The base case termed simple key, is straightforward; we can normalize it.

$$\sum_{i=1}^{Dim} 3^{Dim-i-1}(a_i + 2) \tag{1}$$

Algorithm 1. Key Calculation

Input: key object *keyObj*, input data *inputData*, data fields *fields*
Output: index key *key*
1: T ← keyObj.type
2: **if** T is Simple **then**
3:     *key* ← NORMALIZE(*inputData*, *fields*[0])
4: **else if** T is Sort **then**
5:     *key* ← 0.0
6:     **for** each *f* in *fields* **do**
7:         t ← NORMALIZE(*inputData*, *f*)
8:         *key* ← *key* × 3 + t + 2
9:     **end for**
10: **else if** T is Range **then**
11:     *key* ← CALCULATERADIUS(*keyObj*, *inputData*, *fields*)
12: **end if**

Conversely, we treat sort and range keys as multidimensional cases. The sort key is calculated using multidimensional fields along with an ascending/descending flag. It could demonstrate that sorting vectors through a linear combination that strictly adheres to lexicographic order is unsolvable. Therefore, we employ a weighted sum (as shown in Eq. 1) to approximate lexicographic order as closely as possible, where $a_1, a_2, \ldots, a_{\mathrm{Dim}}$ represents the normalized values. This approach allows us to utilize a 64-bit float to represent a sort item across five fields.

The range key, on the other hand, is derived from a specific range index characterized by two significant fields: the center c and the rate r. The value of the range key is computed using Eq. 2. In this context, we represent the range index as a hypercube, with the center denoting the cube's midpoint and the rate indicating the relative distance to the center in dimension i.

$$\max_{1 \le i \le N} \frac{|x_i - c_i|}{r_i} \tag{2}$$

3.4   Index Recommendation Algorithm

The index recommendation algorithm varies between sort queries and range queries. We will explain each approach separately.

The core idea behind the index recommendation for sort queries is to select a sort index that encompasses all required dimensions in the correct order. There are two exceptional cases to consider: oversize and partial dimensions. An oversized index has stricter requirements, making it acceptable for use, whereas a partial index does not meet our criteria; thus, we will reject it and store it in the cache. The algorithm for this process is outlined in Algorithm 2.

For an N-dimensional range query request, we will traverse all indexes in the cache and calculate the matching dimension D_i and the spatial volume V_i formed by these matching dimensions together with the range query request for

---

Algorithm 2. Sort Index Recommend Algorithm

Input: query command *qcmd*, index cache *cache*
Output: recommend index *idx*
1: maxDim ← 0
2: bestIndex ← nil
3: **for** each i in *cache* **do**
4:     sharedDim ← CALCULATESHAREDDIM(*qcmd*, *i*)   ▷ count of same fields
5:     **if** sharedDim = LEN(qcmd.dims) **then**
6:         **if** sharedDim = LEN(i.dims) **then**
7:             idx ← i   ▷ cache hit, stop searching
8:             **return**
9:         **else**
10:             sharedDim ← LEN(i.dims)
11:             **if** sharedDim > maxDim **then**
12:                 maxDim, bestIndex ← sharedDim, i
13:             **end if**
14:         **end if**
15:     **else**
16:         **if** sharedDim > maxDim **then**
17:             maxDim, bestIndex ← sharedDim, i
18:         **end if**
19:     **end if**
20: **end for**
21: **if** maxDim > LEN(qcmd.dims) **then**
22:     idx ← bestIndex   ▷ cache hit, but oversize
23: **else**
24:     NEWINDEX(*qcmd.dims*)
25:     idx ← SIMPLEINDEX(*qcmd.dims*[0])   ▷ cache miss, use 1D index instead
26: **end if**

---

index i. D_i represents the number of matching dimensions between index i and request, V_i represents the volume of the range where index i and query overlap in the matching dimensions, that is, the volume of a hypercube centered on the index center and with the growth rate as the radius completely within the range of query request. There are three cases of V_i and D_i. They are **perfect match** (exist at least 1 index which meets $D_i = N$ and $V_i > 0$), **partial match** ($D_i < N$ and $V_i > 0$), **no match** ($D_i = 0$ or $V_i = 0$). We classify no matches as failures, while partial matches and perfect matches are considered successes. In the case of multiple matches, we prioritize perfect matches first; if the perfect matches are not available, we then select the partial match with the most matching dimensions and the smallest volume.

Additionally, we employ a heuristic cache to enhance the performance of these algorithms. We operate under the assumption that most queries exhibit temporal locality, meaning that the same query is likely to occur multiple times in the near future. To leverage this, we treat the indexes as cache entries. We utilize the LRU (Least Recently Used) algorithm to establish a maximum limit for the number of sort indexes S and the number of range indexes T.

4   Evaluation

4.1   Experimental Setup

Our experiments were conducted on devices listed in Table 4. In the experiment, a central node runs the back-end module and is responsible for receiving information. In contrast, all nodes in the cluster run the front-end module, handling reporting and query requests to the central node. To increase the cluster size, each node generates fake data using multiple threads for reporting.

Table 4. Devices Setup.

Device	D-1	L-1	L-2	S-1	S-2
OS	Win11 Home	Win11 Home	Win11 Home	Debian/bullseye	Ubuntu18.08
CPU	Intel i5-12500	Intel i5-1135G7	Intel i7-12700H	Cortex-A72	ARMv8
Memory	16 GB	16 GB	16 GB	8 GB	32 GB

We categorized the experiments into two types. The first type, referred to as the basic experiments, was conducted using the D-1 equipment to evaluate the performance of the CMS itself. The second type, the experiments in a distributed environment, utilized all the devices shown in Table 4 to assess performance under the influence of communication. Additionally, we compared CMS with Redis by substituting the CMS core with Redis for this evaluation.

Metrics. We use freshness and latency as our key metrics. Freshness indicates the system's ability to maintain the most up-to-date status of the computility of nodes. We measure freshness by calculating the time difference between the query time and the time when the computility data was collected. Latency refers to the execution time of the query, quantified as the time difference between when the result is obtained and when the query was initiated.

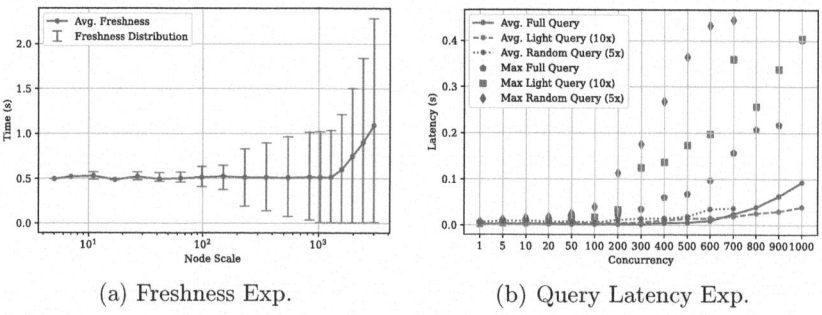

(a) Freshness Exp.   (b) Query Latency Exp.

Fig. 2. Freshness and Query Latency Basic Experiments.

4.2   Basic Experiments

Figure 2(a) illustrates the relationship between freshness and node scale in basic experiments. At more minor scales, the average freshness is approximately 0.5 s. As the scale increases, both the average and maximum freshness also rise. Notably, even at a scale of 3000 nodes, CMS can maintain freshness at approximately 1 s, demonstrating its capability to ensure stable freshness under high concurrency.

Figure 2(b) presents the latency for full, light, and random queries. We scaled the light and random queries multiple times. The latency for all three query types shows a positive correlation with concurrency, maintaining a low latency of around 0.2 s for small to medium concurrency scales (less than 700). In fact, at even larger concurrency scales, CMS achieves an average latency of less than 0.1 s. The random query encompasses both full and light queries, resembling typical daily tasks. The maximum latency for random queries can be controlled within 0.1 s, indicating that CMS performs effectively in handling everyday tasks.

4.3   Experiments in Distributed Environment

Similar to the basis experiments, we conducted experiments on freshness and query latency within a distributed environment.

Figure 3(a) displays the average and distribution of freshness across four query nodes. Despite being situated in different environments, all four nodes maintain comparable freshness levels, demonstrating that CMS is stable in a distributed setting. Moreover, even with a larger node scale, the average freshness remains below 1 s, and the maximum latency is kept under 2 s, indicating that CMS can effectively manage concurrent reports.

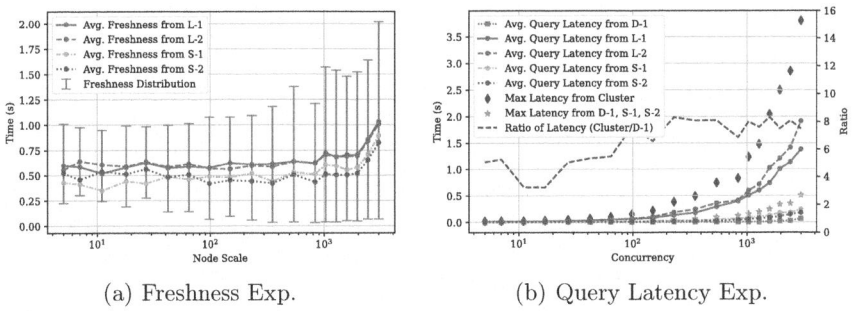

(a) Freshness Exp.   (b) Query Latency Exp.

Fig. 3. Freshness and Query Latency Experiments in Distributed environment.

Figure 3(b) illustrates the query latency at varying levels of concurrency. The latency trend for all nodes increases with higher concurrency. There is a noticeable difference between the maximum latency experienced by the cluster and that of nearby nodes, which is influenced by the geographical distribution of nodes (i.e., network communication). However, the ratio of these two latencies approaches a constant, suggesting that this disparity is not related to concurrency but is instead attributable to network factors. Nevertheless, the maximum average query latency remains within 2 s, with the maximum latency not exceeding 4 s, which is sufficient to meet various usage requirements.

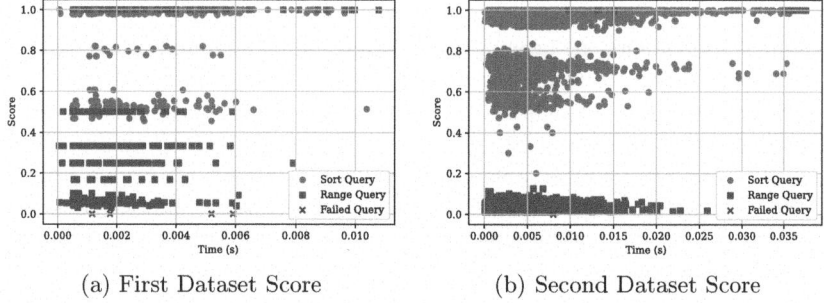

(a) First Dataset Score   (b) Second Dataset Score

Fig. 4. Sort Query Score and Range Query Score of Two Datasets

In addition to experiments on freshness and query latency, we also conducted tests on multidimensional queries. This experiment utilized two distinct test datasets: the first dataset contained a total of 1175 queries, while the second dataset included 8071 queries. We compared the query results with the actual values to calculate the query scores and plotted the correlation distribution between the query scores and response times for both datasets.

We use *accuracy* to evaluate the performance of multidimensional queries. For sorting queries, accuracy reflects the overlap with lexicographical order, where higher accuracy is better. For range queries, accuracy measures the proportion of matching nodes found, with any non-zero result being acceptable; thus, we focus more on the failure rate.

Figure 4(a) displays the results for the first dataset, while Fig. 4(b) presents the results for the second dataset. The accuracy of the sort queries is consistently above 0.9, whereas the accuracy for range queries is 0.2971 and 0.0376 for the two datasets, respectively. Notably, there is no significant difference in response times between the two types of queries; the sort query on the two datasets is 2.499 ms and 5,595 ms, while the range query is 2.014 ms and 3.401 ms. The failure query rates observed in the experiments were 1.205% for the first dataset and 0.038% for the second dataset.

4.4   Comparison Experiments

To assess the query performance of CMS from a broader perspective, we compared its performance with viable alternative solutions. For this comparison, we utilized Redis' ordered collection as the foundational data structure and implemented the necessary query functions using the Go programming language in conjunction with the Redis API. Since our primary focus was on evaluating Redis' query latency and scores, our experiments concentrated exclusively on these two aspects.

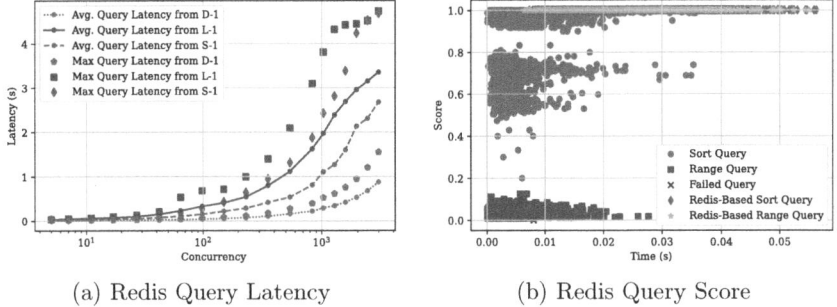

(a) Redis Query Latency   (b) Redis Query Score

Fig. 5. Query Latency and Score in Redis-Based Framework

Figure 5(a) illustrates the query latency for Redis. As concurrency increases, the query time for Redis continues to rise, similar to the trend observed in the CMS framework. However, it is important to note that the average query latency for the Redis implementation is measured in seconds, whereas the average query latency for CMS remains below 1 s. This demonstrates that CMS offers a lower response time and is better suited to meet user needs.

Figure 5(b) presents the query scores based on Redis. In comparison to CMS, the Redis version achieves higher query scores for both sorting and range queries, indicating that it has superior performance in these areas. However, as shown in Table 5, the higher query scores in Redis result in increasing query latency, which is 25.66 ms and 25.13 ms, respectively.

Table 5. Comparison Between CMS and Redis

System	Query Type	Accuracy	Query Latency (ms)	Failure Rate
CMS	Sort Query	0.9309	2.499	–
	Range Query	0.2971	2.014	1.205%
Redis	Sort Query	1.0	25.66	–
	Range Query	1.0	25.13	0%

5   Conclusions

CMS effectively addresses the challenges of storage and multidimensional query technology in computility resource status management. CMS achieves high response speed and accuracy by leveraging multidimensional query indexes, advanced query algorithms, and the BCQL while minimizing time and space consumption. In high concurrency and long-distance scenarios, the average query accuracy of the multidimensional sorting queries and multidimensional range queries of the CMS system reached 0.9386 and 0.2971, respectively. The average query latency is only 2.499 ms and 2.014 ms, while Redis-based got 25.66 ms and 25.13 ms, which are 10.27 and 12.48 times higher than the CMS. The results show that CMS is inferior to Redis in query accuracy but has significant advantages in query response speed compared to Redis.

Acknowledgments. This research was partially supported by the National Natural Science Foundation of China under Grant Nos. 62072434 and U23B2004, and the Innovation Funding of ICT, CAS under Grant No. E361050.

References

1. Backus, J.W., et al.: Revised report on the algorithmic language ALGOL 60. Commun. ACM **6**(1), 1–17 (1963)
2. Barth, W.: Nagios: System and Network Monitoring. No Starch Press (2008)
3. Burns, B., Grant, B., Oppenheimer, D., Brewer, E., Wilkes, J.: Borg, omega, and kubernetes. Commun. ACM **59**(5), 50–57 (2016)
4. ETCD Authors: ETCD: a distributed, reliable key-value store for the most critical data of a distributed system (2024). https://etcd.io
5. Fitzpatrick, B.: Distributed caching with memcached. Linux J. **2004**(124), 5 (2004)
6. Foster, I., Kesselman, C.: Globus: a metacomputing infrastructure toolkit. Int. J. Supercomput. Appl. High Perform. Comput. **11**(2), 115–128 (1997)
7. Hindman, B., et al.: Mesos: a platform for fine-grained resource sharing in the data center. In: Proceedings of the 8th USENIX Symposium on Networked Systems Design and Implementation (NSDI), pp. 1–14 (2011)
8. Jennings, B., Stadler, R.: Resource management in clouds: survey and research challenges. J. Netw. Syst. Manag. **23**, 567–619 (2015)
9. Massie, M.L., Chun, B.N., Culler, D.E.: The ganglia distributed monitoring system: design, implementation, and experience. Parallel Comput. **30**(7), 817–840 (2004)
10. Ousterhout, K., Wendell, P., Zaharia, M., Stoica, I.: Sparrow: distributed, low latency scheduling. In: Proceedings of the 24th ACM Symposium on Operating Systems Principles (SOSP), pp. 69–84 (2013)
11. Prometheus Authors: Prometheus: monitoring system and time series database (2024). https://prometheus.io
12. Pugh, W.: Skip lists: a probabilistic alternative to balanced trees. Commun. ACM **33**(6), 668–676 (1990)
13. Redis Authors: Redis: the real-time data platform (2024). https://redis.io
14. Sun, N., Zhang, Y., Zhang, F.: Commun. CCF. Computility **18**(9), 87 (2022)
15. Verma, A., Pedrosa, L., Korupolu, M., Oppenheimer, D., Tune, E., Wilkes, J.: Large-scale cluster management at Google with Borg. In: Proceedings of the 10th European Conference on Computer Systems (EuroSys), pp. 1–17 (2015)
16. Widenius, M., Axmark, D.: MySQL Reference Manual: Documentation from the Source. O'Reilly Media, Inc. (2002)

Fast Memory Disaggregation with SwiftSwap

Xiangwei Zhang[1], Desheng Wang[1], Weizhe Zhang[1(✉)], Zhiji Yu[1], and Meng Hao[2]

[1] School of Computer Science and Technology, Harbin Institute of Technology, Shenzhen 518055, Guangdong, China
{wangdesheng,wzzhang}@hit.edu.cn
[2] School of Cyberspace Science, Harbin Institute of Technology, Harbin 150001, China
haomeng@hit.edu.cn

Abstract. With the continuous evolution of cloud computing technology, the memory requirements of cloud servers are increasing. Insufficient memory has become the performance bottleneck of many applications. Memory disaggregation has been proposed to solve this problem, which enables computing nodes to utilize the memory of remote memory nodes, thus not only effectively extending the capacity of logical memory, but also significantly improving the resource utilization and elasticity of the whole cluster, providing a more flexible resource allocation scheme for large-scale parallel computing and data processing. However, most of the existing memory disaggregation systems require modification of hardware, operating systems or applications, which are difficult to use. This paper proposes a high-performance memory disaggregation system SwiftSwap, which can directly access remote memory without any modification of hardware, operating system, or application. We design and implement a high performance cache, cache lookup algorithm LDA and cache elimination strategy RM_AwareLRU on the computing node to improve the performance of the system. Through comprehensive evaluation, SwiftSwap has up to 5.1× performance advantage in throughput, 4.8× performance advantage in tail delay, and 6.4× performance advantage against applications running in containers.

Keywords: Cloud computing · Memory disaggregation · Caching strategy

1 Introduction

With the continuous development of cloud computing, computing clusters require more and more memory [17], and the memory size has become the performance bottleneck of many applications [11,15], because once the memory is

© IFIP International Federation for Information Processing 2025
Published by Springer Nature Switzerland AG 2025
X. Chen et al. (Eds.): NPC 2024, LNCS 15527, pp. 219–230, 2025.
https://doi.org/10.1007/978-981-96-2830-8_17

insufficient, the memory access requests of the application will cause a large number of swap in and swap out operations, which will access the disk (swap space) and cause great latency. Because disk read and write performance compared to memory has a huge gap.

As a lightweight and portable software packaging technology, containers encapsulate an application and its runtime environment (dependent libraries, configuration files, etc.) together in an independent unit, and have been widely [8] used in the field of cloud computing. If the container runs out of memory, it will use the swap space (local disk), which will affect the performance of the application or even cause the application to be unable to run (that is, the process is killed by the OOM killer process under the linux system). For example, the performance loss of redis server running under docker is shown In Fig. 1. According to the results in the figure, when the in-memory Working Set is 75%, the performance degradation of redis is at least 27%, and when the value is 25%, the performance of redis is only 31% of that under sufficient Memory.

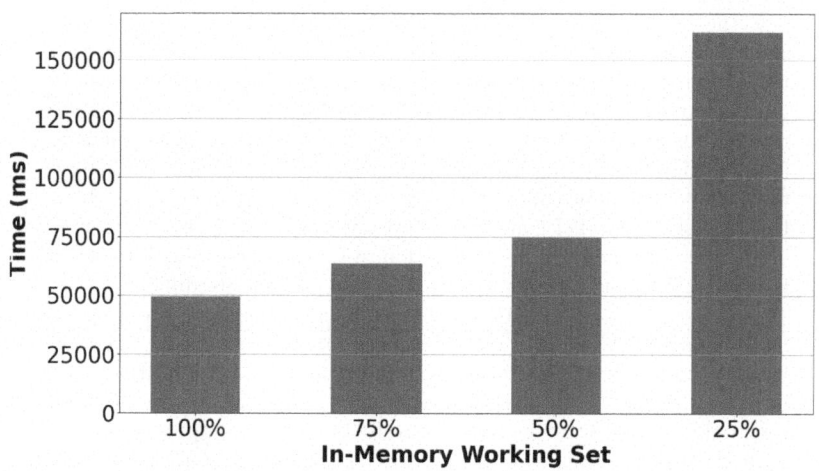

Fig. 1. Performance loss of Redis under insufficient memory.

In recent years, memory disaggregation has been proposed to solve this performance bottleneck, which allows a computing node to use the memory of a remote node when memory is insufficient, and thus can make full use of the memory resources of the whole cluster to improve the resource utilization of the cluster. At the same time, with the development of network technology [5], the current RDMA network can meet the requirements of a large number of memory workloads, and a large number of memory disaggregation cluster have emerged [1,2,6,7,9,13]. However, most of the current solutions are difficult to be easily applied to the existing operating system, these solutions need to re-write or modify the existing application program, redesign and implement the hardware such as modifying the switch, using new hardware, etc., modify the software source code of the current operating system or reconfigure the operating system.

In this paper, we propose a high performance memory disaggregation system called SwiftSwap. The key contributions of SwiftSwap are outlined as follows.

- We design and implement a kernel module SwiftSwap, which does not require any modifications to the existing hardware, operating system and application. Compared with the existing swap-based disaggregated memory, we add a cache in the computing node, and design and implement a high performance cache lookup algorithm and cache elimination strategy, which not only ensure data consistency, but also greatly reduce the performance loss of remote data access.
- By using fio [4], redis [15], and memcached [11] to evaluate the performance of SwiftSwap, the evaluation results show that compared with the current commonly used Network Block Device (NBD) [12] and the default swap of linux system, the performance of SwiftSwap is up to 5.1 times advantage in throughput and 4.8 times advantage in tail delay.

2   Related Work

At present, there are mainly the following schemes for memory disaggregation.

Based on swap. For example, FASTSWAP [1] proposed an algorithm to dynamically adjust the ratio of local memory and remote memory by evaluating the cost of local and remote memory. Hermit [13] proposed asynchronous garbage collection and dynamically adjusted the number of cpu cores used for garbage collection to improve the system performance.

Based on virtualization, such as GiantVM [7] realizes memory disaggregation based on QEMU-KVM, virtualizes IO, CPU and other resources and performs thread scheduling in the client, and schedules the threads sharing data to the same node to reduce the overall network overhead. XMemPod [2] proposed a hierarchical memory expansion framework, that is, memory is extended on the virtual machine and then on the remote memory.

Others, such as MIND [9], use programmable network switches for memory management. DirectCXL [6] proposed to use new hardware to complete resource pooling. AIFM [16] provides developers with C++ standard class-like data structures and interfaces to use remote memory.

Most of the existing memory disaggregation systems need to modify the hardware, operating system or application program, and the development and deployment cost is high. Compared with the existing research, SwiftSwap does not need any changes to the operating system kernel code. At the same time, it also takes into account the locality and system performance. A cache is added to the computing node, and a high performance cache lookup algorithm and cache elimination strategy are designed and implemented to ensure data consistency and low latency.

3   The Overview of SwiftSwap

3.1   Architectural Overview

SwiftSwap is a high performance memory disaggregation system whose main purpose is to efficiently provide cluster memory to applications without requiring any modifications to applications, operating systems, hardware, etc. The architecture of SwiftSwap is shown in Fig. 2. Applications such as memcached, redis, etc. run in the Docker container of the computing node. When Docker doesn't have enough memory, the page fault of the operating system will be triggered, which uses virtual memory through VMM, and then uses SwiftSwap.

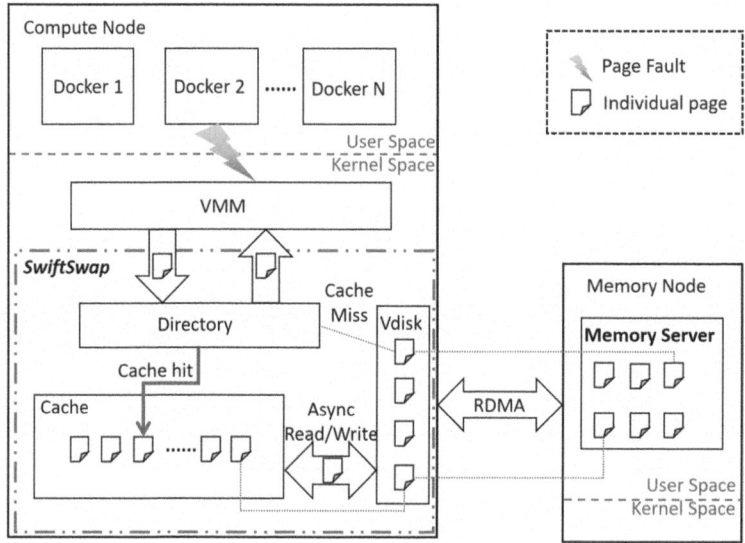

Fig. 2. Architecture of SwiftSwap

The SwiftSwap client on the computing node is an loadable kernel module, running in the kernel space, can access all the resources of the system, when the application uses virtual memory through VMM, SwiftSwap will be used. For the sake of program locality and system performance, SwiftSwap adds a layer of caching to cache remote memory data.

When the VMM requests to read or write virtual memory, it first looks up the entry of the cache according to the address, offset, length and other information of the virtual memory. The entry contains the cache address, specific data, the spinlock corresponding to the cache entry, and the lru list pointer corresponding to the management cache. If the cache hit, it will directly read and write to the local cache, and then the local cache will asynchronously synchronize with the remote memory through rdma to ensure the consistency of system data. If the cache miss, it will first use one-sided RDMA operation to read the remote memory to the local cache. Data is then read and write.

The SwiftSwap server on the memory node runs in user space and is mainly responsible for providing remote memory, memory mapping, memory management, connection management, etc. Specifically, the local memory is pre-allocated for computing nodes according to the local memory usage, which can reduce the overhead of memory initialization. The SwiftSwap server also takes care of managing the RDMA connection and handles requests from the compute node for memory mappings, which bind the virtual address of the compute node to the memory of the memory node.

3.2   Directory Lookup Algorithm

When a read or write request is made to SwiftSwap, it first looks through the directory to see if the cache hit, based on the virtual address, operation, offset, and other information. In this paper, a Directory Lookup Algorithm(DLA) is designed and implemented by considering the cost of cache query, the performance under the condition of multiprocessor, as shown in Algorithm 1.

Algorithm 1. Directory Lookup Algorithm(DLA)

Input: Virtual address to access VADDR, operation OPT, OFFSET
Output: the corresponding entry
1: hashcode=hash(VADDR)
2: index=hashcode%bucketsize
3: entrylist=get_entrylist(index)
4: **for** entry in entrylist **do**
5:     **if** entry.addr==VADDR **then**   ▷ cache hit
6:         **return** entry
7:     **end if**
8: **end for**
9: victim_entry=get_victim_entry(entrylist)   ▷ cache miss
10: **if** victim_entry.Modified **then**
11:     evict victim_entry to remote
12: **end if**
13: **if** OPT==READ **then**
14:     entry=rdma_read(VADDR,OFFSET)   ▷ read remote data
15:     **return** entry
16: **end if**
17: entry=get_entry(VADDR)   ▷ get local entry
18: **return** entry

The DLA accepts as input a virtual address (VADDR) which is intended for access by the application, an operation type (OPT) indicating either a read or write operation, and an OFFSET. It then retrieves the cache entry that corresponds to the provided virtual address. Initially, the VADDR is subjected to a hash function, resulting in the generation of a hashcode. This hashcode is subsequently used to compute an index by performing a modulo operation with the number of buckets' bucketsize, thereby identifying the specific location within the hash table to be queried.

Upon identifying the index, the system retrieves the entrylist, which represents the collection of entries stored at that index. Following the locking, the system iterates through each entry within the entrylist, comparing the address of each entry against the VADDR. In the event that a matching entry is identified, signifying a cache hit, the entry is unlocked and subsequently returned. However, if no matching entry is found upon completing the iteration, a cache miss is deemed to have occurred.

When cache miss, the system initiates the retrieval of data from a remote location. This process commences with a call to the get_victim_entry() function, which is responsible for identifying the least recently used entry (victim_entry) for replacement. If the cache associated with the victim_entry has been modified, the data contained within the victim_entry is written back to the remote memory via RDMA. Conversely, if no modifications have been made, the writing process to the remote is deemed unnecessary. The subsequent action is contingent upon the value of the OPT parameter. If the operation is read, a one-sided RDMA is employed to retrieve the data from the remote location and subsequently obtain the entry. Alternatively, if the operation is write, a cache entry is procured and subsequently inserted into the corresponding cache list.

3.3   Caching Strategy

When the cache miss, the appropriate strategy needs to be selected to evict the cache to remote. This paper proposes a Remote Memory Aware LRU Caching Algorithm (RM_AwareLRU), which takes into account the recent usage of the cache and the state of the cache (whether the cache has been modified or not). This strategy corresponds to the get victim_entry algorithm in line 11 of Algorithm 1, as shown in Algorithm 2.

Algorithm 2. RM_AwareLRU

Input: Less used list Inactive_list, traversed depth Max_depth
Output: entry needs to be evicted
1: **for** entry in Inactive_list and Current_depth<Max_depth **do**
2:      **if** entry.Modified==0 **then**
3:          **return** entry
4:      **end if**
5: **end for**
6: **return** inactive_list[0]   ▷ Least recently used entry

The lru_list in this paper mainly contains two linked lists: one is the recently used cache list active_list, the other is the recently used cache list inactive_list.

Each linked list holds a member pointer p of the corresponding cache entry, and the corresponding entry is obtained by pointer p.

The input to RM_AwareLRU is the least recently used cache table Inactive_list, the maximum traversal depth Max_depth (this is a variable parameter, which is set to 8 in this paper), and the Inactive_list[0] corresponding to the least used entry when selecting the eliminated cache. When traversing the depth of current_depth<Max_depth, if it finds a cache that has not been modified, it will be eliminated first. If the depth of Max_depth is reached, the least recently used cache will be eliminated. The corresponding entry is Inactive_list[0].

Finally, a summary of the interaction between cache and remote memory is given. When a read or write operation to SwiftSwap is initiated, if the cache is hit, the local cache will be operated directly. After the operation is completed, the read or write request will be directly marked as completed, and then asynchronously synchronized to the remote memory through RDMA. If the cache is not alive, it will first select a cache according to RM_AwareLRU to flush to the remote, and then if it is a write operation, it does not need to wait for the flush process, it can directly write data to the new entry, and then mark the request complete, after that, it will also call RDMA to asynchronously complete data synchronization. In the case of a read operation, rdma_read is called to read the remote data into the local cache before the data can be read.

4   Experiments and Evaluation

This part mainly answers the following three questions.

–   How was SwiftSwap setup and deployed in our evaluating environment?
–   How does SwiftSwap itself perform as a virtual block device?
–   What impact does SwiftSwap have on applications running in containers?

4.1   Experimental Setup

Our implementation of SwiftSwap on linux 5.15 contains more than 2600 lines of C code. The computing node is implemented based on infiniband and runs in the kernel space. It mainly creates a virtual block device and sets it as the swap space. The memory node is implemented based on rdma-core [14] and runs SwiftSwap server programs in user space.

Our experiments are mainly carried out in an RDMA cluster with two x86-64 machines, where the memory node is set to use 32 GB of memory, and the application of the computing node runs in the container, while some memory restrictions are made according to different application situations. The RDMA network between the two machines is connected by a direct network cable. Each machine has a kernel version 5.15.0, a 16-core Intel(R) Xeon(R) Gold 5218 CPU @ 2.30 GHz, and the CPU is an Intel(R) Xeon(R) Gold 5218 CPU. The version of the RDMA network card driver is MLNX_OFED_LINUX-5.8-3.0.7.0 (OFED-5.8-3.0.7).

4.2   Benefits as a Block Device

The first step is to evaluate the performance of SwiftSwap itself as a block device. We use fio [4] to conduct a comprehensive test and analysis of block device performance. And compared with Linux original swap and NBD. We selected several commonly used fio test methods, namely sequential read, random read, sequential write, and random write. We ran multiple tests after setting the device to its initial state and calculated the average. The sequential read results are shown in Fig. 3. According to the results, SwiftSwap has about 20.6% performance improvement in bandwidth and IOPS compared with default swap of Linux system, and has about 516.4% performance improvement compared with NBD. And the Tail Latency, especially on p99 and p999, is greatly reduced compared with Linux swap and NBD.

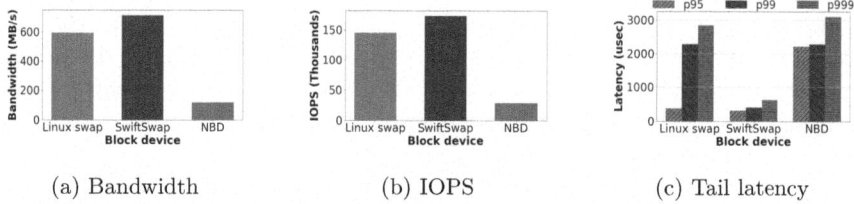

(a) Bandwidth   (b) IOPS   (c) Tail latency

Fig. 3. Evaluation results for sequential reads

Random read results are shown in Fig. 4. According to the results, SwiftSwap has about 57.9% performance improvement in bandwidth and IOPS compared with Linux swap, and about 296.4% performance improvement compared with NBD. Compared with Linux swap and NBD, the Tail Latency is greatly reduced, especially on p95 and p99, and the three are close to each other on p999.

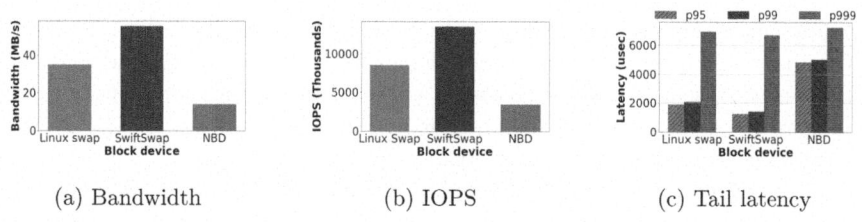

(a) Bandwidth   (b) IOPS   (c) Tail latency

Fig. 4. Evaluation results for random reads

The bandwidth and IOPS of SwiftSwap are 6.1% higher than that of Linux swap and 23.7% higher than that of NBD. The tail latency of SwiftSwap is 15% lower than that of Linux swap and 36% lower than that of NBD (Fig. 5).

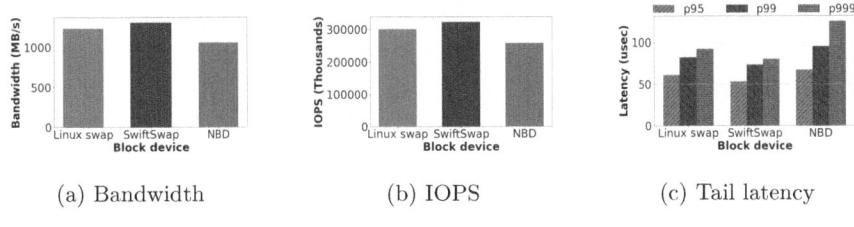

(a) Bandwidth   (b) IOPS   (c) Tail latency

Fig. 5. Evaluation results for sequential writes

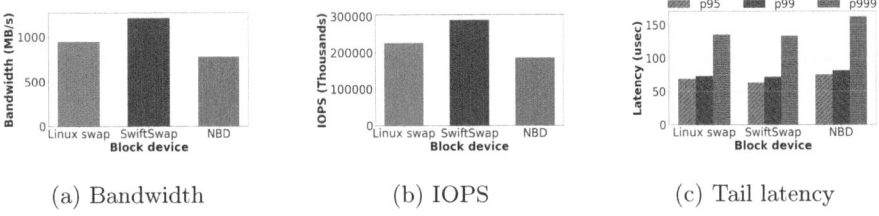

(a) Bandwidth   (b) IOPS   (c) Tail latency

Fig. 6. Evaluation results for random writes

The random write results are shown in Fig. 6. The bandwidth and IOPS of SwiftSwap are increased by about 28.1% compared with Linux swap and about 55.8% compared with NBD, and the tail latency is close to Linux swap.

The experimental results on block devices show that SwiftSwap outperforms nbd by about 516% and linux swap by about 58%.

4.3 Benefits for Applications

In order to evaluate the impact of SwiftSwap on applications running in Docker, we choose Memcached [11], Redis [15], Dacapo bench [3] and commonly used algorithm quicksort as program to conduct performance evaluation.

In this section, we evaluate the impact of SwiftSwap on the application by running the benchmark and setting different memory limits on the container based on the memory requirements of the application, and compare it with Linux swap and NBD. During the experiment in this part, the computing node will only open one swap at the same time, and the swap space set is enough for the application to use. Each experimental data is the average of multiple experimental data.

In the Memcached experiment, we run the Memcached server in Docker and set different container memory Settings, and use mcperf [10] for performance evaluating. We use mcperf to create 100 threads, read a total of 1 GB of data concurrently, and test with different data granularity. The evaluation results are depicted in the following Fig. 7a. According to the results, when data granularity is set to 1 KB, the throughput of SwiftSwap is about 37.8% higher than that of Linux swap, and about 116.9% higher than that of NBD. When data granularity is 4 KB, the throughput of SwiftSwap is 9.1% higher than that of Linux swap and

55.8% higher than that of NBD. When data granularity is 8 KB, the throughput of SwiftSwap is 10.9% higher than that of Linux swap and 63.4% higher than that of NBD.

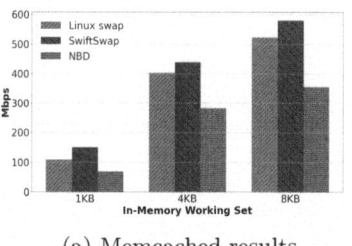

(a) Memcached results.

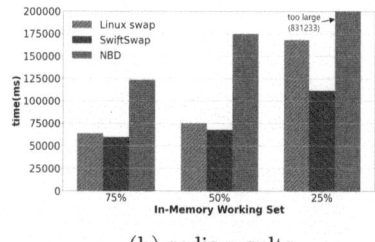

(b) redis results.

Fig. 7. Experimental results for memcached and redis.

In the Redis experiment, we run the Redis server in Docker and limit the server memory, write a script to use the Redis-benchmark to evaluate the performance of Redis and record the test time, and the test results are shown in Fig. 7b. According to the test results, when the In-Memroy Working Set is 75% and 50%, the performance of SwiftSwap is 7.2% and 10.8% higher than that of Linux swap, and the performance is 107.4% and 159.0% higher than that of NBD. When the In-Memroy Working Set is 25%, the performance of SwiftSwap is about 50.6% higher than that of Linux swap, and 645.6% higher than that of NBD.

In the experiments with Dacapo, we set the in-memory size to 75% of the working set and selected four benchmarks: h2, tradesoap, tradebeans, and jython for performance evaluation. The overall results are shown in Fig. 8a.

Under the h2 benchmark, SwiftSwap improves the performance by about 64.4% compared with Linux swap and by about 80.3% compared with NBD. In tradesoap benchmark, SwiftSwap improves the performance by about 142.3% compared with Linux swap and 261.4% compared with NBD. Under the tradebeans benchmark, SwiftSwap improves the performance by about 9.4% compared with Linux swap and 122.1% compared with NBD. Under the jython benchmark, SwiftSwap improves the performance by about 36.7% compared with Linux swap and 370.4% compared with NBD. Overall, SwiftSwap achieves 63.2% performance improvement over Linux swap and 208.5% improvement over NBD. We can see that SwiftSwap achieves significant performance gains on both the h2 and tradesoap benchmarks.

In the quicksort experiment, we run a quicksort program in a container to sort random integers and limit the memory of the container according to the memory required by the application, limiting the memory usage to 75% of the working set size, and record the time of quicksort under different memory. The experimental results are shown in Fig. 8b. On the whole, SwiftSwap improves only 9.3% performance compared with Linux swap and 33.2% performance compared

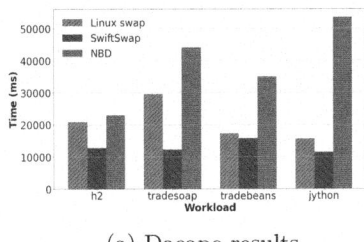

(a) Dacapo results.

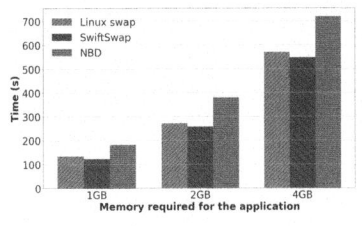

(b) Quicksort results.

Fig. 8. Experimental results for dacapo and redis.

with NBD, probably because memory access in quicksort is more continuous and the cache under Linux is easier to be utilized.

In summary, thanks to the efficient data transfer of RDMA, the cache added in this paper and the cache policy RM_AwareLRU, SwiftSwap can greatly improve the data transfer throughput and the application execution speed compared with the default swap and NBD of Linux. In terms of application performance improvement, compared with Linux swap, SwiftSwap improves the average performance by about 35.6% and the maximum performance by about 142.3%. Compared with NBD, SwiftSwap improves the average performance by about 186.3% and the maximum performance by about 645.6%.

5 Conclusion

This paper proposes a memory disaggregation solution SwiftSwap to efficiently use remote memory without any modifications to hardware, operating system, or application. SwiftSwap adds caches to compute nodes, designs and implements DLA to find cache entries, and caching strategy RM_AwareLRU, which reduces synchronous access to remote memory. We implemented SwiftSwap and conducted a thorough performance evaluation. The evaluation depicts that the advantages of swiftswwap in terms of block device throughput (up to 5.1×), tail latency (up to 4.8×), and application performance (up to 6.4×). In the future, we will optimize the existing framework to achieve high availability of the system.

Acknowledgments. This work was supported in part by the Joint Funds of the National Natural Science Foundation of China (Grant No. U22A2036), in part by the Shenzhen Colleges and Universities Stable Support Program under Grant GXWD20220817124251002, GXWD20231129102636001 and GXWD20231130110352002, in part by the Guangdong Basic and Applied Basic Research Foundation under Grant 2023A1515110271, in part by the Shenzhen Colleges and Universities Scientific Research Startup Foundation for Newly Introducing Advanced Scholars (entitled Research on Hybrid Deployment for Deep Learning Jobs on Intelligent Clusters); in part by the Scientific Research Startup Foundation of Harbin Institute of Technology Shenzhen.

References

1. Amaro, E., et al.: Can far memory improve job throughput? In: Proceedings of the Fifteenth European Conference on Computer Systems, pp. 1–16 (2020)
2. Cao, W., Liu, L.: Hierarchical orchestration of disaggregated memory. IEEE Trans. Comput. **69**(6), 844–855 (2020)
3. Dacapo (2024). https://github.com/dacapobench/dacapobench
4. Fio (2024). https://github.com/axboe/fio
5. Gao, P.X., et al.: Network requirements for resource disaggregation. In: 12th USENIX Symposium on Operating Systems Design and Implementation (OSDI 16), pp. 249–264 (2016)
6. Gouk, D., Lee, S., Kwon, M., Jung, M.: Direct access, high-performance memory disaggregation with DirectCXL. In: 2022 USENIX Annual Technical Conference (USENIX ATC 22), pp. 287–294 (2022)
7. Jia, X., Zhang, J., Yu, B., Qian, X., Qi, Z., Guan, H.: GiantVM: a novel distributed hypervisor for resource aggregation with DSM-aware optimizations. ACM Trans. Archit. Code Optim. (TACO) **19**(2), 1–27 (2022)
8. Keller Tesser, R., Borin, E.: Containers in HPC: a survey. J. Supercomput. **79**(5), 5759–5827 (2023)
9. Lee, S.S., Yu, Y., Tang, Y., Khandelwal, A., Zhong, L., Bhattacharjee, A.: MIND: in-network memory management for disaggregated data centers. In: Proceedings of the ACM SIGOPS 28th Symposium on Operating Systems Principles, pp. 488–504 (2021)
10. mcperf (2024). https://github.com/sivasankariit/mcperf
11. Memcached (2024). https://www.memcached.org
12. Network block device (2024). https://github.com/NetworkBlockDevice/nbd
13. Qiao, Y., et al.: Hermit: low-latency, high-throughput, and transparent remote memory via feedback-directed asynchrony. In: 20th USENIX Symposium on Networked Systems Design and Implementation (NSDI 23), pp. 181–198 (2023)
14. rdma-core (2024). https://github.com/linux-rdma/rdma-core
15. Redis (2024). https://redis.io
16. Ruan, Z., Schwarzkopf, M., Aguilera, M.K., Belay, A.: AIFM: high-performance, application-integrated far memory. In: 14th USENIX Symposium on Operating Systems Design and Implementation (OSDI 20), pp. 315–332 (2020)
17. Sunyaev, A., Sunyaev, A.: Cloud computing. In: Internet Computing: Principles of Distributed Systems and Emerging Internet-Based Technologies, pp. 195–236 (2020)

HASLB: Huge Page Allocation Strategy Optimized for Load-Balance in Parallel Computing Programs

Lei Yue[1], Tao Wu[1], Yang Shen[2], Jin Zhang[1], and Wenzhe Zhang[2(✉)]

[1] School of Computer and Communication Engineering, Changsha University
of Science and Technology, Changsha 410114, China
wutao@stu.csust.edu.cn
[2] College of Computer Science and Technology, National University of Defense
Technology, Changsha 410073, China
{shenyang_23,zhangwenzhe}@nudt.edu.cn

Abstract. Equitable resource allocation is currently considered as a key enabler for achieving complete parallelism in parallel computing. Optimized memory management mechanisms are crucial for load balance in parallel tasks. In some cases, the performance of Linux's huge page management mechanism deteriorates when handling parallel tasks due to the nonhomogeneous allocation of memory resources among parallel processes. This research introduces HASLB, a huge page allocation strategy optimized for parallel programs. HASLB evaluates the status of parallel processes based on the count of huge pages acquired by each process and the number of page faults it encountered. Following the results of the analysis, huge pages are allocated using a method conducive to load balance. The problems in the Linux transparent huge page mechanism are optimized through this strategy, which limits the greedy allocation mechanism in some situations. HASLB achieves a reasonable allocation of memory resources among parallel processes with low overhead, benefiting the load balance of parallel computing programs. In addition, contiguous memory would be protected because of limiting the greedy allocation of huge pages. The parallel benchmark experiments show a maximum performance improvement of 6.4% compared to Linux in the BFS benchmark. In the IS benchmark program, huge page consumption exhibits a 9% reduction.

Keywords: Parallel Computing · Load Balance · Huge Page Allocation

1 Introduction

Huge pages in Linux, available in 2 MB and 1 GB sizes, are designed to reduce memory management overhead and improve performance by decreasing TLB misses, page faults, and address translation overhead. Linux supports huge pages

Published by Springer Nature Switzerland AG 2025
X. Chen et al. (Eds.): NPC 2024, LNCS 15527, pp. 231–242, 2025.
https://doi.org/10.1007/978-981-96-2830-8_18

through two methods: standard huge pages using hugetlbfs [1] and transparent huge pages (THP) [2]. Standard huge pages require explicit user requests and reserve contiguous physical memory, which can complicate programming and exclude older applications. In contrast, THP offers transparent support, allowing applications to benefit from huge pages without code changes, making it popular in high-performance computing studies [3–7].

However, THP's aggressive allocation strategy can lead to performance issues, especially in parallel computing programs. THP allocates huge pages greedily during page faults, causing load imbalances where faster processes receive more huge pages and slower ones receive fewer. This imbalance may arise in environments where contiguous memory is limited, resulting in degraded performance of parallel programs.

To address THP's allocation issues, previous studies [3,5] have focused on reducing memory waste by adjusting page sizes based on memory utilization. However, these methods often introduce high monitoring overhead. The load imbalance caused by THP's strategy in parallel computing has been less explored, with more focus on upgrading hot pages to huge pages, which might improve performance but could also worsen load imbalance in parallel computations.

This research introduces HASLB, an optimized huge page allocation strategy for parallel computing. HASLB ensures even distribution of huge pages among parallel processes, maintaining load balance even in fragmented memory environments. It monitors page faults and huge page allocations within each process, using this data to guide future allocations. Our contributions include:

1) Improved Load Balance: HASLB ensures equitable huge page allocation among parallel processes, enhancing overall efficiency. Experimental results show a performance improvement of about 6.4% in fragmented memory environments compared to Linux, as shown by the BFS benchmark.
2) Dynamic Adjustment Based on Process States: HASLB dynamically adjusts huge page allocation by analyzing process states over time, ensuring fair distribution among processes requiring parallelism and adapting to changes.
3) Memory Fragmentation Mitigation: HASLB reduces memory fragmentation by limiting huge page allocation for faster processes. Preserving contiguous memory areas and reducing the defragmentation. In the IS benchmark [8], HASLB reduces huge page consumption by about 9% compared to Linux.

2   Background and Motivation

2.1   Advantages and Issues of Huge Pages

As computer technology advances, application memory demands have surged, and hardware-supported memory capacity continues to grow. Memory-intensive applications often generate numerous page table entries when using 4 KB base pages, leading to limited TLB coverage and increased TLB misses. In Linux, a TLB miss may require accessing a four-level page table, resulting in five memory accesses compared to one for a TLB hit, creating a significant disparity in address translation overhead. Huge pages can significantly improve TLB hit rates, as a single 2 MB huge page needs just one TLB entry, compared to 512 entries for the same memory size in base pages. This expands TLB coverage and enjoys broad support, with Linux offering transparent huge page (THP) support and hardware vendors like Intel enhancing L2 TLB entries for huge pages [9,10].

However, THP can lead to memory waste and performance issues due to its greedy allocation strategy. When applications encounter page faults, Linux aggressively allocates huge pages, and the khugepaged daemon upgrades base pages to huge pages. This approach often results in poor utilization of huge pages, causing memory waste and fragmentation. Over time, high fragmentation levels can lead to memory compression, which carries significant overhead, and studies [6,11] suggest that using huge pages may sometimes degrade performance compared to base pages.

2.2 THP-Induced Load Imbalance in Parallel Computing

Parallel computing programs maximize system resources and hardware power, speeding up processes and improving efficiency. Huge pages, a valuable resource, should be fully utilized in parallel computing. However, Linux's aggressive allocation strategy often assigns huge pages to processes experiencing page faults, leading to load imbalance. In complex environments, aggressive scheduling can exacerbate this issue, with faster processes obtaining more huge pages and slower processes fewer, especially during memory shortages.

Most parallel computing programs use MPI [12], where processes handle similar tasks and require equal resources. They also rely on synchronization, so faster processes wait for slower ones, making rapid execution less beneficial. THP's greedy allocation strategy further widens this gap, as faster processes get more huge pages and accelerate further, while slower processes lag. This creates a cycle of increasing load imbalance.

2.3 Motivation of the Research

Previous research [5] on huge pages primarily focused on improving memory utilization and reducing fragmentation. Ingens [3] is notable for its management of memory inflation and fragmentation by monitoring utilization and adjusting page sizes, though it introduces some overhead. While Ingens offers a fair allocation scheme for huge pages, it is geared towards parallel virtual machines rather than diverse parallel processes in a thread group. Studies aimed at boosting program performance through huge pages have mostly optimized access to frequently used pages by upgrading them from base to huge pages. However, this approach is not suitable for parallel computing programs, which can lead to uneven workload distribution in parallel programs, as it doesn't account for which process the hot pages belong to, potentially causing unfairness and exacerbating load imbalance.

To address these issues, this research introduces HASLB, a refined huge page allocation strategy designed to improve load balancing in parallel computing. By modifying the Linux kernel to limit the greedy allocation strategy, HASLB reduces the allocation of huge pages to highly efficient processes and promotes their allocation to less efficient ones, balancing memory resources and enhancing load balance. Additionally, HASLB aims to better utilize base pages in memory gaps, reducing fragmentation and preserving contiguous memory.

3   Design for Load Balance Among Parallel Processes

The design of HASLB relies on reserving transparent huge pages. After kernel initialization, the buddy system [13] manages memory. It organizes free blocks into multiple lists based on size, with each list indexed by the number of page frames it manages. The buddy system allocates the smallest suitable block, or a larger one if necessary [14], which supports the reservation of large memory blocks. By limiting the allocation of huge pages for faster processes and reserving them for slower processes, this approach aims to achieve more uniform distribution and better load balance in parallel programs.

In cases of contiguous memory shortages, Linux's default greedy allocation strategy may not fairly distribute huge pages in parallel computing. HASLB addresses this by ensuring fair allocation among multiple processes, overcoming the greedy strategy, which enhancing overall system efficiency in parallel processes.

3.1   Lightweight Monitoring and Sampling

We developed a lightweight monitoring module to record page faults and huge page allocations for parallel processes with minimal overhead. This data is analyzed using a huge page allocation decision model, which then assigns a new allocation ratio for each process. The design of HASLB is shown in Fig. 1.

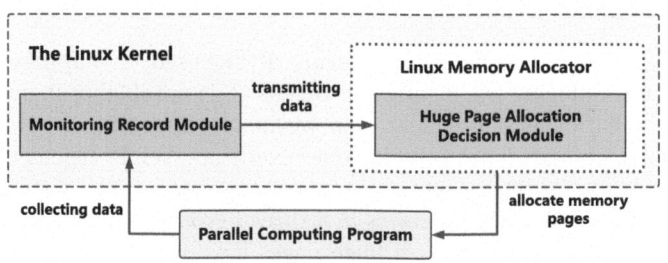

Fig. 1. The overview of HASLB.

Our framework consists of two main parts. A user-space application that specifies the processes in a parallel computing program that need to be monitored. And a kernel-based module that tracks the specified processes. This module collects data on page faults, huge page allocations, and process status (classified as "require huge pages" or "do not require huge pages").

Previous studies [3,15–19] used various monitoring techniques, such as Page Table-Based Memory Access Tracking and Hardware-Based Sampling, which often suffer from high overhead or lack fine-grained sampling of base pages. Our approach focuses on recording performance data during program execution. We define an allocation cycle as either when the total page fault count reaches 25600 or when huge page allocations total 50 pages. After collecting sufficient data, we adjust the allocation ratio for the next cycle. This process, illustrated in Fig. 2, repeats until the program ends.

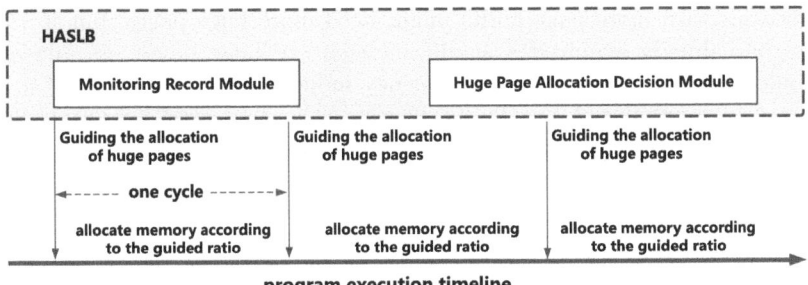

Fig. 2. The working process representation of HASLB.

The performance monitoring module operates in real-time, tracking page faults and huge page allocations with minimal overhead. It gathers and compiles data on page faults and huge page allocations per process, which is then used to adjust allocation ratios of each process for subsequent cycles.

3.2   Huge Page Allocation Strategy for Load Balance

Our research introduces an adaptive allocation mechanism, HASLB, which ensures more equitable huge page distribution than Linux, benefiting load balance in parallel programs. HASLB analyzes data from each allocation cycle to determine process execution speed and memory needs, using this information to allocate huge pages more fairly in subsequent cycles. Our strategy is based on two key designs.

1) **Allocating huge pages based on process states for better load balance.** In MPI programs, processes may have distinct roles, such as computation or data collection, and may not always operate simultaneously or require the same resources. HASLB adjusts huge page allocation dynamically according to the state of each process, ensuring fair distribution among those needing it. For example, during computation, if four processes are running

simultaneously, they will receive huge pages equally. After the computation finishes, if only one process responsible for data collection needs memory, it will receive all the available huge pages.

The need for huge pages is determined by the ratio of page faults for each process compared to the total number of page faults in the cycle. Processes with a page fault ratio below a threshold are marked with state 0, which means that the process does not need to be allocated huge pages and receive base pages only. Processes exceeding the threshold are marked with state 1 and receive an equitable share of huge pages. Huge pages will be allocated fairly among processes in state 1.

2) **Adjust huge page allocation based on each process's page fault proportions and current huge page share.** Building on the design1, we further adjust huge page allocation according to each process's page faults. Processes with more page faults might need more huge pages, but if a process has already acquired a significant share of huge pages, its allocation should be reduced. Page fault frequency indicates memory needs of a process. A high number of page faults suggests either increased memory usage or exhausted huge pages. The number of huge pages a process has reflects how well its needs are met. Faster-running processes often experience more page faults and consume more huge pages. To maintain load balance, huge page allocations should be reduced for faster-running processes and increased for slower-running processes.

The allocation quota of huge pages for process i.

$$b_i = (\frac{A_i}{\sum\limits_{i=0}^{n} A_i} \times (1-q) + \frac{\frac{sum+N}{n} - B_i}{N} \times q) \times N \tag{1}$$

Let b_i be the upper limit of huge pages for process i in the next cycle. A_i is the page fault count for process i this cycle, sum denotes total allocated huge pages, N is the total number of huge pages to be allocated per cycle, and B_i is the number of huge pages already acquired by process i. n is the number of processes, and q, ranging from 0 to 1, balances the impact of page faults and existing huge pages on the allocation.

The page fault proportion affects fair huge page allocation to meet memory needs, while the proportion of already acquired huge pages aims for equity. Setting q to 1 eliminates this effect, which may lead high-load processes to use more base pages and fewer huge pages compared to lower-load processes, which is not ideal. Setting q to 0 results in greedy allocation similar to Linux's approach, which does not promote load balance. In the experiment, we conducted a large number of tests on multiple benchmark programs. Experiments showed that $0.8 < q < 0.9$ achieves the better load balance. For the setting of q, the default setting is 0.85, and we have also developed an interface for users to adjust it. In subsequent work, we will explore methods to automatically adjust the q value to achieve optimal load balancing.

In summary, HASLB uses process status and page fault proportion to determine the allocation of huge pages for the next cycle, ensuring fair distribution and load balance in parallel programs.

4 Experiment

We developed a memory fragmentation program to create a controllable environment for varying fragmentation degree. This program allows precise create fragmentation area and degree, which ensures accuracy in comparative testing. Six benchmark programs—IS (Integer Sort, random memory access), MG (Multi-Grid on a sequence of meshes, long- and short-distance communication, memory intensive), CG (Conjugate Gradient, irregular memory access and communication), BFS (Breadth-First Search), LAS (Large Array Summation), and QuickSort—were used to compare Linux's huge page allocation strategy with HASLB. The first three benchmarks are from NAS Parallel Benchmarks (NBP) [8]. These benchmarks, based on MPI, cover a range of tasks including complex communication, memory-intensive operations, and irregular memory access.

The experiments utilized the Linux kernel version 5.10.194, and the processor of the test platform is ARM64 architecture with 8 cores. The number of processes of the MPI parallel program we tested is set to 2, 4, 6, and 8. The memory size of the test environment is set to 3 GB, 4 GB, 6 GB and 8 GB to test the benchmark programs under different memory conditions. Before the test, 2/3 of the memory is fragmented by the fragmentation program, and huge pages cannot be allocated in the fragmented memory area. Based on the above configuration, we strictly control the variables and conduct a large number of tests to compare the load balancing performance of HASLB and Linux. By testing the IS and MG benchmark programs, we show in detail the differences in the huge page allocation process between HASLB and Linux, as well as the differences in page consumption between HASLB and Linux. For all benchmark programs, we compare the performance of HASLB and Linux as well as the huge page consumption. All test results are presented in Sect. 5.

5 Evaluation

In the experimental setup, the IS benchmark classes was configured to Class C, the number of processes is configured as 4, with iteration counts established at 10, 50, and 100 for various stress tests performed on Linux and HASLB. The average performance metrics were calculated across several test iterations, and Table 1 displays the comparative performance results of HASLB versus Linux.

We set the iteration count to 100 and collected the data. Table 2 compares the huge page consumption between the two strategies, and Fig. 3 shows the trend of huge page allocation for the IS benchmark program. Figure 3 reveals that Linux's greedy allocation results in uneven huge page distribution among the four parallel MPI processes. Initially, each process requests few huge pages,

Table 1. Performance comparison of IS on Linux and HASLB.

Iterations	Time consumption on Linux (s)	Time consumption on HASLB (s)
10	14.90	14.91
50	72.97	71.64
100	139.57	136.97

allowing for a relatively fair distribution. However, after 20 s, a surge in page requests leads to unequal allocation, with some processes rapidly acquiring more pages than others. By the 30-s mark, the system's huge pages are depleted, with Process 2 acquiring the most (155 pages) and Process 4 the least (89 pages). This highlights how Linux's approach can cause load imbalance in parallel programs.

Table 2. Comparison of huge pages consumption of IS on Linux and HASLB.

Benchmark Program	Consumption on Linux	Consumption on HASLB
IS (Class C)	463	421

In contrast, HASLB ensures even huge page allocation among parallel processes, as shown in Fig. 3. At 20 s, as demand increases, HASLB limits allocation of pages to faster processes and redistributes the saved huge pages to slower ones. This continues until all huge pages are consumed, with each process receiving approximately 105 huge pages, ensuring equitable distribution.

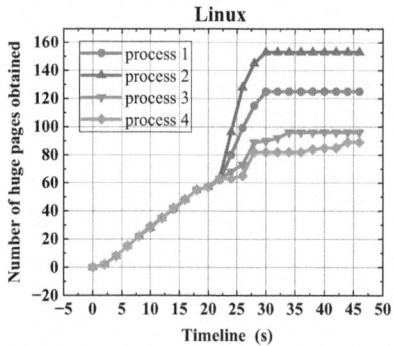 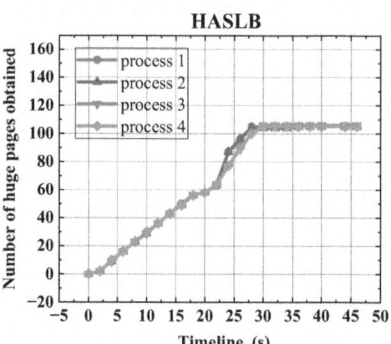

Fig. 3. Comparison of huge page allocation trends on Linux and HASLB.

We also evaluated various MPI-based parallel benchmark programs in a fragmented memory environment. Figure 4 shows that, with Linux as the baseline (100%), HASLB improves performance: a 6.41% gain in the BFS, a 3.34% gain in CG and a 1.87% gain in the IS. The advantage of HASLB is that it can fairly allocate huge pages to parallel processes even in fragmented memory. Therefore, HASLB helps to enhance load balance and overall efficiency.

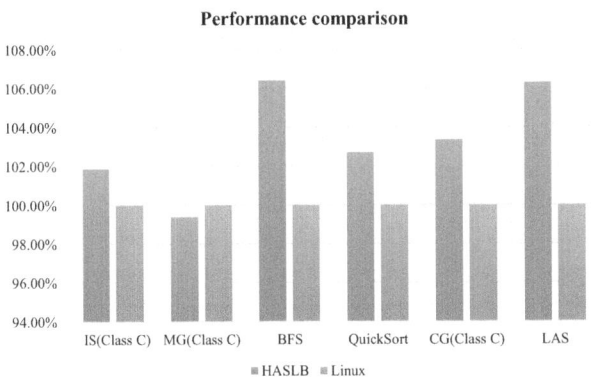

Fig. 4. Performance comparison of various benchmark programs on Linux and HASLB.

The performance of MG on HASLB does not improve compared to Linux, but it significantly reduces huge page consumption. MG (Class C) tests showed a 21% reduction in huge page consumption with HASLB compared to Linux. Figure 5 shows the remaining physical memory after completing the MG operation.

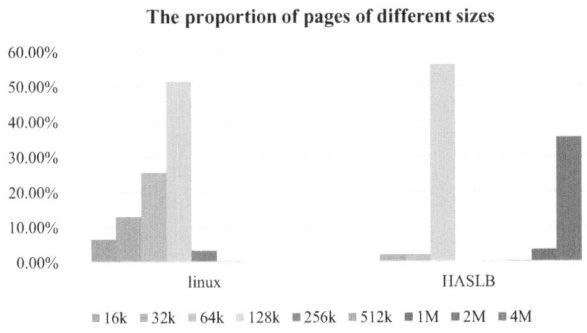

Fig. 5. Comparing Linux and HASLB, after executing MG, the proportion of blocks of different sizes in the remaining memory of the system

On the other hand, HASLB is good for keeping contiguous memory. After executing MG on Linux, contiguous memory is nearly depleted, as shown in Fig. 5. Contiguous blocks of 2 MB or larger are at 0%, while blocks smaller than

512 KB account for over 9%, with 128 KB blocks making up more than 50%. In contrast, running MG on HASLB preserves contiguous memory, with blocks larger than 2 MB making up about 36% of the remaining memory. Blocks of 128 KB are over 50%, similar to Linux. HASLB maintains contiguous memory by controlling huge page allocation while supporting parallel computing performance.

HASLB generally offers better huge page consumption compared to Linux. Figure 6 compares huge page consumption between the two strategies, with Linux set to 100%. HASLB reduces huge page consumption by 21% in the MG benchmark and shows advantages in other benchmarks as well. Lower huge page consumption increases base page usage, protecting contiguous memory and easing defragmentation in fragmented environments.

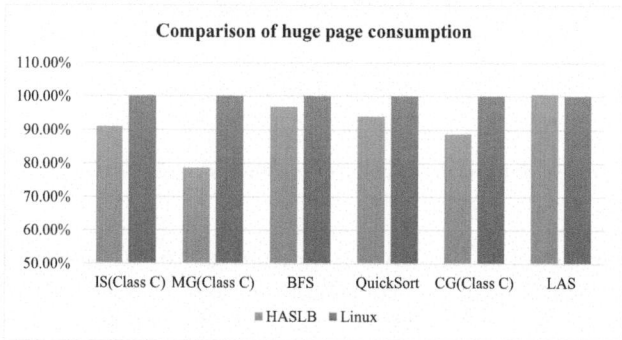

Fig. 6. Comparison of huge page consumption of various benchmark programs on Linux and HASLB.

The experimental results show that HASLB can achieve huge page allocations conducive to load balance when dealing with parallel computing programs. In environments with severe memory fragmentation and a shortage of contiguous memory, HASLB has a performance advantage over Linux. In most cases, HASLB significantly reduces the consumption of contiguous memory compared to Linux.

6   Related Work

Recent research on memory management focuses on optimizing application performance. The study [20] address heterogeneous memory systems by migrating hot pages to faster memory. However, this approach is not always beneficial because it merely migrates hot pages to fast memory without considering which process the hot pages belong to. In parallel computing programs, it may lead to a situation where a large number of pages from one process are migrated to fast memory, resulting in an uneven workload. Merchandiser [21] addresses this issue. Their strategy can fairly distribute memory resources among parallel processes on heterogeneous memory, achieving load balance in parallel programs. This research guides the fair allocation of huge pages on regular systems.

In regular systems [3,6], the strategy typically involves upgrading hot base pages to huge pages to improve performance by enhancing access efficiency. However, these methods may cause load imbalance and face high overhead challenges in monitoring memory utilization. Ingens uses the Linux memory access tracking framework for fine-grained monitoring but with increased overhead, while another study [5] achieves low-overhead monitoring by combining TLB and page table monitoring. However, this approach cannot achieve fine-grained sampling with huge pages and does not consider load balancing among parallel processes.

7   Conclusion

This research introduces HASLB, a new strategy for allocating huge pages to enhance load balance in parallel computing environments. Designed to curb Linux's aggressive memory allocation, HASLB effectively allocates huge pages fairly even in fragmented memory scenarios, outperforming the Linux transparent huge page mechanism. HASLB collects and processes data with very low overhead through simple monitoring. By limiting huge page allocation for faster processes and reserving resources for slower ones, HASLB improves load balance and reduces huge page consumption. It limits unreasonable hugepage allocations and allocating base pages helps preserve contiguous memory and reduce fragmentation.

References

1. Linux Foundation: Hugetlbfs Reaervation. Linux Kernel Documentation. https://www.kernel.org/doc/html/v4.18/vm/hugetlbfs-reserv.html. Accessed 15 May 2024
2. Linux Foundation: Transparent Huge Pages. Linux Kernel Documentation. https://www.kernel.org/doc/html/latest/admin-guide/mm/transhuge.html. Accessed 15 May 2024
3. Kwon, Y., Yu, H., Peter, S., Rossbach, C.J., Witchel, E.: Ingens: huge page support for the OS and hypervisor. SIGOPS Oper. Syst. Rev. **51**(1), 83–93 (2017). https://doi.org/10.1145/3139645.3139659
4. Manocha, A., Yan, Z., Tureci, E., Aragón, J.L., Nellans, D., Martonosi, M.: Architectural support for optimizing huge page selection within the OS. In: Proceedings of the 56th Annual IEEE/ACM International Symposium on Microarchitecture (MICRO '23), pp. 1–14. ACM, New York (2023). https://doi.org/10.1145/3613424.3614296
5. Li, X., Liu, L., Yang, S., Peng, L., Qiu, J.: Thinking about a new mechanism for huge page management. In: Proceedings of the 10th ACM SIGOPS Asia-Pacific Workshop on Systems, pp. 40–46. Association for Computing Machinery (2019). https://doi.org/10.1145/3343737.3343745
6. Panwar, A., Prasad, A., Gopinath, K.: Making huge pages actually useful. SIGPLAN Not. **53**(2), 679–692 (2018). https://doi.org/10.1145/3296957.3173203

7. Hunter, A.H., Kennelly, C., Turner, P., Gove, D., Moseley, T., Ranganathan, P.: Beyond malloc efficiency to fleet efficiency: a hugepage-aware memory allocator. In: USENIX Symposium on Operating Systems Design and Implementation (2021). https://api.semanticscholar.org/CorpusID:235651499

8. NASA Advanced Supercomputing (NAS) Division: NAS Parallel Benchmarks (2023). https://www.nas.nasa.gov/software/npb.html. Accessed 20 Apr 2024

9. 7-cpu.com: Skylake. http://www.7-cpu.com/cpu/Skylake.html. Accessed 10 May 2024

10. 7-cpu.com: Haswell. http://www.7-cpu.com/cpu/Haswell.html. Accessed 10 May 2024

11. Kwon, Y., et al.: Coordinated and efficient huge page management with ingens. In: OSDI (2016). https://doi.org/10.5555/3026877.3026931

12. Open MPI: Open Source High Performance Computing. https://www.open-mpi.org/. Accessed 25 Apr 2024

13. Linux Foundation: Physical Page Allocation. Linux Kernel Documentation. https://www.kernel.org/doc/gorman/html/understand/understand009.html. Accessed 15 May 2024

14. Mauerer, W.: Professional Linux Kernel Architecture, 1st edn. Wiley, Hoboken (2008)

15. Bergman, S., Faldu, P., Grot, B., Vilanova, L., Silberstein, M.: Reconsidering OS memory optimizations in the presence of disaggregated memory. In: Proceedings of the 2022 ACM SIGPLAN International Symposium on Memory Management, pp. 1–14 (2022). https://doi.org/10.1145/3520263.3534650

16. Kim, J., Choe, W., Ahn, J.: Exploring the design space of page management for multi-tiered memory systems. In: Proceedings of the 2021 USENIX Annual Technical Conference, pp. 715–728 (2021). https://www.usenix.org/conference/atc21/presentation/kim-jonghyeon

17. Duraisamy, P., et al.: Towards an adaptable systems architecture for memory tiering at warehouse-scale. In: Proceedings of the 28th ACM International Conference on Architectural Support for Programming Languages and Operating Systems, pp. 727–741 (2023). https://doi.org/10.1145/3582016.3582031

18. Gupta, V., Lee, M., Schwan, K.: HeteroVisor: exploiting resource heterogeneity to enhance the elasticity of cloud platforms. In: Proceedings of the 11th ACM SIGPLAN/SIGOPS International Conference on Virtual Execution Environments, pp. 79–92 (2015). https://doi.org/10.1145/2817817.2731191

19. Lee, T., Monga, S.K., Min, C., Eom, Y.I.: MEMTIS: efficient memory tiering with dynamic page classification and page size determination. In: Proceedings of the 29th Symposium on Operating Systems Principles (SOSP '23), pp. 17–34 (2023). https://doi.org/10.1145/3600006.3613167

20. Dulloor, S.R., et al.: Data tiering in heterogeneous memory systems. In: Proceedings of the Eleventh European Conference on Computer Systems, pp. 1–16 (2016). https://doi.org/10.1145/2901318.2901344

21. Xie, Z., Liu, J., Li, J., Li, D.: Merchandiser: data placement on heterogeneous memory for task-parallel HPC applications with load-balance awareness. In: Proceedings of the 28th ACM SIGPLAN Annual Symposium on Principles and Practice of Parallel Programming, pp. 204–217. Association for Computing Machinery (2023). https://doi.org/10.1145/3572848.3577497

LightFinder: Finding Persistent Items with Small Memory

Lu Cao[1,2], Weiqiang Xiao[1], and Weizhe Zhang[1,2](✉)

[1] Department of Computer Science and Technology, Harbin Institute of Technology,
Shenzhen, China
{caol,weizhe.zhang}@pcl.ac.cn
[2] Peng Cheng Laboratory, Shenzhen, China

Abstract. Detecting persistent items in large-scale data streams efficiently and accurately is a significant challenge, particularly when working with limited memory. Current state-of-the-art methods often require substantial memory resources to maintain high detection accuracy. To address this limitation, we present LightFinder (LF), which leverages a Conservative-Update (CU) strategy to minimize hash collision errors by selectively updating the smallest active counter. Additionally, LF supports detection across varying persistence windows, enhancing detection accuracy and flexibility in skewed data streams. Our analysis reveals that LF excels in detecting persistent items with high accuracy even under stringent memory constraints. Our approach effectively estimates item persistence and maintains robust performance across various persistence windows. Notably, when operating with just 10% of the memory required by On-Off Sketch (OO), LF achieves an Average Absolute Error (AAE) nearly half that of OO (up to 1.5 times lower), and its Average Relative Error (ARE) is reduced by an order of magnitude. This demonstrates LF significantly outperforms existing methods in terms of space efficiency. Our codes are open-sourced on GitHub [1].

Keywords: Data streams · Persistent items · Persistence windows · Sketch

1 Introduction

As big data continues to grow exponentially, processing high-dimensional items within data streams has become increasingly costly and difficult. The challenge of preserving vast quantities of data under limited resources is now more pressing than ever. Defined by their ordered, high-volume, and rapidly arriving sequences, data streams embody complex, high-dimensional items that must undergo compression for efficient processing [5,10]. During compression, these items exhibit three key characteristics: high speed, skewness, and persistence [6,7,22,25]. The ability to analyze and extract these traits through advanced processing techniques is essential for improving data processing capabilities, highlighting the critical importance of research in this area [3,8].

© IFIP International Federation for Information Processing 2025
Published by Springer Nature Switzerland AG 2025
X. Chen et al. (Eds.): NPC 2024, LNCS 15527, pp. 243–255, 2025.
https://doi.org/10.1007/978-981-96-2830-8_19

In modern communication networks, base stations are required to process massive user data streams in real-time, managing millions of item packets per second while maintaining high continuity. To achieve this, item processing algorithms depend on compact data structures that optimize memory efficiency and effectively handle high-load conditions. The inherent skewness within data streams—where the majority of items appear infrequently, and a small subset dominates—introduces significant complexity. This imbalance poses a considerable challenge to real-time feature detection, particularly when operating under constrained memory [18,27]. For example, while 2-bit counters are prone to overflow, 32-bit counters, though preventing overflow, limit the number of available counters, thereby reducing detection accuracy [14–16,21]. The concept of persistence in data streams, which refers to the repeated occurrence of items across non-overlapping time windows, adds another layer of difficulty to real-time identification. The rapid pace of data streams exacerbates the challenge of accurately detecting persistent items without incurring excessive memory consumption [9]. Although persistence is advantageous for maintaining update histories and facilitating efficient querying, its linear space consumption becomes increasingly problematic in scenarios with limited memory and biased data distributions. To address these challenges—namely, the high speed, skewness, and persistence of data streams—the Persistent Sketch method has been proposed [4,13,17], particularly for use cases such as spectrum monitoring and anomaly detection. Consequently, the ability to efficiently query persistent items in environments with limited memory has emerged as a critical research priority.

Key Sketch algorithms for detecting persistent items in high-speed data streams include Small-Space (SS) [12], PIE [2], and On-Off Sketch [26]. The foundational concept behind SS is "sampling and counting" which utilizes a hash table to track item frequencies. However, this method's space efficiency is compromised by the necessity to sample all items, including those that are non-persistent. PIE addresses this by employing a reversible Bloom Filter [23] combined with Raptor codes [19] to encode item IDs for the purpose of identifying persistent items. Despite its effectiveness, PIE suffers from space inefficiency as it encodes both persistent and non-persistent items in each window, leading to wasted space. In contrast, OO distinguishes between persistent and non-persistent items, aiming to optimize space usage by storing only persistent items. However, this approach is not without its limitations; hash collisions in the Count-Min (CM) sketch [20] can result in an overestimation of item persistence. Each of these algorithms grapples with issues related to memory efficiency, especially under constrained memory conditions, and typically operates under the assumption of uniform time window sizes.

To address the constraints of existing methods concerning memory usage and accuracy, contemporary research has increasingly focused on the development of compact data structures for Persistent Sketch and the optimization of counter efficiency. In response to these challenges, we introduce LightFinder (LF), a novel approach designed to facilitate efficient and accurate querying of persistent items within low-memory environments. LF primarily confronts two critical issues: the estimation of persistence and the detection of persistent items. Specifically, LF approximates the persistence value of each item in the data stream and identifies items that exceed a designated persistence threshold.

LF employs a 2D array data structure, where each row is associated with a distinct hash function mapping items to specific counters. Each bucket within this array contains two fields: one for storing the key of a persistent item and another as a flag indicating whether the item has been accessed within the current time window. The flag is initially set to "On" and switches to "Off" once accessed. This design ensures efficient memory usage and mitigates counter overflow. Leveraging the inherent skew in data streams and the periodic nature of item persistence, LF sequentially marks multiple items that map to the same counter. This strategy mitigates errors arising from multiple hashing functions and optimizes the use of memory. The data structure of LF is streamlined to retain only essential information, which enhances its suitability for environments with restricted memory resources. When an item exhibits sufficient persistence across multiple measurement windows, LF capitalizes on this periodic increase by methodically marking items associated with the same counter, thereby collecting code bits to accurately decode and identify the persistent item's identifier. Our key contributions can be summarized as follows:

- Introduction of LF: We introduce LightFinder (LF) as a novel approach for efficiently and accurately estimating persistence and detecting persistent items in environments with limited memory.
- Conservative-Update (CU)-Based Selective Update: LF utilizes a CU-based selective update strategy to achieve high-precision detection of persistent items under constrained memory conditions. Notably, when operating with only $1/10$ of the memory compared to existing methods, LF's Average Absolute Error (AAE) is reduced to half that of the On-Off Sketch (OO)—up to 1.5 times lower—while its Average Relative Error (ARE) is an order of magnitude lower.
- Support for Variable Window Sizes: LF is capable of handling persistence queries across varying window sizes. Evaluations conducted using real network traffic datasets reveal that LF consistently outperforms the existing OO scheme across a range of window sizes.

The paper is structured as follows: Sect. 2 reviews related work, emphasizing the limitations of recent studies in persistence estimation. Section 3 introduces the concept of persistent items and details the design of LightFinder. Section 4 presents experimental results and analysis. Finally, Sect. 5 concludes the paper and future work.

2   Related Work and Observations

Existing methods for detecting persistent items have faced significant challenges in balancing high accuracy with efficient memory usage, motivating the development of our proposed approach. While there have been advancements in signal detection with recent studies such as Small-Space (SS) [12], PIE [2], and On-Off

Sketch (OO) [26], accurately estimating the persistence of all items remains a difficult task.

SS employs a sampling strategy within a hash table to track signal persistence, which helps to reduce time and space overhead. However, this method records a large number of non-persistent signals, leading to inefficient memory usage. To address the limitations of sampling, PIE utilizes Raptor codes to encode signal identifiers, storing these codes instead of the actual IDs. This approach minimizes memory usage and incorporates persistence and frequency weighting, enabling better detection of infrequent but persistent signals. Despite these improvements, PIE's requirement to store codes for all signals—including non-persistent ones—combined with the complexity of the encoding and decoding processes, presents challenges for handling high-speed data streams.

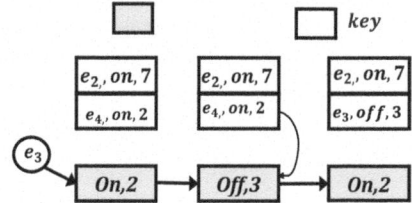

Fig. 1. An insertion example of the On-Off Sketch

Figure 1 OO Sketch improves upon the Count-Min (CM) Sketch by introducing state indicators that monitor counter increments within each time window, effectively filtering out non-persistent signals and retaining only the persistent ones. Its structure consists of a counter array and a key-value bucket array. Each counter features an on/off state, which allows it to increment once per time window, thereby enhancing accuracy and optimizing memory usage. Upon the arrival of a signal, OO maps it to a counter via a hash function. If the counter is in the 'on' state and the signal has not yet been recorded, the flag switches to 'off', and the counter is incremented by one. The counter's value is then compared with the stored value in the key-value pair. If the stored value is lower, both the key and value are updated with the new signal's key and the counter's value. Finally, the counter's state and value are swapped with the replaced key-value pair. However, due to the possibility of multiple signals being mapped to the same counter, OO's replacement strategy may erroneously classify a single occurrence as persistent, thereby reducing detection accuracy, particularly under low-memory conditions.

From these observations, we can draw the following conclusions about existing persistent signal detection methods:

1. *High Accuracy with Limited Memory: Current methods struggle to maintain high detection accuracy when constrained to low-memory environments, particularly when the available memory is less than 100 KB.*
2. *Handling High-Speed Data Streams: Although these methods may achieve low detection errors, the complexity of multiple memory accesses and the associated update processes hinder their capability to manage high-speed data streams effectively, thereby limiting their practical deployment.*

These limitations highlight the need for a more efficient approach to detecting persistent items, which we address with our proposed method.

3   LightFinder Design

Motivated by the inefficiencies observed in existing methods under limited memory and high-speed conditions [24], we designed LightFinder to optimize memory usage and enhance the accuracy and flexibility of detecting persistent items in high-speed, skewed data streams. Persistent Items in Data Streams are characterized by repeating sequences of items. LightFinder employs a novel approach using a Conservative-Update strategy to achieve this goal. Furthermore, LightFinder introduces the capability to support varying persistent window sizes, significantly improving detection performance in dynamic data stream environments. In the design of LightFinder, persistent items are identified as sequences that repeat within L non-overlapping time windows. The persistence of an item e is determined by its appearances across these time windows, with persistence values ranging from 0 to L. An item is classified as α-persistent if it appears in at least αL windows, where α is a user-defined threshold, satisfying the condition $0 < \alpha \leq 1$. This threshold α establishes the criterion for identifying α-persistence, allowing users to set a specific persistence level according to their needs. sLightFinder's flexible approach to handling persistence across varying window sizes, coupled with its Conservative-Update strategy, provides an efficient solution for accurately detecting persistent items, even in scenarios with constrained memory and high-speed, skewed data streams.

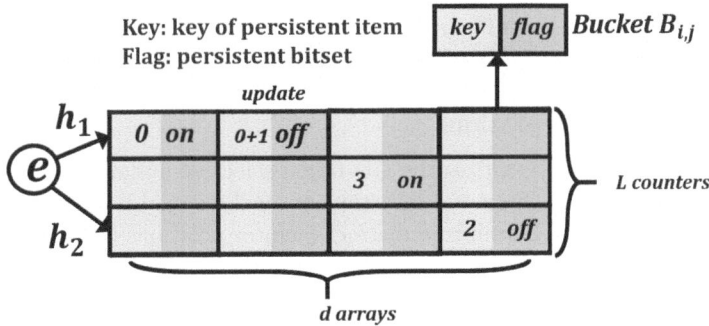

Fig. 2. The data structure of LightFinder

3.1   Data Structure

The data structure employed by LightFinder (LF), as depicted in Figs. 2, consists of a 2D array with d rows and l columns. Each row is associated with a distinct hash function $h_1, h_2, \ldots, h_d$, which maps incoming data items to specific counter columns. Within each bucket $B_{i,j}$, there are two fields: one dedicated to storing the key of a persistent item, and the other to a *flag* that indicates whether the item has been accessed during the current time window. Initially, this *flag* is set to *On* and is switched to *Off* once the item is accessed.

The counters within this 2D array are designed to monitor item persistence, with each row containing multiple counters, the positions of which are determined by the respective hash functions. Upon the arrival of a new item, it is mapped to the counters in each row, and the corresponding *bitset* status is evaluated. The *bitset*, initially set to *On*, indicates whether the item has appeared within the current window. If the *bitset* is *On*, indicating the item's first occurrence, the status is switched to *Off*, and the counter is incremented by one. Conversely, if the *bitset* is *Off*, meaning that the item has already appeared, the counter remains unchanged. LF updates the counters sequentially during the item insertion process.

3.2 CU-Based Selective Update Strategy

The CU-based selective update strategy introduces a subtle yet significantly efficient modification to the traditional CM strategy, known as conservative updating. Unlike the CM strategy, which increments each mapped counter, the CU strategy opts to increment only the smallest counter (or counters, in the event of a tie for the minimum) among those mapped.

The CM strategy encounters issues due to the inherent nature of hash collisions, where the same counter may be mapped to by distinct elements. Incrementing every counter mapped by an element with each operation can substantially amplify the error attributed to cumulative miscounting. In contrast, the CU strategy mitigates this by updating only the smallest counter value among those an element is mapped to during each operation. By doing so, it avoids inflating counters that have already been affected by hash collisions, thus reducing the error associated with cumulative miscounting. This refined approach enhances the accuracy of network traffic analysis by conservatively adjusting the counters and providing a more reliable estimation of traffic patterns.

3.3 LightFinder Operations

Insert: LightFinder (LF) utilizes the CU-based selective update strategy during persistence estimation. Upon the insertion of an item e_i, LF computes d hash functions, which map the item to d distinct counter positions $C_j[h_j(e_i)]$. During this insertion, the LF first identifies the minimum value $\min_{1 \leq j \leq d}(C_j[h_j(e_i)])$ among the d counters. It then updates the counters among the d counters whose count value equals this minimum value and whose bitset is in the *On* state. Afterward, the bitset status is changed to *Off*, and the counter value is incremented to $\min_{1 \leq j \leq d}(C_j[h_j(e_i)]) + 1$.

Query: When querying the persistence of an item e_i, LFbegins by computing the d hash functions to retrieve the corresponding d counters. The persistence of e_i is then estimated by reporting the minimum value among these counters. Formally, the estimated persistence $\hat{p}_i$ is defined as: $\hat{p}_i = \min_{1 \leq j \leq d}(C_j[h_j(e_i)])$.

3.4 A Running Example

Figure 3 illustrates the item insertion in the LightFinder algorithm, showing operations and update rules for multiple items. With $d = 3$, each item maps

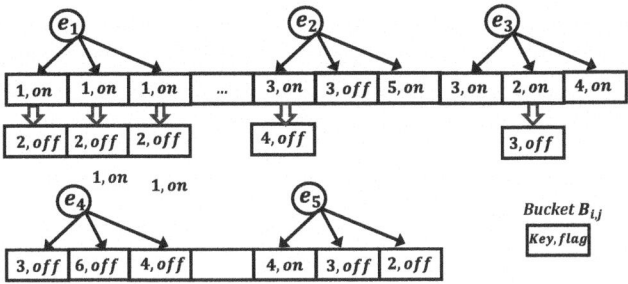

Fig. 3. A running example of LightFinder

to three counters via hash functions, and the counter states are checked. The following outlines the handling steps for each case:

Case 1: e_1 is mapped to three buckets where all window states are *On*, and their count values are equal to 1. The window state is set to *Off*, and the counter is updated to 2.

Case 2: e_2 is mapped to three buckets where all window states are *On*, and their count values are 2, 3, and 4. Update the count value of the bucket with the smallest count value to 3, and set its window state to *Off*.

Case 3: e_3 is mapped to three buckets, among which there are two buckets with the smallest count value, and their window states are *On* and *Off*. Increment the count value of the former by one and set its window state to *Off*.

Case 4: e_4 is mapped to three buckets, and their window states are all *Off*. No updates are made.

Case 5: e_5 is mapped to three buckets, among which the bucket with the smallest count value has its window state set as *Off*. No updates are made.

4   Performance Evaluation

In this section, the experimental settings are presented, and the performance of LightFinder in persistence estimation and identifying persistent items evaluated.

4.1   Experimental Settings

Development: Both LightFinder and On-Off Sketch were implemented in C++ using 32-bit Bob Hash with varying seeds. The experimental parameters are set as $d = 3$ (3 rows) for both OO and LF. For OO, the number of counters per row is defined as $l = \frac{M}{d \times \left(\frac{1}{8}+4\right)}$, while for LF, it is $l = \frac{M}{d \times \left(\frac{1}{8}+2\right)}$, where M represents the total memory size in bytes. All algorithms were executed in a single-threaded environment. We only compared OO because it is the most representative algorithm in this field.

Computation Platform: The experiments were conducted on a six-core Intel i5-8400 processor (2.80 GHz, 6 threads) equipped with 16 GB of DRAM. The processor is configured with 32 KB of L1 cache, 256 KB of L2 cache per core, and a shared 9MB L3 cache. The following metrics were considered:

1. **Recall:** The proportion of true persistent items that are correctly identified out of all actual persistent items.
2. **Precision:** The proportion of correctly identified persistent items out of all items reported as persistent.
3. **F1 Score:** The harmonic mean of Recall and Precision, reflecting the balance between the two. It is calculated as $F1 = \frac{2 \times \text{Recall} \times \text{Precision}}{\text{Recall} + \text{Precision}}$.
4. **AAE (Average Absolute Error):** The mean absolute difference between the true persistence and the estimated persistence of items. It is given by $\text{AAE} = \frac{1}{|\Phi|} \sum_{e_i \in \Phi} \left| P(e_i) - \hat{P}(e_i) \right|$.
5. **ARE (Average Relative Error):** The mean relative difference between the true persistence and the estimated persistence of items. It is calculated as $\text{ARE} = \frac{1}{|\Phi|} \sum_{e_i \in \Phi} \frac{|P(e_i) - \hat{P}(e_i)|}{P(e_i)}$.
6. **Throughput:** The number of insertions processed per second, measured in millions of operations per second (Mops). It is computed as $\frac{N}{T}$, where N is the total number of insertions and T is the total time in seconds.

Datasets consist of the CAIDA anonymized internet trace from 2016 [11], collected at the Equinix-Chicago monitoring center, with each item identified by the source and destination IP addresses. A 5-s monitoring interval was selected, comprising 165K unique items and 2.49M network packets, to maintain consistency with the data used in the Elastic Sketch paper. Each dataset was divided into T window sizes, with $T = 200$, $T = 400$, $T = 800$, and $T = 1600$.

4.2 Persistence Estimation

A thorough comparison between the LightFinder (LF) and On-Off Sketch (OO) methods was conducted to evaluate their performance in persistence estimation. For this assessment, both LF and OO were configured with $d = 3$. The experiments used fixed window sizes of 200 and 1600, with memory allocations varying from 100 KB to 500 KB. Additionally, to address scenarios with limited memory, further evaluations were performed with compact memory settings ranging from 1 KB to 10 KB and a persistence window size of 1600. This specific window size was chosen because OO's capabilities for persistence estimation are confined to this window size alone. Persistence estimation was also evaluated with a fixed 100 KB memory and varying window sizes (200, 400, 800, 1600). With 32-bit counters and 100 KB memory, each row in OO contains 8,274 buckets. For LF, with 16-bit counters and the same memory, each row contains 16,062 buckets. The bitsets were initialized to *On* at the start of each new window.

AAE (Fig. 4): The comparative analysis between LF and OO across a range of memory allocations and window configurations is presented in detail. Figure 4(a)–(b): reveal that LF achieves a significant reduction in AAE, out-

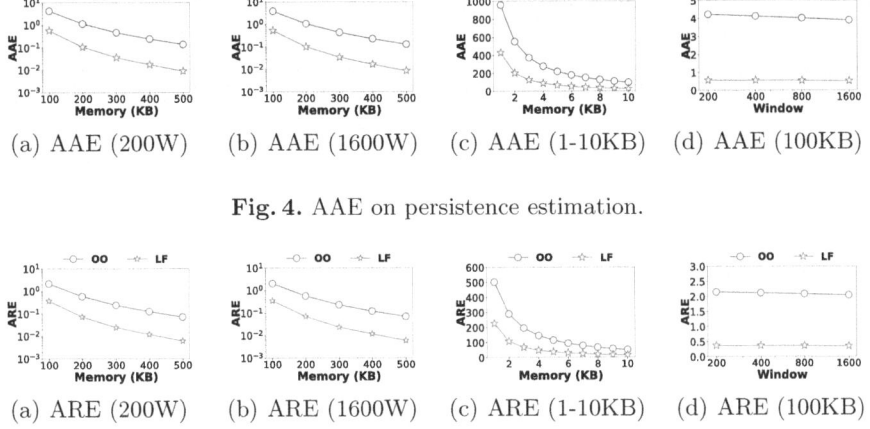

Fig. 4. AAE on persistence estimation.

(a) ARE (200W)   (b) ARE (1600W)   (c) ARE (1-10KB)   (d) ARE (100KB)

Fig. 5. ARE on persistence estimation.

performing OO by approximately 6 to 7 times when tested with window sizes of 200 and 1600. Figure 4(c): delves into performance under stringent memory constraints, specifically within the 1 KB to 10 KB range. The results show that LF maintains a relatively lower AAE at 10 KB, which remains significantly lower than OO's AAE even as memory decreases to 1 KB. This stark contrast highlights LF's effectiveness in low-memory scenarios, where resource constraints significantly impact performance. Figure 4(d): shows that LF's AAE remains stable between 0.5 and 1 across different window sizes with 100 KB memory, while OO exhibits much higher error rates, highlighting LF's robustness in memory-constrained environments.

ARE (Figs. 5): LF consistently achieves lower ARE than OO across various memory and window configurations, with a significant margin in accuracy and stability. Figure 5(a)–(b): Under persistent window sizes of 200 and 1600, LF achieves ARE values approximately one order of magnitude lower than OO across all memory sizes. For example, at 100 KB, LF's ARE is around 0.3, while OO's ARE is around 2. Even as memory increases to 500 KB, LF's ARE remains significantly lower, underscoring its ability to minimize errors effectively. Figure 5(c): In small memory (1–10 KB), LF shows much better accuracy than OO, consistently maintaining lower ARE. This reinforces LF's strength in handling limited memory resources more effectively than OO. Figure 5(d): With a fixed memory size of 100 KB, LF's ARE remains consistently low, ranging between 0.25 and 0.5 across various window sizes, while OO's ARE stays above 2.5. This highlights LF's better accuracy and stability, especially as window sizes increase.

4.3   Finding Persistent Items

The LightFinder (LF) algorithm was systematically compared to the On-Off Sketch (OO) method under a variety of memory capacities and window configurations. Both algorithms were consistently set up with $d = 3$ hash functions. Tests were conducted with memory sizes ranging from 100 KB to 500 KB and window sizes of 200 and 1600. Additional tests were performed with 1–10 KB memory and a 1600 window, with a threshold set to 0.00005, as suggested by the On-Off Sketch authors. For OO, with 32-bit counters and a total memory of M KB, each row occupies M/d KB. Each counter uses 4.125 B (4 B for the counter value and 0.125 B for the flag), resulting in $M/(d \times 4.125)$ counters per row. For LF, with 16-bit counters and the same total memory of M KB, each row occupies M/d KB. Each counter uses 2.125 B (2 B for the counter value and 0.125 B for the flag), resulting in $M/(d \times 2.125)$ counters per row.

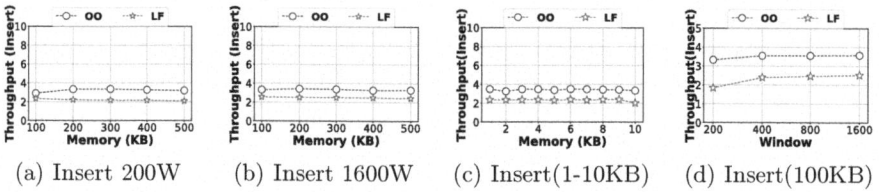

(a) Insert 200W   (b) Insert 1600W   (c) Insert(1-10KB)   (d) Insert(100KB)

Fig. 6. Throughput on persistence estimation.

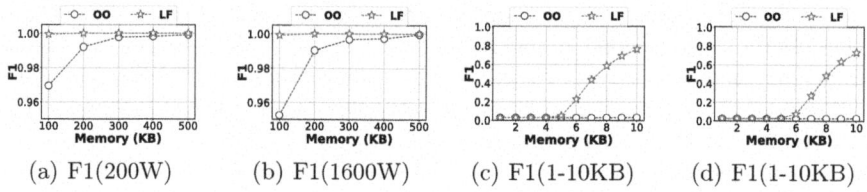

(a) F1(200W)   (b) F1(1600W)   (c) F1(1-10KB)   (d) F1(1-10KB)

Fig. 7. F1-score on finding persistent items.

Throughput (Fig. 6): The comparative analysis of insertion throughput between LF and OO was conducted across different memory and window configurations revealed that LF had slightly lower throughput (2–3) compared to OO (3–4), due to its advanced memory management and hashing strategies aimed at reducing errors. Figure 6(a)–(b): With persistent window sizes of 200 and 1600, LF consistently achieved an F1-score near 1 across all memory sizes, highlighting its superior accuracy and stability compared to OO, which peaked at 0.98 in the 1600 window and 500 KB memory configuration. Figure 6(c): In small memory conditions (1–10 KB), LF's throughput was slightly lower than OO's, but its optimized hashing strategy ensured better accuracy, which is crucial for scenarios with limited memory. Figure 6(d): At a fixed memory size of 100 KB, LF's throughput remained stable as the window size increased, whereas OO showed variability. Despite LF's slightly lower throughput, its reduced error rates and consistent performance make it ideal for accuracy-sensitive applications.

F1-Score (Fig. 7): The results show that LF consistently outperforms OO in F1-score across various memory sizes and persistent window configurations, especially in small memory settings (1–10 KB) where OO struggles. Figure 7(a)–(b): With persistent window sizes of 200 and 1600, LF consistently maintains an F1-score near 1 across all memory sizes. In contrast, OO reaches about 0.93 at 100 KB with the 200 window and improves from 0.9 at 100 KB to around 0.98 at 500 KB with the 1600 window, but it remains below LF. Figure 7(c): In small memory environments (1–10 KB) with a persistent window size of 200, LF quickly surpasses OO, reaching over 0.8 at 8 KB, while OO stays below 0.1 throughout this range. Figure 7(d): Similarly, with a persistent window size of 1600, LF achieves an F1-score around 0.6 at 10 KB, while OO remains nearly flat at 0.

5   Conclusion and Future Work

This paper introduces LightFinder as an innovative approach to improve the adaptability and effectiveness of detecting persistent items, particularly in memory-constrained environments. By eliminating the reliance on the assumption of uniform window sizes, we have effectively mitigated the inefficiencies arising from the skewed distribution of data streams, a challenge that is especially significant in scenarios with limited memory. LightFinder addresses both the estimation of persistence and the detection of persistent items, outperforming established methods such as On-Off Sketch (OO) in terms of both accuracy and resource efficiency. Notably, LightFinder achieves up to a 1.5-fold reduction in Average Absolute Error (AAE) and substantially decreases the Average Relative Error (ARE), making it an optimal solution for environments where memory is a critical constraint. Future research will focus on further optimizing the algorithm's throughput under even more stringent memory conditions and expanding its applicability to a wider array of data stream contexts. All source code is released at Github [1].

Acknowledgments. This work was supported in part by the Joint Funds of the National Natural Science Foundation of China (Grant No. U22A2036), in part by the Shenzhen Colleges and Universities Stable Support Program No. GXWD20220817124251002, in part by the Shenzhen Stable Supporting Program (General Project) (No. GXWD20231130110352002), in part by the Shenzhen Colleges and Universities Stable Support Program under Grant GXWD20231129102636001, and in part by the Guangdong Basic and Applied Basic Research Foundation under Grant 2023A1515110271.

References

1. The source codes of lightfinder and other related algorithms (2025). https://github.com/doubleblind2025/Light-Finder
2. Dai, H., Shahzad, M., Liu, A.X., Zhong, Y.: Finding persistent items in data streams. Proc. VLDB Endow. **10**(4), 289–300 (2016)
3. Estan, C., Varghese, G., Fisk, M.: Bitmap algorithms for counting active flows on high-speed links. IEEE/ACM Trans. Netw. **14**(5), 925–937 (2006)
4. Fan, Z., Hu, Z., Wu, Y., Guo, J., Liu, W., Yang, T.: PISketch: finding persistent and infrequent flows. In: ACM SIGCOMM, pp. 8–14 (2022)
5. Fan, Z., Wang, R.: OneSketch: a generic and accurate sketch for data streams. IEEE Trans. Knowl. Data Eng. **35**(12), 12887–12901 (2023)
6. Gama, F., Marques, A.G., Mateos, G., Ribeiro, A.: Rethinking sketching as sampling: a graph signal processing approach. Signal Process. **169**(C), 107404 (2020)
7. Greenwald, M., Khanna, S.: Space-efficient online computation of quantile summaries. In: SIGMOD '01. Association for Computing Machinery, New York (2001)
8. Greenwald, M., Khanna, S.: Space-efficient online computation of quantile summaries. SIGMOD Rec. **30**(2), 58–66 (2001)
9. Guha, S., Chandrashekar, J., Taft, N.: How healthy are today's enterprise networks? In: Proceedings of the 8th ACM SIGCOMM Conference on Internet Measurement, IMC '08, p. 6. Association for Computing Machinery (2008)
10. Huang, H., Yu, J., Du, Y., Liu, J.: Memory-efficient and flexible detection of heavy hitters in high-speed networks. In: ACM SIGMOD (2024)
11. Center for Applied Internet Data Analysis: The CAIDA traces (2016). http://www.caida.org/data/overview/
12. Lahiri, B., Chandrashekar, J., Tirthapura, S.: Space-efficient tracking of persistent items in a massive data stream. In: DEBS. Association for Computing Machinery (2011)
13. Li, H., Chen, Q., Zhang, Y., Yang, T., Cui, B.: Stingy sketch: a sketch framework for accurate and fast frequency estimation. In: ACM VLDB (2022)
14. Li, M., Chen, D., Dai, H., Xie, R.: Seesaw counting filter: a dynamic filtering framework for vulnerable negative keys. IEEE Trans. Knowl. Data Eng. **35**(12), 12987–13001 (2023)
15. Li, M., et al.: A pareto optimal bloom filter family with hash adaptivity. VLDB J. **32**(3), 525–548 (2023)
16. Li, W., Patras, P.: Tight-sketch: a high-performance sketch for heavy item-oriented data stream mining with limited memory size. In: ACM CIKM (2023)
17. Santos, A., Bessa, A., Musco, C., Freire, J.: A sketch-based index for correlated dataset search. In: ICDE, pp. 2928–2941 (2022)
18. Shi, Q., Xu, Y., Qi, J., Li, W., Yang, T.: Cuckoo counter: adaptive structure of counters for accurate frequency and top-k estimation. IEEE/ACM Trans. Netw. **31**(4), 1854–1869 (2023)
19. Shokrollahi, A.: Raptor codes. IEEE Trans. Inf. Theory **52**(6), 2551–2567 (2006). https://doi.org/10.1109/TIT.2006.874390
20. Ting, D.: Count-min: optimal estimation and tight error bounds using empirical error distributions. In: ACM SIGKDD, pp. 2319–2328 (2018)
21. Wang, H., et al.: Bamboo filters: make resizing smooth. In: IEEE ICDE (2022)
22. Wang, L., Luo, G., Yi, K., Cormode, G.: Quantiles over data streams: an experimental study. In: Proceedings of the 2013 ACM SIGMOD International Conference on Management of Data, SIGMOD '13, p. 12. Association for Computing Machinery (2013)

23. Xiaohuan, Z., Minghui, L.: Large flow identification based on counting bloom filter and space saving. J. Univ. Chin. Acad. Sci. **32**(3), 391 (2015)
24. Yang, T., Gong, J.: HeavyGuardian: separate and guard hot items in data streams. In: Proceedings of the 24th ACM SIGKDD International Conference on Knowledge Discovery and Data Mining (KDD '18), pp. 2584–2593. ACM, New York (2018)
25. Yang, T., Zhang, H., Yang, D.: Finding significant items in data streams, pp. 1394–1405 (2019). https://doi.org/10.1109/ICDE.2019.00126
26. Zhang, Y., Li, J., Lei, Y.: On-off sketch: a fast and accurate sketch on persistence. Proc. VLDB Endow. **13**(11), 2372–2385 (2020). https://doi.org/10.14778/3425879.3425884
27. Zhao, Y., Han, W., Zhong, Z., Zhang, Y., Yang, T., Cui, B.: Double-anonymous sketch: achieving top-k-fairness for finding global top-k frequent items. In: ACM SIGMOD (2023)

MiDedup: A Restore-Friendly Deduplication Method on Docker Image Storage Systems

Lisha Qin[1], Haoliang Tan[1,2], Xiangyu Zou[1], Wenhao Ou[1], Yan Wei[3],
Rubing Huang[4], and Wen Xia[1,2(✉)]

[1] Harbin Institute of Technology, Shenzhen, China
xiawen@hit.edu.cn
[2] Peng Cheng Laboratory, Shenzhen, China
[3] Zhongruan International Technology Service Co., Ltd., Shenzhen, China
[4] Macau University of Science and Technology, Macao, China

Abstract. Docker image storage systems, like Docker registry, often employ deduplication to reduce storage overhead. Existing deduplication methods for these systems detect redundancy at either layer or file level, each with its own advantages and limitations. Layer-level deduplication offers much faster restoration but lower deduplication ratio, as it eliminates duplicate layers while ignoring duplicate files across layers. Conversely, file-level deduplication offers a higher deduplication ratio but slower restoration, as removing duplicate files scatters the files of a layer, leading to multiple disk read I/O during restoration. Our analysis reveals that the slow restoration in file-level deduplication partly stems from ignoring file-layer relationships. In this paper, we propose MiDedup, a new Docker deduplication method. MiDedup detects redundancy at file-level and organizes files into a restore-friendly layout by considering file-layer relationships to enhance restore speed. Our studies also show that duplicated files of one layer are not uniformly distributed across different layers. MiDedup uses this insight to skip deduplicating scattered files to further optimize the file layout for faster restoration. Evaluations indicate that MiDedup achieves restore speeds that are 8–19× faster than file-level deduplication (slightly slower than layer-level one), while maintaining 9–47% higher deduplication ratios than layer-level deduplication.

Keywords: Docker image · File-level deduplication · Restore speed

1 Introduction

Recently, containers [1] have been an effective alternative to Virtual Machines (VMs) [2] for virtualization, both in personal setups and cloud computing environments. In contrast to VMs, containers share the OS kernel but provide isolation by process visibility (via namespaces) and resource allocation (via control groups) [3], which require fewer system resources, exhibit quicker startup times,

© IFIP International Federation for Information Processing 2025
Published by Springer Nature Switzerland AG 2025
X. Chen et al. (Eds.): NPC 2024, LNCS 15527, pp. 256–269, 2025.
https://doi.org/10.1007/978-981-96-2830-8_20

and have lower execution overhead than VMs. As a result, container frameworks like Docker have been widely used in modern cloud platforms [4,5].

As the trend of container popularity grows, the volume of container images is experiencing rapid growth and brings huge storage overhead for image repositories. The vast number of images in public registries is only a fraction, with private images likely numbering much higher. Therefore, major cloud providers like AWS [7], Google [8], and Azure [9], as well as large organizations, are inevitably allocating more storage resources to their image registries, thus usually deployed on the HDD disks for their competitive price [10].

To reduce the data volume and improve the storage efficiency of container images, the Docker registry employs a layer-sharing technique (a.k.a layer-level deduplication), as images are structured into several read-only layers (saved as tarred and compressed file format, i.e., tarball, is also the unit of image transmission and storage), which are shareable among different images. Nevertheless, this method cannot fully leverage compressibility, as completely identical layers are uncommon, and redundancies tend to exist at a finer granularity. Specifically, recent studies reported that ① only 3% of the files in image repositories are unique [14], but ② only 36% of the layers are identical in the 10,000 most popular Docker Hub images [11]. These results mean that many duplicated files remain and are stored in the container image storage systems among different image layers, even configuring layer-sharing techniques.

Thus, some works, like DupHunter [12], propose applying file-level deduplication on Docker images to achieve a 2× higher deduplication ratios. However, directly employing the deduplication scheme increases the GET layer latency by up to 36× [12], which mainly comes from the expensive cost of the files restoring process, i.e., fetching all files required by the specific image layer from the HDD disk. Specifically, according to our observation 2 (detailed in Sect. 3), the layer-sharing technique only requires reading a single file (tarball) from the disk, which could fully utilizes the disk's **Sequential Read I/O** capability during the restoration of an image layer. On the contrary, file-level deduplication requires a great deal of **Random Read I/O** operations to retrieve the files of the image layer being restored. This is primarily due to two reasons: image layers typically comprise massive small files, and file-level deduplication results in the required files, including the small ones, being physically dispersed across the disk.

Actually, the number of read I/O operations during restoration is primarily determined by the file data layout of the image layer being restored. A more sequential layout results in a reduced number of read I/O, consequently leading to a faster restore speed. Specifically, file-level deduplication preserves a random file layout where files are stored in a dispersed manner. The physical address of files depends only on their writing order, without considering the relationship with layers. In contrast, the layer-sharing technique packages and stores all necessary files together in a tarball. This method constitutes a naturally restore-friendly file arrangement; however, it fails to identify and remove duplicate files across layers. To sum up, both file-level and layer-level deduplication methods can only optimize for either restore performance or storage cost with their own file layout design. Thus, a **well-designed data storage layout** for container images should consider both restore performance and storage cost simultaneously.

Inspired by the layer-sharing technique, which compactly stores files within a layer for fast restoration, we have identified a limitation in the file-level deduplication technique: it does not consider the relationship between files and layers during storage. Consequently, files from the same layer may be stored separately. Coupled with the observation in Sect. 3 that there are many unique files exclusive to a specific layer, this suggests an optimal (restore-friendly) file layout for file-level deduplication can be achieved by taking into account the relationship between files and layers. Additionally, the observation in Sect. 3 reveals that duplicated files from one layer are not distributed evenly across different layers. That is, for a given layer, only a few other layers share a significant number of files with it, while other layers either do not share files or share only a small number. This indicates that we can refine the file layout for file-level deduplication, potentially enhancing restoration speed without significantly impacting the deduplication ratio, by preventing the sharing of files with layers that have limited file overlap.

Motivated by the above observations and analyses, in this paper, we propose a novel deduplication method called MiDedup, which eliminates redundancy at the file level while ensuring a **read-optimized optimal file layout** by considering the relationship between image files and layers. MiDedup aims to simultaneously achieve a high deduplication ratio and rapid restore speed. On one hand, it classifies and organizes the files of each layer into two categories: "unique", which comprises files exclusive to that layer, and "share", which encompasses files common to multiple layers. On the other hand, it identifies layers with significant duplicate file content (exceeding a pre-defined threshold) and performs deduplication only against those layers. This prevents the sharing of files with layers that have minimal file overlap, thus optimizing the file layout for faster reads. Our contributions in this paper can be summarized as follows:

- We conclude that the slow restore performance of current file-level deduplication methods on Docker images is partly due to their oversight of the relationship between files and image layers, leading to a random data layout and subsequent random I/O issues.
- By analyzing the relationship between duplicate files and image layers, we find that duplicated files are not randomly distributed across different image layers. Instead, several similar image layers tend to have more duplicate files.
- These findings motivate us to propose a restore-friendly optimal file data layout for deduplication, called MiDedup, which reduces a large number of random I/O operations to a limited count, thereby achieving a balance between data reduction and restore performance.
- Experiments based on public Docker image datasets indicate that our MiDedup significantly increases the deduplication ratio without notably sacrificing restore performance compared with the native layer-sharing technique.

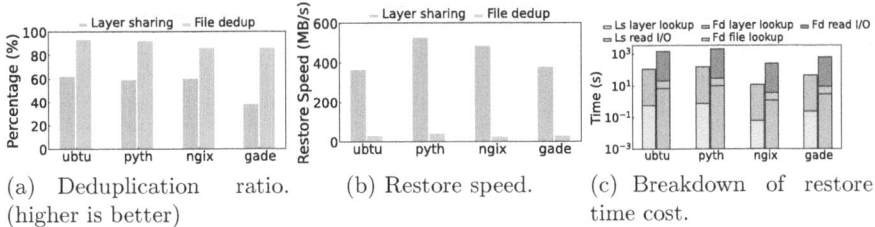

(a) Deduplication   ratio.   (b) Restore speed.   (c) Breakdown of restore
(higher is better)   time cost.

Fig. 1. The dilemma of deduplication ratio and restore speed between layer-sharing (Ls) and file-level deduplication (Fd) on four container images.

2   Background and Related Works

Docker System. Docker is a popular container framework. It automates the creation and deployment of application containers by packaging an application with its runtime dependencies into a container image and then running this image on a host machine [13]. The Docker system consists of several components. Users interact with Docker via the Docker client, which sends commands to the Docker daemon. The daemon is responsible for running containers from locally available images, building new images, and pushing new images to a Docker registry. Additionally, the daemon supports launching containers from images not available locally by pulling the required image via the network from the remote registry, which stores a huge number of container images. Therefore, the ability to quickly retrieve and access image data in an image registry is crucial for rapidly responding to client requests for new image deployments.

Docker Images and Layers. Container images are the basic data units used by Docker to package, distribute, and run applications. Docker images consist of a series of individual layers. A layer contains a subset of the files in the image and often represents a specific component of the image, e.g., codes and libraries. This modular design allows layers to be shared between two images when they depend on the same component. Image layers are read-only and stored as Gzip compressed archival files. When users start a container, the storage driver of Docker creates a new writable layer atop the underlying read-only layers. The top layer becomes unchangeable once the new image is committed.

Data Reduction on Docker Images. Based on the layer-sharing strategy, Skourtis et al. [11] argue that image layer reorganization, which maximizes layer overlap, is beneficial to reducing storage and network consumption. Zhao et al. [12] proposed using file-level deduplication (i.e., DupHunter) in Docker registries to reduce the storage space of massive Docker images, which can achieve a 6.9X higher compressibility than the native layer-sharing scheme. Regarding the restore delay problem caused by deduplication, DupHunter lacks optimization from the deduplication perspective. Instead, it applies caching and pre-constructing image layers based on client behavior to accelerate the process of restoring images, which is orthogonal to and can also be integrated into our MiDedup.

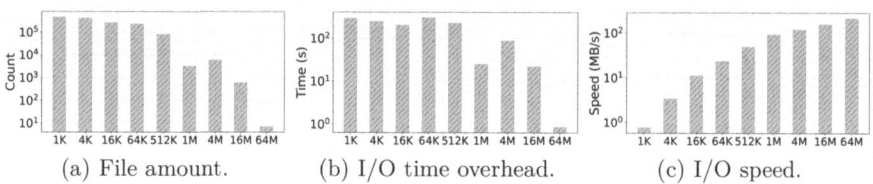

| (a) File amount. | (b) I/O time overhead. | (c) I/O speed. |

Fig. 2. The file amount and restore I/O characteristic of traditional file-level deduplication on Ubuntu images varying different file sizes.

File-Level Deduplication. It is a file-granularity data reduction technique, usually applied in file systems [17], backup storage systems [15,16], and Docker image storage systems [12]. File-level deduplication generates a fingerprint (e.g., SHA256 [19]) for each file to identify and remove duplicated files. Files with the same fingerprint are considered duplicated and stored as one copy.

3   Observations and Motivations

Observation#1: The Dilemma Between Deduplication Ratio and Restore Performance. Generally, applying a finer granularity in the deduplication improves the deduplication ratio. For example, compared to file-level deduplication, the layer-sharing technique (a.k.a. layer-level deduplication) applies a coarser granularity (i.e., image layers) and retains significant redundancy among executable code and libraries, as different developers may import duplicate files. As shown in Fig. 1(a), file-level deduplication achieves a 20%–40% higher deduplication ratio compared to the native layer-sharing technique, significantly reducing storage costs in image registries.

However, a finer granularity in deduplication could lead to inefficient I/Os. For example, compared to the layer-sharing technique (simply reads the compressed layers during restoration), directly applying file-level deduplication in image layers results in up to **20× decrease in restore speed**, as shown in Fig. 1(b). The reason is that file-level deduplication introduces high random I/O costs for accessing all files of the layer during restore layers. In Fig. 1(c), we exhibit the breakdown of the restore time cost of these two methods. Both of them first look up the recipe for layers and files to acquire the location of data and then read the corresponding data from the disk. The main overhead of restoring comes from the read I/O. However, the I/O overhead in file-level deduplication is significantly higher than the layer-sharing technique, which decreases the restoration performance of container images.

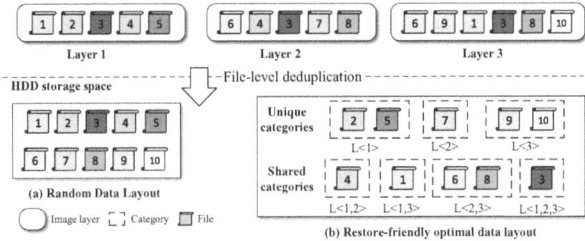

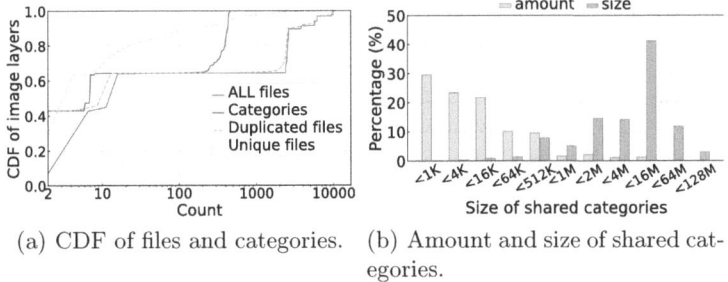

Fig. 3. The random data layout and restore-friendly optimal data layout.

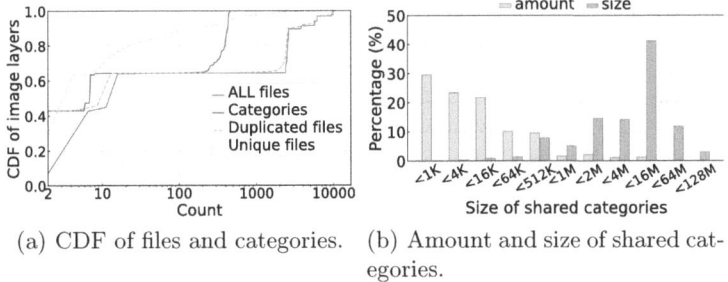

(a) CDF of files and categories.   (b) Amount and size of shared categories.

Fig. 4. Duplicated files are not distributed evenly in Ubuntu container images. This observation is general in other datasets, which are evaluated in the experiment section.

Observation#2: The Inefficient I/O in File-Level Deduplication is Caused by Small and Random Access on Small Files. Traditional file-level deduplication stores all unique files based on their order of appearance, disrupting the natural sequential order within the deduplicated files and resulting in a random file layout. Figure 3(a) provides an example of this. Therefore, when restoring deduplicated files, there requires massive small and random I/O (containing expensive disk seeks) to acquire corresponding files, especially small files. We study the number of files, I/O time cost, and I/O speed for various file sizes during the restoration of the Ubuntu image dataset, and the results are listed in Fig. 2. We find that the number of small files (i.e., "Size <4 KB") accounts for more than 60% of the files, and their I/O speed is only 2.5 MB/s, which occupies over 1/3 of the total overhead of the I/O time and completely fails to take advantage of the sequential read performance of the disk. In contrast, the I/O speed of larger files, such as those bigger than 16 MB, can reach up to 100 MB/s. Thus, limiting the number of read I/O operations, i.e., combining the random I/O of small files into large sequential I/O, when accessing layer files is essential to mitigate the restoration performance decline of file-level deduplication.

Observation#3: The Opportunity of Combining the Small I/O with Appreciable Data Reduction Benefit by Designing the Optimal File Layout. We find that traditional file-level deduplication fails to consider the relationship between files and layers during file storage. This leads to some files belonging to the same layer being stored separately, thereby causing multiple random read operations (many disk seeks) during restoration. Figure 3 provides a simplified example to illustrate this issue. With the traditional file-level deduplication method, the amount of I/O during the restoration of each image layer depends solely on the number of files in that layer. For instance, in a random data layout, layer 3 requires 6 reads. However, if the file-layer relationship is considered in the file data layout, we can make related files consecutive in the storage layout, and the amount of read I/O can be combined. To achieve this, we classify files of one layer into two categories, i.e., unique and shared. The "**unique category**" includes files that belong exclusively to a specific image layer. The "**shared category**" comprises files that are shared among multiple layers.

For example, we use L<1, 2, 3> to denote a category of files collectively owned by layers 1, 2, and 3, with only one copy stored for deduplication. In Fig. 3, files of layer 3 can be classified into four categories to achieve an optimal layout: $\{<3>, <1,3>, <2,3>, <1,2,3>\}$. The first category is the unique category, while the remaining three are shared categories. When restoring layer 3, only 4 reads are required (the same number as the categories, which is less than the 6 reads needed for a random file layout). Here, an obvious benefit is that the optimal file layout could combine all unique files (amounts ranging from 100 to 500 in some layers, as shown in Fig. 4(a)) I/O of a certain layer into one unique category.

As stated above, the restoration performance of a layer with the optimal data layout depends on the number of categories. If duplicated files are uniformly distributed across the categories, the restoration performance of the optimal layout would be comparable to that of a random layout. Particularly, the number of valid categories is calculated as $\sum_{i=1}^{n} \binom{n}{i}$ (where n is the number of layers), which grows significantly as layers amount increases. Therefore, in the worst case, one file in one category is possible. However, we observe that **duplicated files within a layer are not uniformly distributed across different layers**. Specifically, most files within a layer are shared among a small number of categories, which is much less than the amount of files. On one hand, As shown in Fig. 4(a), in Ubuntu image layers, about 40% layers have more than 2500 files, while only 20% layers have more than 300 categories. On the other hand, as shown in Fig. 4(b), in the case of the Ubuntu image, 89% of the files in terms of data volume within a layer are shared among only 6% of the categories, while the remaining 11% of files are shared among 94% of the categories. Consequently, we can break up many small shared categories and migrate files into unique categories for better performance restoration with a minor loss of deduplication ratio.

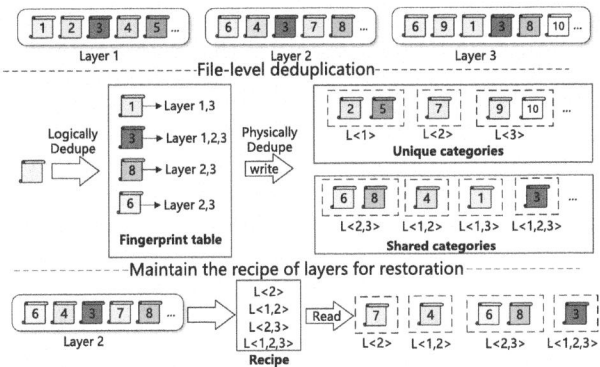

Fig. 5. The overview of deduplication and restoration in MiDedup.

4 Design and Implementation

4.1 Design Overview

Figure 5 presents an overview of MiDedup, which comprises three modules: logical file-level deduplication, physical file-level deduplication, and layer recipe maintenance. The first two modules serve to perform file-level deduplication and preserve a restore-friendly file layout. The third module focuses on ensuring the correct restoration of the image. More specifically, ❶ logical file-level deduplication records the reference relationships between image files and layers for preparation of the optimal file layout. ❷ Physical file-level deduplication classifies files into two categories and reallocates categories with a limited number of shared files to the unique categories. ❸ The layer recipe maintenance module keeps track of the essential categories for each layer, facilitating restoration.

4.2 Implementation

Following are the details of the implementation of MiDedup.

Logically File-Level Deduplication. This part mainly involves logically deduplicating each file to obtain its relationship with layers, such as their attributes of unique files, duplicated files, and referenced image layer sets of duplicated files. Specifically, (1) Docker image layers are stored as packaged and compressed tarballs in the registry, which do not directly support file-level deduplication. Therefore, we first decompress and unpack all layer tarballs and then retrieve the file content by inspecting the headers in the tar format. Notably, we treat the headers of the tar file as unique files, which are typically 512 bytes and difficult to deduplicate due to their variable metadata. (2) Each file is calculated via its content with a cryptographically secure hash signature (e.g., SHA-256), also called a fingerprint [19], for uniqueness identification. After that, we record each file's referenced layers, i.e., the image layer where the processed file is located, and then get a mapping (or called `fingerprint table`) from each file (fingerprint) to the layer sets. Therefore, a unique file only has one referenced layer, while duplicated files may have several ones (at least two).

Physically File-Level Deduplication. This part will classify and write the files into categories according to their relationship with layers to maintain the restore-friendly file layout. Typically, (1) The `fingerprint table` is traversed to get another mapping (`layer-set table`) from layer sets to the duplicated file sets. For example, as shown in Fig. 5, the layer set $\{2, 3\}$ contains duplicated files $\{6, 8\}$. Additionally, we record the total size of each layer set to facilitate the subsequent filtering of smaller shared categories. (2) Here, each slot of the `layer-set table` is the initial "shared categories", recording the duplicated files set commonly owned by a specific layer set. Then, files in a "shared category" should be stored together for deduplication and fast restoration. The unique files are classified into the "unique category" to maintain the optimal and restore-friendly file layout. (3) To reduce the number of categories and thus accelerate restoration, we set a minimum size threshold for "shared category", e.g., 512 KB. Then, the duplicated files in the small "shared category" will be considered unique and rewritten into their "unique category". Experiment results (detailed in Sect. 5.3) show that a reasonable minimum threshold can accelerate the restore performance by $1.5\times$–$2.0\times$ with less than a 3% decline of deduplication ratio. (4) After determining the categories, each of them will be allocated to a file path to write in. Then, re-read each file in the image layers. If it is a unique file or a rewritten file, write it into the corresponding "unique category" and record its address (i.e., position and length). Otherwise, if it is a duplicated file, write it into the corresponding "shared category" upon first identification or perform deduplication and only store the file's address of the "shared category" when the duplicated files repeatedly occur. (5) It is noteworthy that each file will be compressed by the general compressor (e.g., ZSTD [18]) before being written to disk to reduce the storage overhead. Besides, the tar headers of a specific layer will stored in its corresponding "unique category" as well.

Maintain the Recipe of Layers for Restoring. To this end, each image layer records the required categories and the position of each file within these categories, ensuring accurate layer restoration. During restoration, only the relevant categories are required to be read. For example, in Fig. 5, the relevant categories of layer 2 are the unique category $\{<2>\}$ and shared categories $\{<1, 2>, <2, 3>, <1, 2, 3>\}$. This design greatly reduces disk read operations and leverages the sequential read performance compared to traditional file-level deduplication.

5   Performance Evaluation

5.1   Evaluation Setup

Evaluation Platform. We have developed a prototype system capable of applying various deduplication methods to Docker container images. After deduplication, the system can restore any layer from the stored data. We performed our experiments on a workstation running Centos 8.0 with an Intel Core i7-8700@3.2 GHz CPU, 128 GB memory, and 7200rpm HDDs.

Evaluation Methods. To better evaluate our method, i.e., MiDedup, we configure the following four evaluated methods. *Layer-sharing*, which only removes duplicated layers among images. It is effective for restoration but remains a lot of duplicated files. This method can be considered as the native storage method of images in the public Docker image registry [6]. *File-level deduplication*, which stores images at the file granularity, and all duplicated files only store one copy for less storage overhead. It is also the essential storage design in the state-of-the-art high-performance deduplication method, called DupHunter [12], for Docker registries. It is noteworthy that DupHunter introduces other techniques for higher restore speed, which mostly concentrate on the pre-fetching and caching of image data. These optimizations are orthogonal to different storage designs. Thus, we do not set up more experiments in this area. *File-level deduplication+*, which optimizes the native file deduplication by storing all unique files of one layer in one image file, enabling combining all read I/Os of one layer's unique files into one. Duplicated files are saved in the image file when they first occur. This method is set up to demonstrate that trivial optimization struggles to compensate for the huge restore performance gap between file-level deduplication and the native technique of layer-sharing. *MiDedup*, which maintains optimal file layout by classifying files into categories with the technique of filtering the small "shared category" into "unique category".

Configurations. In addition, all methods will compress the remaining data by the local compressor, i.e., ZSTD [18]. The file security hash used to identify uniqueness is configured as SHA256 [19]. To evaluate restore performance, tested datasets are restored from the HDD to the RAM disk (memory) for each image layer. Note that before each restoration of one layer, we always flush the file system cache using the command: "echo 3 > /proc/sys/vm/drop_caches". This setting ensures that every recovery reads the necessary data from the disk. We present the average results of five runs.

Datasets. Six popular types of container images are collected from public Docker registries. We downloaded all available versions of these images (as of

Table 1. Six popular Docker container images on public Docker Hub.

Name	Total Size	Layers	Files	Container Image Description
Ubuntu	36.3 GB	1131	1.5M	Debian-based Linux operating system
MySQL	47.1 GB	1449	0.8M	A high performance relational database
Python	73.8 GB	1949	2.5M	Open source programming language
Nginx	5.3 GB	406	0.2M	Open source web server software
WordPress	42.9 GB	1811	1.2M	A system for website customization
Gradle	16.8 GB	204	0.2M	A automation build tool

March 2024) to evaluate different deduplication methods on Docker registry storage systems. Table 1 displays the characteristics of these datasets, including the number of image layers, files, total size (measured after decompression), etc.

5.2   Overall Performance

Deduplication Ratio. As shown in Fig. 6(a), we compare the deduplication ratio of four methods, which is measured in terms of (original size of images − compressed size after deduplication)/(original size of images), by running four methods to reduce the data volume of images data. This metric indicates the percentage of data reduced by deduplication. The results show that file-level deduplication(+) can further eliminate 11%–48% container images data than the layer-sharing technique, which confirms the effectiveness and necessity of applying more fine-grained deduplication (i.e., file-level) to the container images. This is because many duplicated files remain across different layers, e.g., source codes, documents, and libraries, which heavily exacerbate the storage overhead of the Docker registry. Moreover, MiDedup also removes 9%–47% more image data than layer-sharing but is 1%–10% less than file-level deduplication because here MiDedup set a 2 MB "shared categories" limitation, which transformed some duplicated files of the small "shared categories" into their "unique categories" for a better restore performance. However, for the MySQL, Nginx, and Gradle container image datasets, MiDedup's deduplication ratio is comparable to that of fully file-level deduplication, which exhibits its data reduction capability.

Deduplication Speed. As shown in Fig. 6(b), we compare the deduplication speed of three methods, which is measured in terms of (original size of images)/(total time of deduplication). Here, the time cost of layer-sharing is not considered for the assumption that images are initially stored in the form of layer-sharing. From the results, we can conclude that, compared to file deduplication, MiDedup increases the deduplication time cost by 10%–25%, mainly because it needs to first calculate the category of each file and then write each file into the corresponding category. However, in the image repository, the frequency of image restoration is much higher than the frequency of image creation. For example, some popular images are pulled more than one million times a week [6]. Thus, restore performance is a more critical indicator in the Docker registry.

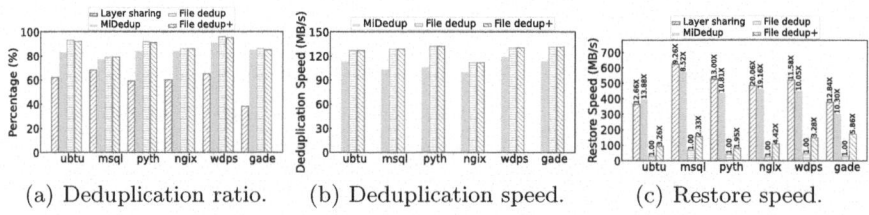

(a) Deduplication ratio.   (b) Deduplication speed.   (c) Restore speed.

Fig. 6. Overall performance of four methods on images. In Figure(a), a higher deduplication ratio is better. In Figure(c), data labels normalize file-level deduplication.

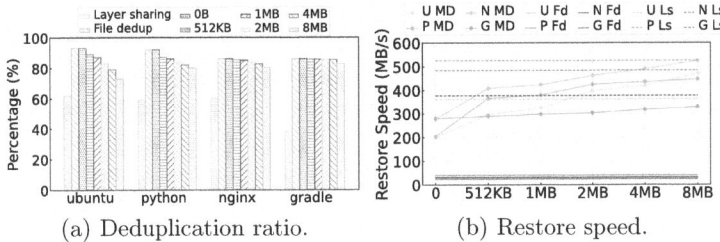

(a) Deduplication ratio.   (b) Restore speed.

Fig. 7. The deduplication ratio (higher is better) and restore speed of different limitation sizes of the shared category. ('U', 'P', 'N', and 'G' denote Ubuntu, Python, Nginx, and Gradle container images, respectively. 'MD', 'Fd', and 'Ls' denote MiDedup, file-level deduplication, and layer-sharing technique, respectively.)

Restore Speed. As shown in Fig. 6(c), we compare the restore speed of four methods, which is measured in terms of (original size of images)/(total time of restoring all compressed image layers one by one). Not surprisingly, layer-sharing achieves the fastest restore speed on nearly all datasets, which is $9\times$– $20\times$ faster than that of directly applying file-level deduplication, which incurs too much random I/O. A trivial optimization of combining files for storage (file-level deduplication+) still results in a $2\times$–$5\times$ decline in restore performance. This slowdown impacts the service capability of image repositories that must frequently respond to image pulls. In contrast, MiDedup provides similar data reduction to file-level deduplication while experiencing only a minimal decline in restore speed, i.e., only 10% slower than reading the entire layer with one disk I/O for each layer restoration when configured with a 2 MB limitation of shared categories. Results show that with optimal file layout, MiDedup acquires the benefit of similar sequential read I/O with layer-sharing.

5.3   Parameter Discussion

In this subsection, we evaluate how the performance of MiDedup varies with different sizes of the "shared categories" limitation. As shown in Fig. 7(a) and 7(b), when the limitation is set to 0 (i.e., all duplicated files are stored in the "shared category"), MiDedup achieves a deduplication ratio equivalent to that of file-level deduplication, but with a restore speed that is $4\times$ faster. The results indicate our optimal file layout can improve restore performance without compromising compressibility at all. Similarly, when the limitation is set to 8 MB, MiDedup achieves a restore speed comparable to the layer-sharing technique (about 5% slower) but with a deduplication ratio that is 8%–40% higher. Considering the balance between the deduplication ratio and restore performance, we set the default threshold of "shared categories" to 2 MB.

6   Conclusion and Future Work

In this paper, we address the decline in restore performance caused by file-level deduplication in Docker image repositories and propose MiDedup, a method that considers the relationships between image files and layers. MiDedup uses a restore-friendly file layout to reduce disk-read operations during restoration. Experiments with six public Docker image datasets show that MiDedup significantly improves the deduplication ratio without compromising restore performance compared to the native layer-sharing technique. In the future, we will explore more fine-grained deduplication techniques, e.g., chunk-level deduplication and delta compression, on the Docker image storage systems.

Acknowledgement. This work was supported in part by the Major Key Project of PCL under Grant PCL2024A05, in part by Shenzhen Science and Technology Program under Grants RCYX20210609104510007, KJZD20230923114610021, and GXWD202311 28111309001, in part by GuangDong Basic and Applied Basic Research Foundation under Grant 2023A1515110072, and in part by the Science and Technology Development Fund of Macau, Macau SAR, under Grant Nos. 0021/2023/RIA1.

References

1. Potdar, A.M., Narayan, D.G., Kengond, S., et al.: Performance evaluation of Docker container and virtual machine. Comput. Sci. **171**, 1419–1428 (2020)
2. Smith, J.E., Nair, R.: The architecture of virtual machines. Computer **38**(5), 32–38 (2005)
3. Rosen, R.: Namespaces and cgroups, the basis of Linux containers, Seville, Spain (2016)
4. Kataru, S.S., Gude, R., Shaik, S., et al.: Cost optimizing cloud based docker application deployment with cloudfront and global accelerator in AWS cloud. In: Proceeding of the 2023 International Conference on Sustainable Communication Networks and Application (ICSCNA), pp. 200–208. IEEE (2023)
5. Zhang, L., Xie, Y., Jin, M., et al.: A novel hybrid model for Docker container workload prediction. IEEE Trans. Netw. Serv. Manag. (TNSM) **20**(3), 2726–2743 (2023)
6. Docker Hub (2024). https://hub.Docker.com/
7. Amazon. Amazon Elastic Container Registry (2024). https://aws.amazon.com/ecr/
8. Google. Google Container Registry (2024). https://cloud.google.com/container-registry/
9. Microsoft. Azure Container Registry (2024). https://azure.microsoft.com/en-us/services/container-registry/
10. Gu, L., Tang, Q., Wu, S., et al.: N-docker: a NVM-HDD hybrid docker storage framework to improve docker performance. In: Proceedings of the 16th IFIP International Conference on Network and Parallel Computing (NPC), pp. 182–194. Springer (2019)
11. Skourtis, D., Rupprecht, L., Tarasov, V., et al.: Carving perfect layers out of Docker images. In: Proceedings of the 11th USENIX Workshop on Hot Topics in Cloud Computing (HotCloud 19) (2019)

12. Zhao, N., Albahar, H., Abraham, S., et al.: DupHunter: flexible high-performance deduplication for docker registries. In: Proceedings of the 2020 USENIX Annual Technical Conference (USENIX ATC 20), pp. 769–783 (2020)
13. Docker (2024). https://www.Docker.com/
14. Zhao, N., Tarasov, V., Albahar, H., et al.: Large-scale analysis of the Docker hub dataset. In: Proceedings of the 2019 IEEE International Conference on Cluster Computing (CLUSTER), pp. 1–10. IEEE (2019)
15. Meyer, D.T., Bolosky, W.J.: A study of practical deduplication. ACM Trans. Storage (TOS) **7**(4), 1–20 (2012)
16. Zou, X., Yuan, J., Shilane, P., et al.: The dilemma between deduplication and locality: can both be achieved? In: Proceedings of the 19th USENIX Conference on File and Storage Technologies (FAST 21), pp. 171–185 (2021)
17. Cao, Z., Wen, H., Ge, X., et al.: TDDFS: a tier-aware data deduplication-based file system. ACM Trans. Storage (TOS) **15**(1), 1–26 (2019)
18. ZSTD lossless compressor (2024). https://github.com/facebook/zstd
19. Muthitacharoen, A., Chen, B., Mazieres, D.: A low-bandwidth network file system. In: Proceedings of the Eighteenth ACM Symposium on Operating Systems Principles (SOSP' 01), pp. 174–187. ACM (2001)

SPLR: A Selective Packet Loss Recovery for Improved RDMA Performance

Pingping Dong[1], Liying Chen[1], Xiaojuan Lu[1], Xin Zhang[2],
Lianming Zhang[1(✉)], Jiawei Huang[3], and Guo Chen[2]

[1] Hunan Normal University, Changsha, China
zlm@hunnu.edu.cn
[2] Hunan University, Changsha, China
[3] Central South University, Changsha, China

Abstract. With the large-scale deployment of RDMA in data centers, distributed applications can efficiently transfer data with very low CPU overhead. However, PFC that ensure RDMA lossless environment brings problems such as head-of-line blocking and pause frame storm, which seriously affects network performance. Lossy RDMA is increasingly a focus, but the timeout problem caused by incast packet loss is still the main cause of high tail delay. In this paper, we propose SPLR, a selective packet loss recovery support for RDMA, which can selectively drop packets that will not result in timeout by anticipating the switch overflow in advance. SPLR comprehensively considers traffic characteristics, congestion mitigation and drop cost, establishing a multi-objective optimization model on the congested port to actively drop the selected packets in flow unit, thus, to achieve lower flow completion time and better performance. Experiments show that SPLR achieves up to 8.64× reduction of 99.9th percentile flow completion time compared to IRN, and other alternatives.

Keywords: Data Center Network · RDMA · Programmable Switch

1 Introduction

Over the years, we have witnessed the rapid development of information industry. Distributed computing has become an important way to support Cloud Computing, Mobile Edge Computing, Mobile Internet and other services, which has become a major computing application area that academic and industrial circles focus on [1]. The operation of distributed computing depends on large-scale data center network, and its performance depends on torage, computing power, network performance and many other aspects. However, compared with computing and storage, network has become a bottleneck in the performance of reduced distributed computing, and has become a focus of academic research.

Currently, TCP/IP, as the mainstream technology of the protocol stack in the data center network, has been unable to meet the requirements of low latency and high throughput of the new generation applications in the data center. RDMA relying on its mechanism for accessing host memory without CPU involvement significantly reduces network delay and is emerging as a representative networking technology for data centers. However, due to the limited hardware resources of NICs [2], deploying a lossless environment seems to be the best way to ensure network performance. RDMA over Converged Ethernet v2 (RoCEv2) builds RDMA on lossless Ethernet, by using Priority-based Flow Control (PFC) [3] to prevent packet loss at the link level . While PFC can be useful in certain scenarios, its disadvantages have been criticized by more and more scholars in recent years [4]. PFC implementation can add complexity to network configurations, leads head-of-line blocking, congestion spreading, deadlock and unfairness, especially in situations where there are frequent incast events. Considering the tradeoffs and complexities associated with PFC, we should put more effort into exploring efficient solutions in the field of lossy network to mitigate the performance damage caused by packet lost.

The redundant retransmissions of GBN (Go-Back-N) [5] makes the impact of the loss of even one packet on network performance magnified by several times. To seek higher loss recovery ability, IRN [4] receives out-of-order packets, and only retransmit the lost packets, improving the transmission efficiency. Nevertheless, in the case of small flow dominance or tail packet loss, IRN still relies on timeouts like GBN, resulting in high tail flow completion time. Switch-assisted loss recovery can benefit timeout avoidance. Recently, Lightning [6] solves the architectural challenge of packet drop at ingress, proposes a switch building block to enhance RoCE's simple loss recovery, which is more convenient. Nevertheless, Lightning still passively withstand the arrival of the burst. In addition, some studies [7] improve the scalability of RDMA.

Based on the above observations, we ask: *Can we create a more friendly loss recovery mechanism for burst flows with more effectively perception and more proactive packet loss strategy?*

Fortunately, there are signs to follow for the dynamics of interaction between traffic characteristics and buffer sharing. On the one hand, we found that the traffic inside data center will fluctuate significantly, and the data arrival frequency of distributed computing services has a certain periodicity, including the peak period with higher rates and the relatively idle valley period. On the other hand, the development of programmable switches enables them to drop packets actively and provide more computing and storage resources [8]. This makes it possible for us to achieve more proactive resource allocation within the switch.

In this paper, we propose SPLR, an accurate and efficient RDMA loss recovery mechanism. SPLR extends the existing packet loss decision mechanism through two modules: **Periodic Overflow Prediction** and **Selective Packet Drop Strategy**. The former predicts the overflow time of congested port in advance, by periodically collecting information (size, hop, etc.) of active flows. Consider that dropping packets on a flow unit is the best way to ensure orderly reception, the latter uses multi-objective optimization decision model to find the flows that are most suitable to be dropped, and sends NACK (Negative Acknowledgment) feedback packet to the source. It is worth noting that, the multi-objective optimization decision model comprehensively considers three key points to determine the sacrificed-flow by alleviating congestion, reducing the waste of link resources and improving the completion time, to search for higher performance benefits.

We test SPLR on a large-scale ns-3 simulations, and compare its performance with GBN, IRN and Lightning, we get some gratifying results. SPLR greatly improves the small flow dilemma in congested ports when incast occurs, resulting in less packet loss and more stable queue length changes. As a result, SPLR significantly reduces 99%-ile FCT (Flow Completion Time) up to 76.1% under incast scenarios, which gives us confidence to let some operations on NICs transfer to switches.

2   Background and Motivation

2.1   Challenge of Incast Congestion

In distributed computing, the computing task is divided into a number of smaller tasks and allocated to a number of small computing nodes for distributed processing, so as to avoid the construction of expensive high performance machines. In this design, the distributed computing needs to feed data out of the physical server, generating many small volume of data communications among tens of thousands of servers. This kind of many-to-one traffic pattern can easily cause queue stacking at ToR switch ports close to the receiver, which we call it *incast congestion*. In distributed applications, up to 99% of traffic is completed within a single RTT, which would bring a sub-RTT level surge in traffic rate. However, both end-to-end congestion control and lossy mechanisms (such as IRN) are still helpless against sudden small flows which is very sensitive to delay.

To this end, we build a simple micro-benchmark using an ns-3-based simulator with a leaf-spine topology that includes 96 hosts, where all links have a capacity of 40 Gbps and a propagation delay of 10 microseconds with a 2:1 oversubscription ratio and 20-to-1 incast degree of incast traffic. Figure 1 illustrates the average latency of all flow and tail latency of incast flow when encountering incast congestion in lossy RDMA, using DCQCN protocol, which is widely deployed in commodity switches, and HPCC protocol, the most advanced congestion control algorithm. In the figure, FCT slowdown is the ratio of the actual flow completion time to the flow completion time of the flow if it were transmitted in isolation without experiencing congestion. Figure 1 indicates that even with the addition of the state-of-the-art congestion control algorithm today's lossy RDMA protocols still suffer from high latency problems. Incast flow FCT slowdown reveals that actual completion times are hundreds of times the theoretical, significantly increasing average and tail latencies by up to 5.3×, harming distributed application service quality.

We examine the switch's packet drop behavior during incast congestion to explain this phenomenon. Many requests in distributed apps, with minimal data, consist of few packets, leading to significant flow completion time increases with

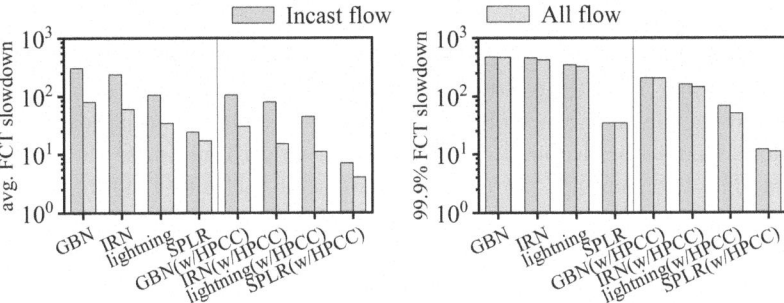

Fig. 1. Incast flow dilemma(DCQCN is used as the congestion control algorithm by default).

packet loss. Host-driven loss recovery triggers timeouts, while switch mechanisms waste link resources. Current mechanisms, unable to predict network status or control speeds, neglect incast congestion, passively waiting for bursts. This incast traffic dilemma, previously avoided, mainly contributes to RDMA latency issues. While lossy RDMA mechanisms have improved, they haven't addressed small flow traffic specifics and packet loss differences.

2.2 Opportunities

However, the idea of Lightning is absolutely a good place to start. We have to admit that the NICs has taken on a very cumbersome part of the RDMA function, and its limited resources prevent us from developing it more complex. On the contrary, the functions implemented inside the switch are relatively simple. With the technological advancement of programmable switches, it is time to let some operations on NICs transfer to switches.

The ability of P4 programmable switch to perform packet processing at line rates makes it possible to identify and respond to microbursts within the network. In addition, both the control plane and the data plane can do things like tag, discard, and prioritize packets [9] to alleviate congestion timely and provide accurate network load reporting.

Inspired by this, is it possible to seek a more active, more accurate, and more effective packet drop decision scheme implemented in the switch?

3 SPLR Design

3.1 Design Principle and Overview

Our primary goals are *reducing the occurrence of packet loss and minimizing the harm of packet loss*. Experience has proved that incast congestion is fast and large [10], making it difficult to prevent. And putting too much weight on NICs is not what we want to see. Therefore, we focus on rapid response to congestion and using switch memory resources properly.

To fully satisfy these goals, SPLR deploys two functional modules on the switch: **Periodic Overflow Prediction** and **Selective Packet Drop Strategy**. The former is dedicated to periodically collect statistics on active flows and predicting the occurrence of buffer overflows. The latter actively selects and sorts flows that to be dropped on the spot, striving to minimize the impact of the loss. The two modules are not independent of each other. Only by relying on the advance prediction of buffer overflow, the active traffic selection module can make the decision of packet loss in advance, instead of passively accepting packet loss. At the same time, the flow information collection function of the prediction module also provides calculation parameters for flow selection. We lead with a brief design rationale to show how SPLR works as shown in Fig. 2, then fill in the details in the rest of this section.

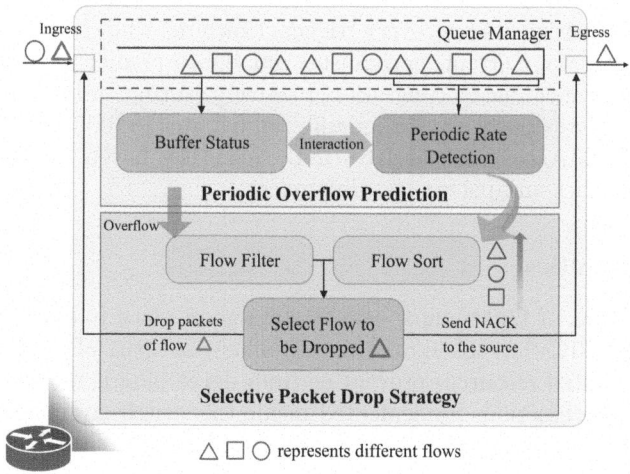

Fig. 2. Overview of SPLR.

3.2   Periodic Overflow Prediction

Microbursts caused by incast flow produce a sudden increase in the queue length within a sub-millisecond time scale and cause buffer exhaustion . Existing lossy mechanisms have been passively subjected to such burst. But do we really have to hand over our arms and surrender to the burst arrival?

The answer is no, P4 programmable switch performing packet processing at line rates, making it possible to quickly capture queue usage and extract packet information in ultra-short cycles [8]. SPLR analyzes the dynamics of the interaction between traffic patterns and switch buffers, detecting bursts in a very short time. Concretely, SPLR predicts whether the buffer is about to overflow and the time until the queue is full by setting a threshold for each port and priority queue. The threshold is determined by the amount of buffers currently occupied and the packet arrival frequency.When the buffer occupancy is small and the packet enqueue frequency is larger than the packet dequeue frequency, the buffer will overflow.

3.3   Selective Packet Drop Strategy in Flow Unit

In order to ensure that the packets arriving at the destination are in order [11], Lightning filters the packets with unexpected sequence until the packets with the expected sequence arrive to switch. We observe that such a strategy makes decisions on a flow unit, meaning that dropping in a packet unit is not justified enough. For this reason, SPLR proposes selective packet drop strategy, which allows for more efficient consolidation of resources that should be "wasted". First, SPLR analyzes the difference in importance of the activity flows that pass through a congested port from the following aspects:

- **Application characteristics of the flow.** For example, in the Ceph storage system, heartbeat flows are used to monitor the normal operation of Ceph nodes. This kind of data flow has the highest transmission priority and is highly sensitive to delay. However, the delay of migration flows won't affect the normal operation of the system and user experience, which have lowest transmission priority.
- **How much the flow contributes to congestion.** Obviously, faster congestion relief is expected. That is to say, dropping the flows that contributes the most to congestion is the fastest way to slow down the flow arrival rate.
- **The cost to drop the flow.**Dropping a flow at the switch, especially if it's the last hop, wastes network link resources. Small flow loss is worse, as tail packet loss triggers conservative RTO retransmissions, risking severe delays [12].
- **The price of the retransmission the flow.** As in the previous point, retransmitting packets takes up bandwidth. Different flows retransmit packets at different price.

Considering the above, we introduce two submodules, flow filter and flow sorter, to select the drop flow.

Flow Filter. Regarding application characteristics, in fact, the flows that are usually more latency-sensitive in distributed applications are the small flows, such as heartbeat flows. Therefore, SPLR will filter out the small flows first when selecting the flow to be sacrificed. In this way, the space left by dropping the large flow of packets can accommodate the small flow of packets passing through quickly.

Flow Sorter. SPLR takes the two key factors of congestion relief and drop cost as indicators, establishing a flow selection multi-objective optimization model as shown in Eq. (1) for egress queue of switch to select the flows that should be dropped the most and maximize the network resource utilization.

$$\max f_1(x) = r_{\text{in}}(x) - r_{\text{out}}(x)$$
$$\min f_2(x) = hop(x) \qquad s.t. \ \ x \in \{1, \cdots, k\} \qquad (1)$$

There are k flows entering the above model, with x indicating their flow ID. First, we use $r_{in}(x) - r_{out}(x)$ to express the flow's contribution to queue growth, where $r_{in}(x)$ is the enqueue rate and $r_{out}(x)$ is the dequeue rate of the packet of flow x. The higher this value, the more this flow contributes to congestion, and the more it is worth to be dropped. Second, since both the cost to drop and the price of retransmission of flow represent the resources consumed to transport the flow, they can be illustrated by the number of switches that this flow has gone through. That is, the fewer *hop* a flow has experienced, the less it costs to drop and retransmit. It is worth noting that the above multi-objective optimization model needs to be solved repeatedly and routinely in the control plane of the switch, so we use custom evolution operators to improve the convergence of the solution algorithm.

After contacting a Pareto optimal solution set that is more suitable to be dropped, the traffic in the solution set is sorted according to the score. Therefore, switch can drop packets in order until the traffic arrival rate is less than the link bandwidth, and sends NACK to source as Lightning does.

4   Evaluation

In this section, we perform ns-3 simulations [13] to evaluate the performance of SPLR and compare it with GBN, IRN, and Lightning.

4.1   Evaluation Setup

1) Simulation Setting: Our ns-3 based simulator uses a 96-host leaf-spine topology, which contains 4 core switches, 12 ToR switches, and 96 servers (8 servers per ToR switch) with a 2:1 over-subscription ratio. All links have 40 Gbps capacity and 10 μs propagation delay. The switch applies dynamic buffer sharing model and set the parameter α [14] to 1.0 with 4.5 MB total buffer, which allows an egress queue to grow up to 2.25 MB (50% of total buffer) at most.

2) Workloads and Metrics: We model a setup based on the traffic patterns observed in the data center under distributed applications. Specifically, we extract the traffic distribution from the data center traffic traces FB_KeyValue and Data_Mining to generate the background flows. These background flows are transmitted between a random pair of hosts and the traffic pattern follows a Poisson process. At the same time, we periodically generate small flows (with 8KB size) of many-to-one model to simulate incast events that are common in data centers, which take up 0.5% of total traffic volume, and a 20-to-1 incast degree as default. FCT slowdown and packet loss rate is used as the primary performance metric to report the transmission performance of each schemes. The queue length of a switch port is adopted to analyze the stability of the algorithm for network congestion control from the micro level.

4.2 Primary Outcomes

We will present the outcomes of SPLR compared to other schemes from the following aspects.

1) Dose SPLR benefit flow completion time?

Figure 3 shows the overall performance of GBN, IRN, Lightning and SPLR with FB_KeyValue workload and Data_Mining workload for background flows, by using DCQCN [15] as congestion control. We run the simulations with 20% to 90% background traffic loads, which represent a lowly to highly loaded network. As we can see, since GBN and IRN receive packet loss feedback from the host, it is easy to trigger timeout retransmission, bringing worse effect than switch-driven loss recovery. In the case of heavy load, the IRN that cannot detect tail loss has similar flow completion time as the GBN. In contrast, switch-driven loss recovery eliminates this timeout, which brings low latency. SPLR introduces selective packet loss on the basis of Lightning to actively select the most appropriate flow for the limited switch buffer, which makes SPLR show better performance. For FB_KeyValue traffic workload, SPLR improves the average and 99-percentile flow completion time slowdowns for overall flow sizes by 23.1%–76.9%, 13.1%–49.9% in lossy RDMA when compared to others. For Data_Mining traffic workload, SPLR improves the average and 99.9% flow completion time slowdowns for overall flow sizes by 48.81%–70.64%, 73.36%–89.83% in lossy RDMA when compared to others. The results show that SPLR is effective in loss recovery.

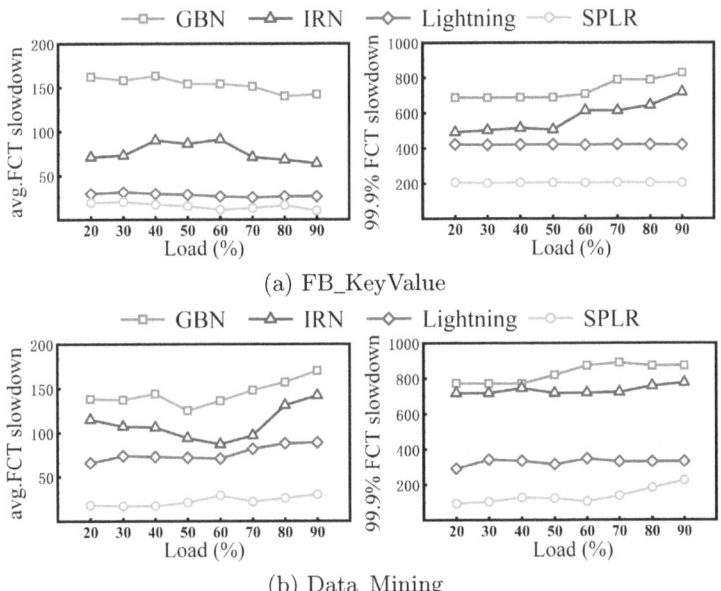

Fig. 3. FCT slowdown of incast traffic under GBN, IRN, lightning, and SPLR, with DCQCN.

2) What about the packet loss rate?

We take FB_KeyValue traffic mode as an example, and calculate the packet loss rate and flow loss rate under different load. As shown in Fig. 4, both the packet loss rate and the flow loss rate increase with aggrandizing load. The first thing we need to know is that, the number of lost packets in the IRN, in theory, is the most accurate reflection of the volume of data that network can bear. The redundant retransmission problem of GBN causes a lot of packet loss. Lightning has a better packet loss rate because it get a faster response by sending NACK directly to the source, which makes the source end suspend the transmission of congestion flow in time. However, SPLR's packet loss rate is 27.99% to 65.23% lower than Lightning's, which can probably be explained by the flow loss rate graph on the right.

We find the selective packet drop mechanism SPLR to be of great help here. GBN, IRN, and Lightning have worse flow loss rates due to indiscriminate flow loss. IRN effectively reduces the congestion duration by introducing BDP (Bandwidth Delay Product) as the rate limit reference value. Lightning responds to congestion more quickly with the help of switches. Therefore, both IRN and Lightning have relatively lower flow loss rates in the final result. In addition, when we compare the packet loss rate and flow loss rate of each loss recovery mechanism, we find that the flow loss rate of this three mechanisms is generally greater than the packet loss rate due to undifferentiated passive packet loss. However, the flow loss rate of SPLR is as low as 0.13%, and only 3.18% under heavy load, which is due to SPLR drops packets in flows to allocate buffer space within the switch and reduce unnecessary packet loss.

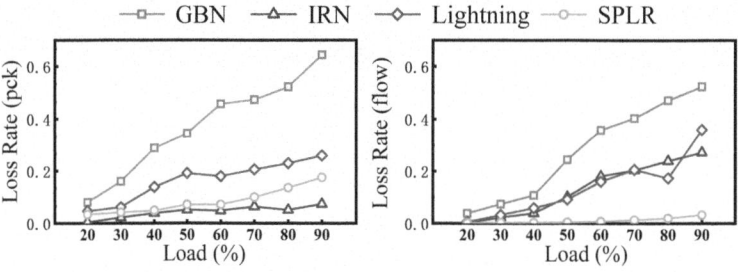

Fig. 4. Packet loss rate and flow loss rate under GBN, IRN, lightning, and SPLR.

3) Does SPLR keep queues stable?

We track the queue length of the switch port subjected to incast for Lightning and SPLR, as shown in Fig. 5. On account of Lightning filters out out-of-order packets, very few flows are still in transit on the switch when incast is serious. In this case, the queue empties quickly and does not recover in a short time. SPLR, however, senses the burst and makes the decision to drop the packet in time, which allows it to slow down the queue growth faster. It is worth noting that SPLR maintains a high link utilization while keeping the queue length from growing, which allows SPLR to transmit more data than Lightning in the time that take to experience the incast.

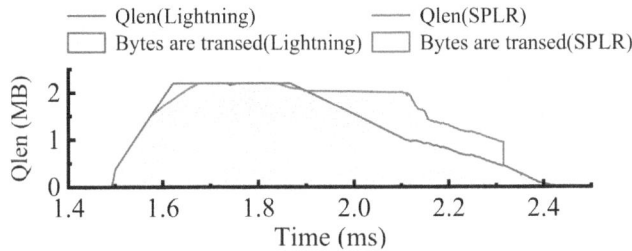

Fig. 5. Length of the queue (being subjected to incast) of Lightning and SPLR.

4.3   Discussion

In this section, we will into the discussion of the effects of SPLR through a series of targeted simulations.

1) SPLR's performance at different incast degree.

In order to evaluate the robustness of SPLR effect under different incast degrees, we conducted comparative tests under 50-to-1, 100-to-1 and 200-to-1 three incast degrees respectively. The results shown in Fig. 6 demonstrate SPLR is more resilient to incast degrees compared others, even after suffering severe incast events. SPLR achieves comparable performance with 4× more incast degree (50 vs. 200).

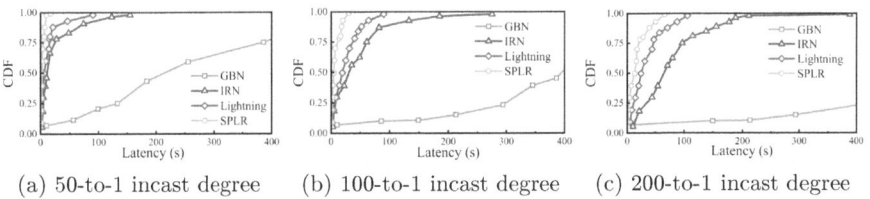

(a) 50-to-1 incast degree   (b) 100-to-1 incast degree   (c) 200-to-1 incast degree

Fig. 6. FCT of GBN, IRN, Lightning and SPLR with increasing incast degree.

2) SPLR's performance in different application scenarios.

We test SPLR performance in a variety of application scenarios, not just in distributed applications. Figure 7 shows the comparison between SPLR and loss recoveries in three other traffic patterns Google_Apps, MS_WebSearch and Facebook_WebServer, in addition to the two distributed applications FB_KeyValue and Data_Mining. Obviously, SPLR performs well in different application scenarios, especially for the tail flow completion time.

3) SPLR's performance under different congestion control algorithms. We compare the performance of SPLR against GBN, IRN and Lightning, under the FB_KeyValue distribution with three classic congestion control algorithms DCQCN and HPCC. The results of tail FCT slowdown for small flow and average FCT slowdown for large flow are reported in Fig. 8. It can be seen

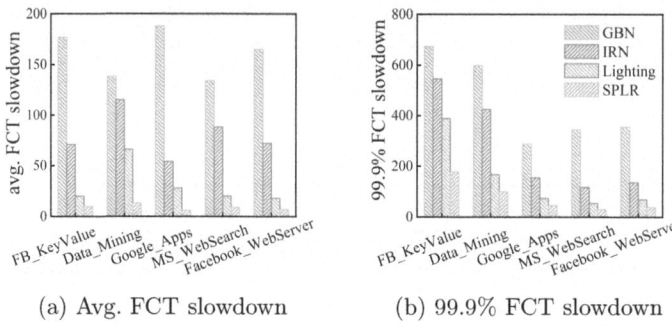

(a) Avg. FCT slowdown   (b) 99.9% FCT slowdown

Fig. 7. performance in different application scenarios.

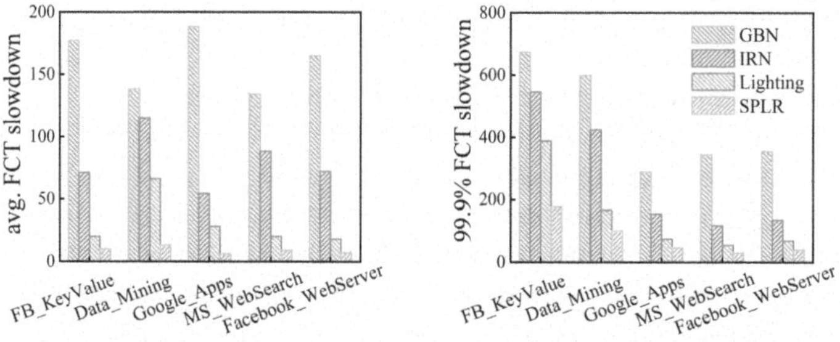

(a) Avg. FCT slowdown   (b) 99.9% FCT slowdown

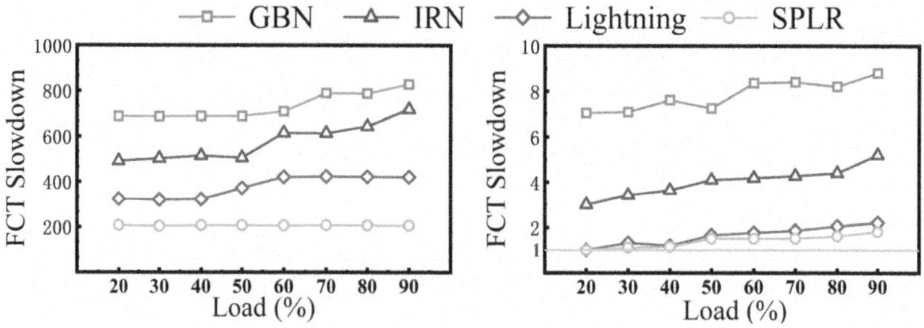

(a) *DCQCN*

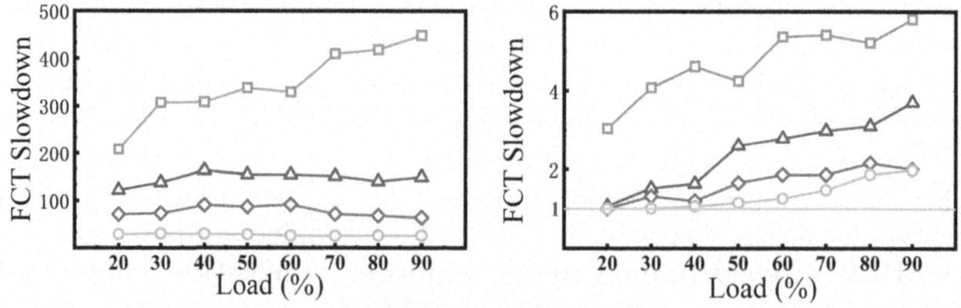

(b) *HPCC*

Fig. 8. Tail FCT slowdown for small flow (left) and avg FCT slowdown for large flow (right) under GBN, IRN, lightning, and SPLR, with *DCQCN* and *HPCC*.

that SPLR helps RDMA to achieve better transmission performance whether with end-to-end signal or INT messages as congestion signals. In particular, the collaboration with HPCC is promising for SPLR to achieve close to the optimal flow completion time.

5 Conclusion

We introduce SPLR, an RDMA loss recovery mechanism optimizing for accuracy and efficiency. SPLR locally selects loss schemes at switch ports using a multi-objective model, actively dropping packets by flow. Results in ns-3 show SPLR allocates buffer resources effectively, reducing tail completion times for small flows, highlighting the network's future role in transmission control.

Acknowledgments. This work was partially supported by the National Natural Science Foundation of China (Nos. 62472170), Hunan Province's Major Science and Technology Research Project (Nos. 2023ZK1080 and 2024QK2009), and Scientific Research Fund of Hunan Provincial Education Department of China (Nos. 22B0102 and 22A0056).

References

1. Dong, F., Guo, X.L., Wang, K., Shen, D., Luo, J.Z., Lui, J.C.: Distributed and optimal RDMA resource scheduling in shared data center networks. In: Proceedings of IEEE Conference on Computer Communications(INFOCOM 2020), pp. 606–615 (2020)
2. Wang, Z.L., et al.: SRNIC: a scalable architecture for RDMA NICS. In: 20th USENIX Symposium on Networked Systems Design and Implementation (NSDI 2023), pp. 1–14 (2023)
3. Priority based flow control. *802.11Qbb* (2011)
4. Radhika, M., Alexander, S., Aurojit, P., Eitan, Z.: Revisiting network support for RDMA. In: 17th USENIX Symposium on Networked Systems Design and Implementation (NSDI 2020), pp. 19–36 (2020)
5. Guo, C., et al.: RDMA over commodity ethernet at scale. In: Proceedings of the ACM Special Interest Group on Data Communication (SIGCOMM 2016), pp. 202–215 (2016)
6. Meng, Q.K., Ren, F.Y.: Lightning: a practical building block for RDMA transport control. In: 2021 IEEE/ACM 29th International Symposium on Quality of Service (IWQOS 2021), pp. 1–10 (2021)
7. Lu, Y.W., et al.: Memory efficient loss recovery for hardware-based transport in datacenter. In: 1st Asia-Pacific Workshop on Networking (APNET 2017), pp. 22–28 (2017)
8. Agrawal, A., Kim, C.: Intel tofino2—a 12.9 tbps p4-programmable ethernet switch. In: 2020 IEEE Hot Chips 32 Symposium (HCS 2020), pp. 1–32(2020)
9. Jose, G., Elie, F.K., Jorge, C., Gautam, S.: A survey on TCP enhancements using p4-programmable devices. Comput. Netw. **212**, 109030 (2022)

10. Zeng, G.X., Chen, L., Yi, B.R., Chen, K.: Cutting tail latency in commodity datacenters with cloudburst. In: Proceedings of IEEE Conference on Computer Communications (INFOCOM 2022), pp. 600–609 (2022)
11. Song, C.H., Xin, Z.K., Raj, J, Inho, C., Li, J.L., Mun, C.C.: Network load balancing with in-network reordering support for RDMA. In: Proceedings of the ACM Special Interest Group on Data Communication (SIGCOMM 2023), pp. 816–831 (2023)
12. Lim, H., Bai, W., Zhu, Y.B., Jung, Y., Han, D.S.: Towards timeout-less transport in commodity datacenter networks. In: 16th European Conference on Computer Systems (EuroSys 2021), pp. 33–48 (2021)
13. Ns3 network simulator. https://www.nsnam.org/. Accessed 22 Oct 2024
14. Choudhury, A.K., Ellen, L.H.: Dynamic queue length thresholds for shared-memory packet switches. IEEE/ACM Trans. Netw. (TON) **6**(2), 130–140 (1998)
15. Zhu, Y.B., et al.: Congestion control for large-scale RDMA deployments. In Proceedings of the ACM Special Interest Group on Data Communication (SIGCOMM 2015), pp. 523–536 (2015)

Emerging Architectures and Systems

A Cluster-Based Platoon Formation Scheme for Realistic Automated Vehicle Platooning

Ziye Liu[1], Chen Chen[1,5(✉)], Qizhong Zhang[5], Zhiyi Wang[2], Yoong Choon Chang[3], Lei Liu[4], Qingqi Pei[1], and Shaohua Wan[6]

[1] School of Telecommunications Engineering, Xidian University, Xi'an, China
cc2000@mail.xidian.edu.cn
[2] State Grid Jilin Province Electric Power Company Limited Information Communication Company, Changchun, China
[3] Lee Kong Chian Faculty of Engineering & Science, Universiti Tunku Abdul Rahman, Bandar Sungai Long, Kajang, Malaysia
[4] Xidian Guangzhou Institute of Technology, Xidian University, Guangzhou, China
[5] Xidian Hangzhou Institute of Technology, Xidian University, Hangzhou, China
[6] Shenzhen Institute for Advanced Study, University of Electronic Science and Technology of China, Shenzhen, China

Abstract. In response to the burgeoning interest in Vehicle-to-Everything (V2X) communications and its pivotal role in enhancing road transportation efficiency and safety, this paper presents a novel scheme for the formation of vehicle platoons, addressing the critical need for realistic implementation strategies. Recognizing the limitations of existing research that often relies on idealized assumptions, this work proposes a platoon formation method utilizing the real-world dataset. The method combines the robustness of Random Forest algorithms for feature selection with the adaptability of Fuzzy K-Means (FKM) clustering to effectively group vehicles with similar characteristics into platoons. This approach ensures the consistency of speed and acceleration within platoons, a crucial aspect for maintaining platoon integrity and stability. Validated through the Kaggle dataset, the scheme not only showcases the feasibility of forming efficient vehicle platoons in realistic scenarios but also introduces a velocity and acceleration-based Cooperative Adaptive Cruise Control (CACC) strategy to prove the formatted platoon stability.

Keywords: V2X · Platooning · Vehicle-Road Cooperation · Fuzzy K-Means · CACC

1 Introduction and Motivation

In the rapidly evolving domain of intelligent transportation systems (ITS), the integration of vehicular communication technology has witnessed unprecedented growth [1,2]. This surge is primarily attributed to significant advancements in

ⓒ IFIP International Federation for Information Processing 2025
Published by Springer Nature Switzerland AG 2025
X. Chen et al. (Eds.): NPC 2024, LNCS 15527, pp. 285–296, 2025.
https://doi.org/10.1007/978-981-96-2830-8_22

communication and autonomous driving technologies. Such progress has propelled vehicle platooning into the limelight of both academic research and practical application, capturing the global interest of technologists and policymakers alike. Vehicle platooning [3] heralded as a cornerstone innovation, aims to radically enhance the efficiency of transportation systems [4]. By optimizing the coordination of vehicle distances and speeds, platooning has the potential to substantially increase road capacity, alleviate traffic congestion, and contribute to environmental sustainability by reducing fuel consumption and carbon emissions [5].

Despite the promising benefits, the practical implementation of vehicle platooning poses considerable challenges, particularly in the formation of vehicle platoons—a process crucial to realizing the theoretical advantages of this technology. Historically, research in this area, as demonstrated in studies by predecessors such as [7,8] and [9], has primarily focused on the development of methodologies to streamline the platoon formation process. In platoon formation, comprehensive strategies that incorporate both large-scale route planning and detailed speed adjustments are crucial [10]. Innovative solutions include the use of cloud computing for dynamic platoon management [11], and the development of queue driving models for autonomous vehicles to improve traffic flow and safety [15]. 5G C-V2X technologies have introduced algorithms for dynamic platoon management and resource allocation that meet stringent communication requirements [6].

However, a significant limitation of these studies is their reliance on idealized assumptions, which treat vehicles merely as homogenous communication nodes without accounting for the inherent variability of vehicles for platooning [2]. These approaches have led to a substantial gap between the theoretical models and their applicability in practical, on-road conditions, where the diverse attributes of individual vehicles play a pivotal role in the dynamics of platoon formation [10]. Meanwhile, The transition from theoretical research to practical implementation of vehicle platooning technology has accelerated through multiple field tests globally. Field tests across various regions have demonstrated the practical implications of vehicle platooning: the UK focused on environmental and safety impacts, the USA examined feasibility on highways, and China evaluated advancements towards global standardization [14]. These tests not only showcased the potential of platooning but also highlighted regional and operational challenges, underscoring the need for adaptable and robust platoon formation strategies. Thus, a precise and efficient method for classifying vehicles into platoons, especially examined by the real-world dataset, is imperative.

Addressing these critical gaps, this study introduces an innovative platoon formation methodology that places a strong emphasis on the practical attributes of vehicles. By leveraging advanced feature selection techniques and FKM clustering, this approach not only acknowledges but also capitalizes on the unique characteristics of each vehicle to facilitate efficient and realistic platoon formation. This method stands distinguished from previous work by its application of real-world data sets, specifically sourced from Kaggle [12], to validate the proposed platoon formation process. To the best of our knowledge, this study is the inaugural effort to employ real-world data sets for the formation of vehicle platoons, providing a robust validation of the proposed methodology and demonstrating its feasibility and effectiveness in practical scenarios. The contributions of this work include:

1) A vehicle platoon formation architecture is proposed under the Vehicle-Road Cooperation (VRC) framework, tailored to real-world scenarios. This architecture facilitates the efficient grouping of vehicles with similar attributes.
2) A platoon formation method based on Random Forest feature selection and FKM clustering is introduced. This method effectively manages the overlap of numerous vehicle characteristics, ensuring vehicles with aligned interests are rapidly grouped into platoons.
3) A comprehensive experimental analysis is conducted to demonstrate the performance of the platoon formation methods. Utilizing the communication-dynamics joint platform PLEXE [13], the results of the formation methods are validated, ensuring the stability of the formed platoons.

The remainder of this paper is structured as follows: Sect. 2 describes the scenario and system model as well as the clustering strategy and CACC strategy for platoon formation. Section 3 evaluates the performance of the proposed strategies through numerical examples. Finally, Sect. 4 concludes the paper.

2 Platoon Formation Approach

2.1 Platooning System Architecture

As shown in Fig. 1, the Vehicle-to-Infrastructure (V2I) communication-enabled VRC system allows Road Side Units (RSUs) to gather and analyze vehicle data, supporting efficient platoon formation. Vehicles are categorized into three tiers—premium, mid-range, and basic—based on attributes like speed, acceleration, and comfort. This categorization helps in managing platoon integrity by aligning vehicles with similar performance characteristics, which is essential for minimizing operational inefficiencies and enhancing safety.

Given the objective of categorizing different vehicles into platoons, clustering naturally emerges as a suitable method. Current clustering methods can be broadly categorized into machine learning-based and novel deep learning-based approaches. However, due to the limited size of the Kaggle dataset (containing data for only 205 vehicles), deep learning-based methods are not feasible as they require large amounts of data for training. The FKM clustering algorithm is used for its ability to handle the overlapping nature of vehicle characteristics, such as engine power and performance, essential for accurate vehicle categorization and effective platoon formation.

In the VRC/V2X system, dynamic data sharing and management are facilitated through the exchange of Basic Safety Messages (BSMs) and Roadside Safety Messages (RSMs). Vehicles broadcast BSMs to indicate their platoon joining intent and share dynamic and static data. RSUs process these messages, use feature selection and clustering algorithms to organize platoons, and communicate platoon details and leader assignments back to the vehicles via RSMs.

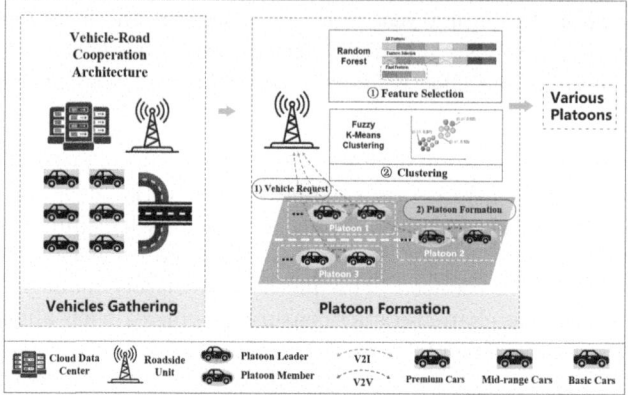

Fig. 1. The proposed platooning formation scheme architecture.

2.2   Random Forest for Identifying Key Features

The fuzzy clustering methods are found comparatively higher as it is expected, due to the iterative fuzzy calculations. To address the serious issue, the random forest algorithm is employed for feature selection first, identifying the most useful features for platoon formation. The random forest algorithm is employed to identify attributes that significantly impact vehicle classification. By aggregating the predictions from numerous decision trees—each constructed from randomly selected attribute subsets—this method not only boosts the model's accuracy but also its ability to discern the importance of various features. Within the random forest model, attribute significance is determined based on the attribute's contribution to improving model accuracy across tree splits. Essentially, the algorithm calculates each attribute's importance by measuring its effectiveness in refining the model's predictive performance. Consequently, attributes that greatly enhance the model's accuracy are considered crucial and are thus selected for the final model formulation.

Given a vehicle dataset with its corresponding features, this is represented as matrix $\mathbf{X}$, encapsulating m vehicles across n features, defined by:

$$\mathbf{X} = \begin{bmatrix} x_{11} & x_{12} & \cdots & x_{1n} \\ x_{21} & x_{22} & \cdots & x_{2n} \\ \vdots & \vdots & \ddots & \vdots \\ x_{m1} & x_{m2} & \cdots & x_{mn} \end{bmatrix}, \tag{1}$$

where m denotes the vehicle count, n the feature count per vehicle, and x_{ij} the jth feature's value for the ith vehicle.

For the random forest model, considering a feature matrix $X \in \mathbb{R}^{n \times m}$ and a target vector $y \in \mathbb{R}^n$, where y indicates the dataset's vehicle prices, with n as the sample count and m the feature count, the model's representation is:

$$\hat{y} = \frac{1}{B} \sum_{b=1}^{B} T_b(\mathbf{X}; \Theta_b), \tag{2}$$

with $\mathbf{X}$ as the feature matrix, Θ_b the bth tree's parameters, and the significance of each tree T_b in feature importance assessment being derived from its contribution to purity gain at feature splits during construction.

The feature f_j's importance score, $I(f_j)$, is given by:

$$I(f_j) = \frac{1}{B} \sum_{b=1}^{B} I_b(f_j), \tag{3}$$

with $I_b(f_j)$ as feature f_j's importance score in the bth tree, determined through the purity gain of that feature at all splits within the tree.

Subsequently, the top K features $\{f_{j_1}, f_{j_2}, \ldots, f_{j_K}\}$, which correlate strongly with the target (vehicle price), are chosen for further analysis. The selected feature subset $\mathbf{X}_{selected} \in \mathbb{R}^{n \times K}$ is described as:

$$\mathbf{X}_{selected} = \mathbf{X}[:, \{j_1, j_2, \ldots, j_K\}], \tag{4}$$

where $\mathbf{X}[:, \{j_1, j_2, \ldots, j_K\}]$ denotes the submatrix obtained by selecting the highest-scoring features from $\mathbf{X}$.

Therefore, $\mathbf{X}_{selected}$ includes the most relevant features for predicting vehicle prices, serving as the basis for subsequent vehicle clustering.

Algorithm 1. Platoon Formation

Input: Vehicle dataset $\mathbf{X}$, Number of platoons c
Output: Platoon members list $= \{p_1, p_2 \ldots p_n\}$
    Initialization: Select features from $\mathbf{X}_{selected}$ using Random Forest. Initialize cluster centers $\mathbf{C} = \{\mathbf{c}_1, \mathbf{c}_2, \ldots, \mathbf{c}_c\}$ and membership matrix U randomly.
1: **repeat**
2:     **for** each data point $i = 1$ to n **do**
3:         **for** each cluster $j = 1$ to c **do**
4:             Calculate u_{ij} according to (5)
5:         **end for**
6:     **end for**
7:     **for** each cluster $j = 1$ to c **do**
8:         Update $\mathbf{c}_j$ according to (6)
9:     **end for**
10: **until** convergence
11: Assign vehicles to platoons based on the highest membership value in U.
12: **for** each platoon j **do**
13:     Calculate distances $d(\mathbf{x}_i, \mathbf{c}_j)$
14:     Compile the Platoon members list $= \{p_1, p_2 \ldots p_n\}$ based on proximity to $\mathbf{c}_j$.
15:     Appoint the platoon leader as the member with the minimum distance to $\mathbf{c}_j$.
16: **end for**

2.3 FKM Clustering for Platoon Formation

Following the feature selection via the random forest model, a pivotal feature subset $\mathbf{X}_{selected}$ is acquired, which significantly influences vehicle price prediction. This subset, embodying essential vehicle attributes for classification, is then utilized to perform FKM clustering, categorizing vehicles into potential platoons. FKM, distinct from traditional k-means, employs a soft clustering mechanism, assigning each vehicle to multiple clusters based on varying membership degrees [16]. This characteristic is particularly beneficial for dealing with the overlapping nature of vehicle features, as observed in the Kaggle dataset analysis.

The primary aim of FKM clustering is to optimize the cluster formation by minimizing the distances between vehicles (data points) and the cluster centroids, all the while considering each vehicle's degree of membership to different clusters. This process, leveraging $\mathbf{X}_{selected}$ derived from the initial random forest assessment, unfolds as follows:

1. Initialize the cluster centroids $\mathbf{C} = \{\mathbf{c}_1, \mathbf{c}_2, \ldots, \mathbf{c}_c\}$, where c denotes the pre-determined number of clusters, representing distinct vehicle platoons.
2. Calculate the membership degree u_{ij} of each vehicle $\mathbf{x}_i$ in $\mathbf{X}_{selected}$ to a centroid $\mathbf{c}_j$, employing the formula:

$$u_{ij} = \frac{1}{\sum_{k=1}^{c} \left(\frac{||\mathbf{x}_i - \mathbf{c}_j||}{||\mathbf{x}_i - \mathbf{c}_k||} \right)^{\frac{2}{m-1}}}, \tag{5}$$

   effectively reflecting the vehicle's potential alignment with each platoon based on its selected features.
3. Update the centroids $\mathbf{c}_j$ to accurately represent the collective position of vehicles within each cluster, weighted by their membership degrees:

$$\mathbf{c}_j = \frac{\sum_{i=1}^{n} u_{ij}^m \mathbf{x}_i}{\sum_{i=1}^{n} u_{ij}^m}, \tag{6}$$

   thereby adjusting the platoon centroids to better match the aggregated characteristics of their respective vehicles.
4. Repeat the calculation of membership degrees and updating of centroids until the centroids stabilize within a specified threshold ε, or until reaching a set number of iterations, ensuring the formation of well-defined and coherent vehicle platoons.

Through this process, vehicles are dynamically grouped into clusters that best represent potential platoons, with each platoon characterized by similar vehicle features and intended functionalities. This nuanced approach facilitates the formation of efficient and cohesive platoons, primed for effective collaboration and enhanced road performance. Algorithm 1, utilizing random forest-based FKM for platoon formation, starts with feature selection via Random Forest, iteratively adjusts clusters based on vehicle features, and selects the nearest vehicle to each cluster center as the leader for efficient platoon organization.

2.4   CACC Strategy

In the CACC system employing Broadcast Mode, the lead vehicle (Vehicle 1) broadcasts its state information, such as acceleration, to the following vehicles (Vehicles 2 through 8). Each vehicle in the platoon adjusts its control input, u_i, based on the lead vehicle's broadcasted acceleration and its own relative position. The control input is formulated as:

$$u_i = k_d(x_{i-1} - x_i - l_{i-1} - 25\,m) + k_s(\ddot{x}_{i-1} - \ddot{x}_i) \tag{7}$$

Here, u_i is the control input for the $i_t h$ vehicle k_d and k_s are the gain factors for distance and acceleration error components, respectively. This control strategy allows each vehicle to maintain a predefined safety distance, in this case, 25 m, from its preceding vehicle, solely using acceleration information to ensure the platoon's cohesive movement. The reliance on broadcasted acceleration data from the lead vehicle facilitates synchronized acceleration adjustments throughout the platoon, enhancing the collective dynamical stability.

Utilizing the vehicle feature data from Kaggle, a simplified model is constructed to assess an automobile's acceleration capability, providing a method that estimates performance based on given parameters. Acceleration capacity $\ddot{x}$ can be approximated by the ratio of *horsepower* to *curbweight*. The higher this ratio, the more horsepower per unit of weight is available to propel the vehicle, theoretically signifying a stronger potential for acceleration.

3   Experiments and Performance Evaluation

3.1   Kaggle Dataset

The dataset allowed us to classify vehicle attributes into basic information, performance metrics, dimensions, weight, and fuel efficiency, as detailed in TABLE1. This categorization includes vehicle make and model, engine specifications, body dimensions, and fuel consumption rates. Highlighting the complexity within these attributes, the analysis points out the challenges in accurately classifying vehicles for platoon formation, especially when distinguishing between low, mid, and high-tier vehicles based on their characteristics. The overlap in attributes among different vehicle tiers complicates this task, underscoring the necessity of a nuanced approach in vehicle classification and platoon strategy development. This exploration emphasizes the diversity and complexity in vehicle attributes, highlighting the importance of considering both individual and interrelated impacts of these attributes for effective vehicle clustering.

3.2   Experimental Setup

The research infrastructure is underpinned by Ubuntu 22.04 and utilizes the processing capabilities of an Intel(R) Core(TM) i9-13900H CPU complemented by 32 GB of RAM. The PLEXE platform, a sophisticated cooperative vehicle simulation framework, is utilized to orchestrate platoon formation and management.

Table 1. The 3 examples of Selected Vehicle Features from car_price.csv

CarName	FuelType	Aspiration	CarBody	DriveWheel	EngineLocation	WheelBase	EngineType
bmw x4	gas	std	sedan	rwd	front	103.5	ohc
audi 5000 s (diesel)	gas	turbo	hatchback	4wd	front	99.5	ohc
nissan nv200	gas	std	sedan	fwd	front	97.2	ohc
CarName	CylinderNumber	EngineSize	FuelSystem	HorsePower	CityMPG	HighwayMPG	
bmw x4	six	209	mpfi	182	16	22	
audi 5000 s (diesel)	five	131	mpfi	160	16	22	
nissan nv200	four	120	2bbl	97	27	34	

The experimental platoon comprises 8 vehicles within PLEXE, an enhancement to Veins that enriches the SUMO and Veins environment to simulate platooning systems with higher fidelity. The platoon is configured with 8 members, ensuring communication within the fleet and between the platoon leader and RSUs via the 802.11p standard, as illustrated in Fig. 2. The simulation parameters specific to platoon scenarios in PLEXE are presented in Table 2.

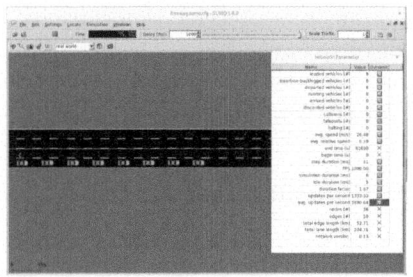

Fig. 2. Diagram of platoon experiments on PLEXE platform.

Table 2. Platoon Simulation Parameters in PLEXE

Parameter	Value
Cruising speed	95 km/h
Braking vehicle deceleration	8 m/s^2
Platoon size	8 cars
Simulation time step	10 ms
Min/max acceleration	-8 to 3 m/s^2

3.3 Performance Evaluation of Platoon Formation

In this study, the FKM algorithm is configured to align with the vehicle classification tiers detailed in the System Model. The number of clusters is defined as three, corresponding to the high, medium, and low categories. The fuzziness parameter is set to 2, providing a moderate level of cluster overlap. To ensure the process iterates sufficiently for stable cluster formation, the maximum number of iterations is set at 100, while the convergence threshold is established at 0.001 to halt iterations when changes become negligible. Lastly, the seed for the random number generator is fixed at 42, facilitating result reproducibility across different runs.

The random forest algorithm assesses feature relevance in price prediction, refining the inputs for FKM clustering. After one-hot encoding categorical variables and discarding overfit-prone features like "CarName" and "CarID," the data is segmented into features and target variables—prices—and standardized to neutralize scale disparities. A random forest regressor, composed of 100 trees with a set seed of 42, forecasts prices on the training set. It gauges feature significance through internal ranking, highlighting engine size, curb weight, horsepower, and car width as the most predictive attributes, with correlation coefficients of 0.874, 0.835, 0.808, and 0.759, respectively. These coefficients markedly surpass those of other variables, as delineated in Fig. 3.

In Fig. 4, the clustering outcomes from the FKM algorithm are exhibited for both selectively chosen features and the comprehensive feature set. On the selected features, the clustering results display data points that are densely grouped, underscoring the algorithm's proficiency in establishing well-defined clusters. The data points, color-coded to represent distinct clusters, show minimal overlap, indicating precise cluster demarcation. On the full features, a more scattered arrangement of data points with increased overlap is revealed, signifying a weaker distinction among clusters.

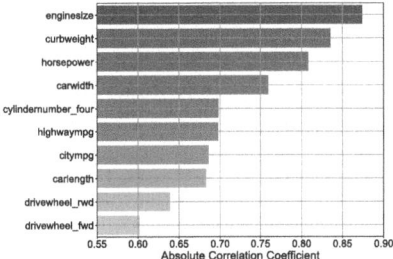

Fig. 3. Top 10 features correlated with the price of vehicles.

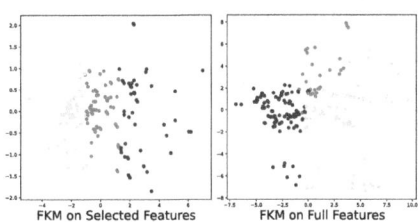

Fig. 4. The visualization of FKM clustering results.

Table 3. The evaluation of clustering methods

Method	Selected Features		
	Silhouette Coefficient	Davies-Bouldin	Calinski-Harabasz
Proposed method	**0.468**	**0.773**	**202.43**
K-means	0.373	0.972	197.69
DBSCAN	0.517	0.597	144.25
Agglomerative Hierarchical	0.367	0.674	192.17

In Table 3, the proposed method is compared, which leverages FKM clustering informed by a random forest-based feature selection process, with three established clustering techniques: K-means, DBSCAN, and Agglomerative Hierarchical Clustering. The result presented in Table 3 encapsulates the comparative evaluation of clustering algorithms using selected features from a Kaggle dataset.

The assessment utilizes three metrics: Silhouette, Davies-Bouldin, and Calinski-Harabasz (CH) scores, where higher Silhouette and CH scores, combined with a lower Davies-Bouldin score, indicate better clustering performance. the proposed method, which implements FKM clustering informed by a feature selection process via random forests, achieves a CH score of 202.43, which is higher than the other clustering method. It's noteworthy that the CH index, in particular, is more favorable towards hard clustering approaches, due to its sensitivity to cluster separation and compactness. The FKM algorithm, augmented by feature selection, demonstrates a marked advantage in managing the numerous overlapping features present in the Kaggle dataset. This suggests that the proposed method's capability to discern subtle distinctions within the data is enhanced, affirming the utility of feature selection in improving the performance of clustering algorithms, especially when dealing with complex datasets where features exhibit significant overlap.

The Random Forest-informed FKM clustering method is applied to classify 24 randomly selected vehicles from the Kaggle dataset into three platoons, aiming to analyze their intra-platoon acceleration capabilities, as presented in Fig. 5. This analysis assessed the mean acceleration ratio and its variance across 20 trials to gauge the performance consistency of each platoon. Results indicate distinct and consistent mean acceleration ratios across the platoons, demonstrating the clustering method's effectiveness in grouping vehicles with similar acceleration traits. Specifically, Platoon 1 exhibited the lowest mean acceleration ratio, showing conservative acceleration behavior; Platoon 2 had a moderate ratio; and Platoon 3 had the highest ratio, indicating the most aggressive acceleration. Variance analysis revealed low variance in Platoon 1 and 2, suggesting high consistency in acceleration performance among their vehicles. In contrast, Platoon 3 showed higher variance, likely due to its more aggressive acceleration profiles. These findings affirm the clustering algorithm's efficacy in forming platoons with uniform performance characteristics, crucial for maintaining stability and safety within the platoon system.

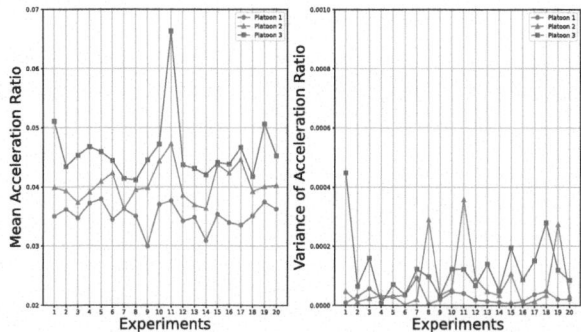

Fig. 5. The evaluation of the platoon acceleration performance.

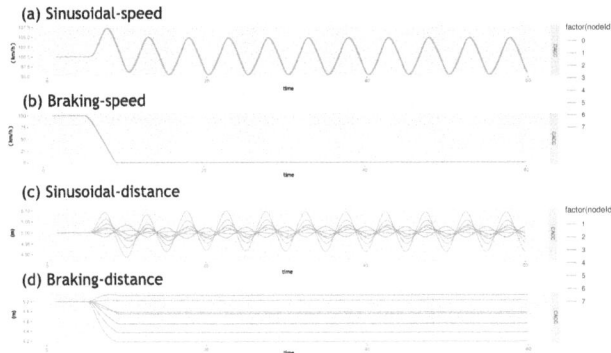

Fig. 6. The Platoon experiments on the PLEXE platform.

To validate the CACC strategy outlined in Sect. 2.4, simulations are conducted on the PLEXE platform, incorporating visible light communication. These tests assessed vehicle platoon dynamics under sinusoidal speed variations and emergency braking scenarios, as depicted in Fig. 6. Results demonstrated that platoon members adeptly synchronized with the lead vehicle's acceleration changes, maintaining cohesion and consistent spacing during speed fluctuations. In emergency braking tests, all vehicles decelerated uniformly, quickly reducing speed to zero and keeping a safe distance between each other, confirming the platoon's ability to ensure safety. Overall, the experiments validated the effectiveness of the clustering algorithms in achieving stable and safe platoon operations under various driving conditions.

4   Conclusion

This paper introduces a cluster-based platoon formation scheme that uses real-world data to enhance automated vehicle platooning. The method combines Random Forest for feature selection with FKM clustering, resulting in platoons with stable and consistent behavior across different driving scenarios. Although the Kaggle dataset is effective, its limited size suggests the need to investigate how the method performs with larger datasets and in more diverse environments. Additionally, future research will examine communication aspects and consider integrating 5G networks and edge computing for real-time platoon management, which would further improve the scalability and adaptability of the proposed scheme in dynamic vehicular environments.

Acknowledgements. This work is supported by the 2023 science and technology project 'Research and application of multi communication system fusion networking technology for typical scenarios in power grids' 2023JBGS-11 of State Grid Jilin Electric Power Company.

References

1. Li, H., Chen, C., Shan, H., Li, P., Chang, Y.C., Song, H.: Deep deterministic policy gradient-based algorithm for computation offloading in iov. IEEE Trans. Intell. Transp. Syst. (2023)
2. Yu, S., Gong, X., Shi, Q., Wang, X., Chen, X.: EC-SAGINs: edge-computing-enhanced space-air-ground-integrated networks for internet of vehicles. IEEE Internet Things J. **9**(8), 5742–5754 (2021)
3. Deng, Z., Yang, K., Shen, W., Shi, Y.: Cooperative platoon formation of connected and autonomous vehicles: toward efficient merging coordination at unsignalized intersections. IEEE Trans. Intell. Transp. Syst. (2023)
4. Chen, C., Wang, C., Li, C., Xiao, M., Pei, Q.: A V2V emergent message dissemination scheme for 6g-oriented vehicular networks. Chin. J. Electron. **32**(6), 1179–1191 (2023)
5. Wan, S., Gu, R., Umer, T., Salah, K., Xu, X.: Toward offloading internet of vehicles applications in 5G networks. IEEE Trans. Intell. Transp. Syst. **22**(7), 4151–4159 (2020)
6. Pu, L., Chen, X., Mao, G., Xie, Q., Xu, J.: Chimera: an energy-efficient and deadline-aware hybrid edge computing framework for vehicular crowdsensing applications. IEEE Internet Things J. **6**(1), 84–99 (2018)
7. Luo, S., Chen, X., Zhou, Z., Chen, X., Wu, W.: Incentive-aware micro computing cluster formation for cooperative fog computing. IEEE Trans. Wireless Commun. **19**(4), 2643–2657 (2020)
8. Elbert, R., Knigge, J.-K., Friedrich, A.: Analysis of decentral platoon planning possibilities in road freight transport using an agent-based simulation model. J. Simul. **14**(1), 64–75 (2020)
9. Xiao, T., Chen, C., Dong, M., Ota, K., Liu, L., Dustdar, S.: Multi-agent reinforcement learning-based trading decision-making in platooning-assisted vehicular networks. IEEE/ACM Trans. Netw. (2023)
10. Hou, J., et al.: Large-scale vehicle platooning: Advances and challenges in scheduling and planning techniques. Engineering (2023)
11. Danquah, W.M., Altilar, D.T.: Data partitioning and scheduling schemes for federated platoon-based vehicular cloud. Veh. Commun. **38**, 100529 (2022)
12. Kaggle, Kaggle car price dataset (2020). https://www.kaggle.com/datasets/hellbuoy/car-price-prediction
13. Segata, M., et al.: Multi-technology cooperative driving: an analysis based on PLEXE. IEEE Trans. Mob. Comput. **22**(8), 4792–4806 (2023)
14. Noruzoliaee, M., Zou, B., Zhou, Y.J.: Truck platooning in the us national road network: a system-level modeling approach. Transp. Res. Part E: Logistics Transp. Rev. **145**, 102200 (2021)
15. Chen, C., Xiao, T., Qiu, T., Lv, N., Pei, Q.: Smart-contract-based economical platooning in blockchain-enabled urban internet of vehicles. IEEE Trans. Industr. Inf. **16**(6), 4122–4133 (2019)
16. Zhao, X., Nie, F., Wang, R., Li, X.: Improving projected fuzzy k-means clustering via robust learning. Neurocomputing **491**, 34–43 (2022)

AnaNET: Anatomical Network for Aggregated Time Series Forecasting in Multi-layered Architecture

Tiancheng Zhang[1], Cheng Zhang[2], Shuren Liu[1], Xiaofei Wang[1(✉)], and Shaoyuan Huang[1]

[1] Tianjin University, Tianjin, China
{zhangtiancheng,shurenliu,xiaofeiwang,hsy_23}@tju.edu.cn
[2] Tianjin University of Finance and Economics, Tianjin, China
zhangcheng@tjufe.edu.cn

Abstract. Data centers have become crucial infrastructure, continuously providing services for large-scale distributed computing, computational networks, and large model training. Accurate prediction of future power consumption in data centers is essential for ensuring system efficiency and energy management. However, data centers often employ multi-layered architectures and consist of heterogeneous devices, leading to highly complex and chaotic time-series information, making overall power consumption prediction challenging. To address this issue, this paper analyzes the complexity of aggregated time series from both horizontal and vertical perspectives, tackling the challenges posed by data aggregation in multi-layered architectures. We introduce AnaNET, an innovative analytical network designed specifically to dissect and model the complex and chaotic nature of power consumption. AnaNET utilizes a novel frequency decomposition and inverse progressive decomposition method, isolating and analyzing different periodic patterns within the aggregated data. AnaNET demonstrated approximately 22% relative improvement across six real-world time-series datasets. Code is available at: https://github.com/hihiztc1/AnaNET_NPC.

Keywords: Time series forecasting · Multi-Layered architecture · Data centers

1 Introduction

As critical infrastructure for large-scale distributed computing, computing power networks, and large model training, data centers are becoming increasingly important. However, their massive energy consumption makes them significant contributors to carbon emissions. By 2030, the data center industry is expected to account for 8% of global carbon emissions [2]. Accurate prediction of future

© IFIP International Federation for Information Processing 2025
Published by Springer Nature Switzerland AG 2025
X. Chen et al. (Eds.): NPC 2024, LNCS 15527, pp. 297–309, 2025.
https://doi.org/10.1007/978-981-96-2830-8_23

power consumption in data centers is crucial for providing data support for energy-saving strategies and ensuring stable, safe power usage to avoid risks such as equipment failures, fires, and power outages, which can lead to business interruptions, data loss, and significant economic losses [5].

Data centers typically utilize multi-layer architectures, comprising multiple racks, rooms, and buildings, filled with various heterogeneous devices such as heating, ventilation, and air conditioning (HVAC), communication, and computing equipment. The data center shown in Fig. 1 serves as an example where a multi-layered structure abundant in time series data can be observed. Based on the mode of data generation, these time series can be divided into two categories: **At**omic **T**ime **S**eries (AtoTS) and **Agg**regated **T**ime **S**eries (AggTS). This phenomenon is also common in industrial [13] and network [7] domains.

AtoTS: Time series directly generated by sensors, referred to as AtoTS, typically contains a limited number of periodic patterns reflecting the characteristics of the monitored object and their environment.

AggTS: In a multi-layered architecture like data centers, AggTS data are produced by collecting multiple AtoTS. These AtoTS are often reported to higher levels within the architecture and aggregated to form new time series data with collective characteristics.

If AtoTS reflects an individual characteristic and a local environment, AggTS, which aggregates multiple AtoTS, synthesizes group characteristics and overall environmental feedback. As a result, AggTS datasets may integrate various periodic frequencies, leading to potential chaotic phenomena.

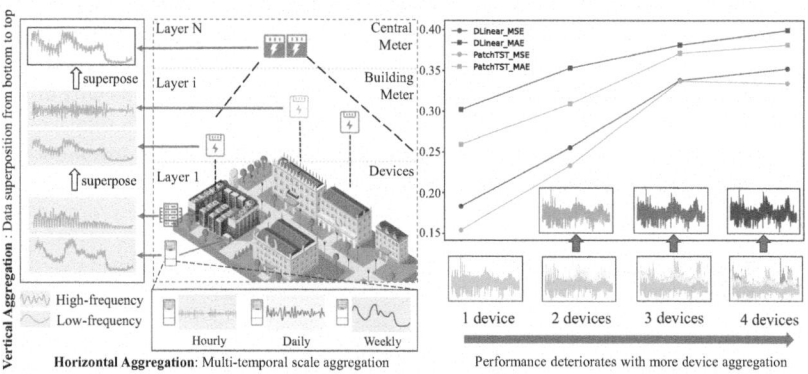

Fig. 1. Time series aggregation process in a multi-layered architecture (left), and the predictive performance of different models for AggTS (right).

To address the chaos phenomena in AggTS, this paper analyzes the aggregation of periodic patterns within AggTS, considering it as a behavior occurring in both horizontal and vertical dimensions.

Horizontal Aggregation. The same device shows distinct multi-periodic characteristics over time due to influences from monitored objects and societal habits. Different fluctuation patterns appear at various observation granularities. For instance, as shown in Fig.1, air conditioning electricity consumption varies daily and weekly. These multi-periodic features pose challenges for prediction. Many studies[14,17,18] attempt to address this by using seasonal-trend decomposition, extracting trends for larger time periods (weeks, months, years) and treating smaller time periods as seasonal variations. This helps models to better handle the multi-periodic issues across different time scales.

Vertical Aggregation. In addition to horizontal aggregation, vertical aggregation further complicates the prediction challenges. In a multi-layered architecture, data progressively aggregates from the lower levels to the top, involving the integration of information from multiple data sources to form an AggTS. During this process, the periods in AggTS become complex and intertwined. Most existing model architectures and seasonal-trend decomposition techniques struggle to effectively handle such data, resulting in poor forecasting performance for multi-layered aggregated time series data, as shown in Fig. 1.

The major challenge for AggTS prediction is dealing with its complex and chaotic periodic patterns. It is crucial to design modules better suited than seasonal-trend decomposition to disentangle these patterns and effectively stack these modules to fit multi-layered architectures. This paper introduces AnaNET, which incorporates frequency decomposition modules to separate the intertwined high and low frequency periods in AggTS. By stacking modules in the reverse direction of data aggregation, AnaNET decomposes and models AggTS, simplifying it into basic frequency components for precise predictions.

In summary, the main contributions of this study are as follows:

1. Unlike most works utilizing seasonal-trend decomposition, we propose **a refined frequency decomposition module (FD)** that effectively separates entangled periods in AggTS data. FD is an improvement over traditional frequency decomposition methods, adeptly decomposing multivariate time series and making it well-suited for integration into deep learning models.
2. To address dual aggregation behaviors in multi-layer scenarios, **a progressive reverse dissection framework** is proposed. It continuously decomposes complex sequences into simpler frequency components to facilitate more precise temporal dependency discovery.
3. AnaNET is introduced, significantly enhancing performance in the complex task of AggTS prediction. Our method achieves around a **29%** improvement in MSE across six datasets, demonstrating its effectiveness.

2   Related Work

Energy consumption and forecasting have become critical issues for data centers, especially with the rise of distributed computing and large models, leading to the global expansion of large-scale data center construction and the proposal of various management systems. Dynamo [15] studied Facebook's data centers, offering solutions based on multiple levels and constraints. ANT-Man [6] examines power consumption dynamics across granularities. In power management systems, forecasting is vital for informing future decisions and scheduling. Recently, more efforts have been directed toward tackling the challenges of time series forecasting involving complex periodic patterns.

Pyraformer [10] uses a pyramidal attention module to capture temporal dependencies across resolutions, identifying both short- and long-term patterns. However, its coarser resolutions struggle to capture short-term patterns crucial for accurate forecasting. Autoformer [14] addresses intricate temporal patterns by progressively decomposing and eliminating trend components to focus on seasonal dependencies. DLinear [17] combines trend and seasonal decomposition with linear layers, outperforming previous Transformer-based methods. These methods focus on horizontal decomposition, neglecting the complexity of vertical aggregation in multi-layered scenarios.

PatchTST [12] segments time series into patches, excelling at capturing longer semantic information. However, its single-token patch representation may miss intricate periodic patterns, particularly in AggTS. TSMixer [3], with its fully MLP-based architecture, delivers strong univariate and superior multivariate forecasting. MV-DTSF [16] converts time series into binary images, leveraging a visual backbone to capture temporal dependencies, but struggles to model complex power consumption effectively.

Despite their inspiring results, they still struggle with the mutual overlapping of different periods. Furthermore, in multi-layered scenarios like data centers, which are filled with various heterogeneous devices, entanglement and chaotic characteristics are particularly prominent. A more suitable model for these conditions is yet to be proposed.

3   Methodology

Notations and Problem Definition. In practice, time series forecasting often uses rolling predictions with a look-back window of length T, processing multiple T-length historical data as inputs:

$$X = \{\mathcal{X}_t = [x_t, ..., x_{t+T-1}] | t < \mathcal{T} - T + 1, x \in \mathbb{R}^d\} \tag{1}$$

Where $\mathcal{T}$ is the last observable time index and x represents the historical data at a given time step. The model aims to predict the next P time steps:

$$\widehat{Y} = \{\hat{y}_{t+T}, ..., \hat{y}_{t+T+P-1}\} = Model(X) \tag{2}$$

Frequency Decomposition (FD). As explained in the introduction, multilayered scenarios tend to exhibit periodic pattern aggregation in dual dimensions.

To explore more suitable decomposition methods for AggTS, we first utilized the Lyapunov exponent [11] and Fast Fourier Transform (FFT) to measure the chaos degree and potential frequency patterns in the time series. Lyapunov

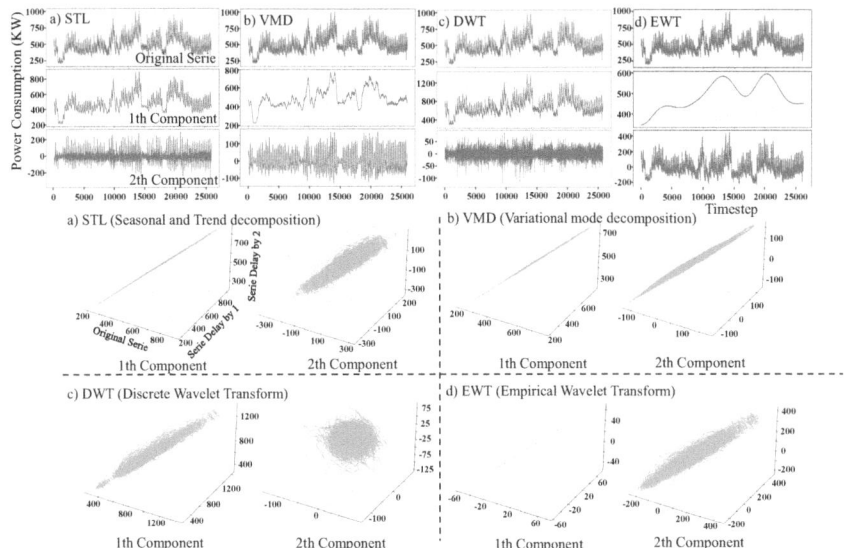

Fig. 2. Decomposition results of different methods on the DCP_A.

exponents indicate the presence of chaotic modes. We calculate these exponents through phase space reconstruction using the delay method [8], where higher positive values suggest greater chaos. FFT reveals potential frequencies within the time series. We decomposed the raw data, selected the six most dominant frequency components in each 96-segment part, and counted those exceeding 30% of the segments. The results are in Table 1 of the experiment section.

We compared different decomposition methods using the DCP_A dataset, standardizing the number of components to two for consistency. The decomposition results are shown in Fig. 2. Compared to other methods, Variational Mode Decomposition (VMD) [4] effectively decomposes the chaotic original sequence into two components with lower chaos. While VMD effectively disentangles chaotic time series, it has two major flaws hindering its integration into deep models: it is limited to one-dimensional time series and incurs high computational costs. In this paper, we developed a torch-based Frequency Decomposition module, inspired by VMD principles. This module supports multi-dimensional time series with low computational overhead, making it suitable for deep models.

FD first constructs a variational problem. The input time series $\mathcal{X} \in \mathbb{R}^{T \times D}$, where D is the embedding dimension, is decomposed into high-frequency element $\mathcal{H} \in \mathbb{R}^{T \times D}$ and low-frequency element $\mathcal{L} \in \mathbb{R}^{T \times D}$. $\mathcal{H}$ and $\mathcal{L}$ must be finite bandwidth IMFs with a central frequency. The goal is to minimize the sum of their estimated bandwidths, with the constraint that their sum equals the original series $\mathcal{X}$. The corresponding constraint variational expression is:

$$\min_{\{\mathcal{H},\mathcal{L}\},\{\mathcal{H}_\omega,\mathcal{L}_\omega\}} \left\{ \left\| \partial_t \left[(\delta(t) + j/\pi t) * \mathcal{H}(t) \right] e^{-j\mathcal{H}_\omega t} \right\|_2^2 + \right.$$

$$\left. \left\| \partial_t \left[(\delta(t) + j/\pi t) * \mathcal{L}(t) \right] e^{-j\mathcal{L}_\omega t} \right\|_2^2 \right\}$$

$$\text{s.t. } \mathcal{H} + \mathcal{L} = \mathcal{X} \tag{3}$$

Here, $\mathcal{H}_\omega$ and $\mathcal{L}_\omega$ are the center frequencies of the high-frequency and low-frequency elements. $\delta(t)$ is the Dirac function. The Lagrange multiplier λ transforms the problem into an unconstrained one. The ADMM [1] iterative algorithm is used to obtain the iterative formulas for $\mathcal{H}$, $\mathcal{L}$, $\mathcal{H}_\omega$, and $\mathcal{L}_\omega$.

$$\widehat{\mathcal{H}}^{n+1}(\omega) \leftarrow \frac{\widehat{\mathcal{H}}(\omega) - \widehat{\mathcal{L}}(\omega) + \widehat{\lambda}(\omega)/2}{1 + 2\alpha\left(\omega - \mathcal{H}_\omega\right)^2}$$

$$\widehat{\mathcal{L}}^{n+1}(\omega) \leftarrow \frac{\widehat{\mathcal{L}}(\omega) - \widehat{\mathcal{H}}(\omega) + \widehat{\lambda}(\omega)/2}{1 + 2\alpha\left(\omega - \mathcal{L}_\omega\right)^2}$$

$$\mathcal{H}_\omega^{n+1} \leftarrow \frac{\int_0^\infty \omega \left| \widehat{\mathcal{H}}^{n+1}(\omega) \right|^2 d\omega}{\int_0^\infty \left| \widehat{\mathcal{H}}^{n+1}(\omega) \right|^2 d\omega} \tag{4}$$

$$\mathcal{L}_\omega^{n+1} \leftarrow \frac{\int_0^\infty \omega \left| \widehat{\mathcal{L}}^{n+1}(\omega) \right|^2 d\omega}{\int_0^\infty \left| \widehat{\mathcal{L}}^{n+1}(\omega) \right|^2 d\omega}$$

$$\widehat{\lambda}^{n+1}(\omega) \leftarrow \widehat{\lambda}^n(\omega) + \gamma\left(\widehat{\mathcal{X}}(\omega) - \sum_k \widehat{u}_k^{n+1}(\omega) \right)$$

Here, α is the penalty factor affecting the bandwidth of each IMF. $\widehat{\mathcal{H}}^{n+1}(\omega)$, $\widehat{\mathcal{L}}^{n+1}(\omega)$, $\widehat{\mathcal{X}}(\omega)$, and $\widehat{\lambda}(\omega)$ are the Fourier transforms of $\mathcal{H}^{n+1}(t)$, $\mathcal{L}^{n+1}(t)$, $\mathcal{X}(t)$, and $\lambda(\omega)$, respectively. Formulas (4) will be iterated multiple times, updating until $\left| \widehat{\mathcal{H}}^{n+1} - \widehat{\mathcal{H}}^n \right| 2^2 / \left| \widehat{\mathcal{H}}k^n \right| 2^2 + \left| \widehat{\mathcal{L}}^{n+1} - \widehat{\mathcal{L}}^n \right| 2^2 / \left| \widehat{\mathcal{L}}k^n \right| 2^2 < \varepsilon$, where ε is a minimum value set to $5e - 5$.

3.1   Model Structure

To address AggTS from multi-layer data fusion, the model uses an encoder-decoder framework (Fig. 3). Historical time series data of length T is embedded and fed into the encoder to extract latent high-frequency components. These components are then input into the corresponding layer's decoder to learn temporal patterns and serve as input for the next layer's encoder.

The decoder operates in two pathways: historical data is decomposed into a simpler trend part and a more complex seasonal part via a seasonal-trend decomposition module [14]. The latter halves of these parts, with placeholders matching the forecast length P, are used for multi-step forecasting. In the first pathway, the trend part is combined with low-frequency components from subsequent frequency decomposition modules. In another pathway, the seasonal part is embedded and input for dependency learning. The final output is the superposition of layer-by-layer low-frequency components and the reconstructed high-frequency components.

Next, we will focus on the internal structure of the encoder and decoder.

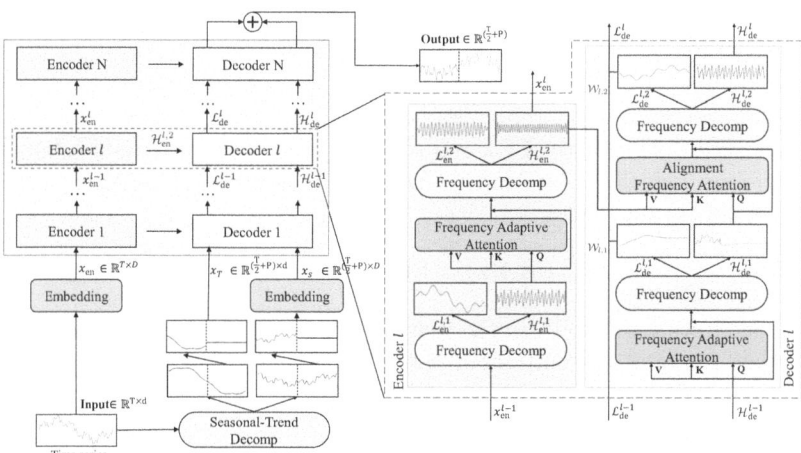

Fig. 3. The architecture of AnaNET. The process of the model's operation is explicitly displayed.

Encoder. The encoder consists of two moudles: FD for frequency breakdown and Frequency Adaptive Attention for learning patterns. It splits the time series into high-frequency and low-frequency components and focuses on latent patterns in high-frequency components to aid the decoder. Formalized as:

$$
\begin{aligned}
\mathcal{L}_{en}^{l,1}, \mathcal{H}_{en}^{l,1} &= \text{FD}\left(\mathcal{X}_{en}^{l-1}\right) \\
\mathcal{L}_{en}^{l,2}, \mathcal{H}_{en}^{l,2} &= \text{FD}\left(\mathcal{H}_{en}^{l,1} + \text{FAA}\left(\mathcal{H}_{en}^{l,1}\right)\right) \\
\mathcal{X}_{en}^{l} &= \mathcal{H}_{en}^{l,2}
\end{aligned}
\tag{5}
$$

where $\mathcal{L}_{en}^{l,i}, \mathcal{H}_{en}^{l,i}, i \in \{1,2\}$ represents the low-frequency and high-frequency components after the i-th FD module in the l-th layer respectively.

Frequency Adaptive Attention Module (FAA). The FAA uses FFT to convert high-frequency components into the frequency domain, identifying major frequencies to represent the time series. A key question in using FFT is which fourier components should be chosen to represent the time series. Selecting all fourier components often leads to over-fitting and reduction of calculation efficiency. Another wise approach is to make random selections [18]. Although random selection ensures efficient computation, there is still a possibility of missing the significant period, resulting in the loss of important information. In AnaNET, we prefer to select M major components to retain essential information while maintaining computational efficiency.

Assuming a time series $\mathcal{X} \in \mathbb{R}^{T \times D}$ denoted as $(x_1, x_2, \ldots, x_T)$, we can transform it via FFT into $(\mathcal{C}1, \mathcal{C}2, \ldots, \mathcal{C}f)$, where $f = T//2$. Each $\mathcal{C}f$ is a complex number representing the amplitude and phase of each component. Due to frequency domain conjugacy, only the first half of the fourier components are considered. FAA calculates the average amplitude of $\mathcal{C}$ across the D dimensions and selects M components with larger amplitudes. This process can be defined as:

$$M = \text{Select-M} \ (\ \text{Avg} \ (\ \text{Amp} \ (\ \text{FFT} \ (\mathcal{X})))) \tag{6}$$

Here, $\text{FFT}(\cdot)$ denotes the FFT and $\text{Avg}(\cdot)$ averages the amplitude values from D dimensions, calculated by $\text{Amp}(\cdot)$. $M \in \mathbb{C}^{M \times D}$ represents the M components with the largest amplitudes.

$$FAA(x) = \text{FFT}^{-1} (\boldsymbol{W}\boldsymbol{M}) \tag{7}$$

To enable AnaNET to learn the weights between different components, $\boldsymbol{M}$ is multiplied by a randomly initialized parameterized kernel $\boldsymbol{W}$. The result is then transformed back to the time domain via inverse FFT as the output of FAA.

Decoder. Similar to the encoder, the decoder contains two FD modules and one FAA module. It differs by including a unique AFA module, which captures latent high-frequency patterns from the corresponding encoder layer. Decoder has two data channels for low-frequency and high-frequency components. The first channel combines the output from the previous decoder layer with low-frequency components decomposed by FD and passes it to the next layer. The second channel uses FAA and AFA to learn time series patterns and reconstruct high-frequency components. The process is formalized as follows:

$$\begin{aligned}
\mathcal{L}_{\text{de}}^{l,1}, \mathcal{H}_{\text{de}}^{l,1} &= \text{FD} \ (\mathcal{H}_{\text{de}}^{l-1} + \text{FAA} \ (\mathcal{H}_{\text{de}}^{l-1})) \\
\mathcal{L}_{\text{de}}^{l,2}, \mathcal{H}_{\text{de}}^{l,2} &= \text{FD} \left(\mathcal{H}_{\text{de}}^{l,1} + \text{AFA} \left(\mathcal{H}_{\text{de}}^{l,1}, \mathcal{H}_{\text{en}}^{l,2} \right) \right) \\
\mathcal{H}_{\text{de}}^{l} &= \mathcal{H}_{\text{de}}^{l,2} \\
\mathcal{L}_{\text{de}}^{l} &= \mathcal{L}_{\text{de}}^{l-1} + \mathcal{P}_{l,1} \cdot \mathcal{L}_{\text{de}}^{l,1} + \mathcal{P}_{l,2} \cdot \mathcal{L}_{\text{de}}^{l,2}
\end{aligned} \tag{8}$$

where $\mathcal{L}_{\text{de}}^{l,i}$ and $\mathcal{H}_{\text{de}}^{l,i}$ represent the low-frequency and high-frequency components after the i-th FD module in the l-th layer, respectively. $\mathcal{P}_{l,i}$ is the projector for the i-th low-frequency element, mapping it to the input vector dimensions.

Alignment Frequency Attention Module (AFA). Unlike the canonical transformer, we use the AFA to obtain information from the corresponding high-frequency components in the encoder to guide period discovery in the decoder. The queries from the i-th decoder layer are denoted as $\boldsymbol{q}_i^{de} \in \mathbb{R}^{(\frac{T}{2}+P) \times D}$. The keys and values from the i-th encoder layer's high-frequency components are denoted as $\boldsymbol{k}_i^{en} \in \mathbb{R}^{T \times D}$ and $\boldsymbol{v}_i^{en} \in \mathbb{R}^{T \times D}$. Similar to FAA, M major fourier components are selected to represent queries, keys, and values, denoted as:

$$
\begin{aligned}
\boldsymbol{Q}_i^{de} &= \text{Select-M} \left(\text{FFT} \left(q_i^{de} \right) \right) \\
\boldsymbol{K}_i^{en} &= \text{Select-M} \left(\text{FFT} \left(k_i^{en} \right) \right) \\
\boldsymbol{V}_i^{en} &= \text{Select-M} \left(\text{FFT} \left(v_i^{en} \right) \right)
\end{aligned} \tag{9}
$$

where, $\boldsymbol{Q}$, $\boldsymbol{K}$ and $\boldsymbol{V} \in \mathbb{C}^{M \times D}$. The result of AFA is defined as:

$$
\text{AFA}(q_i^{de}, k_i^{en}, v_i^{en}) = \text{FFT}^{-1} \left(\text{Padding} \left(\sigma \left(\boldsymbol{Q}_i^{de} \cdot \boldsymbol{K}_i^{en\top} \right) \cdot \boldsymbol{V}_i^{en} \right) \right) \tag{10}
$$

4   Experiments

Datasets. To comprehensively validate the effectiveness of the proposed model for prediction of AggTS in multi-layer scenarios, we collected aggregated power AggTS data from three real data centers, denoted as DCP. The ETTm dataset includes oil temperature data from two different transformers. To consider the overall oil temperature of transformers in a given area and simulate the aggregation process, we combined them into an aggregated dataset named ETTm_MIX for evaluating the model's performance. We measure these datasets in Table 1. It can be observed that the degree of chaos and the number of potential cycles in AggTS are multiples of those in AtoTS (Fig. 4).

Table 1. The measurement of different datasets.

Dataset	Class	L. E.	M. F.
DCP_A	AggTS	0.0139	68
DCP_B	AggTS	0.0134	75
DCP_C	AggTS	0.0129	45
ETTm_MIX	AggTS	0.0074	28
ECL	AtoTS	0.0062	30
ETTm2	AtoTS	0.0061	24

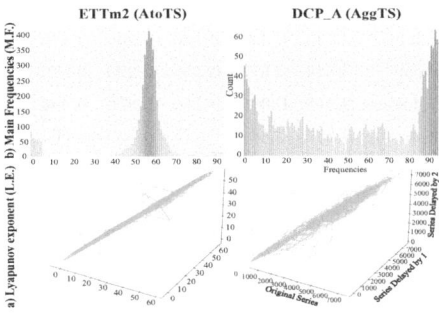

Fig. 4. Measurement results visualization.

Baselines. We select six state-of-the-art (SOTA) models as comparison, including three transformer-based models: PatchTST [12], Pyraformer [10], Autoformer [14] and two MLP-based model: DLinear [17], TSMixer [3] and one vision-based model: MV-DTSF [16]. These models have demonstrated robust performance in time series forecasting.

Implementation. In experiments, both prediction and input lengths are set to 96. Datasets are split into training, validation, and test sets in a 7:1:2 ratio, with standardization applied. We used Adam [9] optimization with an initial learning rate of 10^{-4}, halving each epoch, and a batch size of 32. All experiments were conducted in PyTorch on two NVIDIA GeForce RTX 3090 GPUs.

4.1   Main Results

Table 2 shows that while current SOTA models excel on AtoTS, they fall short with the chaotic and complex AggTS. In contrast, the proposed model outperforms them, improving MSE by **29.4%** and MAE by **14.7%** on average. Notably, DCP_A, with the highest Lyapunov exponent, benefits significantly from the proposed model. This improvement likely stems from our specially designed FD and inverse decomposition architecture, which effectively eliminate interference between multiple frequencies and allow for more accurate capture of temporal dependencies.

Table 2. Forecasting in AggTS and AtoTS. A lower MSE or MAE indicates a better prediction. The best results are in **bold**.

Datasets	AggTS								AtoTS			
	DCP_A		DCP_C		DCP_B		ETTm_MIX		ETTm2		ECL	
Metrics	MSE	MAE	MSE	MAE	MSE	MAE	MSE	MAE	MSE	MAE	MSE	MAE
AnaNET	**0.178**	**0.320**	**0.141**	**0.260**	**0.314**	**0.416**	**0.042**	**0.156**	**0.064**	0.192	**0.274**	0.387
TSMixer	0.473	0.500	0.144	0.264	0.571	0.522	0.048	0.157	0.121	0.240	0.288	**0.379**
MV-DTSF	0.427	0.457	0.155	0.278	0.566	0.502	0.051	0.158	0.131	0.249	0.348	0.412
PatchTST	0.333	0.429	0.146	0.266	0.472	0.478	0.045	0.157	0.069	0.189	0.337	0.414
Dlinear	0.544	0.573	0.155	0.290	0.576	0.551	0.044	0.157	0.073	0.198	0.402	0.462
Pyraformer	0.318	0.419	0.150	0.276	0.494	0.501	0.050	0.163	0.071	0.195	0.409	0.469
Autoformer	0.367	0.468	0.275	0.407	0.665	0.617	0.153	0.297	0.065	**0.189**	0.360	0.445

4.2   How AnaNET work: Ablation Study and Model Analysis

We conducted ablation studies to highlight the importance of the reverse decomposition architecture. In Table 3, S denotes seasonal-trend decomposition and F denotes frequency decomposition. AnaNET includes five decomposition stages, and we systematically removed each module to assess its contribution. The results show a noticeable performance decline when any module is excluded, with the efficiency dropping further as more modules are removed. This trend underscores the complexity of periodic patterns in AggTS data and validates the effectiveness of the reverse progressive decomposition approach.

Table 3. Ablation study of decomposition, gradually removing the decomposition module from the model. (-x%) indicates the percentage of performance drop.

Decomp.	SFFFF	SFFF	SFF	SF	S	-
DCP_A	**0.178**	0.188	0.188	0.184	0.198	0.228
		(-5.6%)	(-5.3%)	(-3.4%)	(-10.1%)	(-22%)
DCP_C	**0.141**	0.142	0.145	0.145	0.147	0.301
		(-0.3%)	(-2.4%)	(-2.4%)	(-3.7%)	(-53.0%)

Parameter Sensitivity: In AnaNET, the hyperparameter M in FAA and AFA defines the number of Fourier components used for time series representation. In Fig. 5, we contrast the performance of AnaNET across various datasets under different values of M. We observe that a larger M leads to better results, but beyond a certain value, the efficiency gains start to diminish. For computational efficiency, it is ultimately set to 64.

The hyperparameter α in Eq. (4) controls the bandwidth of each IMF. Our FD shows stable performance across different α values, as illustrated in Fig. 5, leading us to fix α at 2000 for the experiments.

Time and Memory Consumption: We conducted experiments on DCP_A under input-96-predict-96, measuring the spatiotemporal cost and accuracy of each model. As shown in Fig. 6, when dealing with chaotic datasets, AnaNET achieves the best performance among all SOTAs models with minimal space increase and moderate time consumption.

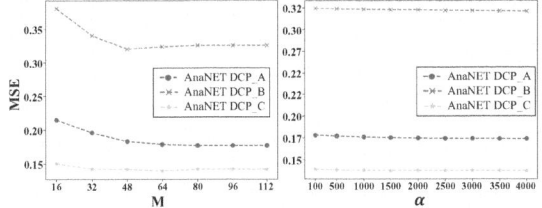

Fig. 5. Parameter sensitivity.

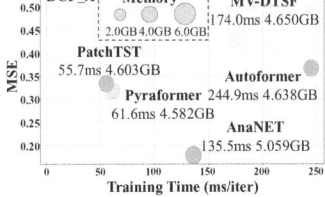

Fig. 6. Time and memory usage.

5   Conclusion

We proposed AnaNET, a deep model designed for predicting complex power consumption in multi-layered architectures like data centers, which house vast amounts of heterogeneous devices. The upper-layer time series data in these architectures, referred to as Aggregated Time Series (AggTS), are characterized by complex and chaotic periodic patterns resulting from both vertical and horizontal aggregation. To address this, AnaNET employs a frequency decomposition and inverse progressive decomposition method, specifically tailored for forecasting complex AggTS data. This approach effectively separates intertwined periodic patterns, enabling precise predictions. Experimental results demonstrate that AnaNET outperforms existing six methods on six datasets.

Acknowledgments. This work is supported in part by National Science Foundation of China under Grant No. 62072332, in part by China NSFC (Youth) through Grant No. 62306208, in part by Tianjin Natural Science Foundation (Youth) Tianjin Natural Science Foundation General Project No. 23JCQNJC00920, in part by the Tianjin Xinchuang Haihe Lab under Grant No.22HHXCJC00002.

References

1. Boyd, S., Parikh, N., Chu, E., Peleato, B., Eckstein, J., et al.: Distributed optimization and statistical learning via the alternating direction method of multipliers. Found. Trends® Mach. Learn. **3**(1), 1–122 (2011)
2. Cao, Z., Zhou, X., Hu, H., Wang, Z., Wen, Y.: Toward a systematic survey for carbon neutral data centers. IEEE Commun. Surv. Tutorials **24**(2), 895–936 (2022)
3. Chen, S.A., Li, C.L., Arik, S.O., Yoder, N.C., Pfister, T.: TSMixer: an all-MLP architecture for time series forecast-ing. Trans. Mach. Learn. Res. (2023)
4. Dragomiretskiy, K., Zosso, D.: Variational mode decomposition. IEEE Trans. Signal Process. **62**(3), 531–544 (2014)
5. Hong, T., Pinson, P., Wang, Y., Weron, R., Yang, D., Zareipour, H.: Energy forecasting: a review and outlook. IEEE Open Access J. Power Energy **7**, 376–388 (2020)
6. Hou, X., Li, C., Liu, J., Zhang, L., Hu, Y., Guo, M.: Ant-man: towards agile power management in the microservice era. In: International Conference for High Performance Computing, Networking, Storage and Analysis, pp. 1–14. IEEE (2020)
7. Huang, S., Wang, Z., Zhang, H., Wang, X., Zhang, C., Wang, W.: One for all: Unified workload prediction for dynamic multi-tenant edge cloud platforms. In: Proceedings of the 29th ACM SIGKDD Conference on Knowledge Discovery and Data Mining. KDD 2023, pp. 788–797 (2023)
8. Josiński, H., Świtoński, A., Michalczuk, A., Wojciechowski, K.: Phase space reconstruction and estimation of the largest lyapunov exponent for gait kinematic data. In: AIP Conference Proceedings, vol. 1648, p. 660006. AIP Publishing LLC (2015)
9. Kingma, D.P., Ba, J.: Adam: a method for stochastic optimization. In: International Conference on Learning Representations (2015)
10. Liu, S., et al.: Pyraformer: low-complexity pyramidal attention for long-range time series modeling and forecasting. In: International Conference on Learning Representations (2021)
11. Lyapunov, A.M.: The general problem of the stability of motion. Int. J. Control **55**(3), 531–534 (1992)
12. Nie, Y., Nguyen, N.H., Sinthong, P., Kalagnanam, J.: A time series is worth 64 words: long-term forecasting with transformers. In: International Conference on Learning Representations (2023)

13. Wen, Q., Yang, L., Zhou, T., Sun, L.: Robust time series analysis and applications: An industrial perspective. In: Proceedings of the 28th ACM SIGKDD Conference on Knowledge Discovery and Data Mining. KDD 2022, pp. 4836–4837 (2022)

14. Wu, H., Xu, J., Wang, J., Long, M.: Autoformer: decomposition transformers with auto-correlation for long-term series forecasting, vol. 34, pp. 22419–22430 (2021)

15. Wu, Q., et al.: Dynamo: Facebook's data center-wide power management system. In: Proceedings of the 43rd International Symposium on Computer Architecture. ISCA 2016, pp. 469–480. IEEE Press (2016). https://doi.org/10.1109/ISCA.2016.48

16. Yang, L., Fan, X., Zhang, Z.: Your time series is worth a binary image: machine vision assisted deep framework for time series forecasting. arXiv preprint arXiv:2302.14390 (2023)

17. Zeng, A., Chen, M., Zhang, L., Xu, Q.: Are transformers effective for time series forecasting? In: Proceedings of the AAAI Conference on Artificial Intelligence, vol. 37, pp. 11121–11128 (2023)

18. Zhou, T., Ma, Z., Wen, Q., Wang, X., Sun, L., Jin, R.: Fedformer: frequency enhanced decomposed transformer for long-term series forecasting. In: International Conference on Machine Learning, pp. 27268–27286. PMLR (2022)

Deep Reinforcement Learning for Large-Scale Scientific Workflow Scheduling with Improved Structure Feature Extraction and Sampling

Xumai Qi, Dongdong Zhang$^{(\boxtimes)}$, Taotao Liu, and Hongcheng Wang

School of Computer Science and Technology, Tongji University, Shanghai, China
{2111137,ddzhang,ttliu,wanghc}@tongji.edu.cn

Abstract. In recent years, deep reinforcement learning (DRL) has been widely explored to schedule workflows in cloud computing. However, the previous studies pay less attention to the complex workflow structure and the DRL sampling efficiency, so that the scheduling performance deteriorates for large-scale scientific workflow scheduling, especially when there are multiple quality of service (QoS) requirements. To tackle this problem, we propose a DRL-based scheduling algorithm with improved structure feature extraction and sampling strategy. Firstly, we introduce graph attention network to extract workflow structure features better to improve scheduling performance of large-scale scientific workflows with DRL. Secondly, we design a DRL sampling strategy based on genetic algorithm, which generates suboptimal initial sample trajectories for the DRL agent to accelerate the training process. Experiments on Pegasus workflow dataset show that the proposed method can get better QoS results and faster training speed in simulated cloud environment.

Keywords: Cloud Computing · QoS · Large-Scale Scientific Workflow · Graph Neural Network · Reinforcement Learning · Genetic Algorithm

1 Introduction

Since more and more scientific fields have become data-driven, the demand for the massive scientific computation is increasing. Nowadays, cloud computing technology has brought great convenience for users to obtain high-performance computing resources. Under this background, the scheduling of large-scale scientific workflows on cloud computing platforms has become an important study topic.

In recent years, many studies have been exploring the utilization of deep reinforcement learning (DRL) to solve the workflow scheduling problem. Yang et al. [1] was the first to propose a model-based reinforcement learning in the distributed and cloud-based system to schedule scientific workflow. The DRL-based model proposed by Yu et al. [2] optimized multiple QoS objectives. Yu et al. [3] designed a method based on deep-Q-network to select fault-tolerant policies, in order to achieve dependable workflow

© IFIP International Federation for Information Processing 2025
Published by Springer Nature Switzerland AG 2025
X. Chen et al. (Eds.): NPC 2024, LNCS 15527, pp. 310–323, 2025.
https://doi.org/10.1007/978-981-96-2830-8_24

scheduling. These studies were tested on small or medium scale workflow (usually consisting 50–500 tasks), and showed good performance. However, these studies only utilize explicit raw information of the tasks and workflows to be the state information for their DRL models. There exist complex sequential and parallel dependencies relationships among the tasks, especially for large-scale scientific workflows [4].

Some researchers have noticed that the workflow is a graph structure, and introduced graph neural network (GNN) to their DRL scheduling model to extract the structural features. Decima [5] was the first to introduce GNN into DRL model in order to extract global embeddings of the workflow, then the DRL model could make decisions with the global embedding. However, this model cannot schedule in the environment with heterogenous computing resources, and the size of the workflows that it can handle is still limited due to its reliance on relatively simple message passing neural network. Zhou et al. [6] and Song et al. [7] respectively use basic message passing neural network and graph convolution network (GCN) [8] to extract the feature of workflows as DAGs, generating the embeddings for both task nodes and the whole environment. But the GNN modules utilized in these studies still has limitations. The basic message passing neural networks have low computation efficiency on large graphs, and GCNs are not efficient enough to preserve local information of graphs. These methods may not be as effective in large-scale scientific workflow scheduling tasks, particularly when multiple quality of service (QoS) requirements are involved. In addition, the sampling efficiency of existing DRL scheduling methods restricts its training speed on large-scale workflows.

To address this challenge, many studies resort to heuristic or meta-heuristic rules. Dong et al. [9] applied heterogeneous earliest finish time algorithm (HEFT) [10], which is a classic heuristic algorithm for workflow scheduling, to their DRL model. HEFT took on the decision-making regarding resource allocation, this allows the DRL model to concentrate on determining fault-tolerance policies, thereby reducing the complexity of the decision space. Xie et al. [11] proposed an improved two-stage genetic algorithm (GA) to optimize makespan in workflow scheduling problems. Several problem-specific evolution operators based on heuristic rules were proposed to improve the optimality. But its experiments were only conducted on small and medium-sized scale scientific workflows. Qin et al. [12] proposed several problem-specific evolution operators for memetic algorithm to solve workflow scheduling problem with multiple objectives. However, getting an optimal solution with GA has high time complexity, especially in large-scale workflow scheduling because of huge search space. Therefore, there is still a need to enhance the sampling efficiency of DRL.

In this paper, we propose a DRL-based scheduling algorithm with improved structure feature extraction and sampling strategy. We first formulate the large-scale scientific workflow scheduling problem in a cloud environment, aiming to optimize QoS objectives including makespan, energy cost, and reliability. Then, we introduce a graph attention network (GAT) to extract the structural features of task nodes for the DRL model. Leveraging the feature representation with structural information obtained by GNN, the DRL model can exhibit improved performance. Next, we design a DRL sampling strategy based on genetic algorithm. GA is used to get sub-optimal solutions. With these solutions, initial sampling trajectories for the DRL model can be generated. This approach reduces the need for excessive exploration in the large workflow, thereby enhancing training efficiency. The overall DRL model is trained by proximal policy optimization (PPO).

The contributions of this paper are as follows:

- A DRL framework to solve large-scale scientific workflow, with a GAT based feature module in DRL model to extract the task node features and global features for the large-scale scientific workflow, which can optimize makespan, energy cost and reliability.
- A GA and DRL hybrid training strategy for large-scale scientific workflow, improving the sampling efficiency when training.
- Simulated experiments on Pegasus workflows, which show that our method outperforms the baselines.

2   Proposed Method

2.1   Problem Formulation

The overall architecture of the DRL-based scheduling model and where the proposed approach fits into it is illustrated in Fig. 1. In the cloud computing environment, users upload jobs of scientific computing applications in the form of workflows. The scheduling model is responsible for determining the execution order of tasks in a workflow, and then assigning them to the appropriate computing resources. Finally, the results of the computation should be fed back to the user.

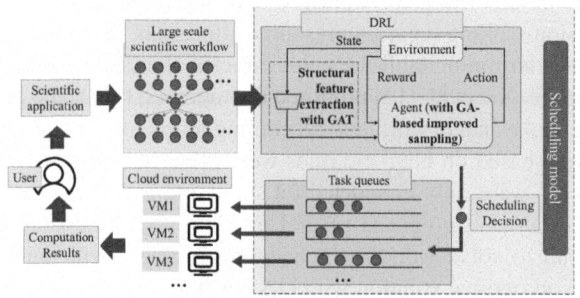

Fig. 1. The overall architecture of the DRL-based scheduling model.

We use a DAG $G(T, E)$ to model the relationship of tasks in a workflow. In a workflow with n tasks, $T = \{t_1, t_2, \ldots, t_n\}$ is the set of tasks. The directed edge set $E = \{e_{ij} | 1 \leq i, j \leq n\}$ represent the precedence relationships between tasks. A task can be started only after all its predecessors have finished execution and data transmission. The attributions of task t_i include average runtime r_i and result data size d_i. The attributions of each task are known in advance before scheduling. Additionally, for the convenience of calculation and simulation, we assume that each workflow only has one entrance task and one exit task. If there are more than a task node without any predecessor, a pseudo start node would be created, with all the nodes without predecessor to be its successors. Similarly, a pseudo exit node would be generated for the nodes without successors. Both the average runtime and the data size of the pseudo task nodes are set to 0.

In cloud computing environment, there are many computing resources available, usually virtual machine (VM) instances. Each VM can only process one task at a time. There is a virtual task queue for each VM. Note that the queue is still part of the scheduling model with only containing the task indexes, it's not part of the VM. When a task is allocated to a VM, it is pushed into the queue tail. The tasks in the queue are executed one by one. The VMs are linked through network to transmit the task data. Assume that a transmission is started as soon as the precedence task is finished, and one VM can receive multiple transmission synchronously. If a task and its successor are allocated to different VMs, it would take an amount of time to transmit data. Otherwise if they are allocated to the same VM, there is no transmission. For VM_k, its attributions include computing capacity c_k, average fault probability f_k and power factor u_k.

$ET(t_i, VM_k)$ is the execution time of task t_i running on VM_k and can be calculated as (1). Define $ST(t_i)$ and $FT(t_i)$ to be the start time and finish time of task t_i, and $Alc(t_i)$ is the VM that t_i is actually allocated to, we can get (2).

$$ET(t_i, VM_k) = \frac{r_i}{c_k} \tag{1}$$

$$FT(t_i) = ST(t_i) + ET(t_i, Alc(t_i)) \tag{2}$$

Assume $CT(t_i, VM_k, VM_{k'})$ is the time required for the result data of t_i to transmit from VM_k to $VM_{k'}$, the precedence constraint between a task and its predecessors is in (3):

$$ST(t_i) \geq FT(t_j) + CT(t_j, Alc(t_j), Alc(t_i)), \forall t_j \in \text{predecessors of } t_i, \tag{3}$$

The effect of spatial distance on the transmission time can be negligible in a cloud environment, so the bandwidth B can be assumed as constant. Then the transmission time can be calculated as (4):

$$CT(t_i, Alc(t_i), Alc(t_j)) = CT(t_i) = \frac{d_i}{B}. \tag{4}$$

Once t_i is scheduled, its start and finish time can be estimated. It is waiting for in the VM's queue. Assuming $t_{i'}$ is directly in front of t_i in the queue, the estimated start time $EST(t_i)$ is as shown in (5). Each task's EST in a queue can be calculated recursively.

$$EST(t_i) = \max_{t_j \in \text{predecessors of } t_i} (FT(t_j) + CT(t_j), FT(t_{i'})) \tag{5}$$

Similar with [13], we quantify $D(t_i, VM_k)$, the reliability of t_i on VM_k, with Poisson distribution, as shown in (6). The power model of energy consumption $C(t_i, VM_k)$ is (7):

$$D(t_i, VM_k) = e^{-f_k \times ET(t_i, VM_k)}. \tag{6}$$

$$C(t_i, VM_k) = ET(t_i, VM_k) \times c_k u_k. \tag{7}$$

We define the decision point to be the moment when at least one task is schedulable. At the decision point, the scheduling model chooses a task among all schedulable tasks, and allocate it to a proper VM, without violating the precedence constraints among the tasks mentioned above. The goal is to minimize the workflow's overall makespan MP, energy cost EC, maximize reliability RB. Their definition are shown in (8) (9) (10):

$$MP = \max_{t_i T}(FT(t_i)), \tag{8}$$

$$RB = \prod_{t_i T} D(t_i, Alc(t_i)), \tag{9}$$

$$EC = \sum_{t_i T} C(t_i, Alc(t_i)). \tag{10}$$

2.2 Deep Reinforcement Learning with Graph Attention Network

We use Markov Decision Process (MDP) to model the scheduling of a workflow. MDP can be described as a four-tuple $M = \{s, a, P, R\}$, in which s is the set of states, a is the set of actions, P is the transition probability function and R is the reward function.

State. State is the DRL agent's observation of the workflow and cloud environment. One state includes the global information including, the information of each task and each VM. Global information includes the current timestamp, total reliability and energy consumption of the tasks that are already scheduled. Information of task t_i includes some static attributions: r_i, d_i; and dynamic information: whether scheduled, started or already finished. Estimated finish time if started. Information of VM_k includes its c_k, f_k, u_k, as well as the estimated finish time of its queue.

Given the explicit information of a state, we still need structural information about the dependency relationships. For a task t_i, we collect its information, as well as all VMs' information and the workflow's global information together, into a raw feature vector v_i. GAT [14] is introduced to extract the feature. Define a GAT network with L layers, the node feature vector $h^l(t_i)$ can be calculated by (11). Note that $h^0(t_i) = v_i$.

$$h^l(t_i) = \sigma\left(\sum_{t_j \in N(t_i)} \alpha_{i,j} W h^{l-1}(t_j)\right) + h^{l-1}(t_i), 1 \leq l \leq L \tag{11}$$

where $N(t_i)$ represents the set of neighborhood tasks of t_i, l is the current network layer. σ is the activation function, W is the weight matrix, and $\alpha_{i,j}$ is the attention coefficients between t_i and t_j. $\alpha_{i,j}$ can be calculated by normalizing the weights of edges with softmax.

Then the global feature $H(G)$ of workflow G can be obtained by processing the node features with a pooling layer, as shown in (12):

$$H(G) = \underset{t_i \in T}{\text{pooling}}(h^L(t_i)) \tag{12}$$

Action. In our model, an action is to choose a task among all the schedulable tasks. Then it would be added to one VM's queue according a greedy policy. The greedy policy is to choose the VM with the minimum growth in total estimated finish time and energy cost, and the maximum decrease in reliability. We regard a task to be "schedulable" if (I) all predecessors have been scheduled and (II) at least one of its predecessors has started. Condition (I) guarantees that the finish time of the predecessors can be predicted. Thus, we have plentiful information to make an action. Condition (II) prevents the agent from making decision too early, because we want the scheduling to be real-time. If there is no schedulable task in the workflow, this current step would be skipped, until there is at least one schedulable task. A multi-layer perceptron (MLP) policy network would calculates the probability of choosing each schedulable task according to their node feature vector. Then a new action would be sampled. Consider the current time is τ, and p_i is the probability to choose the currently schedulable task t_i, the action a_τ can be calculated by (13) (14). r is a random number satisfying $r \in [0,1)$.

$$p_i = \underset{j \text{ is schedulable}}{\text{softmax}}(\text{MLP}_1(h^L(t_i))) \tag{13}$$

$$a_\tau = \underset{i \text{ is scheduable}}{\arg\max}\ (\sum_{j \text{ is scheduable}} p_j > r) \tag{14}$$

Reward and Transition Probability. The DRL agent learns to solve an MDP without prior knowledge about P nor R. P is implicit in the environment. R_τ, the reward at time τ, should be the weighted value of the estimated increasement in finish time and energy cost, and the decrease in reliability. The reward can be calculated by (15). In (15), C_1, C_2 and C_3 are constant weight coefficients. RB_τ and EC_τ are the overall reliability and energy cost of all the scheduled tasks at time τ. EFT_τ is the estimated finished time of all the scheduled tasks at τ. The positive sign before each term means that this term should be maximized, and the negative sign means that the term should be minimized.

$$R_\tau = C_1\frac{RB_\tau - RB_{\tau-1}}{RB_\tau} - C_2\frac{EFT_\tau - EFT_{\tau-1}}{EFT_\tau} - C_3\frac{EC_\tau - EC_{\tau-1}}{EC_\tau} \tag{15}$$

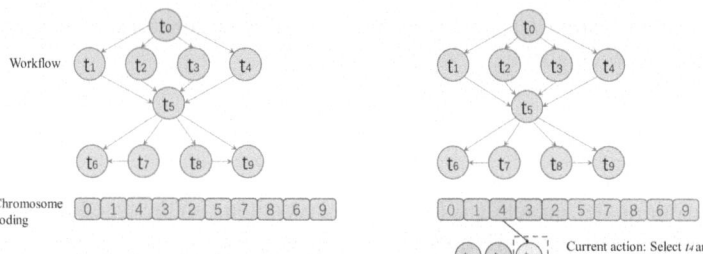

(a) An example of the chromosome coding

(b) The conversion between the GA individual and the DRL action.

Fig. 2. Chromosome coding and its conversion to DRL action. In (b), The currently schedulable tasks are marked in blue, the scheduled in yellow and the unschedulable in green. Now the schedulable tasks are t_2, t_3, t_4., and the first one in the chromosome is t_4. So, the current action is "select t_4 from $\{t_2, t_3, t_4\}$". Similarly, in the next step, the schedulable tasks are t_2, t_3, and the first schedulable task is t_3. So, the action is "select t_3 from $\{t_2, t_3\}$". (Color figure online)

2.3   Training with GA-Based Sampling Strategy

Algorithm 1. The crossover operator.
Input:
Two individuals I_a and I_b, and their length *len*.
Output:
Two new individuals $I_{a'}$ and $I_{b'}$.
1:   *CxPoint*←*RandInt*[0, *len*);
2:   $I_{a'}$←*SubString*(I_b, 0, *CxPoint*);
3:   $I_{b'}$←*SubString*(I_a, 0, *CxPoint*);
4:   **for each** *i* **in** [*CxPoint*, *len*):
5:      **if** task $I_a[i]$ **is not in** $I_{a'}$:
6:          append $I_a[i]$ to the end of $I_{a'}$;
7:      **end if**
8:      **if** task $I_b[i]$ **is not in** $I_{b'}$:
9:          append $I_b[i]$ to the end of $I_{b'}$;
10:    **end if**
11: **end for**

Algorithm 2. The mutation operator.
Input:
An individual *I*.
Output:
A new individual *I'*.
1:   Randomly choose a task t_i;
2:   *MutPoint*←the index of t_i in *I*;
3:   *start, end*←*MutPoint*
4:   **while** *start*≥0 & *I*[*start*]∉*pre*(t_i):
5:      *start*←*start*−1;
6:   **end while**
7:   **while** *end*≥0 & *I*[*end*]∉*su*(t_i):
8:      *end*←*end*+1;
9:   **end while**
10: *MutPoint'*←*RandInt*[*start, end*);
11: *I'*← *I*.
12: Swap(*I'*[*MutPoint*], *I'*[*MutPoint'*]).

Our motivation to introduce GA-based sampling is to improve the sampling efficiency of DRL when learning to schedule large-scale workflows. The low sampling efficiency problem is caused by the sparse reward information and the time-consuming sampling in large-scale workflow environment. In the predecessors' work on DRL-based workflow scheduling, at each step, the agent selects a task as an action based on the current workflow state, and gets a reward as feedback calculated by the estimated gains and losses in the objectives. Each $\{s_\tau, a_\tau, R_\tau\}$ tuple is a sample. Based on the samples obtained from repeated interaction with the environment, the DRL model updates its policy. But the reward information is sparse because an accurate feedback can only be obtained after scheduling the whole workflow. So, when beginning training, the agent samples nearly blindly with little reward information. Besides, sampling in large-scale workflow is time-consuming. These lead to low sampling and training efficiency.

To tackle the problem above, we propose a GA-based sampling strategy for DRL training. Although GA has high time complexity and might fall into local optimum, it is faster than training a DRL model to get sub-optimal solutions. Motivated by [15], at the beginning of training, DRL updates the policy with the samples generated by the GA, rather than the ones obtained by interacting with the environment. The sub-optimal schedules generated by GA would be converted to $\{s_\tau, a_\tau\}$ pairs, forming a sampling trajectory. These trajectories would be added to the experience pool of the training of the DRL model. These sub-optimal solutions contain more useful reward information. This saves the agent from doing much blind and time-consuming sampling.

Chromosome Coding. As shown in Fig. 2, a GA individual is decoded as the sequence of task indexes in order of execution, which is a topological sort of the workflow, in order not to violate the precedence constraints. It's similar with the priority list used in list-based workflow scheduling algorithms. At each decision point, the first schedulable task in the sequence is chosen to be scheduled. Given a workflow, the individual and the action can be easily interconverted to each other as illustrated in Fig. 2(b).

Evolution Operators. To keep the individuals feasible after the evolution operations, the dependency constraints among the tasks must not be violated. That is, the individuals still must be a topological sort. Motivated by [16]. Two evolution operators, crossover (Algorithm 1) and mutation (Algorithm 2), are additionally designed.

2.4 DRL Training

The training is based on PPO [17]. As an actor-critic DRL model, it contains an actor network calculating the policy, and a critic network estimating the value function. The action loss can be calculated by (16). In (16), policy $\pi_\theta(a_\tau|s_\tau)$ is the probability to execute a_τ under state s_τ, exactly p_i in (13).

$$
L_\tau^A = \begin{cases} \min(\frac{\pi_\theta(a_\tau|s_\tau)}{\pi_\theta'(a_\tau|s_\tau)}), 1+ \in A_\tau, A_\tau \geq 0 \\ \min(\frac{\pi_\theta(a_\tau|s_\tau)}{\pi_\theta'(a_\tau|s_\tau)}), 1- \in A_\tau, A_\tau < 0 \end{cases} \tag{16}
$$

A_τ is the advantage function, determining whether the current action a_τ should be preferred, and it can be calculated by (17). γ is the discount factor which set 1.0.

$$
A_\tau = \sum_{\tau'} \gamma^{\tau'} \sigma_{\tau+\tau'} = \sum_{\tau'} \gamma^{\tau'} (R_{\tau'+\tau} + \gamma V(s_{\tau'+\tau+1}) - V(s_{\tau'+\tau})) \tag{17}
$$

The value function $V(s_\tau)$ is calculated by critic network, as shown in (18). The critic loss can be calculated by mean square error in (19).

$$
V(s_\tau) = \mathrm{MLP}_2(H(G_\tau)), \tag{18}
$$

$$
L_\tau^C = E[(\sum_{\tau'} \gamma^{\tau'} R_{\tau+\tau'} - V(s_{\tau'}))^2] \tag{19}
$$

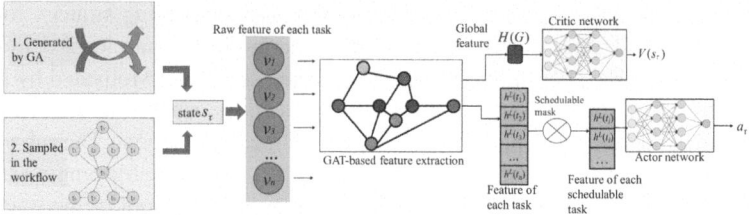

Fig. 3. Training process of the DRL model.

Algorithm 3. Training of the proposed model.
___
Input:
Scientific workflows $G(T, E)$, VMs
Output:
A DRL Scheduling model that can generate solutions.
1:   Randomly initialize an initial GA population *pop*;
2:   Initialize the weights and parameters of GA and DRL network;
3:   Run GA on *pop* for by calling Algorithm 1 and Algorithm 2 to get *pop'*;
4:   Convert the individuals in *pop'* into $\{s, a\}$ trajectories, add them to the experience buffer;
5:   **for each** *trajectory* **in** the experience pool **do**
6:       Estimate reward R of each $\{s, a\}$ pair in *trajectory*;
7:       Calculate the loss functions by (16)(19) and update the DRL network with the loss;
8:   **end for**;
9:   Initialize a workflow state s_0;
10: **for** *index* = 0, 1, 2, ..., *ep* **do:**
11:     **for** τ = 0, 1, 2, ..., **do**
12:         Calculate the current policy by (14);
13:         Estimate reward R_τ;
14:         Add tuple $\{s_\tau, a_\tau, R_\tau\}$ to the experience pool;
15:     **end for**;
16:     Calculate the loss functions by (16)(19) and update the DRL network with the loss;
17: **end for**.

Figure 3 shows the overall training. Firstly, some topological sorts of the workflow are randomly generated as GA's initial population. After running GA several episodes, select the suboptimal individuals in the population and convert them to sampling trajectories. Add these trajectories to the DRL model's experience buffer, then start training. At the beginning of training, the agent is constrained to follow the trajectories, then it explores the scheduling policies on its own. These steps are illustrated in Algorithm 3.

3   Experiment and Discussion

In this section, experiments are conducted to verify the performance of the proposed method. The baseline include the classical HEFT [10], GA only, and DRL models with different workflow feature extractors: explicit raw task information, GAT [14], a 4-layer GCN [8] and DAGNN [18], which is a GNN model specifically for DAG.

3.1   Workflow and Simulation Environment

We adopt the scientific workflows in Pegasus project [19], which is widely used as the testbench to test the performance of workflow scheduling algorithms. It provides many real-world scientific workflow applications, including CyberShake, LIGO, Montage and

SIPHT. The CyberShake workflow is compute-intensive and used to characterize earthquake hazards in a region. LIGO workflow is compute-intensive, generating and analyzing gravitational waveforms. Montage workflow is communication-intensive, to create custom mosaics of the sky. SIPHT workflow is used to automate the search for untranslated RNAs. In Pegasus, 9.09% of the workflows in CyberShake, LIGO and Montage, and 37.5% of the SIPHT workflows have more than 1000 tasks. 40 SIPHT workflows have more than 5000 task nodes. We choose these workflows to conduct experiments. The average runtime and data size of tasks are also provided by Pegasus.

The simulation and training are conducted on an Ubuntu 20.04 server with RTX3090 graphic cards and 64-core 2.70 GHz Xeon6226 CPU. We have implemented a simulation environment based on Gym, which is a library for developing interactive environment for training and testing DRL agents. In the Gym environment, the simulation process of scientific workflow execution on cloud platform is implemented based on SimPy, a discrete-event simulation framework on standard Python 3 platform.

3.2   The Effect of GA-Based Sampling

Table 1. The training time, FLOPs per episode, inference time, and average cumulative episode reward for the DRL methods to train scheduling on SIPHT workflow. The "training time" in is the total time required for the DRL model to con-verge, including simulation time and network weight update time. The "FLOPs per episode" is used to measure the total computation amount of calculating new actions and updating network weights of the DRL model in an episode during the training process. Both training time and FLOPs per episode is used to measure the training efficiency of the DRL model.

	Training time	FLOPs per episode	Inference time	Average episode reward
Raw feature	13.9 h	6.85M	<1 ms	−735.8
Ours with GAT	50.2 h	33.4M	<1 ms	**−720.4**
Ours with GCN	53.2 h	36.9M	<1 ms	−755.0
Ours with DAGNN	>100 h	13.7G	332 ms	−763.3

Table 1 compares the training time, FLOPs (floating point operations) per episode, inference time, and average cumulative episode reward of each kind of DRL-based method to train scheduling on the SIPHT workflow. Table 1 clearly shows that the training is quite time-consuming, while the inference speed is fast. So, improving sampling strategy is necessary. It also preliminarily shows that GAT as the feature extractor has better optimization performance than raw features and GCN, while they share similar training time and FLOPs per episode. Additionally, it is evident in Table 1 that the DRL model with DAGNN as feature extractor performs badly in cumulative reward (note that cumulative reward is the higher the better). Its training and inference speed are also much slower. We analyze that the network structure and number of parameters of

DAGNN appear to be excessively bulky when handling graphs of such scale. In fact, it's initially proposed for DAGs in the knowledge graph area, where the graphs are even larger than scientific workflows. Besides, its message passing mechanism based on topological batching for directed edges exhibits high time complexity. According to the above reasons, the following experiments no longer considers DAGNN.

Table 2. Training results on GA-based sampling.

Start training from	None	50th	100th	500th
Average episode reward	−720.4	−717.7	−724.8	−725.0
Training runtime time	50.2 h	30.0 h	17.6 h	26.6 h
GA + Training runtime	50.2 h	30.8 h	19.1 h	34.1 h

We apply NSGA-II [20], the classical multi-objective GA to assist sampling, and choose the schedules with the minimum weighted rewards as the samples. If the population size is set to 100, crossover rate $= 0.25$, mutation rate $= 0.15$, when scheduling a SIPHT workflow with 1000 tasks, it takes about 100 generations (1.5 h) for GA to converge. Though these schedules generated by GA might not be optimal, running a GA is obviously much less time-costing than training a DRL model.

Respectively, DRL models (PPO + GAT) are trained with the initial samples converted from populations at 50th, 100th and 500th generation as the initial samples. As shown in Table 2, compared to training directly from scratch, the model trained with GA sampling exhibit faster training. It also shows that simply increasing the generations of GA cannot help to improve the result and speed of DRL training. Based on our analysis, with the increase of iteration rounds, the diversity of individuals within the genetic algorithm population decreases, which might not be conducive to the exploration of reinforcement learning agents.

3.3 The Performance of Optimizing QoS Objectives

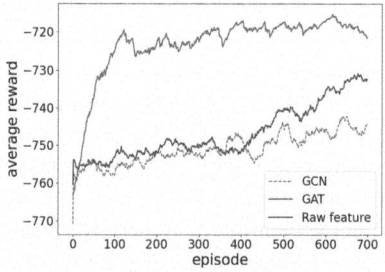

Fig. 4. The cumulative reward during training. Note that the x-axis label is the training episode instead of the training time.

We measure the performance of scheduling algorithms with multiple QoS objectives with the following metrics:

Objective Values. We compare the losses/gains in each objective to the baselines.

Hypervolumes. We introduce this metric because it's difficult to compare the performance of the algorithms if the results are not Pareto dominated by the others. It calculates the volume among a set of schedules and a reference point in the objective space. Because the workflow is complex, the true Pareto front is unknown, this approach can better compare the solutions. The reference point set to the worst extreme value of each objective. After DRL training reaches convergence, we generate multiple schedules, which is regarded as a solution set of the workflow, and its hypervolume is calculated.

Figure 4 displays the fluctuating curves of the values of the average cumulative reward per episode as the training processes on the SIPHT workflow when using different GNN as the feature extractor for the DRL model. It can be observed that the convergence of the DRL model based on GCN is quite slower.

Table 3 further exhibits the objectives (makespan, energy cost, reliability) and hypervolume of each model on each type of workflows. Note that the difference in reliability is small, because the fault rate f_k is set low. The DRL models is better than HEFT in energy consumption and reliability, although HEFT still outperforms DRL models in makespan. Because HEFT is mainly designed for optimizing makespan only. But there is exception: DRL models still outperform HEFT in makespan in CYBERSHAKE (155.5 for GAT, 156.2 for GCN, while it's 160.0 for HEFT). This further illustrates the effectiveness of DRL in workflow scheduling involving multiple QoS objectives.

It can be observed from Fig. 4 that GAT generally outperforms those methods with explicit feature, which is as expected. Obviously, the models using explicit features would fail to extract structural features in large-scale scientific workflows, resulting in limited ability of scheduling. These DRL models can only make decisions based on the explicit information that they observe currently, and cannot gain insight into the global state of the workflow based on the structural information, so that they cannot perform some compromise policies. Also, compared with the DRL model using GCN to extract feature, GAT performs better. Based on analysis, this is because GCN has limited ability to handle structural information of workflow. In GCN, each node is only connected to its neighboring nodes. This means it may not fully capture the global relationships and structural information between tasks in the workflow, while the attention coefficient between each pair of tasks can be learned. It can also explain why GAT cannot perform as good as GCN on Montage workflows in some objectives (while GAT's hypervolume is still better): The task nodes in Montage are more directly interconnected. Besides, the workflow is a DAG, while GCN is less applicable to directed graphs.

Table 3. Average results of the objectives hypervolume and on the workflows.

		HEFT	raw feature	GCN	GAT
SIPHT	*MP*	1403	1510	1778	1419
	EC	1.821×10^5	1.829×10^5	1.878×10^5	1.819×10^5
	RB	0.730	0.700	0.751	0.756
	Hypervolume	N/A	1.40×10^7	1.78×10^7	2.02×10^7
LIGO	*MP*	1347	1437	1443	1429
	EC	1.936×10^5	1.956×10^5	1.954×10^5	1.692×10^5
	RB	0.737	0.738	0.741	0.745
	Hypervolume	N/A	3.68×10^7	3.69×10^7	3.70×10^7
MONTAGE	*MP*	71.00	72.03	72.61	71.82
	EC	8940	8890	8810	8877
	RB	0.967	0.971	0.973	0.971
	Hypervolume	N/A	6.41×10^3	6.63×10^3	6.55×10^3
CYBERSHAKE	*MP*	160.0	177.2	156.2	155.5
	EC	2.21×10^4	2.25×10^4	2.18×10^4	2.17×10^4
	RB	0.968	0.985	0.990	0.990
	Hypervolume	N/A	7.21×10^4	6.82×10^4	7.27×10^4

4 Conclusion

In this paper, we propose a DRL-based scheduling algorithm with improved structure feature and sampling. We incorporate a graph attention network into the DRL model to extract the complex structure feature of the workflow, so that the scheduling performance can be improved with DRL on large-scale scientific workflow. We also design a hybrid training strategy with GA and DRL to improve sampling efficiency. GA is employed to generate suboptimal initial sample trajectories for the DRL agent, thus expediting the training process. Experiments conducted on Pegasus workflow dataset demonstrate that our method yields superior QoS results as well as training efficiency. As future work, we will try to improve our method by combining more heuristic rules, so that it can be applied to more dynamic environments with other QoS requirements.

Acknowledgement. This research is funded in part by National Key R&D Program of China (No. 2021YFB3301900).

References

1. Yang, Z., Nguyen, P., Jin, H., Nahrstedt, K.: MIRAS: model-based reinforcement learning for microservice resource allocation over scientific workflows. In: 2019 IEEE 39th International Conference on Distributed Computing Systems (ICDCS), pp. 122–132. IEEE (2019)

2. Yu, X., Wu, W., Wang, Y.: Integrating cognition cost with reliability QoS for dynamic work-flow scheduling using reinforcement learning. IEEE Trans. Serv. Comput. **16**(4), 2713–2726 (2023)
3. Yu, X., Wu, W., Wang, Y.: Dependable workflow scheduling for microservice QoS based on deep Q-network. In: 2022 IEEE International Conference on Web Services (ICWS), pp. 240–245. IEEE (2022)
4. Bharathi, S., Chervenak, A., Deelman, E., Mehta, G., Su, M-H., Vahi, K.: Characterization of scientific workflows. In: 2008 third Workshop on Workflows in Support of Large-Scale Science, pp. 1–10. IEEE (2008)
5. Mao, H., Schwarzkopf, M., Venkatakrishnan, S.B., Meng, Z., Alizadeh, M.: Learning schedul-ing algorithms for data processing clusters. In: Proceedings of the ACM Special Interest Group on Data Communication, pp. 270–288 (2019)
6. Zhou, Y., Li, X., Luo, J., Yuan, M., Zeng, J., Yao, J.: Learning to optimize dag scheduling in heterogeneous environment. In: 2022 23rd IEEE International Conference on Mobile Data Management (MDM), pp. 137–146. IEEE (2022)
7. Song, Y., Li, C., Tian, L., Song, H.: A reinforcement learning based job scheduling algorithm for heterogeneous computing environment. Comput. Electr. Eng. **107**, 108653 (2023)
8. Wu, F., Souza, A., Zhang, T., Fifty, C., Yu, T., Weinberger, K.: Simplifying graph convolutional networks. In: International Conference on Machine Learning, pp. 6861–6871. PMLR (2019)
9. Dong, T., Xue, F., Tang, H., Xiao, C.: Deep reinforcement learning for fault-tolerant workflow scheduling in cloud environment. Appl. Intell. **53**(9), 9916–9932 (2023)
10. Topcuoglu, H., Hariri, S., Wu, M.-Y.: Performance-effective and low-complexity task scheduling for heterogeneous computing. IEEE Trans. Parallel Distrib. Syst. **13**(3), 260–274 (2002)
11. Xie, Y., Gui, F.-X., Wang, W.-J., Chien, C.-F.: A two-stage multi-population genetic algo-rithm with heuristics for workflow scheduling in heterogeneous distributed computing environments. IEEE Trans. Cloud Comput. **11**(2), 1446–1460 (2021)
12. Qin, S., Pi, D., Shao, Z., Xu, Y., Chen, Y.: Reliability-aware multi-objective memetic algorithm for workflow scheduling problem in multi-cloud system. IEEE Trans. Parallel Distrib. Syst. **34**(4), 1343–1361 (2023)
13. Zhao, L., Ren, Y., Xiang, Y., Sakurai, K.: Fault-tolerant scheduling with dynamic number of replicas in heterogeneous systems. In: 2010 IEEE 12th International Conference on High Performance Computing and Communications (HPCC), pp. 434–441. IEEE (2010)
14. Veličković, P., Cucurull, G., Casanova, A., Romero, A., Lio, P., Bengio, Y.: Graph attention networks. arXiv preprint arXiv:171010903 (2017)
15. Chien, C.-F., Lan, Y.-B.: Agent-based approach integrating deep reinforcement learning and hybrid genetic algorithm for dynamic scheduling for Industry 3.5 smart production. Comput. Industr. Eng. **162**, 107782 (2021)
16. Zhu, Z., Zhang, G., Li, M., Liu, X.: Evolutionary multi-objective workflow scheduling in cloud. IEEE Trans. Parallel Distrib. Syst. **27**(5), 1344–1357 (2015)
17. Schulman, J., Wolski, F., Dhariwal, P., Radford, A., Klimov, O.: Proximal policy optimization algorithms. arXiv preprint arXiv:170706347 (2017)
18. Thost, V., Chen, J.: Directed acyclic graph neural networks. arXiv preprint arXiv:210107965 (2021)
19. Deelman, E., Vahi, K., Juve, G., Rynge, M., Callaghan, S., Maechling, P.J., et al.: Pegasus, a workflow management system for science automation. Futur. Gener. Comput. Syst. **46**, 17–35 (2015)
20. Deb, K., Pratap, A., Agarwal, S., Meyarivan, T.: A fast and elitist multiobjective genetic algorithm: NSGA-II. IEEE Trans. Evol. Comput. **6**(2), 182–197 (2002)

Global Color-Aware Arbitrary Style Transfer with Discrete Wavelet Transform

Bochao Chen[1], Junhao Tan[2], Xiaoqiang Li[1($\boxtimes$)], and Songwen Pei[2]

[1] School of Computer Engineering and Science, Shanghai University,
Shanghai 200444, China
xqli@shu.edu.cn
[2] School of Optical-Electrical and Computer Engineering, University of Shanghai
for Science and Technology, Shanghai 200093, China
swpei@usst.edu.cn

Abstract. The purpose of image arbitrary style transfer is to apply a given artistic or photorealistic style to a target content image. While existing methods can effectively transfer style information, the variability in color brightness features between the style and content images can significantly impact the quality of the style transfer. Specifically, traditional arbitrary style transfer relies on an encoder-decoder architecture of spatial-aware neural networks operating in the RGB domain, which typically preserves only local color brightness information and lacks a global color perception compared to the wavelet frequency domain. In this paper, we address the issue of insufficient global color perception in images from the perspective of image enhancement. We propose **G**lobal **C**olor-aware **A**rbitrary **S**tyle **T**ransfer with Discrete Wavelet Transform (GCAST), which achieves a balance between the global color characteristics of style images and the local details of content images. Our approach involves an encoder that integrates preliminary feature encoding through cross-layer attention fusion, while the decoder modifies frequency features using a wavelet-based adjustment block. To maintain a balance between content and style in the stylized images, we design a comprehensive loss function that incorporates multiple restoration loss, double style loss, and noise regularization loss. Extensive experiments comparing our method with state-of-the-art techniques demonstrate that our proposed model generates stylized images with superior results in terms of global color perception and human perceptual studies.

Keywords: Wavelet Transform · Cross-Layer Attention Fusion · Arbitrary Style Transfer

---

B. Chen and J. Tan—Contribute equally to this work.

1   Introduction

The aim of arbitrary style transfer is to effectively combine arbitrary content images with the distinctive stylistic patterns of a specific art style image. The pioneering work of Gatys et al. [5] introduces an optimization-based approach. This method utilizes pre-trained deep neural networks to iteratively enhance the similarity of content and style features. While this approach has been influential [16,27,30], it has inherent limitations, most notably its time-consuming nature. This shortcoming prompted Johnson et al. [12] to explore feedforward networks for the direct and rapid generation of stylized images. More recently, Transformer-based approaches [4,31] have also contributed to neural style transfer by employing self-attention mechanisms and positional encoding. Although existing algorithms can achieve style transfer, the arbitrary style transfer task still encounters the issue of migration bias due to insufficient global color perception. When there is a significant disparity in color brightness between the content and the styled image, various degradation phenomena often arise, including low visibility, low contrast, and high noise levels, which impede the effective execution of neural style transfer [3,10,18].

Therefore, we propose a novel framework motivated by RAST [19] to address the issue of inadequate global color perception in style transfer from the perspective of image enhancement. During style transfer, significant discrepancies in the color brightness features between the content image and the stylized image can lead to the loss of color feature details during the transfer process, resulting in distortion of the stylized image's overall effect. Our objective is to integrate more global stylized color features into the content features while preserving the local details (*e.g.*, contour) of the content features.

We begin by performing cross-layer attention fusion of downsampled, multi-sized content and style image features to capture and characterize richer, deeper texture and color features. Unlike traditional arbitrary style transfer methods that operate in the RGB domain, we globally fuse the color features of the stylized image derived from SANet [32] in the frequency domain. This process is enhanced by the additional extraction of low-frequency information through a multi-level wavelet transform neural network, which includes a Wavelet-based Adjustment Block (WAB). This approach enlarges the perceptual field and better preserves the global color of style images while maintaining the local texture details of content images. Extensive experiments, both qualitative and quantitative, demonstrate the superior performance of our proposed framework in terms of content preservation and style embedding. The contributions of this paper are summarized as follows:

(1) We propose an arbitrary style transfer model based on discrete wavelet transform that enhances global color perception. A Cross-layer Attention Fusion (CAF) mechanism is introduced in the encoder for initial feature extraction, while the Wavelet-based Adjustment Block (WAB) employed in the decoder balance between color characteristics of style with the local details of content images.

(2) We have developed a comprehensive loss function to address the issue of unstable training associated with traditional loss functions, ensuring consistency in content between the output image and the input image.

The remainder of the paper is structured as follows: Sect. 2 reviews related work, Sect. 3 describes the proposed GCAST and its key loss functions, Sect. 4 presents the experiments and evaluations, and Sect. 5 offers the conclusions.

2   Related Work

2.1   Image Style Transfer

Image Style Transfer has gained significant attention recently. Initially introduced as a stroke-based rendering algorithm [7], it evolved to address the image analog problem [8] by learning transformations between image pairs. Traditional methods like Gaussian filters [6] and bilateral filters [25] focus on low-level features but struggle with image structure preservation. In contrast, Gatys et al. [5] proposed a neural network-based method that combines content and style features using a convolutional neural network and Gram matrix, achieving style transformation through iterative optimization, albeit with high computational costs.

Arbitrary style transfer methods have developed flexible feed-forward architectures using a unified model for various styles. AdaIN [10] and DIN [11] combine content and style feature statistics through conditional instance normalization, but dynamic affine parameter generation can cause distortions. To address this, some methods use an encoder-decoder architecture with feature transformation and fusion. Attention mechanisms [26] have also been introduced, such as SANet [32] for aligning style and content features, AdaAttN [18] for adaptive attention normalization, CAST [34] for utilizing extensive style information, RAST [19] for tackling content leakage, and QuantArt [9] for high visual fidelity through vector quantization. Existing Image Style Transfer methods primarily focus on local color luminance and often neglect global color perception. To address this, we propose Global Color-aware Arbitrary Style Transfer with Discrete Wavelet Transform (GCAST) to enhance global color perception.

2.2   Wavelet Transform

Wavelet transform [20] has been widely used in signal processing for its effectiveness and reversibility. The discrete wavelet transform (DWT) decomposes signals into subbands of different frequencies, while the inverse DWT reconstructs the original signal. Recently, wavelet transform has been integrated with deep neural networks for various computer vision tasks. For example, Veena et al. [22] used wavelet filters and a least squares approach for image denoising, and Ji and Jung [14] used deep convolutional neural networks to enhance image contrast and reduce noise in wavelet coefficients.

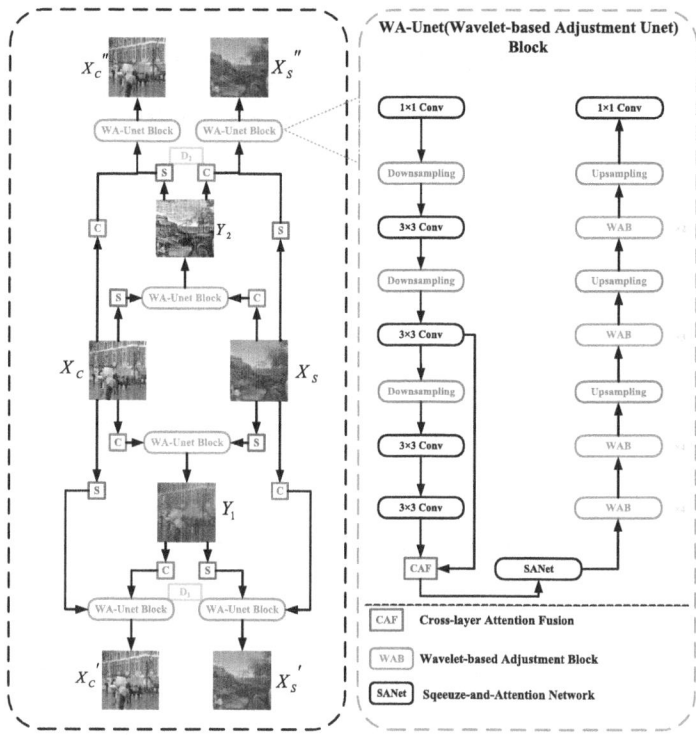

Fig. 1. The GCAST framework features a Wavelet-based Adjustment Block (WAB) that is utilized multiple times for both stylization and image restoration by sharing the same parameters. Additionally, the model incorporates two external discriminators, D1 and D2, which facilitate the transfer process from content to style and from style to content, respectively.

3   GCAST

3.1   Overall Framework

The primary structure of the framework is illustrated in Fig. 1. The Wavelet-based Adjustment Block (WAB) serves as a transfer module that takes the content image X_c and the style image X_s as inputs, producing a stylized image Y_1 that blends the content of X_c with the style of X_s. Subsequently, we feed the stylized image Y_1 and the content image X_c back into the WAB. If the WAB functions correctly, the resulting output should closely resemble the original content image $X_c{}'$. The mathematical representation of this process is as follows:

$$\mathcal{W}(X_c, X_s) = Y_1, \mathcal{W}(Y_1, X_c) = X_c' \approx X_c, \qquad (1)$$

where $X_c{}'$ denotes the restored content image, which should closely resemble the original content image X_c. Furthermore, the style image can be reconstructed by treating X_s as the content image and Y_1 as the style image, resulting in the restored style image X_s', which should be similar to the original style image X_s. By interchanging the roles of X_c and X_s, we can generate a total of four restored images, all of which should approximate the original input images. Consequently, the framework produces multiple restored images as follows:

$$
\begin{aligned}
\mathcal{W}(X_c, X_s) &= Y_1, \mathcal{W}(X_s, Y_1) = X_s' \approx X_s, \\
\mathcal{W}(X_s, X_c) &= Y_2, \mathcal{W}(Y_2, X_s) = X_s'' \approx X_s, \\
\mathcal{W}(X_s, X_c) &= Y_2, \mathcal{W}(X_c, Y_2) = X_c'' \approx X_c,
\end{aligned}
\tag{2}
$$

where X_c', X_c'', X_s' and X_s'' denote the restored content and style images, respectively.

3.2 Wavelet-Based Adjustment Unet (WA-Unet)

Previous arbitrary style transfer methods typically extract content and style features in the RGB domain, which fails to balance the global color features necessary for style identification with the local texture features essential for content identification. To address this limitation, we have developed an encoder-decoder Wavelet-based Adjustment UNet Block to generate stylistic images, as illustrated in Fig. 1. Specifically, we utilize the pretrained VGG-19 [24] network as the encoder to obtain preliminary stylish feature maps. Given the convolutional neural network's (CNN) limitations in capturing long-range dependencies and deep multi-scale cross-layer features, we have designed a Cross-layer Attention Fusion (CAF) module that fuses the outputs from the 3rd and 5th layers of VGG-19. In the decoder, we replace traditional convolutional layers with our proposed Wavelet-based Adjustment Block (WAB) to jointly extract the global color features of style images and the local detail/contour features of content images, ultimately generating stylistic images.

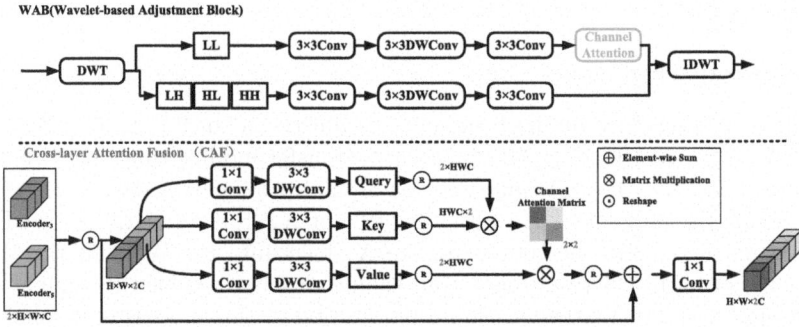

Fig. 2. The details of proposed Wavelet-based Adjustment Block (WAB) and Cross-Layer Attention Fusion (CAF) module.

Wavelet-based Adjustment Block (WAB). Given the briefly introduction in Sect. 2.2, the discrete wavelet transform (DWT) can decompose input image $I \in \mathbb{R}^{H \times W \times C}$ into global color-dominated low-frequency I_{LL} component and local detail-dominated high-frequency $\{I_{LH}, I_{HL}, I_{HH}\}$ components, which can be expressed as:

$$I_{LL}, \{I_{LH}, I_{HL}, I_{HH}\} = 2D - DWT(I). \tag{3}$$

The low-frequency component is sensitive to global color features, ensuring style consistency, while the high-frequency component is sensitive to local detail features, ensuring content preservation. Following three convolutions block (3×3 Conv, 3×3 DWConv, 3×3 Conv), low-frequency and high-frequency components are extracted locally into I'_{LL} and $I'_{LH}, I'_{HL}, I'_{HH}$. To further explore the channel-wise color diversity of the low-frequency component, we introduce a Channel Attention mechanism, which will be discussed in the CAF module, to obtain I''_{LL}. Finally, an Inverse Discrete Wavelet Transform (IDWT) operation is utilized to restore the output image I_{output}.

$$I_{output} = 2D - IDWT(I''_{LL}, I'_{LH}, I'_{HL}, I'_{HH}). \tag{4}$$

Cross-layer Attention Fusion (CAF). The CAF module fuses the 3rd and 5th output of VGG-19 to obtain cross-layer multi-scale deep features, effectively eliminating redundant features while preserving distinct characteristics. As illustrated in Fig. 2, we utilize channel concatenation features ($F \in \mathbb{R}^{H \times W \times 2C}$) from $Encoder_3$ and $Encoder_5$. We apply 1×1 convolutions and 3×3 depth-wise convolutions to generate the Query $Q \in \mathbb{R}^{2 \times HWC}$, Key $K \in \mathbb{R}^{HWC \times 2}$, Value $V \in \mathbb{R}^{2 \times HWC}$ followed by a reshaping operation. Subsequently, Q and K are used to compute the layer channel attention matrix $A \in \mathbb{R}^{2 \times 2}$. Finally, V is multiplied by the channel attention matrix A, scaled by a factor α and added to F to produce the output F_{out}, which can be expressed as:

$$F_{output} = W_{1 \times 1} Channel - Attention(Q, K, V) + F,$$
$$Channel - Attention(Q, K, V) = V softmax(\frac{QK}{\alpha}). \tag{5}$$

3.3 Loss Function

To ensure accurate transfer, we have designed the multiple restoration loss L_{mr} and the double style loss L_{ds} to maintain content invariance and style implementation, respectively. We utilize perceptual loss [13] as the foundational function for assessing content consistency. According to Eq. 6, the differences in style features can be determined by the mean and standard deviation of the feature map, where γ_i represents the i-th layer of the VGG-19 network. Additionally, Eq. 7 explains how to calculate the variance of content features, with the Relu3_1 and Relu5_1 layers being employed to extract content features, as discussed in Sect. 3.2.

$$\Delta s(X_1, X_2) = \begin{aligned} &\sum_{i=1}^{5} \| \, \mathbb{E}(\gamma_i(X_1)) - \mathbb{E}(\gamma_i(X_2)) \, \|_2 \\ &+ \sum_{i=1}^{5} \| \, \sigma(\gamma_i(X_1)) - \sigma(\gamma_i(X_2)) \, \|_2, \end{aligned} \tag{6}$$

$$\Delta c(X_1, X_2) = \| \, \gamma_{3\_1}(X_1) - \gamma_{3\_1}(X_2) \, \|_2 + \| \, \gamma_{5\_1}(X_1) - \gamma_{5\_1}(X_2) \, \|_2 . \tag{7}$$

Utilizing these functions, we developed the multiple restoration loss $\mathcal{L}_{mr}$ to minimize the content variance between the restored image and the input image, as well as to assess the differences among various restored images. The equation for the multiple restoration loss $\mathcal{L}_{mr}$ is presented below:

$$\mathcal{L}_{mr} = \Delta c(X_c', X_c) + \Delta c(X_s'', X_s) + \Delta s(X_s', X_s) + \Delta s(X_c'', X_c). \tag{8}$$

To prevent the stylized image from closely resembling the content image, we introduce the double style loss $\mathcal{L}_{ds}$. This loss function is designed to maximize the stylistic differences between the content image and the stylized image. Our objective is to enhance the stylistic discrepancies between Y_1 and X_c, as well as between Y_2 and X_s. The equation for the style difference loss $\mathcal{L}_{ds}$ is presented below:

$$\mathcal{L}_{ds} = \Delta s(Y_1, X_c) + \Delta s(Y_2, X_s). \tag{9}$$

In addition to the previously mentioned loss functions, we incorporate four established loss functions: identity loss [32], external adversarial loss [2], and total variation (TV) loss [1]. The identity loss $\mathcal{L}_{id}$, introduced by SANet, is utilized to enhance content preservation and improve the accuracy of style implementation. Furthermore, we include the external adversarial loss $\mathcal{L}_{adv}$ to capture human-perceived style features. We manage the transformations between content and style using two multi-scale discriminators [28], denoted as D1 and D2. Lastly, we employ TV loss to regularize the noise in feature differences between content and style images, ensuring a smoother transition of color features.

The ultimate loss function $\mathcal{L}$ can be summarised as follows,

$$\mathcal{L} = \lambda_1 \mathcal{L}_{mr} + \lambda_2 \mathcal{L}_{ds} + \lambda_3 \mathcal{L}_{id} + \lambda_4 \mathcal{L}_{adv} + \lambda_5 (TVLoss(X_c) + TVLoss(X_s)), \tag{10}$$

where the loss weights are set to $\lambda_1 = 2$, $\lambda_2 = -2$, $\lambda_3 = 1$, $\lambda_4 = 5$ and $\lambda_5 = 0.01$.

4   Experiments

4.1   Datasets

Our proposed GCAST is trained using the COCO [17] dataset as the content dataset and WikiArt[1] as the style dataset.

COCO Dataset. The COCO2017 dataset comprises 118,287 training images, 5,000 validation images, and 40,670 test images. Given the richness of this extensive training data, which may lead to overfitting in style transfer applications, a subset of 10,000 images was randomly selected for content use.

---

[1] https://www.wikiart.org/.

WikiArt Dataset. WikiArt paintings is a publicly available dataset that represents one of the largest online collections of artworks. This collection includes images of 81,449 diverse paintings created by 1,119 artists, spanning from antiquity to modernity.

In addition, to ensure an even distribution of style images across each category, we selected the works of 20 artists and extracted 500 images from each artist, resulting in a total of 10,000 style images.

4.2   Implementation Details

We trained GCAST on a server equipped with three Tesla A10 GPUs, using a batch size of 2. The input images were uniformly resized to 512 pixels and cropped into 256×256 patches, demonstrating that our method is free from size constraints. The Adam optimizer [15] was employed with a momentum of 0.9 for 160,000 iterations. The initial learning rate was set to 1×10^{-4} and was gradually decreased using a cosine annealing schedule, reaching a minimum of 1×10^{-6}.

| Content | Style | **Ours** | RAST | SANet | QuantArt | CAST | AdaAttn |

Fig. 3. The qualitative comparison of five state-of-the-art methods for artistic image style transfer reveals that our model is superior in terms of stylistic color representation, minimizing distortion and blurring while preserving more contour information from the original content. (Color figure online)

Table 1. Quantitative comparisons of five state-of-the-art methods for artistic image style transfer.

Method	Ours	RAST	SANet	CAST	QuantArt	AdaAttn
LPIPS(X_c,X'_c) ↓	0.195	**0.187**	0.455	0.324	0.446	0.385
LPIPS(X_s,X'_s) ↓	**0.189**	0.250	0.436	0.423	0.268	0.296
SSIM ↑	0.439	0.359	0.279	0.301	0.387	**0.487**
PSNR ↑	**19.891**	15.759	16.856	17.041	14.456	19.058
User score ↑	**4.13**	4.00	3.00	3.33	3.20	3.66
Inference Time(ms/img) ↓	10	6	6	8	5	112

4.3 Qualitative Comparisons

As illustrated in Fig. 3, we selected five state-of-the-art arbitrary style transfer models: RAST [19], SANet [32], CAST [34], QuantArt [9], AdaAttn [18]. GCAST demonstrates greater sensitivity to the global distribution of salient colors in the style, enabling it to achieve enhanced vibrancy and coherence when applied to content. Specifically, GCAST excels in managing significant color brightness differences between content and style images, effectively understanding global color information and complex content structures. Other models struggle: RAST retains content features but has poor stylistic embedding (rows 1, 3, and 4); SANet fails to retain content efficiently (rows 2, 3, and 5) and introduces color distortions (rows 1, 2, and 3); QuantArt loses content detail (rows 1 and 2) and performs poorly in style implementation (rows 2, 3, and 5); CAST compromises edge detail (rows 1, 2, and 5); and AdaAttn loses content information (rows 2 and 3) while introducing distortions (rows 2, 3, and 5). Overall, GCAST outperforms other methods in style transfers, preserving content and embedding style effectively.

4.4 Quantitative Comparisons

We further quantitatively compare the performances of five state-of-the-art methods in artistic image style transfer. To assess the disparity between the generated image and the content and style images, we utilize the LPIPS [33] loss. When calculating metrics, if the generated image Y is used in conjunction with either the content or style image, the resulting loss is typically large and does not accurately reflect performance. Therefore, we evaluate the feature gap between the content image X_c, style image X_s, and the restored images X'_c, X'_s to assess content preservation and style consistency performance, respectively. The Structural Similarity Index Measure(SSIM) [29] evaluates the overall similarity between the content and stylized images in terms of brightness, contrast, and structure. Additionally, the Peak Signal-to-Noise Ratio(PSNR) [23] provides an objective assessment of image quality based on pixel differences between the content and stylized images.

Table 1 shows that RAST achieves the best content preservation on the LPIPS(X_c,X'_c) metric (row 2), with GCAST in second place. GCAST ranks first in the LPIPS(X_s,X'_s) metric (row 3), indicating superior style embedding due to its multiple recovery architecture and cross-layer attentional fusion with wavelet adjustments. GCAST ranks second in SSIM (row 4) for strong content structure maintenance and first in PSNR (row 5) for excellent pixel-level content preservation. However, GCAST ranks fifth in inference time (row 7), indicating higher time complexity from its advanced mechanisms, which could be optimized in future work.

User Study. To conduct a more comprehensive analysis of the effects of style transfer, we performed a user perception study involving 15 participants. This study aimed to evaluate users' sensory perceptions of the generated results from 10 pairs of content and style images. Participants were instructed to assess the results based on the following criteria: (i) Do the generated results retain the outline and details of the content image? (ii) Does the style of the generated results align with that of the style image? (iii) Are the generated results ambiguous? (iv) Do the generated results exhibit color distortion? The final average ratings are presented in Table 1, utilizing a Likert scale [21] that ranges from 1 (worst) to 5 (best). As shown in Table 1, our model achieves the highest scores.

5 Conclusion

In this work, we propose a Global Color-aware Arbitrary Style Transfer with Discrete Wavelet Transform (GCAST), which integrates global color features from style images with local detail features from content images. We place greater emphasis on the global color-aware stylistic features, as they are essential for enhancing the generated output. Our approach involves the design of a Wavelet-based Adjustment UNet, an Encoder-Decoder network. Specifically, we introduce a Cross-layer Attention Fusion mechanism (CAF) in the encoder for initial feature extraction, while the Wavelet-based Adjustment Block (WAB) employed in the decoder balance between color characteristics of style with the local details of content images.

Acknowledgments. The authors would like to thank the anonymous reviewers for their invaluable comments. Any opinions, findings and conclusions expressed in this paper are those of the authors and do not necessarily reflect the views of the sponsors.

References

1. Chan, S.H., Khoshabeh, R., Gibson, K.B., Gill, P.E., Nguyen, T.Q.: An augmented Lagrangian method for total variation video restoration. IEEE Trans. Image Process. **20**(11), 3097–3111 (2011). https://doi.org/10.1109/TIP.2011.2158229
2. Chen, H., et al.: Artistic style transfer with internal-external learning and contrastive learning. In: Advances in Neural Information Processing Systems, vol. 34, pp. 26561–26573. Curran Associates, Inc. (2021)

3. Deng, J., Luo, G., Zhao, C.: UCT-GAN: underwater image colour transfer generative adversarial network. IET Image Process. **14**, 3613–3622 (2020). https://api.semanticscholar.org/CorpusID:228997783

4. Deng, Y., Tang, F., Dong, W., Ma, C., Pan, X., Wang, L., Xu, C.: Stytr^2: image style transfer with transformers (2022). https://arxiv.org/abs/2105.14576

5. Gatys, L.A., Ecker, A.S., Bethge, M.: Image style transfer using convolutional neural networks. In: 2016 IEEE Conference on Computer Vision and Pattern Recognition (CVPR), pp. 2414–2423 (2016). https://doi.org/10.1109/CVPR.2016.265

6. Gooch, B., Reinhard, E., Gooch, A.: Human facial illustrations: creation and psychophysical evaluation. ACM Trans. Graph. **23**(1), 27–44 (2004). https://doi.org/10.1145/966131.966133

7. Hertzmann, A.: Painterly rendering with curved brush strokes of multiple sizes. In: Proceedings of the 25th Annual Conference on Computer Graphics and Interactive Techniques, pp. 453–460. SIGGRAPH 1998, Association for Computing Machinery, New York, NY, USA (1998). https://doi.org/10.1145/280814.280951

8. Hertzmann, A., Jacobs, C.E., Oliver, N., Curless, B., Salesin, D.H.: Image analogies, pp. 327–340. SIGGRAPH 2001, Association for Computing Machinery, New York, NY, USA (2001). https://doi.org/10.1145/383259.383295

9. Huang, S., An, J., Wei, D., Luo, J., Pfister, H.: Quantart: quantizing image style transfer towards high visual fidelity. In: 2023 IEEE/CVF Conference on Computer Vision and Pattern Recognition (CVPR), pp. 5947–5956 (2022). https://api.semanticscholar.org/CorpusID:254877300

10. Huang, X., Belongie, S.: Arbitrary style transfer in real-time with adaptive instance normalization (2017). https://arxiv.org/abs/1703.06868

11. Jing, Y., et al.: Dynamic instance normalization for arbitrary style transfer. ArXiv **abs/1911.06953** (2019). https://api.semanticscholar.org/CorpusID:208138280

12. Johnson, J., Alahi, A., Fei-Fei, L.: Perceptual losses for real-time style transfer and super-resolution (2016). http://dblp.uni-trier.de/db/conf/eccv/eccv2016-2.html#JohnsonAF16, cite arxiv:1603.08155

13. Johnson, J., Alahi, A., Fei-Fei, L.: Perceptual losses for real-time style transfer and super-resolution (2016). https://arxiv.org/abs/1603.08155

14. Jung, Z.J.C.: Subband adaptive enhancement of low light images using wavelet-based convolutional neural networks (2021)

15. Kingma, D., Ba, J.: Adam: a method for stochastic optimization. Comput. Sci. (2014)

16. Li, Y., Wang, N., Liu, J., Hou, X.: Demystifying neural style transfer. In: Proceedings of the Twenty-Sixth International Joint Conference on Artificial Intelligence, IJCAI-17, pp. 2230–2236 (2017). https://doi.org/10.24963/ijcai.2017/310

17. Lin, T.-Y., et al.: Microsoft COCO: common objects in context. In: Fleet, D., Pajdla, T., Schiele, B., Tuytelaars, T. (eds.) ECCV 2014. LNCS, vol. 8693, pp. 740–755. Springer, Cham (2014). https://doi.org/10.1007/978-3-319-10602-1_48

18. Liu, S., et al.: Adaattn: revisit attention mechanism in arbitrary neural style transfer. In: 2021 IEEE/CVF International Conference on Computer Vision (ICCV). pp. 6629–6638. IEEE Computer Society, Los Alamitos, CA, USA (2021). https://doi.org/10.1109/ICCV48922.2021.00658

19. Ma, Y., Zhao, C., Basu, A., Li, X.: Rast: restorable arbitrary style transfer via multi-restoration. In: 2023 IEEE/CVF Winter Conference on Applications of Computer Vision (WACV), pp. 331–340 (2023). https://doi.org/10.1109/WACV56688.2023.00041

20. Mallat, S.: A theory for multiresolution signal decomposition: the wavelet representation. IEEE Trans. Pattern Anal. Mach. Intell. **11**, 674–693 (1989). https://api.semanticscholar.org/CorpusID:2356353
21. Nicholls, M.E.R.: Likert Scales. Corsini Encyclopedia of Psychology (2010)
22. Raghavendra, C., Sivasubramanian, S., Kumaravel, A.: Improved image compression using effective lossless compression technique. Clust. Comput. **22**(2), 3911–3916 (2018). https://doi.org/10.1007/s10586-018-2508-1
23. Setiadi, D.R.I.M.: PSNR vs SSIM: imperceptibility quality assessment for image steganography. Multimedia Tools Appl. **80**(6), 8423–8444 (2020). https://doi.org/10.1007/s11042-020-10035-z
24. Simonyan, K., Zisserman, A.: Very deep convolutional networks for large-scale image recognition. CoRR **abs/1409.1556** (2014). https://api.semanticscholar.org/CorpusID:14124313
25. Tomasi, C., Manduchi, R.: Bilateral filtering for gray and color images. In: Sixth International Conference on Computer Vision (IEEE Cat. No.98CH36271), pp. 839–846 (1998). https://api.semanticscholar.org/CorpusID:14308539
26. Vaswani, A., et al.: Attention is all you need. In: Advances in Neural Information Processing Systems. vol. 30. Curran Associates, Inc. (2017)
27. Wang, P., Li, Y., Vasconcelos, N.: Rethinking and improving the robustness of image style transfer. 2021 IEEE/CVF Conference on Computer Vision and Pattern Recognition (CVPR) pp. 124–133 (2021), https://api.semanticscholar.org/CorpusID:233209896
28. Wang, T.C., Liu, M.Y., Zhu, J.Y., Tao, A., Kautz, J., Catanzaro, B.: High-resolution image synthesis and semantic manipulation with conditional GANS. 2018 IEEE/CVF Conference on Computer Vision and Pattern Recognition, pp. 8798–8807 (2017). https://api.semanticscholar.org/CorpusID:41805341
29. Wang, Z., Bovik, A.C., Sheikh, H.R., Simoncelli, E.P.: Image quality assessment: from error visibility to structural similarity. IEEE Trans. Image Process. **13**, 600–612 (2004). https://api.semanticscholar.org/CorpusID:207761262
30. Wilmot, P., Risser, E., Barnes, C.: Stable and controllable neural texture synthesis and style transfer using histogram losses. ArXiv **abs/1701.08893** (2017)
31. Wu, X., Hu, Z., Sheng, L., Xu, D.: Styleformer: real-time arbitrary style transfer via parametric style composition. In: Proceedings of the IEEE/CVF International Conference on Computer Vision (ICCV), pp. 14618–14627 (2021)
32. Zhang, Q.L., Yang, Y.B.: Sa-net: shuffle attention for deep convolutional neural networks. In: ICASSP 2021 - 2021 IEEE International Conference on Acoustics, Speech and Signal Processing (ICASSP), pp. 2235–2239 (2021). https://doi.org/10.1109/ICASSP39728.2021.9414568
33. Zhang, R., Isola, P., Efros, A.A., Shechtman, E., Wang, O.: The unreasonable effectiveness of deep features as a perceptual metric. In: 2018 IEEE/CVF Conference on Computer Vision and Pattern Recognition, pp. 586–595 (2018). https://doi.org/10.1109/CVPR.2018.00068
34. Zhang, Y., et al.: Domain enhanced arbitrary image style transfer via contrastive learning. In: ACM SIGGRAPH 2022. Association for Computing Machinery (2022). https://doi.org/10.1145/3528233.3530736

Incentivizing Crowdsensing
for DT-Enabled Metaverse

Dongdong Ye[1], Xumin Huang[1,2]($\boxtimes$), Yuan Wu[2,3], Jiawen Kang[1],
Weifeng Zhong[1], and Dusit Niyato[4]

[1] School of Automation, Guangdong University of Technology, Guangzhou, China
huangxumin@gdut.edu.cn
[2] State Key Laboratory of Internet of Things for Smart City, University of Macau,
Taipa, Macau, China
[3] Department of Computer and Information Science, University of Macau,
Taipa, Macau, China
[4] Collge of Computing and Data Science, Nanyang Technological University,
Singapore, Singapore

Abstract. Digital Twin (DT) has been proposed as a key enabling technology to produce a digital clone of the physical world and facilitate the convergence of the physical and virtual worlds for building a real-world Metaverse. For physical-virtual synchronization, crowdsensing is applied to employ Internet of Things (IoT) devices to sense physical objects and collect status information for timely updating the associated DTs. However, an incentive mechanism is necessitated to stimulate the devices to perform sensing tasks while meeting task requirements such as Age of Information (AoI) requirements. Thus, we adopt a contract theoretic approach to design an incentive mechanism for the devices that are classified into several types and the type parameters are unknown to others. The contract consists of a set of contract items with each contract item representing a device type, which specifies the required data updating frequency and monetary reward. We formulate an optimal contract design problem subject to feasible constraints including the average AoI requirement for each device type. Furthermore, we solve the problem by transforming it into a convex optimization problem that can be directly tackled by the existing methods. Finally, we provide numerical results to demonstrate the effectiveness and efficiency of our scheme.

Keywords: Digital twin-enabled Metaverse · crowdsensing · AoI · contract theory

1 Introduction

Metaverse has been conceived as an immersive successor to the mobile Internet and enables users to participate in a variety of online activities such as gaming, socializing, studying, shopping and traveling through interacting with each other

X. Chen et al. (Eds.): NPC 2024, LNCS 15527, pp. 336–347, 2025.
https://doi.org/10.1007/978-981-96-2830-8_26

and surrounding virtual objects in the virtual worlds [1]. Different virtual service providers (VSPs) have developed many virtual businesses that allow users to fully immerse themselves in the virtual life [2]. For example, users can play virtual reality (VR) or augmented reality (AR) games such as Horizon worlds, take an immersive tour of Korea in ZEPETO World, receive online education from Metaverse, MOOC and enjoy AR experience in autonomous driving.

To build a real-world Metaverse, the seamless convergence of the physical and virtual spaces is important. We need to acquire digital representations of physical objects and reshape them into the virtual space to make the Metaverse combine the reality with virtual together. To this end, digital twin (DT), which aims at enabling a systematic and fully digitalized modeling system, provides a promising solution. By producing accurate DTs of the physical entities and simulating these DTs, the DT technology is useful to predict and estimate their dynamics and evolutions during the entire life cycles, which can be exploited to understand, predict, optimize and control physical networks [3]. DT provides an efficient approach to create virtual objects that have the same features of the physical objects in real life, and generate a digital clone of the real world for constructing the Metaverse. DT-enabled Metaverse brings immersive experiences to users in the virtual worlds [4]. However, a huge amount of diverse data, e.g., status information of the physical objects, should be collected and analyzed to update their DTs. To achieve real-time synchronization between the virtual and physical worlds, a VSP can adopt the crowdsensing technique to employ a variety of Internet of Things (IoT) devices as data collectors to collectively sense the physical objects in a cost-efficient manner. Nevertheless, the VSP necessitates an incentive mechanism to provide proper incentives for all data collectors while considering the task requirements such as timeliness of their collected data.

Recently, research efforts have been devoted to different optimization schemes for the Metaverse. On one hand, users require available bandwidth to access the Metaverse and computing resources to run their Metaverse applications. The bandwidth allocation problem among the users was studied by using auction or game theories in [5, 6], respectively. The computing resource trading problem was studied for the vehicular Metaverse when a vehicle employed neighbour vehicles with underutilized computing resources to complete a large-scale rendering task for the construction of the vehicular Metaverse [7]. Researchers have proposed DT-enabled Metaverse and investigated the performance improvements according to different optimization goals. A group of unmanned aerial vehicles was employed by several VSPs to perform data collection and assist the VSPs in synchronizing the DTs [8]. In this work, both the association between the data collectors and VSPs and the synchronization intensity control problem among the VSPs were addressed from a game theoretic perspective. A timely and secure crowdsensing scheme was presented to provide reliable and up-to-date data sources for the Metaverse [9]. To promote the use of crowdsensing, the authors also took into account an age of information (AoI) optimization goal to optimize the data collection, transmission, and processing operations. AoI has been utilized as a performance metric to quantitatively assess the freshness of received data in a time-critical data delivery system. Many schemes based on AoI were introduced to achieve the freshness-aware crowdsensing. For example, AoI was used to model the waiting time cost of a publisher of tasks. An AoI-based queuing game method was further presented for the task publisher to dynamically adjust the monetary reward for the data collectors, so as to stimulate the data collectors to complete their tasks timely [10]. A joint AoI optimization and privacy-preserving scheme was presented to collect and process the sensing data with both data freshness and security guarantee [11]. In particular, the average AoI value of all collected data was formulated and minimized by optimizing spectrum access strategies among all data collectors. Furthermore, a task publisher was assumed to only utilize and store the latest data from each data collector in the local cache and build a queue to replace the data [12]. The average AoI of each data collector's data in an $M/M/1$ First Come-First-Service (FCFS) queue and data collectors' social influences with each other were jointly considered to determine data updating frequencies and reward of the data collectors.

Compared with the above works, we focus on the incentive mechanism design for crowdsensing in the DT-enabled Metaverse by using a contract-theoretic approach. To implement virtual businesses in the virtual world, a VSP employs several IoT devices to detect physical objects of interest and utilize the collected data as synchronized data to maintain the associated DTs. We particularly consider an information asymmetry scenario where all devices are classified into multiple types according to the sensing cost parameters; however, the VSP does not know exactly a type of each device. Facing the information asymmetry, the VSP designs a contract-based incentive mechanism to encourage diverse devices to accept sensing tasks. The contract consists of a set of contract items with each contract item representing a device type, which specifies the required data updating frequency and monetary reward. Moreover, we refer to [12] to define the concept of AoI and calculate the average AoI value for each type of device. We also consider the social benefit of a device gained from other devices. On the VSP side, we formulate a VSP satisfaction function with respect to a device type. The utility of the VSP is calculated by the total degree of satisfaction minus the total monetary cost. As a decision maker, the VSP aims to maximize the utility subject to feasible constraints such as the average AoI requirement for each device type. To tackle the optimal contract design problem, we first simplify the original problem by reducing the complicated constraints, and transform the problem into a convex optimization problem that can be solved by using the block coordinate descent (BCD) method.

The main contributions of this paper are summarized as follows.

- We propose the integration of crowdsensing and DT for building the real-world Metaverse. A hierarchical architecture is presented to introduce the network functionalities.
- We design a contract-based crowdsensing scheme in DT-enabled Metaverse. The VSP employs contract theory to design a proper contract so as to incentivize the devices to accept the contract items based on the true types while maximizing the utility of the VSP.

- We present an efficient solution to achieve the optimal contract design. Through proper problem simplification and reformulation, we can adopt the BCD method to tackle the problem and derive an optimal contract.

2 System Model and Problem Formulation

2.1 Network Model

We propose a hierarchical architecture for the DT-enabled Metaverse, comprising three layers: IoT, DT, and Metaverse (see Fig. 1). At the IoT layer, VSPs use crowdsensing to gather physical data. The DT layer processes this data into digital twins, while the Metaverse layer enables real-time user interactions with these virtual counterparts. Then, we provide more details of the hierarchical architecture as follows.

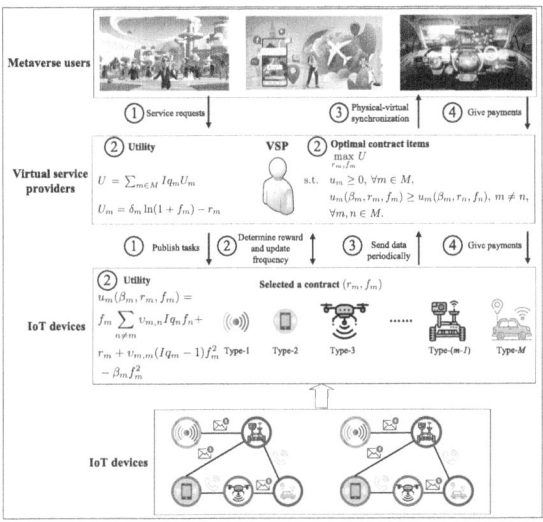

Fig. 1. The three-layer architecture of the DT-enabled Metaverse

A Metaverse user first requests services such as gaming, tourism, or vehicular mixed reality from a VSP. In response, the VSP designs a corresponding sensing task and broadcasts its specific requirements to a set of IoT devices. The VSP collaborates with the devices to develop an incentive scheme, which indicates the data update frequency for each device and promising reward. Once the task is assigned, the devices begin sensing activities, continuously collecting data from specified areas. The data is packaged into fixed-size packets. Simultaneously, the devices upload the latest data to the VSP according to the pre-setting data update frequency. The VSP consistently processes the incoming data from each device, performs data cleaning, updates the associated DTs, and delivers the updated DTs to the Metaverse user. The VSP periodically compensates the IoT devices according to the agreed-upon strategy, continuing until the entire sensing task is finalized.

2.2 AoI Requirement

We consider a crowdsensing system that consists of a VSP and multiple IoT devices. The VSP recruits a set of devices to perform the sensing tasks. The VSP utilizes the latest data from each device to update the DTs and maintains a queue for cleaning the data from a device. For all devices, their queues are assumed to follow a typical M/M/1 queue under the FCFS serving policy. For simplicity, we consider the collection time per data sample and processing rates of the queues among all devices are identical, denoted by τ and γ respectively. Referring to [12], we define the AoI of a data sample α as the time difference between the current time t and the creation time t_0 of this data sample, i,e, $\alpha = t - t_0$, which refers to the sum of the data collection time, waiting time and processing time in the queue. Given a time interval of observation $\triangle t$, we evaluate the average AoI value of this data sample, $\bar{\alpha} = \frac{1}{\triangle t} \int_0^{\triangle t} \alpha(t) dt$. According to [13], we can calculate the average AoI value of the device's data in the queue with a single source as follows.

$$\bar{\alpha} = \frac{(\rho - 1)(\rho^2 - \gamma \rho \tau) + 1}{(1 - \rho)\rho\gamma}, \tag{1}$$

where $\rho = f/\mu$ and f refers to arrival rate of the queue, i.e., data update frequency of the device.

2.3 Device Model

We present a utility function for a device as follows. The device optimizes the data update frequency f to improve the utility function, including the monetary reward given by the VSP, social benefit from other devices and data collection cost. The work [14] formulates a convex data collection cost function on f, i.e., βf^2, where β is an individual sensing cost parameter of the device and is private information. Furthermore, we classify all devices into discrete M types according to their sensing cost parameters. The set of device types is denoted as $\mathcal{M}$ and the elements are sorted in descending order, $\beta_1 \geq \beta_2 \geq \cdots \geq \beta_M$. According to historical knowledge, the ratio of type-m devices is q_m. The promising reward and data update frequency requirement for a type-m device are r_m and f_m, respectively. To make the reward model more realistic, inspired by [14], we consider the social network influence of a type-n device on the type-m device, which is denoted by $v_{m,n}$. To model the social network influence between a type-m device and a type-n device are positive only when both devices' effort levels are positive, a product form function in [14] is adopted to express the influence by $v_{m,n}f_m f_n$. When considering all pair of device's types, the influence is $\sum_{m \in M} \sum_{n \in M} v_{m,n} f_m f_n$. To simplify the analysis without loss of generality, we consider $v_{m,n} = v_{n,m}$ and $v_{m,m} > 0$ and the influence is reduced to $\Phi_m = f_m \sum_{n \neq m} v_{m,n} I q_n f_n + v_{m,m}(I q_m - 1) f_m^2$. As a result, the type-$m$ device's utility is

$$u_m = r_m + \Phi_m - \beta_m f_m^2. \tag{2}$$

Let $R_m = \Phi_m + r_m$ and we have $u_m = R_m - \beta_m f_m^2$.

2.4   VSP Model

The VSP optimizes the monetary reward for each type of device to maximize the utility, which is equal to its satisfaction degree minus the monetary cost. Since the VSP hopes the collected data is as fresh as possible, the satisfaction degree with the device increases with the increase of the data update frequency, we use a logarithmic function to describe the diminishing return of VSP's satisfaction degree regarding a type-m device with the increase of f_m, i.e., $\delta_m \ln(1 + f_m)$, $\delta > 0$ is a factor indicating the scale of the satisfaction degree and can also be adjusted to coordinate with the control strategy on the synchronization intensity. Note that the logarithmic function has been widely used in the crowd-sensing applications. Then, the VSP's utility gained from the type-m device is $U_m = \delta_m \ln(1 + f_m) - r_m$. Since there exist I devices with M types, the total utility of the VSP is $U = \sum_{m \in M} I q_m U_m$ which refers to the tradeoff between the physical-virtual synchronization intensity requirement and monetary cost in crowdsensing.

In crowdsensing for a DT-enabled Metaverse, the VSP faces information asymmetry regarding device types. To overcome the problem, contract theory is applied by the VSP to design a contract with M contract items associated with M device types. Each item specifies data update frequency and reward, which should meet the Individual Rationality (IR) and Incentive Compatibility (IC) constraints to ensure truthful type selection.

Definition 1. *(Individual Rationality) Each contract item is required to provide a nonnegative utility for the device type, i.e.,*

$$R_m - \beta_m f_m^2 \geq 0, \ \forall m \in \mathcal{M}. \tag{3}$$

Definition 2. *(Incentive Compatibility) A type-m device would rather choose the contract item (f_m, d_m) fitting its own type instead of any other contract items (f_m, d_m), $m \in \mathcal{M}$, and $m \neq n$, i.e.,*

$$R_m - \beta_m f_m^2 \geq R_n - \beta_m f_n^2, \ \forall m, n \in \mathcal{M}, \ m \neq n. \tag{4}$$

For the VSP, the optimal contract design problem is to optimize $\boldsymbol{f} = \{f_m\}_{m \in \mathcal{M}}$ and $\boldsymbol{R} = \{R_m\}_{m \in \mathcal{M}}$ to maximize U while meeting the feasible con-straints.

Problem 1: $\max_{\boldsymbol{f}, \boldsymbol{R}} U$

s.t.   Constraints in (3) and (4),

$$f_m \geq 0, R_m \geq 0, \ \forall m \in \{1, \ldots, M\}, \tag{5}$$

$$\bar{\alpha}_m \leq \alpha_{\max}, \ \forall m \in \{1, \ldots, M\},$$

$$\sum_{m \in M} I q_m f_m \leq F_{\max}.$$

Here, $\alpha_{\max}$ is the maximum of the average AoI value, and $F_{\max}$ is used to ensure that the total data update frequency of all devices will not exceed the upper limit.

3   Contract-Based Incentive Mechanism

Since there are M IR constraints and $M(M-1)$ IC constraints in **Problem 1**, it is difficult to directly solve the complex problem with complicated constraints. In the following, we first reduce the number of constraints to simplify the original problem based on **Lemma 1**.

Lemma 1. *A feasible contract item with asymmetric information should meet the following conditions:*

$$R_1 - \beta_1 f_1^2 \geq 0, \tag{6a}$$

$$R_m - \beta_m f_m^2 \geq R_{m-1} - \beta_m f_{m-1}^2, \ \forall m \in \{2, \ldots, M\}, \tag{6b}$$

$$R_m - \beta_m f_m^2 \geq R_{m+1} - \beta_m f_{m+1}^2, \ \forall m \in \{1, \ldots, M-1\}, \tag{6c}$$

$$0 \leq f_1 \leq f_2 \leq \cdots \leq f_M, \ 0 \leq R_1 \leq R_2 \leq \cdots \leq R_M. \tag{6d}$$

Proof. Please refer to [15].   □

The constraint (6a) related to the IR constraints ensures the nonnegative utility for each device type. Constraints (6b), (6c) and (6d) are relevant with IC constraints. Constraints (6b) and (6c) indicate that the IC constraints can be reduced to Local Downward Incentive Compatibility (LDIC) and Local Upward Incentive Compatibility (LUIC) with monotonicity, respectively [15]. Constraint (6d) specifies that a device of a lower type is given more monetary rewards to provide a higher data update frequency. As a result, **Problem 1** can be reformulated as **Problem 2** with **Lemma 1**, which is shown as follows.

$$\textbf{Problem 2:} \ \max_{f,R} U$$

$$\begin{aligned}
\text{s.t.} \quad & R_1 - \beta_1 f_1^2 = 0, \\
& R_m - \beta_m f_m^2 = R_{m-1} - \beta_m f_{m-1}^2, \\
& \forall m \in \{2, \ldots, M\}, \\
& f_m \geq 0, \ R_m \geq 0, \ \forall m \in \{1, \ldots, M\}, \\
& \bar{\alpha}_m \leq \alpha_{\max}, \ \forall m \in \{1, \ldots, M\}, \\
& \sum_{m \in M} Iq_m f_m \leq F_{\max}.
\end{aligned} \tag{7}$$

Based on the first two constraints in **Problem 2**, the optimal solution of R_m denoted as R_m^* is calculated by the iterative method in a serial way and we have

$$R_m^* = \begin{cases} \beta_m f_m^2 + \sum_{1 \leq j \leq m-1} \left(\beta_j f_j^2 - \beta_{j+1} f_j^2 \right), 2 \leq m \leq M \\ \beta_1 f_1^2, m = 1 \end{cases} \tag{8}$$

By substituting (10) into U in **Problem 2**, the problem is reformulated as

Problem 3: $\max_{f} U = \sum_{m \in M} U_m$ (9)

$$\text{s.t.} \quad f_m \geq 0, \ \forall m \in \{1, \ldots, M\}, \tag{9a}$$

$$\bar{\alpha}_m \leq \alpha_{\max}, \ \forall m \, \{1, \ldots, M\}, \tag{9b}$$

$$\sum_{m \in M} I q_m f_m \leq F_{\max}, \tag{9c}$$

where $U_m = I q_m \delta_m \ln(1 + f_m) - I b_m f_m^2 + I^2 q_m^2 \Phi_m$. Here, for $1 \leq m < M$, we have $b_m = q_m \beta_m + (\beta_m - \beta_{m-1}) \sum_{j=m+1}^{M} q_j$; for $m = M$, we have $b_m = q_m \beta_m$. Let $U_{\text{new}} = -U$ and **Problem 3** is transformed into a new **Problem 4** with the minimization objective $\min_f U_{\text{new}}$. We further have **Lemma 2** as follows.

Lemma 2. *Given* $\boldsymbol{f}_{-m} = \{f_1, \ldots, f_{m-1}, f_{m+1}, \ldots, f_M\}$, $f_m < \gamma, \forall m \in M$ *and* $-\frac{I q_m \delta_m}{(1+f_m)^2} - 2I b_m + 2I q_m \upsilon_{m,m}(I q_m - 1) > 0, \forall m \in M$, **Problem 4** *is a convex problem with respect to* f_m.

Proof. First, we compute the second-order derivatives of U_{new} with respect to f_m and have $\frac{\partial^2 U_{\text{new}}}{\partial f_m^2} = -\frac{I q_m \delta}{(1+f_m)^2} - 2I b_m + 2I q_m \upsilon_{m,m}(I q_m - 1) > 0$. U_{new} is strictly convex with respect to $f_m, \forall m \in M$ when $\boldsymbol{f}_{-m}$ is given. In other words, U_{new} is a block multi-convex with respect to $\boldsymbol{f}$. Second, constraints (9a) and (9c) refer to two sets of linear constraints. Third, $\bar{\alpha}_m = \frac{\gamma \tau - \rho_m}{\gamma} + \frac{1}{(1-\rho_m)\rho_m \gamma}$. We compute the second-order derivative of $\bar{\alpha}_m$ with respect to f_m. Based on $f_m < \gamma, \forall m \in \mathcal{M}$,

we have $\frac{\partial \bar{\alpha}_m^2}{\partial f_m^2} = \left[\frac{2\left(\frac{2f_m}{\gamma} - 1\right)^2}{\left(\frac{f_m}{\gamma} - \frac{f_m^2}{\gamma^2}\right)^3} + \frac{2}{\left(\frac{f_m}{\gamma} - \frac{f_m^2}{\gamma^2}\right)^2} \right] \frac{1}{\mu} > 0$ Constraint (9b) is also a

convex set. To summarize, **Problem 4** is a convex problem in f_m. $\qquad\square$

At this time, we refer to [16] and apply the BCD method to solve **Problem 4**. The BCD method is performed in an iterative manner and the main steps of this method are shown as follows. Initialization: we set the initialization parameters $\beta_m, \delta_m, q_m, \upsilon_{m,n}, \forall m, n \in M$ and $\gamma, \epsilon, I, M, \tau$ and $z = 1$ and $\eta = 10^{-5}$. Iteration: given z, looping the iteration from 1 to M. In each iteration, given $\boldsymbol{f}_{-m}^{z-1,*}$, a standard convex optimization tool is used to solve **Problem 4** and obtain $f_m^{z,*}$. After M iterations, we obtain $\boldsymbol{f}^{z,*}$. Termination: if $|\boldsymbol{f}^{z,*} - \boldsymbol{f}^{z-1,*}| \leq \eta$, the algorithm is terminated and output $\boldsymbol{f}^*$ and derive $\boldsymbol{R}^*$ by substituting $\boldsymbol{f}^*$ into Eq. (8). Otherwise, proceed to the next iteration, $z = z+1$. In addition, the total time complexity, denoted as $\mathcal{O}\left(z_{\max} \cdot \sum_{m=1}^{M} c_m\right)$ where $z_{\max}$ is the total number of iterations until convergence and c_m is the time complexity of optimizing each block m, is well-suited for the DT-Enabled Metaverse.

Table 1. Parameter Setting in the Simulation.

Parameter	Setting
Serving rate	$\gamma = 1$
Data update frequency	$f \in (0, \gamma)$ per minute
Social network influence	$v \in [0.01, 0.2]$
Upper limit of the average AoI	$\alpha_{\max} = 7$

4   Numerical Results

In this section, we evaluate the performance of our scheme for crowdsensing in DT-enabled Metaverse. For simplicity, we choose $M = 5$ devices and $I = 5$ types and the sensing cost parameter β follows the uniform distribution among $[0, 1]$. Referring to [12, 17], we adopt the simulation parameters shown in Table 1.

To highlight the superiority of our scheme, we compare our scheme with two baseline schemes, as shown in Fig. 2. Our scheme utilizes a contract-based incentive mechanism under asymmetric information and with consideration of the social benefits of the devices. The traditional schemes neglect the social benefits and include:

- Stackelberg game under asymmetric information (SG) : a type-m device is the game follower and its utility $u_m = pf_m - \beta_m f_m^2$ while the VSP plays as a game leader and utility is $U = \sum_{m \in \mathcal{M}} I q_m [\delta_m \ln(1 + f_m) - pf_m]$ where p is the decision of the VSP and refers to monetary payment per data update frequency paid to all devices [18].
- Contract theory under asymmetric information (CA): This scheme is similar to our scheme, but the social benefits of the devices $\{\phi\}_{\forall m}$ are not considered.
- Contract theory under complete information (CC): This is an ideal scenario where the optimal contract design is performed without the information asymmetry such that each contract item is designed to make each device of any type obtain zero utility $u_m = r_m - \beta_m f_m^2 = 0, \forall m$.

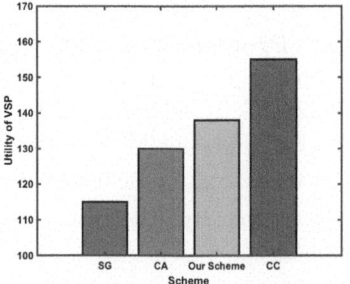

Fig. 2. Performance comparison among different schemes.

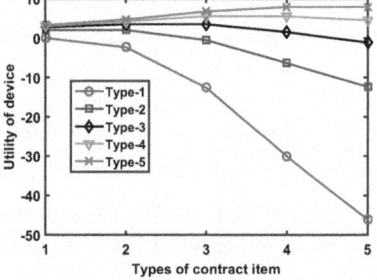

Fig. 3. Validation of contract properties.

The CC scheme achieves the highest utility for the VSP by setting each device's utility to zero and minimizing the monetary reward paid to them, maximizing the VSP's utility. Our scheme outperforms both the SG and CA schemes. In our scheme, the VSP has a monopoly position in the contract design, maximizing its utility under IR and IC constraints. In contrast, the SG scheme offers a sub-optimal solution by optimizing both VSP and device utilities to reach Stackelberg equilibrium. Compared to the CA scheme, our scheme incorporates social benefits in the utility function, which is helpful to reduce the monetary cost and improve the VSP's utility. Compared to the SG and CA schemes, our scheme obtains the higher utility for the VSP and the utility improvements reach approximately 21% and 2%, respectively.

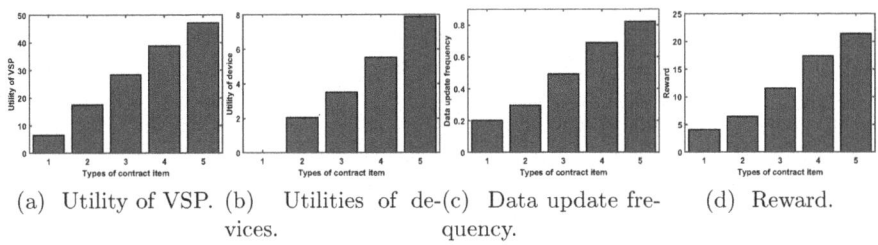

(a) Utility of VSP. (b) Utilities of de-(c) Data update fre-(d) Reward.
vices.   quency.

Fig. 4. System performance with respect to different device types under our scheme.

Figure 3 shows the validation of the IC and IR constraints in the proposed contract-based incentive mechanism. We evaluated the utilities of different devices with diverse types when selecting different contract items from the VSP. From the figure, we validate that our contract design satisfies the IR and IC constraints. A device with an arbitrary type achieves the maximal utility with a nonnegative value only when accepting the contract item matched with the type. The process of selecting the contract items indirectly discloses the types of devices to the VSP. This means that the contract-theoretic approach is effective to tackle the information asymmetry problem for the VSP.

We further validate the theoretical analysis for our contract design in **Lemma 1**. Figure 4 shows the utilities of the VSP and devices, data update frequency, and monetary reward with respect to different device types. Devices with higher types can get higher and positive utilities. In particular, the utility of the devices with the lowest type is zero. At the same time, devices with the higher types need to be given with more monetary reward to increase the data update frequencies. The numerical results are consistent with the previous analysis in **Lemma 1**.

5 Conclusion

We designed a contract-based incentive mechanism for crowdsensing in a DT-enabled Metaverse. A VSP recruited IoT devices to collect sensing data of physical objects for updating the DTs. Devices were classified by private sensing cost parameters, and the VSP utilized the contract theoretic approach to incentivize them with different types to accept the contract items according to their true types. The contract incorporated social benefits from other devices and average AoI requirements. By simplifying the coupled constraints, the optimal contract design problem was transformed into a convex optimization problem that can be solved by using the BCD method. Numerical results showed that compared with the baseline scheme, our scheme is superior to improve VSP's utility. Limited sensing nodes hinder data collection, reducing the quality of DT-enabled Metaverse services. As highlighted in [19], generative AI technologies, particularly large language models, can enhance data generation, potentially adding $2 trillion in value. Future research should explore integrating generative AI with mobile crowdsensing to enhance service quality.

Acknowledgements. This work was supported by Guangzhou Basic Research Program under Grant 2023A04J0340 and Grant 2023A04J1704, in part by Guangdong Basic and Applied Basic Research Foundation under Grant 2024A1515011795, in part by Key Project in Higher Education of Guangdong Province under Grant 2024ZDZX1046, and in part by MYRG-GRG2023-00083-IOTSC-UMDF. Dusit Niyato's work was supported in part by National Research Foundation, Singapore, and Infocomm Media Development Authority under its Future Communications Research & Development Programme, Defence Science Organisation (DSO) National Laboratories under the AI Singapore Programme (FCP-NTU-RG-2022-010 and FCP-ASTAR-TG-2022-003), in part by Singapore Ministry of Education (MOE) Tier 1 (RG87/22), and in part by the NTU Centre for Computational Technologies in Finance (NTU-CCTF).

References

1. Wang, Y., et al.: A survey on metaverse: fundamentals, security, and privacy. IEEE Commun. Surv. Tutor. **25**(1), 319–352 (2022)
2. Wang, H., et al.: A survey on the metaverse: the state-of-the-art, technologies, applications, and challenges. IEEE Internet Things J. **10**(16), 14 671–14 688 (2023)
3. Wu, Y., Zhang, K., Zhang, Y.: Digital twin networks: a survey. IEEE Internet Things J. **8**(18), 13 789–13 804 (2021)
4. Aloqaily, M., Bouachir,O., Karray, F., Al Ridhawi, I., El Saddik, A.: Integrating digital twin and advanced intelligent technologies to realize the metaverse. IEEE Consum. Electron. Mag. **12**(6), 47–55 (2022)
5. Xu, M., Niyato, D., Kang, J., Xiong, Z., Miao, C., Kim, D.I.: Wireless edge-empowered metaverse: a learning-based incentive mechanism for virtual reality. In: ICC 2022-IEEE International Conference on Communications. IEEE, pp. 5220–5225, 2022
6. Huang, X., et al.: Joint user association and resource pricing for metaverse: distributed and centralized approaches. In: 2022 IEEE 19th International Conference on Mobile Ad Hoc and Smart Systems (MASS). IEEE, pp. 505–513, 2022
7. Jiang, Y., et al.: Reliable distributed computing for metaverse: a hierarchical game-theoretic approach. IEEE Trans. Veh. Technol. **72**(1), 1084–1100 (2022)
8. Han, Y., et al.: A dynamic hierarchical framework for iot-assisted digital twin synchronization in the metaverse. IEEE Internet Things J. **10**(1), 268–284 (2022)

9. Wang, W., Yang, Y., Xiong, Z., Niyato, D.: Footstone of metaverse: a timely and secure crowdsensing. IEEE Netw. (2023)
10. Gao, H., et al.: Dynamic task pricing in mobile crowdsensing: an age-of-information-based queueing game scheme. IEEE Internet Things J. **9**(21), 21 278–21 291 (2022)
11. Yang, Y., Zhang, B., Guo, D., Xu, R., Su, C., Wang, W.: Age of information optimization for privacy-preserving mobile crowdsensing. IEEE Trans. Emerg. Top. Comput. **12**(1), 281–292 (2023)
12. Xu, Y., et al.: Aoi-guaranteed incentive mechanism for mobile crowdsensing with freshness concerns. IEEE Trans. Mob. Comput. **23**(5), 4107–4125 (2023)
13. Yates, R.D., Kaul, S.K.: The age of information: real-time status updating by multiple sources. IEEE Trans. Inf. Theory **65**(3), 1807–1827 (2018)
14. Cheung, M.H., Hou, F., Huang, J.: Make a difference: diversity-driven social mobile crowdsensing. In: IEEE INFOCOM 2017-IEEE Conference on Computer Communications, pp. 1–9. IEEE, 2017
15. Hou, Z., Chen, H., Li, Y., Vucetic, B.: Incentive mechanism design for wireless energy harvesting-based internet of things. IEEE Internet Things J. **5**(4), 2620–2632 (2017)
16. Xu, Y., Yin, W.: A block coordinate descent method for regularized multiconvex optimization with applications to nonnegative tensor factorization and completion. SIAM J. Imag. Sci. **6**(3), 1758–1789 (2013)
17. Xiao, M., Xu, Y., Zhou, J., Wu, J., Zhang, S., Zheng, J.: Aoi-aware incentive mechanism for mobile crowdsensing using stackelberg game. In: IEEE INFOCOM 2023-IEEE Conference on Computer Communications, pp. 1–10. IEEE, 2023
18. Huang, X., et al.: Service reservation and pricing for green metaverses: a stackelberg game approach. IEEE Wirel. Commun. **30**(5), 86–94 (2023)
19. Huang, X., et al.: Federated learning-empowered AI-generated content in wireless networks. IEEE Network **38**(5), 304–313 (2024)

Intelligent Telemetry: P4-Driven Network Telemetry and Service Flow Intelligent Aviation Platform

Jing Gao[1,2] , Fanqin Zhou[1(✉)] , Mianxiong Dong[2], Lei Feng[1] ,
Kaoru Ota[2], Zijian Li[3], and Jiawei Fan[3]

[1] State Key Laboratory of Networking and Switching Technology,
Beijing University of Posts and Telecommunications, Beijing 100876, China
fqzhou2012@bupt.edu.cn
[2] Department of Information and Electronic Engineering,
Muroran Institute of Technology, Muroran 050-8585, Japan
[3] School of Computer Science (National Pilot Software Engineering School), Beijing
University of Posts and Telecommunications Address Beijing, 100876 Beijing, China

Abstract. To address the current challenges in network monitoring and management, such as poor real-time performance, high cost, low accuracy, and slow fault detection and recovery, a P4-driven network telemetry and resource scheduling platform is designed and presented in this paper. This platform embeds telemetry information within data packets, achieving real-time monitoring and anomaly detection of network states. It significantly enhances the granularity and timeliness of network monitoring and employs a path rerouting mechanism for rapid network recovery. The platform boasts high scalability and customizability, allowing on-demand adjustment of telemetry strategies and parameters. It provides low-overhead, business-level telemetry information, offering comprehensive support for diverse services and advancing network management and service quality. This work provides a technical foundation for constructing the next generation of intelligent, efficient, and reliable networks through continuous research and practical application.

Keywords: P4-driven network telemetry · On-demand adjustment · Resource scheduling

1 Introduction

Data centers face increasingly complex network environments, making traditional monitoring methods inadequate for fine-grained management [1]. With predominantly east-west traffic and critical applications requiring high service quality, conventional node and link monitoring offers only coarse-grained resource awareness, hindering quick fault detection and network recovery [2,3].

Published by Springer Nature Switzerland AG 2025
X. Chen et al. (Eds.): NPC 2024, LNCS 15527, pp. 348–359, 2025.
https://doi.org/10.1007/978-981-96-2830-8_27

In-band Network Telemetry (INT) is a promising technology for fine-grained business awareness. However, traditional telemetry methods lack flexibility [4]. Administrators can only activate telemetry when needed and deactivate it after collecting sufficient data, generating unnecessary data, and increasing the network burden [5].

Advancements in programmable technology, such as P4-based programmable switches, enable customizable packet processing logic, allowing flexible, on-demand INT with minimal overhead [6]. This improves network intelligence and responsiveness [7,8]. Existing telemetry schemes mostly rely on static, fixed collection strategies, typically providing only coarse-grained resource state information, making it difficult to achieve fine-grained business awareness.

The main contributions of this paper are as follows: first, we propose an on-demand telemetry method leveraging the flexibility of the P4 programming language, dynamically adjusting telemetry strategies based on actual business needs, thereby significantly improving the efficiency and effectiveness of telemetry. Second, we implement network anomaly detection and business rerouting based on business telemetry data, supporting precise monitoring and optimization of business flows, which enhances the overall network service quality. Finally, we propose and implement a P4-driven network telemetry and intelligence platform based on bmv2, demonstrating in an intuitive way on-demand business telemetry, anomaly detection, and rerouting functionalities.

The rest of the paper is organized as follows. Section 2 provides a comprehensive review of the related work. Section 3 describes the research methodology, detailing the fine-grained on-demand telemetry mechanism, the P4 data plane-based in-band network telemetry, anomaly monitoring, and quick rerouting mechanisms. Section 4 discusses module function and system design, covering the telemetry control subsystem, anomaly detection subsystem, and task scheduling subsystem, along with their core functions and system function design. Section 5 presents the implementation and results. Section 6 concludes the paper and discusses limitations and future research directions.

2   Related Work

Over the past few decades, traditional network measurement technologies have been developed and refined, falling into three categories: active measurement, passive measurement, and hybrid measurement [4]. Active measurement technology involves injecting probe packets into the network for related measurements, with representative schemes including Ping and Traceroute [5]. However, because it requires the injection of additional probe packets, it increases the network load, and the routing paths of the probe packets do not match those of the business packets, failing to accurately reflect the network state faced by the observed business [6]. Passive measurement technology records and analyzes existing traffic within the network to obtain measurement results, with representative schemes including NetFlow, sFlow, and IPFIX [7]. Yet, due to limitations in switch performance and net-work bandwidth, the measurement granularity is coarse, and deployment across management domains is challenging. Hybrid measurement schemes combine the advantages of active and passive measurements. With the advent of software-defined networking (SDN), fine-grained network management has become possible [2,8], but its centralized control plane limits scalability, and the data plane's limited functionality makes implementing new measurement features difficult. Therefore, traditional network measurement technologies struggle to fully meet the needs of modern large-scale networks.

The emergence of the programmable data plane (PDP) [2,9] has provided a new design space for network telemetry solutions. P4-based programmable chips are one of the PDP technology routes [10]. PDP allows customization of packet operations and access to internal device states, making it possible to implement network measurements directly in the data plane [11]. Consequently, in-band network telemetry (INT) has garnered widespread attention in both industry and academia in recent years. Unlike traditional network measurement technologies, in-band network telemetry combines packet forwarding with network measurement, where forwarding nodes (such as switches and smart network interface cards (NICs)) collect internal network states and insert telemetry data into packets [12]. Thus, in-band network telemetry boasts strong real-time capabilities, fine measurement granularity, and rich measurement states.

This paper is based on the P4 programmable switch in-band network telemetry technology, addressing the coarse granularity of traditional network measurement technologies. After conducting network telemetry, the accuracy and operability of the measurements are improved by adjusting the operations on demand. Simultaneously, the proposed platform adds network anomaly detection and a rapid rerouting algorithm based on backup paths, enabling quick network state recovery.

3   Functional Requirements and Mechanisms

The technical approach adopted mainly encompasses four key components: a fine-grained on-demand telemetry mechanism for applications, an in-band network telemetry mechanism based on the P4 data plane, an anomaly monitoring mechanism based on network telemetry, and a quick rerouting mechanism based on backup paths.

3.1   Fine-Grained On-Demand Telemetry for Applications

As network scale and complexity increase, traditional network telemetry methods face challenges due to their lack of flexibility and unnecessary resource overhead. These methods often fail to meet the demands of efficient management in modern networks.

This paper proposes a fine-grained, on-demand telemetry method tailored for business applications. It allows telemetry tasks to be issued on-demand, targeting specific business needs and adjusting telemetry activities dynamically. This approach constrains overall resource overhead by deploying intelligent telemetry control modules at network nodes, capable of real-time network status sensing. These modules activate or deactivate telemetry functions based on predefined strategies, providing higher frequency and detailed monitoring for critical applications and conserving resources for ordinary ones.

3.2 In-Band Network Telemetry Based on P4 Data

This paper investigates the in-band network telemetry mechanism based on the P4 data plane. Initially, users define packet processing logic using the P4 programming language, including performance metrics such as latency, packet loss rate, and queue length. When packets traverse the P4-based data plane, switches insert the required telemetry information into the packet headers or payloads according to the pre-defined P4 code. As these packets travel through the network, each node further inserts or updates the telemetry information, ultimately reaching a centralized telemetry data collection point, typically a network controller or a dedicated monitoring server. The telemetry message collector is shown in Fig. 1.

The P4 Telemetry Metadata Values Used. The P4.org specification provides recommended values for telemetry metadata, which can be obtained by implementing INT. The telemetry metadata specified in the guidelines theoretically allows INT to define and collect any internal device information, including:

P4.org has developed an open source software switch called bmv2 (behavioral model version 2) designed to be a target for P4 programs. Based on bmv2, we adopted the following metadata: Switch id, ingress port, egress port, ingress timestamp, egress timestamp, hop latency, and queue occupancy.

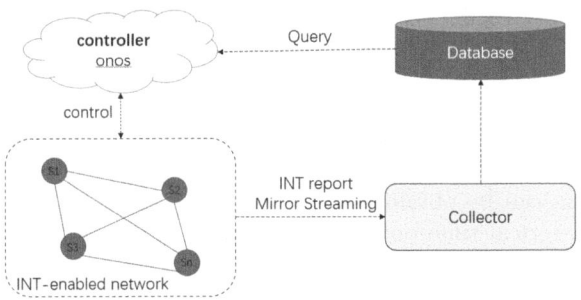

Fig. 1. Telemetry message collector.

In-Band Network Telemetry in Postcard Model. We choose the postcard model as the telemetry mode of INT, which is divided into three steps: the definition of metadata set, the acquisition of network resource metadata and the processing of metadata collector.

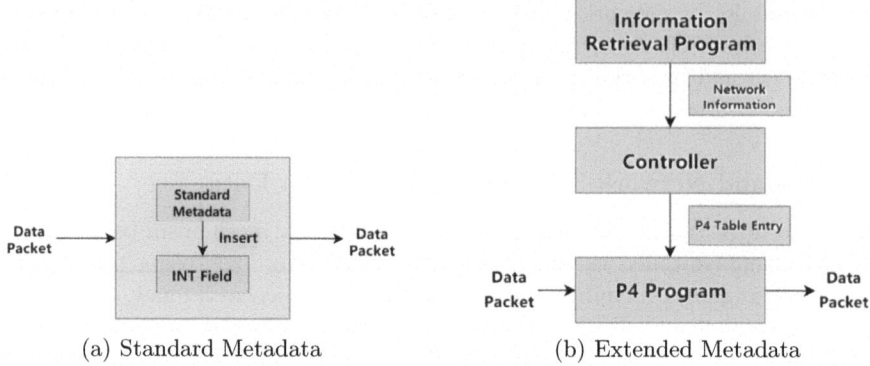

(a) Standard Metadata   (b) Extended Metadata

Fig. 2. Network telemetry metadata

Metadata Set Definition. Metadata, also known as intermediary data or relay data, refers to data about data. It primarily describes the properties of data, supporting functions such as indicating storage locations, historical data, resource discovery, and file records. Metadata acts as an electronic catalog, essential for describing and archiving data content or features to facilitate data retrieval.

Network Resource Metadata Acquisition. For standard metadata structures, a P4-based programmable switch automatically generates a standard metadata structure during the packet processing flow. This structure records the switch's state information from when the packet enters the switch to when it is forwarded out to the corresponding port, including ingress port number, egress port number, queue length, ingress timestamp, and egress timestamp. This metadata can be directly acquired. Extended metadata includes information such as received packet count, received byte count, ingress port dropped byte count, egress port dropped byte count, network path, and link latency. They can be obtained through calculation based on the acquired basic metadata.

Collector Processes the Collected Metadata. For example, the "received byte count" metadata can be obtained by calculating the total received bytes from the previous historical time point to the current historical time point. For the "link latency" metadata, it can be derived by calculating the timestamps of the links traversed by the packet to determine the link latency.

Packet Parsing and Processing. In the packet parsing and processing flow of a P4-based programmable switch, a standard metadata structure is generated for each packet entering the pipeline. This structure records the switch's state information before the packet enters the switch to after it is forwarded out of the corresponding port, including the ingress port number, egress port number, queue length, ingress timestamp, egress timestamp, and other network node information. For telemetry tasks that require collecting the above node information, the relevant fields can be directly read from the standard metadata during packet processing and then inserted into the corresponding INT fields. This process completes the insertion of network state and resource telemetry information for the switch node, as illustrated in Fig. 2(a). For network information beyond the standard metadata, we consider using the local controller of the switch to pass it into the P4 switch by issuing P4 table entries. The telemetry scheme for network information beyond the standard metadata is illustrated in Fig. 2(b).

3.3 Anomaly Monitoring Mechanism Based on Network Telemetry

To overcome the limitations of traditional active and passive monitoring, which struggle with timely anomaly detection and recovery in large-scale data centers, this paper proposes an unsupervised anomaly detection algorithm based on graph attention network reinforcement learning based on network telemetry. This method accurately pinpoints anomaly locations, ensuring transmission performance.

This method achieves accurate, business-level detection of network anomalies and faults by predefining events for various application queues involved in end-to-end transmission, ensuring comprehensive and precise monitoring. All switch nodes in the end-to-end path are considered monitoring targets.

3.4 Quick Rerouting Mechanism Based on Backup Paths

Network node or link failures can disrupt service flows. Traditional routing algorithms have long convergence times and cannot quickly perform on-demand scheduling, resulting in poor user-level transmission performance. Each subtask can have multiple next-hop alternatives, allowing the construction of multiple backup routes to restore services.

In data centers, simultaneous rerouting of multiple services can disrupt computational and network resources, affecting stability. Hence, rational planning and the quick selection of backup routes are crucial to ensuring business reliability [13]. This paper uses a fast rerouting method based on backup paths, leveraging telemetry-derived insights into business and resource states to provide precise guidance for alternative path planning and quick rerouting decisions.

4   System and Functional Design

4.1   System Architecture Design

The system architecture design is shown in Fig. 3. The telemetry control subsystem flexibly enables or disables telemetry functions based on actual service needs. For critical business traffic, telemetry can be instantly activated for real-time network monitoring, ensuring high reliability and service quality. Conversely, for non-critical business or low-traffic periods, telemetry can be disabled to reduce resource overhead, reducing the processing burden on network devices.

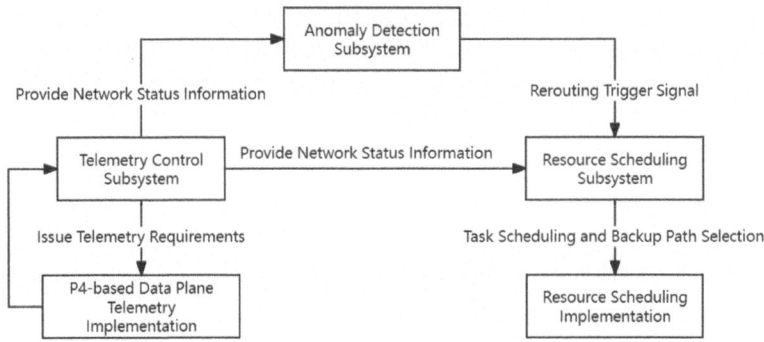

Fig. 3. System architecture.

P4-based data plane telemetry customizes packet processing logic using the P4 programming language, embedding telemetry information directly into packets for real-time, fine-grained network status monitoring.

The anomaly detection subsystem monitors the network environment in real-time and detects anomalies, initiating rerouting signals when necessary. This subsystem interacts with the anomaly monitoring front-end and the programmable data plane to acquire real-time network status information, quickly identifying issues such as increased latency, packet loss, and abnormal bandwidth utilization. Upon receiving rerouting signals, the Task Scheduling Subsystem activates the path rerouting mechanism, adjusting data packet transmission paths to avoid

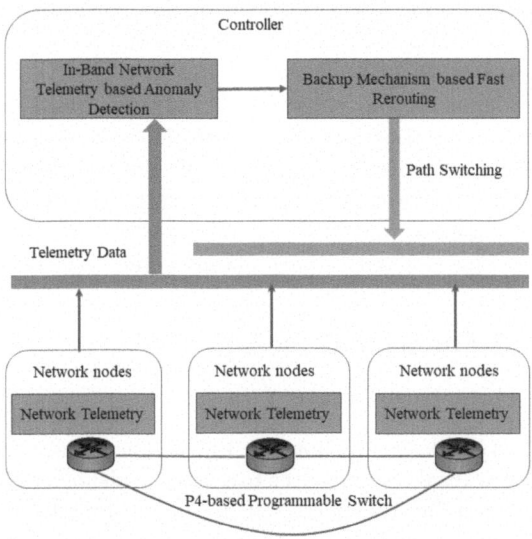

Fig. 4. The core function diagram of the experimental platform.

affected network nodes or links, ensuring data transmission continuity and stability. The resource scheduling function translates planning schemes into scheduling instructions supported by the experimental system's hardware facilities. The platform is based on the P4 programmable data plane provided by the bmv2 experimental platform.

4.2   System Functional Design

This subsection introduces the main functional design of the system, including in-band telemetry, anomaly detection, and resource scheduling functions. The core functional architecture of the experimental platform is shown in Fig. 4.

In-Band Telemetry Function. The in-band telemetry function mainly includes two parts: telemetry demand management and telemetry implementation, as shown in Fig. 5. The telemetry task management function encompasses the configuration, modification, issuance, activation, and suspension of telemetry tasks, ultimately handing over the execution to switches deployed in facilities to implement telemetry. The telemetry implementation function includes the implementation on network node devices, which mainly refers to the data plane telemetry function based on the P4 data plane, as well as the telemetry collector function.

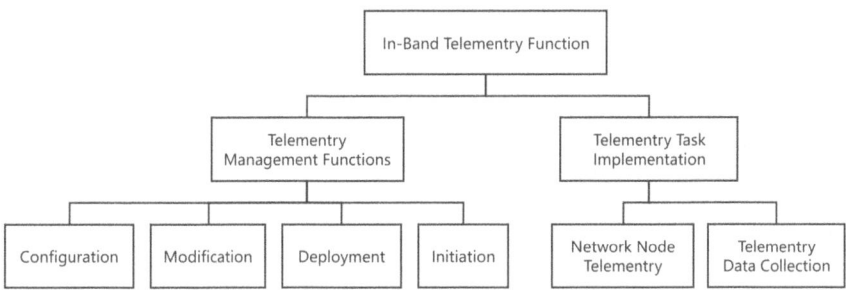

Fig. 5. In-Band Telemetry Function.

Anomaly Detection Function. The anomaly detection function analyzes network state anomalies based on telemetry data. It primarily includes the preprocessing of telemetry data, converting it into a format that the anomaly detection algorithm module can handle, as shown in Fig. 6. The anomaly detection algorithm then performs real-time anomaly detection based on the processed data. Upon detecting an anomaly, the anomaly information management function records the anomalous events and notifies other relevant modules, such as the frontend, to display the latest anomaly information. Additionally, relevant anomalies trigger the resource scheduling function, activating the backup path switching to implement rerouting.

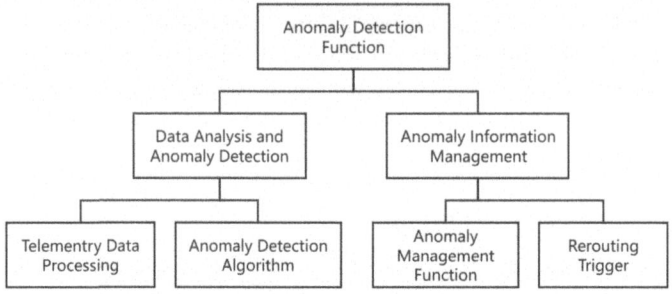

Fig. 6. Anomaly detection function.

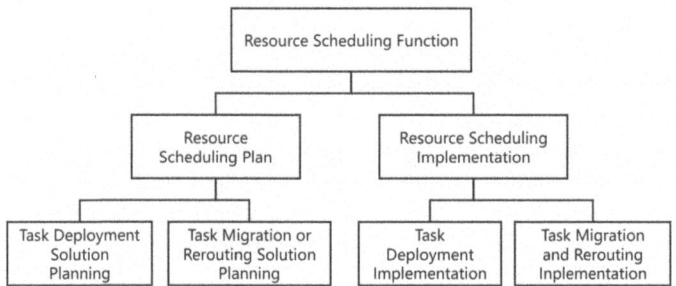

Fig. 7. Resource scheduling function.

Resource Scheduling Function. The resource scheduling function is primarily based on the network resource status data obtained from telemetry, as well as the business structure and resource demand data. Initially, it plans the deployment of business tasks, assigning each subtask to the appropriate nodes for execution. Figure 7 shows the resource scheduling function composition. During the operation of the business, if anomalies in node or link resource status occur, the resource scheduling function will reroute or migrate the tasks to ensure the quality of service.

5   Implementation and Results

The functions of the implemented platform are shown in Fig. 7. They include integrated monitoring, telemetry management, telemetry data analysis, anomaly detection, and platform management.

Figure 8 displays the integrated monitoring interface. The left side shows the resource status of the device, including node status and network status. The middle section shows the status of business operation, showing the end-to-end flow of business across the network, the current telemetry tasks in the system, and the latest telemetry data. Simultaneously, the Integrated monitoring

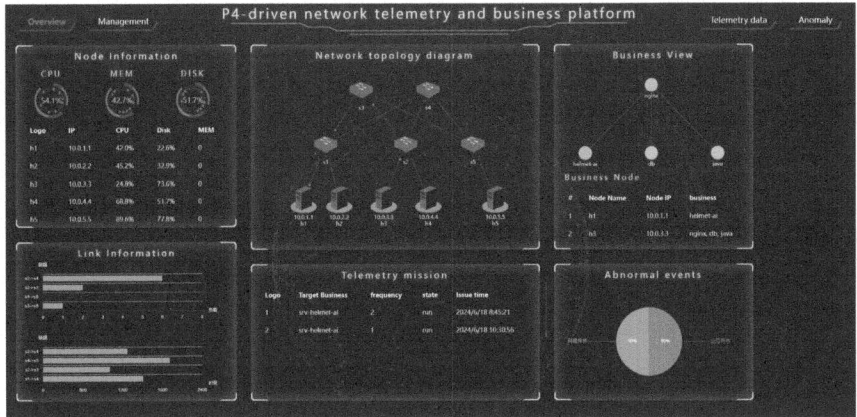

Fig. 8. Integrated monitoring interface.

interface also displays the detected anomalies during telemetry. On the right side, users can select a business and view its flow information within the network, as well as the resource information of the nodes and links it passes through.

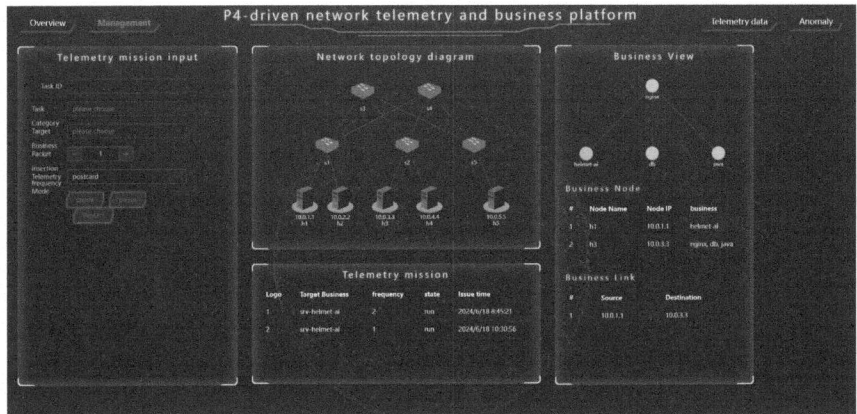

Fig. 9. Telemetry management interface.

The telemetry management interface, as shown in the Fig. 9, primarily displays fine-grained, business-oriented telemetry. It enables lifecycle management of telemetry tasks, including creation, initiation, and suspension, among other management functions. Additionally, it allows users to set the frequency of telemetry packet insertion.

The anomaly management interface, as shown in the Fig. 10, primarily displays the anomalies detected by the system. It provides statistics on the types of anomalies affecting nodes, links, and business operations. The interface lists anomaly information from newest to oldest, with the rightmost section showing the current facility anomalies. Users can also select a target business to display the flow direction of its traffic.

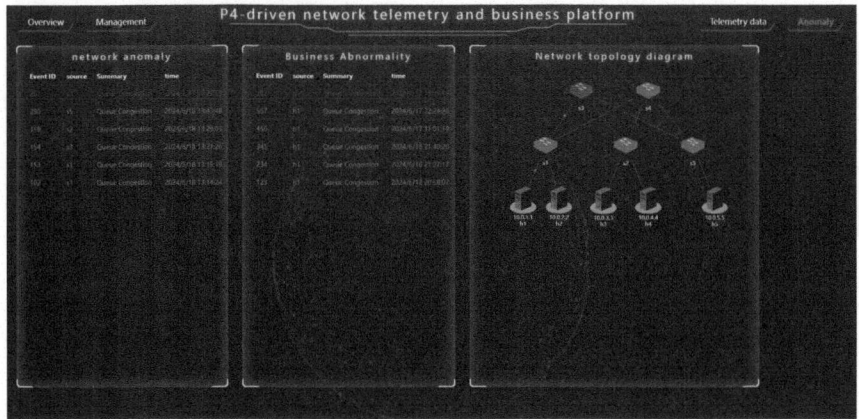

Fig. 10. Anomaly management interface.

6   Conclusion

The paper employs a P4-driven network telemetry and resource scheduling platform, leveraging the customizable P4 data plane to obtain fine-grained telemetry data during packet forwarding. The fine-grained on-demand telemetry mechanism selects critical business operations for detailed monitoring, collects rich telemetry metadata through the P4 data plane, and uses AI techniques for anomaly detection and rapid fault localization. A quick rerouting mechanism based on backup paths ensures rapid network service recovery. As technology continues to improve, the P4-driven network telemetry and resource scheduling platform will demonstrate robust advantages and broad application prospects in various fields.

Acknowledgments. This work was supported by National Natural Science Foundation of China (U22B2031) and China Fundamental Research Funds for the Central Universities (2024RC05), partially supported by JSPS KAKENHI (JP22K11989, JP24K14910), and JST, PRESTO (JPMIPR21P3), Japan JIST ASPIRE (JPM-JAP2344), the Soroptimist Japan Foundation. This work was also supported by the China Scholarship Council (202306470058).

References

1. Tan, L.Z.: An understanding of in-band network telemetry. SDNLAB. https://www.sdnlab.com/23822.html. Accessed 23 July 2024
2. Yuan, G., Dong, D., Qi, X.: MPICC: multi-path INT-based congestion control in data-center networks. In: IFIP International Conference on Network and Parallel Computing, pp. 256–268. Springer International Publishing, Cham (2021)
3. Morton, A.: Active and passive metrics and methods (with hybrid types in-between). IETF, Fremont (2016). https://www.rfc-editor.org/rfc/rfc7799.html
4. Dai, M., Cheng, G., Zhou, Y.Y.: Survey on measurement methods in software-defined networking. Ruan Jian Xue Bao/J. Softw. **30**(6), 1853–1874 (2019). (in Chinese with English abstract)
5. Bifulco, R., Rétvári, G.: A survey on the programmable data plane: abstractions, architectures, and open problems. In: Proceedings of the 19th IEEE Int'l Conference on High Performance Switching and Routing (HPSR), pp. 1–7. IEEE, Bucharest (2018). https://doi.org/10.1109/HPSR.2018.8850761
6. Han, S., Jang, S., Choi, H., Lee, H., Pack, S.: Virtualization in programmable data plane: a survey and open challenges. IEEE Open J. Commun. Soc. **1**, 527–534 (2020)
7. Bosshart, P., et al.: P4: programming protocol-independent packet processors. ACM SIGCOMM Comput. Commun. Rev. **44**(3), 87–95 (2014)
8. Chowdhury, S.R., Boutaba, R., François, J.: Lint: accuracy-adaptive and lightweight in-band network telemetry. In: 2021 IFIP/IEEE International Symposium on Integrated Network Management (IM), pp. 349–357. IEEE
9. Fu, M., Liu, Q., Liu, J.: A learning-based service function chain early fault diagnosis mechanism based on in-band network telemetry. IEICE Trans. Inf. Syst. **105**(2), 344–354 (2022)
10. Zhang, C., Dong, M., Ota, K.: Fine-grained management in 5G: DQL based intelligent resource allocation for network function virtualization in C-RAN. IEEE Trans. Cogn. Commun. Netw. **6**(2), 428–435 (2020)
11. Zhou, R., Dong, D., Huang, S., Zhou, Z.: Taming congestion and latency in low-diameter high-performance datacenters. In: Network and Parallel Computing: 18th IFIP WG 10.3 International Conference, NPC 2021, Paris, France, 3–5 November 2021, Proceedings 18, pp. 229–242 (2021)
12. Dong, M., Ota, K., Liu, A., Guo, M.: Joint optimization of lifetime and transport delay under reliability constraint wireless sensor networks. IEEE Trans. Parallel Distrib. Syst. **27**(1), 225–236 (2015)
13. Misa, C., Durairajan, R., Rejaie, R., Willinger, W.: DynATOS: a network telemetry system for dynamic traffic and query workloads. I IEEE/ACM Trans. Netw. (2024)

L²SCD: Low-Latency Serverless Computing Dispatcher via Programmable Network Hardware

Song Liu, Yangyu Luo, Jiapei Xu, Xinjing Yuan$^{(\boxtimes)}$, and Jianzhong Zhang

College of Computer Science, and DISSec, Nankai University, Tianjin, China
1120190174@mail.nankai.edu.cn

Abstract. The serverless computing dispatcher receives many requests in user space and distributes them to worker nodes. These requests traverse between kernel space and user space, which increases the dispatching latency. For workflows with extremely short execution times that are invoked thousands of times per second, this latency significantly affects their completion time. Therefore, minimizing dispatching latency is crucial to ensuring the responsiveness of workflows. Drawing on the capabilities of modern programmable network devices, we introduce a serverless computing dispatcher that runs on DPU and programmable switches. At the DPU, the dispatcher uses DPDK to extract request information and add it to the packet header. At the programmable switch, the dispatcher executes the dispatching algorithm and forwards the request to the appropriate function at line speed, avoiding the request in the kernel space and user space transmission time and reducing scheduling latency. Experiments demonstrate that, in high concurrency scenarios, **L²SCD** significantly reduces the average and P99 latency of single function invoking, improving performance by 15× and 27×, compared to two baselines on average, respectively.

Keywords: Serverless · Cloud Computing · In-Network Computing

1 Introduction

Serverless computing is one of the most widely used paradigms in cloud computing. Currently, several commercial cloud service providers, including AWS Lambda [1], Azure Functions [2], and Google Cloud Functions [3], provide serverless computing services. Moreover, this paradigm is widely applied in domains such as machine learning [4], video processing [5], and the Internet of Things [6]. This paradigm decomposes a monolithic application into loosely coupled functions, organized into workflows and hosted in containers. Developers are relieved from managing infrastructure like servers and virtual machines, allowing them to focus on implementing the application and reducing operational overhead.

© IFIP International Federation for Information Processing 2025
Published by Springer Nature Switzerland AG 2025
X. Chen et al. (Eds.): NPC 2024, LNCS 15527, pp. 360–370, 2025.
https://doi.org/10.1007/978-981-96-2830-8_28

Serverless computing is rapidly developing and attracting substantial attention from both industry and academia.

However, serverless computing still faces several challenges, among which end-to-end latency is particularly critical, especially in latency-sensitive scenarios [7]. In addition to the latency required for function execution, the end-to-end latency in serverless computing primarily consists of cold start and request dispatching. In a serverless computing system, the dispatcher is responsible for invoking functions. For each workflow request, the dispatcher triggers function invocations multiple times, depending on the number of functions included in the workflow. Upon receiving a user request or a packet containing a function's return value, the dispatcher invokes the corresponding function. For example, in a workflow composed of n chained functions, a single request triggers at least $2n+1$ times network stack traversals by the dispatcher. This characteristic significantly increases the dispatcher's load. Furthermore, the dispatchers of current mainstream serverless computing platforms [8,9,11] run in the user space of the operating system, and their processing speed depends on the server's CPU. Although server CPUs can perform complex computations at high speed, when handling a large number of scheduling tasks, the frequent traversal of data packets containing user requests or function return values through the kernel network stack increases the CPU load, leading to a significant increase in request processing latency. For workflows with execution times of only a few hundred milliseconds, the dispatcher's latency often becomes the main source of end-to-end latency under high concurrent request loads [10,12]. Experiments on Knative [11] and OpenWhisk [8] show that when performing stress tests with a request rate of 1K requests per second (RPS) on a workflow containing only a single function, the average dispatching latency on both platforms approaches 50 ms, with the network stack traversal time averaging 40 ms, accounting for approximately 80% of the total time. Moreover, the more functions a workflow has, the greater the dispatching latency [12].

Both academia and industry are exploring solutions at the software and hardware levels to mitigate the impact of packet traversal within the network protocol stack. For instance, SPRIGHT [13] applies eBPF and shared memory in serverless computing to reduce the number of layers packets that must traverse in the kernel network stack, thereby reducing CPU load. However, eBPF and shared memory are confined to a single server, meaning all function containers must be deployed on the same server, which restricts system flexibility. DPDK enables user-space execution of the kernel network stack, avoiding frequent context switching between kernel and user spaces, which reduces CPU resource wastage. Nevertheless, DPDK still occupies CPU resources even when no packets require processing. On the other hand, works such as EZpath [14], DeeP4R [15], and P4Hauler [16] utilize programmable switches to perform in-network computation, which prevents packets from traversing the kernel network stack, leading to significantly lower processing latency. Speedo [12] offloads the serverless computing dispatcher into a smart NIC, successfully avoiding the latency caused by the network protocol stack. However, Speedo assumes that communication between the dispatcher and function containers and between users and the dispatcher uses UDP protocol. Considering that TCP is the dominant protocol in data center and internet communications today, this assumption limits Speedo's deployment flexibility.

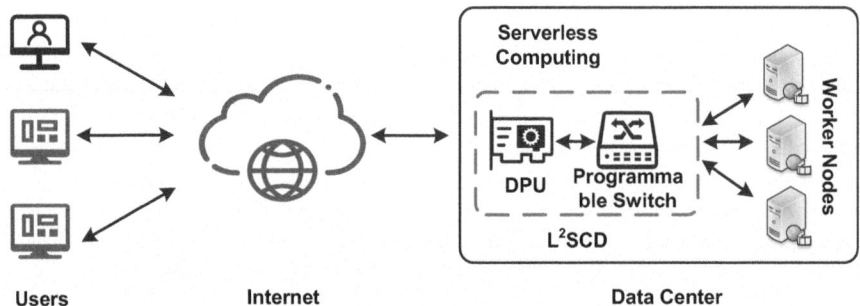

Fig. 1. L²SCD overview

Based on those insights, we propose a serverless computing dispatcher based on programmable network devices, named **L²SCD**, as shown in Fig. 1. An innovative approach in **L²SCD** decomposes the dispatcher into two components: a request parser and a request forwarder, deployed on the BlueField-2 DPU and the Tofino programmable switch. Utilizing a lightweight user-space protocol stack implemented with DOCA-DPDK, the request parser efficiently handles user connections, request decryption, and workflow ID extraction. After completing these tasks, the parser writes the workflow ID into the options field of the IP header and sends the modified packet to the request forwarder. The request forwarder, running on the Tofino programmable switch, is responsible for efficiently routing requests to the appropriate function container based on the workflow ID. Thanks to the advantages of the programmable switch, the dispatcher can perform routing at line speed, significantly reducing processing latency. The main contributions of this paper are summarized as follows:

- We propose the **L²SCD** serverless computing dispatcher, which splits the dispatcher into a request parser and a request forwarder, deployed on the DPU and programmable switch, respectively. This architecture leverages the strengths of both devices to reduce dispatching latency
- By implementing a lightweight user-space protocol stack with DOCA-DPDK development library in the request parser, we minimize kernel-mode overhead. Routing on the programmable switch further reduces CPU load and network processing latency.

Experiments demonstrate that, compared to traditional methods, **L²SCD** significantly reduces the average and P99 latency(tail latency) of individual function dispatching. In 5K RPS concurrency scenarios, **L²SCD** achieves performance improvements of 15× and 27× on average latency and 2× and 2.7× on P99 latency, compared to 2 different serverless systems, respectively.

2 Background

2.1 Serverless Computing Dispatcher

The Dispatcher plays an important role in serverless computing. When a serverless computing platform receives a user request and processes it through several steps: first, the platform performs preprocessing operations, including session establishment, authentication, and workflow lookup. Then, based on factors such as node load, data availability on the nodes, function affinity, and the startup cost of the function, the platform determines the worker node where the target function will be executed. These steps are collectively known as dispatch operations, and the component responsible for handling them is called the Dispatcher. When a function within a workflow is completed, the Dispatcher checks the function dependencies of that workflow to identify and invoke the next function to be executed. In serverless computing platforms, the Dispatcher runs in the operating system's user space, requiring function invocation requests to traverse the network protocol stack in kernel space. As request concurrency increases, this traversal leads to increased dispatching latency, which impacts the end-to-end latency of all workflows [10, 12].

2.2 Programmable Network Hardware

The programmable switch is highly efficient at processing packets at a line rate with immense throughput, which helps reduce latency and conserve CPU resources. It provides hardware acceleration for key data center applications such as distributed storage [17], cloud gateways [18], and network function virtualization [19]. However, their inability to handle encrypted data or establish TCP connections limits their applicability in serverless computing dispatcher, which require decryption and workflow ID extraction to function effectively. In contrast, Data Processing Units (DPU) like Nvidia BlueField-2 offer much greater programmability along with limited packet forwarding capabilities. DPU is designed to handle more complex computational tasks, making it well-suited for offloading tasks in serverless computing environments [20]. BlueField-2, in particular, is equipped with a general-purpose ARM CPU, a high-performance network interface card, and specialized hardware accelerators. This configuration allows it to run its own operating system and function similarly to an independent server. The flexibility and capability of DPUs like BlueField-2 make them a more suitable choice for managing serverless computing tasks compared to the more rigid programmable switch.

3 System Design and Implementation

L²SCD leverages the strengths of both programmable switches and DPU by innovatively splitting the dispatcher into the request parser and the request forwarder deployed on the DPU and the programmable switch. The architecture of

L²SCD is illustrated in Fig. 2. The request parser, running on the BlueField-2 DPU, uses a lightweight user-space kernel protocol stack to establish connections with users, decrypt requests, and add the workflow ID to the IP header's option field. This setup enables the request forwarder, located on the programmable switch, to obtain the workflow ID without decrypting the data packet, thereby facilitating efficient function invocation. The request forwarder collaborates with both the control plane and the data plane to achieve efficient scheduling operations. In this setup, the request parser only needs to process each workflow request once, while the request forwarder handles multiple invocations. Therefore, the request parser is better suited for deployment on the DPU, while the request forwarder is more appropriately placed on the programmable switch.

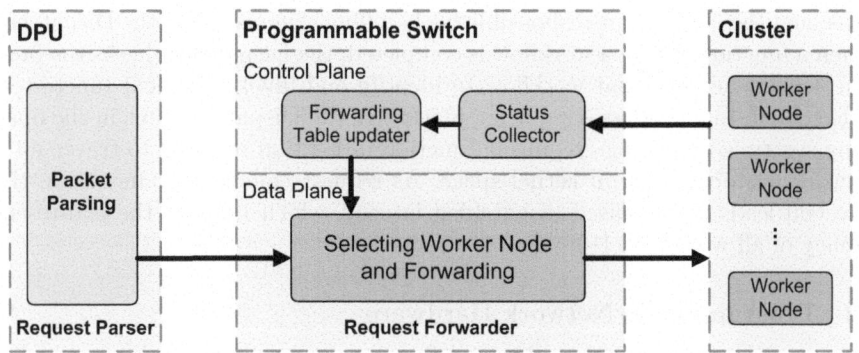

Fig. 2. **L²SCD** architecture

3.1 Request Parser in DPU

The request parser runs on the ARM CPU of the BlueField-2 DPU. It utilizes the DOCA-DPDK library to implement a lightweight user-space TCP/IP protocol stack, accelerating packet processing, as shown in Fig. 3. Since the request parser does not rely on the full kernel protocol stack for packet parsing, **L²SCD** reduces the overhead associated with kernel-mode context switching and interrupt handling by operating in user space. The polling mechanism of DOCA-DPDK further enhances packet processing speed. Although DOCA-DPDK requires dedicated CPU resources on the DPU during operation, it does not burden the server's CPU. When a user request arrives, the parser receives the user's data packet and establishes a TCP connection. It then parses the request to obtain the corresponding workflow ID. Next, the request parser establishes a TCP connection to a virtual IP address (the address of the request forwarder) and forwards the user request. During this process, the request parser inserts the workflow ID into the option field of the IP header of all packets and re-encapsulates these packets. This allows the request forwarder on the programmable switch to easily extract the workflow ID during the parsing stage and use it in subsequent processing without needing to perform additional decryption.

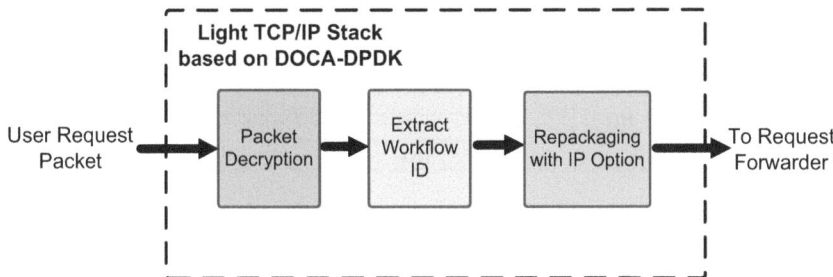

Fig. 3. The packet parsing process in DPU

Additionally, the request parser maintains two flow mapping table entries for each user request, corresponding to the external-facing IPv4 flow state machine and the internal system-facing IPv4 flow state machine. As packets enter the up and down stream ring buffers of the forwarder, they are handled by two different DPDK threads (optimized through thread affinity), which update the respective flow state machines. Utilizing the multi-threaded programming acceleration model of the DOCA-DPDK library, packets flowing in different directions are processed by independent, lock-free DPDK ring buffers (rte-ring buffers) to ensure system internal order and consistency. In a multi-core, high-speed network environment, memory barrier techniques are employed to synchronize multiple cores and threads, further enhancing performance and reducing latency.

L²SCD deploys the request parser on the DPU, addressing the issue of programmable switches being unable to decrypt and retrieve the workflow ID by rewriting packet headers. Additionally, it employs a lightweight user-space protocol stack, significantly reducing processing latency.

3.2 Request Forwarder in Programmable Switch

The request forwarder located on the programmable switch is divided into the control and data planes, as shown in Fig. 4. The data plane is primarily responsible for packet processing and forwarding, while the control plane collects load information from various worker nodes and executes the load balancing algorithm. Since the data plane cannot handle complex computational tasks, the control plane computes the results and updates the data plane's tables to achieve load balancing.

When a packet sent by the request parser arrives, the data plane first determines whether it is a regular packet or a load status update packet. If it is a load status update packet, the data plane forwards it to the control plane for

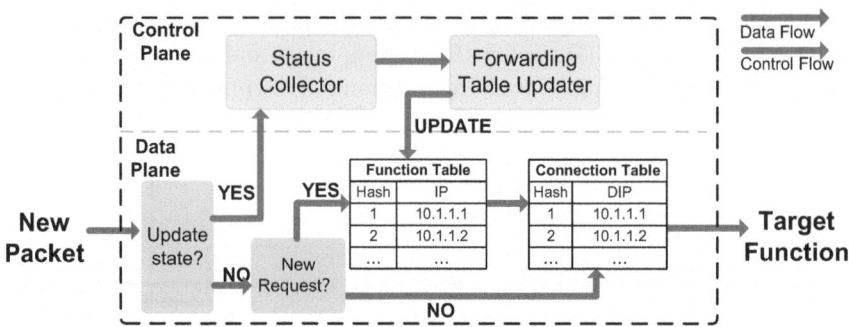

Fig. 4. Packet forwarding process in programmable switch

status updates. Due to the limitations of programmable switch programming, deploying complex load-balancing algorithms directly on the data plane is challenging. Additionally, relying solely on simple stateless load balancing on the programmable switch could lead to uneven server loads. Therefore, we deploy more complex load-balancing algorithms in the forwarding table updater on the control plane, which maintains the status of each server. Upon receiving status update information from the data plane, the control plane recalculates the load balancing strategy and updates the data plane's tables accordingly.

For regular packets, the data plane further determines whether they are request packets or response packets by examining the five-tuple. Response packets contain the final result of the workflow, and the data plane simply forwards them back to the original sender. Request packets include those sent by the user or by functions within the workflow to invoke other functions. To ensure continuity and consistency of requests, the data plane first calculates a hash value from the five-tuple fields in the request information to determine if the request is new. If it is a new request, the data plane records the hash value and uses it to look up the target server from a table.

After selecting the target server, the data plane stores the hash value along with the target server in a forwarding cache table to ensure that subsequent packets from the same request are sent to the same server. Even if the server pool or load-balancing strategy changes, all packets from the same connection will continue to be forwarded to the same server. When the connection ends, the data plane clears the relevant data from the forwarding cache table and deletes the cached hash value, allowing the next request to be treated as a new request and assigned a target server accordingly.

4   Evaluation

We implemented **L²SCD** on the NVIDIA BlueField-2 DPU and the Tofino programmable switch, then compared its dispatching performance against TinyFaaS and OpenFaaS. TinyFaaS is a lightweight serverless computing platform designed for the Internet of Things (IoT), while OpenFaaS is a mainstream open-source serverless computing platform. We selected workflows containing a single function as well as those with multiple function chains as our application workloads to demonstrate the scheduling superiority of **L²SCD** across different application types. The key parameter of interest is system load, measured by the number of requests per second (RPS) arriving at the system. Our primary evaluation metrics are scheduling latency and throughput. Dispatching latency refers to the net network path latency, excluding the CPU processing time on the worker nodes (i.e., function execution time), while throughput refers to the end-to-end system throughput.

The experimental topology is a dumbbell topology composed of a client, a server with a DPU, a programmable switch, and function servers. The client is connected to the DPU-equipped server via a 100G NIC. Both the client and the DPU-equipped server have the same configuration, with 16-core i7-10700 processors (2.9 GHz) and 32 GB of memory. The DPU-equipped server is connected to the function servers via the programmable switch. The function servers are equipped with 64-core Intel Xeon processors (2.3 GHz) and 256 GB of memory.

4.1 Single-Function Workflow

We initiated a single-function workflow request, gradually increasing the load while measuring the average and P99 latency as well as throughput at different load levels for the platforms under test.

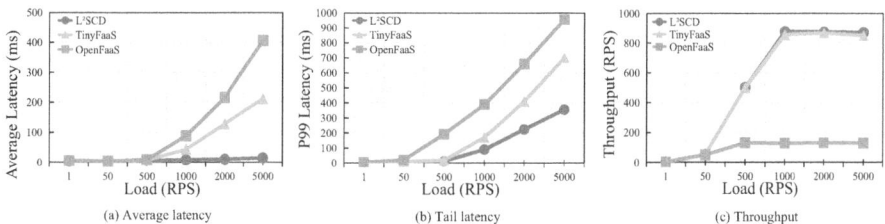

(a) Average latency   (b) Tail latency   (c) Throughput

Fig. 5. Dispatching latency and throughput for Single-Function Workflow

Figure 5 shows the comparisons of average latency, P99 latency, and throughput at different load levels between **L²SCD**, TinyFaaS, and OpenFaaS. **L²SCD** achieves comparable throughput to TinyFaaS after offloading. Our approach demonstrates more stable latency performance, with average latency remaining under 15 ms (14.19 ms) even at 5K RPS, whereas TinyFaaS, without offloading the dispatcher, experiences an average latency of 211.35 ms at the same load, a nearly 15-fold difference. Additionally, our method results in significantly lower P99 latency, with a P99 latency of 355 ms at 5K RPS, compared to 700 ms for TinyFaaS, representing approximately a 2x improvement. Furthermore, **L²SCD** shows a significant throughput advantage over OpenFaaS under high concurrency, with OpenFaaS saturating at 200 RPS. In comparison with OpenFaaS, our work exhibits a 27-fold reduction in average latency at 5K RPS, along with a 2.7-fold reduction in P99 latency.

4.2   Multi-Function Workflow

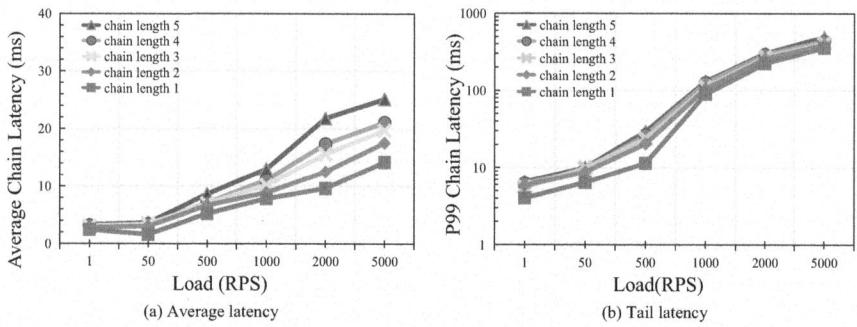

Fig. 6. Dispatching latency for Multi-Function Workflow

This section presents the performance of **L²SCD** in the context of work-flows. In a workflow or function invocation chain, dispatching latency accumulates across the sequence of functions triggered by a single user request. Here, we present the performance of our hardware Dispatcher when handling workflows. We deployed a simple chain of functions running no-op operations, gradually increasing the chain length from 1 to 5, and measured the scheduling latency. Figure 6 displays the results, showing that the length of the chain directly impacts the invocation latency. Nonetheless, the overall scheduling latency remains at an acceptable level. For a chain length of 5, our system achieves an average invocation latency of 25.13 ms, thanks to our ability to maintain very low latency for individual function invocations.

5   Conclusion

We present **L²SCD**, a low-latency serverless computing dispatcher built upon the BlueField-2 DPU and Tofino programmable switch. **L²SCD** effectively offloads dispatcher tasks from the server's CPU, minimizing the overhead associated with kernel-space traversals. Our evaluation demonstrates that **L²SCD** offers high performance on dispatching compared to TinyFaaS and OpenFaaS.

Acknowledgments. This work was supported in part by the National Natural Science Foundation of China (No. 62172241, No. 62402247).

References

1. AWS Lambda. https://aws.amazon.com/lambda
2. Azure Functions. https://azure.microsoft.com/en-au/products/functions
3. Google Cloud Functions. https://cloud.google.com/functions
4. Fu, Y., et al.: ServerlessLLM: low-latency serverless inference for large language models. In: 18th USENIX Symposium on Operating Systems Design and Implementation (OSDI 24), pp. 135–153 (2024)
5. Hou, B., Yang, S., Kuipers, F.A., Jiao, L., Fu, X.: Eavs: edge-assisted adaptive video streaming with fine-grained serverless pipelines. In: IEEE Conference on Computer Communications (INFOCOM 23), pp. 1–10 (2023)
6. Golec, M., Gill, S.S., Parlikad, A.K., Uhlig, S.: HealthFaaS: ai-based smart healthcare system for heart patients using serverless computing. IEEE Internet Things J. **10**(21), 18469–18476 (2023)
7. Szalay, M., Matray, P., Toka, L.: Real-time faas: towards a latency bounded serverless cloud. IEEE Trans. Cloud Comput. **11**(2), 1636–1650 (2022)
8. Openwhisk. https://openwhisk.apache.org/
9. Pfandzelter, T., Bermbach, D.: Tinyfaas: a lightweight faas platform for edge environments. In: IEEE International Conference on Fog Computing (ICFC 22), pp. 17–24 (2022)
10. Fuerst, A., Rehman, A., Sharma, P.: Ilúvatar: a fast control plane for serverless computing. In: Proceedings of the 32nd International Symposium on High-Performance Parallel and Distributed Computing (HPDC 23), pp. 267–280 (2023)
11. knative. https://knative.dev/docs
12. Daw, N., Bellur, U., Kulkarni, P.: Speedo: fast dispatch and orchestration of serverless workflows. In: Proceedings of the ACM Symposium on Cloud Computing (SOCC 22), pp. 585–599 (2022)
13. Qi, S., Monis, L., Zeng, Z., Wang, I.C., Ramakrishnan, K.K.: Spright: extracting the server from serverless computing! High-performance ebpf-based event-driven, shared-memory processing. In: Proceedings of the ACM SIGCOMM 2022 Conference, pp. 780–794 (2022)
14. Zha, Z., Wang, A., Guo, Y., Li, Q., Sun, K., Chen, S.: EZPath: expediting container network traffic via programmable Switches. In: IFIP Networking Conference (IFIP Networking 22) ,pp. 1–8 (2022)
15. Gupta, S., Gosain, D., Kwon, M., Acharya, H. B.: Deep4r: deep packet inspection in p4 using packet recirculation. In: IEEE Conference on Computer Communications (INFOCOM 23), pp. 1–10 (2023)
16. Tajbakhsh, H., Parizotto, R., Schaeffer-Filho, A., Haque, I.: P4Hauler: an accelerator-aware in-network load balancer for applications performance boosting. IEEE Trans. Cloud Comput. (2024)
17. Wang, Q., Lu, Y., Xu, E., Li, J., Chen, Y., Shu, J.: Concordia: distributed shared memory with in-network cache coherence. In: 19th USENIX Conference on File and Storage Technologies (FAST 21), pp. 277–292 (2021)
18. Pan, T., et al.: Sailfish: accelerating cloud-scale multi-tenant multi-service gateways with programmable switches. In: Proceedings of the 2021 ACM SIGCOMM 2021 Conference, pp. 194–206 (2021)

19. Chen, X., et al.: LightNF: simplifying network function offloading in programmable networks. In: 2021 IEEE/ACM 29th International Symposium on Quality of Service (IWQOS 21), pp. 1–10 (2021)
20. Choi, S., Shahbaz, M., Prabhakar, B., Rosenblum, M.: λ-nic: interactive serverless compute on smartnics. In: Proceedings of the ACM SIGCOMM 2019 Conference Posters and Demos, pp. 151–152 (2019)

LBoDSN: An In-Network Load Balancing Mechanism for Lossless Data Center Networks Based on Direct Switch Notification

Qingyu Shi[1,2]([✉]), Fangxue Jiang[1], Huang Huang[2], Xiaocui Li[1,2],
Chuang Li[1,2]([✉]), Wenzhi Cao[1,2], and Limei Liu[1,2]

[1] School of Advanced Interdisciplinary Studies, Hunan University of Technology
and Business, Changsha, China
qingyushi@hust.edu.cn, chuangli@hutb.edu.cn
[2] Xiangjiang Laboratory, Changsha, China

Abstract. With the extensive deployment of Remote Direct Memory Access (RDMA) in lossless data center networks (DCNs), enhancing the RDMA load balancing performance for distributed AI training and HPC applications becomes particularly critical. However, existing load balancing schemes either suffer difficulty in responding to congestion in sub-RTT time, or cannot accurately detect and reroute flows that are on the verge of creating path congestion for Priority-based Flow Control (PFC) enabled lossless DCNs. In this paper, we propose LBoDSN, an in-network load balancing mechanism for lossless DCNs based on direct swtich notification, to address above challenges. LBoDSN monitors ingress queue length evolution at destination switches to predict the triggering time of PFC pause, and accurately identifies congested flows based on the congestion contribution level before PFC pause, then further proactively sends the flow congestion notification (FCN) to source switches for fast rerouting. The FCN contains a flow ID that identifies the congested flow, and a path ID that identifies the target path to which the congested flow will be rerouted. And after rerouting, the Congestion Notification Packet (CNP) of the old path is selectively discarded at source switches to improve transmission performance, while out-of-order packets are reordered at the destination switch. The experimental results show that under realistic workloads, LBoDSN achieves 9–64% and 20–80% better than CONGA for the average and tail Flow Completion Times (FCTs), respectively. Compared with ConWeave, LBoDSN achieves around 8% better performance for the average and tail FCTs while significantly reducing switch queue usage for reordering.

Keywords: Data center networks · Lossless networks · Network load balancing

© IFIP International Federation for Information Processing 2025
Published by Springer Nature Switzerland AG 2025
X. Chen et al. (Eds.): NPC 2024, LNCS 15527, pp. 371–382, 2025.
https://doi.org/10.1007/978-981-96-2830-8_29

1   Introduction

Modern data centers are typically using RoCEv2 [23] or InfiniBand [1] to construct RDMA lossless networks to support distributed storage, high-performance computing (HPC), and distributed AI training [4,5,7,12,20]. To further improve the transmission performance of lossless networks in data centers, researchers have proposed a series of transmission control and load balancing schemes to optimize the RDMA communication between servers [13,15,16,19]. Among them, the goal of load balancing schemes is to evenly distribute the network traffic between nodes across multiple paths, as there are multiple end-to-end paths between any two server racks in data center network topologies (e.g., leaf-spine). However, current studies have shown that Equal Cost Multiple Path (ECMP) forwarding [8], as the standard load balancing strategy in DCNs, falls short due to hash collisions and its inability to adapt to dynamic traffic [3,19,21]. Therefore, numerous schemes have proposed new load balancing mechanisms to optimize network performance, such as congestion sensing, packet spraying, flowlet scheduling, etc. Moreover, it is often necessary to consider the impact of PFC mechanism on the load balancing in lossless networks, where downstream network devices notify upstream network devices to pause/send packets based on the local queuing length through PFC pause/resume frames [9,10,19].

In recent years, though many schemes utilized in lossy networks in data centers, such as CONGA [3] and LetFlow [21], can improve the multi-path transmission efficiency in lossless networks, they easily aggravate PFC pausing and PFC congestion spreading without considering the PFC mechanism, leading to suboptimal performance. And thus some load balancing mechanisms for lossless networks have been implemented in programmable switches, greatly improving transmission performance by considering the PFC mechanism. Several schemes implemented in source switches perform load balancing based on probe information such as link utilization and delay (e.g., ConWeave [19]). Besides, some other schemes at destination switches monitor ingress queue length to predict the PFC pause time and actively notify the source switch to perform load balancing before PFC pause (e.g., RLB [9]).

However, current load balancing schemes for lossless network still have two drawbacks that lead to performance losses: 1) the schemes implemented in source switches usually takes one round-trip time (RTT) at least to perceive congestion signals and cannot timely respond to congestion; 2) the schemes monitoring congestion at destination switches do not accurately identify the congested flow causing path congestion and the congestion notification information sent to the source switch is not precise enough, which may reroute uncongested flows and cause suboptimal performance.

Therefore, we proposes a novel in-network load balancing mechanism for lossless DCNs using direct switch notification based on programable switches, denoted as LBoDSN, to address above challenges. LBoDSN monitors ingress queue length evolution at destination switches to predict the triggering time of PFC pause, and identifies congested flows based on the congestion contribution level before PFC pause, then further proactively sends the flow congestion notification (FCN) to source switches for fast rerouting. The FCN contains a flow ID that identifies which flow should be rerouted, and a path ID that identifies which path should be rerouted to. And after rerouting, the CNP (Congestion Notification Packet) [23] of the old path is selectively discarded at source switches to improve transmission performance, while out-of-order packets are reordered at the destination switch. In summary, we have made three principal contributions:

- According to our analysis, we meticulously analyze the limitations of existing load balancing schemes for lossless networks in data centers and reveal the need for faster and more precise load balancing mechanism.
- We propose LBoDSN, a lossless network load balancing mechanism for data centers based on DSN. LBoDSN enables quick sensing of the congested flow and the target path to which the congested flow will be rerouted before PFC pause. LBoDSN provides sub-RTT rerouting time and more precise rerouting for RDMA flows. Besides, after rerouting, LBoDSN prevents the impact of CNPs of the old path on the transmission rate and guarantees packet reordering.
- We implemented LBoDSN using NS3 [2], a widely-used network simulation platform, and conducted a performance comparison against existing lossless network load balancing schemes including CONGA, LetFlow, DRILL, and ConWeave. The experimental results demonstrate the effectiveness of LBoDSN in reducing the FCT and the switch queue usage.

2   Related Work and Motivation

Existing lossless networks in PFC-enabled data centers usually employ the hop-by-hop flow control mechanism. When the switch ingress port queue length exceeds the PFC pause threshold, it sends a PFC pause message to the upstream switch's relevant port (or priority queue) to pause data transmission, and when the ingress port queue length decreases to the PFC resume threshold, it sends a PFC resume message to the upstream switch to resume data transmission. However, as PFC pause is based on ports or queues, the coarse-grained feedback on congestion can lead to issues such as congestion spreading [9,19]. Although existing load balancing schemes are capable of sensing PFC pause events, they still have negative impacts on performance due to their untimely and imprecise in sensing congestion and making load balancing decisions.

Link utilization-based load balancing schemes (e.g., CONGA [3], HULA [11]) cannot sense the PFC pause/resume message, where a path with low link utilization due to PFC pausing maybe classified as a good path without congestion. Delay-based load balancing schemes (e.g., Hermes [22], ConWeave [19]) need one RTT time at least to receive congestion signals and the probe reply can be blocked by PFC pause, which causes slow responds to congestion. Some solutions (e.g., Proteus [10]) sense path states using RTT and link utilization at the source switch to guide initial path selection and makes more fine-grained rerouting decisions using sub-RTT level signals (e.g., cumulative sojourn time) when encountering PFC pause events. Moreover, some schemes implemented in destination switches (e.g., RLB [9]) can predict the trigger time of PFC pause to sense congestion faster than the above described schemes. However, current mechanisms cannot distinguish which flows cause path congestion before PFC pause, and may schedule uncongested flows to other suboptimal paths, resulting in performance loss.

Furthermore, the existing schemes for lossless DCNs do not pay attention to the impact of the congestion feedback signal CNP (Congestion Notification Packet) [23] from multiple paths on the transmission rate after rerouting. Because the sender with DCQCN enabled adjusts sending rate according to CNPs from the receiver, the flow sending rate after rerouting can be affected by CNPs generated before rerouting.

Therefore, it is very necessary to study how to sense congestion within one RTT time and reroute flows leading to path congestion before PFC pause, as well as to avoid the effect of CNPs on transmission rate of old path. In this paper, we proposes LBoDSN to solve above problems. The design of LBoDSN is detailed in the next section.

3   Design

3.1   Overview of LBoDSN

LBoDSN is an in-network load balancing mechanism based on programable switches for lossless DCNs. LBoDSN incorporates congestion sensing at the destination switch to identify congested flows and directly notifies the source switch to perform load balancing, as shown in Fig. 1. The algorithm of this scheme is specifically deployed on both source and destination switches. It consists of two main components, namely congestion perception and rerouting decision module at the destination switch and rerouting execution module at the source switch.

The Congestion perception and rerouting decision module encompasses several key functions: predicting PFC pauses, identifying congested flows, selecting rerouting path, and sending flow congestion notification (FCN). The FCN contains a flow ID that identifies the congested flow, and a path ID that identifies the target path to which the congested flow will be rerouted. The functions of rerouting execution module include the allocation of new flows, management of FCNs, and handling of CNPs. Besides, LBoDSN reroutes congested flows to specified paths according to the information of FCNs received at the source switch.

3.2   Congestion Perception and Rerouting Decision

This module initially checks whether the ingress queue length exceeds a given threshold at the current rate and only performs predictions when network congestion occurs. Upon detecting congestion, LBoDSN follows a streamlined process: (1) it predicts if the ingress queue length exceeds a predefined threshold below the PFC pause level; (2) activates the congestion flow identification mechanism; and (3) dispatches a direct notification to the upstream source switch.

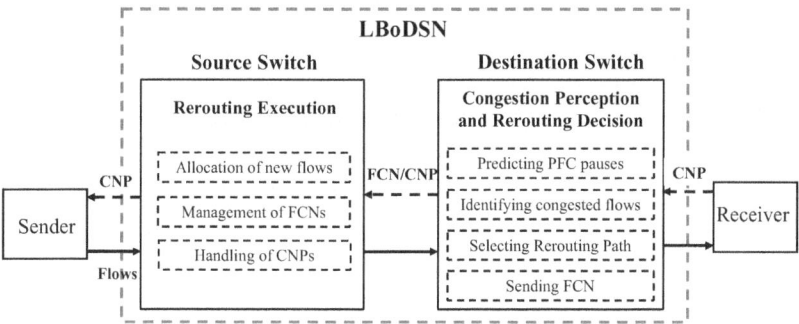

Fig. 1. LBoDSN overview.

Predicting PFC Pauses. This function predicts the onset of PFC pause by monitoring the rate of increase in the ingress queue length at the destination switch. Specifically, the scheme leverages flow monitoring techniques on programmable switches to obtain data such as link latency and queue length. We assume that an $n : 1$ ratio is used to simulate the incast scenario and n flows are forwarded simultaneously from the source switch to the same destination switch. LBoDSN triggers PFC pause prediction mechanism after t_d that is the link delay for transmitting FCNs from the destination switch to the source switch when the ingress queue length increases to Q_{th}. The packet arrival rate at the destination switch ingress port can be denoted as λ_t and the forwarding rate as μ_t. The queue length threshold Q_{th} is calculated as Eq. (1) shows:

$$Q_{th} = (Q_{PFC} - (\lambda_t - \mu_t) \cdot t_d) \cdot \varepsilon \tag{1}$$

where Q_{PFC} is the threshold for triggering a PFC pause in the ingress port queue of the destination switch, ε is a multiplicative factor between 0 and 1. When C is the link bandwidth, we can predict the range of the Q_{th} value, which can be expressed in Eq. (2):

$$Q_{th} \in [\lfloor t_d \cdot C \rfloor, \lfloor (Q_{PFC} - C \cdot t_d) \cdot \varepsilon \rfloor] \tag{2}$$

In our experimental results, the above Q_{th} threshold is effective and robust in our simulations when we set the multiplicative variable ε around 0.8.

Identifying Congested Flows. When the ingress queue length of the destination switch increases to Q_{th}, the congested flow causing a large accumulation of the queue length are immediately identified. Specifically, inspired by FlowSail [14], LBoDSN calculates the flow congestion contribution threshold F_{cc} at the destination switch to identify the congested flow as Eq. (3) shows, where each flow is assigned the same weight, i.e.:

$$F_{cc} = Q \gg \lceil \log_2 Q_T[qInd].fNum \rceil \tag{3}$$

where Q represents the transient ingress queue length of the destination switch, Q_T is the queue table maintained with the switch, $qInd$ is the index of the indicated queue, and $fNum$ is the number of flows in this queue. When the queued size of a flow in current ingress queue exceeds the flow congestion contribution threshold F_{cc}, this flow is identified as a congested flow with a high contribution to the imminent triggering of the PFC pause, and its $flowID$ is recorded as one of the carry information for the next FCN. Besides, since it takes at least one RTT time for the FCN to arrive at the source switch and the packet after rerouting to arrive at the destination switch, LBoDSN generates at most one new FCN in one RTT time for the same ingress port at the destination switch to ensure stable load balancing performance.

Selecting Rerouting Path. In the next step, LBoDSN selects the rerouting path for the congested flow at the destination switch. Concretely, LBoDSN leverages the well-known power-of-two-choices technique [17,22] to avoid the herd behavior, and LBoDSN defines the new overall path delay T_d to sense the least load path, which is expressed in Eq. (4):

$$T_d = T_{path} + T_{PFC} \tag{4}$$

where T_{path} represents the original path delay monitored by the destination switch and T_{PFC} represents the delay required for PFC resume. When the congested flow is identified, calculating the overall path delay T_d for each path. For the ingress queue that is in PFC pause, based on the queue length trend and the PFC resume threshold, we can predict the time required for PFC resume, that is:

$$T_{PFC} = \frac{Q - Q^*_{PFC}}{-\Delta L} + T_{re\_flight} \tag{5}$$

where Q is the transient queue length of ingress port of destination switch, Q^*_{PFC} is the PFC resume threshold of ingress queue at the destination switch, and T_{re_flight} measured by INT [15] is the time for the PFC resume frame to arrive at the source switch. ΔL denotes the growth gradient of the ingress queue length of the destination switch. For flows that are not in the PFC pause path, T_{PFC} is 0.

Sending Congestion Notification. When LBoDSN has predicted the impending PFC pause and identifies the congested flow and rerouting path at the destination switch, the next step is to send the FCN to the source switch, which can be generated by packet mirroring replication of the programmable switch. The FCN packet contains a flow ID that identifies the congested flow, a path ID that identifies the target path to which the congested flow will be rerouted, and a one-bit congestion tag with value of 1. If the ingress queue length drops below the Q_{th} threshold and the queue growth gradient is small, LBoDSN sends the FCN containing the current path ID and the congestion tag with value of 0 to the source switch to inform this path is in an uncongested state.

3.3   Rerouting Execution

Rerouting execution implemented at the source switch needs to mange new flows and the congestion feedback information of FCNs and CNPs. The new flow

Table 1. Outcome of path classification using FCN and link utilization.

FCN	Link Utilizaiton	Reason	Characterization
No FCN or FCN with a congestion tag of 0	Low/Moderate	No PFC pause and under-utilized link	Uncongested path
	High	Fully-utilized link with no congested flow	
FCN with a congestion tag of 1	Low/Moderate	Prone to cause PFC pause and congestion is easing	Undetermined path
FCN with a congestion tag of 1	High	Prone to cause PFC pause and congestion is happening	Congested path

selects its transmission path according to a random algorithm based on path classification. Besides, the congested flow is identified by the FCN, which contains its flow ID and a path ID that identifies the target path to which it will be rerouted. Moreover, LBoDSN selectively discards CNPs of old path at the source switch to prevent the CNP generated by the old path affecting the transmission efficiency of flows in the new path after rerouting.

Allocation of New Flows. When the source switch selects paths for new flows arriving at the switch, LBoDSN leverages a random selection method based on path classification to evenly allocate new flows to different paths as much as possible. Firstly, we classify parallel paths into the following three types based on the congestion feedback of FCNs and link utilization: (1) uncongested path that has not received an FCN or has received an FCN with a congestion tag of 0; (2) undetermined path that has received an FCN with a congestion tag of 1 and has low or moderate link utilization; (3) congested path that has received an FCN with a congestion tag of 1 and has full link utilization. Table 1 summarizes the outcome of path classification and the reasons behind them.

For each new flow, LBoDSN first tries to randomly select a rerouting path from the set of uncongested paths. If the set is empty, LBoDSN further checks the set of undetermined paths. If that fails as well, LBoDSN makes a random selection of a path from among those possessing the three least loaded local queues.

Management of FCNs. When the network is congested, the source switch generally receives FCNs from the destination switch. The rerouting execution module will manage FCNs according to the relative congestion tag value. If the congestion tag value is 1, the path will be recorded as having received the FCN with a congestion tag of 1 as Table 1 shows. Besides, LBoDSN extracts flow id fx and path id Px from the FCN, modifies the flow fx routing path to Px, and the subsequent packets of flow fx will be forwarded from path Px. If the congestion tag value is 0, the flow is recorded as a state of cleared congestion, and when all the congested flows in this path have entered the state of cleared congestion, the path state will be recorded as having received the FCN with a congestion tag of 0.

Handling of CNPs. After rerouting, LBoDSN selectively discards CNPs of old paths (denoted as stale CNPs in the following sections) at source switches to improve transmission performance, while out-of-order packets are reordered at the destination switch like ConWeave [19].

First, we distinguish stale CNPs through a direct notification from destination switches. Specifically, after rerouting, the source switch adds a one-bit special tag to the tail of the first packet on the new path as a notification message based on the INT technique [15]. When the notification message reaches the destination switch, the destination switch firstly replicates the message by using the ingress mirroring technique and mapping its source-destination IP address, while removing the payload and adding the same tag with the source packet to generate a notification reply message to the source switch. When the next CNP of this flow arrives at the source switch, verify whether its notification reply message has been returned. If not, the CNP is regarded as a stale CNP and will be selectively discarded at the source switch. Otherwise, it will be forwarded to the sender.

The above selectively discarding stale CNPs is applied to avoid that congestion control algorithms over-adjust the flow rate in new paths after rerouting. Considering that the sender under the DCQCN protocol reduces the flow rate based on CNPs and increases the flow rate according to timers and byte counters, discarding all stale CNPs will result in excessive growth of the flow rate, which causes congestion on the new path. And not discarding stale CNPs at all will result in too low flow rate, which causes under-utilization of bandwidth on the new path. Therefore, we implement a model that discards stale CNPs based on probability to smooth the flow rate control at the sender side. Firstly, calculate the average $avgCNP$ of stale CNPs, as Eq. (6) shows:

$$avgCNP = (1 - w_q) \cdot avgCNP + w_q \cdot W \qquad (6)$$

where W is actual number of stale CNPs for this flow, $w_q (0 \leqslant w_q \leqslant 1)$ is a weight value. Meanwhile, we set a threshold T and calculate the discarding probability p of stale CNPs, as Eq. (7) shows:

$$p = \frac{\max P \cdot avgCNP}{T} \qquad (7)$$

where $maxP$ is the maximum discarding probability of stale CNPs. When the number of stale CNPs does not exceed the threshold T, the stale CNP is discarded with the discarding probability p, and the discarding probability p increases linearly with the number of arriving stale CNPs. When the number of stale CNPs reaches the threshold T, stale CNPs will be all discarded.

4   Evaluation

For performance evaluation, we compare LBoDSN with the state-of-the-art load balancing mechanisms to investigate the enhancement in performance with NS3 large-scale simulations [2].

Topology: We construct an 8×8 leaf-spine network topology in NS3, featuring 100 Gbps links and a server count of 128 (16 servers for each leaf switch).

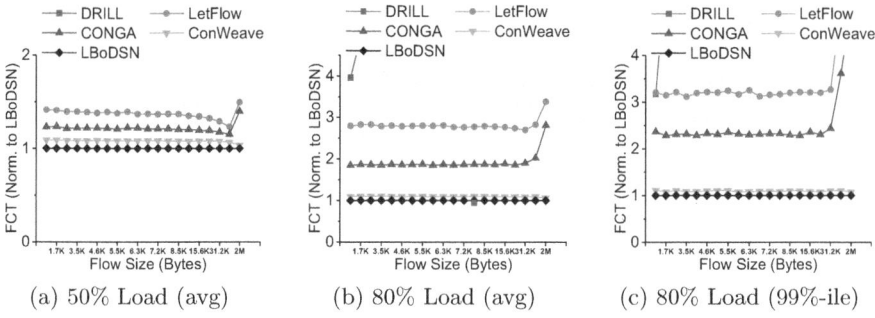

Fig. 2. FCT for the AliCloud storage workload (normalized to LBoDSN).

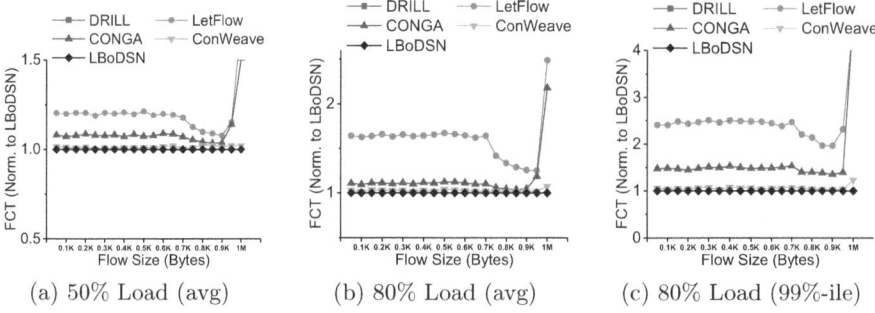

Fig. 3. FCT for the Meta Hadoop workload (normalized to LBoDSN).

This design ensures eight distinct equal-cost paths between any host pair, interconnected through diverse switches. Consequently, we implement a 2:1 oversubscription ratio at the leaf level to meet standard configurations in common DCNs [3].

Workloads: We utilize two realistic workloads (AliCloud storage [15,19] and Meta Hadoop [18,19]) derived from operational data centers to simulate traffic dynamics for our evaluations. To replicate these workloads, we generate flows between randomly selected senders and receivers within various leaf switches, following Poisson processes.

Schemes Compared: We compare LBoDSN with ConWeave [19], CONGA [3], Letflow [21], and DRILL [6]. ConWeave performs fine-grained load balancing for RDMA flows in the switch and reorders the out-of-order packets through the in-network reordering mechanism. CONGA and LetFlow implements flowlet switching in the switches, where we choose a flowlet time gap of 100µs. DRILL employs per-packet load balancing based on local queue utilization in switches. In all schemes, we use DCQCN [23] as the standard congestion control scheme and PFC mechanism for lossless DCNs.

Metrics: Similar to previous work, we adopt the average and tail Flow Completion Time (FCT) as the principal metric for evaluating performance, where we normalize the FCT to LBoDSN in order to better visualize the results.

4.1 Reduction in FCT

We conducted experiments under average traffic loads of 50% and 80% in different workloads, corresponding to a moderately and highly congested network, respectively. We show the average and tail FCTs in Fig. 2 and Fig. 3. In some of the test results, the performance metrics for DRILL are omitted, as incorporating their FCTs would necessitate a large adjustment to the scale for proper representation.

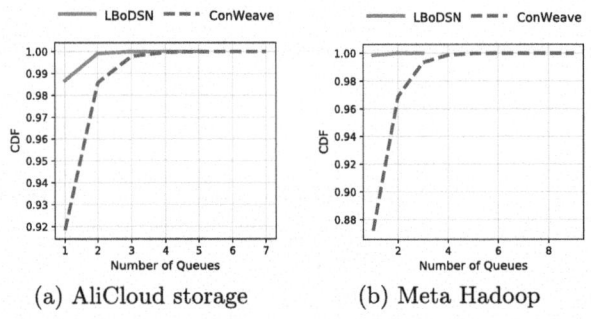

(a) AliCloud storage   (b) Meta Hadoop

Fig. 4. Number of queues usage per egress port (80% Avg.Load).

As Fig. 2 and Fig. 3 show, LBoDSN outperforms all other schemes. LBoDSN achieves around 8% better performance than ConWeave for the average and tail FCTs. LBoDSN predicts the triggering time of PFC pause and identifies congested flows based on the congestion contribution level before PFC pause at destinations, then further proactively sends FCNs to source switches for fast rerouting. ConWeave detects path congestion based on continuous RTT monitoring at source switches and does not distinguish the congestion state of different flows on the congested path to make differentiated load balancing decisions. Therefore, LBoDSN can sense congested flows and select rerouting path faster at the destination switch than ConWeave. And LBoDSN solves the performance damage caused by stale CNPs, thereby improving the transmission performance. Besides, LBoDSN performs 9–64% and 20–80% better than CONGA for the average and tail FCTs, respectively. Compared with LetFlow, LBoDSN improves the average and tail FCTs by 18–70% and 29–83%, respectively. The results show that LBoDSN can effectively improve the performance by sensing the trend of PFC pause and rerouting congested flows in advance. CONGA and LetFlow distribute flowlets at source switches but cannot sense PFC pause/resume events, which degrades performance for lossless DCNs. For example, a path with low link utilization because of PFC pausing is mistaken for a good path in CONGA. Therefore, LBoDSN can outperform CONGA and LetFlow in our experiments.

4.2 Reduction in Queues Usage

Rerouting at the source switch will produce out-of-order packets. As RDMA is highly sensitive to out-of-order packets in lossless DCNs [19], LBoDSN employs the same mechanism as ConWeave to reorder out-of-order packets at the destination switch, which requires switch queues for reordering. Queues are a valuable hardware resource for switches and using too many queues may affect other services. Therefore, we monitor the number of queues used per switch egress port for schemes in our experiments to check the feasibility of LBoDSN.

As Fig. 4 shows, under both workloads, LBoDSN uses fewer queues than Con-Weave and up to five additional queues. This is because LBoDSN only reroutes congested flows which have a large probability of causing path congestion or PFC pause, and ConWeave reroutes flows more frequently. Compared with Con-Weave, LBoDSN achieves more fine-grained congestion sensing and more cautious rerouting decisions. Therefore, LBoDSN can reduce the queue usage of switches to achieve less hardware resource consumption.

5 Conclusion

In this work, we propose LBoDSN, which realizes in-network load balancing for lossless DCNs using direct switch notification based on programable switches. LBoDSN monitors ingress queue length evolution at destination switches to predict the triggering time of PFC pause, and identifies congested flows based on the congestion contribution level before PFC pause, then further proactively sends the FCN to source switches for fast rerouting. Besides, after rerouting, the CNP of the old path is selectively discarded at source switches to improve transmission performance, while out-of-order packets are reordered at destination switchs. Simulation experiments under realistic workloads strongly confirm the effectiveness of LBoDSN in reducing the FCT and the switch queue usage.

Acknowledgments. This work was supported by the National Key Research and Development Program of China (2021YFC3300603, 2023YFC3306204); the National Natural Science Foundation of China (62376092); the MOE (Ministry of Education in China) Project of Humanities and Social Sciences (23YJCZH183); the Natural Science Foundation of Hunan Province of China (2022JJ40129, 2023JJ40236); the Open Project of Xiangjiang Laboratory (23XJ01012, 22XJ03014); and the Interdisciplinary Research Project of Hunan University of Technology and Business (2023SZJ16).

References

1. Infiniband trade association. infinibandtm architecture specification volume 1 release 1.3. March 2015
2. NS3. https://www.nsnam.org/. Accessed 13 Aug 2024
3. Alizadeh, M., et al.: CONGA: distributed congestion-aware load balancing for datacenters. In: Proceedings of the ACM SIGCOMM, pp. 503–514 (2014)

4. Bai, W., et al.: Empowering azure storage with RDMA. In: Proceedings of the USENIX NSDI, pp. 49–67 (2023)
5. Gao, Y., et al.: When cloud storage meets RDMA. In: Proceedings of the USENIX NSDI, pp. 519–533 (2021)
6. Ghorbani, S., Yang, Z., Godfrey, P.B., Ganjali, Y., Firoozshahian, A.: DRILL: micro load balancing for low-latency data center networks. In: Proceedings of the ACM SIGCOMM, pp. 225–238 (2017)
7. Guo, C., et al.: Rdma over commodity ethernet at scale. In: Proceedings of the ACM SIGCOMM, pp. 202–215 (2016)
8. Hopps, C.: Analysis of an equal-cost multi-path algorithm. RFC 2992 (2000)
9. Hu, J., He, Y., Wang, J., Luo, W., Huang, J.: RLB: reordering-robust load balancing in lossless datacenter networks. In: Proceedings of the ACM ICPP, pp. 576–584 (2023)
10. Hu, J., et al.: Enabling load balancing for lossless datacenters. In: Proceedings of the IEEE ICNP, pp. 1–11 (2023)
11. Katta, N., Hira, M., Kim, C., Sivaraman, A., Rexford, J.: HULA: scalable load balancing using programmable data planes. In: Proceedings of the ACM SOSR, p. 10 (2016)
12. Lao, C., et al.: ATP: in-network aggregation for multi-tenant learning. In: Proceedings of the USENIX NSDI, pp. 741–761 (2021)
13. Li, W., et al.: Flow scheduling with imprecise knowledge. In: Proceedings of the USENIX NSDI, pp. 95–111 (2024)
14. Li, W., Zeng, C., Hu, J., Chen, K.: Towards fine-grained and practical flow control for datacenter networks. In: Proceedings of the IEEE ICNP, pp. 1–11 (2023)
15. Li, Y., et al.: HPCC: high precision congestion control. In: Proceedings of the ACM SIGCOMM, pp. 44–58 (2019)
16. Lu, Y., et al.: Multi-Path transport for RDMA in datacenters. In: Proceedings of the USENIX NSDI, pp. 357–371 (2018)
17. Mitzenmacher, M.: The power of two choices in randomized load balancing. IEEE Trans. Parallel Distrib. Syst. (TPDS) 12(10), 1094–1104 (2001)
18. Roy, A., Zeng, H., Bagga, J., Porter, G., Snoeren, A.C.: Inside the social network's (datacenter) network. In: Proceedings of the ACM SIGCOMM, pp. 123–137 (2015)
19. Song, C.H., Khooi, X.Z., Joshi, R., Choi, I., Li, J., Chan, M.C.: Network load balancing with in-network reordering support for rdma. In: Proceedings of the ACM SIGCOMM, pp. 816–831 (2023)
20. Taranov, K., Byan, S., Marathe, V., Hoefler, T.: Kafkadirect: zero-copy data access for apache kafka over rdma networks. In: Proceedings of the ACM SIGMOD, pp. 2191–2204 (2022)
21. Vanini, E., Pan, R., Alizadeh, M., Taheri, P., Edsall, T.: Let it flow: resilient asymmetric load balancing with flowlet switching. In: Proceedings of the USENIX NSDI, pp. 407–420 (2017)
22. Zhang, H., Zhang, J., Bai, W., Chen, K., Chowdhury, M.: Resilient datacenter load balancing in the wild. In: Proceedings of the ACM SIGCOMM, pp. 253–266 (2017)
23. Zhu, Y., et al.: Congestion control for large-scale rdma deployments. In: Proceedings of the ACM SIGCOMM, pp. 523–536 (2015)

LDChain: A Lightweight and Scalable Blockchain System for Dynamic IoT Scenarios

Jianrong Wang[1], Yuxuan Cao[1], Dengcheng Hu[1], Qi Li[2(✉)], Sen Li[3], Xuewei Li[1], and Xiulong Liu[1]

[1] College of Intelligence and Computing, Tianjin University, Tianjin, China
{wjr,caesar,hdc,lixuewei,xiulong_liu}@tju.edu.cn
[2] School of Electrical and Information Engineering,
Tianjin University, Tianjin, China
qi.li@tju.edu.cn
[3] School of Future Technology, Tianjin University, Tianjin, China
senli@tju.edu.cn

Abstract. As a distributed ledger, blockchain inherently guarantees data consistency. However, when applied to the Internet of Things (IoT), existing solutions employing blockchain systems struggle to address the scalability demands posed by the dynamic mobility of heterogeneous devices. To this end, we propose Lightweight DAG Chain (LDChain), a lightweight and scalable blockchain system tailored for IoT scenarios. LDChain connects weak nodes and strong nodes through a hierarchical DAG consensus algorithm. For weak nodes, we introduce a transaction-based DAG consensus mechanism utilizing a snapshot synchronization strategy to cater to the dynamic nature of weak nodes and the scalability demands of the system. The integrated snapshot synchronization strategy, based on the second latest block transaction selection algorithm, reduces the storage and computational overhead for resource-restricted devices. For strong nodes, we devise a block-based DAG consensus mechanism and a repackaging strategy, which resolves transaction conflicts across regions by managing conflicting transactions through a priority queue. We implement a prototype of LDChain and conduct experiments in a network environment comprising 10 cloud servers, simulating several strong nodes and weak nodes. The experimental results show that our system achieves a throughput exceeding 7000 transactions per second (TPS) and a transaction confirmation latency of 1.3 s with 100 nodes.

Keywords: Blockchain · Hierarchical DAG consensus · System scalability · Dynamic IoT scenarios

1 Introduction

1.1 Motivation and Problem Statement

The Internet of Things (IoT) encompasses sensing, computing, and communication technologies [1]. Diverse IoT services and applications become integral to

© IFIP International Federation for Information Processing 2025
Published by Springer Nature Switzerland AG 2025
X. Chen et al. (Eds.): NPC 2024, LNCS 15527, pp. 383–395, 2025.
https://doi.org/10.1007/978-981-96-2830-8_30

everyday life [2,3]. IoT devices are characterized by low-power operation and extensive deployment, enabling various systems [4,5]. Efficient and secure data processing and sharing are critical in IoT [6]. Addressing data consistency across multiple devices is a crucial challenge for IoT [7].

Blockchain offers a robust solution to the aforementioned challenges [8]. Consensus algorithms are pivotal in maintaining consistency and significantly influence system performance within blockchain frameworks. However, due to the limited storage space [9], computing resources [10], and communication capabilities [11] of IoT devices, traditional consensus algorithms encounter several issues. For example, Proof of Work (PoW) [12,13] suffers from lower throughput and higher transaction confirmation latency. Practical Byzantine Fault Tolerance (PBFT) [14,15] exhibits limited scalability and is unsuitable for large-scale IoT environments. Consequently, there is a pressing demand for a lightweight and scalable blockchain system designed to meet the needs of IoT applications.

1.2   Limitations of Prior Arts

Previous studies contributed to enhancing system performance. [16–20] improved throughput by optimizing the PBFT consensus process in IoT scenarios. PoBT [21] achieved faster transaction and block verification for IoT blockchain. However, these efforts did not address the problem of device mobility in IoT scenarios, which complicates their continuous participation in the consensus process, thereby impacting system consistency and stability.

Several studies optimized the impact of device mobility. B-DSPA [22] addressed dynamic entry and exit of devices but lacked real-time awareness of device status. DR-BFT [23] ameliorated the quorum method to accommodate device mobility. However, the frequent turnover of devices necessitates incessant updates to the quorum structure, incurring computational operations with time complexity of $O(n \ logn)$. Another solution [24] addressed inefficiencies stemming from device mobility by performing device calculations and selections for network sharding. Each device must broadcast to obtain information about neighboring devices constantly, and the continual variation of network sharding also brings recurrent computations. Nevertheless, the introduction of mechanisms in the mentioned solutions increases computational and communication overhead, rendering these solutions unsuitable for resource-restricted devices. Meanwhile, they still restrict the number of participating consensus devices, leading to lower system throughput as the network scales, and limiting scalability.

Furthermore, the above studies inadequately account for the capabilities and specific characteristics of diverse devices within IoT environments. The heterogeneity of devices, each possessing varying computational, storage, and communication capabilities, hinders the effectiveness of singular consensus algorithms and associated systems within the practical context of IoT.

1.3   Proposed Approach

We propose Lightweight DAG Chain (LDChain), a lightweight DAG blockchain system tailored for IoT's master-slave network. The core of LDChain is hierarchical DAG consensus. Considering the heterogeneity of nodes, we categorize nodes like base stations, which possess substantial computing, storage, and communication capabilities, as strong nodes. Conversely, nodes with constrained resources, like vehicles, are classified as weak nodes. Weak nodes generate transactions and communicate locally in their region to achieve transaction-based DAG consensus at the weak node layer, accommodating dynamic joining and exiting of resource-restricted devices. Strong nodes aggregate transactions from weak nodes within their respective areas and communicate among themselves to establish global block-based DAG consensus at the strong node layer.

1.4 Challenges and Solutions

There are two main challenges in implementing our proposed LDChain:

The First Challenge is Maintaining the Participation of Resource-restricted Devices in the Consensus. The surge in transaction data not only intensifies computational costs but also surpasses the IoT devices' storage capacity. Hence, we devise a snapshot synchronization strategy by optimizing the data structure of transactions and blocks, as well as modifying the random walk approach. Weak nodes can synchronize with the confirmation blocks issued by strong nodes, thus deleting locally confirmed transaction data and reducing computational load. Next, synchronization rules are formulated to involve lagging nodes in consensus and maintain data consistency via the second latest confirmation block. Lastly, a reissuing mechanism is designed to enhance transaction efficiency.

The Second Challenge is How to Address the Issues of Cross-regional Conflicts in the Strong Node Layer. Cross-regional transaction conflicts in the consensus of strong nodes within the same round can hinder voting on previous round blocks. To tackle this challenge, we establish transaction priorities and devise a repackaging strategy. When transaction conflicts arise between blocks, nodes repackage transactions based on the maintained conflict transaction priority queue. Newly packaged blocks are subsequently issued for re-voting and confirmation.

1.5 Main Contribution

Overall, our main contributions are as follows:

- We propose LDChain, a novel blockchain system designed for IoT scenarios, which offers high performance and minimal storage overhead while retaining core blockchain advantages. We categorize IoT nodes into weak and strong types, applying transaction-based DAG consensus and block-based DAG consensus to each type, respectively.
- We design a snapshot synchronization strategy to reduce the storage and computational overhead of weak nodes. We enhance system performance by implementing a new random walk method for optimizing the selection of unapproved transactions. Additionally, we resolve cross-regional conflicts among strong nodes with a repackaging strategy that prioritizes transactions.

– We implement LDChain and conduct various evaluations to manifest its stability, efficiency, and scalability. In the experiment, we use 10 cloud servers to
simulate 10 strong nodes, with each server also simulating an equal number
of weak nodes. Our experiment demonstrates a system capable of achieving
over 7000 TPS and 1.3 s of confirmation latency across a total of 100 weak
nodes while ensuring minimal storage cost fluctuations.

2   System Overview

In this section, we introduce an overview of LDChain.

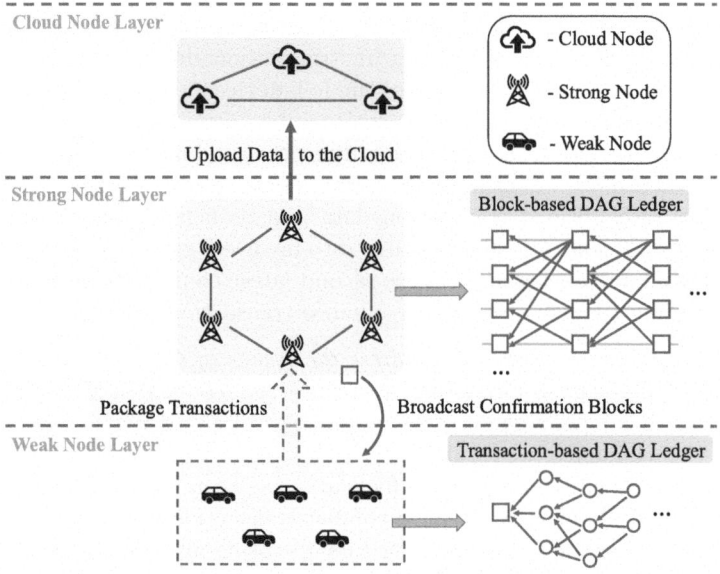

Fig. 1. LDChain Hierarchy.

Figure 1 illustrates the hierarchical structure of our system, comprising the
weak node layer, the strong node layer, and the cloud node layer arranged from
bottom to top. Weak nodes denote resource-restricted IoT devices like drones
and vehicles, characterized by constrained computing, storage, and communication resources. They are numerous, highly mobile, and capable of dynamically
entering and leaving specific areas. Strong nodes, on the other hand, represent
resource-rich IoT devices that are fewer in number and fixed at specific locations,
typically including base stations and roadside units.

The system workflow unfolds as follows. Weak nodes generate transactions,
broadcast them, collaborate with other weak nodes locally to achieve regional
consensus and establish a transaction-based DAG ledger structure. Strong nodes

aggregate transactions from weak nodes that have attained regional consensus within their respective areas into proposal blocks. They then coordinate with strong nodes across regions to achieve global consensus, thus forming a block-based DAG ledger structure. Subsequently, strong nodes broadcast confirmation blocks to weak nodes, enabling them to perform snapshot synchronization. The cloud nodes aid in storing block data, alleviating storage demands on strong nodes. However, this also incurs additional communication and transmission overhead. Our research centers on the strong node and weak node layers.

3   Design of Weak Node Layer

The hierarchical DAG consensus forms the foundation of LDChain. This section offers a detailed exposition of the transaction-based DAG consensus implemented at the weak node layer. We design an asynchronous mechanism tailored for transactions within the DAG framework to accommodate the dynamic characteristics of weak nodes, thereby optimizing system performance.

3.1   Transaction-Based DAG Consensus

A transaction comprises a header and a body. Our focus is on transaction headers. The header includes data items such as the parent transaction hash, the hash of the latest confirmation block, the transaction body hash, and nonce.

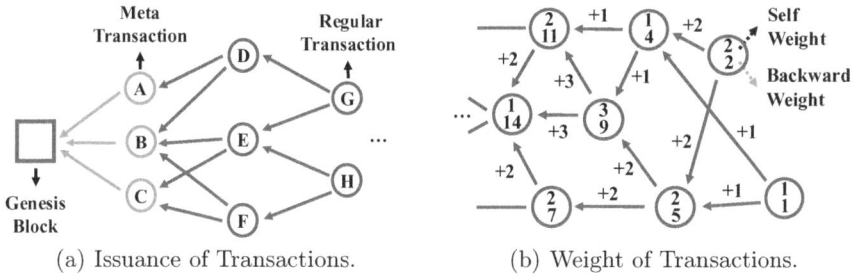

(a) Issuance of Transactions.   (b) Weight of Transactions.

Fig. 2. Transaction-based DAG.

In each region, strong nodes initialize by issuing a genesis block upon system startup. As shown in Fig. 2(a), the genesis block serves as the parent node for meta transactions (e.g., A, B, and C), while regular transactions (e.g., D to H) reference preceding transactions. Before issuance, weak nodes must complete PoW. It's noteworthy that the PoW difficulty is relatively low, enabling weak nodes to complete it quickly. The transaction's self-weight, W_{i_s}, is proportional to the PoW conducted. Besides PoW, weak nodes must approve two unapproved transactions to issue a regular transaction.

We introduce backward weight, $W_{i_{back}}$, which is defined as the sum of a transaction's self-weight and the combined self-weight of all transactions that directly or indirectly approve it:

$$W_{i_{back}} = W_{i_s} + \sum W_{i_{approved}} \tag{1}$$

In Fig. 2(b), the circle represents the transaction. The upper number indicates the transaction's self-weight, whereas the lower number indicates its backward weight. The numbers on the directed edges illustrate the accumulation of backward weights within the graph. Each transaction's self-weight applies to all transactions that it directly or indirectly approves.

3.2 Snapshot Synchronization Strategy

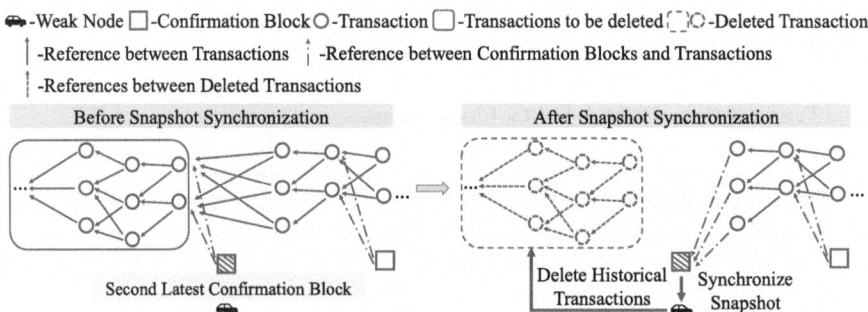

Fig. 3. Snapshot Synchronization Strategy.

To mitigate the resource constraints faced by weak nodes, we propose a snapshot synchronization strategy. As depicted in Fig. 3, weak nodes can synchronize a snapshot starting from the second latest confirmation block and subsequently purge local historical transactions. It should be noted that, weak nodes have the flexibility to select any non-latest confirmation block for snapshot synchronization. Upon receiving the latest confirmation block and completing the snapshot synchronization process, if a weak node attempts to issue a transaction and finds that some nodes have deleted the corresponding parent transaction, it becomes impossible for these nodes to verify the transaction's validity or compute associated transaction attributes.

In LDChain, we tolerate a slight lag caused by weak nodes due to network latency. When a node's latest maintained confirmation block differs by at least two blocks from those of other nodes in the system, we consider it significantly lagging. Transactions approved by such lagging nodes are relatively old at the time of issuance, making it difficult to obtain approval and regional confirmation from other nodes. This situation increases the number of unconfirmed transactions in the system, thereby affecting transaction confirmation latency. As a result, upon a node's discovery that its previously issued transactions remain unconfirmed within the region after two confirmation blocks, it has the option to reissue these transactions.

3.3   Transaction Selection Algorithm

We employ the Markov Chain Monte Carlo (MCMC) algorithm [25] for selecting two unapproved transactions. Two particles are placed on the latest confirmation block and directed toward unapproved transactions. The transactions reached by these particles are then selected for approval. When transaction x directly verifies transaction y, the transition probability of particles moving from transaction y to x is defined as follows:

$$P_{yx} = f(k(W_{y_b} - W_{x_b})) \cdot (\textstyle\sum_z f(k(W_{y_b} - W_{z_b})))^{-1} \tag{2}$$

where $k > 0$, f denotes a monotonically decreasing function. W_{x_b} signifies the backward weight of transaction x, W_{y_b} denotes the backward weight of transaction y, and z represents all transactions that approve y. We do not emphasize the configuration of correlation functions and parameters in transition probability. Comprehensive research on this subject was conducted in [26] and [27].

We introduce the transaction confidence ratio, C_i, to ascertain when a transaction achieves regional confirmation. The calculation of the transaction confidence ratio is as follows:

$$C_i = \sum_{irt} Q_{irt} \cdot (\sum_{aut} Q_{aut})^{-1} \tag{3}$$

where irt denotes all unapproved transactions identified by transaction i through the transaction selection algorithm, and aut represents all unapproved transactions. Strong nodes execute the transaction selection algorithm multiple times during transaction packaging. Once a transaction's confidence ratio exceeds a specified threshold (e.g., 90%), it is deemed regionally confirmed. Currently, strong nodes can package confirmed transactions in the proposal block.

Based on the assumption of an assiduous honest majority [28], system security is ensured. The snapshot synchronization alters only the starting point of the random walk during unapproved transaction selection, with the parameters of the random walk in the algorithm and the confirmed transactions having no impact on system security [28]. Thus, as long as malicious nodes possess less than 50% of the computing power, double-spending attacks will be unsuccessful.

4   Design of Strong Node Layer

This section presents a detailed introduction to block-based DAG consensus within the strong node layer. Based on the synchronous network, we design a block-based DAG consensus that operates in a round manner.

4.1   Block-Based DAG Consensus

The proposal block includes multiple transactions forming a Merkle Tree. Its header contains the parent block hash, Merkle Tree root hash, mining difficulty, and the current round number. The confirmation block comprises consensus proposal blocks from each round, with its body formed by merging multiple Merkle Trees of proposal blocks. Its header includes the confirmation block hash, the root hash of the overall Merkle Tree, and the current round number.

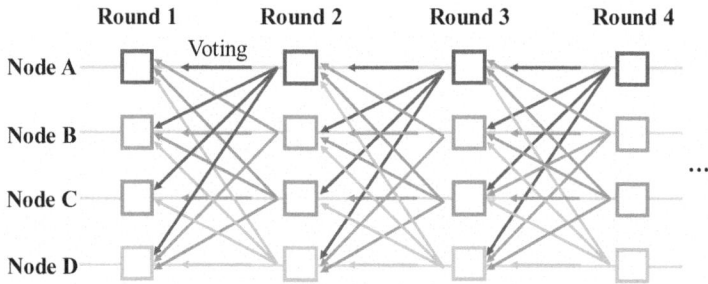

Fig. 4.   Block-based DAG.

Figure 4 illustrates that each node issues a proposal block in every round and casts votes on blocks from other nodes in the preceding round. A proposal block contains all regionally confirmed transactions from the local region of the node that remain unpackaged. Each strong node derives the voting results based on the header information of the proposal blocks.

Assuming there are n strong nodes in the system, a proposal block achieves global confirmation if it garners more than $n/2$ votes. Upon completing a consensus round, each strong node must consolidate all proposal blocks into a confirmation block and distribute it to all weak nodes within its local network.

4.2   Repackaging Strategy

Under the proposed consensus architecture, when cross-regional transaction conflicts occur, strong nodes may lack sufficient votes. Ensuring consensus becomes critical amidst cross-regional transaction conflicts. Hence, we propose a solution for cross-regional conflict resolution.

Each transaction is assigned a transaction priority, denoted as R_i, which is calculated as follows:

$$R_i = w_1 T_i + w_2 B_i + w_3 S_i \tag{4}$$

where T_i is the transaction timestamp, B_i is the account balance, S_i is the transaction type, and w_1, w_2, and w_3 are their corresponding weights. Transactions are categorized as either smart contract transactions or other transactions, with smart contracts allowed to define transaction type priority parameters for specific transactions. The weights of each item can be adjusted based on different system deployments to accommodate various scenarios.

Each node maintains multiple priority queues for conflicting transactions, assuming varying transaction priorities. When there are conflicting transactions between blocks, nodes selectively package and reissue transactions from the top position of conflicting transaction priority queues. In the subsequent consensus round, each node votes for the repackaged transaction upon block issuance. Proposal blocks from all honest nodes adhering to the repackaging strategy can be confirmed. If malicious nodes fail to follow the repackaging strategy and do not receive sufficient endorsements, their proposal blocks are invalidated.

Overall, the proposed innovative consensus employs a repackaging strategy to mitigate potential conflicts arising from malicious nodes that issue conflicting transactions across regions. In the context of numerous heterogeneous IoT devices, the system can leverage the support of strong nodes to implement identity authentication management, thereby reducing associated security threats.

5   Evaluation and Analysis

In this section, we evaluate the performance of LDChain.

5.1   Experimental Environment

We conduct simulation tests on LDChain to simulate varying numbers of devices in the network by adjusting node counts. The system is implemented using over 2000 lines of Java code, demonstrating a comprehensive and robust development effort. The experiment utilizes 10 cloud servers, each equipped with 2 CPU cores (AMD EPYC Bergamo processor, Rui frequency 3.1 GHz), 4 GB of memory and a 10MB/s bandwidth, running Ubuntu Server 22.04 LTS 641 operating system.

5.2   Experimental Setup

In the experiment, we define the transition probability as follows:

$$P_{yx} = e^{(-0.03 \cdot (W_{y_b} - W_{x_b}))} \cdot \left(\sum_{z} e^{(-0.03 \cdot (W_{y_b} - W_{z_b}))} \right)^{-1} \qquad (5)$$

where the decreasing function $f(x) = exp(-x)$, and the coefficient $k = 0.03$.

The experiment utilizes 10 cloud servers as strong nodes, with each server concurrently simulating an equal number of weak nodes, ranging from 10 to 100 in total. We vary the number of weak nodes in our experiments to measure storage cost, throughput, and transaction confirmation latency within the system, thereby analyzing the effectiveness of the system in IoT scenarios. It is important to note that, compared to other studies, our research demonstrates superior performance. To clearly and intuitively illustrate the effectiveness of the snapshot synchronization strategy, we focus solely on comparing these metrics with and without the snapshot synchronization strategy.

5.3 Experimental Results and Analysis

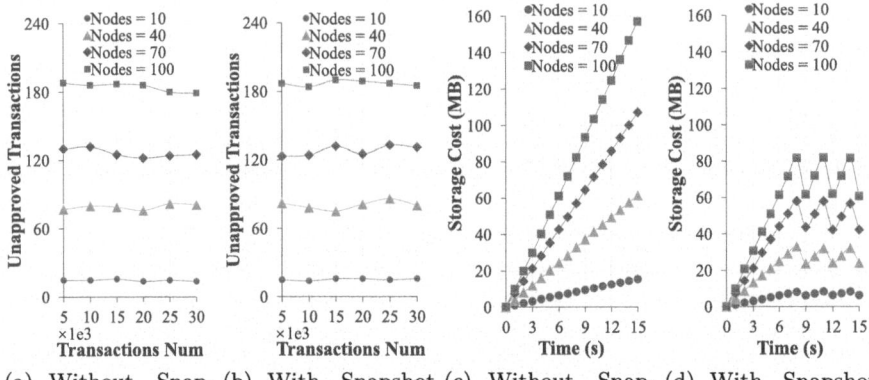

Fig. 5. Unapproved Transactions and Storage Costs under Different Numbers of Nodes.

Initially, we simulate the count of unapproved transactions in the system. Figure 5(a) illustrates the unapproved transaction count across varying total transaction numbers without employing the snapshot synchronization strategy, while Fig. 5(b) depicts results with the snapshot synchronization strategy applied. The experimental results indicate that the count of unapproved transactions remains consistent, demonstrating the system's stability. This count correlates with the number of weak nodes: with 10 weak nodes, there are approximately 16 unapproved transactions, increasing to around 190 with 100 weak nodes.

Subsequently, we evaluate the storage overhead of weak nodes. Figure 5(c) illustrates a continuous increase in transaction quantity over time. Without the snapshot synchronization strategy, storage overhead will persistently escalate. For 100 weak nodes, the storage overhead increases by about 10MB per second. When storage overhead reaches the limit of weak nodes, they are unable to store additional transaction data to maintain system operation. In Fig. 5(d), with the snapshot synchronization strategy in place, the storage cost for an individual node fluctuates narrowly across each synchronization round, as only specific confirmation blocks and associated transactions require storage. With 100 weak nodes, the storage overhead for a single node ranges between 60 MB and 90 MB.

Regarding throughput, we calculate the system's throughput across various transaction quantities. Figure 6(a) and Fig. 6(b) show that as the number of nodes increases, the system's TPS continuously improves, indicating strong scalability. Without using the snapshot synchronization strategy, an increase in total transactions raises the computational cost of random walks and transaction attributes. With an equal total transaction quantity, fewer nodes result in

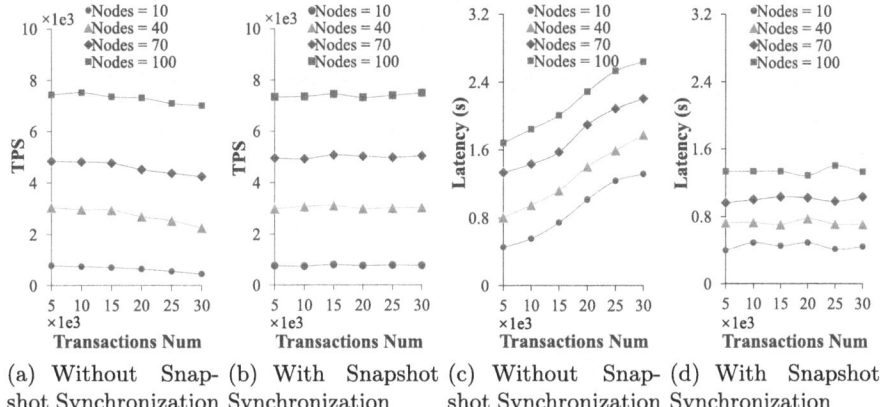

(a) Without Snap- (b) With Snapshot (c) Without Snap- (d) With Snapshot
shot Synchronization Synchronization   shot Synchronization Synchronization

Fig. 6. TPS and Latency under Different Numbers of Nodes.

more random walk steps, significantly reducing TPS when the number of nodes is low. For instance, with 10 weak nodes, increasing total transaction quantity from 5000 to 30000 decreases TPS by 42%. Conversely, when employing snapshot synchronization strategies, the corresponding transaction count fluctuations in relevant computations are minimal, thereby ensuring stable TPS. With 100 weak nodes, the system achieves approximately 7400 TPS.

Finally, we compute the average confirmation latency of transactions achieving global confirmation. According to Fig. 6(c), without using snapshot synchronization, transaction confirmation latency increases as transaction quantity accumulates. As total transaction quantity increases from 5000 to 30000, transaction confirmation latency under various weak node numbers escalates from 57% to 190%. The snapshot synchronization strategy causes the transaction quantity saved by each weak node to fluctuate within a defined range. Consequently, transaction confirmation latency remains consistent across different total transaction quantities, as depicted in Fig. 6(d). Moreover, varying numbers of weak nodes impact the number of transactions included in proposal blocks between strong node rounds. Specifically, when the total number of weak nodes reaches 100, transaction confirmation latency peaks at approximately 1.3 s.

6   Conclusion

We proposed an efficient hierarchical consensus blockchain system based on the master-slave network architecture of the Internet of Things. We devised a transaction-based consensus mechanism for weak nodes and a block-based consensus mechanism for strong nodes, tailored to node mobility and heterogeneity, achieving high throughput and minimal transaction confirmation latency. Additionally, we implemented a snapshot synchronization strategy to reduce storage and computational overhead for weak nodes and resolved cross-regional conflict transactions in strong nodes consensus using a repackaging strategy. Experimental analysis confirmed that our system achieves a throughput of 7400 with 100 weak nodes, and transaction confirmation latency averages around 1.3 s.

References

1. Chiang, Y., et al.: Management and orchestration of edge computing for IoT: a comprehensive survey. IEEE Internet Things J. **10**(16), 14307–14331 (2023)
2. Zhou, X., Ge, S., Liu, P., Qiu, T.: DAG-based dependent tasks offloading in MEC-enabled IoT with soft cooperation. IEEE Trans. Mob. Comput. **23**(6), 6908–6920 (2024)
3. Hua, H., Li, Y., Wang, T., Dong, N., Li, W., Cao, J.: Edge computing with artificial intelligence: a machine learning perspective. ACM Comput. Surv. **55**(9), 1–35 (2023)
4. Fu, R., et al.: Smart sensing and communication co-design for IIoT-based control systems. IEEE Internet Things J. **11**(3), 3994–4014 (2024)
5. Khor, J.H., Sidorov, M., Ong, M.T., Chua, S.Y.: Public blockchain-based data integrity verification for low-power IoT devices. IEEE Internet Things J. **10**(14), 13056–13064 (2023)
6. Sun, D., et al.: A comprehensive survey on collaborative data-access enablers in the IIoT. ACM Comput. Surv. **56**(2), 1–37 (2023)
7. Yu, J., Yan, B., Qi, H., Wang, S., Cheng, W.: An efficient and secure data sharing scheme for edge-enabled IoT. IEEE Trans. Comput. **73**(1), 178–191 (2023)
8. Xu, R., Lan, Q., Pokhrel, S.R., Li, G.: A knowledge graph-based survey on distributed ledger technology for IoT verticals. ACM Comput. Surv. **56**(2), 1–36 (2023)
9. Yang, L., Liao, Y., Cheng, X., Xia, M., Xie, G.: Efficient edge data management framework for IIoT via prediction-based data reduction. IEEE Trans. Parallel Distrib. Syst. **34**(12), 3309–3322 (2023)
10. Shi, T., Cai, Z., Li, J., Gao, H., Qiu, T., Qu, W.: An efficient processing scheme for concurrent applications in the IoT edge. IEEE Trans. Mob. Comput. **23**(1), 135–149 (2022)
11. Xia, D., Zheng, X., Liu, L., and Ma, H.: Parallel cross-technology transmission from IEEE 802.11 ax to heterogeneous IoT devices. In: 2023 IEEE Conference on Computer Communications (INFOCOM), pp. 1–10. IEEE (2023)
12. Xu, J., Wang, C., Jia, X.: A survey of blockchain consensus protocols. ACM Comput. Surv. **55**(13s), 1–35 (2023)
13. Garay, J., Kiayias, A., and Shen, Y.: Proof-of-work-based consensus in expected-constant time. In: Annual International Conference on the Theory and Applications of Cryptographic Techniques, pp. 96-125. Springer (2024)
14. Luo, H., Yang, X., Yu, H., Sun, G., Lei, B., Guizani, M.: Performance analysis and comparison of non-ideal wireless PBFT and RAFT consensus networks in 6G communications. IEEE Internet Things J. **11**(6), 9752–9765 (2024)
15. Othmen, R. B., Abbessi, W., Ouni, S., Badreddine, W., and Dequen, G.: Simulation of optimized cluster based PBFT blockchain validation process. In: 2023 IEEE Symposium on Computers and Communications (ISCC), pp. 1317–1322. IEEE (2023)
16. Lao, L., Dai, X., Xiao, B., and Guo, S.: G-PBFT: a location-based and scalable consensus protocol for IoT-blockchain applications. In: 2020 IEEE International Parallel and Distributed Processing Symposium (IPDPS), pp. 664–673. IEEE (2020)

17. Xu, G.: SG-PBFT: a secure and highly efficient distributed blockchain PBFT consensus algorithm for intelligent Internet of vehicles. J. Parallel Distrib. Comput. **164**, 1–11 (2022)
18. Chen, X., Xue, G., Yu, R., Wu, H., Wang, D.: A vehicular trust blockchain framework with scalable byzantine consensus. IEEE Trans. Mob. Comput. **23**(5), 4440–4452 (2023)
19. Tang, F., Xu, T., Peng, J., Gan, N.: TP-PBFT: a scalable PBFT based on threshold proxy signature for IoT-blockchain applications. IEEE Internet Things J. **11**(9), 15434–15449 (2023)
20. Qushtom, H., Mišić, J., Mišić, V.B., Chang, X.: A two-stage PBFT architecture with trust and reward incentive mechanism. IEEE Internet Things J. **10**(13), 11440–11452 (2023)
21. Biswas, S., Sharif, K., Li, F., Maharjan, S., Mohanty, S.P., Wang, Y.: PoBT: a lightweight consensus algorithm for scalable IoT business blockchain. IEEE Internet Things J. **7**(3), 2343–2355 (2020)
22. Tao, Q., Ding, H., Jiang, T., Cui, X.: B-DSPA: a blockchain-based dynamically scalable privacy-preserving authentication scheme in vehicular ad hoc networks. IEEE Internet Things J. **11**(1), 1385–1397 (2024)
23. Fan, Y., Wu, H., Paik, H.Y.: DR-BFT: a consensus algorithm for blockchain-based multi-layer data integrity framework in dynamic edge computing system. Futur. Gener. Comput. Syst. **124**, 33–48 (2021)
24. Zhang, X., Li, R., Zhao, H.: A parallel consensus mechanism using PBFT based on DAG-lattice structure in the Internet of Vehicles. IEEE Internet Things J. **10**(6), 5418–5433 (2022)
25. Andrieu, C., Thoms, J.: A tutorial on adaptive MCMC. Stat. Comput. **18**, 343–373 (2008)
26. Fan, C., Ghaemi, S., Khazaei, H., Chen, Y., Musilek, P.: Performance analysis of the IOTA DAG-based distributed ledger. ACM Trans. Model. Perform. Eval. Comput. Syst. **6**(3), 1–20 (2021)
27. Zhang, X., Zhu, X., Ali, I.: Performance analysis of IOTA tangle and a new consensus algorithm for smart grids. IEEE Internet Things J. **11**(4), 6396–6411 (2024)
28. Bramas, Q.: The stability and the security of the Tangle (2018). https://hal.science/hal-01716111/

MEGA: Mesh-Aligned 3DGS Towards Geometry-Preserving Online Reconstruction

Ke Luo, Shengyuan Ye, Tao Ouyang$^{(\boxtimes)}$, and Zhi Zhou

School of Computer Science and Engineering, Sun Yat-sen University,
Guangzhou 510006, China
{luok7,yeshy8}@mail2.sysu.edu.cn, {ouyt33,zhouzhi9}@mail.sysu.edu.cn

Abstract. 3D Gaussian Splatting (3DGS) has recently emerged as a significant advancement in 3D scene reconstruction, offering real-time, high-resolution, and photorealistic rendering. Despite these advantages, 3DGS often compromises geometric accuracy for visual fidelity. In contrast, geometrically precise representations such as voxel grids, point clouds, and meshes are widely used in robotics, particularly with the increasing availability of high-accuracy LiDAR and LiDAR-Inertial-Visual (LIV) systems. Recent research has utilized LiDAR priors to initialize 3D Gaussians. However, the optimization processes in 3DGS can distort the original geometric information. Furthermore, existing methods mainly focus on offline 3DGS training, which cannot fully exploit the real-time capabilities of LIV systems. To address these limitations, we introduce MEGA, an edge-assisted online reconstruction approach with mesh-aligned 3DGS. MEGA facilitates online 3DGS training by leveraging incrementally available posed frames, colored LiDAR points, and triangle mesh faces from LIV systems. It employs a novel mesh-aligned representation to dynamically populate 3D Gaussians based on triangle mesh faces. Additionally, it introduces an image-to-geometry alignment technique to resolve inconsistencies between frames and LiDAR priors. Extensive evaluations demonstrate that MEGA achieves superior rendering quality while preserving precise geometric information.

Keywords: 3DGS · Online Reconstruction · Edge Computing

1 Introduction

3D Gaussian Splatting (3DGS) [6] has recently emerged as a significant advancement in 3D scene reconstruction. Its real-time, high-resolution, and photorealistic rendering capabilities have led to widespread adoption across various applications. However, since 3DGS is primarily optimized for visual fidelity, it can lead to over-fitting to visual appearances [21], which in turn compromises geometric accuracy. In contrast, geometrically precise 3D scene representations, such as voxel grids, point clouds, and meshes, are commonly used in robotics [8,10,23]. As high-accuracy LiDAR technology becomes more widely deployed and LiDAR-Inertial-Visual (LIV) systems mature [11], these geometrically precise representations, referred to as LiDAR priors, are becoming increasingly accessible.

Given the similar point-based structure of 3DGS and LiDAR priors, recent studies have begun to leverage the latter for the initialization of 3D Gaussians [3,9,22,25]. While LiDAR priors have been effective in these studies, we have observed that the optimization and densification processes used by 3DGS can disrupt the original precise geometric information. Furthermore, most existing studies use LiDAR priors only for offline 3DGS training, which overlooks the potential benefits of real-time LIV systems. Another line of research focuses on 3DGS-enabled simultaneous localization and mapping (SLAM) [5,14]. Although these methods successfully achieve simultaneous pose tracking and 3DGS training, they often compromise on resolution to enable real-time processing and require high-performance GPUs at the device side, which limits their deployment on low-power mobile robotic platforms.

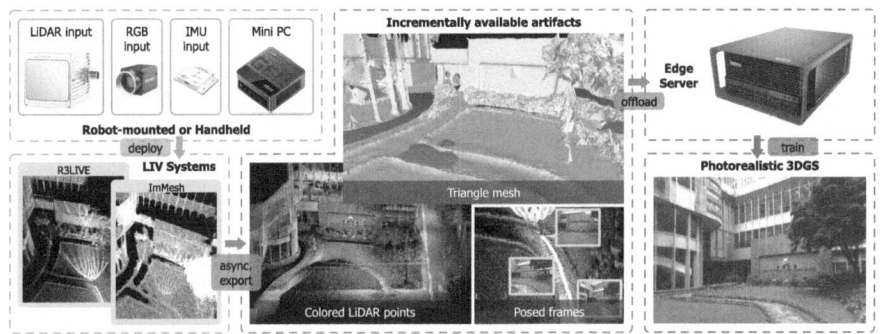

Fig. 1. Edge-assisted online reconstruction with LIV systems and 3DGS.

To achieve photorealistic yet geometry-preserving online reconstruction, this work introduces MEGA, an edge-assisted approach with mesh-aligned 3DGS. As depicted in Fig. 1, MEGA enhances 3DGS training by utilizing incrementally available artifacts, such as posed frames, colored LiDAR points, and triangle mesh faces, from LIV systems deployed on robot-mounted or handheld devices. These incremental artifacts are asynchronously exported and offloaded to an edge server, allowing the LIV systems to continue real-time operation without interruption. At the same time, the edge server uses these offloaded artifacts for online 3DGS training. Specifically, it employs a novel mesh-aligned representation to construct 3D Gaussians based on triangle mesh faces, and it further refines the parameter deduction of these 3D Gaussians to continuously preserve precise geometric information. Additionally, an image-to-geometry alignment technique is introduced to address inconsistencies between posed frames and LiDAR priors.

The contributions of this work are summarized as follows:

- We propose a novel mesh-aligned 3DGS representation that allows for the construction of 3D Gaussians using incrementally available triangle mesh faces while preserving their inherent geometric characteristics.
- We introduce an image-to-geometry alignment design to address subtle inconsistencies between posed frames and the underlying geometric structure, enabling the reconstruction of smooth and high-fidelity surfaces.
- We implement MEGA, a comprehensive edge-assisted approach that integrates the above designs towards geometry-preserving online reconstruction. Extensive evaluations on representative datasets show that MEGA achieves superior rendering quality, preserves accurate geometric information, and supports deployment on low-power mobile platforms with edge assistance.

2   Background and Related Work

2.1   Conventional 3D Scene Representations

We first introduce 3D scene representations commonly utilized in robotics.

Voxel grid is a straightforward extension of 2D image, where each voxel resembles a generalized pixel in 3D space, spanning a unit of 3D volume instead of 2D area. While dense voxel grids are easy to implement, they can consume excessive resources due to the cubic growth of storage with increasing resolution [15], limiting their usage in high-resolution and/or large-scale 3D scenes.

Point cloud, on the other hand, encompasses a set of sparse 3D points. The point cloud format is broadly adopted by range sensors like multi-beam LiDAR, which represent the distances and intensities of nearby obstacles in different directions as a point cloud during each scan. While point clouds are efficient 3D scene descriptors for applications like SLAM [8,11], their disjoint nature hinders visual performance, often resulting in many tiny holes due to the lack of points.

Mesh is the fundamental scene modeling tool in most existing 3D applications [10]. Mesh employs a set of spatially distributed polygonal faces (e.g., triangle faces) to model object surfaces. While high-fidelity meshes still require human efforts from 3D modeling experts, recent research [10,18] has demonstrated significant improvements in automatic online meshing with LiDAR odometry. Despite the distinct designs of the above representations, they are not mutually exclusive. In fact, many practical algorithms combine their usage to jointly benefit from their advantages. For example, VoxelMap [23] uses adaptively-sized voxels to manage LiDAR points and exploits them to summarize voxel-wise planar features, facilitating subsequent triangle face construction [10].

2.2   Learning-Based 3D Scene Representations

Building on the foundation of conventional 3D scene representations, recent advancements have introduced learning-based methods. These novel approaches, such as Neural Radiance Field (NeRF) and 3DGS, have garnered considerable attention due to their remarkable ability to achieve photorealistic rendering and capability to learn from ubiquitous camera captures.

NeRF [16] is similar to a continuous version of voxel grid: while a voxel grid stores features in discrete voxels, NeRF uses a compact neural network (NN) to predict features given any position and viewing direction. When rendering a designated view, NeRF performs ray marching and conducts alpha composition to obtain pixel colors. The entire rendering process is differentiable, allowing image-based supervision to guide the NN towards a high-fidelity representation. However, as a massive number of NN evaluations are required during ray marching, NeRF can be time-consuming in terms of both training and rendering.

3DGS [6] realizes the properties of continuous volumetric rendering like NeRF while reducing training time and achieving real-time rendering speed at high resolution. Instead of using implicit NNs, 3DGS adopts an explicit structure similar to point clouds and meshes. Specifically, 3DGS represents a scene with a set of 3D Gaussians, where each 3D Gaussian is akin to an ellipsoid with position, shape, orientation, anisotropic color, and Gaussian distribution-based intensity (refer to the upper right corner of Fig. 2(c) for illustration). Photorealistic rendering is achieved by composing ray-Gaussian intersections with directional colors and position-dependent intensities. The rendering process is also differentiable, allowing 3D Gaussians to be supervised by image ground truths.

(a) point cloud depth and rendering   (b) mesh depth and rendering   (c) 3DGS depth, rendering, and ellipsoid

Fig. 2. Visual comparison among explicit 3D scene representations.

Figure 2 provides a visual comparison among explicit 3D scene representations obtained with existing works [6,10,11], including point cloud, mesh, and 3DGS. Regarding rendering quality, the point cloud rendering appears rough and exhibits many tiny holes. The mesh rendering is smoother but looks smudgy due to the insufficient number of faces to model complicated objects. In contrast, the 3DGS rendering presents the best quality with photorealistic appearances. Regarding depth quality, both point cloud and mesh can recover decent scene geometry, given their high-accuracy LiDAR inputs and motion-compensated mapping. However, 3DGS generates disordered depth despite being photorealistic.

2.3   Related Work

Recent research has integrated LIV systems into 3DGS training, leveraging their produced geometrically precise LiDAR priors and posed frames. For instance, DrivingGaussian [25] and StreetGaussians [22] utilize LiDAR priors to initialize

3D Gaussians and regulate their positions in large-scale urban scene reconstruction. LIV-GaussMap [3] builds on VoxelMap [23] for real-time localization and mapping, employing surface Gaussians derived from voxels to initialize 3D Gaussians. Gaussian-LIC [9] introduces an incremental expansion strategy for 3DGS based on posed frames and colored LiDAR points from Coco-LIC [8] to enable online reconstruction. Although these studies demonstrate the effectiveness of incorporating LiDAR priors into 3DGS training, their application is primarily limited to the initialization of 3D Gaussians. Since 3DGS training is optimized for rendering quality, subsequent optimization steps can lead to over-fitting of 3D Gaussians to visual appearances [21], thereby compromising geometric accuracy, as illustrated in Fig. 2(c).

Concurrently, pioneering studies [2,12,19] have proposed integrating 3DGS with meshes to facilitate real-time manipulation, adaptation, and dynamic deformation. However, these studies mainly focus on independent entities rather than complete scenes and they do not address online reconstruction.

3   MEGA Design and Implementation

3.1   Overview of MEGA

To address the compromise in geometric accuracy observed in existing works, this study proposes MEGA, an edge-assisted approach for photorealistic yet geometry-preserving online reconstruction with mesh-aligned 3DGS. The mesh-aligned 3DGS method consists of two key designs: (1) 3D Gaussians are constructed by inheriting geometric characteristics from triangle mesh faces, and their subsequent parameter deduction is revised to preserve accurate geometric information (§3.2). (2) An image-to-geometry alignment technique is introduced to mitigate inconsistencies between visual appearances and the underlying geometric structure, facilitating geometrically consistent optimization (§3.3).

MEGA integrates these designs to formulate a comprehensive online reconstruction approach. As illustrated in Fig. 1, LIV systems are deployed on a robot-mounted or handheld mini PC to process multi-modal sensor inputs, generating posed frames, colored LiDAR points, and triangle mesh faces in real-time. These incrementally available artifacts are exported from the LIV systems and offloaded to the edge server asynchronously, without disrupting the real-time processing loops at the device side. Simultaneously, the 3DGS training framework deployed on the edge server consumes these artifacts to expand and optimize a 3DGS model, where the mesh-aligned 3DGS representation and image-to-geometry alignment aid in achieving geometry-preserving reconstruction.

3.2   3D Gaussian Initialization and Parameter Deduction

As described in Sect. 2.2, 3DGS employs an explicit structure similar to point clouds and meshes. Additionally, 3D Gaussians share substantial similarities with triangle mesh faces, given the ability to collapse into flat 2D Gaussians for planar appearances and the learnable scaling and orientation parameters to approximate the coverage of triangle faces. These similarities bridge 3DGS to the underlying geometric structure by allowing 3D Gaussians to inherit characteristics beyond positions. Inspired by these observations, we propose a mesh-aligned representation for populating 3D Gaussians during training.

As illustrated in Fig. 3(a), to construct a 3D Gaussian based on a triangle face, we first propose 3D axes for the face. The z-axis aligns with the face's normal vector, the x-axis is defined by the direction from the face's centroid (c) to its farthest corner, and the y-axis is determined following the right-hand rule. Next, a 3D Gaussian is constructed by inheriting these 3D axes, and its scaling parameters are selected to achieve similar coverage to the face. To ensure that the constructed 3D Gaussian preserves the face's geometric characteristics, we constrain its movement and rotation as illustrated in Fig. 3(b). Specifically, the 3D Gaussian's position is deduced by adding drifts to the centroid along the x-axis ($d_x \overrightarrow{x}$) and y-axis ($d_y \overrightarrow{y}$), while its rotation is restricted around the z-axis by applying an additional rotation degree (represented as quaternion q_z) to the original orientation (represented as quaternion q).

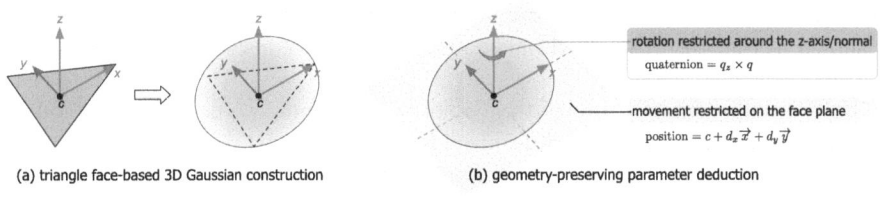

(a) triangle face-based 3D Gaussian construction   (b) geometry-preserving parameter deduction

Fig. 3. Illustration of a mesh-aligned 3D Gaussian.

The revised parameter deduction for 3D Gaussians ensures that they can only move within planes determined by their corresponding triangle mesh faces and they always conform to the original normal directions. Notably, the scaling along the z-axis is minimized to mimic the planar appearances of faces, and the movement along the z-axis is limited to a sufficiently small range, facilitating the depth ordering of 3D Gaussians in the same plane.

3.3 Image-to-Geometry Alignment

In LIV systems, LiDAR points and camera frames typically undergo different processing flows due to their distinct data acquisition mechanisms, formats, and potential lack of hardware synchronization [8,11]. Despite being in the same 3D coordinate system, LiDAR mapping and camera tracking poses can exhibit inconsistencies. While some works [5,14] focus on 3DGS-enabled SLAM methods that incorporate frame pose optimization into 3DGS training, they cannot fully leverage the precise LiDAR inputs. Meanwhile, we observe that the inconsistencies between LiDAR mapping and camera tracking poses are usually small, making an additional tracking module unnecessary.

| (a) point cloud rendering (PCR) | (b) PCR over ground truth | (c) warped ground truth | (d) PCR over warped ground truth |

Fig. 4. Illustration of image warping for geometric consistencies. *The thin black areas outside the red lines in sub-figure (c) indicate the empty regions caused by image warping. For better visibility, please zoom in to observe these effects.* (Color figure online)

To address this, we propose an image-to-geometry alignment technique that mitigates inconsistencies by warping images instead of modifying tracking poses. Figure 4 illustrates this technique. Specifically, Fig. 4(a) shows a geometrically precise point cloud rendering (PCR). Figure 4(b) overlays the PCR on the ground truth image with a 50% opacity, and the yellow box in the zoomed-in part highlights a mismatched area. After slight warping w.r.t. the ground truth image, as shown in Fig. 4(c), the fused image achieves better consistencies, as indicated by the green box in Fig. 4(d).

For implementing the image-to-geometry alignment, we use the open-source homography optimization module provided by Kornia [17], which can learn a 3×3 homography matrix for each pair of source and target images through gradient descent. In each image-to-geometry alignment step, we render training views with the latest set of 3D Gaussians and use these renderings as target images, while the ground truth images serve as source images. With the mesh-aligned representation, the renderings effectively preserve geometric structure. The homography optimization module then tunes the transformation matrices to warp the ground truth images towards mitigating inconsistencies. Since the renderings are only used as target images, no 3D Gaussian is involved in the homography optimization process. Moreover, homography matrices are the only optimizable parameters, ensuring the efficiency of the alignment step. During online training, image-to-geometry alignment steps are scheduled periodically per training view (e.g., once after every ten visits to a training view).

4   Performance Evaluation

We have fully implemented the proposed MEGA approach based on the reference implementation of 3DGS [7], utilizing two LIV systems, R^{3}LIVE [11] and ImMesh [10], for camera pose tracking and online meshing, respectively.

To the best of our knowledge, there was no publicly available open-source implementation targeting online 3DGS training with LIV systems at the time of writing. Therefore, we conducted both online and offline experiments to extensively evaluate MEGA. First, we incorporated the designs of MEGA, including the mesh-aligned representation and image-to-geometry alignment, with the density control strategy proposed in 3DGS to create an offline mode and evaluated it against the latest geometry-oriented offline 3DGS methods [1,4], as well as a straightforward offline reproduction of Gaussian-LIC [9]. Next, we examined the performance of MEGA for online reconstruction by comparing it against the offline mode. Specifically, the online mode constructs 3D Gaussians based on the incremental triangle mesh faces without extra densification and performs training steps alongside camera pose tracking and online meshing procedures.

4.1   Experimental Setup

Baseline Methods: We compared MEGA with the following baseline methods:

- **3DGS** corresponds to the original 3DGS implementation [7]. We utilized the same posed frames and colored points exported from R^{3}LIVE for 3DGS initialization and optimization.
- **Coco-LIC** resembles an offline version of Gaussian-LIC [9]. While Gaussian-LIC is the most relevant work to MEGA, its implementation has not been open-sourced yet. However, Coco-LIC [8], the tracking module it relies on, is publicly available. We enhanced Coco-LIC to export posed frames and colored points and supplied them to 3DGS. Additionally, we carefully calibrated the frame selections to ensure that **Coco-LIC** uses the same set of frames as other methods relying on R^{3}LIVE. Since Gaussian-LIC does not modify the core rendering pipeline of 3DGS, this reproduction can be regarded as a straightforward offline version of Gaussian-LIC.
- **2DGS** [4] and **PGSR** [1] are two recent works focusing on 3DGS-based surface reconstruction. In addition to the visual quality the original 3DGS is optimized for, they introduce regularization terms to recover scene geometry, such as depth distortion and normal consistency. Similar to **3DGS**, we employed the posed frames and colored points exported from R^{3}LIVE for their initialization and optimization.
- **2DGS+** and **PGSR+** are variants of **2DGS** and **PGSR**, respectively. They exploit the homography matrices resulting from MEGA to warp ground truths, potentially increasing the geometric consistencies among frames.

Datasets: We followed Gaussian-LIC [9] for the selection of datasets, including *hku_campus_seq_00*, *degenerate_seq_00*, *hkust_campus_02 (top 150 seconds)* from the R^{3}LIVE dataset [11], *hku2* from the FAST-LIVO dataset [24], and *botanic_1018_00*, *botanic_1018_09* from the BotanicGarden dataset [13]. Specifically, we excluded *LiDAR_Degenerate* and *Visual_Challenge* scenes from the FAST-LIVO dataset because the LIV systems we utilized are not optimized for scenarios with significant degeneration. While improving the robustness of the underlying camera pose tracking and online meshing modules is possible, it is beyond the scope of this work.

Metrics: Since MEGA involves image-to-geometry alignment steps, the renderings of MEGA can exhibit slight offsets from the ground truths, invalidating traditional image quality metrics like PSNR and SSIM. Therefore, we introduced an additional warping process before calculating PSNR and SSIM metrics. This warping process employs the same homography optimization module used in the image-to-geometry alignment to transform the ground truths. Additionally, we found that the warping process also benefits baseline methods. Hence, we report warped PSNR and SSIM for all methods.

For learning-based metrics, we used Q-Align [20] as an alternative. Q-Align leverages the latest advancements in large multi-modality models and achieves state-of-the-art performance in image quality assessment. Furthermore, Q-Align does not rely on reference images, allowing it to assess image quality purely based on the renderings, thus eliminating the need for an extra warping process over ground truths.

Experimental Platform: The evaluation was conducted on a realistic platform with a mini PC and an edge workstation. The mini PC features an AMD Ryzen 7 8845HS CPU, which is low-power yet sufficient for running LIV systems in real-time. The edge workstation is equipped with a powerful Intel Core i9-13900K CPU and an NVIDIA RTX4090 GPU, allowing for training 3DGS at full speed. The mini PC communicates with the edge workstation through a Wi-Fi 6 router.

4.2 Quantitative Comparison

Table 1 summarizes the quantitative results comparing MEGA with baseline methods. The results demonstrate that MEGA consistently achieves superior image quality across all datasets, ranking first in most cases regarding different datasets and metric types, proving the efficacy of its mesh-aligned designs.

Table 1. Quantitative comparison of MEGA with baselines on three datasets. **1** 2 3 *highlight the top-3 metric values.*

	R³LIVE			FAST-LIVO			BotanicGarden		
	PSNR↑	SSIM↑	Q-Align↑	PSNR↑	SSIM↑	Q-Align↑	PSNR↑	SSIM↑	Q-Align↑
3DGS	21.51	0.76	2.40	28.77	0.79	2.47	14.57	0.45	2.38
Coco-LIC	20.82	0.72	2.23	28.31	0.77	2.33	14.40	0.43	2.40
2DGS	21.45	0.76	2.37	28.51	0.79	2.41	14.87	0.48	2.17
PGSR	22.16	0.76	2.47	28.60	0.80	2.54	13.16	0.37	2.40
2DGS+	22.91	0.82	2.53	28.77	0.81	2.39	15.24	0.49	2.15
PGSR+	23.38	0.81	2.59	29.32	0.82	2.50	13.25	0.38	2.29
MEGA	23.34	0.82	2.53	30.66	0.86	2.73	17.95	0.57	2.51

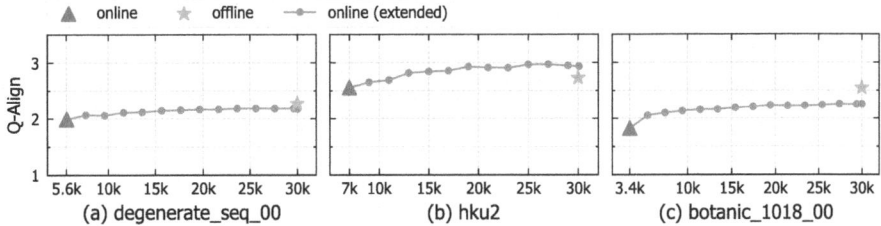

Fig. 5. Comparison of MEGA under different deployment modes and training steps.

Additionally, we find that Coco-LIC generally performs slightly worse than 3DGS (R³LIVE). Nonetheless, Coco-LIC proves to be more robust in scenes with significant degeneration. Both 2DGS+ and PGSR+ achieve better PSNR and SSIM than their counterparts, highlighting the effectiveness of the image-to-geometry alignment employed in MEGA. Notably, PGSR and PGSR+ achieve remarkable PSNR in the R³LIVE dataset due to their additional exposure compensation module, which is not present in other methods.

Figure 5 compares the Q-Align metric values achieved by the online and offline modes of MEGA on the *degenerate_seq_00*, *hku2*, and *botanic_1018_00* scenes. For the online mode, we extended the optimization procedures, training each model until 30k steps after online meshing finished and taking a snapshot every 2k steps, to showcase the trend in metric values. The results indicate that the online mode achieves Q-Align metric values close to the offline mode, suggesting that online training steps alone can already learn reasonable scene representations. Further training steps result in a stable increase in metric values, allowing for the fitting of fine-grained details exhibited in the scenes.

Remarkably, the online mode achieves comparable Q-Align metric values without densification, i.e., 3D Gaussians are simply derived from triangle mesh faces, confirming the efficacy of the mesh-based construction. In the *hku2* scene shown in Fig. 5(b), the online mode even surpasses the offline mode with extended training. This is possible because the online mode has access to all posed frames and maintains a set of key frames based on their position and orientation. In contrast, the offline mode simply takes every fifth frame as a key frame, following the setting in Gaussian-LIC [9]. In the *botanic_1018_00* scene shown in Fig. 5(c), the online mode shows a relatively larger gap compared to the offline mode. This can be attributed to the fact that the botanic scene exhibits many tiny tree leaves, which are challenging to model using a small number of 3D Gaussians, thus requiring denser 3D Gaussians and longer training steps.

4.3 Visual Comparison

Figure 6 provides a visual comparison of MEGA in both its offline and online modes. Unlike 3DGS that exhibits disordered geometry (Fig. 6(a)), MEGA consistently preserves the accurate geometry inherited from the online meshing module and presents a decent scene appearance with online training alone, as shown in Fig. 6(c). Further training steps after the completion of meshing allow the online mode to fit intricate scene details, as demonstrated in Fig. 6(d), approaching the high-fidelity representation achieved by the offline mode (Fig. 6(b)).

(a) 3DGS (30,000)   (b) MEGA (offline, 30,000)   (c) MEGA (online, 5,634)   (d) MEGA (online, 30,634)

Fig. 6. Visual comparison of 3DGS, MEGA (offline), and MEGA (online) on the *degenerate_seq_00* scene. *The number in each sub-caption indicates the training steps.*

Figure 7 illustrates a visual comparison for the ablation of the image-to-geometry alignment and mesh-aligned parameter deduction designs. Figure 7(a) and (b) showcase the renderings obtained without and with image-to-geometry alignment, respectively. The slight inconsistencies between LiDAR priors and posed frames lead to rough surfaces, while the image-to-geometry alignment effectively mitigates these inconsistencies, resulting in smooth and high-fidelity surfaces. Figure 7(c) and (d) showcase the renderings obtained without and with mesh-aligned parameter deduction, respectively. Without the geometric regulation provided by parameter deduction, the optimization process is more prone to over-fitting visual appearances with incorrect geometry. For instance, the texture of the drainage channel is represented incorrectly in Fig. 7(c), while it is accurately aligned to the ground in Fig. 7(d).

(a) MEGA w/o alignment   (b) MEGA w/ alignment   (c) MEGA w/o param. deduction   (d) MEGA w/ param. deduction

Fig. 7. Visual comparison for the ablation of alignment and parameter deduction.

5   Conclusion

This study introduces MEGA, an edge-assisted online reconstruction approach that features a novel mesh-aligned representation for incremental 3D Gaussian construction and an image-to-geometry alignment design to address inconsistencies between posed frames and LiDAR priors. Furthermore, the edge-assisted pipeline enables MEGA to be deployed on low-power mobile robotic platforms. Extensive evaluations demonstrate that MEGA achieves superior rendering quality without compromising geometric accuracy.

Acknowledgments. This work was supported in part by Guangdong S&T Programme (Grant No. 2024B0101020004); Guangdong Basic and Applied Basic Research Foundation (No. 2023B1515120058); Guangzhou Basic and Applied Basic Research Program (No. 2024A04J6367).

References

1. Chen, D., et al.: PGSR: planar-based gaussian splatting for efficient and high-fidelity surface reconstruction. CoRR arxiv:2406.06521 (2024)
2. Gao, L., et al.: Mesh-based gaussian splatting for real-time large-scale deformation. CoRR arxiv:2402.04796 (2024)
3. Hong, S., et al.: Liv-gaussmap: lidar-inertial-visual fusion for real-time 3d radiance field map rendering. CoRR arxiv:2401.14857 (2024)
4. Huang, B., Yu, Z., Chen, A., Geiger, A., Gao, S.: 2d gaussian splatting for geometrically accurate radiance fields. In: SIGGRAPH (2024)
5. Keetha, N., et al.: Splatam: splat, track & map 3d gaussians for dense rgb-d slam. In: CVPR (2024)
6. Kerbl, B., Kopanas, G., Leimkühler, T., Drettakis, G.: 3d gaussian splatting for real-time radiance field rendering. ACM Trans. Graph. **42**(4), 139:1–139:14 (2023)
7. Kerbl, B., Kopanas, G., Leimkühler, T., Drettakis, G.: Reference implementation of 3DGS (2023). https://github.com/graphdeco-inria/gaussian-splatting
8. Lang, X., et al.: Coco-lic: continuous-time tightly-coupled lidar-inertial-camera odometry using non-uniform b-spline. IEEE Rob. Autom. Lett. **8**(11), 7074–7081 (2023)
9. Lang, X., et al.: Gaussian-lic: photo-realistic lidar-inertial-camera SLAM with 3d gaussian splatting. CoRR arxiv:2404.06926 (2024)
10. Lin, J., et al.: Immesh: an immediate lidar localization and meshing framework. IEEE Trans. Rob. **39**(6), 4312–4331 (2023)
11. Lin, J., Zhang, F.: R^{3}live: a robust, real-time, rgb-colored, lidar-inertial-visual tightly-coupled state estimation and mapping package. In: ICRA. IEEE (2022)
12. Liu, I., Su, H., Wang, X.: Dynamic gaussians mesh: consistent mesh reconstruction from monocular videos. CoRR arxiv:2404.12379 (2024)
13. Liu, Y., et al.: Botanicgarden: a high-quality dataset for robot navigation in unstructured natural environments. IEEE Rob. Autom. Lett. **9**(3), 2798–2805 (2024)
14. Matsuki, H., Murai, R., Kelly, P.H.J., Davison, A.J.: Gaussian splatting SLAM. In: CVPR (2024)
15. Mescheder, L.M., Oechsle, M., Niemeyer, M., Nowozin, S., Geiger, A.: Occupancy networks: learning 3d reconstruction in function space. In: CVPR (2019)
16. Mildenhall, B., Srinivasan, P.P., Tancik, M., Barron, J.T., Ramamoorthi, R., Ng, R.: Nerf: representing scenes as neural radiance fields for view synthesis. In: ECCV (2020)

17. Riba, E., Mishkin, D., Ponsa, D., Rublee, E., Bradski, G.: Kornia: an open source differentiable computer vision library for pytorch. In: Winter Conference on Applications of Computer Vision (2020)
18. Ruan, J., Li, B., Wang, Y., Sun, Y.: Slamesh: real-time lidar simultaneous localization and meshing. In: ICRA. IEEE (2023)
19. Waczynska, J., Borycki, P., Tadeja, S.K., Tabor, J., Spurek, P.: Games: mesh-based adapting and modification of gaussian splatting. CoRR arxiv:2402.01459 (2024)
20. Wu, H., et al.: Q-align: teaching lmms for visual scoring via discrete text-defined levels. In: ICML (2024)
21. Xiong, H., Muttukuru, S., Upadhyay, R., Chari, P., Kadambi, A.: Sparsegs: real-time 360° sparse view synthesis using gaussian splatting. CoRR arxiv:2312.00206 (2023)
22. Yan, Y., et al.: Street gaussians for modeling dynamic urban scenes. In: ECCV (2024)
23. Yuan, C., Xu, W., Liu, X., Hong, X., Zhang, F.: Efficient and probabilistic adaptive voxel mapping for accurate online lidar odometry. IEEE Rob. Autom. Lett. **7**(3), 8518–8525 (2022)
24. Zheng, C., Zhu, Q., Xu, W., Liu, X., Guo, Q., Zhang, F.: FAST-LIVO: fast and tightly-coupled sparse-direct lidar-inertial-visual odometry. In: IROS. IEEE (2022)
25. Zhou, X., Lin, Z., Shan, X., Wang, Y., Sun, D., Yang, M.H.: Drivinggaussian: composite gaussian splatting for surrounding dynamic autonomous driving scenes. In: CVPR (2024)

MTEE: Multiscale Temporal Entropy Evaluation Paradigm for Heterogeneous Complex Datasets

Ledong An[1], Chenyang Wang[2], Shaoyuan Huang[1], Yang Guo[4], Cheng Zhang[3], Chao Qiu[1(✉)], and Xiaofei Wang[1]

[1] College of Intelligent and Computing, Tianjin University, Tianjin, China
chao.qiu@tju.edu.cn
[2] College of Computer Science and Software Engineering, Shenzhen University, Shenzhen 518060, Guangdong, China
chenyangwang@ieee.org
[3] Tianjin University of Finance and Economics, Tianjin, China
zhangcheng@tjufe.edu.cn
[4] China Mobile (Suzhou) Software Technology Company Limited, Suzhou 215163, China
guoyang@cmss.chinamobile.com

Abstract. The rapid advancements in time-series forecasting have led to the emergence of datasets with increasingly diverse characteristics. Researchers typically focus on designing robust algorithms to handle these datasets. However, model performance can vary across different datasets. Existing studies commonly use Mean Absolute Error (MAE) and Mean Squared Error (MSE) to evaluate model performance. These metrics often need to fully account for the impact of dataset quality on forecast accuracy and reliability, leading to insufficient explanations of model forecasts and even dataset dependence. Furthermore, the lack of dataset evaluation makes it difficult to determine whether forecast results are influenced by data characteristics or model architecture, significantly hindering model improvement. To address this problem, this study proposes a new dataset evaluation paradigm-Multiscale Temporal Entropy Evaluation Paradigm. This paradigm aims to tackle the problem of data feature ambiguity affecting model forecast interpretability. By evaluating nine time-series datasets from domains such as weather, economics, transportation, and networks and comparing these evaluations with the forecast results from six different models, this study demonstrates the effectiveness of this method in explaining the relationship between dataset features and model performance.

Keywords: Dataset Evaluation · Entropy · Time series Forecasting

© IFIP International Federation for Information Processing 2025
Published by Springer Nature Switzerland AG 2025
X. Chen et al. (Eds.): NPC 2024, LNCS 15527, pp. 409–420, 2025.
https://doi.org/10.1007/978-981-96-2830-8_32

1   Introduction

As the application of time series forecasting expands, datasets with various types and complexities continue to emerge. Researchers often focus on developing robust algorithms to address these datasets. However, the diverse patterns and noise within these datasets present challenges for model forecasts. Therefore, evaluating datasets before developing models is crucial. Choosing appropriate datasets can significantly improve model performance and ensure forecast accuracy. For example, traditional models such as ARIMA [3] perform well with short-term linear data, while deep learning models such as LSTM [6] excel with nonlinear datasets. Transformer and their variants, such as Fedformer, Autoformer, Pyraformer, and DynEformer [8,9,18–20,22], have also shown significant success with long-term time series data. Despite their success, these models typically rely on Mean Absolute Error (MAE) and Mean Squared Error (MSE) to evaluate forecasts. **However, this evaluation method may overlook the fact that the quality of the dataset itself can also affect model forecasts. Without evaluating dataset, it is difficult to discern whether the forecast results are influenced by the characteristics of the dataset or the model architecture, which could lead to problems such as dataset dependence [17].**

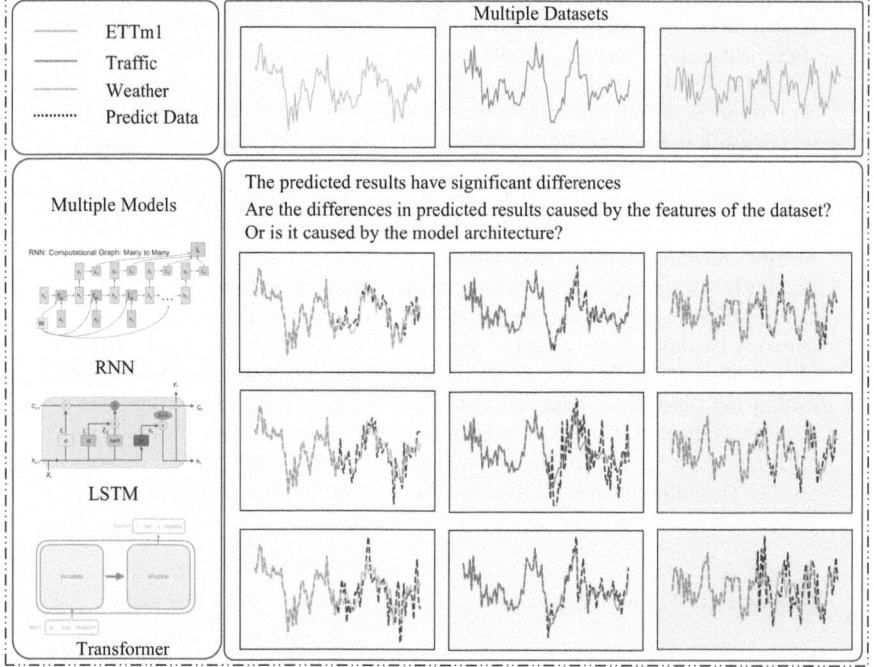

Fig. 1. Ambiguity in Dataset Features Hinders the Interpretability of Model Forecast Results.

As shown in Fig. 1, we select three datasets, ETTm1, Traffic, and Weather, and perform a simple forecast using RNN [12], LSTM, and Transformer. The forecast from these models varies significantly across the different datasets. These differences might be due to the characteristics of the datasets or the models themselves. However, without a detailed analysis of data features, it is challenging to identify the root cause of these differences, posing a significant obstacle to evaluating model performance.

There is an urgent need to develop a universal data evaluation method to address the challenge of insufficient interpretability of model forecasts due to unclear data features. Such a method would enhance researchers' understanding of the intrinsic relationships between dataset features and model forecasts. Several key dataset evaluation metrics have been proposed, *e.g.*, Zhang, G *et al.* [21] demonstrated that evaluating seasonality and trends can significantly improve neural network prediction accuracy. Raubitzek*et al.* [15] investigated the impact of data complexity on model performance, while Miloš B. *et al.* [1] emphasized the importance of information density within datasets. However, these metrics often focus on individual features and lack a comprehensive evaluation of multiple features, limiting their effectiveness in analyzing complex time series data. Mirna *et al.* [14] compared various independent evaluation metrics and highlighted the critical role of complex feature patterns in identifying data distribution patterns, suggesting that assessing dataset complexity can significantly enhance model forecasting performance.

Entropy [16] provides a comprehensive and nuanced analysis of data features compared to single-metric evaluations due to its ability to capture complex patterns and dynamic characteristics. Permutation entropy [11] assesses the nonlinear dynamic features of time series by reflecting system chaos through the complexity of permutation sequences. Sample entropy [23] measures the complexity and regularity of time series by quantifying uncertainty through the degree of matching in short-term time series. These entropy-based methods are less sensitive to time dimensions and struggle to directly evaluate time-specific features such as trends, complexity, periodicity, and information density. Therefore, there is a need to further optimize existing evaluation methods to address their limitations in time series assessment. This paper proposes an approach that integrates entropy with multiscale and time window techniques to evaluate time-series performance, thereby overcoming entropy's limitations in capturing temporal dimensions. This approach assesses datasets from four critical perspectives: periodicity, trend, complexity, and information density. It provides a more comprehensive and detailed evaluation of time series characteristics, offering valuable insights for model pre-evaluation. The innovations of this paper are as follows:

– Propose the Multiscale Temporal Entropy Evaluation Paradigm to overcome the limitations of relying solely on metrics such as MAE and MSE to measure model performance. This paradigm can reflect the objective characteristics of time-series datasets from multiple perspectives, thereby enabling the pre-evaluation of model performance.

- Time-series datasets can be evaluated across various time scales using multiscale and time window methods. This approach enables a comprehensive assessment of both long-term trends and short-term fluctuations, allowing the dynamic characteristics within the data to be effectively captured.
- Identifying the characteristics of different datasets and explaining the differences in model performance, this method can comprehensively evaluate various features of time series and evaluate model performance through these features, demonstrating high generalization ability.

2   Related Work

Time-series forecasting is a long-standing and continuously evolving research field. Researchers have proposed various methods for evaluating time-series datasets to address different scenarios. SVM [2] was highly regarded for its performance in handling high-dimensional data, strong generalization ability, and robustness. However, its performance was limited in time-series evaluation, which required high continuity and smoothness. The main reasons for this included its sensitivity to parameters, high computational complexity, and limitations in handling nonlinearly separable and nonstationary data.

Lyapunov [10] provided critical dynamic feature information based on rigorous mathematical theory, but its application was limited, especially in the presence of significant noise or irregularities. ARIMA excelled in handling linear data by relying mainly on the linear relationship of time series, but its applicability was limited to non-stationary series or data with complex structures. Fourier Transform [4] converted time-domain signals into frequency-domain representations, showing the frequency components of the signal, but was ineffective for non-stationary time-series or signals whose frequency characteristics changed over time. Furthermore, ETS [5] and Holt-Winters [7] were widely used for the analysis of time series datasets. These methods primarily smoothed time series through weighted averaging, which was suitable for capturing trends and seasonality in time series but limited in forecasting high-frequency and complexly changing time series.

Entropy is a robust tool that operates independently of data distribution assumptions, making it applicable to various time series datasets. However, traditional entropy metrics do not incorporate the time dimension, which limiting their direct use in time-series forecasting and analysis. To mitigate this limitation, researchers have proposed several enhancements. For example, permutation entropy [11] is used to analyze permutation patterns within sequence data, effectively capturing local structures and ordering rules. Nevertheless, the information content may need to be more accurate in short sequences or sequences with frequent repetitions. Sample entropy [23] is tailored for nonstationary and nonlinear time series, considering the distribution characteristics of the samples at different time points. However, it is susceptible to sample selection and may be influenced by abrupt changes or outliers. Fuzzy entropy [13], another variation, incorporates the concepts of fuzziness and uncertainty in time series. Despite this, it has high computational complexity and is sensitive to parameter selection, which may hinder its performance when dealing with large-scale data.

Given these challenges, there is an urgent need to propose a more generalized data evaluation method. This method should efficiently and robustly handle complex, variable information density, sparse, and uneven time series datasets. Entropy can be combined with multiscale and time window methods as a powerful tool independent of data distribution assumptions. It can more comprehensively capture the intrinsic by conducting multi-level, multi-time scale analysis.

3   Methodology

In this section, we improve the Shannon entropy formula by introducing multiscale and time window methods, forming a new theoretical framework. This framework retains the core advantage of entropy in measuring information uncertainty while addressing the limitations of traditional entropy, which often fails to fully capture the changes and complexities of data over time. It allows for the decomposition and analysis of time series datasets at different scales, thereby comprehensively capturing the multi-level structure and dynamic characteristics of the data, as shown in Fig. 2.

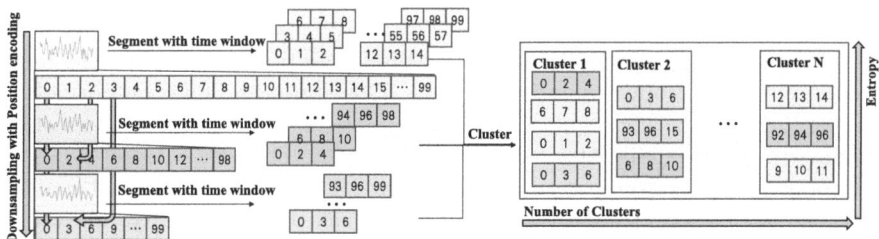

Fig. 2. Multiscale Temporal Entropy schematic diagram.

Building upon this new theoretical framework, regularization terms can be integrated to account for the diverse characteristics of time series. This approach facilitates a comprehensive evaluation of trends, periodicity, complexity, and information density within the data.

3.1   Multiscale Temporal Entropy Evaluation Paradigm

We first perform downsampling on the initial time series to segment it into subsequences at various time scales. This downsampling process allows us to observe data trends across different scales, revealing details that might be obscured within the overall pattern. Subsequently, we apply a time window method to further process these downsampled subsequences, dividing them into multiple clusters. This clustering process helps us better capture the local dynamic features of the time series, particularly sudden events or short-term fluctuations that the overall trend might overshadow. The specific steps are as follows:

For a given time series $\{x_1, x_2, \ldots, x_N\}$, with subsampling scale τ, window length W, generate downsampled subsequences. For each window position k, the window contains:

$$\{w_k^{(\tau)}, w_{k+1}^{(\tau)}, \ldots, w_{k+W-1}^{(\tau)} \mid w_k^{(\tau)} = x_{k\tau+1}\} \tag{1}$$

where $\{w_k^{(\tau)}\}$ is the downsampled sequence obtained by taking every τ-th sample from the original time series $\{x_1, x_2, \ldots, x_N\}$.

We calculate the entropy within each window to quantify the uncertainty and complexity of the information for that period. These windows span different parts of the entire time series, allowing us to capture dynamic changes and information characteristics at various scales. We obtain the multiscale temporal entropy by averaging the entropy values across all window positions. This method effectively integrates information across different scales of the time series, thereby revealing the overall complexity and structural characteristics of the time series. The specific steps are as follows:

$$H_\tau(X) = \frac{1}{M} \sum_{k=1}^{M} \left[-\sum_{j=k}^{k+W-1} \left(\frac{\text{count}(w_j^{(\tau)})}{W} \log \frac{\text{count}(w_j^{(\tau)})}{W} \right) \right] \tag{2}$$

To address the diverse characteristics of datasets, we propose an enhanced multiscale temporal entropy evaluation method. This approach builds on Formula 2 by incorporating specific regularization terms for different features, each corresponding to a particular metric. We calculate a comprehensive entropy value by performing a weighted aggregation of the results. This enhanced method enables a detailed evaluation of features such as periodicity, trend, stability, and information density across multiple scales, thereby revealing deeper characteristics and complexities of the data. The specific steps are as follows:

$$H_\tau^{\text{MTE}}(X) = \alpha \cdot \frac{1}{M} \sum_{k=1}^{M} \left[-\sum_{j=k}^{k+W-1} \left(\frac{\text{count}(w_j^{(\tau)})}{W} \log \frac{\text{count}(w_j^{(\tau)})}{W} \right) \right] + \beta \cdot H_\tau^{(F)}(X) \tag{3}$$

where α is the coefficient for the temporal entropy component, β is the coefficient for the regularization term, M is the total number of windows, and $H_\tau^{(F)}(X)$ is the entropy of the regularization term for the specific feature F.

3.2   EEMD-Multiscale Temporal Entropy

Seasonality is a common feature in time series, referring to patterns that repeat at regular intervals. This repetitiveness often reflects certain regular behaviors or periodic processes, such as seasonal changes, day-night cycles, economic cycles, and so on. Ensemble Empirical Mode Decomposition (EEMD) is an improved method of Empirical Mode Decomposition (EMD). By introducing white noise and averaging multiple decomposition results, EEMD overcomes the mode mixing problem inherent in EMD. With its strong adaptability, multiscale decomposition capability, and noise resistance, EEMD offers unique advantages for analyzing seasonality in time series. It can accurately extract the seasonal components within the data and quantify the energy distribution of these components, providing an effective method for seasonality analysis in time series. Combining the EEMD transformation with the original formula. The specific steps are as follows:

First, decompose the time series $x_1, x_2, \ldots, x_N$ using Ensemble Empirical Mode Decomposition (EEMD) to obtain m intrinsic mode functions (IMFs). For each IMF, calculate the ratio of its energy to the total energy, denoted as p_i:

$$p_i = \frac{\sum_{t=1}^{N}(\mathrm{IMF}_i(t))^2}{\sum_{j=1}^{m}\sum_{t=1}^{N}(\mathrm{IMF}_j(t))^2}, \quad i = 1, 2, \ldots, k \tag{4}$$

Building upon the multiscale time entropy paradigm, introduce EEMD decomposition and calculate the entropy by considering the energy proportion of each IMF. The transformed formula are as follows:

$$H_\tau^{EEMD}(X) = \frac{1}{M}\sum_{k=1}^{M}\left(-\sum_{i=1}^{m}\frac{\sum_{t=1}^{N}(\mathrm{IMF}_i(\tau,t))^2}{\sum_{j=1}^{m}\sum_{t=1}^{N}(\mathrm{IMF}_j(\tau,t))^2}\log\frac{\sum_{t=1}^{N}(\mathrm{IMF}_i(\tau,t))^2}{\sum_{j=1}^{m}\sum_{t=1}^{N}(\mathrm{IMF}_j(\tau,t))^2}\right) \tag{5}$$

where $\mathrm{IMF}_i(\tau,t)$ is the subsequence of the i-th IMF at scale τ, and p_i denotes the energy proportion of the i-th IMF.

3.3   VEMSE-Multiscale Temporal Entropy

Trend is an essential feature in time series, characterized by sustained patterns of increase, decrease, or stability over a longer time frame. Unlike seasonality, which reflects periodic patterns, trends represent the time series' global characteristics and are observed at larger time scales. Variational Embedding Multiscale Sample Entropy (VEMSE) is an advanced algorithm for analyzing multichannel systems, addressing the imbalance in traditional Multiscale Sample Entropy (MMSE) with embedding dimensions and data length. By integrating multiscale analysis and variational embedding, VEMSE captures long-term trends in time series data more accurately. Changes in entropy values across different scales and embedding dimensions quantify the time series trend. Trends cause significant entropy changes at larger scales, enabling effective extraction and quantification of trend characteristics.

In VEMSE, the embedding dimension m_j for each subsequence $y_j^{(\tau)}$ varies rather than being fixed. Therefore, based on the original formula, we introduce a unique embedding dimension m_j for each subsequence and recalculate the probability distribution and entropy values accordingly. Therefore, the formula for addressing trendiness can be expressed as:

$$H_\tau^{\mathrm{VEMSE}}(X) = \frac{1}{M}\sum_{k=1}^{M}\left[-\sum_{j=k}^{k+W-1}\left(\frac{\mathrm{count}(y_j^{(\tau,m_j)})}{W}\log\frac{\mathrm{count}(y_j^{(\tau,m_j)})}{W}\right)\right] \tag{6}$$

3.4   RCMPE-Multiscale Temporal Entropy

In time series analysis, complexity typically refers to the combined expression of the chaotic, random, and nonlinear characteristics of the time series. Complex time series exhibit dynamic changes, non-linear features, and a certain degree of randomness, making their forecast and analysis challenging. Refined Composite Multiscale Permutation Entropy (RCMPE) is a further development based on Multiscale Permutation Entropy (MPE). RCMPE combines the advantages of multiscale analysis and permutation entropy, allowing for a more refined capture of time series' nonlinear dynamic characteristics and complexity. By calculating the permutation entropy at different time scales and combining the results, RCMPE provides a more comprehensive description of the sequence complexity. It can thoroughly evaluate the complexity of time series, avoiding the excessive simplification or smoothing of time scales seen in traditional methods. RCMPE is suitable for analyzing complex and non-linear time series, effectively addressing sequences with multiple dynamic features. The formula is expressed as follows:

$$H_{\tau,\delta}^{\mathrm{RCMPE}}(X) = \frac{1}{M} \sum_{k=1}^{M} \left[-\frac{1}{N_k} \sum_{j=1}^{N_k} \left(\frac{\mathrm{count}(P_k^{\tau,j})}{W} \log \frac{\mathrm{count}(P_k^{\tau,j})}{W} \right) \right] \quad (7)$$

where δ is the delay parameter, M is the number of scales, and $P^{\tau,j}$ is the k-th permutation of the j-th subsequence at scale τ.

3.5   MTPE-Multiscale Temporal Entropy

In time series analysis, Information Density describes the distribution and variation of information within time series data, revealing trends, seasonality, and complexity. The challenges in analyzing information density include the nonlinearity and nonstationarity of time series, multiscale characteristics, noise and outliers, and computational complexity. Multiscale Tsallis Permutation Entropy (MTPE) has significant advantages in analyzing information density because the Tsallis entropy is a nonadditive entropy that better handles complex systems with long-range dependencies and fractal characteristics. MTPE can capture the multifractal characteristics and underlying patterns of time series at different time scales. By introducing the concept of permutation entropy, it enhances resistance to noise and outliers. Additionally, the adjustable parameter q in the Tsallis entropy makes the computation more flexible, allowing it to adapt to different types of time series. Introducing the MTPE framework into the original formula, the formula is shown as follows:

$$H_{\tau}^{\mathrm{MTPE}}(X) = \frac{1}{M} \sum_{k=1}^{M} \left[\frac{1}{q-1} \left(1 - \sum_{j=k}^{k+W-1} \left(\frac{\mathrm{count}(w_j^{(\tau)})}{W} \right)^q \right) \right] \quad (8)$$

where W is the width of each sliding window, τ is the time delay, q is the adjustable parameter of Tsallis entropy.

4   Experiments

This paper selects six representative time-series forecasting models as benchmarks: Fedformer, Pyraformer, Informer, Autoformer, Reformer, and ETSformer. Additionally, nine datasets from various domains, such as networking, traffic, weather, energy, and economics, were chosen. We used the multiscale temporal entropy evaluation method to assess the seasonality, trend, stability, and information density of these time series. To effectively test the regularization term designed for specific features, we set α to 0 and compared the multiscale temporal entropy evaluation results with the MAE (Mean Absolute Error) and MSE (Mean Squared Error) of each model across different datasets. All experiments were conducted in PyTorch on two NVIDIA GeForce RTX 3090 GPUs.

4.1   Dataset

This paper selects edge cloud upload bandwidth workload data, ECW-08 and ECW-09, from commercial crowdsourced edge clouds. The edge cloud infrastructure includes 5,174 heterogeneous devices that are self-built, recruited, and user-rented, supporting over 40 typical applications. Additionally, ECW-New App is chosen, referring to workload sequences of applications that have never appeared in ECW, to verify the method's ability to evaluate network datasets. Furthermore, the ETTm1 and ETTm2 datasets record the operational data of power transformers, which can be used for energy consumption and equipment maintenance forecasting. ECL provides electricity consumption information, aiding in energy demand forecasting and load management. The Exchange dataset contains exchange rate data from multiple countries, which can be used for financial market forecasting and risk management. The Traffic dataset offers traffic flow information suitable for traffic flow forecasting and optimization. Lastly, the Weather dataset records various meteorological parameters, providing rich data sources for weather forecasting and climate research. Evaluating these datasets can verify the generalization ability of time series analysis methods.

4.2   Main Results

Table 1 summarizes the forecasting results of six mainstream models on various datasets, including two metrics: MSE and MAE. Table 2 presents the evaluation results of the multiscale temporal entropy evaluation method, specifically including the calculated results for seasonality, trend, stability, and information density. By comparing and analyzing the results of the models on these datasets from Table 1 and Table 2, it is further validated that the multiscale temporal entropy evaluation method can effectively identify the characteristics of the datasets and evaluate model performance effectively. There are significant differences in the performance of different models on different datasets. Through the multiscale temporal entropy evaluation method, we can better understand the reasons behind these differences.

Table 1. The MAE and MSE of the model's forecasting results.

Model	Metric	ETTm1	ETTm2	ECL	Weather	Traffic	Exchange	ECW-08	ECW-ne*	ECW-09
Fedformer	MSE	**0.034**	0.061	0.193	0.217	**0.587**	0.148	0.084	0.077	0.158
	MAE	**0.140**	0.187	0.308	0.296	**0.366**	0.278	0.161	0.210	0.212
Pyraformer	MSE	**0.070**	0.064	0.386	0.197	**0.607**	0.085	0.094	0.139	0.197
	MAE	**0.201**	0.190	0.449	0.281	**0.392**	0.204	0.178	0.292	0.204
Informer	MSE	0.084	0.071	0.274	0.300	**0.719**	**0.847**	0.072	**0.049**	0.191
	MAE	0.232	0.195	0.368	0.384	**0.391**	**0.752**	0.147	**0.150**	0.193
Autoformer	MSE	**0.063**	0.104	0.201	0.266	**0.613**	0.197	0.078	0.081	0.136
	MAE	**0.189**	0.249	0.317	0.366	**0.388**	0.323	0.145	0.210	0.199
Reformer	MSE	0.293	0.096	0.312	0.689	**0.732**	**1.065**	0.720	0.493	0.099
	MAE	0.470	0.236	0.402	0.596	**0.423**	**0.829**	0.134	0.566	0.124
ETSformer	MSE	0.375	0.088	0.187	0.197	**0.607**	0.085	0.093	0.124	0.123
	MAE	0.398	0.234	0.304	0.281	**0.392**	0.204	0.169	0.275	0.209

Table 2. Results of the multiscale temporal entropy evaluation method.

Characteristic	ETTm1	ETTm2	ECL	Weather	Traffic	Exchange	ECW-08	ECW-ne*	ECW-09
Trend	0.399	0.531	0.806	0.436	**1.179**	0.174	0.673	0.753	0.926
Seasonal	**0.824**	0.953	0.983	1.155	**1.307**	0.703	1.223	1.080	0.946
Info density	0.813	0.808	0.775	0.770	**0.814**	0.776	0.811	**0.687**	0.806
Complex	1.594	1.139	1.286	1.357	**1.389**	**1.629**	1.379	1.600	1.384

4.3 Effectiveness Analysis of Multiscale Temporal Entropy Evaluation Method

For the multiscale temporal entropy evaluation method, the magnitude of the characteristic values reflects the complexity of the dataset in terms of seasonality, trend, stability, and information density. Smaller characteristic values indicate that the dataset is relatively simple regarding these features, making it easier to evaluate and forecast. Therefore, datasets often perform better on models designed to target these features. The visualization analysis is shown in Fig. 3. For models improved to capture seasonality, such as Fedformer, Autoformer, and Pyraformer, these models exhibit excellent forecasting performance on datasets with robust seasonality assessments, such as ETTm1, ETTm2, ECW-09, and Exchange. However, due to the high complexity of the Exchange dataset, models designed for complexity, like Informer and Reformer, do not perform as well. Similarly, the ECW-New App dataset is highly complex, resulting in lower forecasting accuracy with Reformer. However, because it performs best regarding

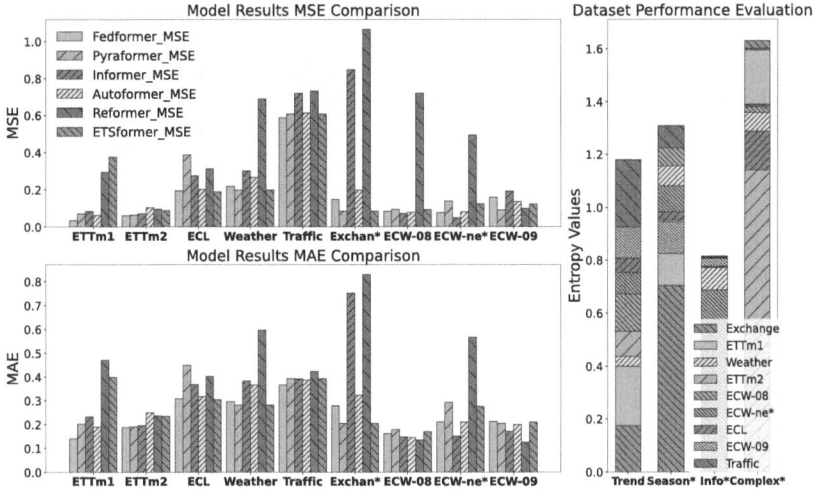

Fig. 3. Analysis of the Effectiveness of Multiscale Temporal Entropy Evaluation Results and Model Forecasting Results.

information density, the Informer model, which incorporates time fusion encoding to enhance temporal information perception, performs exceptionally well. In contrast, the Traffic dataset performs poorly across all four evaluation metrics, with the MAE and MSE of its model forecasts significantly lower than those of other datasets. These results validate the effectiveness of the proposed method, as it reflects the objective characteristics of the datasets through evaluation.

5   Conclusion

This paper provides an objective assessment of datasets by designing targeted regularization terms. It explains the performance differences of models on these datasets and validates the effectiveness of the multiscale temporal entropy evaluation paradigm in time series analysis. The paper also demonstrates the high generalizability of dataset performance assessment. Future work could optimize the multiscale temporal entropy evaluation method by designing new regularization terms and applying it to a wider range of datasets. Additionally, it could explore the application of the multiscale temporal entropy evaluation method in other time series tasks, such as anomaly detection and pattern recognition. This would provide new insights for the selection and evaluation of time series forecasting models and advance the development of time series analysis methods.

Acknowledgments. This work is supported in part by the Tianjin Natural Science Foundation under Grant No. 23JCYBJC00780, the National Natural Science Foundation of China under Grant No. 62072332, and the Tianjin Xinchuang Haihe Lab under Grant No. 22HHXCJC00002.

References

1. Stojanović, M.B., Božić, M.M., Stanković, M.M., Stajić, Z.P.: A methodology for training set instance selection using mutual information in time series prediction. Neurocomputing **141**, 236–245 (2014)
2. Awad, M., et al.: Support vector machines for classification. In: Efficient Learning Machines: Theories, Concepts, and Applications for Engineers and System Designers, pp. 39–66 (2015)
3. Box, G.E.P., et al.: Time series analysis, forecasting, and control. Holden-Day, Incorporated (1990)
4. Cooley, J.W., et al.: The fast fourier transform and its applications. IEEE Trans. Educ. **12**(1), 27–34 (1969)
5. Gardner, E.S., Jr.: Exponential smoothing: the state of the art. J. Forecast. **4**(1), 1–28 (1985)
6. Graves, A., et al.: Long short-term memory. In: Supervised Sequence Labelling with Recurrent Neural Networks, pp. 37–45 (2012)
7. Holt, C.C.: Forecasting seasonals and trends by exponentially weighted moving averages. Int. J. Forecast. **20**(1), 5–10 (2004)
8. Huang, S., et al.: One for all: unified workload prediction for dynamic multi-tenant edge cloud platforms, pp. 788–797 (2023)
9. Liu, S., et al.: Pyraformer: Low-complexity pyramidal attention for long-range time series modeling and forecasting. In: International Conference on Learning Representations (2021)
10. Lyapunov, et al.: The general problem of the stability of motion (1994)
11. Ma, C., et al.: Early fault diagnosis of rotating machinery based on composite zoom permutation entropy. Reliabil. Eng. Syst. Saf. **230**, 108967 (2023)
12. Medsker, L.R., et al.: Recurrent neural networks. Des. Appl. **5**(64–67), 2 (2001)
13. Pandey, K., et al.: Selecting features by utilizing intuitionistic fuzzy entropy method. Decis. Mak. Appl. Manag. Eng. **6**(1), 111–133 (2023)
14. Ponce-Flores, M., et al.: Time series complexities and their relationship to forecasting performance. Entropy **22**(1), 89 (2020)
15. Raubitzek, S., Neubauer, T.: Combining measures of signal complexity and machine learning for time series analyis: a review. Entropy **23**(12) (2021). https://doi.org/10.3390/e23121672
16. Shannon, C.E.: A mathematical theory of communication. Bell Syst. Techn. J. **27**(3), 379–423 (1948)
17. Shmueli, G., et al.: Predictive analytics in information systems research. MIS Q. **35**(3), 553–572 (2011)
18. Vaswani, A., et al.: Attention is all you need. Adv. Neural Inf. Process. Syst. **30** (2017)
19. Wang, C.R., et al.: Heterogeneous edge caching based on actor-critic learning with attention mechanism aiding. IEEE Trans. Netw. Sci. Eng. **10**(6), 3409–3420 (2023)
20. Wu, H., et al.: Autoformer: decomposition transformers with auto-correlation for long-term series forecasting. Adv. Neural. Inf. Process. Syst. **34**, 22419–22430 (2021)
21. Zhang, G.P., Qi, M.: Neural network forecasting for seasonal and trend time series. Eur. J. Oper. Res. **160**(2), 501–514 (2005)
22. Zhou, T., et al.: Fedformer: frequency enhanced decomposed transformer for long-term series forecasting. In: International Conference on Machine Learning, pp. 27268–27286. PMLR (2022)
23. Zhuang, D., et al.: The iba-ismo method for rolling bearing fault diagnosis based on vmd-sample entropy. Sensors **23**(2), 991 (2023)

nHAS: Neural-Compensated Hybrid Adaptive Scheduling for Cloud Gaming

Qianyun Gong[1], Jiapei Xu[1], Jianxin Shi[1], Xinjing Yuan[1], Jingdong Xu[1], Guanyu Gao[2], and Lingjun Pu[1(✉)]

[1] College of Computer Science, and DISSec, Nankai University, Tianjin, China
`pulingjun@gmail.com`
[2] Nanjing University of Science and Technology, Nanjing, China

Abstract. Cloud gaming, as one of the most promising live-streaming services, has garnered great attention by reducing client hardware requirements. However, it faces major challenges in maintaining high-quality user experience due to varying network conditions. From a network adaptation perspective, existing adaptive strategies can be categorized into adaptive bitrate (ABR)-based and adaptive frame rate (AFR)-based schemes. While ABR adapts well to bandwidth, it introduces redundant key frames, reducing video quality. AFR, on the other hand, avoids redundant key frames but has limited bandwidth adaptability. To tackle network variation and ensure high-quality experiences in cloud gaming, we propose nHAS, a hybrid adaptive live streaming scheduling system with neural compensation. nHAS integrates a deep reinforcement learning (DRL)-guided hybrid adaptive algorithm that dynamically optimizes bitrate and adjusts the resolution and frame rate to minimize redundant data. Additionally, to compensate for the impact of low frame rate and low resolution on video quality, we design a lightweight neural-compensated module tailored to the real-time and content-homogeneity characteristics of cloud gaming. Extensive evaluations demonstrate that nHAS increases video multi-method assessment fusion (VMAF) score and quality of experience (QoE) by 1.97 and 12.4% over the baseline.

Keywords: Neural compensation · Adaptive bitrate · Adaptive frame rate · Cloud gaming

1 Introduction

Cloud gaming is designed to offload the heavy storage, processing, and rendering of large-scale games to cloud servers, thereby reducing the hardware requirements on the client side. Meanwhile, it involves streaming live game videos from servers to clients. However, fluctuating and limited bandwidth presents non-trivial streaming challenges for a high-quality, low-latency user experience [1,2]. Firstly, the growing demand for video streaming applications in recent years, such as holographic telepresence, video conferencing, and virtual reality, is crowding out the available bandwidth for cloud gaming. Secondly, the rising

X. Chen et al. (Eds.): NPC 2024, LNCS 15527, pp. 421–434, 2025.
https://doi.org/10.1007/978-981-96-2830-8_33

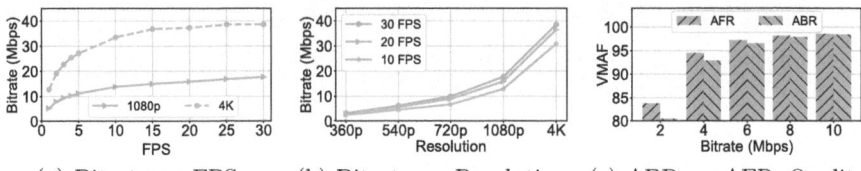

(a) Bitrate vs. FPS.   (b) Bitrate vs. Resolution.   (c) ABR vs. AFR. Quality.

Fig. 1. Analysis of video streaming for cloud gaming Genshin.

expectations from users for quality of experience (QoE) require higher network bandwidth. Thirdly, time-varying networks make it difficult for cloud gaming applications to utilize bandwidth resources effectively.

Existing live streaming systems attempt to optimize the user experience through adaptive bitrate (ABR) schemes [3–5], adaptive frame rate (AFR) schemes [6,7], congestion control strategies [8], and video enhancement technologies [1,9]. From the network adaptation perspective, these methods can be categorized into ABR-based and AFR-based schemes. ABR algorithms adapt well to bandwidth variations but introduce redundant key frames. Since different bitrates correspond to different optimal resolutions, ABR typically adjusts the bitrate by altering the resolution. This adjustment would artificially introduce additional key frames, rather than responding to regular video scene changes, which significantly reduces encoding efficiency and content quality (Sect. 2). Conversely, AFR algorithms avoid introducing additional key frames, yet their adaptability to varying bandwidth is limited, as residual information for higher frame rate content is more sparse (Sect. 2). Although there are some joint decision methods for ABR and AFR [6,10], they primarily focus on reducing frame latency without considering the impact of redundant key frames on video quality or the differences in bandwidth adaptability between ABR and AFR.

To this end, we advocate a hybrid ABR-AFR streaming scheduling method specifically for cloud gaming that fully leverages the distinct characteristics of ABR and AFR. However, there are still challenges in implementing this strategy in practice: (1) How to balance bitrate and frame rate decisions to accommodate different network variations? The impact of frame rate and resolution on video quality depends not only on available bandwidth but also on video content, making it challenging to identify the best settings. (2) How to maintain a high QoE even when the network is inadequate? If the bandwidth is insufficient, selecting video content with a low bitrate and frame rate would not only result in a poor viewing experience but would also cause the *stuttering* problem [6].

In this work, we propose nHAS, a hybrid adaptive live-streaming scheduling approach with neural compensation, designed to balance network adaptability and video quality in cloud gaming. To optimize the hybrid decisions, we develop the deep reinforcement learning (DRL)-guided Encoding Parameter Control (DRL-EPC) module, which operates in two stages. In the first stage, DRL optimizes the most network-sensitive parameter, bitrate, using cross-layer observations. In the second stage, leveraging the encoder's perception of video complexity, we adjust the resolution and frame rate to minimize redundant information. Additionally, to compensate for the impact of low frame rates and resolution on QoE, a video quality compensation module is needed. While some existing works [1,9,11] focus on real-time video quality enhancement, they do not account for the specific characteristics of cloud gaming. In nHAS, we design a Neural video quality Compensation module (NComp) tailored to the real-time nature and content homogeneity of cloud gaming. Our key contributions include:

- We propose nHAS, a neural-compensated hybrid adaptive live streaming scheduling strategy that effectively combines ABR and AFR approaches to enhance both network adaptability and video quality, addressing the limitations inherent in existing methods.
- We design the DRL-EPC algorithm to dynamically optimize bitrate and adjust resolution and frame rate, minimizing redundant data and maintaining high video quality under various network conditions.
- To mitigate the adverse impacts of low frame rates and resolutions on user QoE, we deploy the NComp module on the client side. NComp is tailored to the real-time and content-homogeneity characteristics of cloud gaming, providing real-time quality compensation to ensure a satisfactory user experience even under suboptimal network conditions.
- We implement a prototype system of nHAS. Extensive evaluations demonstrate that nHAS reduces latency, and packet loss rates by 21.1%, and 38.4%, respectively, while improving QoE by 12.4% and increasing the video multimethod assessment fusion (VMAF) score by 1.97 over the baseline.

2   Motivation

Bandwidth Adaptability of ABR vs. AFR. Video encoding involves several processes, including motion estimation, motion compensation, discrete cosine transform, quantization, and entropy coding. Among these, motion estimation and compensation are particularly critical, as they significantly reduce a large amount of temporal redundancy by predicting and compensating for motion. However, vanilla video compression alone is insufficient to ensure optimal streaming performance under fluctuating network conditions. Adaptation mechanisms like ABR or AFR are necessary to manage network variations. ABR achieves adaptability by selecting from a bitrate ladder with various bitrate-resolution combinations, as different bitrates correspond to different optimal resolutions. By lowering the resolution, ABR reduces spatial information, leading to a significant reduction in data transmission. For example, as shown in Fig. 1(a), our analysis[1] of the Genshin cloud gaming platform demonstrates that dropping from 1080p to 540p can reduce the bitrate by an average of 64.4%. In contrast, AFR adapts to bandwidth variations by adjusting the frame rate. Although reducing the frame rate decreases temporal redundancy, its impact on video size is limited due to the substantial compression already achieved through motion estimation and compensation. For instance, Fig. 1(b) shows that reducing from 30 FPS to 15 FPS decreases the bitrate by only about 4.5%-15.3%.

---

[1] For detailed experimental setup in this section, see Sect. 4.1.

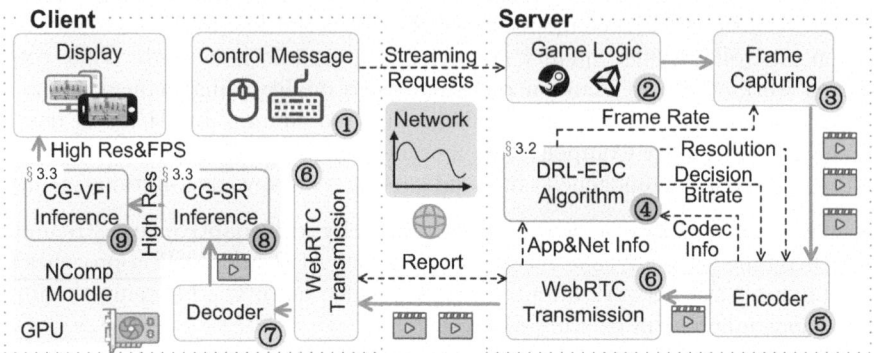

Fig. 2. Overview of nHAS.

Video Quality of ABR vs. AFR. In video encoding, serialized frames are categorized as key frames and non-key frames. Key frames are independently encoded, containing complete image data, making them larger in size. Non-key frames, in contrast, rely on motion estimation and compensation, using predictive information from surrounding frames to significantly reduce data size. ABR algorithms often adjust video resolution in response to network variations, which results in the introduction of new key frames. These key frames are not driven by content changes but are instead added to reinitialize the reference frame sequence for the new resolution, leading to increased redundant data and reducing the effective information density per unit of data, which decreases video quality. In contrast, AFR algorithms adapt by adjusting the frame rate without generating new key frames. Existing reference frames are reused, avoiding the redundancy introduced by ABR. As a result, AFR retains more effective information at the same bitrate, leading to relatively higher video quality than ABR. As shown in Fig. 1(c), this difference is especially significant at low bitrates, where the VMAF score for AFR is 3.34 points higher than that of ABR at 2 Mbps.

In summary, ABR has stronger bandwidth adaptability than AFR, but it introduces redundant key frames, which reduces video quality compared to AFR.

3   System Design

The overall system architecture of nHAS is shown in Fig. 2. The server receives keyboard and mouse inputs from the client and captures the game screen (①-③). Simultaneously, the DRL-EPC algorithm adjusts bitrate, resolution, and frame rate using cross-layer information. It combines the strengths of ABR and AFR while minimizing redundant data transmission to maintain video quality (④). The encoder then encodes the video based on DRL-EPC's decisions and transmits it to the client via WebRTC (⑤, ⑥). On the client side, the received video stream is decoded (⑦). To compensate for the negative impact of low frame rates and resolutions on QoE, the NComp module improves resolution

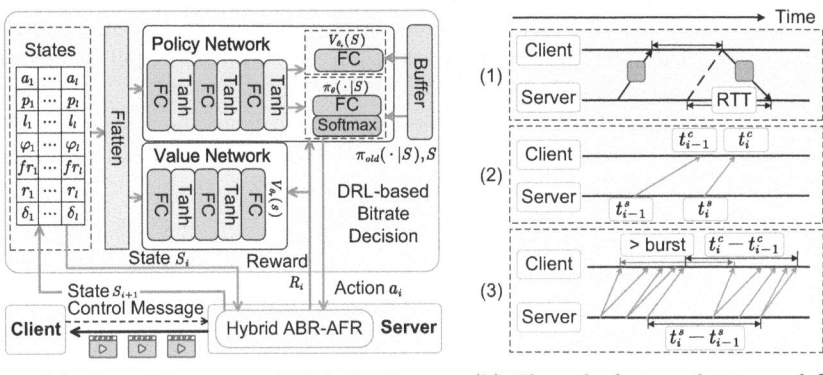

(a) The architecture of DRL-EPC.   (b) The calculation of rtt φ and δ.

Fig. 3. The DRL-EPC algorithm.

and frame rate using super-resolution for cloud gaming (CG-SR, ⑧) and video frame interpolation for cloud gaming (CG-VFI, ⑨). CG-SR and CG-VFI are designed specifically for cloud gaming, leveraging its real-time nature and content homogeneity. Finally, the optimized video frames are then displayed on the client device. The following sections will detail the two core modules of nHAS: the DRL-FEC algorithm and the NComp module.

3.1 DRL-Guided Encoding Parameter Control (DRL-EPC)

As discussed in Sect. 2, ABR adapts better to bandwidth, while AFR retains more effective information per unit of data, leading to higher video quality. To combine these strengths, we design a DRL-guided encoding parameter control algorithm. Specifically, to avoid an excessively large decision space and lengthy decision times, we first use DRL to only identify the most network-sensitive factor, the bitrate, by utilizing cross-layer states. Based on this decision, the encoder-assisted hybrid ABR-AFR algorithm adjusts resolution and frame rate, ensuring network adaptability while minimizing redundant information. In nHAS, the hybrid ABR-AFR control module is treated as part of the environment, while DRL continuously interacts with it to learn its behavior over time.

DRL-Based Bitrate Decision. nHAS combines the strengths of ABR and AFR, reducing redundant data transmission while ensuring network adaptability. However, the interdependence between frames during encoding poses significant challenges to decision-making, as the encoding and transmission of the current frame depend on previous ones. We address this by modeling the process as a Markov decision process and employing DRL for decision-making. To reduce the decision space and time, we focus DRL on the most network-sensitive factor, bitrate, while treating frame rate and resolution adjustments as part of the environment, as shown in Fig. 3(a). Based on the phasic policy gradient (PPG) [12], we develop the DRL-based bitrate decision algorithm, detailed as follows.

Observation. We incorporate cross-layer information from the network, codec, and application layers as states to enhance decision-making. The state is represented as $S_t = \{a_t, p_t, l_t, \varphi_t, fr_t, r_t, \delta_t\}$, capturing from the past l time slices before current time t. The design of each layer's state is outlined as follows:

(1) Application layer states. The variables a_t, p_t, l_t, and φ_t represent the decision bitrate, received Real-time Transport Protocol (RTP) packet count, packet loss rate, and RTT, respectively. As shown in Fig. 3(b-1), the RTT φ_t is calculated as $\varphi_t = c_t - s_t - d_t$, where c_t is the current timestamp, s_t is the timestamp when the server sends the report, and d_t is the duration between receiving and sending the report.

(2) Codec layer states. fr_t is the frame rate, and r_t is the codec bitrate.

(3) Network layer states. As shown in Fig. 3(b-2), δ_t represents the difference between the arrival interval of two consecutive RTP groups at the client and the departure interval at the server, given by $\delta_t = (t_i^c - t_{i-1}^c) - (t_i^s - t_{i-1}^s)$, where t_i^c and t_i^s are the timestamp of the i-th RTP group's arrival at the client and departure from the server, respectively. However, the RTP group may be split into different packets, and in case of post-congestion recovery, queued packets might be sent in a burst, denoted by ζ. As a result, we need to re-group the packets by combining packets sent within the same ζ into one group. Additionally, if the arrival interval between two packets is shorter than ζ and results in a negative latency interval, these packets are also re-grouped into one group. In Fig. 3(b-3), if a packet's arrival time exceeds ζ compared to the first packet in the current group, it is re-grouped into the orange group.

Bitrate Decision. Upon the arrival of each control message, the RL agent takes an action $a_t \in \mathcal{A} : \{a^1, a^2, \cdots a^{|\mathcal{A}|}\}$ based on the current state S_t, determining the decision bitrate for the corresponding time slice.

Objective. The goal of nHAS is to minimize redundant information while maximizing QoE. The reward is formulated as $R_t = \alpha_1 \cdot p_t + \alpha_2 \cdot r_t - \alpha_3 \cdot l_t - \alpha_4 \cdot \varphi_t - \alpha_5 \cdot (r_t - a_t)^+$. The detailed meaning of each part can be found above. We emphasize the last item $(r_t - a_t)^+$ to help reduce the sudden occurrence of key frames, thereby reducing redundant information and maintaining video quality.

Neural Network Architecture. Our design employs a policy network π and a value network V, both sharing the same parameters θ. As shown in Fig. 3(a), both networks have three fully connected layers. Additionally, the policy network incorporates a value head and a policy head for parameter sharing.

Training Methodology. The actor-critic networks face a trade-off between using shared or separate networks for training. Shared parameters improve feature

---

Algorithm 1: Hybrid ABR-AFR Control.

---

input : a_t, fr^{max}, r_{t-1}, fr_{t-1};
output: resolution res_t, frame rate fr_t;

/* Step1: frame rate adaptation.   */

1   $b^f_{t-1} \leftarrow r_{t-1}/fr_{t-1}$, $\Delta fr \leftarrow |a_t - r_{t-1}|/b^f_{t-1}$;
2   **if** $a_t \leq r_{t-1}$ **then**
3      $\Delta fr = \min(fr^{max} - fr_{t-1}, \Delta fr)$;
4      $fr_t \leftarrow fr_{t-1} - \Delta fr$;

5   **else**
6      $fr_t \leftarrow \min(fr_{t-1} + \Delta fr, fr^{max})$;

7   Update frame sample rate $sr_t \leftarrow fr_t$;
     /* Step2: resolution adaptation.   */
     /* Encode until $t+1$ with RC_RESIZE_ALLOWED based on sr_t and b_t.   */
8   $res_t, r_t \leftarrow$ RC_RESIZE_ALLOWED(sr_t, a_t).

---

utilization while causing conflicts between the policy and value objectives. To address this, we decouple the training of the policy and value networks while sharing parameters by alternating between a policy phase (training the policy network) and an auxiliary phase (knowledge distillation from the value network). In the policy phase, we introduce policy entropy to encourage exploration, while the remaining optimization follows proximal policy optimization (PPO). The auxiliary phase preserves knowledge in the value network while maintaining policy network information through a joint loss function, $L^{joint} \leftarrow L^{aux} + \beta_{clone}\hat{\mathbb{E}}_t[KL[\pi_{\theta_{old}}(\cdot|S_t), \pi_\theta(\cdot|S_t)]]$, where $L^{aux} = \frac{1}{2}\hat{\mathbb{E}}_t[(V_{\theta_\pi}(s_t) - \hat{V}^{targ}_t)^2]$. The KL divergence ensures the policy does not deviate too far.

Hybrid ABR-AFR Control. nHAS aims to adapt to the network while minimizing redundant data transmission. With DRL-based bitrate optimized for network adaptability, the focus shifts to reducing transmission redundancy. Since ABR tends to transmit more redundant data compared to AFR, the hybrid ABR-AFR control algorithm prioritizes adjusting the frame rate and only modifies the resolution when the frame rate cannot accommodate the current bandwidth. Additionally, as video complexity affects final quality, the encoder assists in making the final decision. The detailed process is shown in Algorithm 1.

Algorithm 1 takes several inputs: the decision bitrate a_t from the DRL algorithm, the maximum frame rate fr^{max} (we set it to 30 FPS), the previous codec bitrate r_{t-1}, and the previous frame rate fr_{t-1}. It outputs decisions on the current frame rate fr_t and resolution res_t. Initially, it calculates the previous average bitrate per frame b^f_{t-1} (L1). Based on the difference between a_t and r_{t-1}, it estimates the frame rate change Δfr using a linear model for robustness. Given the effectiveness of frame rate adjustments on reducing redundant data transmission, the algorithm prioritizes aligning the frame rate fr_t with a_t (L2-L6) and updates the video frame sampling rate sr_t accordingly (L7). To

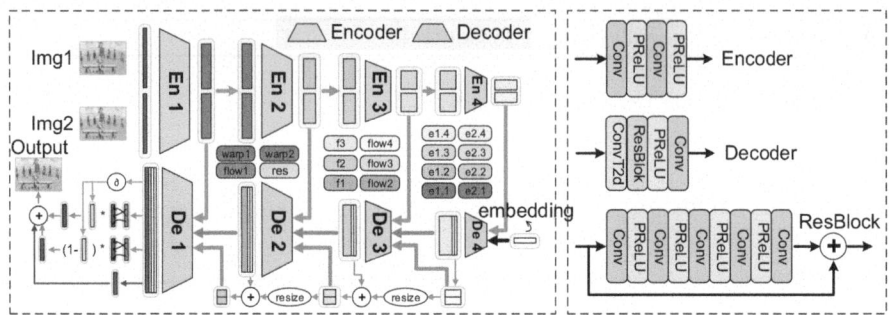

Fig. 4. The architecture of CG-VFI.

prevent limited AFR adaptation to bandwidth variations, we use the LibVPX configuration option RC_RESIZE_ALLOWED to fine-tune the resolution based on video content complexity and a_t (L8). Since we prioritize adjusting the frame rate, there are almost no redundant key frames in most cases.

3.2   Neural Video Quality Compensation (NComp)

To mitigate stuttering from low frame rates and quality degradation from low resolution, we design a neural-based quality enhancement module specifically for cloud gaming, taking its content homogeneity and real-time nature into account. NComp includes the CG-VFI and CG-SR modules, which activate only when low frame rates or resolutions are detected.

CG-VFI. Current neural VFI methods fall short of meeting the high frame rate demands of cloud gaming. For instance, interpolating from 30 FPS to 60 FPS requires inserting 30 frames per second, with an inference time under 33 ms, which existing models cannot achieve [13–15]. We design CG-VFI based on an encoder-decoder model IFRNet [15], to overcome this. As shown in Fig. 4, CG-VFI takes adjacent frames as input and outputs the intermediate frame. The input frames first go through the encoder for feature extraction, which prepares the decoder to gradually reconstruct the intermediate frame. Compared to the original IFRNet, the advantages of our CG-VFI include:

(1) *Reduced computational burden.* We apply a pruning algorithm based on the sum of absolute values of filter weights [16] to reduce the number of channel feature maps. The pruning ratio, adjustable based on the client's computing power, can shrink the model size by up to 90% with only a minimal 0.2dB difference in performance loss compared to IFRNet.

(2) *Removal of traditional frame upscaling methods.* IFRNet originally uses bilinear interpolation for SR before VFI, which can degrade the quality of subsequent frames. Since SR might be activated independently in nHAS, bilinear interpolation is inadequate for high-quality upscaling. Therefore, we replace bilinear interpolation with advanced neural-based models.

(3) *Loss function simplification.* The original IFRNet loss function incorporates an optical flow distillation loss, which addresses brightness variations caused by lighting changes and prevents objects from falling into local minima within repetitive textures. Given the content homogeneity characteristic of video content in cloud gaming, these concerns are less pronounced in nHAS. Consequently, we remove this specific loss component from our model.

CG-SR. For the same game, its video content is homogeneous. To this end, we design a content-aware lightweight SR model, called CG-SR, by modifying the existing SRVC [17]. The main modifications include:

(1) *Single stream transmission.* Unlike the dual-stream approach of SRVC, which transmits the video stream alongside real-time trained neural network models, CG-SR simplifies the process. Leveraging the homogeneity of cloud gaming content, CG-SR pre-deploys the model on the client side, transmitting only the video stream and eliminating the need for real-time model training.
(2) *Optimized patch processing.* SRVC processes video by dividing each frame into 5×5-pixel patches, which is computationally intensive. CG-SR reduces the number of patches and increases their size, employing batch processing to accelerate computation while maintaining enhancement quality.
(3) *Streamlined network architecture.* SRVC uses a network consisting of five convolutional layers and one upsampling layer. CG-SR streamlines this by reducing the filter count based on the sum of absolute filter weights [16].

4   Evaluation

4.1   Experimental Setup

Implementation. We develop a nHAS prototype based on WebRTC ($\sim$3500 lines in total). The testbed comprises two components, both implemented in Python. (1) The server, equipped with an RTX 3090 GPU, consists of stream transmission modified on aiortc, traffic control via Linux TC tool, and the DRL-EPC algorithm. (2) The client, equipped with an RTX 3080 GPU, consists of stream transmission and CG-SR/CG-VFI inferring.

Video Dataset. To align client-received frames with original gameplay in real-time, we pre-record gameplay using Fraps at 30 FPS and 1080p resolution. After that, we get a video dataset of about 60 h, 70% of which is used for training and 30% for testing.

Network Traces. (1) FCC, broadband network traces; (2) Lumos5G [18], 5G traces; (3) Genshin, collected commercial cloud gaming traces. Here, 70% of the traces in the datasets are used for training and 30% for testing.

430   Q. Gong et al.

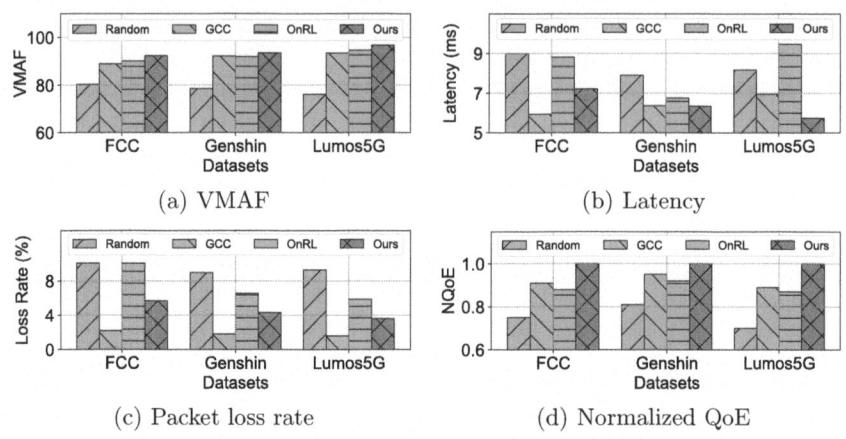

(a) VMAF   (b) Latency

(c) Packet loss rate   (d) Normalized QoE

Fig. 5. Performance comparison of different algorithms.

Baselines. (1) GCC, the default congestion control algorithm for WebRTC, is used in applications like Google Meet, with conservative bitrate decisions. (2) OnRL [19], a reinforcement learning-based algorithm for real-time communication congestion control that learns online. (3) Random, a method that randomly selects a target bitrate within the specified bandwidth ranges.

Metrics. (1) QoE, based on the model from [7]. It is calculated as $QoE = \sum_{n=1}^{N} q_n - \mu \sum_{n=1}^{N} T_n - \sum_{n=1}^{N-1} |q_{n+1} - q_n|$, where n is the frame index, N is the total number of testing frames and T_n is frame-level latency. According to [7], μ is set to 4.3, and q_n is frame quality measured in structural similarity index (SSIM). (2) Packet loss rate. (3) Frame-level latency. (4) Viewing quality metrics include peak signal-to-noise ratio (PSNR), SSIM, and VMAF. We focus on VMAF as it can estimate user perceptual video quality levels [20].

Training for CG-SR and CG-VFI. (1) CG-SR uses the Adam optimizer ($\beta_1 = 0.9$, $\beta_2 = 0.999$) with a learning rate of 1×10^{-3}, trained over 200 epochs for performance optimization. (2) CG-VFI employs the AdamW optimizer ($\beta_1 = 0.9$, $\beta_2 = 0.999$) with an initial learning rate of 1×10^{-4}, reduced to 1×10^{-5} through cosine annealing, and is trained over 300 epochs.

Training for DRL. The hyperparameters are set as $\alpha_1 = 110, \alpha_2 = 1, \alpha_3 = 500, \alpha_4 = 100, \alpha_5 = 1$. And $\mathcal{A}$ is {2Mbps, 4Mbps, $\cdots$, 40Mbps}. We use the Adam optimizer ($\beta_1 = 0.9$, $\beta_2 = 0.999$) with a learning rate of 5×10^{-4}. The auxiliary phase is executed at a ratio of 1:32 compared to the policy phase.

4.2 Performance Evaluation

Figure 5 compares the performance of nHAS with baseline methods across different datasets. A key feature of nHAS is its ability to ensure high video quality by

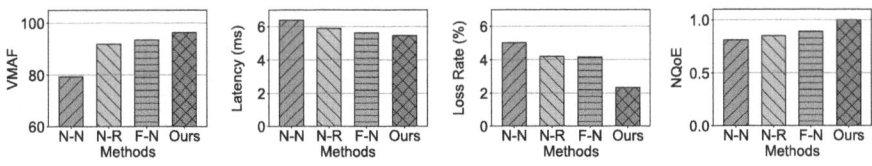

Fig. 6. The performance of DRL-EPC algorithm.

reducing redundant keyframe transmission and deploying NComp module on the client side. As shown in Fig. 5(a), nHAS achieves significantly higher VMAF, with improvements of 15.87, 2.71, and 1.97 points over Random, GCC, and OnRL, respectively. Moreover, nHAS excels in latency and packet loss rate, ranking just below GCC in Fig. 5(b) and (c). This performance is largely attributed to nHAS's hybrid ABR-AFR module, which prioritizes AFR adjustments and notably reduces sudden bitrate spikes, thus alleviating network congestion. In addition to managing network congestion, the neural network compensation module in nHAS ensures consistent video quality, leading to more stable video quality. Consequently, nHAS offers stable performance, low latency, and high video quality, resulting in a normalized QoE (NQoE) improvement of 33.22%, 9.17%, and 12.42% over Random, GCC, and OnRL, respectively.

4.3   Ablation Experiment

Performance of DRL-EPC. To evaluate the performance of DRL-EPC, we compare the following methods: (1) No frame rate or resolution adaptation (N-N), (2) No frame rate adaptation but with resolution adaptation (N-R), (3) Frame rate adaptation without resolution adaptation (F-N), and (4) Frame rate and resolution adaptation (Ours, F-R). As shown in Fig. 6, F-R outperforms the others across all metrics. Specifically, compared to N-R, F-R reduces redundant key frames leading to a 44.6% decrease in packet loss rate, a 7.3% reduction in latency, and an enhancement in VMAF by 4.51 points. This demonstrates the significant benefits of the hybrid AFR-ABR control.

Performance of NComp. We assess the performance of the NComp by evaluating CG-VFI, CG-SR, and SR-VFI (the combination of SR with VFI).

Table 1. The performance of CG-VFI (15 FPS→30 FPS).

Method	Inference Time (ms)	PSNR	SSIM	VMAF
CG-VFI (Ours)	**25.05**	33.42	0.9856	92.34
IFRNet	52.99	34.23	0.9871	93.16

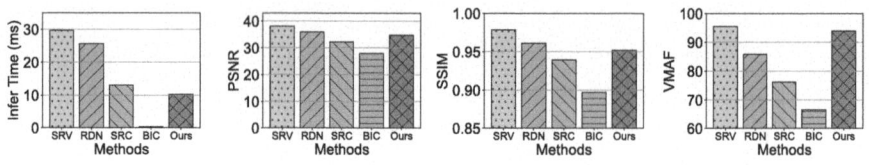

Fig. 7. The performance of CG-SR.

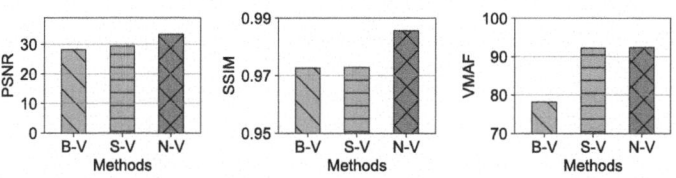

Fig. 8. The performance of SR-VFI.

Performance of CG-VFI. As shown in Table 1, we compare CG-VFI with IFR-Net [15]. CG-VFI reduces inference time by 62% compared to IFRNet, remaining under 33 ms, enabling real-time frame interpolation from 30 FPS to 60 FPS. VMAF value is only 0.82 points lower than IFRNet, showing that CG-VFI achieves notable inference time reduction with minimal quality loss.

Performance of CG-SR. We compare CG-SR with state-of-the-art fast inference SR models, including SRVC (SRV) [17], RDN [21], SRCNN (SRC) [22], and traditional BICUBIC (BIC), as shown in Fig. 7. Although CG-SR is slightly inferior to RDN in PSNR and SSIM, it achieves a VMAF score of 93.93 and has the shortest inference time among all neural-based models, at just 10.26 ms.

Performance of SR-VFI. To demonstrate that combining CG-SR and CG-VFI does not interfere with or degrade video quality, we compare three methods: (1) B-V: Upscales 540p to 1080p using BICUBIC, then doubles the frame rate from 15 FPS to 30 FPS with CG-VFI. (2) S-V (Ours): Uses CG-SR for upscaling from 540p to 1080p, then CG-VFI to double the frame rate. (3) N-V: Directly processes 1080p videos to double the frame rate without SR. As shown in Fig. 8, B-V achieves a VMAF of 78.13, largely due to quality loss during BICUBIC upscaling, which is further degraded by frame interpolation. S-V shows a little decrease in PSNR compared to N-V but achieves nearly identical VMAF, demonstrating the effective synergy between CG-SR and CG-VFI.

5   Related Work

Optimization of Interactive Video Streaming. Existing methods for optimizing interactive video transmission focus on adaptive bitrate algorithms [3–5], congestion control [8], forward error correction [9,23], and video quality enhancement [1,9]. However, most of these methods overlook redundant key frames, which reduce information density per unit of data and degrade video quality. While adjusting the frame rate [6,7] can avoid introducing redundant data, existing AFR algorithms have limited network adaptability. So we propose nHAS, which combines the strengths of ABR and AFR to ensure bandwidth adaptation while minimizing redundant data transmission.

Intelligent Enhancement for Video Streaming. Video enhancement technologies such as SR, neural codecs, and image prediction are gradually being applied to video streaming. For example, Rosevin [20] integrates ABR and SR scheduling at the edge to optimize long-term QoE for distributed users. Similarly, Grace [9] and Gemino [11] utilize neural codecs to optimize video conferencing. However, optimizations tailored specifically for cloud gaming, particularly those focusing on lightweight, client-side deployment, remain scarce. To bridge this gap, nHAS introduces a lightweight real-time video enhancement module.

6 Conclusion

In this paper, we measure and analyze the network adaptability and video quality of ABR and AFR. To combine their strengths, we propose nHAS, a neural-compensated hybrid ABR-AFR video scheduling scheme for cloud gaming. Extensive experiments conducted on a prototype system demonstrate that nHAS performs well in terms of QoE and VMAF while ensuring performance in terms of latency and packet loss rate.

Acknowledgments. This work was supported in part by the National Natural Science Foundation of China (No. 62172241, No. 62402247).

References

1. Wu, J., Guan, Y., Mao, Q., et al.: ZGaming: zero-latency 3D cloud gaming by image prediction. In: SIGCOMM (2023)
2. Alhilal, A., Braud, T., Han, B., et al.: Nebula: reliable low-latency video transmission for mobile cloud gaming. In: WWW (2022)
3. Tashtarian, F., Bentaleb, A., Amirpour, H., et al.: ARTEMIS: adaptive bitrate ladder optimization for live video streaming. In: NSDI (2024)
4. Zhang, D., Zhu, H., et al.: DSJA: Distributed server-driven joint route scheduling and streaming adaptation for multi-party realtime video streaming. TMC (2023)
5. Xiao, X., Yan, M., Zuo, Y., et al.: From ember to blaze: swift interactive video adaptation via meta-reinforcement learning. In: INFOCOM (2023)
6. Meng, Z., Wang, T., Shen, Y., et al.: Enabling high quality real-time communications with adaptive frame-rate. In: NSDI (2023)
7. Wang, F., Li, Q., Shi, W., et al.: Reparo: QoE-aware live video streaming in low-rate networks by intelligent frame recovery. In: MM (2023)
8. Wang, S., Yang, S., Kong, X., et al.: Pudica: toward near-zero queuing delay in congestion control for cloud gaming. In: NSDI (2024)

9. Cheng, Y., Arapin, A., Zhang, Z., et al.: Grace: loss-resilient real-time video communication using data-scalable autoencoder. NSDI (2024)
10. Yin, W., Lu, B., Zhao, Y., et al.: SAFR: a real-time communication system with adaptive frame rate. In: MobiSys Workshop (2023)
11. Sivaraman, V., Karimi, P., Venkatapathy, V., et al.: Gemino: practical and robust neural compression for video conferencing. NSDI (2024)
12. Cobbe, K.W., Hilton, J., Klimov, O., et al.: Phasic policy gradient. In: ICML (2021)
13. Meyer, S., et al.: Phase-based frame interpolation for video. In: CVPR (2015)
14. Niklaus, S., Mai, L., Wang, O.: Revisiting adaptive convolutions for video frame interpolation. In: WACV (2021)
15. Kong, L., Jiang, B., Luo, D., et al.: IFRNet: intermediate feature refine network for efficient frame interpolation. In: CVPR (2022)
16. Lin, M., et al.: HRank: filter pruning using high-rank feature. In: CVPR (2020)
17. Khani, M., Sivaraman, V., Alizadeh, M.: Efficient video compression via content-adaptive super-resolution. In: ICCV (2021)
18. Narayanan, A., Ramadan, E., Mehta, R., et al.: Lumos5G: mapping and predicting commercial mmwave 5G throughput. In: IMC (2020)
19. Zhang, H., Zhou, A., Lu, J., et al.: OnRL: improving mobile video telephony via online reinforcement learning. In: MobiCom (2020)
20. Zhang, X., Xu, H., Zou, L., et al.: Rosevin: employing resource-and rate-adaptive edge super-resolution for video streaming. In: INFOCOM (2024)
21. Zhang, Y., et al.: Residual dense network for super-resolution. In: CVPR (2018)
22. Dong, C., Loy, C.C., He, K., et al.: Learning a deep convolutional network for image super-resolution. In: ECCV (2014)
23. Meng, Z., Kong, X., Chen, J., et al.: Hairpin: rethinking packet loss recovery in edge-based interactive video streaming. In: NSDI (2024)

QDPformer: Quantum-Driven Workload Prediction Model Based on Transformer

Zixuan Cui[1], Shaoyuan Huang[1], Cheng Zhang[2], Xudong Li[3],
Xiaofei Wang[1(✉)], Chao Qiu[1], and Dusit Niyato[4]

[1] Tianjin University, Tianjin, China
{zixuancui,hsy_23,xiaofeiwang,chao.qiu}@tju.edu.cn
[2] Tianjin University of Finance and Economics, Tianjin, China
zhangcheng@tjufe.edu.cn
[3] China Mobile (Suzhou) Software Technology Co., Ltd., Suzhou, China
lixudong3@cmss.chinamobile.com
[4] Nanyang Technological University, Singapore, Singapore
dniyato@ntu.edu.sg

Abstract. Workload prediction is critical to ensuring quality of service in distributed edge cloud platforms (ECP). However, this task faces multiple challenges due to the inherent uncertainties within ECP. On the one hand, ECP aggregates heterogeneous infrastructure resources, whose static attributes are difficult to effectively represent and utilize. On the other hand, the dynamic switching of applications deployed on edge servers leads to diverse workload patterns. These uncertainties make server workload prediction in ECP challenging. Inspired by quantum theory in modeling uncertainty, we make an important attempt to design a Quantum-Driven workload Prediction model based on Transformer (QDPformer). Specifically, we introduce fundamental concepts such as quantum states and density matrices to model various uncertain features in ECP. Additionally, we present an improved quantum attention mechanism based on quantum measurement and quantum evolution that enables QDPformer to simulate dynamic changes in servers, significantly enhancing the model's predictive performance. Experimental results on real ECP datasets show that QDPformer achieves up to a 24.52% reduction in mean squared error (MSE) compared with the baseline models.

Keywords: Workload Prediction · Quantum Theory · Edge Cloud Platforms · Transformer

1 Introduction

Workload prediction is crucial for resource management and load balancing, especially for distributed edge cloud platforms (ECP). It can provide assistance for application deployment by predicting server workloads, avoiding additional overhead caused by excessive or insufficient resource allocation [2].

Figure 1 presents a schematic diagram of a typical ECP architecture. As illustrated, ECP integrates highly heterogeneous edge node resources distributed

Published by Springer Nature Switzerland AG 2025
X. Chen et al. (Eds.): NPC 2024, LNCS 15527, pp. 435–447, 2025.
https://doi.org/10.1007/978-981-96-2830-8_34

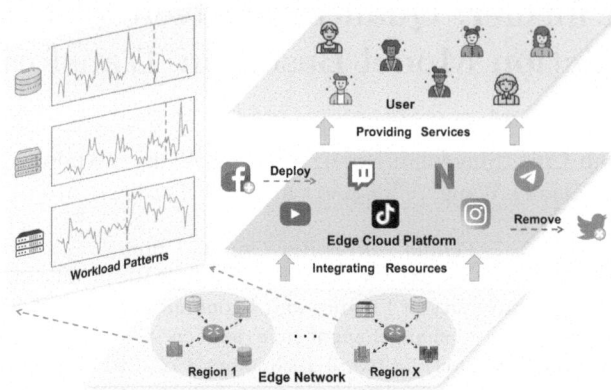

Fig. 1. The architecture of edge cloud platform.

across different regions to provide edge computing services and solutions for applications deployed on it, accommodating various scenarios.

However, workload prediction in ECP faces significant challenges due to uncertainties in several key areas:

Heterogeneous Infrastructure Resources. To satisfy the application requirements of different scenarios, servers in ECP are usually heterogeneous, with different hardware architectures, computing capabilities, and characteristics.

Dynamic Workload Patterns. ECP hosts a variety of applications with diverse resource demands. Additionally, applications on servers may change dynamically, resulting in uncertain workload patterns.

These uncertainties coupled together lead to difficulties in predicting workloads in ECP. Existing time series prediction models, such as RNN, LSTM, and Transformer, may not achieve optimal performance in workload prediction because they struggle to effectively utilize server attribute information and may perform poorly when encountering previously unseen workload patterns [10,12].

The emergence of quantum theory has, to a certain extent, alleviated the problem of uncertainty that traditional theories cannot systematically explain, making it well-suited for ECP with complex uncertain features. Currently, several studies have made significant progress in addressing uncertainties in various scenarios by combining quantum theory with neural networks [5,6,13]. Inspired by this, we have designed a Quantum-Driven workload Prediction model, QDP-former, which is based on the Transformer architecture due to its flexibility, extensibility, and excellent performance. QDPformer utilizes mathematical concepts from quantum theory in a quantum-like manner to model and address the challenges of uncertainties in workload prediction.

In summary, the main contributions of our research are as follows:

– We model workload patterns and static attributes in ECP in a quantum-like manner, leveraging concepts from quantum theory, including quantum states, density matrices, and quantum measurement.

- We introduce an improved quantum attention mechanism that simulates dynamic fluctuations in server workloads over time, thereby enhancing prediction accuracy and generalization capability.
- We propose a novel workload prediction model, QDPformer, and validate its performance on real ECP datasets. Compared with five baseline models, QDPformer achieves up to a 24.52% reduction in MSE.

2   Preliminaries

2.1   Problem Definition

The main purpose of workload prediction is to accurately predict the workload of ECP servers over a future period of time so as to provide decision-making recommendations for resource management. Since ECP contains multiple servers and introduces static attributes such as server geographic location, memory size, and disk size into the prediction process, the problem can be defined as a multivariate multi-series prediction problem.

QDPformer employs a sliding window (of length T) for prediction. By using the server's historical workload data as input, it predicts the workload for a future period. The input series can be represented as:

$$X = \left\{ \mathcal{X}_t^n = \left[\chi_t^n, \chi_{t+1}^n, ..., \chi_{t+T-1}^n \right] \right\}, \tag{1}$$

where $t \leq \mathcal{T} - T + 1$, $n \in [1, N]$ and $x_i^n \in \mathbb{R}^{d_t}$. $\mathcal{T}$ is the index of the time when the workload was last measured, N is the number of workload series (i.e., the number of servers in ECP) and d_t is the dynamic feature dimension ($d_t > 1$).

The static attributes, such as ISP, memory size, disk size, and the number of CPUs, are represented by $S = \left\{ S^n | n \in [1, N], s^n \in \mathbb{R}^{d_s} \right\}$, where d_s is the static feature dimension. The prediction process can be expressed as:

$$\hat{\mathcal{Y}}_t^n = f(\mathcal{X}_t^n, S^n), \tag{2}$$

where $\hat{\mathcal{Y}}_t^n = \left\{ \hat{y}_t^n, ..., \hat{y}_{t+L-1}^n \right\}$ is the predicted workload series, L is the prediction length, and f is the prediction model.

2.2   Quantum Theory

Quantum States. Quantum theory is a physical theory that describes the behavior of fundamental particles in the microscopic world. In quantum theory, quantum states are used to describe the state of a quantum system. Quantum states can be in pure or mixed states. A pure state is one in which the system is in a definite quantum state, which can be represented by a state vector $|\psi\rangle$ in Hilbert space. It can also be expressed as a density matrix: $\rho = |\psi\rangle\langle\psi|$.

For a quantum system in a mixed state, its density matrix can be represented as:

$$\rho = \sum_i p_i |\psi_i\rangle\langle\psi_i|, \tag{3}$$

where p_i is the probability that the system is in the i_{th} pure state $|\psi_i\rangle$ and satisfies $\sum_i p_i = 1$. ρ is symmetric, positive semidefinite, and of trace 1.

Evolution. In quantum theory, the state of a system does not remain unchanged but evolves over time [6]. A unitary operator U is used to describe the evolution. U is a complex unitary matrix satisfying $UU^H = I^2$. The evolution process can be represented as follows:

$$\hat{\rho} = U\rho U^H. \tag{4}$$

Measurement. According to Gleason's Theorem [5,13], we can calculate the probability of observing $|\psi\rangle$ in the space of density operators ρ using the projector $|\psi\rangle\langle\psi|$:

$$p_\psi(\rho) = \langle\psi|\rho|\psi\rangle = tr(\rho|\psi\rangle\langle\psi|). \tag{5}$$

The observed probability $p_\psi(\rho)$ is a non-negative real-valued scalar because both ρ and $|\psi\rangle\langle\psi|$ are Hermitian.

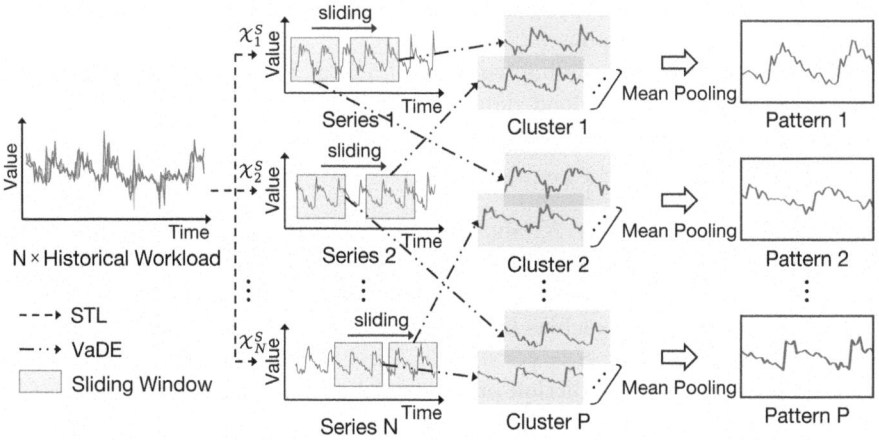

Fig. 2. The process of clustering workloads.

3   Model Design

3.1   Workload Pattern Clustering

As shown in Fig. 2, we introduce the temporal decomposition technique, Seasonal and Trend decomposition using Loess (STL), to unveil various workload patterns within the historical workload data from N servers in ECP. The decomposition process can be represented as follows:

$$\text{STL}(\mathcal{X}) \rightarrow \mathcal{X}^S, \mathcal{X}^T, \mathcal{X}^R, \tag{6}$$

where $\mathcal{X}$ is the workload series, and $\mathcal{X}^S$, $\mathcal{X}^T$, and $\mathcal{X}^R$ represent the seasonal component, trend component, and residual component, respectively. The seasonal component is retained due to its distinct temporal features.

Next, VaDE [4] is used to cluster the seasonal components of the workload. The seasonal components are input to the model through a sliding window of length T_w. This method consists of encoder, decoder, and Gaussian Mixture Model (GMM). The clustering process can be represented as follows:

$$Z_t = \text{Encoder}(\mathcal{X}_t^S),$$
$$C = \text{GMM}(Z_t), \tag{7}$$
$$\hat{\mathcal{X}}_t^S = \text{Decoder}(Z_t),$$

where Encoder and Decoder consist of multiple fully connected layers, Z_t represents the encoding vector of the workload series, and C is the clustering result.

Then, workload series from the same category are compressed into a single series through an average pooling operation. The process is as follows:

$$\mathcal{P} = \left\{ P_i = \left[\text{MeanPooling}(\mathcal{X}_t^{S,n}) \mid \mathcal{X}_t^{S,n} \in C_i \right] \right\}, \tag{8}$$

where $i \in [1, 2, ..., P]$. P_i represents workload patterns with representative features extracted from historical workload data.

3.2   Feature Pool

To enhance the model's accuracy, we construct a feature pool using the concept of density matrix to extract the characteristics of workload patterns from the series to be predicted. As shown in Fig. 3, we regard the workload patterns P_i obtained from clustering as a quantum system in a pure state and map them to high-dimensional embedding vectors $\boldsymbol{P_i}$ through a fully connected network. The vector representation of a quantum pure state must be a unit vector; therefore, each embedding vector needs to be normalized as follows:

$$|P_i\rangle = \frac{\boldsymbol{P_i}}{\|\boldsymbol{P_i}\|_2}. \tag{9}$$

The construction of the feature pool can be represented as:

$$\rho_f = \sum_{i=1}^{P} p_i |P_i\rangle\langle P_i|, \tag{10}$$

where $\sum_i p_i = 1$. ρ_f is the feature pool, which is symmetric. The value of p_i corresponds to the probability of pattern P_i in the input series, calculated as follows:

$$\rho_x = \sum_{j=1}^{b} \frac{1}{b} |\mathcal{X}_t\rangle\langle\mathcal{X}_t|, \tag{11}$$

$$p_i = \langle P_i|\rho_x|P_i\rangle = \text{tr}(\rho_x|P_i\rangle\langle P_i|), \tag{12}$$

where ρ_x is the density matrix representation of the input series, $|\mathcal{X}_t\rangle$ is the embedding vector of the input series. b denotes the batch size during each iteration of neural network training.

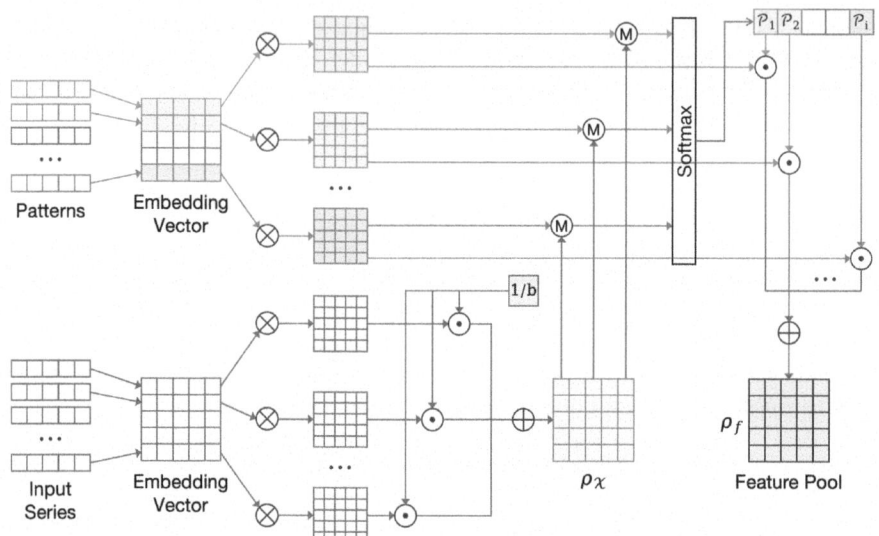

Fig. 3. Construction of the feature pool. $\otimes$ denotes the outer product of a vector. $\oplus$ denotes the element-wise addition. $\odot$ denotes the point-wise product. Ⓜ means the measurement operation according to Eq. 12.

3.3   QDPformer

The overview of QDPformer is shown in Fig. 4. QDPformer is based on the Transformer architecture but additionally includes a Static Attribute Layer (the SA Layer) and a Feature Pool Layer (the FP Layer), each designed to extract useful information from static attributes and workload patterns, respectively.

Encoder. The encoder block consists of the Input & Positional Encoding layer and the Encoder layer. The former maps the input workload series into embedding vectors of dimension d_{model} and introduces positional information. The latter is used to learn deeper features. These layers all adhere to the original Transformer model and uses sine and cosine functions to embed time-step information into the input series.

FP Layer. As shown in Fig. 5, the FP layer learns from workload patterns, where the Q-Embedding module maps input series into Hilbert space, creating their density matrix representations. The Q-Embedding & Measurement (QEM) module constructs the feature pool, with more details in Sect. 3.2. This process can be represented as:

$$\rho_x = \text{Q-Embedding}(\mathcal{V}_t), \tag{13}$$

$$\rho_f, P_i = \text{QEM}(\rho_x, \mathcal{P}), \tag{14}$$

$$\text{Padding} = \text{Linear}(P_i), \tag{15}$$

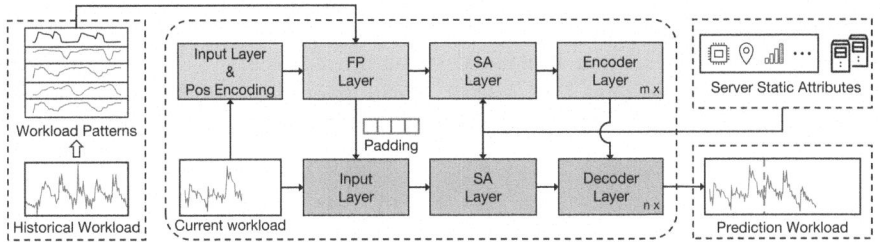

Fig. 4. The architecture of QDPformer.

where $\mathcal{V}_t \in \mathbb{R}^{b \times T \times d_{model}}$ denotes the embedding vector of the workload. Notably, we map the workload pattern P_i with the highest probability p_i through a linear layer to pad the decoder's input to enhance prediction accuracy.

To extract more effective information from the feature pool ρ_f and inspired by the multimodal fusion in QLM [6], we design an improved quantum attention (Q-Attention) mechanism, which expands the original two heads to h heads:

$$\rho = \text{Q-Attention}(\rho_x, \rho_f). \tag{16}$$

The details of Q-Attention are shown in Fig. 6. ρ_x is fed into a Q-Linear layer to get the output Q, and ρ_f is fed into h Q-Linear layers to get the outputs K and V. The Q-Linear is a linear layer designed for the density matrix, analogous to quantum evolution:

$$Q = U_1 \rho_x U_1^H, \tag{17}$$

$$K = U_2 \rho_f U_2^H, \tag{18}$$

$$V = U_3 \rho_f U_3^H, \tag{19}$$

where U_1, U_2, and U_3 are unitary matrices so Q, K, and V are also density matrices. Then, we can calculate the attention score between K and Q:

$$s_i = \text{tr}(K_i Q), \tag{20}$$

$$\alpha_i = \text{Softmax}(s_i). \tag{21}$$

The output is obtained by weighted summation of V:

$$\rho = \sum_{i=1}^{h} \alpha_i V_i, \tag{22}$$

where $\rho \in \mathbb{R}^{d_{dm} \times d_{dm}}$. Following [13], we extract the diagonal elements of ρ, denoted $\mathcal{V}_{diag}^f \in \mathbb{R}^{d_{dm}}$, and integrate them with the input series through linear mapping and a residual mechanism to maintain dimension consistency:

$$\Gamma_f = \text{Expand}(\mathcal{V}_{diag}^f) \in \mathbb{R}^{b \times d_{dm}}, \tag{23}$$

$$\mathcal{E}_f = \text{Flatten}(\text{Linear}(\Gamma_f)) \in \mathbb{R}^{b \times T \times d_{model}}, \tag{24}$$

$$\mathcal{V}_{t-f} = \text{Norm}(\mathcal{V}_t + \text{Dropout}(\mathcal{E}_f)) \in \mathbb{R}^{b \times T \times d_{model}}. \tag{25}$$

The Expand operation extends the dimension of $\mathcal{V}_{diag}^f$ from d_{dm} to $b \times d_{dm}$ to obtain Γ_f, which is then Flattened to obtain $\mathcal{E}_f \in \mathbb{R}^{b \times T \times d_{model}}$ consistent with the input dimensions. The Add & Norm layer then combines $\mathcal{V}_t$ and $\mathcal{E}_f$, encapsulating workload pattern information.

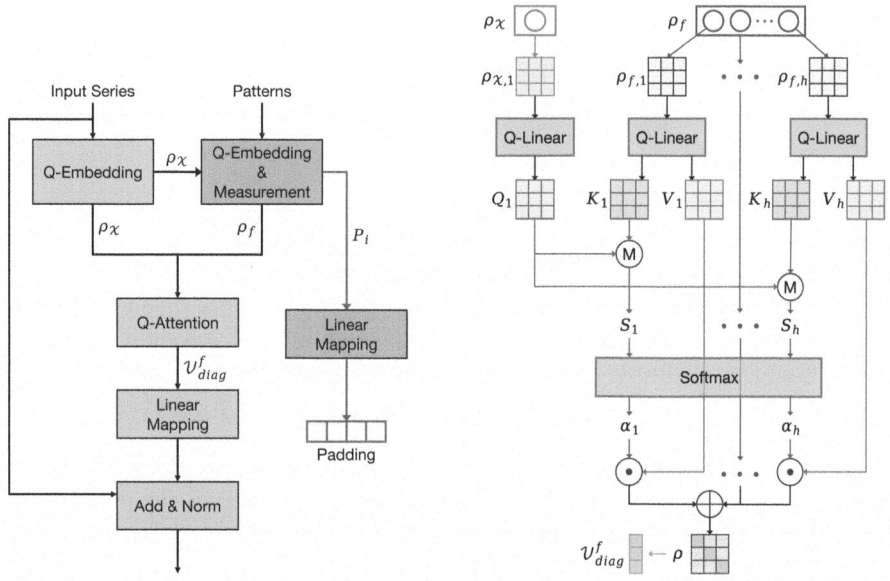

Fig. 5. FP Layer.   **Fig. 6.** Q-Attention module.

Server workloads in ECP are influenced by factors such as user behavior and business requirements, introducing variability and uncertainty. By adopting the quantum attention mechanism, which simulates dynamic changes, QDPformer's predictive performance is effectively improved, especially for new data.

SA Layer. This layer is similar to the FP layer, with the only difference being that it embeds the static attributes $\mathcal{X}_t^{sa}$ into the workload series through the Q-Embedding layer (instead of the QEM module) and is represented as follows:

$$\mathcal{V}_{t-f-s} = \text{SA Layer}(\mathcal{V}_{t-f}, \mathcal{X}_t^{sa}), \tag{26}$$

$$\mathcal{V}_{enc}^m = \text{Encoder}(\mathcal{V}_{enc}^{m-1}), \tag{27}$$

where $\mathcal{X}_t^{sa} \in \mathbb{R}^{b \times d_s}$ and d_s are the dimension of the static attributes. The encoder consists of a stack of m similar modules with an attention mechanism. When $m = 1$, $\mathcal{V}_{enc}^{m-1}$ refers to $\mathcal{V}_{t-f-s}$, which is the output of the SA Layer.

Decoder. The decoder block predicts future workload series and comprises three layers: the input layer, the SA layer, and n stacked decoder layers, formalized as follows:

$$\mathcal{X}_t^{dec}[:, -L:, 0] = \text{Padding}, \tag{28}$$

$$\mathcal{L}_t = \text{Linear}(\mathcal{X}_t^{dec}), \tag{29}$$

$$\mathcal{L}_{t-s} = \text{SA Layer}(\mathcal{L}_t, \mathcal{X}_t^{sa}), \tag{30}$$

$$\mathcal{D}_{enc}^n = \text{Decoder}(\mathcal{D}_{enc}^{n-1}, \mathcal{V}_{enc}^m), \tag{31}$$

where $\mathcal{X}_t^{dec} \in \mathbb{R}^{b \times (T+L) \times d_t}$. When $n = 1$, Decoder's input D_{enc}^{n-1} refers to $\mathcal{L}_{t-s}$. The output of the decoder will finally pass through a linear layer to obtain the predicted workload.

4 Experiments

4.1 Datasets

We utilized an open-source edge cloud upload bandwidth workload dataset (ECW[1]), collected from a commercial ECP with geographically dispersed and heterogeneous servers. ECW includes upload bandwidth workloads for 797 servers over 720 h, comprising 16 feature dimensions: 12 static attributes (e.g., geographic location, number of CPUs, memory size, disk size) and 4 dynamic attributes (e.g., upload bandwidth, time). Additionally, ECW provides three supplementary datasets under different scenarios: ECW-App Switch (workloads during application switches), ECW-New App (workloads from previously unseen applications), and ECW-New Infras (workloads on new infrastructures). These datasets exhibit high dynamic uncertainties. ECW is divided into 80% training and 20% validation sets. All models are trained and tested on ECW and then inferred on the supplementary datasets to verify robustness and generalization.

4.2 Experiment Settings

Consistent with [3], all datasets use a batch size of 256, input workload series length of $T = 48$, and predicted length of $L = 24$. When clustering workloads, the STL decomposition period is set to 24, and seasonal components are input to the VaDE model through a sliding window of length $T_w = T$. QDPformer, implemented in PyTorch, comprises two Encoder layers and one Decoder layer. It is trained using the ADAM optimizer with an initial learning rate of 10^{-4}. Evaluation metrics include mean squared error (MSE) and mean absolute error (MAE). Experiments were conducted on a Tesla V100-SXM2 (32 GB memory), each run three times and averaged.

4.3 Baselines

We compared our model with several baseline time series prediction models: **Deep AR** utilizes RNN-based sequence modeling for end-to-end time series prediction [7]. **MQRNN** combines deep neural networks with quantile regression

---

[1] https://github.com/hsy23/KDD23_DynEformer.

Table 1. Comparison of prediction models on four datasets.

Dataset	QDPformer		DynEformer		Autoformer		Informer		Deep Trans.		MQRNN		DeepAR	
Metric	MSE	MAE	MSE	MAE	MSE	MAE	MSE	MAE	MSE	MAE	MSE	MAE	MSE	MAE
ECW	**0.067**	**0.138**	0.069	0.144	0.076	0.139	0.072	0.147	0.073	0.151	0.083	0.154	1.088	0.736
App Switch	**0.060**	**0.172**	0.077	0.193	0.113	0.236	0.083	0.199	0.162	0.297	0.418	0.496	0.633	0.588
New App	**0.064**	**0.190**	0.080	0.203	0.076	0.191	0.083	0.206	0.172	0.303	1.907	0.989	0.557	0.568
New Infras.	**0.157**	**0.245**	0.359	0.401	0.208	0.304	0.223	0.317	0.342	0.407	-	-	0.945	0.704

The '-' indicates that the model's performance is significantly below par.

to capture complex patterns and provide confidence intervals [10]. **Deep Transformer** employs the self-attention mechanism within the Transformer architecture for temporal forecasting [12]. **Autoformer** integrates decomposition blocks and an autocorrelation mechanism instead of self-attention to enhance prediction accuracy [11]. **Informer** is a Transformer-based model designed to optimize efficiency and performance in both long-term and short-term forecasting tasks [14]. **DynEformer** focuses on workload prediction in ECP using pre-trained global pooling to learn workload patterns [3].

4.4   Experiment Results

To determine the optimal number of clusters P, we calculated the Bayesian Information Criterion (BIC) values of the VaDE model based on ECW, using negative BIC values for clarity (where larger values indicate a better fit). As shown in Fig. 7, the BIC value peaks at $P = 400$, indicating that 400 is the preferred number of clusters.

Overall Performance. Table 1 compares the prediction accuracy of the models on four datasets using MSE and MAE metrics. The experimental results show that QDPformer achieves best performance compared with the baseline models. Although the improvement on ECW is not significant, QDPformer reduces MSE by 22.08%, 15.79%, and 24.52% on the App Switch, New APP, and New Infras datasets respectively, compared with the best results of the baseline models. This result demonstrates the superior generalization performance of QDPformer in scenarios with complex uncertainties.

Training Details. To further illustrate the effectiveness and stability of QDPformer, we compare the training and validation losses of QDPformer and DynEformer across several training epochs. Both models utilize MSE as the evaluation metric. As shown in Fig. 7, the training and validation losses for QDPformer steadily decline with increasing epochs and stabilize at lower levels compared to DynEformer, indicating better fitting capability. Moreover, since ECW consists of concatenated workload data from 797 servers, there are fluctuations in the training and validation losses. In contrast, the variance in QDPformer's loss is significantly smaller due to the unique quantum theory-based modeling approach, further demonstrating the robustness of our proposed model.

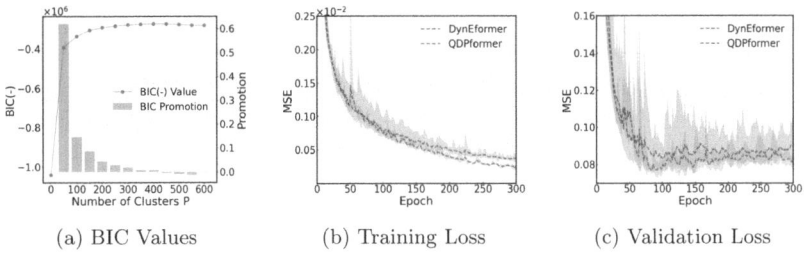

(a) BIC Values   (b) Training Loss   (c) Validation Loss

Fig. 7. BIC values and performance evaluation.

5   Related Work

Classic time series prediction methods for workload prediction are primarily based on mathematics and statistics [7,9,10]. In recent years, deep learning models have performed much better in the field of time series prediction. These models include recurrent neural networks (RNN), convolutional neural networks (CNN), and the Transformer models [12,14].

However, the inherent uncertainties due to heterogeneous infrastructure and frequently switching applications make workload prediction in ECP more complex than single time series prediction tasks. Although some studies have optimized time series models for server workload prediction [1,3], they still face challenges in modeling uncertainties. Therefore, we seek inspiration from quantum physics to construct neural network prediction models.

Quantum theory, as a fundamental scientific theory, is no longer limited to describing physical phenomena in the microscopic world. Particularly in the field of NLP, researchers have made significant progress by combining quantum theory with neural networks to construct quantum language models that represent the uncertainties in complex semantic information [5,6]. Additionally, Singh et al. have demonstrated the effectiveness of integrating quantum methods with neural networks for workload prediction [8]. In contrast, we innovatively combine quantum theory with the Transformer model and preprocess workload data using clustering, making it more suitable for ECP with complex patterns.

6   Conclusion

In this paper, we have proposed QDPformer, a novel workload prediction model based on the Transformer architecture. QDPformer incorporates quantum theory concepts, including quantum states, quantum measurement, and quantum evolution, to effectively model and learn uncertain features in ECP. Experimental results on real datasets have demonstrated QDPformer's superior performance in workload prediction for ECP, with MSE reduced by up to 24.52% compared with the baseline models. The integration of quantum theory in workload prediction presents significant research potential and warrants further exploration.

Acknowledgments. This work is supported in part by National Science Foundation of China under Grant No. 62072332, in part by China NSFC (Youth) through Grant No. 62306208, in part by Tianjin Natural Science Foundation (Youth) Tianjin Natural Science Foundation General Project No. 23JCQNJC00920, in part by the Tianjin Xinchuang Haihe Lab under Grant No. 22HHXCJC00002.

References

1. Bao, L., Yang, J., Zhang, Z., Liu, W., Chen, J., Wu, C.: On accurate prediction of cloud workloads with adaptive pattern mining. J. Supercomput. **79**(1), 160–187 (2023)
2. Duc, T.L., Leiva, R.G., Casari, P., Östberg, P.O.: Machine learning methods for reliable resource provisioning in edge-cloud computing: a survey. ACM Comput. Surv. (CSUR) **52**(5), 1–39 (2019)
3. Huang, S., Wang, Z., Zhang, H., Wang, X., Zhang, C., Wang, W.: One for all: unified workload prediction for dynamic multi-tenant edge cloud platforms. In: Proceedings of the 29th ACM SIGKDD Conference on Knowledge Discovery and Data Mining, pp. 788–797 (2023)
4. Jiang, Z., Zheng, Y., Tan, H., Tang, B., Zhou, H.: Variational deep embedding: an unsupervised and generative approach to clustering. In: Proceedings of the 26th International Joint Conference on Artificial Intelligence, pp. 1965–1972 (2017)
5. Li, Q., Wang, B., Melucci, M.: CNM: an interpretable complex-valued network for matching. arXiv preprint arXiv:1904.05298 (2019)
6. Li, Z., Zhou, Y., Liu, Y., Zhu, F., Yang, C., Hu, S.: QAP: a quantum-inspired adaptive-priority-learning model for multimodal emotion recognition. In: Findings of the Association for Computational Linguistics: ACL 2023 (2023)
7. Salinas, D., Flunkert, V., Gasthaus, J., Januschowski, T.: Deepar: probabilistic forecasting with autoregressive recurrent networks. Int. J. Forecast. **36**(3), 1181–1191 (2020)
8. Singh, A.K., Saxena, D., Kumar, J., Gupta, V.: A quantum approach towards the adaptive prediction of cloud workloads. IEEE Trans. Parallel Distrib. Syst. **32**(12), 2893–2905 (2021)
9. Van Der Voort, M., Dougherty, M., Watson, S.: Combining kohonen maps with arima time series models to forecast traffic flow. Transp. Res. Part C Emerg. Technol. **4**(5), 307–318 (1996)
10. Wen, R., Torkkola, K., Narayanaswamy, B., Madeka, D.: A multi-horizon quantile recurrent forecaster. arXiv preprint arXiv:1711.11053 (2017)
11. Wu, H., Xu, J., Wang, J., Long, M.: Autoformer: decomposition transformers with auto-correlation for long-term series forecasting. Adv. Neural. Inf. Process. Syst. **34**, 22419–22430 (2021)
12. Wu, N., Green, B., Ben, X., O'Banion, S.: Deep transformer models for time series forecasting: the influenza prevalence case. arXiv preprint arXiv:2001.08317 (2020)

13. Zhang, P., Niu, J., Su, Z., Wang, B., Ma, L., Song, D.: End-to-end quantum-like language models with application to question answering. In: Proceedings of the AAAI Conference on Artificial Intelligence, vol. 32 (2018)
14. Zhou, H., Zhang, S., Peng, J., Zhang, S., Li, J., Xiong, H., Zhang, W.: Informer: beyond efficient transformer for long sequence time-series forecasting. In: Proceedings of the AAAI Conference on Artificial Intelligence, vol. 35 (2021)

RFaaS: Function Scheduling Across Heterogeneous Clusters

Zhihang Tang[1,2], Yiming Li[1], Zezheng Mao[1], Laiping Zhao[1($\boxtimes$)], and Keqiu Li[1]

[1] College of Intelligence and Computing, Tianjin University, Tianjin 300072, China
{tangzhihang,laiping}@tju.edu.cn
[2] Intelligent Computing Infrastructure Innovation Center, Zhejiang Lab,
Hangzhou 311121, China

Abstract. The rapid development of cloud computing has attracted a diverse migration of applications. Serverless computing, with its abstract resource management, on-demand billing, and dynamic scaling, has become a popular cloud computing paradigm. X86 signifies traditional computility, while RISC-V symbolizes new potential. Making the most of existing traditional computing resources while exploring the potential of new computility will be a key challenge. The x86 and RISC-V hybrid computility supply will continue for a long time. Task management under diverse instruction set architectures is a critical issue that needs addressing in this evolving landscape. Current research predominantly concentrates on homogeneous instruction set clusters. In this paper, we propose RFaaS, a function job scheduling methodology tailored for RISC-V + X86 heterogeneous instruction set clusters, leveraging the OpenFaaS serverless computing platform. We delve into the affinity traits of function jobs in RISC-V + X86 amalgamated instruction set clusters and devise an affinity classifier alongside an architecture-aware scheduling algorithm. Our methodology dissects scheduling decisions into resource fulfillment and affinity alignment, underpinned by a meticulously crafted update algorithm to uphold and refine job affinities. Experimental results show that RFaaS can provide at least 3x performance improvement and 2.4x throughput increase compared to existing solutions.

Keywords: Heterogeneous Clusters · Serverless Computing · Function Scheduling · RISC-V

1 Introduction

The rapid development of cloud computing has attracted a diverse migration of applications. Serverless computing, known for its high level of abstraction in resource and programming management, on-demand billing, and dynamic scaling, has become a popular cloud computing paradigm. But with the processor architectures continue to evolve, the trend toward heterogeneous clusters is becoming increasingly evident. Heterogeneous clusters [1], comprising a variety of hardware components, allow for greater

X. Chen et al. (Eds.): NPC 2024, LNCS 15527, pp. 448–460, 2025.
https://doi.org/10.1007/978-981-96-2830-8_35

flexibility and efficiency in handling a variety of workloads, not only bolster the development and deployment aptitudes of cloud applications but also lay the groundwork for performance enhancements. Nonetheless, the distinct operational attributes of disparate hardware elements within heterogeneous clusters, coupled with the divergent tasks executed on different hardware nodes, escalate the intricacy surrounding resource allocation and scheduling determinations.

The X86 architecture represents traditional computility, has captured a significant share of the server market (e.g., achieved 88% in 2023 [2]). RISC-V [3] is a fifth-generation RISC (Reduced Instruction Set Computing) architecture, represents emerging and exploratory computility, has garnered significant attention due to its open-source nature, simplicity, modularity, and scalability, According to relevant agency forecasts, it is expected that RISC-V processors will occupy nearly a quarter of the global market share by 2030. In the foreseeable future, fully utilizing traditional computing resources while exploring the potential of new computility will be a key challenge. Therefore, X86 and RISC-V hybrid computing offerings will continue for a long time. In this trend, exploring and improving task management mechanisms under heterogeneous instruction set architectures has become a difficult problem that we must solve.

Existing works mainly focus on the homogeneous instruction set cluster, which can effectively allocate resources and schedule the homogeneous instruction set, but lacks the analysis on the impact of the heterogeneous instruction set [4],cannot exploited the characteristics of different instruction set clusters. This may result in poor execution performance and thus violating the SLO (service level objective) of the job. For example, OpenFaaS [5] is a popular Serverless framework, but has hardware inawareness shortcomings which may lead to latency sensitive functions being deployed on weaker hardware, and scheduling policy limitations.

In this paper, we will explore the function job scheduling problem of heterogeneous instruction set cluster based on X86 + RISC-V. This hardware combination selection aims to show how cross-node heterogeneity and intra-node heterogeneity should work together efficiently in concrete practice, and provide examples for heterogeneous computing research on representative hardware platforms. However, it is not easy to achieve, mainly due to the following challenges: Firstly, the computing efficiency and computing characteristics of heterogeneous cluster based on X86 + RISC-V are significantly different from those of traditional cluster, so it is necessary to profile it to obtain rich computing characteristics; Secondly, how to design an efficient scheduling algorithm according to the computing power characteristics of heterogeneous clusters to improve the utilization rate of computing power resources of heterogeneous clusters?

To address challenges above, our main contributions are as follows:

- We analyze the deployment problems and execution characteristics of jobs on RISC-V + X86 clusters, and profile the functional job characteristics of heterogeneous instruction sets.
- We design RFaaS, a function job scheduling method for RISC-V + X86 heterogeneous instruction set clusters, aimed at improving throughput while ensuring job execution times.

- We implement the prototype system of RFaaS, and evaluate its performance. Experimental results show that RFaaS can provide at least 3x performance improvement and a 2.4x throughput increase compared to existing solutions.

2   Background and Motivation

X86 is a traditional architecture with a Complex Instruction Set Computing (CISC) design, is known for its widespread use in personal computers and servers. In contrast, RISC-V is an emerging open-source architecture following a Reduced Instruction Set Computing (RISC) approach, offers simplicity and flexibility. One significant difference in function execution lies in the complexity of instruction sets: X86's CISC design allows for more complex instructions per operation, while RISC-V's RISC design favors a simpler and more streamlined approach to function execution.

To explore the relationships between different functions in RISC-V + X86 heterogeneous cluster scenarios and enhance the scheduling efficiency of heterogeneous instruction set clusters, we analyzed the characteristics of function tasks for two architectures. We selected some of the most popular current processor-level benchmarks (such as microbench [6], ServerBench [7], DeathStarBench [8], FunctionBench [9]) to test machines in both architectures. Combined with the experiments of Zorun et al. [10]. The test environment configuration is the same as in Sect. 4.2.

Figure 1 shows the results of a computationally structured microbench test, the Performance of RISC-V is low, with almost all functions performing less than half as well as on X86. The reason for the above results is mainly due to the differences in processor levels. It can be concluded that existing RISC-V processors still lack the same performance as mainstream cloud vendors' processors, showing disadvantages in compute-intensive tasks.

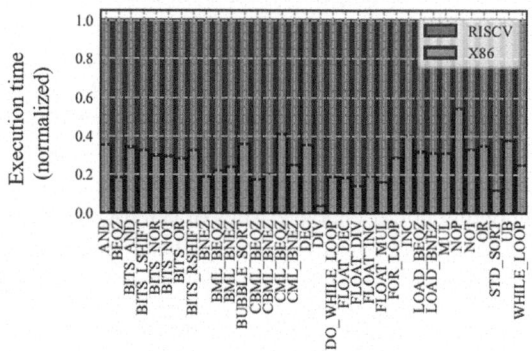

Fig. 1. Computational benchmark compares two architectures

In order to explore suitable tasks and fully leverage the advantages of RISC-V architecture, we make a more detailed exploration of the above benchmark. The first is that because RISC-V has simple instruction set makes context switching and interrupt handling more efficient, it may have an advantage when making operations with heavy system calls. The experimental results in Fig. 2 show that, almost all system calls show better results on RISC-V than on X86. That is because although X86 processors have more mature hardware optimization technology, but if the function involves system calls, the execution of the function will not only occur on the CPU, but will involve interrupts, context switches, IO waiting and other scenarios, and in these scenarios, RISC-V architecture has some unique designs (for example, simple instruction set of RISC-V makes context switching and interrupt handling more efficient), so RISC-V architecture may have advantages when performing operations with a large number of system calls. Therefore, according to the characteristics of RISC-V + X86 heterogeneous cluster, designing a suitable function job scheduling method has certain research value.

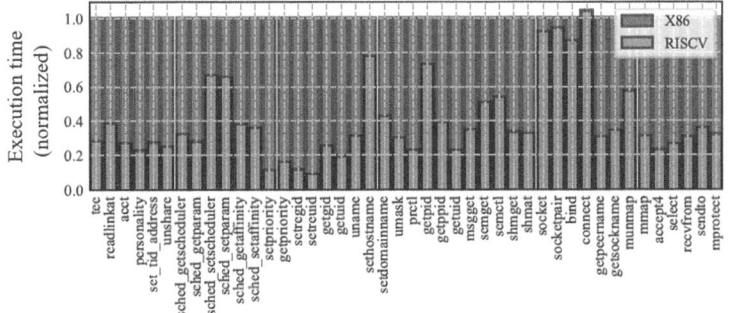

Fig. 2. Comparison of common system execution time between two architectures

3   RFaaS Design

3.1   Overview

The basic design idea of RFaaS is to optimize system performance by using the features and characteristics of different instruction set machines (such as system call time) combined with characteristics such as job affinity.

Figure 3 shows the overall design architecture of RFaaS. When a function is deployed in a cluster, RFaaS will characterize a single run of the function in an offline manner, record and maintain data from various dimensions during job execution ❶, and then train and maintain a classification model based on the results ❷. For online services, job requests that arrive at the gateway will enter classifier ❸. The classifier uses a trained classification model to classify the requested function to obtain its affinity, and places the job into the corresponding classification queue. The classifier will also dynamically update the classification model based on its offline characterization results. When a request enters the classification queue, it cannot determine its final deployment location because the classifier cannot perceive the status of the cluster, especially the queuing situation of the job. After passing through the classifier, the request will be sent to the scheduler module ❹. The scheduler module will periodically synchronize the cluster status ❺ and use heartbeat detection and other methods to check whether the service is

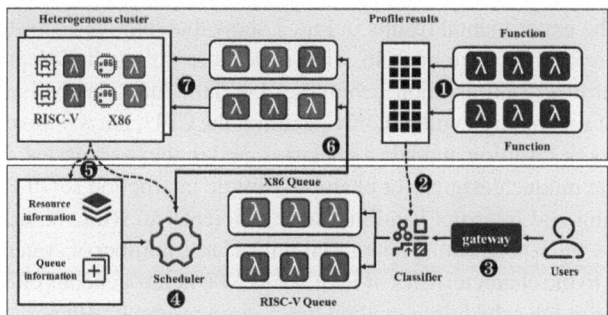

Fig. 3. RFaaS system architecture

alive. Finally, combined with the final completion time and other information carried by the job, the job will be sent to the queue maintained by the corresponding node ❻, and the node will decide which job to run on its own ❼.

3.2 Affinity Classifier

Metric Selection: We selected a series of performance metrics through correlation analysis, using Pearson [13], Kendall [14], and Spearman [15] correlation coefficients to evaluate the correlation between the target placement node and various metrics. Higher coefficients indicate stronger correlations. Table 1 shows the correlation scores between the target placement node and metrics under the three correlation analysis methods, based on metrics with a correlation score greater than 0.1. We selected 10 highly correlated metrics as inputs for the classification model.

Application Profile: We used tools like perf, sar, and strace to profile jobs. However, not all collected metrics can be directly applied to the model. If the correlation between metrics is low, it may lead to model overfitting, affecting generalization and accuracy. On the other hand, high input dimensionality can prolong model training and prediction time, increasing operational costs. Therefore, it is necessary to extract performance metrics highly correlated with inherent characteristics.

Incremental Model: To continuously optimize and update the classification model for optimal performance, we used online incremental learning [16]. Initially, we built a small workload metric dataset and corresponding labels to train the predictor. During execution, the predictor continuously expands the dataset by inserting new metrics and deployment nodes. This allows the model to self-update, improving prediction accuracy and handling dynamic changes effectively.

Model Selection: We summarized the characteristics of several popular incremental machine learning models, such as IKNN [17], ISVR [18], and IMLP [19], and used these models to build the classification model. We tested the accuracy results of k-nearest neighbor (KNN), logistic regression (LR), random forest regression (RFR), support vector machine (SVR), and multilayer perceptron (MLP) predictors. The evaluation metrics include Mean Absolute Error, Mean Squared Error, R2 (Coefficient of Determination),

Table 1. Correlation Scores Between Target Placement Node and Metrics.

Metric	Pearson Coefficient	Kendall Coefficient	Spearman Coefficient
Branch Mispredictions	0.416	0.603	0.738
CPU Migrations	0.337	0.314	0.361
CPU Clock Speed	0.183	0.649	0.792
Page Faults	0.114	0.580	0.662
Context Switches	0.382	0.669	0.797
Branch Instructions	0.256	0.701	0.857
CPU Utilization	0.283	0.197	0.231
Disk IO	0.427	0.295	0.346
Network Bandwidth	0.431	0.438	0.566
System Call Time Ratio	0.965	0.866	0.944
Branch Mispredictions	0.416	0.603	0.738
CPU Migrations	0.337	0.314	0.361

and Explained Variance Score. Among these, RFR significantly outperformed the other methods, achieving an accuracy as high as 99.8%. Therefore, we ultimately chose RFR as the algorithm for the classification model.

3.3 Architecture Aware Gittins Priority Scheduling Algorithm

Analysis of Request Scheduling Problem: Due to resource heterogeneity, sensitivity variations between requests and resources, and potential request concurrency, finding an optimal scheduling scheme for timely requests is highly complex. This complexity arises from the need to consider factors like resource heterogeneity, job sensitivity, node preferences, and request timing. Overcoming these challenges requires an intelligent scheduling algorithm and resource allocation strategy that maximizes cluster resource usage while meeting job SLO.

The Multi-Architecture Cluster Function Scheduling (MA-CFS) problem is defined as follows: Given the different architecture of server set $\{S_1, S_2, ..., S_m\}$ and a variety of different affinity function $\{f_1, f_2, ..., f_n\}$. Each server has a different resource capacity, and each function has different resource requirements. For the heterogeneous cluster composed of these multi-architecture servers, it is required to accurately identify each function and allocate resources reasonably in order to ensure the maximum degree of job SLO.

MA-CFS Problem Modeling: The objective function of MA-CFS problem can be set as follows: $min \frac{\sum_{i=1}^{F}(d_i-b_i)}{F}$, where F represents the set of all requests, d_i represents the time when the execution of the request i starts, and d_i represents the time when the execution of the request i finishes.

This is a Linear Programming (LP) problem with many constraints. First of all, in order to ensure the request latency requirements, time d_i must ensure that the request has been completed no more than the requested deadline e_i, so we can draw the following constraints: $1 \leq d_i \leq e_i, \forall i \in F$. For the start of each request execution time b_i must be less than the request has been completed time e_i, so we can draw the following constraints: $1 \leq b_i \leq e_i, \forall i \in F$. For each request, the start execution time b_i must also be less than the request completion time d_i, so the following constraints can be derived: $b_i \leq d_i, \forall i \in F$. We also define the two binary variables x_{ij}^t and y_{ij}, x_{ij}^t indicates whether job i is running on server j at time t, and y_{ij} indicates whether job i is running on server j. The constraints related to these two variables and the relationship between them can be obtained: $x_{ij}^t \in \{0,1\}$, $y_{ij} \in \{0,1\}$. $x_{ij}^t \leq y_{ij}, \forall i \in F, \forall j \in S, \forall t = 1,2, ..., e_i$. To ensure that any request i is processed by only one server j at the same time, the following constraints can be obtained: $\sum_{j=1}^{S} y_{ij} = 1, \forall i \in F$. For each server, it is necessary to ensure that the sum of memory resource m_i^j and CPU resource c_i^j used by request i allocated on the server at any time t does not exceed the maximum server resource R_{mem}^j and R_{cpu}^j, so the following constraints can be obtained: $\sum_{i=1}^{F} \sum_{j=1}^{S} x_{ij}^t \cdot m_i^j \leq R_{mem}^j, \forall i \in F, \forall j \in S, \forall t = 1,2, ..., e_i, \sum_{i=1}^{F} \sum_{j=1}^{S} x_{ij}^t \cdot c_i^j \leq R_{cpu}^j, \forall i \in F, \forall j \in S, \forall t = 1,2, ..., e_i$.

Architecture-Aware Gittins Priority Scheduling Algorithm, AGPSA: The Architecture-Aware Gittins Priority Scheduling Algorithm (AGPSA) addresses the NP-hard MA-CFS problem by minimizing execution and queuing times. The algorithm schedules jobs without relying on precise duration estimates. When a request arrives, the job classifier assesses its affinity based on job characteristics, and the most compatible node is selected. If it's the job's first execution, the algorithm initializes the Gittins weight to 1.0. The algorithm then checks if the node's resources suffice; if so, the job runs immediately. If not, the job is queued with priority based on its cut-off and queuing times. Periodic checks determine if the job's Gittins weight exceeds a threshold for execution; otherwise, it waits.

Algorithm 1: Gittins weight update algorithm

Input: Job set J
Output: Job set J.
1:    **foreach** $job \in J$ **do**
2:        marking index completed on time?
3:        number of job executions times
4:        scheduling threshold α
5:        improve threshold β
        //wheatherJob is completed on time
6:        **if** $job.realEndtime < job.endTime$ **then**
7:          index=1;
8:        **end**
9:        times++
        //update Gittins index
10:       **if** $index == 1$ **then**
11:         **if** job.gittinsIndex$< \beta$ **then**
12:           $job.gittinsIndex \leftarrow job.gittinsIndex*2;$
13:         **end**
14:         **else**
15:           $job.gittinsIndex \leftarrow job.gittinsIndex +0.05;$
16:         **end**
17:         job.gittinsIndex $\leftarrow$ job.gittinsIndex / *Number of calls;*
18:       **end**
19:       **else**
20:         **if** $job.gittinsIndex == 1.0$ **then**
21:           $Job.gittinsIndex = \alpha;$
22:         **end**
23:         **else**
24:           $job.gittinsIndex \leftarrow job.gittinsIndex - 0.05;$
25:         **end**
26:       **end**
27:     **end**
28:     **return** Job set J

4 Evaluation

4.1 System Implementation

We implemented RFaaS based on the OpenFaaS [5] serverless computing platform using approximately 4400 lines of Java code and 2000 lines of Python code. OpenFaaS is an open source serverless computing platform that simplifies the process of function deployment.

4.2 Experimental Setup

We employed two physical clusters, one based on X86 and the other on RISC-V architecture, as our experimental setups. Each node was equipped with 8 GB RAM and 32 GB storage. The processor frequencies of X86 machines and RISC-V machines are 2.5 GHz and 1.5 GHz respectively. In order to ensure the fairness of the experimental results, we reduced the frequency of X86 processors to the same as that of RISC-V machines. We selected test functions from FunctionBench [20] and DeathStarBench [8] benchmark suites. Given the lack of a serverless platform tailored for RISC-V + X86 heterogeneous clusters, we adapted OpenFaaS, a server-agnostic platform, as a benchmark. To showcase the effectiveness of our proposed scheme, we implemented variants of RFaaS alongside OpenFaaS for comparison.

At present, there is no work to provide a serverless computing platform for RISC-V + X86 heterogeneous instruction set cluster, so we ported the existing server-unaware computing platform OpenFaaS as a benchmarking scheme. In order to reflect the effectiveness and advancement of the proposed scheme, we also implements variants of RFaaS, RFaaS⁻ and OpenFaaS.

4.3 RFaaS Component Evaluation

Classifier Effect Evaluation: We adjusted the input vector S described in formula (1), set it as zero vector, and fed the modified input into different machine learning models, thus obtaining each machine learning classification model of RFaaS after removing the index of kernel state time, and denoting it as RFaaS-wo-sc. In addition, Since the inherent execution characteristics of system calls inevitably lead to some redundancy between the kernel mode time indicator and other indicators, such as disk I/O and network bandwidth, this paper further evaluates the effect of removing disk I/O and network bandwidth two indicators and three indicators. The resulting classifier versions are denoted as RFaaS-wo-dn and RFaaS-wo-scdn.

Figure 4 illustrates the impact of excluding the kernel-state time measure on the accuracy of different machine learning classifiers. The KNN and LR models saw accuracy drops of 14% and 12%, respectively, while the RFR model experienced only an 8% decrease. This decline is expected, given the high correlation coefficient (0.965) of kernel-state time. KNN's heavy reliance on local data structure weakens its spatial recognition when a core feature is removed, and LR loses accuracy due to its dependence on linear correlations. In contrast, RFR's multi-decision tree strategy compensates for missing key features, making it the most resilient. Additionally, the comparison between RFaaS-wo-dn and RFaaS-wo-scdn indicates that kernel-state time, disk I/O, and network bandwidth, though somewhat redundant, are not entirely independent, with kernel-state time having a more significant effect on classifier performance.

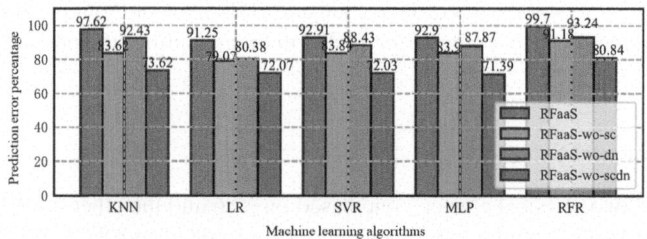

Fig. 4. Classification accuracy under different machine learning models

Scheduler Effectiveness Evaluation: Before evaluating scheduling algorithms, we first evaluated the way machine learning algorithms are used to predict time directly in existing work [16] to verify that "predictors of job execution times cannot make accurate predictions."

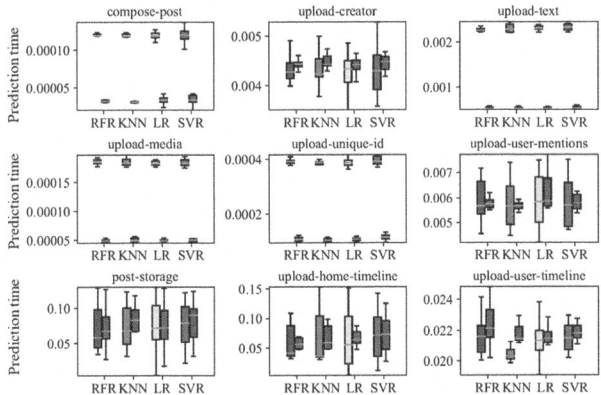

Fig. 5. Prediction of machine learning predictor

Figure 5 compares the prediction results of nine social network functions using four machine learning models: RFR, KNN, LR, and SVR. Each model, trained on the features listed in Table 1 and based on input size, is evaluated on both RISC-V and x86 architectures. The box plots illustrate that, while the prediction time can effectively indicate the optimal execution node for some functions (e.g., compose-post, upload-text), it fails to do so for others (e.g., upload-creator, post-storage), particularly with the RFR model, where classification errors range from 23% to 60%.

To evaluate the AGPSA scheduling algorithm, we integrated a classifier into Open-FaaS to identify function affinity, leading to two OpenFaaS variants: OpenFaaS-RRLB and OpenFaaS-FCFS, based on Round Robin Load Balancing (RRLB) and First Come First Service (FCFS) algorithms, respectively.

4.4 Overall RFaaS Evaluation

Overall Job Completion Time Evaluation: Figure 6 shows a comparison of the job completion time of all functions of RFaaS, RFaaS$^-$ and OpenFaaS solutions under three different loads. These functions are all from the previously mentioned applications, among which CP, UC, UUM and other functions with capital abbreviations are all components of social network applications. CP, UT, UM, UUI, CAP, matmul, float, dd, json belong to X86 affinity functions, UC, UUM, PS, UUT, UHT belong to RISC-V affinity functions.

Figure 6(a) shows that RFaaS and RFaaS$^-$ outperform OpenFaaS significantly in handling sparse workloads, reducing job completion times by at least half. This is due to OpenFaaS's inefficient classifier, which relies on Docker Swarm's default polling

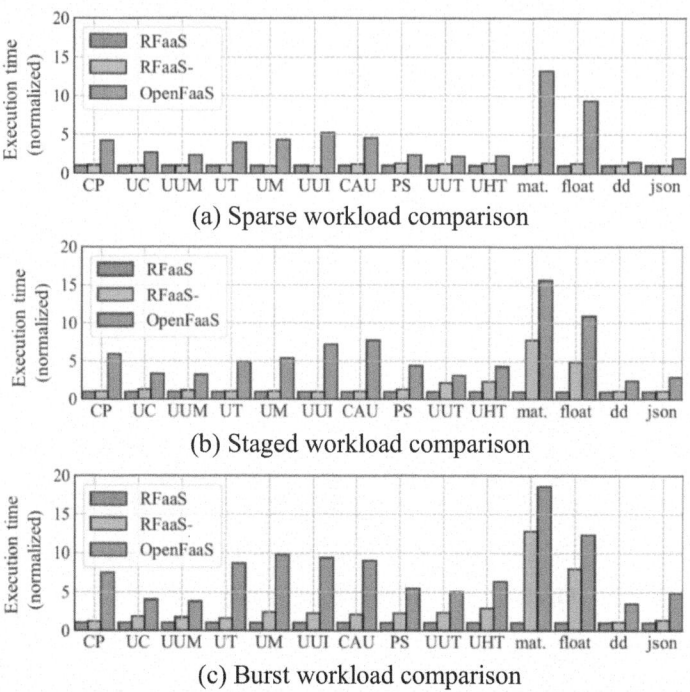

(a) Sparse workload comparison

(b) Staged workload comparison

(c) Burst workload comparison

Fig. 6. Different solutions compare job completion times under three workloads

load balancing, leading to poor scheduling and inefficiency, especially when functions with high affinity for x86 architecture are run on RISC-V nodes. Figure 6(b) reveals an even greater performance advantage for RFaaS under staged workloads, as OpenFaaS's polling strategy increases scheduling errors and queue blocking, prolonging execution times. However, RFaaS⁻ starts to show misclassification under high loads, impacting longer tasks like matrix multiplication. Figure 6(c) demonstrates that these issues are more pronounced under burst workloads.

Overall Throughput Evaluation: Throughput is a key metric for platform capability. This section compares the throughput of RFaaS, RFaaS⁻, and OpenFaaS under three production loads. Figure 7(a) shows that RFaaS improves throughput by 3.54x, 3.64x, and 3.85x over OpenFaaS, and by 1.04x, 1.15x, and 1.33x over RFaaS⁻. RFaaS achieves higher throughput due to its job classifier and efficient scheduling algorithm, which accurately identifies request affinity and avoids assigning jobs to slow nodes. In contrast, RFaaS⁻ lacks effective classification, leading to reduced scheduling accuracy under heavy loads. Figure 7(b) illustrates that RFaaS improves throughput by 3.35x to 3.6x compared to OpenFaaS across various SLO settings.

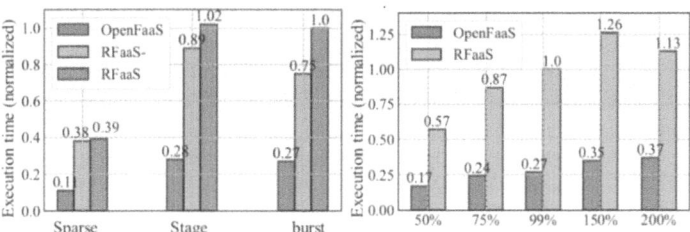

(a) Throughput comparison of different solutions (b) Throughput comparison of different SLOs

Fig. 7. Throughput comparison

4.5 Results and Analysis

According to the complete evaluation of RFaaS, the performance of RFaaS and comparison methods is mainly measured by classifier accuracy, scheduling algorithm accuracy, component cost, job completion time and throughput. The following experimental conclusions can be obtained:

(1) The technical selection of RFaaS in each component is the optimal solution, in which the classifier can reach 99.7% accuracy, and can accurately identify the affinity of the job; The designed scheduling algorithm can guarantee the scheduling success rate of 63.6% even under a large number of sudden workloads. The importance of the selected system call time ratio index is verified. The accuracy of classifiers that removed this index decreased by up to 14%.
(2) RFaaS also fully guarantees the completion time of the job, regardless of the type of load, RFaaS has shown far better performance than OpenFaaS, and can provide at least 3 times the performance lead for each function; RFaaS also provides the largest throughput increase, at least 2.4x, compared to existing OpenFaaS solutions.

5 Conclusion

Aiming at the problem of job deployment on RISC-V + X86 cluster and the characteristics of job running on RISC-V + X86 cluster, in this paper,we designed a function job scheduling method RFaaS for RISC-V + X86 heterogeneous instruction set cluster. RFaaS includes two main components: a job affinity classifier based on system call time ratios and an architecture-aware Gittins priority scheduling algorithm. Through component testing and overall testing of RFaaS, it is verified that the job classifier and job scheduler can maximize throughput compared with existing solutions while guaranteeing job execution time.

References

1. Li, X., Mitchell, S., Fang, Y., Li, J., Perez-Ramirez, J., Lu, J.: Advances in heterogeneous single-cluster catalysis. Nat. Rev. Chem. **7**(11), 754–767 (2023)
2. Gartner. Market Share Analysis: Servers, Worldwide, 2023 (2024)

3. Waterman, A., Lee, Y., Patterson, D., Asanovi, K.: The RISC-V Instruction Set Manual. Volume 1: User-Level ISA, Version 2.0 (2014)
4. Zhao, L., Li, F., Qu, W., et al.: Aiturbo: unified compute allocation for partial predictable training in commodity clusters. In: Proceedings of the 30th InternationalSymposium on High-Performance Parallel and Distributed Computing, pp. 133–145 (2021)
5. Le, D.-N., Pal, S., Pattnaik, P.K.: OpenFaaS. Cloud Computing Solutions: Architecture, Data Storage, Implementation and Security, pp. 287–303 (2022)
6. RISC-V Linux kernel analysis. https://gitee.com/tinylab/riscv-linux
7. Yu, T., Liu, Q., Du, D., et al.: Characterizing serverless platforms with serverlessbench. In: Proceedings of the 11th ACM Symposium on Cloud Computing, pp. 30–44 (2020)
8. Gan, Y., Zhang, Y., Cheng, D., et al.: An open-source benchmark suite for microservices and heir hardware-software implications for cloud & edge systems. In: Proceedings of the Twenty-Fourth International Conference on Architectural Support for Programming Languages and Operating Systems, pp. 3–18 (2019)
9. Shahrad, M., Fonseca, R., Goiri, I., et al.: Serverless in the wild: characterizing and optimizing the serverless workload at a large cloud provider. In: 2020 USENIX Annual Technical Conference (USENIX ATC 2020), pp. 205–218 (2020)
10. Benchmarking RISC-V: VisionFive 2 vs the world (2024). https://blog.bitsofnetworks.org/riscv-performance-power-usage/
11. Jindal, A., Gerndt, M., Chadha, M., et al.: Function delivery network: extending serverless computing for heterogeneous platforms. Softw. Pract. Exp. $51(9)$, 1936–1963 (2021)
12. Yu, G., Chen, P., Zheng, Z., et al.: FaaSDeliver: cost-efficient and QoS-aware function delivery in computing continuum. IEEE Trans. Serv. Comput. (2023)
13. Sedgwick, P.: Pearson's correlation coefficient. BMJ 345 (2012)
14. Abdi, H.: The Kendall rank correlation coefficient. Encyclopedia of Measurement and Statistics, pp. 508–510. Sage, Thousand Oaks (2007)
15. De Winter, J.C., Gosling, S.D., Potter, J.: Comparing the Pearson and Spearman correlation coefficients across distributions and sample sizes: a tutorial using simulations and empirical data. Psychol. Methods $21(3)$, 273 (2016)
16. Zhao, L., Yang, Y., Li, Y., Zhou, X., Li, K.: Understanding, predicting and scheduling serverless workloads under partial interference. In: Proceedings of the International Conference for High Performance Computing, Networking, Storage and Analysis, pp. 1–15 (2021)
17. Cover, T., Hart, P.: Nearest neighbor pattern classification. IEEE Trans. Inf. Theory $13(1)$, 21–27 (1967)
18. Smola, A.J., Schölkopf, B.: A tutorial on support vector regression. Stat. Comput. 14, 199–222 (2004)
19. Hornik, K., Stinchcombe, M., White, H.: Multilayer feedforward networks are universal approximators. Neural Netw. $2(5)$, 359–366 (1989)
20. Kim, J., Lee, K.: Practical cloud workloads for serverless FaaS. In: Proceedings of the ACM Symposium on Cloud Computing, pp. 477–477 (2019)

RV-CVP: A Flexible Variable Precision RISC-V ISA Extension for Convolutional Neural Network

Jingyi Zhu[2,4], Di Zhao[2,3]([✉]), Weifeng Zhang[1]([✉]), Zhijie Jia[2], Boran Liu[2], and Guokai Chen[2]

[1] Alibaba Group, Hangzhou, China
weifeng.z@alibaba-inc.com, weifeng.zhang@ocproject.net
[2] Institute of Computing Technology, CAS, Beijing, China
zhaodi@ict.ac.cn
[3] University of Chinese Academy of Sciences, Beijing, China
[4] Peking University, Beijing, China

Abstract. Convolutional neural network (CNN) performs well in several research fields and achieves high accuracy. With the development of CNNs, various hardware acceleration methods have been proposed. Instruction Set Architecture (ISA) based acceleration methods are gaining attention by providing flexibility and efficiency. Meanwhile, for mobile or embedded environments, there is a preference for variable precision quantization data to meet different accuracy or performance requirements. In this paper, we design a new RISC-V ISA extension, named RV-CVP, which supports variable precision specifically for CNNs. It has 3 computational instructions for CNNs and 3 memory access instructions that closely match the computation. We implement the RV-CVP extension on the open-source processor NutShell. Then a CNN programming library is developed, which allows flexible use of the RV-CVP instructions and building CNN models. Finally, we implement our design in simulation and FPGA platforms and evaluate the code density, performance, hardware resource usage, and power consumption. The results show that the RV-CVP extension improves instruction density by up to 1.678x and program performance by up to 42.06x at the single operator level. While on real CNN models, the RV-CVP extension improves performance by 3.8x–4.4x. The code is available at https://gitee.com/OpenBPU/RV-CVP.

Keywords: RISC-V · Variable Precision · Convolutional Neural Network

1 Introduction

Convolutional neural network (CNN) is a typical kind of forward artificial neural network, which performs well in research fields such as image recognition, speech detection, and natural language processing, and achieves high accuracy [4, 5, 6, 19]. With the development of CNNs, the increase in data size puts high demands on computation and data access bandwidth.

© IFIP International Federation for Information Processing 2025
Published by Springer Nature Switzerland AG 2025
X. Chen et al. (Eds.): NPC 2024, LNCS 15527, pp. 461–473, 2025.
https://doi.org/10.1007/978-981-96-2830-8_36

ISA-based acceleration methods are attracting interest for their flexibility and efficiency. Chen et al. introduced DianNao and DaDianNao [2, 3], high-performance acceleration chips with specialized VLIW designs, but these require numerous computational units and are challenging to program. Liu et al. proposed Cambricon [8], an ISA for ANNs, yet it lacks CNN optimization. Lou et al. suggested an ISA extension for CNNs [10], using matrices as the basic operation, which is not compatible with standard CPU pipelines. Most prior research centers on specific data precisions, like 32-bit FP and 16-bit fixed-point, with limited support for multiple precisions. Lower precision data can enhance throughput and energy efficiency, with precision varied based on accuracy/performance needs [11].

Based on the above problems and the current situation, we design a new RISC-V ISA extension, named RV-CVP, which supports variable precision specifically for CNNs. We implement the extension on the open-source processor NutShell. The main work of this paper is summarized as follows:

- We investigate and abstract core quantized CNN operations into instructions, proposing 3 CNN-specific computational and 3 memory access instructions, with variable precision support for 4 different bit-precision data types.
- We implement the RV-CVP extension on NutShell, with specialized arithmetic units for each instruction.
- We create a software framework for RV-CVP, supporting its instructions and CNN data structures/operators, and port LeNet-5 for testing.
- We implement our design in simulation and FPGA platforms, analyze and evaluate the code density, performance, power consumption, etc. The results show that the RV-CVP extension is flexible and energy efficient.

2   Related Works

2.1   Introduction of RISC-V ISA Extension

The basic form of RISC-V instruction set includes only a base integer instruction set. The more advanced instruction functions are encapsulated as standard extensions, and these extensions can be optionally implemented when designing the processor.

RISC-V ISA defines several standard extensions that extend the functions of the base integer instruction set (I). Some familiar extensions are: integer multiplication and division extension (M), control and status register extension (Zicsr), single-precision floating-point extension (F), double-precision floating-point extension (D), atomic instructions extension (A), compressed instructions extension (C). There are also some newer extensions, such as vector operations extension (V) and so on [9].

In addition to the standard extensions, the RISC-V ISA also reserves a portion of the instruction code space for supporting custom extensions. The instruction set specification reserves four coding spaces, custom-0 to custom-3, for user-defined instruction extensions.

2.2   The Basic Operations of Quantized CNN

CNNs consist of some basic operations: convolution, pooling, activation, and full connection [1]. In this paper, We concern the forms of 2D convolution, pooling, activation under quantization. Assuming q is the quantized value, f is the original floating point value, s is the mapping factor (scaling factor), and z is the quantized zero point, then we have

$$f = s(q - z) \tag{1}$$

Assuming that the convolution weight is w, the bias is b, the input is x, and the output value is y. After quantification we have

$$s_y\left(q_y - z_y\right) = \sum_{i=1}^{n} s_w(q_{wi} - z_w)s_x(q_{xi} - z_x) + s_b(q_b - z_b) \tag{2}$$

$$q_y = \frac{s_w s_x}{s_y} \sum_{i=1}^{n}(q_{wi} - z_w)(q_{xi} - z_x) + \frac{s_b}{s_y}(q_b - z_b) + z_y \tag{3}$$

Here bias is usually quantified directly as int32, and $s_b = s_w s_x$, $z_b = 0$. Since the zero point of weight is usually quantized as 0, following form can be introduced:

$$q_y = \frac{s_w s_x}{s_y}\left(\sum_{i=1}^{n} q_{wi}(q_{xi} - z_x) + q_b\right) + z_y \tag{4}$$

$$q_y = \frac{s_w s_x}{s_y}\left(\sum_{i=1}^{n} q_{wi}q_{xi} - z_x \sum_{i=1}^{n} q_{wi} + q_b\right) + z_y \tag{5}$$

The operation form of full connection is similar to convolution, so the quantization form is the same as convolution.

For pooling, the maximum pooling is not changed under quantization. And for average pooling, we have

$$s_y\left(q_y - z_y\right) = \frac{1}{n} \sum_{i=1}^{n} s_x(q_{xi} - z_x) \tag{6}$$

$$q_y = \frac{s_x}{s_y}\left(\frac{1}{n} \sum_{i=1}^{n} q_{xi} - z_x\right) + z_y \tag{7}$$

For the ReLU activation function, we have

$$q_y = max(q_x, z_x) \tag{8}$$

Now we can quantize the entire network and perform inference on the quantized CNNs according to the above equation.

3   RV-CVP ISA Extension Design

In this section, we first introduce the overall architecture and instruction format of the RV-CVP extension, then introduce the new vector register file and precision register, and finally introduce the functions of each instruction in detail.

31 24	23 20	19 15	14 12	11 7	6 0
00000000	length	00000	func	rd	opcode
	k		CONV	dst_addr	

31 24	23 20	19 15	14 12	11 7	6 0
00000000	length	rs1	func	rd	opcode
	k	algorithm	POOL	dst_addr	

31 25 24 20	19 15	14 12	11 7	6 0
0000000 rs2	rs1	func	rd	opcode
ReLU zero_point	src_data	ACT	dst_addr	

31 20	19 15	14 12	11 7	6 0
imm[11:0]	rs1	func	00000	opcode
src_addr		LOADV.W		

31 27 26 24 23 20	19 15	14 12	11 7	6 0
00000 tag length	rs1	func	rd	opcode
vtag k src_addr		LOADV.D	vec_addr	

31 27 26 24 23 20	19 15	14 12	11 7	6 0
00000 tag length	rs1	func	00000	opcode
vtag k src_addr		LOADV.P		

Fig. 1. The Format of RV-CVP Instructions.

3.1 The Overall Architecture of RV-CVP

After studying and analyzing the core operations of CNNs, the most intensive and basic operations are abstracted as instructions. 3 computational instructions are designed, namely convolution (conv), pooling (pool), and activation (act). To meet the requirement of easy integration with the processor pipeline, the convolution and pooling instructions are designed as one instruction to handle only one window of computation. The memory access structure of the CNNs takes into account the convolution optimization algorithm mentioned previously. Based on that, the direct vector loading instruction (loadv.d) and the partial vector loading instruction (loadv.p) are designed for data loading. Finally, an additional precision loading instruction (loadv.w) is designed to support variable precision.

The RV-CVP extension still satisfies the RISC architecture, where computation and access are independent. Notice that the RV-CVP extension has only load instructions but no store instructions. That is because the computation result of the convolution and pooling instructions is a single element. The result is stored in a general-purpose register and then written back to memory via standard store instructions. The RV-CVP instructions' format is shown in Fig. 1.

3.2 Variable Precision Related Register Design

To support CNN operations with variable precision, we introduce vector register file and precision registers. The register has 8 bits in total, the high 4 bits represent the precision of the main vector, and the low 4 bits represent the precision of the convolution kernel. One-hot encoding is used in the Vwidth register, which supports 16-bit, 8-bit, 4-bit, and 2-bit main vector data, and 8-bit, 4-bit, 2-bit, and 1-bit convolution kernel data.

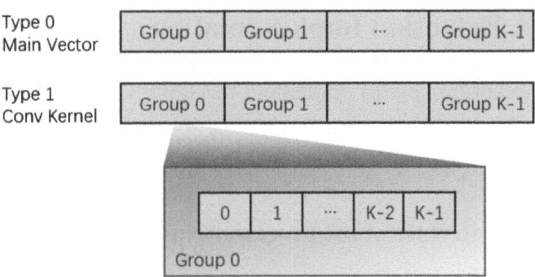

Fig. 2. The Structure of Vector Register File.

We use the RV64 architecture and therefore 8 global Vwidth registers are used with a total of 64 bits. Global Vwidth registers are written by a dedicated instruction loadv.w. loadv.w is similar to the ld instruction in the standard instruction set, and loads 64 bits of data from the target address and writes it to the 8 global Vwidth registers.

The vector register file is designed to store a windowed amount of CNN data, and its structure is shown in Fig. 2. The vector registers are divided into two types, the main vector and the convolution kernel. Each type has K groups, where K is the maximum window size supported in hardware. Each group corresponds to a row of the window and contains K identical registers. The registers of the main vector type are 16-bit and the registers of the convolution kernel type are 8-bit. Each group has one private Vwidth register, which is half the size of the global Vwidth register.

3.3 Functions of RV-CVP Instructions

Loadv.d loads data in one column of the convolution or pooling window. It reads the global Vwidth register indexed by vtag to obtain the data precision to determine the column vector length. The vector is then loaded and deposited into the target Fig. 2: Structure of Vector Register File group of the vector register. When the data precision is less than the vector register bit width, the high bit is filled with 0.

loadv.p is designed to improve access efficiency. For example, the convolution window is calculated from left to right. There is data duplication between the two windows. Loadv.p instruction loads a column vector and deposits it into group k-1 of the vector register, where k is the window size, while the data of group 1 to k-1 slides toward the previous group.

The function of the computational instructions is relatively simple compared to the access instructions. Conv takes the first k elements of the first k groups of the main vector register and the kernel register, performs the vector inner product operation, and writes the result to the rd register.

Pool takes the first k elements in the first k groups of the main vector register, performs the maximum or average pooling operation according to the algorithm specified by rs1, and writes the result to the rd register.

Act supports only the ReLU algorithm, which compares the input data with zero point and returns the maximum value.

4 RV-CVP ISA Extension Implementation

In this section, we describe how to implement the RV-CVP extension on the NutShell processor. We first introduce the overall architecture of NutShell, and then introduce several important modules in the variable precision hardware implementation.

4.1 The Overall Architecture of the Processor NutShell

The RV-CVP extension implementation is based on the open-source NutShell processor, whose overall architecture is shown in Fig. 3. The NutShell processor consists of a front-end and a back-end, with the front-end responsible for fetching, decoding, and issuing, and the back-end responsible for executing and writing back. We place the RV-CVP instruction processing unit (CVPU) at the execution level, which exists as a separate functional unit. The CVPU is composed of three parts: Vector Register File, Vector Memory Unit (VMU), and CNN Arithmetic Unit. The memory access instructions are executed by the VMU and the computational instructions are executed by the CNN Arithmetic Unit. The vector register file is responsible for storing the data and passing it to the CNN Arithmetic Unit.

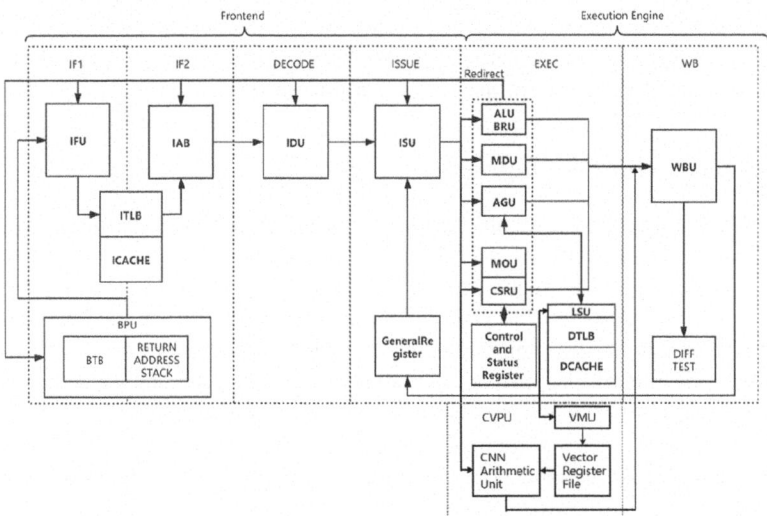

Fig. 3. The Overall View of NutShell with RV-CVP Extension

4.2 Convolution Arithmetic Unit

The size of the convolution arithmetic unit depends on the maximum window size K. In our design, K = 5, because usually the convolution kernel size does not exceed 5 × 5. According to the definition of the convolution instruction, it needs to compute the multiplication and summation of up to 25 pairs of data. We use the classical but efficient Wallace tree multiplier. The structure of the Wallace tree multiplier consists of Booth encoder, switch, Wallace tree array, and adder. The Booth encoder splits the multiplication into multiple additions, producing a series of partial products. The Wallace tree converts the sum of multiple numbers into the sum of 2 numbers.

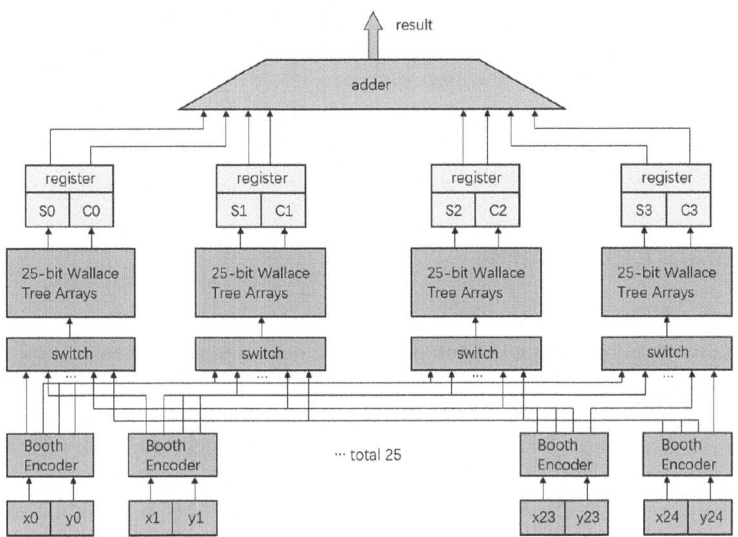

Fig. 4. The Structure of Convolution Arithmetic Unit.

As shown in Fig. 4, instead of using 25 separate multipliers, we combine the partial products of all multiplications and feed them into a larger Wallace tree array to complete the multiplication and summation computations at the same time.

When using low-precision convolution kernels, fewer groups of 25-bitWallace tree arrays are required. We reuse the 4 groups of maximum precision to reduce the hardware cost. For the case where the convolution window is less than 5, in order to reuse the existing structure as much as possible and save resources, we choose to use the computational structure with $k = 5$ and fill the data in the empty position with 0.

4.3 Average Pooling Arithmetic Unit

Average pooling can be divided into two steps, first calculating the sum of all the data in the window, and then dividing by the amount of data. The summation can be easily implemented through an addition tree, but the division is more complicated. If the usual multi-cycle divider is used, the latency of the instruction is too large. Consider that the division here is the integer case and there are only a limited number of divisors: 1, 4, 9, 16, 25. Among them, case 1 does not need calculation, and cases 4 and 16 can be achieved directly by shifting. The idea is to calculate by approximation and let cases 9 and 25 be achieved by a combination of simple operations.

According to the nature of the division, the result remains the same when both the dividend and divisor are multiplied by a non-zero integer. When the divisor is large, the difference between the result of dividing by the divisor plus or minus one and the original result can be less than one, and the two are identical after rounding. Based on the above properties, let's take the case of dividing by 9 as an example. Assuming sum is the summation result, the division result can be written as

$$result = \frac{sum}{9} = \frac{sum}{2^3+1} = \frac{sum(2^3-1)(2^6+1)(2^{12}+1)}{(2^3+1)(2^3-1)(2^6+1)(2^{12}+1)} \approx \frac{1864135sum}{2^{24}} \tag{9}$$

This result is fully accurate within sum $<= 2^{28}$, which matches the data range of 16-bit maximum precision of the input data. For the case of dividing by 25, a similar method can be used. Note that the division by 25 needs to be split into two divisions by 5, otherwise it will not meet the accuracy range.

5 Software Environment

For complex algorithms like CNN, it is difficult to program directly in assembly and not conducive to debugging and maintaining. We need a high-level interface to use the RV-CVP instructions. The idea is to implement a C intrinsic for each instruction using inline assembly.

Once the C intrinsic for each instruction is implemented, a high-level CNN programming library is needed to build and run CNN models. Here we implement a simple but relatively complete library, which is mainly shown in Table 1, including basic data structures, input and output APIs, operator APIs, and utility APIs.

The basic data structures include image_t supporting input and intermediate images of the network, kernel_t supporting convolutional kernel weights, and fc_filter_t supporting full connection parameters. The input APIs are divided into two categories: random generation and import from existing data. The operator APIs are divided into two categories: using RV-CVP instructions and using standard instructions. In addition, there is a set of APIs with the same name and MP suffix as the APIs in the table, which support different precision for different columns in the same image.

Table 1. The Overall View of the CNN Programming Library.

Basic Data Structures	image_t	kernel_t	fc_filter_t
Input and Output APIs	RandomInitImage InitImage SetOutput	RandomInitKernel InitKernel SetOutputKernel	RandomInitFcFilterArray InitFcFilterArray SetOutputFcFilter
Operator APIs	Convolution Activation StdIns_Convolution StdIns_AvgPooling	MaxPooling Flatten StdIns_MaxPooling StdIns_Activatio	AvgPooling Dense
Utility APIs	Transpose	MergeImage	Rescale

6   Evaluation and Result

6.1   Evaluation Through Simulation

To evaluate the performance and the efficiency of the RV-CVP extension, we design a series of performance evaluation programs in the simulation environment using the CNN programming library mentioned in the previous section.

We write performance evaluation programs for convolution, pooling, and activation operators to evaluate the performance of single operators at different data precision. Each performance evaluation program is divided into two parts, a baseline program consisting of standard instruction operators, and a comparison program consisting of RV-CVP operators. These two parts are run independently, performing the same computation on the same input image, and then the instructions of the program and the cycles the program executed are counted.

The former measures the memory space occupied by a program. The instruction density improvement ratio and execution time speedup of RV-CVP compared to the baseline are calculated as shown in Table 2.

The first group is the convolution performance. The RV-CVP program has 1.338x–1.667x instruction density and 19.02x–42.06x speedup compared to the baseline, which is more obvious at low precision. That is because standard instructions do not support low-precision data of less than 8 bits, which requires additional shifting and bit operations, increasing the number of instructions and execution time.

Table 2. The Performance Test Results of Convolution Operator.

Test Program	Instruction Density Improvement Ratio	Baseline Cycles	RV-CVP Cycles	Execution Time Speedup
conv 16-bit	1.338	138859	7300	19.02
conv 8-bit	1.500	218681	6283	34.81
conv 4-bit	1.667	249854	5940	42.06
conv 2-bit	1.480	200583	5810	34.52
pool 16-bit	1.678	124233	7064	17.59
pool 8-bit	1.542	112720	6427	17.54
pool 4-bit	1.613	143254	6657	21.52
pool 2-bit	1.613	150491	6679	22.53
act 16-bit	1.368	13457	3646	3.691
act 8-bit	1.297	11173	1899	5.884
act 4-bit	1.600	15691	1132	13.86
act 2-bit	1.600	15742	797	19.75

The second group is the pooling performance the instruction density and computational performance of RV-CVP compared to the baseline are improved by about 1.6x and 17x–21x. From the structure of the pooling units in the previous section, it is clear that the pool instructions are not optimized for precision, so the performance improvement is not significant relative to the precision change.

The third group is the activation performance. The results are similar to convolution, with higher performance improvement at low precision. The instruction density improvement is about 1.3x–1.6x; the speedup is about 3.6x–19.7x. One activation instruction can compute more data at low precision, so the total number of cycles can be effectively reduced.

6.2 Evaluation Through FPGA

Finally, we implement our design on FPGA to evaluate the power consumption and hardware resource usage of the RV-CVP extension. The platform is the Alveo U250 board, and it is synthesized and implemented by Xilinx Vivado. According to the implementation report, the hardware resource usage on FPGA is shown in Table 3.

In Table 3, we compare our design with the existing accelerators. The first thing to note is that different accelerators have different design goals and different preferences, and it is difficult to effectively and comprehensively measure an accelerator using performance or some other single standard alone. It is more reasonable to consider an accelerator under multiple standards to evaluate its strengths and weaknesses. In addition, while the previous studies are mostly standalone hardware accelerators, our work is a functional extension internal to the CPU. It is a relatively fair approach to remove the impact of the original CPU part and only consider the contribution of the RV-CVP extension.

In terms of Giga Operations Per Second (GOPS), previous studies achieve better performance than ours. The main reason for the performance difference is the architecture. The previous studies are mostly dedicated hardware accelerators, and it has the advantage of maximizing performance but consumes huge hardware resources. Our work, on the other hand, is a functional extension of the CPU, with the acceleration unit located inside the pipeline. The size of the data processed per instruction is only on the level of a convolution window. The advantage is that the hardware resource expense is quite small. The RV-CVP module uses only 6 DSPs and 8264 LUTs, much less than the amount used in the previous studies.

Table 3. The Comparison to Previous Implementations.

	Zhang et al. [11]	Guan et al. [7]	Gong et al. [12]	Gong et al. [12]	Lou et al. [9]	Ours	
						RV-CVP Module	Total
Platform	Virtex7 VX485T	Stratix-V GSMD	Zynq 7020	Virtex-7 690t	Artix7 XC7A100T	Alveo U250	
Model	AlexNet	VGG-19	LeNet-5	AlexNet	LeNet-5	LeNet-5	
Frequency(MHz)	100	150	200	150	100	300	
Data Precision	32-bit float	16-bit fixed	16-bit fixed	16-bit fixed	32-bit float	16/8/4/2-bit fixed	
LUT	186251	42349	38136	305118	24780	8264	63463
FF	205704	N/A	42618	281841	33594	342	69742
BRAM	1024	919	242	2192	29.5	0	73
DSP	2240	1036	205	2980	121	6	25
Power(W)	18.61	25	2.15	30.4	0.331	0.100	

Taking flexibility as the standard, our work has a greater advantage. Our design decomposes the CNN computation into the most basic operations, which can flexibly support many different networks without the limitation of network size. On the other hand, real CNN applications require OS support, meaning that the CPU is indispensable. Dedicated hardware accelerators require additional consideration of connection to the CPU or bus. Our design is CPU-based and directly supports the OS.

Taking power consumption as the standard, our work is at a high level. Our design is based on the NutShell CPU, but the complex logic of the CPU leads to higher LUT and FF hardware resource usage, which increases the overall design power consumption. However, it can be seen that the power consumption of the RV-CVP extension is very small, only 0.1 W. It indicates that the RV-CVP extension can obtain several times performance improvement with only a small increase in power consumption, which is energy efficient.

In terms of data precision, our design is more advantageous. While previous studies only involve traditional 32-bit floating point or 16-bit fixed point data, our work supports multiple variable fixed point precision. Meanwhile, we implement low precision CNN operations, which are not available in normal NN frameworks, making the CNNs more flexible.

7   Conclusion

Based on the computational characteristics of CNNs and the research of convolution optimization algorithms, we abstracted a series of basic operations into instructions. Then the RV-CVP ISA extension is designed according to the RISC-V specification. We implement the RV-CVP extension on the open-source NutShell processor. Then a CNN programming library is developed through inline assembly in C, which allows flexible use of the RV-CVP instructions and building CNN models. Finally, based on simulation and FPGA implementations, we evaluate the performance of the processor with the RV-CVP extension. The results show that RV-CVP provides significant improvements in instruction density and program performance. Compared to baseline programs using the standard instructions, the RV-CVP extension improves instruction density by up to 1.678x and program performance by up to 42.06x at the single operator level. While on real CNN models, the RV-CVP extension improves performance by 3.8x–4.4x. In addition, compared to some previous accelerators, our work has major advantages in flexibility, hardware resource usage, and variable precision support.

Acknowledgments. This study is funded by Alibaba Innovative Research (14873829).

Disclosure of Interests. The authors have no competing interests to declare that are relevant to the content of this article.

References

1. Chellapilla, K., Puri, S., Simard, P.: High performance convolutional neural networks for document processing. In: Tenth International Workshop on Frontiers in Handwriting Recognition. Suvisoft (2006)
2. Chen, T., et al.: Diannao: a small-footprint high-throughput accelerator for ubiquitous machine-learning. ACM SIGARCH Comput. Archit. News **42**(1), 269–284 (2014)
3. Chen, Y., et al.: Dadiannao: a machine-learning supercomputer. In: 2014 47th Annual IEEE/ACM International Symposium on Microarchitecture, pp. 609–622. IEEE (2014)
4. Collobert, R., Weston, J., Bottou, L., Karlen, M., Kavukcuoglu, K., Kuksa, P.: Natural language processing (almost) from scratch. J. Mach. Learn. Res. **12**(ARTICLE), 2493–2537 (2011)
5. Egmont-Petersen, M., de Ridder, D., Handels, H.: Image processing with neural networks—a review. Pattern Recogn. **35**(10), 2279–2301 (2002)
6. Goodfellow, I., Bengio, Y., Courville, A.: Deep learning. MIT Press (2016)
7. Guan, Y., et al.: FP-DNN: an automated framework for mapping deep neural networks onto FPGAS with RTL-HLS hybrid templates. In: 2017 IEEE 25th Annual International Symposium on Field-Programmable Custom Computing Machines (FCCM), pp. 152–159. IEEE (2017)
8. Liu, S., et al.: Cambricon: an instruction set architecture for neural networks. In: 2016 ACM/IEEE 43rd Annual International Symposium on Computer Architecture (ISCA), pp. 393–405. IEEE (2016)
9. Lou, W., Wang, C., Gong, L., Zhou, X.: RV-CNN: flexible and efficient instruction set for CNNs based on RISC-V processors. In: International Symposium on Advanced Parallel Processing Technologies, pp. 3–14. Springer (2019)
10. Zhang, C., Li, P., Sun, G., Guan, Y., Xiao, B., Cong, J.: Optimizing FPGA-based accelerator design for deep convolutional neural networks. In: Proceedings of the 2015 ACM/SIGDA International Symposium on Field-Programmable Gate Arrays, pp. 161–170 (2015)

11. Lee, J., Kim, C., Kang, S., Shin, D., Kim, S., Yoo, H.-J.: UNPU: a 50.6 TOPS/W unified deep neural network accelerator with 1B-to-16B fully-variable weight bitprecision. In: 2018 IEEE International Solid-State Circuits Conference- (ISSCC), pp. 218–220. IEEE (2018)
12. Gong, L., Wang, C., Li, X., Chen, H., Zhou, X.: MALOC: a fully pipelined FPGA accelerator for convolutional neural networks with all layers mapped on chip. IEEE Trans. Comput. Aided Des. Integr. Circuits Syst. **37**(11), 2601–2612 (2018)

Understanding the Inference Performance of Spatial Temporal Diffusion Transformer

Yu Li, Yuanxin Wei, Jiangsu Du$^{(\boxtimes)}$, Dan Huang$^{(\boxtimes)}$, and Nong Xiao

School of Computer, Sun Yat-sen University, Guangzhou, China
{liyu256,weiyx25}@mail2.sysu.edu.cn,
{duiiangsu,huangd79,xiaon6}@mail.sysu.edu.cn

Abstract. Spatial Temporal Diffusion Transformer (ST-DiT) has emerged as a new trend in generative diffusion models on text-to-video generation. As ST-DiT demonstrates great capabilities in practical scenarios, the demand for its inference increases significantly. However, due to the lack of performance studies and its distinct features, such as multi-dimensional attention mechanism, compared to transformer-based language model, our understanding of its inference workload is still limited. This paper aims to conduct an in-depth performance analysis on ST-DiT inference workloads, and provides comprehensive investigation on the identified performance problems, such as diverse performance constraints and varying memory footprint. We propose a resource-aware performance modeling method for ST-DiT and summarize its performance characteristics. Finally, this work conducts extensive experiments to validate our analysis and delivers valuable insights for efficient ST-DiT model deployment.

Keywords: Diffusion Transformer · Performance Profiling · Inference Workload

1 Introduction

In recent years, the realm of AIGC (Artificial Intelligence Generated Content) has experienced a remarkable surge in growth, such as OpenAI's Sora [1] and DALL-E3 [2]. Diffusion model [3] is a kind of generation model widely used in text-to-video generation. A diffusion model defines a Markov chain of diffusion steps, enabling the generation of desired data samples from initial noise. One mainstream implementation adopts the Transformer architecture [4] due to its considerable performance and scalability, namely, Diffusion Transformer (DiT) [5]. Building on this, Spatial Temporal DiT (ST-DiT) is proposed, which facilitates video generation [6] through a multi-dimension attention mechanism.

As ST-DiT models extend the attention mechanism from 1-dimension to temporal and spatial dimensions, their performance characteristics differ from those of transformer-based language models. Specifically, their computation volume,

© IFIP International Federation for Information Processing 2025
Published by Springer Nature Switzerland AG 2025
X. Chen et al. (Eds.): NPC 2024, LNCS 15527, pp. 474–487, 2025.
https://doi.org/10.1007/978-981-96-2830-8_37

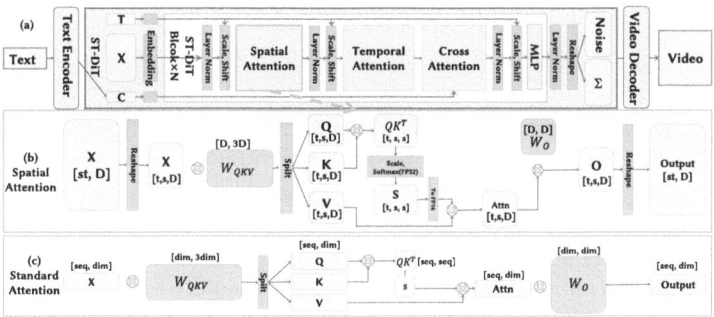

Fig. 1. Illustration of the process of text-to-video generation and a comparison of the spatial attention in ST-DiT with the standard attention in Transformer.

memory access volume and memory footprint change with two dimensions. This will affect the hardware utilization of inference tasks, presenting different performance characteristics. Although the inference performance of transformer-based language models has been extensively analyzed in recent years [7], that of ST-DiT models remains understudied. Therefore, it is non-trivial to promote the inference efficiency of ST-DiT models on devices such as GPUs.

This paper aims to investigate the performance of ST-DiT model inference workloads. We conduct an in-depth theoretical analysis and identify the performance bottleneck under specific hardware devices and task requirements with the roofline model. For example, generating a 4-second video at resolution of 720p on the NVIDIA A100 is memory-bound, meaning the inference process is limited by bandwidth. Furthermore, we propose a resource-aware performance modeling method for ST-DiT models and summarize their distinct features such as large activations. Finally, we conduct extensive experiments to validate our analysis. To the best of our knowledge, our work is the first to provide a systematic analysis of the performance characteristics for ST-DiT inference workloads.

2   Background

2.1   Process of Text-to-Video Generation

The process of generating a video ($[frames, height, width]$) described by a text consists of three parts: text encoder, diffusion model and video decoder. They are executed in the order shown in Fig. 1(a), and we use the notations listed in Table 1 to illustrate the process. First, the text is encoded as a 2-D condition C ($[L, D]$). Then, three inputs including the initial noise X ($[frames', height', width']$) in latent space [8], the diffusion time step T and C, enter the ST-DiT model together. The size of X in the latent space is usually the size of the real video scaled by the scaling factor ($[f_1, f_2, f_3]$), that is, $[frames', height', width'] = [\frac{frames}{f_1}, \frac{height}{f_2}, \frac{width}{f_3}]$. Next, they are calculated separately by the corresponding embedding layer, where the X is patched to

$[\frac{frames'}{p_1}, \frac{height'}{p_2}, \frac{width'}{p_3}]$, and then tokenized and flattened to $[s \times t, D]$. $[p_1, p_2, p_3]$ is the patch size, $t = \frac{frames'}{p_1}$, and $s = \frac{height'}{p_2} \times \frac{width'}{p_3}$. Ranges of s and t will be listed in Sect. 4.

During the whole process, ST-DiT takes the responsibility to predict noise and denoise the initial random noise step by step. It is the most critical and time-consuming part, usually performing more than 100 steps to generate the final results. Each step is an inference process with the same computational characteristics, thus we focus on one step for performance analysis in this paper.

Finally, the output of ST-DiT model will be calculated by the video decoder, which can restore the video representation in latent space to the real video.

2.2   Structure of ST-DiT Model

An ST-DiT model primarily consists of N sequential ST-DiT blocks with the same structure, which are mainly composed of four modules: spatial attention, temporal attention, cross attention and MLP. Figure 1(b) illustrates the spatial attention, which performs the attention mechanism only on the spatial dimension. Within the spatial attention, the data layout of X will be reshaped to $[t, s, D]$ for computation, finally it will be reshaped back to $[s \times t, D]$. Similarly, the temporal attention performs the attention mechanism on the temporal dimension only, with the input being $[s, t, D]$. Cross attention captures the relationship between text condition and video, whose Query is calculated by X with shape of $[s \times t, D]$, while Key and Value are calculated by C.

Comparing spatial attention in ST-DiT (Fig. 1(b)) with standard attention (Fig. 1(c)), we observe that, without considering the batch size dimension, the intermediate activations of spatial attention are three-dimensional, whereas that of standard attention are two-dimensional. Besides, spatial attention necessitates tensor reshaping operation at both its beginning and end.

Table 1. Meaning of Notions.

Notion	Meaning	Notion	Meaning
B	batch size	h	number of attention heads
D	hidden size of ST-DiT model	d	hidden size of attention head
N	number of ST-DiT block	s	spatial dimension
L	max text length	t	temporal dimension
dim	hidden size of standard Transformer	seq	sequence length

2.3   Roofline Model

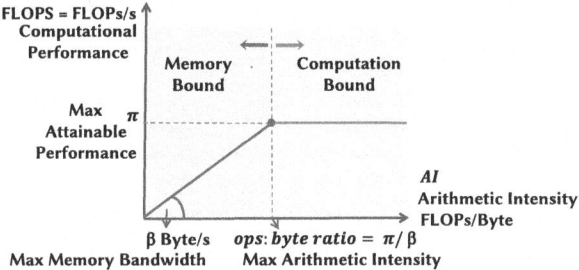

Fig. 2. A Roofline model.

The roofline model [9] serves as an effective theoretical framework to identify the performance bottleneck while deploying a model on specific hardware, which characterizes the relationship between the hardware features (e.g., compute capability and bandwidth) and the arithmetic intensity (AI) of operators. The compute capability of hardware is measured by how many floating-point operations can be performed per second (FLOPS), and AI is the ratio of floating-point operations (FLOPs) performed to the bytes transferred during execution. Therefore, the roofline is defined as following, where bw represents the memory bandwidth of the hardware:

$$\text{FLOPS Attainable} \leq \min(\text{Peak FLOPS, Peak bw} \times \text{AI}) \tag{1}$$

Figure 2 illustrates a roofline model, where π denotes the peak FLOPS and the slope β reflects the peak bandwidth of the hardware. Based on that, we can calculate ops:byte ratio of the hardware, which reflects how many FLOPs it can complete for every byte of memory it accesses at peak performance. By comparing the arithmetic intensity of the operator with this ratio, we can identify the performance bottleneck of an operator. If it falls in the red area, it is memory-bound on this hardware, and if it falls in the green area, it is compute-bound.

3 Performance Analysis of ST-DiT Inference Workload

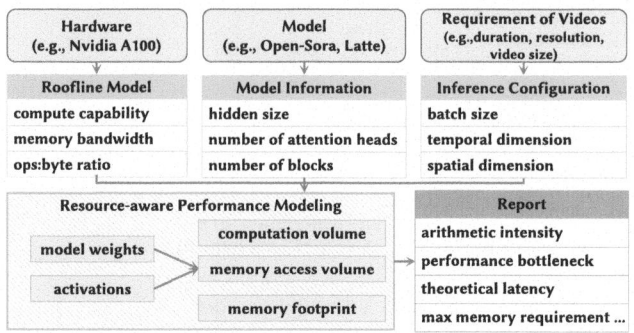

Fig. 3. Overview of the Performance Analysis Process.

In this section, we first give a quantitative analysis of ST-DiT model workload from three perspectives: computation volume, memory access volume, and memory footprint. Based on the quantitative analysis, we present the resource-aware performance modeling approach. Finally, we summarize the computational characteristics of ST-DiT model. The process is shown in Fig. 3.

3.1 Quantitative Analysis

Due to the identical structure of blocks within a model, we will present a detailed quantitative analysis of a single ST-DiT block, thereby elucidating the characteristics of the entire model.

Computation Volume. An ST-DiT block primarily consists of three typical operators: GELU (in MLP), Softmax and GEMM. Table 2 lists the input and output shapes of each operator. Taking GEMM (QK^T in Spatial attention) as an example, multiplying two matrices with shapes of $[Bt, h, s, d]$ and $[Bt, h, d, s]$ respectively will results in $2Bs^2tD$ FLOPs.

Table 2. Computational Characteristics of Key Operators

Operators	Input Shape	Output Shape	FLOPs	Memory Access (bytes)	AI
GELU	[B, st, 4D]	[B, st, 4D]	$52BstD$	$16BstD$	3.25
Softmax	[Bt, h, s, s]	[Bt, h, s, s]	$3Bhs^2t$	$8Bhs^2t$	0.375
GEMM(linear)	[Bt, s, D], [D, 3D]	[Bt, s, 3D]	$6BstD^2$	$8BstD + 6D^2$	$\approx D$
GEMM(QK^T)	[Bt, h, s, d], [Bt, h, d, s]	[Bt, h, s, s]	$2Bs^2tD$	$4BstD + 2Bhs^2t$	$\ll d$

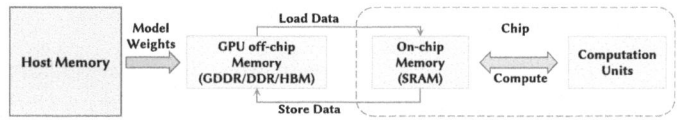

Fig. 4. Execution of an operation on hardware.

Memory Access Volume. The storage structure of a GPU includes on-chip memory like SRAM which is low-capacity and high-bandwidth and off-chip memory like HBM which is high-capacity and relatively low-bandwidth. As shown in Fig. 4, before the inference process, the entire model weights are first loaded into HBM from host memory. When an operator starts executing, the required data will be loaded from HBM to SRAM for computation, and the results will be stored in HBM after computation. Therefore, one operator execution requires two data transfer processes.

Given the above process, we can calculate memory access volume in bytes for each operator with respect to its shapes of input and output. We summarize all memory access volume in Table 2. Note that, for Softmax, the model requires FP32 [10], and other operators are configured with FP16. Taking GELU as an example, the shape of input and output tensors are both $[B, st, 4D]$. Thus, the memory access volume of the two tensors is $16BstD$ bytes. As for attention modules, two different types of GEMM are involved. The first type is the linear layer, where the input is multiplied by the model weights. Before computation, GPU needs to load the weights and the input from HBM. As for the second type, it relates to the matrix multiplication between two intermediate tensors like QK^T. Therefore, both Q and K need to be loaded.

Memory Footprint. Memory footprint is the amount of memory that a model uses during execution, including model weights and intermediate activations.

For model weights, calculating Q, K, V and the output projection in each attention module requires four weights in shape of $[D, D]$. MLP comprises two linear layers, with weights in shape of $[D, 4D]$ and $[4D, D]$ respectively. Therefore, the total weights for an ST-DiT block needs $40D^2$ bytes memory in FP16.

As for intermediate activations, taking the spatial attention as an example, for calculating Q, K, V, saving the input X needs $2BstD$ bytes. Then QK^T needs $4BstD$ bytes for saving Q and K as well as $4Bhs^2t$ bytes for the result. For $Softmax(QK^T) \times V$, saving two input tensors needs $2Bhs^2t + 2BstD$ bytes and $2BstD$ bytes for output. Therefore, attention activations of spatial attention need $10BstD + 6Bhs^2t$, which is $O(s^2t)$. Similarly, the activations for temporal attention require $10BstD + 6Bht^2s$ bytes, which is $O(st^2)$. We calculate that for cross attention and MLP as well, and their memory footprint are both $O(st)$.

Finally, we summarize the quantitative analysis of computation volume, memory access volume and memory footprint in one ST-DiT block in Table 3.

Table 3. Quantitative analysis of one ST-DiT block.

Layer	FLOPs	Memory Access (bytes)	Memory Footprint (bytes)
Spatial Attention	$(4BD + 5Bh)s^2t + 8BD^2st$	$24Bhs^2t + 24BDst$	$6Bhs^2t + 10BstD + 8D^2$
Temporal Attention	$(4BD + 5Bh)t^2s + 8BD^2st$	$24Bht^2s + 24BDst$	$6Bht^2s + 10BstD + 8D^2$
Cross Attention	$(4BD^2 + 4LBD + 4LBh)st$	$(16BD + 32LBh)st$	$(8BD + 8BLh)st + 8D^2$
MLP	$(52BD + 16BD^2)st$	$36BDst + 16D^2$	$20BstD + 16D^2$

3.2 Resource-Aware Performance Modeling

Based on quantitative analysis and the specific hardware information, we first leverage the roofline model to identify the performance bottleneck during the inference process. Then, we model the inference performance from two aspects: inference latency and memory footprint.

Performance Bottleneck Identification. According to Table 3, we can obtain the computation volume and memory access volume of each module, thereby calculating their arithmetic intensity. To identify the performance bottleneck, we compare it with the ops:byte ratio of the hardware, as in Eq. 2. Furthermore, we can determine a model's bound type using the same method.

$$AI = \frac{\text{FLOPs}}{\text{Memory Access Volume}} \begin{cases} < ops : byte\ ratio, & \text{memory-bound} \\ > ops : byte\ ratio, & \text{compute-bound} \end{cases} \quad (2)$$

Latency Modeling. The execution time of an operator is primarily influenced by memory access time, computation time, and the degree of overlap between these two processes. As the degree of overlap is difficult to define, we estimate its execution time based on whether it is limited by computation or memory access. If it is compute-bound, its latency is dominated by computation time. On the contrary, it is dominated by memory access time. Therefore, we can compare its computation time and memory access time, and then take the maximum value as the estimated theoretical execution time of the operator.

We extend this approach to the entire model to estimate the inference latency per request. The amount of computation and memory access for four main modules in the ST-DiT block can be obtained from Table 3. Then, we sum up execution time of each module and multiply it by the number of blocks (N) to estimate the total latency of the entire model, defined as:

$$Latency = N \times \sum_{module} max(\frac{FLOPs_{module}}{FLOPS}, \frac{M_{module}}{bw}) \quad (3)$$

where $FLOPs_{module}$ and M_{module} respectively represents total computation volume and memory access volume of a module, and bw is the peak bandwidth.

Memory Requirement Modeling. As mentioned in Sect. 3.1, we obtain the conclusion that in cross attention and MLP, the memory footprint is $O(st)$, while in spatial attention and temporal attention, the memory footprint is $O(s^2t)$ or $O(st^2)$. Obviously, spatial or temporal attention will result in the peak memory footprint of the entire model. Consequently, we can calculate the total memory required as follows, where $40ND^2$ is the memory footprint of model weights.

$$Peak\ Memory = 40ND^2 + 10BstD + 6Bh \times max(s^2t, st^2) \qquad (4)$$

3.3 Performance Characteristics of Inference Workload

To compare characteristics between ST-DiT model and Transformer model in NLP, we convert its spatial and temporal dimensions into a single dimension (seq). For a two-second video ($t = 16$) at 144p ($s = 108$), seq equals 1728. An extended scenario of a one-minute video ($t = 480$) at 720p ($s = 3600$) significantly expands seq to nearly 2 million. This highlights ST-DiT's notably longer sequence lengths compared to Transformer model, leading to distinct computational characteristics. Given Table 2 and Table 3, we summarize three key computational features emerged between ST-DiT and Transformer models.

Feature 1: The attention mechanism is dominant in both computation and memory access, instead of MLP. It can be observed from Table 3 that, regardless of computation volume or memory access volume, the three attention mechanisms occupy the majority part of the entire model. Therefore, the execution time of attention mechanism is longer than that of the MLP.

Feature 2: The intermediate activations are dominant in memory access, instead of model weights. As shown in Table 2, the memory access volume of intermediate activations is $O(s^2t)$ or $O(st^2)$, while that of model weights is $O(D^2)$. For most inference tasks, s^2t and st^2 are larger than D^2, resulting in intermediate activations dominating memory access. However, for Transformer models, the weights and KV cache are usually dominant [7], since it generates tokens one by one and results in $seq = 1$ during the decoding phase.

Feature 3: The memory requirements of different modules are extremely unbalanced. Observing Table 3, the peak memory requirements for temporal and spatial attention are respectively $O(s^2t)$ and $O(st^2)$, which are much lager than that of the other two modules (cross attention and MLP), whose memory requirements are $O(st)$. This phenomenon can lead to serious memory fragmentation issue, which we will analyze in Sect. 4.

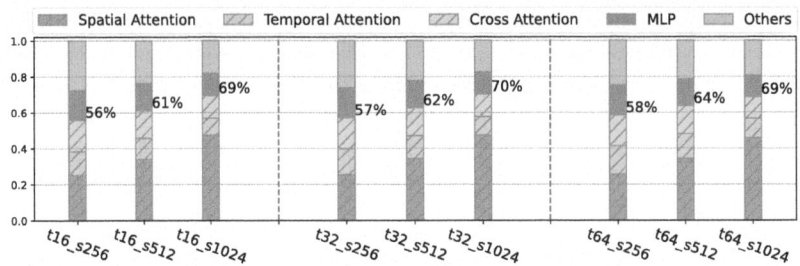

Fig. 5. The inference time breakdown per ST-DiT Block on A100.

4 Evaluation

4.1 Setup

Table 4. GPU Configurations

Device	FP16 Tensor Core	Bandwidth	Memory	ops:byte
V100	112 TFLOPS	900 GB/s	16 GB	116
A10	125 TFLOPS	600 GB/s	24 GB	194
A100	312 TFLOPS	1555 GB/s	40 GB	187
RTX 4090	330 TFLOPS	1008 GB/s	24 GB	305

Hardware: We evaluate inference performance of ST-DiT model on diverse GPUs listed in Table 4. We use FP16 for ST-DiT inference.

Model: We choose Open-Sora-v1.1 [10] (700M) for the evaluation, where $D = 1152$, $L = 200$, $h = 16$ and $N = 28$. For fair comparison, we use the same configuration for Transformer model. All the results mentioned below are the average values of 50 diffusion steps.

4.2 Execution Time Breakdown per ST-DiT Block

We conduct multiple experiments on A100 GPU with different s and t. Figure 5 presents the time breakdown in an ST-DiT block.

It is observed that the three attention mechanisms dominate the execution time, consistently accounting for over 60%, which aligns with **Feature 1**. Among them, the spatial attention consumes the most time. With a fixed t (16, 32 or 64), increasing s markedly increases the time proportion of both spatial attention and the overall attention mechanism. Conversely, constant s with rising t yields only a slight increase in temporal attention's time proportion. As analyzed in Sect. 3.1, with constant t, spatial attention's memory access volume scales as $O(s^2)$ while $O(s)$ for other modules. Similarly, constant s and growing t result in $O(t^2)$ memory access volume for temporal attention, while $O(t)$ for others. This quadratic vs. linear scaling drives attention mechanisms' increased time proportion, with the influence of s outweighing t due to its larger values.

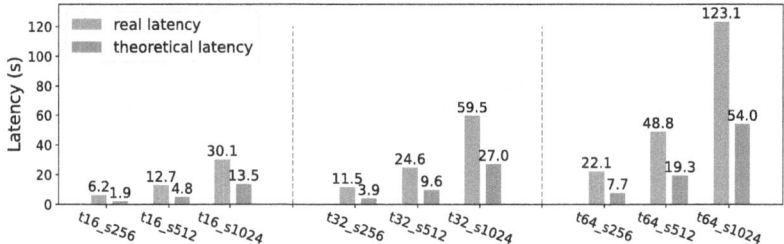

Fig. 6. Inference latency with different inputs on A100.

4.3 Inference Latency

According to Fig. 6, an increase in s and t will result in an increase in inference latency. However, since t is much smaller than s, the effect on inference latency brought by t is minor compared to that brought by s.

There is a certain gap between the actual measured latency and the theoretically estimated latency. This is due to multifaceted reasons (e.g., environmental factors) that the GPU's bandwidth and compute capability often cannot be maximized. Despite this, the trends in performance growth remain aligned. Thus, we can use the inference latency obtained through theoretical analysis to compare different GPUs' hardware performance and guide the model deployment.

4.4 Performance Bottleneck Identification

Open-Sora-v1.1 supports generating 2–16 s videos with the resolutions ranging from 144p to 720p, corresponding to t ranging from 16 to 128, and s ranging from 108 to 3600. Based on the analysis in Sect. 3.1, we can calculate the arithmetic intensity of the entire model. Figure 7 shows the corresponding changes in arithmetic intensity as the temporal and spatial dimensions vary.

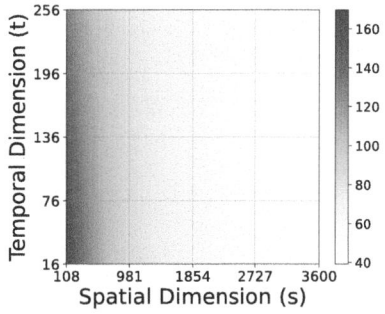

Fig. 7. Arithmetic Intensity of ST-DiT

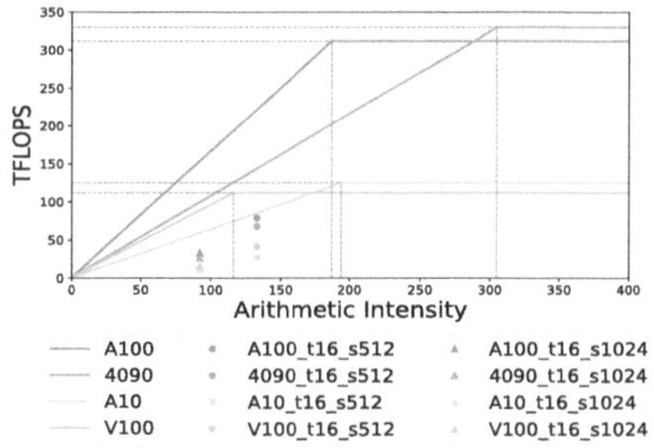

Fig. 8. Roofline Model of ST-DiT.

Figure 7 illustrates that, for the majority of s and t dimensions, the arithmetic intensity of the ST-DiT model is typically lower than 100. As s and t increase, there is a noticeable decline in the overall arithmetic intensity, with s exerting a more significant influence. As shown in Table 4, GPUs with FP16 tensor core exhibit strong compute capability, with an ops:byte ratio higher than 100. Since most of the arithmetic intensity is lower than the ops:byte ratio of GPUs, ST-DiT model is typically memory-bound in our configurations. As the demand for video quality increases, the s and t dimensions increase, leading to a lower arithmetic intensity, and this will make the model more memory-bound.

Figure 8 presents the roofline model of the four NVIDIA GPUs listed in Table 4, with markers of different shapes indicating the performance of the ST-DiT model on these GPUs. Except for the case of V100_t16_st512, all other cases fall within the corresponding memory-bound area, validating the above analysis that ST-DiT is typically memory-bound in our configurations. Besides, for the same model executed on different GPUs, the performance ordering is A100 > 4090 > v100 > A10, which is consistent with the device bandwidth ordering. This provides us with inspiration for choosing GPU devices when deploying ST-DiT models, that is, GPU memory bandwidth is key.

4.5　Batching Effect

Batching serves as an effective optimization approach for Transformer inference, which handles multiple inference requests while loading model weights and KV cache only once. We evaluated the batching effect of the Transformer model and the ST-DiT model on A100. As illustrated in Fig. 9(a), as the batch size (B) increases, the latency of the Transformer model does not increase proportionally, illustrating the benefits brought by the batching optimization. Whereas for the SD-DiT model, the inference latency is almost proportional to B.

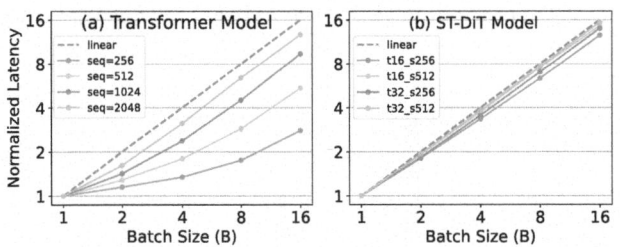

Fig. 9. Inference latency normalized to batch size $= 1$.

We tend to figure out the reasons based on the different performance characteristics of these two models. Increasing B will proportionally increase the model's computation volume and memory access volume of intermediate activations, while the memory access volume of model weights remains unchanged. For the Transformer model where the memory access volume is dominated by model weights, when seq is small, increasing B will lead to an increase in computation volume, while memory access remains relatively constant. In this case, there

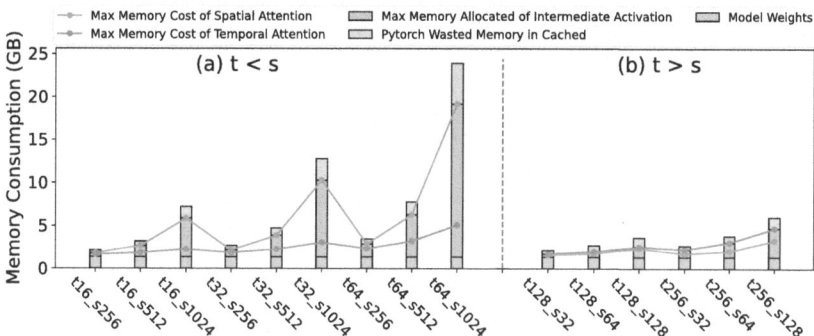

Fig. 10. Memory Consumption.

exists an increase in arithmetic intensity, and the model can more effectively utilize hardware computing resources, thereby improving inference performance. On the other side, for the ST-DiT model, the intermediate activations dominate the memory access volume rather than weights (**Feature 2**), and increasing B will increase the memory access volume. Therefore, batching has relatively little impact on the arithmetic intensity of the ST-DiT model, making the batching optimization ineffective for the ST-DiT model.

4.6 Memory Consumption

Figure 10(a) and (b) respectively illustrate the scenarios where $t < s$ and $t > s$. The memory footprint during the inference process is determined by intermediate activations and model weights. When $t < s$, the memory footprint of spatial attention is also the peak memory footprint of the entire inference process. Conversely, when $t > s$, temporal attention reaches the peak memory footprint. As s or t increases, the gap in peak memory footprint between the two attention modules becomes more obvious, and the memory consumption of intermediate activations exceeds that of model weights. This verifies **Feature 2**.

Additionally, Fig. 10 demonstrates the serious GPU fragmentation issue caused by the imbalanced memory requirements of different modules (**Feature 3**). For the case t64_s1024, there is nearly 5 GB memory reserved but not allocated. If a task tries to allocate another contiguous memory of such size and the GPU's available memory is not enough, it is possible to cause out-of-memory issue.

5 Optimization and Related Work

Kernel Fusion. Considering the memory-bound characteristic of ST-DiT models in most cases, an optimization approach is to maximize the bandwidth utilization of data loading process at once, such as fusion kernel. One existing method is Flash Attention [11], which consolidates original operations of attention including QK^T, Softmax, and *attention score* $\times V$ into a single kernel. This approach eliminates multiple times of intermediate activations transfer.

Sequence Parallelism. Sequence parallelism splits the sequence along the s or t dimension and deploys sub-tasks across multiple GPUs, with the aim of reducing the memory requirement of a single GPU. DeepSpeed-Ulysses [12] splits input to different devices for computation and use all-to-all operation to synchronize results. Ring Attention [13] makes each device calculate while communicating within a ring, which can overlap the computation and communication.

Co-design. Since ST-DiT inference requires hundreds of diffusion steps, many works combine algorithm-level design to reduce the number of diffusion steps, thereby improving efficiency. Distrifusion [14] leverages the similarity between the input from adjacent diffusion steps, and inferences different parts of an image on multiple devices for simultaneous computation. Agarwal, S. et al. [15] propose an approximate caching technique that can reduce the diffusion steps by reusing the intermediate noise states.

6 Conclusion

Faced with the increasing demand for ST-DiT model inference and the lack of its performance study, our work conducts an in-depth theoretical analysis of ST-DiT's systematic performance and figures out its distinct features. Furthermore, leveraging the roofline model, we identify the performance bottleneck on specific hardware and inference tasks, and conduct extensive experiments to validate our analysis. This work would profound significance for understanding of ST-DiT inference workload and provide guidance for further performance optimization.

Acknowledgments. This work is supported by National Key R&D Program of China under Grant 2022ZD0115304, the Fundamental Research Funds for the Central Universities, Sun Yat-sen University: 23xkjc016, the National Natural Science Foundation of China under Grand No.62402534 and the GuangDong Basic and Applied Basic Research Foundation: 2023A1515110117.

References

1. OpenAI. Sora: Creating video from text (2024)
2. OpenAI. Dall-e 3 (2023)
3. Ho, J., Jain, A., et al.: Denoising diffusion probabilistic models (2020)
4. Vaswani, A., Shazeer, N.M., et al.: Attention is all you need. In: Neural Information Processing Systems (2017)
5. Peebles, W., Xie, S.: Scalable diffusion models with transformers. In: Proceedings of the IEEE/CVF International Conference on Computer Vision (ICCV), pp. 4195–4205 (2023)
6. Ma, X., Wang, Y., et al.: Latte: latent diffusion transformer for video generation. arXiv, abs/2401.03048 (2024)

7. Yuan, Z., Shang, Y., et al.: LLM inference unveiled: survey and roofline model insights (2024)
8. Rombach, R., Blattmann, A., et al.: High-resolution image synthesis with latent diffusion models (2022)
9. Williams, S., Waterman, A., et al.: Roofline: an insightful visual performance model for floating-point programs and multicore architectures (2008)
10. Zheng, Z., Peng, X., et al.: Open-sora: democratizing efficient video production for all (2024)
11. Dao, T., Fu, D.Y., et al.: Flashattention: fast and memory-efficient exact attention with IO-awareness. arXiv, abs/2205.14135 (2022)
12. Jacobs, S.A., Tanaka, M., et al.: Deepspeed ulysses: system optimizations for enabling training of extreme long sequence transformer models. arXiv, abs/2309.14509 (2023)
13. Li, S., Xue, F., et al.: Sequence parallelism: long sequence training from system perspective (2022)
14. Li, M., Cai, T., et al.: Distrifusion: distributed parallel inference for high-resolution diffusion models (2024)
15. Agarwal, S., Mitra, S., et al.: Approximate caching for efficiently serving diffusion models (2023)

Author Index

The manufacturer's authorised representative in the EU is Springer
Nature Customer Service Centre GmbH, Europaplatz 3, 69115 Heidelberg,
Germany. If you have any concerns regarding our products, please
contact ProductSafety@springernature.com

Printed and bound by CPI Group (UK) Ltd, Croydon, CR0 4YY
29/04/2026
02099551-0007